Cloud Computing's Transformative Power in Computing Environments

Aisha Hassan Abdalla Hashim
International Islamic University, Malaysia

Zeinab E. Ahmed
University of Gezira, Sudan

Othman O. Khalifa
International Islamic University, Malaysia

Rashid A. Saeed
Taif University, Saudi Arabia

IGI Global
Scientific Publishing
Publishing Tomorrow's Research Today

Vice President of Editorial — Melissa Wagner
Director of Acquisitions — Mikaela Felty
Director of Book Development — Jocelynn Hessler
Production Manager — Mike Brehm
Cover Design — Jose Rosado

Published in the United States of America by
IGI Global Scientific Publishing
701 East Chocolate Avenue
Hershey, PA, 17033, USA
Tel: 717-533-8845
Fax: 717-533-7115
Website: https://www.igi-global.com E-mail: cust@igi-global.com

Library of Congress Cataloging-in-Publication Data

Names: Hashim, Aisha A., 1965- editor http://id.loc.gov/rwo/agents/n2024040016 | Ahmed, Zeinab E., 1984- editor http://id.loc.gov/rwo/agents/n2024040015 | Khalifa, Othman, 1962- editor http://id.loc.gov/rwo/agents/n2025011745 | Saeed, Rashid A., 1974- editor http://id.loc.gov/rwo/agents/n2011072667
Title: Cloud computing's transformative power in computing environments / edited by Aisha Hashim, Zeinab Ahmed, Othman Khalifa, Rashid Saeed.
Description: Hershey, PA : IGI Global Scientific Publishing, [2026] | Includes bibliographical references and index. | Summary: "This book provides a deep understanding of the transforming ability of cloud computing technologies in computing environments. It focuses on understanding the principles, practical implementations, and future trends in cloud computing. It covers the fundamental concepts, service models, and deployment architectures of cloud computing"-- Provided by publisher.
Identifiers: LCCN 2025000179 (print) | LCCN 2025000180 (ebook) | ISBN 9798369399842 h/c | ISBN 9798369399859 s/c | ISBN 9798369399866 ebook
Subjects: LCSH: Cloud computing--Industrial applications | Computer networks--Industrial applications | Computer networks--Technological innovations
Classification: LCC QA76.585 .C58455 2025 (print) | LCC QA76.585 (ebook) | DDC 004.67/82--dc23/eng/20250317
LC record available at https://lccn.loc.gov/2025000179
LC ebook record available at https://lccn.loc.gov/2025000180
British Cataloguing in Publication Data
A Cataloguing in Publication record for this book is available from the British Library.

Table of Contents

Detailed Table of Contents

This chapter offers an in-depth review of the revolutionary development of cloud computing, from its theoretical underpinnings to its current position as a vital component of modern infrastructure for information technology. The historical trends, significant turning points, and technological advancements in the discipline are reviewed in this chapter. It explores the beginnings of cloud computing, how service models have changed over time, the effects of virtualization, and how new technologies are being incorporated. Readers will gain a profound appreciation for how cloud computing has transformed the operations and innovation of organizations by comprehending the historical background and recent developments.

The cloud computing era is currently in the IT industry. With its Internet-based foundation, cloud computing boasts the most potent processing architecture. Hardware, software, and internet infrastructure are all interconnected and integrated to form this system. It offers several advantages over grid computing and other computing systems. Cloud computing architecture is a fundamental framework that enables the delivery of various computing services over the Internet. This architecture comprises a front-end platform, back-end platforms, a cloud-based delivery model, and the network infrastructure that connects these components. The architecture is designed to provide scalable, flexible, and cost-effective solutions for a wide range of applications, from data storage and processing to software development and deployment. This chapter investigates the intricate details of cloud computing architecture, exploring its components

This chapter provides a comprehensive overview of cloud deployment models, including public, private, hybrid, and community clouds, and their profound impact on modern IT infrastructure and the development of inclusive IoT smart systems. The selection of an appropriate cloud model significantly influences critical aspects such as data sovereignty, scalability, resource utilization, and crucially, the accessibility features for individuals with disabilities. We examine the distinct characteristics, advantages, and disadvantages of each model, highlighting how they cater to diverse organizational needs, from cost optimization and rapid provisioning in public clouds to enhanced security and control in private environments. The discussion also addresses the complexities and benefits of hybrid and community cloud approaches, emphasizing their role in enabling flexible, compliant, and collaborative computing solutions. Understanding these models is essential for making informed strategic decisions that foster innovation and ensure equitable access to technology.

Cloud computing has revolutionized the way businesses access and utilize computational resources, providing unparalleled cost efficiency, scalability, and flexibility. Infrastructure as a Service (IaaS), Platform as a Service (PaaS), and Software as a Service (SaaS) comprise the three primary cloud service models; this chapter offers a thorough examination of each. We explore the characteristics, use cases, advantages, and disadvantages of each model, emphasizing the varying degrees of control and responsibility that cloud providers and consumers share.

In addition, the chapter delves into significant future trends, such as the increased integration of Artificial Intelligence functionalities, the paramount importance of robust cloud security measures, the convergence of edge and cloud computing, advancements in resource optimization, and the increasing adoption of cloud-native and serverless architectures. It is imperative for organizations to comprehend these models and emergent trends in order to effectively leverage the transformative power of the evolving cloud landscape.

Cloud computing is a primary driver for digital transformation, driving agility, scalability, and efficiency enhancements across industries. This chapter introduces cloud computing benefits such as flexibility, cost reduction, and accelerated innovation. Cloud strategies such as Hybrid, Multi-Cloud, and a Cloud-Native approach to fit the business needs will be explored. Some industry-specific impacts concerning healthcare, finance, and manufacturing processes will be vividly brought forth. While cloud adoption is a beneficial decision, it can also pose threats such as security, compliance, and integration challenges that will be addressed through mitigation strategies. The future trends in cloud computing that will be discussed include AI-driven cloud services, Edge computing, and Serverless architectures. Real-world case studies will fortify the argument on successful practical applications as effective references for businesses to leverage cloud computing.

This chapter explores the key security threats and vulnerabilities at different levels, such as SaaS, PaaS and IaaS in cloud computing and provides their solutions. It will comprehensively analyze common security risks such as data breaches, unauthorized access and compliance issues. Discuss all security issues such as application security, data security, network security issues, authentication and authorization issues. It explains various data security techniques such as Cryptography, Steganography, Homomorphic cryptography, Quantum cryptography, DNA cryptography, Machine learning and Deep learning, Multi-factor authentication, and Blockchain to describe

Blockchain is a decentralized and distributed digital ledger that records transactions across multiple computers. It consists of a continuously growing list of blocks, where each block contains a set of transactions and a reference to the previous block. The blockchain ensures the immutability and integrity of the recorded transactions by using cryptographic hashes and consensus mechanisms. Cloud computing is a service available over the network. Users can access and store data and applications remotely rather than on local servers or personal computers. Cloud computing offers resource pooling by letting users share the same physical resources dynamically according to their demands, often through virtualization. Cloud computing offers flexible, scalable resources, it can address blockchain's limitations in scalability and transaction speeds by act as a backup for blockchain data, enabling faster recovery and reduced latency. Synergy between cloud computing and blockchain offers significant potential for innovation across numerous sectors

The main idea of cloud computing is being widely promoted as the solution to current ongoing IT problems. In recent years the approach towards IT investment and management is constantly changing. At the same time, cloud computing has developed as a foundation of the contemporary technologies which enables the users

operation of sensor nodes is often constrained by limited energy resources. Efficient wireless energy harvesting (WEH) is a promising solution that can extend the operational lifetime of these nodes. Managing cloud services on sensor nodes plays a critical role in optimizing energy consumption and ensuring effective integration of WEH technologies.

Abhipsha Das, School of Computer Engineering, Kalinga Institute of Industrial Technology, Bhubaneswar, India
Swayam Yadav, School of Computer Engineering, Kalinga Institute of Industrial Technology, Bhubaneswar, India
Neetu Dey, School of Computer Engineering, Kalinga Institute of Industrial Technology, Bhubaneswar, India
Aayushma Gautam, School of Computer Engineering, Kalinga Institute of Industrial Technology, Bhubaneswar, India
Hitesh Mohapatra, School of Computer Engineering, Kalinga Institute of Industrial Technology, Bhubaneswar, India

Load balancing is vital in cloud computing for efficiently distributing workloads and preventing resource bottlenecks. This review explores using Genetic Algorithms (GAs), known for their optimization strength, to improve load balancing by minimizing task execution times and boosting resource utilization. The GA-based approach adapts to changing tasks and conditions, evolving solutions through iterative natural selection processes. This paper examines the key principles and real-world applications of this method, showing its potential to transform traditional load balancing and enhance cloud system performance and scalability.

Rehab Ibrahim Ahmed Omer, International Islamic University Malaysia, Malaysia

This chapter explores how cloud-based predictive analytics is transforming supply chain management by improving efficiency, accuracy in demand forecasting, and strategic decision-making. It discusses the benefits of integrating cloud computing with advanced analytics to enhance real-time data visibility, streamline operations, and enable proactive decision-making across the supply chain. Through detailed use cases, the chapter explains the practical applications of predictive and prescriptive analytics for optimizing inventory levels, forecasting demand fluctuations, and

Preface

In the past decade, cloud computing has transitioned from a disruptive technology to a foundational infrastructure that underpins nearly every sector of our digital society. As organizations increasingly seek flexible, scalable, and efficient computing solutions, cloud computing has emerged as the driving force behind innovation, operational agility, and digital transformation. This edited volume, *Cloud Computing's Transformative Power in Computing Environments*, is a comprehensive collection of research contributions that explore the evolving architecture, deployment strategies, and applications of cloud technologies while addressing the ethical, security, and integration challenges posed by emerging technologies such as AI, blockchain, IoT, and edge computing.

The goal of this book is twofold: first, to present readers with foundational and technical insights into cloud computing; and second, to explore its strategic application across industries and disciplines. Each chapter delves into specific aspects of cloud computing, from architectural frameworks to AI-integrated solutions, providing a multidisciplinary perspective that bridges theory and practice. The book brings together researchers, technologists, and academics from diverse regions and disciplines to provide a truly global and contextualized exploration of cloud computing's transformative power.

CHAPTER OVERVIEW

Chapter 1: Essential Concepts in Cloud Computing

Fatima Ahmed Abdalla and Noor Asiah Rashid present a historical and conceptual overview of cloud computing, tracing its roots, technological evolution, and foundational models. This chapter serves as a springboard for understanding subsequent discussions.

Chapter 2: Cloud Computing Architecture

This chapter, also authored by Fatima Ahmed Abdalla and Noor Asiah Rashid, dives into the structural design of cloud computing, detailing its front-end and back-end components and the internet infrastructure that links them, while discussing advantages over legacy systems.

Chapter 3: Cloud Deployment Models

Azana Hafizah Mohd Aman and her co-authors explore public, private, hybrid, and community clouds. The chapter focuses on strategic decision-making, particularly regarding accessibility, scalability, and compliance in enterprise and IoT contexts.

Chapter 4: Cloud Service Models

This chapter outlines the core service models - SaaS, PaaS, and IaaS- while forecasting emerging trends like AI integration and serverless architecture. It equips organizations to choose appropriate service models for their evolving needs.

Chapter 5: Cloud Computing's Role in Digital Transformation

Salaheldin Edam illustrates how cloud adoption accelerates innovation across industries, including healthcare and manufacturing. He presents real-world cases and forecasts trends such as edge computing and AI-enabled services.

Chapter 6: Cloud Security and Privacy

Rubi Kadyan and her co-authors address the pressing issues of data protection, regulatory compliance, and multi-layered security using modern techniques like quantum cryptography, machine learning, and blockchain.

Chapter 7: Blockchain-Based Security for Cloud Data Storage

Mamoon Saeed and colleagues examine how blockchain can be harnessed to secure cloud data, using mechanisms like smart contracts and distributed consensus to strengthen integrity, confidentiality, and transparency.

Chapter 8: Smart Clouds: Integrating AI, ML, and Blockchain

C.V. Suresh Babu and Sakthivel K. present an integrated framework for intelligent cloud platforms that combine analytics, blockchain, and automation to meet the growing demand for secure and data-driven cloud services.

Chapter 9: Synergizing Cloud and Blockchain Architectures

Sheraz Maki Mohd Ahmed and collaborators explore the complementarity of cloud scalability and blockchain immutability. The chapter provides insights into how this synergy can transform sectors like healthcare, finance, and governance.

Chapter 10: Integrated 5G and Edge Computing Framework

Ashok P. and a multidisciplinary team discuss how the convergence of 5G, edge computing, and cloud can address latency-sensitive IoT applications. This chapter highlights innovations that redefine network performance and resource management.

Chapter 11: Enhancing IoT through Cloud Computing

Salaheldin Edam and co-authors examine how cloud computing enhances IoT through efficient data handling, global scalability, and real-time analytics, paving the way for resilient and intelligent ecosystems.

Chapter 12: Managing Cloud Services on Sensor Nodes for Wireless Energy Harvesting

Muhammed Zaharadeen Ahmed and colleagues highlight the importance of energy-aware cloud service management on sensor nodes. The chapter focuses on integrating wireless energy harvesting to extend the lifespan of smart applications.

Chapter 13: Load Balancing in Cloud Computing with Genetic Algorithms

Abhipsha Das and her co-authors delve into optimization techniques, especially Genetic Algorithms, for efficient load balancing. This chapter proposes an adaptive and scalable approach for handling dynamic cloud workloads.

Chapter 14: Cloud-Based Predictive Analytics in Supply Chains

Rehab Ibrahim Ahmed Omer presents the transformative role of predictive analytics in supply chain optimization. Through cloud integration, companies gain real-time visibility and improved decision-making capabilities.

Chapter 15: Unbundling Cloud Computing in the Construction Industry

Sururah Bello and co-authors analyze the interplay of cloud computing and emergent technologies such as BIM and IoT in the construction sector. This chapter provides a roadmap for digital transformation within one of the world's largest and most traditional industries.

As we navigate an era defined by digitization and rapid technological evolution, this book offers a timely, essential resource for students, professionals, and decision-makers. We invite readers to explore the nuanced intersections of cloud computing with emerging technologies, security challenges, and real-world applications—and to envision the future of computing shaped by the cloud.

Aisha Hassan Abdalla Hashim
International Islamic University, Malaysia

Zeinab E. Ahmed
University of Gezira, Sudan

Othman O. Khalifa
International Islamic University, Malaysia

Rashid A. Saeed
Taif University, Saudi Arabia

Chapter 1
Essential Concepts in Cloud Computing

Fatima Ahmed Mohamed Abdalla
https://orcid.org/0009-0006-0756-4185
University Geomatika Malaysia, Malaysia

Noor Asiah Rashid
University Geomatika Malaysia, Malaysia

ABSTRACT

This chapter offers an in-depth review of the revolutionary development of cloud computing, from its theoretical underpinnings to its current position as a vital component of modern infrastructure for information technology. The historical trends, significant turning points, and technological advancements in the discipline are reviewed in this chapter. It explores the beginnings of cloud computing, how service models have changed over time, the effects of virtualization, and how new technologies are being incorporated. Readers will gain a profound appreciation for how cloud computing has transformed the operations and innovation of organizations by comprehending the historical background and recent developments.

INTRODUCTION TO CLOUD COMPUTING

By understanding these fundamental concepts, readers can grasp the essentials of cloud computing and its potential to transform their business or personal computing experiences. Several concepts and definitions can aid our understanding of cloud computing. The key concepts include the basic definition of cloud computing, service models, deployment models, essential characteristics, and future cloud computing evolution, so this chapter discusses all the mentioned topics and discusses the root

DOI: 10.4018/979-8-3693-9984-2.ch001

of cloud computing. The two primary justifications for using cloud computing CC are dependability and convenience. Cloud services are delivered via the Internet, so privacy and security must be the priority (Shahab Shamshirband et. Al. 2020). The main characteristics of Cloud Computing are categorized by the following elements:

- On-demand self-service: Consumers can automatically request the service based on their needs, without interacting with the service provider.
- Easy-to-access standardized mechanisms: Access to the service should always be possible from the Internet when policies permit.
- Resource pooling and multi-tenancy: sharing resources among multiple tenants can increase utilization and reduce operational costs.
- Rapid elasticity: the ability to scale resources in and out provides flexibility to provision resources on demand.
- Measured service: monitoring service conditions and measuring them enables resource optimisation.
- Auditability and certifiability: services should provide logs and trails that allow the traceability of policies to ensure their correct application is enforced (Radošević & Hongyu Pei-Breivold, 2014). Figure 1 shows the visual representation of Cloud Computing.

Figure 1. Cloud Computing Visual (https://www.spiceworks.com/tech/cloud/articles/what-is-cloud-computing/)

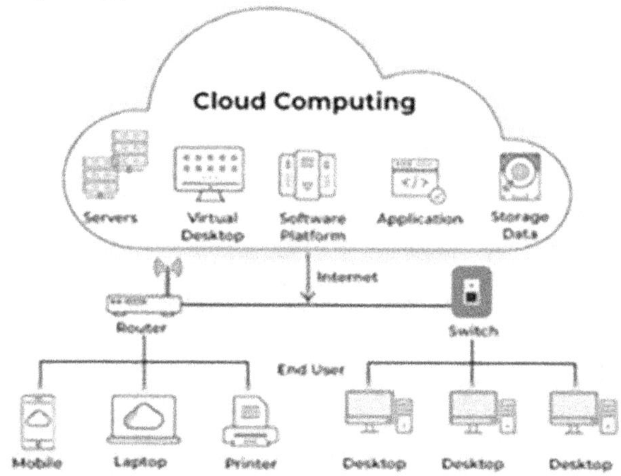

a) Definition and Overview

According to Mell and Grance (2011), and this is the most accepted definition of Cloud computing, cloud computing is a paradigm that enables users to access and store data and applications on distant servers instead of local hardware. According to Armbrust et al. (2010), this technology offers flexibility, scalability, and cost-effectiveness by allowing users to access computational resources via the Internet. However, the most adopted definition of cloud computing is by Mell and Grance (2011) in academia. Infrastructure as a Service (IaaS), Platform as a Service (PaaS), and Software as a Service (SaaS) are the three paradigms into which cloud services are commonly divided (Zhang, Cheng, & Boutaba, 2010). IaaS enables companies to scale their infrastructure up or down in response to demand by providing virtualized computer resources via the Internet. PaaS offers a platform that lets users create, execute, and oversee applications without having to deal with the hassle of constructing and maintaining the supporting infrastructure. SaaS makes high-quality software available to a large audience by delivering software programs over the Internet on a subscription basis (Mell & Grance, 2011; Zhang, Cheng, & Boutaba, 2010).

b) Historical Context and Evolution

The concept of cloud computing has evolved significantly over time. Its roots can be traced back to the 1960s when computer scientist John McCarthy opined that "computation may someday be organized as a public utility" (McCarthy, 1961). The advent of the internet in the 1990s and advancements in virtualization technologies in the 2000s propelled the development of cloud computing (Foster et al., 2008). In the early stages, companies like Google and Amazon began to harness the power of distributed computing to manage their vast amounts of data and traffic, paving the way for the modern cloud computing landscape (Armbrust et al., 2010). This transformation was driven by a need for greater efficiency, flexibility, and cost savings in managing IT resources (Buyya et al., 2009).

Cloud computing has transformed the way individuals and organizations access and utilize technology. This chapter delves into the evolution of cloud computing, tracing its origins from early computing concepts to its status as a cornerstone of modern IT infrastructure. The evolution of a data center into a private cloud is a transformation of the business process streamlining with IT operation from a data center to the cloud, where the user discovers the operation much more effectively and efficiently. Cloud computing is slowly becoming the Internet's lifeblood. Most Internet users use popular but common websites like Facebook, LinkedIn, and Twitter, all of which rely on cloud computing. In addition to this, individuals use cloud storage-dependent apps like YouTube, Gmail, and others. (Rafat Ara, at.el 2020).

c) Early Concepts and Foundations (1960s-1990s)

When we consider the cloud, we often fail to recall the times before the 21st century. Given everything, it has indeed been an absurd decade or so during which the concept truly began to shape into the colossal, universal, and astonishing behemoth we recognise today. However, the foundational ideas of the cloud have existed for many years and, believe it or not, can be traced back to the 1950s with centralised computing. In those early days, centralised computing systems were massive machines and, remarkably, quite expensive, far too costly to even contemplate acquiring and maintaining one for every single employee (Babita Bhagat et al., 2021).

As stated above, the origins of cloud computing can be found in the 1960s, a time when networking and computer technology advanced significantly. Future advancements in networking and computing were made possible by the concepts put out by visionaries such as J.C.R. Licklider regarding a worldwide computer network that would enable users to access data and programs from any location.

d) ARPANET and Networking Innovations

To get to the origins of the Internet, we must go back in time to 1957. You may not recall, but it was the International Geophysical Year, a year dedicated to gathering information about the upper atmosphere during a period of intense solar activity. Eisenhower announced in 1955 that, as part of the activities, the USA hoped to launch a small satellite into Earth orbit. The Kremlin announced that it hoped to do likewise. Planning in America focused on a sophisticated three-stage rocket, but in Russia, they took a more direct approach. Strapping four military rockets together, on 4 October 1957, the USSR launched Sputnik I (a 70 kgs bleeping sphere the size of a medicine ball) into Earth orbit (Kirstein, 1999).

The evolution of the Internet began with the launch of Sputnik I in 1957, which prompted the U.S. to establish the Advanced Research Projects Agency (ARPA). ARPA initiated pioneering computing research, leading to the concept of computer networking. Key contributors such as John Licklider and Leonard Kleinrock envisioned a "Galactic Network," where messages were divided into packets for flexible, secure transmission. This vision culminated in the 1969 launch of ARPANET, connecting UCLA and Stanford. ARPANET quickly expanded to link multiple universities, marking the dawn of true computer networking (Jacksi & Abass, 2019).

During the 1970s and early 1980s, networking advanced significantly. Innovations like email, host-to-host communication, and TCP/IP protocols made the system more powerful and scalable. By adopting TCP/IP in 1982, ARPANET laid the groundwork for what would become the Internet. Government-funded networks like NSFNet expanded access across educational institutions, while open protocols encouraged global collaboration and technological innovation. Meanwhile, private and academic sectors began developing new services and networking tools, leading to increasing international adoption and the birth of early internet services like Usenet and Bitnet (Schafer & Serres, 2016).

The final transformation occurred with the World Wide Web, proposed by Tim Berners-Lee at CERN in 1989. The introduction of HTTP, HTML, and web browsers like Mosaic revolutionised how users accessed and shared information. What had been a tool for scientists became a mainstream platform for communication, commerce, and content. Commercial web activity surged as user-friendly interfaces, improved infrastructure, and widespread PC use drove explosive growth. By the mid-1990s, the Web expanded rapidly, with millions of hosts and websites, ushering in the digital age and fundamentally reshaping global society (The National Science and Media Museum, 2025).

e) Virtualization and Time-Sharing

The advent of virtualization technology in the 1970s made it possible for several users to share a primary computer's resources. This resource sharing was made possible by IBM's virtual machine operating system, which offered separate environments for various users. The future of cloud computing was greatly influenced by this time-sharing concept, which emphasised effective resource use. Mobile cloud computing (MCC), a new computing paradigm that is significant today, allows mobile devices to offload computations to the remote cloud, thereby reducing their limits (Shahab Shamshirband, et al. 2022).

f) The Birth of the World Wide Web

The early 1990s marked a significant turning point with the advent of the World Wide Web. This innovation revolutionised how data could be accessed and shared globally, creating a fertile environment for cloud computing to emerge. Companies like Salesforce began offering Software as a Service (SaaS), which allowed users to access applications over the Internet rather than installing them locally (Devadiga et al., 2021).

g) The Emergence of Cloud Computing (2000-2011)

In the early 2000s, the term "cloud computing" became well-known as businesses realised how scalable and affordable it might be. Amazon Web Services (AWS) and Elastic Compute Cloud: In 2002, Amazon introduced AWS, which offers core cloud services like computing and storage. The 2006 launch of Elastic Compute Cloud (EC2), which enables users to rent virtual servers on demand, was especially revolutionary. This signaled a dramatic change away from more rigid IT infrastructure paradigms and towards more adaptable cloud-based solutions. Because these services allow businesses to rent storage and processing capacity on demand, they set the groundwork for scalable, cost-effective infrastructure.

h) Google's Contributions

Google also significantly advanced cloud computing. With the release of Google App Engine in 2008, programmers could create and host apps on Google's infrastructure. This further proved that cloud platforms are a viable option for hosting services and apps. Because cloud computing makes it possible to access computer services globally through the internet, it has revolutionized data access and storage. Databases, networking, servers, software, storage, analytics, AI, ML, and BI are some of these services. Pay-as-you-use mechanisms in its design facilitate cost effectiveness, scalability, and innovation. Third-party providers, including Google Cloud Platform (GCP), Microsoft Azure, and AWS, offer cloud services. In addition to highlighting current market trends and opportunities, this study investigates these suppliers (Borra, 2024).

i) The Rise of Public Cloud Services

By 2011, the term "cloud computing" was well-known and widely used in a variety of sectors. A proliferation of cloud service providers resulted from organisations embracing public cloud services due to their cost-effectiveness, scalability, and flexibility. When cloud providers introduced cutting-edge services like machine learning, big data analytics, and IoT (Internet of Things) support, the potential applications for cloud computing expanded (Hassan et al., 2022).

j) Cloud Model Evolution (2012-Present)

Several service models were developed as cloud computing advanced to accommodate a range of business requirements. As mobile devices become more and more common in daily life, Mobile Cloud Computing (MCC) has become a paradigm to solve the limited processing capabilities and energy constraints of mobile devices by allowing computation to be offloaded into the distant cloud. Numerous studies have examined MCC's privacy and security concerns, as well as how the combination of cloud and mobile computing has exacerbated these concerns. Shahab Shamshirband and colleagues, 2020

Scaling and deploying applications become easier as serverless computing and containerization become more widely used. Because public cloud services enable businesses to develop more rapidly and efficiently, they have become indispensable to efforts at digital transformation. Previously, providers focused on improving security, compliance, and global reach to overcome the issues that had hindered adoption.

By 2025, 95% of emerging workloads are going to be housed on the cloud, predicts Gartner. Organizations must modify their tactics to take advantage of the flexibility and affordability that come with cloud computing to stay competitive. Forecasts suggest that worldwide spending on cloud services infrastructure will surpass $1 trillion by 2024, propelled by several dominant patterns, including the growing need for cutting-edge platforms and as-a-service solutions, especially those that include artificial intelligence. Cloud computing is becoming more widely acknowledged by businesses as a strategic tool for promoting innovation, improving agility, and attaining success in a variety of industries, in addition to being a way to cut costs. The increasing use of advanced AI, particularly ChatGPT, and the rising cost of cloud computing are driving trends in cloud computing. To increase productivity and improve client relations, businesses are actively moving their operations to cloud-based systems.

Businesses will continue to use cloud services to gain access to cutting-edge technologies, increasing their overall operational efficiency in the process. Because cloud computing eliminates the need to construct or purchase costly infrastructure, which is essential for enabling these resource-intensive operations, it makes new technologies more accessible (Sapkal et al., 2024). This chapter functions as an essential introduction, offering the fundamental information required to comprehend the more complex and wide-ranging concepts in cloud computing. Key elements, including service types (IaaS, PaaS, and SaaS), deployment patterns (public, private, hybrid, and community), and enabling technologies (distributed systems, virtualization, internet connectivity, and scalability) are all skillfully covered by the writers. Regardless of readers past knowledge, this comprehensive overview guarantees that they gain a foundational understanding of the important terms and procedures that are mentioned in the following chapters.

3. CLOUD COMPUTING MILESTONES

The development of Grid computing was developed in the mid-1990s to offer shared access to supercomputers and other high-performance computing resources. Grid computing was a precursor of cloud computing (Foster & Kesselman, 1999). According to Berman, Fox, and Hey (2003), this technique established the fundamental ideas of resource sharing, scalability, and remote access that are essential to cloud computing. The goal of grid computing was to fuse the processing capacity of several geographically separated computers into a virtual supercomputer. Research undertakings and intricate scientific calculations that needed a lot of processing power were made easier by this method (Foster & Kesselman, 1999; Berman, Fox, & Hey, 2003). Figure 2 shows the cloud computing milestones.

Figure 2. Cloud Computing Milestones (https://www.cogentinfo.com/resources/the-evolution-of-cloud-computing-trends-and-emerging-technologies-shaping-2025)

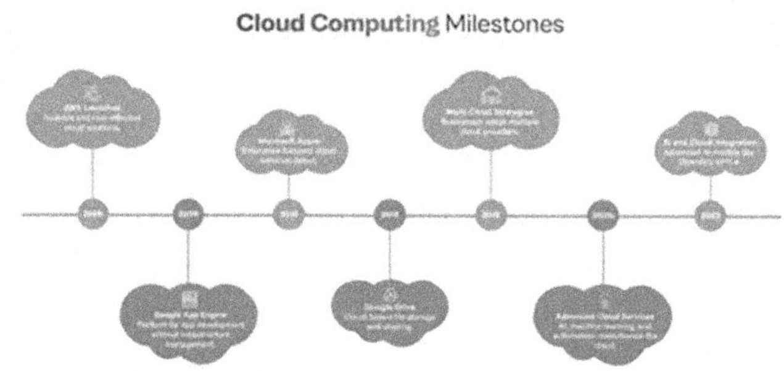

a) Virtualisation Technologies' Role

Cloud computing was made possible by virtualization technologies like VMware and Xen, which allowed several virtual machines to operate on a single physical machine (Rosenblum & Garfinkel, 2005). This development made it easier to create flexible, on-demand services and enabled more effective use of computing resources (Barham et al., 2003). Because the hardware layer was abstracted by virtualisation, several operating systems and apps could share resources on a single server. According to Rosenblum and Garfinkel (2005), this solution not only increased resource utilisation but also offered improved security and isolation for various workloads. Cloud computing's foundation was its capacity to scale up or down in response to demand and dynamically assign resources (Barham et al., 2003).

b) The Origin of Infrastructure as a Service (IaaS)

IaaS, or infrastructure as a service, was created to meet the need for affordable and scalable computer resources. With the introduction of Elastic Compute Cloud (EC2) by Amazon Web Services (AWS) in 2006, consumers may access virtualised computer resources online (Barr, 2006). This was a significant step forward for cloud computing since it allowed companies to access and grow their infrastructure as needed (Buyya et al., 2009). By introducing a pay-as-you-go subscription model, Infrastructure as a Service (IaaS) reduced the need for large upfront investments in physical equipment. As a result, startups and small firms now have access to powerful computing skills that allow them to compete with larger enterprises (Barr, 2006; Buyya et al., 2009).

4. CLOUD SERVICE MODEL EVOLUTION

The development of cloud service models has completely changed how people and organisations use, manage, and access computer resources. From the beginning of simple infrastructure services to the present day of complex, managed platforms, the development of cloud service models has been characterised by constant innovation and modification to satisfy a wide range of intricate requirements.

Three main paradigms are used by cloud computing to supply services: Software as a Service (SaaS), Platform as a Service (PaaS), and Infrastructure as a Service (IaaS). From managing raw computer resources to implementing fully complete software solutions, these models address a wide range of user needs. With distinct benefits and solutions for problems, each model reflects a varying degree of abstraction and control over the underlying infrastructure (Babita Bhagat et al., 2021).

Infrastructure as a Service (IaaS): Early Stages

The fundamental cloud service concept, Infrastructure as a Service (IaaS), offers virtualised computer resources via the internet. IaaS allows customers to provision and maintain basic computing components like virtual machines, storage, and networking without having to buy real hardware. Businesses can optimise costs and increase flexibility by using this strategy to scale resources up or down in response to demand (Krintz, 2017).

In 2006, Amazon Web Services (AWS) introduced its Elastic Compute Cloud (EC2), making it one of the first IaaS providers. EC2 opened the door for a new age of cloud computing by enabling users to rent virtual servers and change capacity in real time (Amazon Web Services, 2023). Other software behemoths like Microsoft

Azure and Google Cloud Platform (GCP) were influenced by AWS's success in creating their own IaaS products, which further cemented the model's acceptance and popularity.

c) Service-Based Platform (PaaS)

Platform as a Service (PaaS) was created in response to the growing demand for increasingly complex solutions that abstracted the maintenance of the underlying infrastructure as cloud technology developed. By providing a complete platform for creating, executing, and maintaining applications, PaaS offers a higher level of abstraction. Operating systems, development tools, middleware, and databases are all included in this approach, which frees developers from worrying about maintaining their hardware and software so they can concentrate on writing code and creating apps (TechTerms, 2023).

One of the earliest PaaS products was the Google App Engine, which debuted in 2008. It streamlined the development process and sped up time-to-market by enabling developers to create and launch web apps utilising the infrastructure provided by Google. Other well-known PaaS solutions with distinctive features and capabilities catered to various development requirements are IBM Bluemix, Heroku, and Microsoft Azure App Services. With Platform as a Service (PaaS), developers may construct programs and apps and distribute them over a network without having to install or manage the production environment. Software-defined servers and associated resources can be rented by clients using PaaS to run pre-existing software or develop and test the newest. The customer has no control over the operating systems, servers, networks, or storage in the cloud. The client oversees the programs and their configuration, nevertheless (Chnar Mustafa Mohammed & Subhi R. M. Zeebaree,2021). PaaS is an excellent fit for startups and small businesses for the following two basic reasons. First off, it's reasonably priced, allowing smaller companies to use state-of-the-art equipment without breaking the bank (Comptia.org, 2024).

PaaS is evolving along with technology these days. Amazon Web Services (AWS) is a cloud provider that offers physical data centers and servers as well as technical services, including databases, storage, and processing power. Because Platform as a Service, or PaaS, removes the need to build solutions, it helps teams save time and money. Instead, they can focus on determining which features and features are most appropriate for the required solution and then choose a pre-built platform that provides the essential characteristics of the desired code (https:u-next.com,2022). An example of PaaS in cloud computing is as below:

SAP Cloud

Instead of being a platform in and of itself, SAP Cloud is a vast suite of applications that enables you to create apps in several industries. SAP Cloud now has just over 1300 apps, all of which are available online. comprises some SAP cloud-based services, all of which are designed to assist businesses in increasing output, fostering innovation, and streamlining processes. For instance, SAP HANA Cloud supports time series, vector, relational, document store, graph, and geospatial data. One of the main characteristics is the ability to use generative AI to develop applications.

Microsoft Azure

Microsoft Azure is an infrastructure and cloud computing platform designed by Microsoft to build, distribute, and manage services and apps via a global network of data centres under Microsoft management. Along with supporting a wide range of programming languages, tools, and frameworks—including both Microsoft-specific and third-party applications and systems—it offers both PaaS and IaaS services. The enormous scalability of Azure Storage allows a user to store and handle hundreds of terabytes of data, supporting the big data scenarios needed by media, financial, and scientific applications. For a small business website, the user can also save the minimal quantities of data needed (Pandit & Pandit, 2021)

It is a fully functional cloud computing platform from Microsoft that offers a range of services for developing, deploying, and managing applications and services through data centres managed by Microsoft. With Microsoft Azure, you may write code in Node.js, PHP, or ASP.NET. It helps companies build the simplest possible capacity to easily move all their apps and infrastructure. It provides mobile services as well as extensive business analytics apps. (Microsoft). Office 365 and Dynamics 365, among other Microsoft services and products, can be integrated with Microsoft Azure. Microsoft Azure is a cost-effective architecture that is adaptable to serve a wide range of services since it provides the infrastructure for a variety of services, hybrid capabilities, strong security features, resource scalability based on demand, and a globally accessible network.

Google App Engine

Google App Engine is a Platform as a Service (PaaS), representing Google's internal infrastructure as a cloud platform. It stands apart from other cloud platforms due to its unique attributes, allowing for the hosting of web applications in Google-managed data centres. Applications are executed virtually across multiple servers and data centres. The architecture of GAE is highly complex, as it incorporates over a million servers distributed geographically around the globe ((Mahesh K et al., 2019)

Google App Engine, which is a part of Google Cloud, offers highly scalable tools and apps that you can include in your company. Numerous languages are supported by Google App Engine, which is very easy to use and compatible with many APIs. Because Google manages the infrastructure, you can focus on developing code. This is a crucial aspect that may lead a developer to utilise additional tools like cloud monitoring, cloud logging, and diagnostic error reporting. In the meantime, Google provides choices for application security, such as an App Engine firewall and managed SSL/TLS certificates.

Oracle Cloud Platform

Oracle Cloud Infrastructure (OCI) is a full suite of public cloud services that let users create and execute a variety of applications in a high-performance, scalable, secure, and highly available setting. (Corporation, 2022). The Oracle Cloud Platform is mostly utilised by businesses. Both Oracle and non-Oracle applications can run well on Oracle Cloud Platform's servers. It is very safe and provides great flexibility with APIs. Dedicated cloud and artificial intelligence, machine learning and developer tools, multi-cloud and hybrid cloud, and Oracle Cloud Infrastructure (OCI) are some of the main features of the Oracle Cloud Platform. Oracle Cloud Platform enables multi-cloud scenarios and integrates with other cloud providers like AWS and Google Cloud. Additionally, it includes prebuilt models and tools for increasing the intelligence of apps.

IBM Cloud Foundry

IBM Cloud Foundry is an open-source PaaS example that has been steadily rising to prominence and offers some useful capabilities. Some of the languages that IBM Cloud Foundry supports are Python, Ruby, PHP, and Java. IBM Cloud Foundry offers a platform-as-a-service (PaaS) for developing, testing, and launching apps, providing an infrastructure-free environment. Ibm.com. Regarding cloud computing, by moving outdated apps to the cloud, this platform helps with their update (IBM, 2023).

Red Hat OpenShift

It is a platform that greatly simplifies the process of developing and releasing apps. The user is never constrained by the platform's capabilities due to its compatibility with numerous APIs. Red Hat OpenShift offers several capabilities, including a straightforward user interface that can be utilised by internal security teams to prevent unauthorised access and deter intrusions (Red Hat, 2024). For OpenShift Dedicated, Red Hat offers a written product life cycle so that partners and customers can efficiently plan, implement, and maintain their platform-based applications. To be as transparent as possible, Red Hat discloses its life cycle and may deviate from these guidelines when disagreements emerge.(Red Hat, 2025)

AWS Lambda

With AWS Lambda, a serverless computing solution from Amazon Web Services (AWS), you can run your code without having to worry about maintaining or configuring servers. Complementary services to various AWS services that can be integrated and include serverless architecture are provided by the AWS cloud (amazon.com/docs.aws). With features like high availability, optimised performance, and minimal server maintenance, AWS is incredibly fault-tolerant and built to protect user programs from machine language errors, guaranteeing error-free and flawless operation (Amazon Web Services, 2024).

Software as a Service (SaaS)

Software as a Service (SaaS) is one of the most well-known and consumer-facing cloud service models. Users no longer need to install and maintain software on their local devices thanks to SaaS, which distributes software programs via the internet. SaaS applications can be accessed by users via web browsers, which makes them easy and available from any location with an internet connection. Customer Relationship Management (CRM) software was transformed by Salesforce, a leader in the SaaS industry, by providing it as a cloud-based service. Businesses of all sizes can now use robust software without having to make a sizable upfront investment thanks to this strategy, which democratized access to cutting-edge CRM technologies. Other well-known SaaS programs that have become essential components of contemporary corporate operations are Adobe Creative Cloud, Microsoft Office 365, and Google Workspace.

d) Function as a Service (FaaS) and Serverless Computing

Serverless computing, or Function as a Service (FaaS), is an advancement of cloud service models that further abstracts server management. FaaS enables programmers to create and implement discrete functions or code segments that are run in reaction to events. The underlying infrastructure is automatically managed by the cloud provider, which scales resources up or down in response to demand.

One of the earliest FaaS products, AWS Lambda, was released in 2014 and helped popularise the serverless computing concept. By only charging users for the actual computation time used by their functions, FaaS lowers operational overhead and expenses, which makes it a desirable choice for microservices architectures and event-driven applications (Amazon Web Services, 2023).

e) Hybrid and Multi-Cloud Strategies

Many businesses are choosing hybrid and multi-cloud strategies as cloud computing becomes more widely used to maximise performance, lower risk, and stay away from vendor lock-in. By combining private and public cloud resources, a hybrid cloud enables companies to keep sensitive data on-site while using public cloud services' scalability and affordability for other workloads. Using several cloud service providers to satisfy various business requirements or improve resilience is known as a multi-cloud strategy. Organisations can increase flexibility and reduce reliance on a single cloud provider by dividing workloads among many clouds. By selecting the most appropriate cloud services for workloads, this method also helps firms maximise overall performance and cost-effectiveness.

f) Edge Computing

One notable development in cloud service models is the emergence of edge computing. By bringing processing capacity closer to the data source, edge computing lowers latency and permits real-time processing. For Internet of Things (IoT) applications, where device-generated data needs to be handled rapidly and effectively, this approach is especially pertinent.

On the other hand, cloud computing offers a great deal of flexibility regarding computing power and data storage. Some providers offer access to services using the pay-as-you-go formula, which lowers initial investments by providing precise billing based on the amount of time and computational capacity needed. Easy-to-use services are made possible by cloud providers' user-friendly graphical interfaces and handling of hardware upkeep. The flexibility to easily expand storage spaces and change components, even temporarily, is what gives the design its scalability and is essential for handling workload surges (Andriulo et al., 2024)

By reducing the need to send massive amounts of data to centralised cloud data centres, edge computing improves user experience and facilitates the expansion of IoT devices. Organisations can now install and maintain edge apps with ease thanks to major cloud providers' integration of edge computing features into their offerings. Edge computing and cloud computing are indeed complementary technologies that work well together to provide a comprehensive solution for modern data processing and administration. At the network's edge, edge computing closes the source of data production and handles data locally. This reduces delay and bandwidth usage. Following processing, the information can be transferred to the cloud for further analysis, long-term storage, or integration with other data sources. Real-time processing is necessary for immediate actions based on sensor data and other real-time data processing needs. After the first edge processing, the data can be aggregated and moved to the cloud for batch processing, machine learning, and advanced analytics. Retail, health care, and smart cities all make extensive use of edge computing. Edge computing can process real-time data from sensors and traffic lights, while cloud computing handles analytics and general city administration. While medical records are stored on the cloud and

g) Machine learning and artificial intelligence as a service (MLaaS and AIaaS)

Cloud computing and artificial intelligence (AI) have advanced quickly, leading to the creation of AI as a Service (AIaaS), a cloud-based approach that enables developers and enterprises to take advantage of AI capabilities without requiring a lot of processing power or specialized knowledge. A game-changing paradigm in cloud computing is Artificial Intelligence as a Service (AIaaS), which allows consumers and enterprises to access AI-powered solutions without having to make large investments in infrastructure and knowledge. AIaaS makes AI more accessible by offering on-demand access to a variety of AI-powered services, including computer vision, natural language processing, machine learning models, and predictive analytics. A scalable, affordable, and easily available solution, AIaaS is being used by businesses more and more for automation, decision-making, and data analysis. (Ikwueze, 2024).

Cloud services for artificial intelligence (AI) and machine learning (ML) have emerged because of the growing demand for these technologies. Pre-built models, tools, and infrastructure are offered by AIaaS and MLaaS for creating, honing, and implementing AI and ML applications. These services enable businesses to use cutting-edge AI and ML technologies without the need for expensive gear or specialised knowledge. Examples of AIaaS and MLaaS products that enable companies to leverage the potential of AI and ML for a range of use cases, such as computer vision, natural language processing, and predictive analytics, include Amazon SageMaker, Google AI Platform, and Microsoft Azure Machine Learning.

h) Containers and Kubernetes

Many technologies, such as Kubernetes and Docker containerization technologies, have significantly changed how developers build and implement web applications nowadays. With the introduction of Docker in 2013, it became simpler to package applications and their dependencies. The resulting containers are lightweight and capable of operating in any environment. The "it works on my machine" problem is lessened by this feature because the containers operate consistently throughout the developer's local environment, on-premises servers, and the cloud. (Pahl et al., 2019). Docker containers are smaller, start up faster, use less resources than virtual machines, and have a shared host operating system kernel because they are designed to be lightweight, nimble, and limited. Docker and Kubernetes collaborate as a container orchestrator.

The procedures of container distribution, growth, and operation across clusters are managed by Kubernetes, even if Docker provides the methods for building the containers and using them in processes. By maintaining and distributing the application components among available resources, Kubernetes does this through load balancing for applications (Brendan Burn et al., 2022). Kubernetes oversees monitoring the state of the containers, including the potential to restart built-in containers when necessary or expand their analytical capacity in response to an increase in requests from the load-balanced IP addresses that were received. The Kubernetes system is ideal for large systems with multiple microservices-based sub-applications because of this degree of automation.

Containerization, which outlines how to put an application and its requirements in a single vessel, is a strong feature of modern cloud computing. In the end, this has altered the way web applications are created, implemented, and managed in many contexts. Pre-containerization, which involved redistributing the apps and services, resulted in inconsistent platforms and compatibility problems that decreased productivity (Pahl et al., 2019). To solve these issues, containers package the software along with all its associated libraries and customisations, as well as the anticipated contexts. Business solutions were made possible by Docker's containerization recommendations, which introduced lighter containers that are simple to build, deploy, and maintain. By running apps in a Docker container on top of the host operating system, Docker containerises programs. As far as the kernel is concerned, it is like other containers; however, neither one contains the other's content nor does it. Docker containers' flexibility in resource availability makes this method less expensive than traditional virtual machines(Alsaffar & Alezzy, 2022)" Docker is a popular tool used by developers in businesses today to create and implement scalable apps. Since containerization has become more and more widespread, it is necessary to operate several containers in different states. This led to the development of the most dependable and well-liked container orchestration platform, Kubernetes.

A program called Kubernetes was created to supervise the operation of apps on a group of computers running in containers. Its purpose is to make it easier to deploy these applications across the available computers and scale the running applications. Therefore, using Kubernetes to help orchestrate containers enables complicated microservices configuration and guarantees high availability through load balancing (Brendan Burn et al., 2022). Another reason for choosing containerization is the requirement for a flexible method of deploying apps across many cloud platforms. An effective and feasible method for moving applications from on-site infrastructure to cloud-based infrastructure is required by enterprises, as different cloud providers offer a variety of services and infrastructures. Containerization provides this flexibility because apps may be packaged once and installed anywhere, regardless of the hardware's structure. Customers who employ hybrid or multi-cloud computing have found this functionality particularly helpful since it reduces the likelihood of vendor lock-in and is less expensive. (Bangar Raju Cherukuri, 2024).

Cloud service models have advanced with the use of orchestration and containerisation technology. Applications and their dependencies are packaged into separate parts by containers, which provide consistency across various environments. The deployment, scaling, and administration of containerised applications are automated by the open-source container orchestration platform Kubernetes. By improving scalability and portability, containers and Kubernetes let businesses develop and implement apps more effectively. The adoption of containerisation and orchestration is made easier by cloud providers' managed Kubernetes services, such as Google Kubernetes Engine (GKE), Amazon Elastic Kubernetes Service (EKS), and Azure Kubernetes Service (AKS).

i) Quantum Cloud Computing

A new field called “quantum cloud computing” uses the concepts of quantum computing to tackle challenging issues that traditional computing is unable to handle. Researchers and developers can investigate quantum algorithms and applications by using quantum cloud services, which give access to quantum computers and development tools.

Examples of quantum cloud solutions that open the door to innovations in domains including material science, cryptography, and optimisation include IBM Quantum Experience, Microsoft Azure Quantum, and Google Quantum AI. Even though it is still in its infancy, quantum cloud computing has the potential to transform computing power and solve problems that conventional computers cannot. The dynamic nature of technology and the constant push for innovation are reflected in the development of cloud service models. Every development stage, from the early IaaS model to the more sophisticated AIaaS and quantum cloud computing, has given people and companies new possibilities and capacities. The future is full of exciting opportunities to improve accessibility, scalability, and efficiency in the digital world as cloud technology develops. A new area that has the potential to completely transform computing power is quantum cloud computing. Organisations can address complicated issues that are now unsolvable with traditional computers by utilising the concepts of quantum computing. Advances in domains like simulation, optimisation, and cryptography will be made possible by quantum cloud services.

Because quantum computing is a cost technology that reacts rapidly to changes in its surroundings, it can operate in very faraway locations. It is possible to install quantum computers in a highly isolated data centre and have them service the server's endpoints. Researchers can use a platform service that allows them to use quantum algorithms and applications under the concept known as quantum cloud computing (Golec, Muhammad, et al. 2024)

j) Cloud Architecture

Cloud computing is a model for enabling universal, on-demand and convenient network access to a shared pool of configurable computing resources (e.g., networks servers, storage, applications, and services) that can be rapidly provisioned and released with minimal management effort or service provider interaction" .".oud computing can be seen as network- enabled services that provide scalable, QoS guaranteed services on demand that can be accessed over the Internet. Cloud computing allows for the sharing of resources over the Internet. These resources are shared using infrastructure provided by a cloud service provider (CSP).

The cloud consumer accesses the resources, which are scalable and ubiquitous, on-demand as–you–use and pay– as–you–go basis. Cloud computing also enables a level of abstraction between the required computing resource and the underlying Cloud computing is a model that facilitates universal, on-demand, and convenient network access to a shared pool of reconfigurable computing resources (such as servers, networks, storage, apps, and services) that can be quickly provisioned and released with little management work or interaction from service providers. One way to think of cloud computing is as network-enabled services that offer scalable, quality-of-service (QoS) guaranteed services that are available over the Internet whenever needed. Resources can be shared online thanks to cloud computing.

Cloud service providers (CSPs) provide the infrastructure for sharing these resources. The cloud consumer has access to resources that are widely available, scalable, and pay-as-you-go or on-demand. A degree of abstraction between the necessary computing resources and the underlying use architecture, including storage, networks, and services, is also made possible by cloud computing. The client and server, as well as the three main service delivery types, are all included in cloud computing. The hardware or software abstraction layer used to connect to cloud services is called a cloud client. The three main service delivery methods are offered by the CSPs via servers.

Although there are many kinds of service delivery, the three main ones are Software-as-a-Service (SaaS), Infrastructure-as-a-Service (IaaS), and Platform-as-a-Service (PaaS). Through the infrastructure that a cloud service provider provides, PaaS offers a computing platform for users to use. A CSP's platform can be used by the user to create, test, and launch an application. The necessary software does not need to be installed by the user. The CSP offers the customer infrastructure in the form of servers, storage, and processing power in IaaS. The user does not need to invest in expensive IT infrastructure, which is an advantage. Services are available on demand and are expandable. Additionally, the consumer uses and pays for the food they consume. With SaaS, a CSP gives a customer access to an application via the Internet. Essentially, the user is not required to buy or install this software. The consumer has remote access to software that is managed from a central location using a network-based system.

In cloud computing, cloud architecture refers to the various components and configurations that make up a system. Front-end platform components (Ara Shapla et al., 2020): This part of the cloud architecture that communicates with users is made up of:

- Web Browser: People use web browsers or mobile apps to access cloud services.
- Devices including PCs, tablets, and smartphones that make use of cloud services, are known as client devices.

The infrastructure and services that support cloud computing are referred to as the back-end platform. These include:

- Servers are real or virtual computers that run applications and store data.
- Storage: Systems that store data include object storage and databases.
- The components that ensure connectivity between different cloud infrastructure components are known as networking elements.
- Data centers house the physical infrastructure used by cloud providers (Nanda Banger et al., 2022).

Cloud-Based Delivery: This describes the methods used to supply cloud services, including:

- Virtualised computer resources can be accessed online using Infrastructure as a Service (IaaS). Google Compute Engine and AWS EC2 are two examples.
- A platform for developing, testing, and deploying applications is offered by Platform as a Service (PaaS). Google App Engine and Microsoft Azure are two examples.
- Online software packages are offered by Software as a Service (SaaS). Google Workspace and Microsoft 365 are two common examples.

To cut expenses, the design must consider several factors, including scalability, elasticity, reliability, security, and cost-effectiveness.

k) Cloud Migration

Cloud migration is the process of moving information, applications, and other digital assets from an organization's on-premises data centre to a cloud provider's data centre. This change may have several benefits, such as lower costs, increased performance, and scalability (oracle.com). There may be many benefits, even if cloud migration is a significant project that requires careful planning and execution. The following actions are necessary for successful cloud migration:

1. Assessment: Examine the current IT infrastructure to see if data and apps can be moved to the cloud.
2. Planning: Develop a comprehensive migration plan that addresses resources, due dates, and potential risks.
3. Testing: Conduct thorough testing to ensure that programs and data operate as intended in the cloud environment.
4. Execution: Follow the plan while moving data and apps to ensure minimal disruption to operations.
5. Optimisation: Monitor the cloud environment and make the required modifications to enhance efficiency and save expenses.

Several challenges could arise because of the migration process:

1. Data security: Ensuring that data is transferred and stored on the cloud securely.
2. Downtime: Reduce downtime during the relocation process to avoid business disruptions.
3. Compatibility refers to confirming that apps and data are appropriate for the cloud environment.

3. THE FUTURE EVOLUTION OF CLOUD COMPUTING

Cloud computing has completely changed how companies function by providing scalable, adaptable, and reasonably priced options for managing, processing, and storing data. Cloud computing has tremendous prospects for the future as technology develops more, which could further change sectors and improve corporate procedures. One of the major developments influencing the direction of cloud computing in the future is the use of multi-cloud and hybrid cloud strategies. To improve resilience, minimise vendor lock-in, and maximise performance, businesses are increasingly using numerous cloud providers1. The best of both worlds in terms of scalability and cost-effectiveness is provided by hybrid cloud solutions, which integrate public and private clouds. A multi-cloud strategy involves the use of cloud services from many cloud providers, such as AWS, Google Cloud, and Microsoft Azure, within the same IT architecture. Figure 3 shows the cloud computing service model.

Figure 3. Cloud Service Model https://x.com/miota_teknologi/status/1456533608420675585)

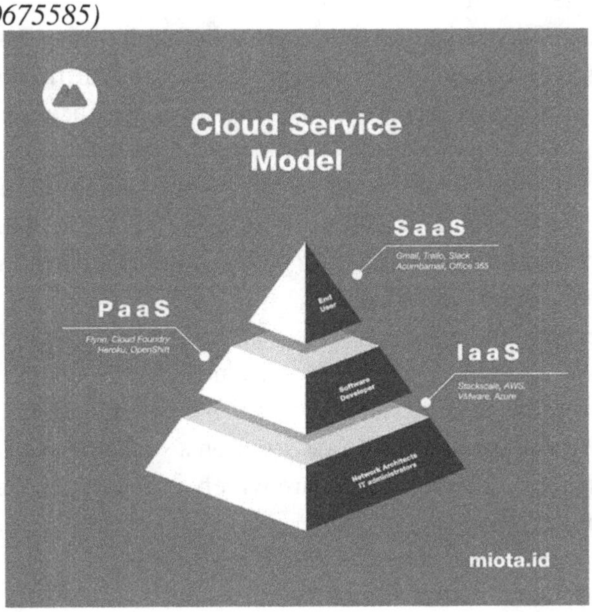

a) Serverless Computing

Although traditional infrastructure management still poses major operational issues, cloud computing has completely changed how businesses deploy and maintain their apps. Serverless computing has become a paradigm shift in this regard, radically changing the way developers work with cloud infrastructure. Serverless computing is a major departure from traditional cloud deployment tactics since it removes the need for server administration and introduces a pay-per-use model. Through automatic scaling and event-driven execution models, this architectural approach has gained significant support in recent years, promises to optimize resource use while reducing operational complexity.

Another new trend that is anticipated to gain popularity in the upcoming years is serverless computing. This paradigm change improves agility, scalability, and cost-effectiveness by enabling developers to create and execute applications without having to worry about maintaining server infrastructure. Developers can produce more inventive and effective solutions by putting more emphasis on inventions than infrastructure management.

The main tenet of serverless architecture is the implementation of an advanced layer of automation that manages the underlying hardware difficulties, hence eliminating the need for direct server control. Organizations can concentrate on application logic rather than infrastructure issues thanks to this abstraction layer's intelligent management of container orchestration, network setups, and system maintenance. A smooth operating environment is produced by the implementation, which includes automatic resource provisioning, security patch management, and system upgrades (Nagendra & Kundavaram, 2024).

With serverless computing, users can save money by just paying for the compute time they need. No costs for resources that are not used. Without requiring human intervention, it automatically adjusts resources based on workload, ensuring optimal performance. Well-known serverless solutions, such as AWS Lambda, Google Cloud Functions, and Microsoft Azure, are widely utilised in batch processing and event-driven applications.

b) Data Governance and Privacy

Strong data governance procedures and adhering to legal standards will be more crucial as cloud computing develops. Establishing trust in cloud settings requires protecting user privacy and data security. To preserve data integrity and adhere to legal requirements, organisations must put in place thorough data governance rules.

c) Containerization and Microservices

Microservices and containerisation are revolutionising the creation and implementation of applications. These methods expedite development, allowing for better resource utilisation and effective scaling1. Developers can construct more modular and robust systems by dissecting apps into smaller, more manageable components (The Cloud Native Experts, 2024).

Containerisation is a lightweight kind of virtualisation that encapsulates an application and its dependencies in a single, portable container. This makes it possible for programmers to ensure that an application runs consistently across different environments. Consistency is one of containerization's key benefits, ensuring that applications run consistently across development, testing, and production environments.

- Isolation: Each container runs independently to prevent conflicts between apps.
- Portability: Containers can be run on any system with a compatible container runtime, such Docker or Kubernetes.

The microservices architecture approach organises an application as a collection of loosely connected services, each responsible for a certain business function. Independent development, implementation, and scaling of microservices is possible.

The advantages of microservices are that Modularity allows for the division of a monolithic application into smaller, easier-to-manage components. Variety in frameworks and technology allows for the creation of a wide range of services. Scalability: The ability to grow individual services independently based on demand. Because of cloud computing's resiliency, a single service failure may not always affect the entire application. Additionally, speed in continuous integration and deployment (CI/CD) enables faster cycles for development and deployment (Bangar Raju Cherukuri, 2024).

Microservices and Containerization Work Together

Microservices architecture is a method for developing software systems structured as a collection of small, autonomous services. Each service is self-contained, focuses on a single business capability, and communicates with other services through well-defined APIs. This design enhances modularity, making the application easier to understand, develop, and test, while also increasing the resilience of its architecture to changing requirements(The Cloud Native Experts, 2024). Combining containerisation and microservices creates a powerful approach to application development and implementation:

- Containers simplify the deployment process by enabling the consistent deployment of microservices in a range of scenarios.
- Enhanced Scalability: Each microservice can be containerized and scaled separately based on its load.

Microservices and Containerization Tools

Developers can use Docker, a popular containerization tool, to design, distribute, and run applications in containers. Using the open-source Kubernetes container orchestration technology, containerised applications may be automatically deployed, scaled, and managed. Istio: A service mesh providing traffic management, security, and microservices monitoring (Verma & Jain, 2015).

d) Elevating Cloud Security

Multi-cloud and hybrid environment security will be a major concern as cloud systems grow more complicated. To protect sensitive data, centralised identity and access management (IAM) solutions must be put in place, and data must be encrypted both in transit and at rest. Organisations may preserve user confidence and safeguard their data by implementing enhanced security measures (Pradhan Kulkarni & BasuMallick, 2021).

Privacy is a fundamental human right that demands that personal information be utilised and protected correctly. It encompasses both the right to privacy and the right to be left alone. Data propagation, trans-border data flow, unauthorised use of cloud services, exploitation of personal data, and dynamic provisioning are some of the ways that implementing cloud computing concepts undermines privacy. Additional privacy concerns include regulating data retention, deleting data that is outsourced, and violating privacy awareness (Abdulsalam, Y.S.; Hedabou, 2022).

The security and privacy issues become more complicated when granting user permission in an environment with little to no user interface because of unauthorised data usage permission and inefficient processing of personal information, which is commonly disregarded during the design phase. Regarding cloud security implementation, there are issues with data security policies for users in the cloud environment (Abdulsalam, Y.S.; Hedabou, 2022).

e) Cloud Computing Storage

Cloud storage is one form of data storage that safely stores digital data. With its remote data management, backup, and maintenance capabilities, and network accessibility, this solution facilitates collaboration and sharing on projects. Important characteristics of cloud storage include being scalable, efficient, secure, reliable, automatic, available, multi-tenant, and affordable (Ara, Rafat, 2020). Here are a few providers of cloud storage:

- **IDrive:** Well-known cloud storage and backup service IDrive offers a range of choices to satisfy business, enterprise, and personal needs.
- **pCloud:** pCloud is a secure cloud storage service that offers a range of services for both personal and business use.(S. Logapriya & S. Niraimathi, 2016)
- **OneDrive:** OneDrive, a cloud storage solution from Microsoft, enables you to save, access, and share files from any place (Ara Shapla et al., 2020)
- **Box:** Cloud storage designed for businesses with cutting-edge security and collaboration tools.
- **Google Drive:** This popular cloud storage service enables users to save, access, and distribute files from any device with an internet connection (Pradhan Kulkarni & BasuMallick, 2021).

f) AI-Driven Cloud Management

Cloud management is becoming more and more reliant on artificial intelligence (AI). Cloud management systems powered by AI can improve security, optimise resource allocation, and automate repetitive tasks2. Businesses may increase productivity and reduce expenses in their cloud operations by utilising AI. In recent years, two of the most significant advancements in the rapidly evolving world of technology have been artificial intelligence (AI) and cloud computing. These concepts are impacting how businesses grow and operate, despite their seeming disparities. Artificial intelligence (AI), on the other hand, gives cloud services automation and intelligence, increasing their intelligence, adaptability, and user responsiveness. By employing AI algorithms to evaluate vast amounts of data, extract insights, and generate predictions, cloud platforms may enhance speed, security, and user experience (Jeyaraman & Muthusubramanian, 2022).

In addition to optimising existing cloud services, AI is fostering innovation by making it easier to develop new, intelligent capabilities. For instance:

1. Data Analytics AI-powered: AI systems can analyse massive datasets stored on cloud servers, identifying patterns, trends, and relationships that people might overlook. This information facilitates data-driven decision-making and strategic planning, which increases competitive advantage and company expansion.
2. self-contained Cloud Administration: AI-powered autonomous cloud management solutions can automate routine tasks like provisioning, monitoring, and optimisation. By using machine learning and predictive analytics, these platforms can continuously learn and adapt to changing conditions, ensuring optimal performance and efficiency.
3. Virtual assistants and chatbots AI-powered: Cloud-based AI-powered chatbots and virtual assistants are transforming customer support and service. These intelligent agents can boost efficiency and convenience by answering queries, aiding, and even doing activities on users' behalf.

g) Green Cloud Computing

Green computing, also known as sustainable IT or green IT, is the practice of organising, using, and discarding computer resources in a way that minimises their negative environmental effects. The main objective of green computing is energy efficiency by reducing computer and data centre energy consumption in addition to using renewable energy and sustainable materials and reusing e-waste. Energy-efficient hardware refers to the use of components and technology that consume less power. Recycling initiatives, which include implementing programs to recycle obsolete equipment and reduce electronic waste, are also part of the strategic strategy to implement green computing.

Using cloud infrastructure and services in a way that reduces carbon emissions, energy consumption, and electronic waste is called "green cloud computing." It aims to create a more sustainable digital world using server virtualisation, energy-efficient technology, and renewable energy sources. IBM.com. One of the approaches to implementing green cloud computing is server virtualisation, which involves combining multiple virtual servers onto fewer physical systems to maximise resource consumption (IBM, 2024)

An increasingly important factor in cloud computing is sustainability. By using renewable energy sources and optimising energy use, green cloud computing aims to lessen the environmental effect of data centers2. To reduce their carbon footprint and help create a more sustainable future, businesses are implementing eco-friendly procedures.

h) Generative AI and Robotics

Robotics and generative AI are revolutionising several sectors by making it possible to build intelligent systems that can carry out challenging tasks. To boost automation, increase decision-making, and spur innovation, these technologies are being incorporated into cloud platforms2. Generative AI may do everything from creating realistic language, music, and images to designing new products or solving difficult problems in novel ways.

Generative AI refers to computational techniques that may generate seemingly unique, meaningful content (e.g., text, images, or audio) from training data. Examples such as Copilot, GPT-4, and Dall-E 2 show how the widespread use of this technology is currently revolutionising our way of working and communicating with each other. (Stefan Feuerriegel and others, 2023). The generative AI tool ChatGPT astonished everyone with its enhanced capacity to carry out extremely complex jobs. Teachers' perspectives regarding ChatGPT's exceptional ability to perform difficult tasks in the field of education are divided, as this AI advancement seems to be revolutionising current educational processes in 2023, Baidoo-anu and Owusu Ansah.

Applications include transitional knowledge work activities and information technology (IT) help desks, were generative AI assists with regular tasks like medical aid and recipe preparation. Generative AI might boost the global gross domestic product (GDP) by 7% and replace 300 million knowledge worker jobs, according to industry sources (Stefan Feuerriegel, et al., 2023). Creating realistic writing, music, and images, as well as designing new products or finding creative answers to difficult problems, are all possible with robotics. The intriguing confluence of generative AI and robotics will produce innovative applications:

The development of generative AI-based adaptive strategies and behaviours for robots to improve their adaptability in changing environments is known as robotic creativity. AI-powered design optimisation can produce and improve robotic designs to boost efficiency and performance. Generative AI's ability to transform businesses to increase efficiency, create new experiences, and be more inventive is AWS's main selling point. Companies of all sizes develop generative AI applications that provide novel experiences for both workers and clients by utilising large language models (LLMs) and foundation models (FMs). Developing and expanding generative AI that is customised for your data, use cases, and clients is made easy by AWS, which offers enterprise-grade security and privacy, access to premier FMs, and applications that leverage generative AI. (AWS, 2024). The more we rely on robotic and artificial intelligence technology, the more ethical considerations customers and service providers must make. (R. Belk, 2020).

The use of cloud computing is rapidly growing. Future innovations and changes are anticipated to bring about several changes. The top 10 cloud computing trends and predictions for the future are as follows:

Figure 4. 10 Future Trends and Predictions of Cloud Computing (https://www.clouddefense.ai/future-of-cloud-computing/)

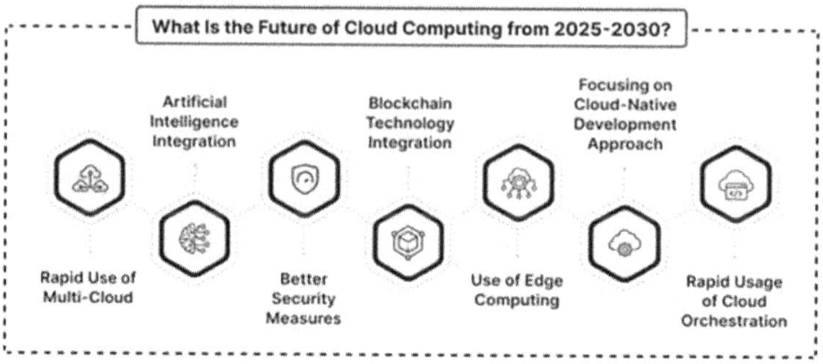

5. SUMMARY

Cloud computing has drastically changed our access to and utilisation of computer resources. This topic is dynamic, as seen by its evolution from virtualisation and grid computing technologies to the range of service models available today. Public Cloud: An online platform where services are provided by third-party suppliers like AWS, Google Cloud, and Microsoft Azure. Through the combination of private, public, and on-premises cloud infrastructure, hybrid and multi-cloud computing provides greater flexibility. The future of business and technology will undoubtedly be greatly influenced by cloud computing. Cloud computing's affordability, scalability, and flexibility make it a vital tool for businesses of all sizes. Developers can focus on building code with serverless since the cloud provider takes care of infrastructure maintenance. Clouds will continue to develop as new technologies and paradigms emerge, fostering innovation and transforming industries globally. There will be new inventions in the future, and each one will undoubtedly involve advanced technologies with AI integration, machine learning, the Internet of Things, and big data analytics. Particularly in cloud computing, data security and compliance standards must be considered immediately to ensure data protection.

Artificial intelligence (AI), machine learning (ML), and deep learning (DL) have revolutionised the field of sophisticated robotics in recent years. AI, ML, and DL are revolutionising advanced robotics by increasing robot intelligence, efficiency, and adaptation to difficult tasks and environments. Advanced robotics applications of AI, ML, and DL include autonomous navigation, natural language processing, object recognition and manipulation, and predictive maintenance. Another use for these technologies is the development of collaborative robots or cobots, that can work alongside humans and adapt to changing situations and roles (Soori Mohsen, 2023)

Cloud computing and AI together represent a paradigm shift in how companies employ technology to drive innovation and growth. By using AI, cloud services are becoming more intelligent, efficient, and adaptable, creating new growth opportunities in several industries.

REFERENCES

Alsaffar, A. S., & Alezzy, A. H. (2022). A Lightweight Portable Multithreaded Client-Server Docker Containers. *Technium*, *4*(10), 31–43. DOI: 10.47577/technium.v4i10.7722

Andriulo, F. C., Fiore, M., Mongiello, M., Traversa, E., & Zizzo, V. (2024). Edge Computing and Cloud Computing for Internet of Things: A Review. In *Informatics* (Vol. 11, Issue 4). Multidisciplinary Digital Publishing Institute (MDPI). https://doi.org/DOI: 10.3390/informatics11040071

Ara Shapla, R., Roy, S., & Kumar Prodhan Jatiya Kabi Kazi Nazrul, U. (2020). *Cloud Computing: Architecture, Services, Deployment Models, Storage, Benefits and Challenges*. https://www.researchgate.net/publication/341788106

Banger, N., & Pallavi, K. (2022). A Review Paper on Cloud Computing Architecture, Types, Advantages and Disadvantages. *International Journal of Advanced Research in Science. Tongxin Jishu*, •••, 14–22. DOI: 10.48175/IJARSCT-3144

Bhagat, B., Khobragade, S., & Arudka, A. (2021). The Evolution of Cloud Computing. *Journal of Networking Security*, *9*(1). Advance online publication. DOI: 10.37591/JoNS

Borra, P. (2024). An Overview of Cloud Computing and Leading Cloud Service Providers. [IJCET]. *International Journal of Computer Engineering and Technology*, *15*(3), 122–133. DOI: 10.17605/OSF.IO/5HQ4M

Burn, B., Beda, J., Hightower, K., & Evenson, L. (2022). *Kubernetes Up & Running: Dive into the Future of Infrastructure* (Third). O'Reilly Media, Inc.

Cherukuri, B. R. (2024). Containerization in cloud computing: Comparing Docker and Kubernetes for scalable web applications. *International Journal of Science and Research Archive*, *13*(1), 3302–3315. DOI: 10.30574/ijsra.2024.13.1.2035

Corporation, O. (2022). *OCI Oracle Cloud Infrastructure for the Modern Enterprise*.

Devadiga, A., Kumar, S., Rachhadiya, M., & Sahitya, A. (2021). *Integrated Development Environment on Cloud*. https://ssrn.com/abstract=3867647 DOI: 10.2139/ssrn.3867647

Hassan, J., Shehzad, D., Habib, U., Aftab, M. U., Ahmad, M., Kuleev, R., & Mazzara, M. (2022). The Rise of Cloud Computing: Data Protection, Privacy, and Open Research Challenges - A Systematic Literature Review (SLR). *Computational Intelligence and Neuroscience*, *2022*, 1–26. Advance online publication. DOI: 10.1155/2022/8303504 PMID: 35712069

Ikwueze, C. (2024). *Artificial Intelligence as a Service: A Systematic Review of Literature from the Customer's Perspective*. University of Oulu.

Jacksi, K., & Abass, S. M. (2019). Development History Of The World Wide Web. *Article in International Journal of Scientific & Technology Research*. www.ijstr.org

Jeyaraman, J., & Muthusubramanian, M. (2022). The Synergy of Data Engineering and Cloud Computing in the Era of Machine Learning and AI TransUnion-USA 2 Discover Financial Services-USA. *Issue 1 Journal of Knowledge Learning and Science Technology Journal Homepage, 1*, 2959–6386. https://doi.org/DOI: 10.60087/jklst.vol1.n.p75

Kirstein, P. T. (1999). Early experiences with the Arpanet and Internet in the United Kingdom. *IEEE Annals of the History of Computing*, *21*(1), 38–44. DOI: 10.1109/85.759368

Logapriya, S., & Niraimathi, S. (2016). Data Storage in Cloud Computing. *IJSRSET*, *2*(2), 1990–2395.

Mahesh, K., Laxmaiah, M., & Sharma, Y. K. (2019). A comparative study on google app engine amazon web services and microsoft windows azure. [IJCET]. *International Journal of Computer Engineering & Technology*, *10*(1), 54–60.

Nagendra, V., & Kundavaram, K. (2024). *Serverless Computing: A Comprehensive Analysis of Infrastructure Abstraction in Modern Cloud Computing*. *6*(6). www.ijfmr.com

Pahl, C., Brogi, A., Soldani, J., & Jamshidi, P. (2019). Cloud container technologies: A state-of-the-art review. *IEEE Transactions on Cloud Computing*, *7*(3), 677–692. DOI: 10.1109/TCC.2017.2702586

Pandit, P., & Pandit, P. D. (2021). *Cloud Computing Case Study on Microsoft Azure*. https://doi.org/DOI: 10.13140/RG.2.2.22421.86245

Pradhan Kulkarni, N., & BasuMallick, C. (2021). *What Is Cloud Storage? Denition, Types, Benets, and Best Practices Cloud storage allows users to store digital data les on virtual servers*. https://www.spiceworks.com/tech/cloud/articles/what-is-cloud-storage/

Radošević, I., & Hongyu Pei-Breivold, S. (2014). *School of Innovation*. Design and Engineering Architecting for the Cloud.

Red Hat, Inc. (2025). *OpenShift Dedicated 4 Introduction to OpenShift Dedicated.*

Sapkal, A., Heisnam, L., & Kusi, S. S. (2024). Evolution of Cloud Computing: Milestones, Innovations, and Adoption Trends. *International Research Journal of Engineering and Technology*. www.irjet.net

Schafer, V., & Serres, Alexandre. (2016). *Histories of the internet and the web.* Living Books about history.

The Cloud Native Experts. (2024, April 15). *What Are Containers?* https://www.aquasec.com/cloud-native-academy/docker-container/microservices-and-containerization/

The National Science and Media Museum. (2025). *History of The Internet*. Taken from the Science + Media Museum, UK1. https://www.scienceandmediamuseum.org.uk/objects-and-stories/short-history-internet

Verma, R., & Jain, P. (2015). *Containerization in Cloud: Docker, Kubernetes, and Beyond Introduction to Containerization*. https://www.researchgate.net/publication/385002203

Chapter 2
Cloud Computing Architecture:
Investigating the Complex Details of Cloud Computing Architecture

Fatima Ahmed Mohamed Abdalla
https://orcid.org/0009-0006-0756-4185
University Geomatika Malaysia, Malaysia

Noor Asiah Rashid
University Geomatika Malaysia, Malaysia

ABSTRACT

The cloud computing era is currently in the IT industry. With its Internet-based foundation, cloud computing boasts the most potent processing architecture. Hardware, software, and internet infrastructure are all interconnected and integrated to form this system. It offers several advantages over grid computing and other computing systems. Cloud computing architecture is a fundamental framework that enables the delivery of various computing services over the Internet. This architecture comprises a front-end platform, back-end platforms, a cloud-based delivery model, and the network infrastructure that connects these components. The architecture is designed to provide scalable, flexible, and cost-effective solutions for a wide range of applications, from data storage and processing to software development and deployment. This chapter investigates the intricate details of cloud computing architecture, exploring its components

DOI: 10.4018/979-8-3693-9984-2.ch002

1. INTRODUCTION

To reach the essence of cloud computing we must revisit the following concept of cloud computing. The National Institute of Standards and Technology (NIST) has proposed the most widely accepted definition of cloud computing. The NIST defines Cloud computing as a distributed computing architecture that concentrates server resources on a scalable platform, delivering computing resources and services as needed, anytime and anywhere (Mell & Grance, 2011). Cloud computing builds increasing cost trends for driving the cost out of the delivery of services while increasing the speed and agility with which services are deployed. It shortens the time from sketching out an application architecture to actual deployment. Cloud computing incorporates virtualization, on-demand deployment, Internet delivery of services, and open-source software. From one perspective, cloud computing is nothing new because it uses approaches, concepts, and best practices that have already been established. From another perspective, everything is new because cloud computing changes how we invent, develop, deploy, scale, update, maintain, and pay for applications and the infrastructure on which they run. This chapter examines the trend of cloud computing architecture, cloud-based delivery models, and network infrastructure (Nanda Banger et al., 2022).

Cloud computing architecture implies a significant change in how businesses deploy and operate apps and services. Makes it possible to distribute computer services—such as servers, storage, databases, networking, software, and analytics—through the Internet, providing economies of scale, flexible resources, and quicker innovation. Through an examination of its components, deployment strategies, and best practices for maximizing security and performance, this chapter dives into the finer points of cloud computing architecture. All types of organizations use cloud computing systems to store data in the cloud, allowing them to access their systems at any time. Cloud computing architecture is divided into two parts: the Front End and the Back End. Both parts are connected through the Internet. There are many ways to describe cloud architecture, but the best way to conceptualize a cloud is through its various layers. Figure 1 shows the basic architecture of cloud computing (Pallis, 2010).

Figure 1. Basic cloud computing architecture

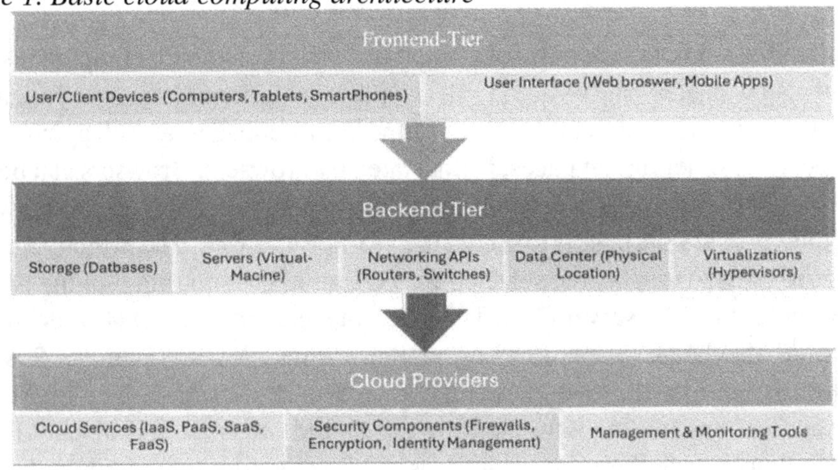

Complete cloud architecture is not a singular concept. Resources and services are accessed using a client-server approach, characterized by a request and response system, as follows:

2. FRONT-END TIER

In cloud computing architecture, front-end platforms include everything end users directly interact with. This covers client software and devices that make cloud services accessible. Mobile applications, online browsers, and API interfaces are the main elements of front-end platforms (Ara Shapla et al., 2020). The front-end section of cloud computing includes various applications and interfaces necessary for different cloud-based services. This is invented using client-side apps, like a web browser like Google Chrome or Internet Explorer. Data storage, servers, virtualization software, and other hardware and software components comprise cloud infrastructure. It also gives end-users a graphical user interface via which they may do their jobs. (Katkar et al., 2022). The frontend platform's function is that users can access cloud services through the frontend platform. It converts user requests into a format that the backend can understand and provides the user with the results in an easy-to-use way. The frontend platform makes sure that users' interactions with cloud services are efficient and seamless (G. Kumar et al., 2014)

a) Web Browsers

A web browser is a piece of software that makes it possible for computer users to find and visit websites. The basic HTML (Hypertext Markup Language) coding that enables us to view images, text, videos, and audio on webpages, as well as hyperlinks that direct us to other online pages, is translated by browsers. Browsers can be used to access files in file systems or information from web servers on private networks, even if their primary purpose is to access the World Wide Web. The primary function of the browser is to display the selected web resource, just putting it in the browser window and asking the server for it. Typically, the resource is an HTML document, but it could also be an image, PDF, or another format. A URI (Uniform Resource Identifier) is used by the user to specify the resource's location. The HTML and CSS specifications outline how the browser should interpret and display HTML files. The World Wide Web Consortium, or W3C, is the web's standards body and is responsible for maintaining these specifications. Chrome, Firefox, Internet Explorer, Opera, and Safari are the most popular web browsers (Jadhav & Vidyapeeth, 2013).

Cloud computing has a deep-rooted dependence on the Internet and Web technologies. Web technology is often used as a cloud service's realization medium and management interface. Web browsers are a crucial interface for users accessing cloud services (Devadiga et al., 2021). They enable users to interact with web applications hosted in the cloud. Modern browsers support a variety of technologies, such as HTML5, CSS3, and JavaScript, which are essential for creating responsive and dynamic web applications. Additionally, web browsers ensure compatibility with various operating systems and devices, providing seamless user experience across platforms. Web browsers also incorporate features such as sandboxing, which isolates web applications from the underlying system, enhancing security. Browser extensions and plugins further extend functionality, enabling users to customize their browsing experience and improve productivity (Ara Shapla et al., 2020).

b) Mobile Applications

Mobile cloud computing is the form of cloud computing in combination with mobile devices. Mobile devices are increasingly becoming an essential part of human life as the most effective and convenient communication tools that are not restricted by time and place. However, mobile devices are facing many challenges in their resources (e.g., battery life, storage, and bandwidth) and communications (e.g., mobility and security) (C Shravanthi, 2014)

Mobile applications have become an integral part of cloud computing, allowing users to access services on the go. Cloud-based mobile apps leverage backend services hosted in the cloud to provide seamless user experiences, data synchronization, and real-time updates (Ananta et al., 2022a). These applications are designed to work across various mobile operating systems, such as Android and iOS, ensuring broad accessibility (Wu & Plakhtii, 2021). Mobile applications often utilize cloud storage to manage user data, allowing for continuous data access and backup. Features like push notifications and offline access enhance user engagement and reliability, making mobile cloud apps indispensable tools for modern users.

Advantages of Mobile Cloud Computing

Mobile cloud services are among the newest and most innovative technologies in the world. Applications for mobile cloud computing are becoming more prevalent in daily life.

- Information technology is notably underutilized in the healthcare industry, especially when it comes to operational efficiency. Most healthcare professionals and organisations continue to use paper medical records, which restricts patient-physician coordination and collaboration(Ananta et al., 2022b).
- Mobile devices allow users access to cloud services anywhere and anytime.
- Mobile cloud services can provide information about a user's location, context, and requested services to improve user experience. Each mobile device has advantageous storage, computing, sensing, and power resources.
- Mobile computing can help to overcome some problems of Cloud Computing, such as solving the problem of WAN latencies by using Cloudlet (C Shravanthi, 2014)

c) API Interfaces

Application Programming Interfaces (APIs) play a pivotal role in front-end platforms by facilitating communication between client applications and cloud services. APIs provide standardized methods for accessing various functionalities and data hosted in the cloud, enabling integration and interoperability between different systems (Williams, 2021). They serve as the building blocks for creating modular and reusable software components. APIs also support various authentication and authorization mechanisms, ensuring secure access to cloud resources. With RESTful and GraphQL APIs being the most common types, developers can choose the appropriate API based on their application's needs and complexity.

The API concept is not new. It likely emerged in 1968 as 'a collection of code routines that provide external users with data and data functionality.' Since APIs are general technological solutions, they can serve various purposes. Consequently, we can adopt a more recent and expanded explanation of APIs, defining them as 'the calls, subroutines, or software interrupts that comprise a documented interface, allowing an application program to use the services and functions of another application, operating system, network operating system, driver, or other lower-level software program'(Angel et al., 2022; Saeidnia et al., 2021). From a software engineering perspective, APIs serve as the interfaces to the various components that a developer can assemble to create an application. An application developer utilises APIs to construct an application by combining different software libraries to achieve a specific goal. While the concept of programmatic interfaces as a collection of methods exported by a particular code library is not new, the advent of the web, especially Web 2.0, introduced the notion of web APIs to denote those APIs that operate over the internet. Web APIs provide developers with the essential building blocks needed to create web-based software applications. Since we are particularly focused on web APIs, in the rest of this document, the term 'API' will refer specifically to web APIs unless indicated otherwise (Santoro et al., 2019).

3. BACK-END TIER

Back-end platforms in cloud computing architecture comprise the infrastructure and services that power cloud applications. These platforms handle data processing, storage, security, and orchestration. The key components of back-end platforms include servers, storage systems, databases, and middleware. The different computers, servers, and data storage devices that make up the "cloud" of computing services are located at the back end of the system. Almost any computer software, from data processing to video games, may theoretically be a part of a cloud computing system. Every program often has its dedicated server. The system is administered by a central server, which keeps an eye on client requests and traffic to make sure everything functions properly. It requires specialized software known as middleware and adheres to a set of guidelines known as protocols. Computers on a network can communicate with one another thanks to middleware. Servers don't always operate at maximum capacity.

In other words, processing power that is not being used is being wasted. It is possible to make a physical server appear to be several servers, each with its operating system. It is referred to as server virtualization. Through server virtualization, the requirement for additional physical machines is decreased by optimizing the performance of individual servers. Demand for a large amount of storage space is likely to be strong for a cloud computing company with a large clientele. For some businesses, hundreds of digital storage devices are necessary. At least twice as many storage devices are needed by cloud computing systems to store all their client's data.

That's because, like all computers, these gadgets malfunction from time to time. Every client's data must be copied by a cloud computing system (Sareen, 2013).

a) Servers

In cloud computing, servers are essential since they serve as the foundation of the infrastructure that provides different cloud services. Servers are used to store, process, and administer data and applications in a cloud computing environment. They may be virtualised versions of physical hardware or actual equipment (Namasudra, 2018)

Important Features of Cloud Computing Servers:

1. **Virtualisation:** This is one of the core concepts of cloud computing. A single physical server can host multiple virtual servers, also known as virtual machines (VMs), due to virtualization technology. Each virtual machine operates its operating system and applications, acting as an independent server. This improves flexibility, scalability, and resource utilization. Furthermore, virtualization simplifies application deployment and management(Liu et al., 2011).
2. **Scalability:** Cloud servers are built with scalability in mind. Depending on demand, resources like CPU, memory, and storage can be dynamically distributed. Businesses may scale their infrastructure up or down as needed thanks to this elasticity, which guarantees cost-effectiveness and peak performance. For instance, more virtual servers can be made available to manage the increased demand during periods of high usage(Mell & Grance, 2011)
3. **Redundancy and Reliability:** To ensure high availability and reliability, cloud servers are configured with redundancy. Multiple servers and data centers typically store duplicate copies of data and applications. To minimize downtime and prevent data loss, the cloud system can quickly switch to a backup server in case of a hardware failure or other issues (Surbiryala & Rong, 2019)
4. Cloud server types include:
    - Computer servers: These servers offer the processing power needed to run programs and handle data. They are frequently employed for jobs like database administration, website hosting, and intricate computation (Pradhan Kulkarni & BasuMallick, 2021).
    - Storage Servers: The purpose of these servers is data storage. From small files to massive databases, they provide scalable storage options for a variety of data kinds.

- Application servers: By hosting and maintaining applications, these servers enable users to access and utilise software via the internet. Web servers, database servers, and email servers are a few examples (Yamato, 2018).

5. **Security:** Cloud servers are outfitted with strong security protocols to safeguard apps and data. Identity and access management (IAM), intrusion detection systems, firewalls, and encryption are all included in this. Additionally, cloud companies use compliance standards to guarantee data protection and satisfy legal requirements (Ts et al., 2020)
6. Management and Monitoring: Cloud service providers offer a variety of tools and platforms for managing and keeping an eye on cloud servers. Performance monitoring, resource allocation, automation, and troubleshooting are some of the features that these products provide. This makes it possible for IT managers to effectively oversee the cloud infrastructure and guarantee peak performance (Alayda et al., 2020).

Ahmad Dar, (2018) stated that the positive aspects of cloud servers are compromises of the following:

- Cost-effectiveness: Cloud servers save companies money by removing the need to purchase and maintain physical infrastructure. Pay-as-you-go pricing enables businesses to only pay for the resources they really utilise.
- Flexibility: Cloud servers are easily reconfigured to accommodate evolving business requirements. This adaptability fosters creativity and quick development cycles.
- Accessibility: Cloud servers facilitate remote work and collaboration by being reachable from any location with an internet connection.
- Resilience: Cloud servers' redundancy and dependability features guarantee high availability and little downtime

In cloud computing, servers are crucial parts that offer the infrastructure required to provide a variety of cloud services. For both people and enterprises, cloud servers provide a dependable, adaptable, and affordable solution through virtualisation, scalability, redundancy, and strong security features.

b) Storage Systems

Cloud storage is a system for storing data where digital data, including documents, images, videos, and other types of media, is kept on third-party virtual or cloud servers. Individuals can move data to an off-site storage system and retrieve it whenever they need to. Cloud storage systems offer scalable and reliable storage solutions for data generated by applications. These systems use distributed storage technologies to ensure data redundancy and availability. Examples include object storage, block storage, and file storage (S. Logapriya & S. Niraimathi, 2016); the following is a list of cloud storage from (Pradhan Kulkarni & BasuMallick, 2021). Public Cloud Storage: Third-party companies offer public cloud storage online. It is open to all users and usually uses a pay-as-you-go model. Google Cloud Storage, Microsoft Azure Storage, and Amazon S3 are a few examples. Because public cloud storage is affordable and expandable, it is perfect for companies of all kinds.

Private Cloud Storage: In which this type of storage is dedicated to a single company, private cloud storage can be hosted by a third-party supplier or on-site. It is appropriate for businesses with strict security or compliance requirements since it provides improved security and control over data. Hybrid Cloud Storage: Public and private cloud storage options are combined in hybrid cloud storage. It enables businesses to benefit from the cost-effectiveness and scalability of public clouds while retaining control and security of private clouds. Businesses with different workloads and storage requirements can benefit from this arrangement. Multi-Cloud Storage: To address requirements and prevent vendor lock-in, multi-cloud storage entails utilising several cloud storage providers. It provides redundancy, flexibility, and the opportunity to maximise performance and cost by utilising the strengths of many providers.

Every form of cloud storage offers benefits and is appropriate for various use cases based on the requirements and objectives of the company. Cloud storage provides several advantages, comprising increased accessibility, a lot of storage space, low prices, and data backup. There are many types of cloud storage (Pradhan Kulkarni & BasuMallick, 2021)

d) Databases

The cloud database stores information from various data centers situated in different locations. This distinguishes the structure of the cloud database from that of a relational database management system, which is inherently more complex. Numerous nodes across a cloud database are designed for query services, accommodating data centers located in diverse geographical areas, including corporate data centers. This connectivity is essential for easy and comprehensive access to the database through cloud services(Al Shehri, 2013).

Databases in the cloud provide robust data management capabilities, supporting various data models such as relational, NoSQL, and in-memory databases. Cloud databases offer features like automated backups, scalability, and high availability, making them ideal for modern applications (E. S. Kumar et al., 2021). Relational databases, such as Amazon RDS, use structured query language (SQL) for managing data, while NoSQL databases, like Amazon DynamoDB, are optimized for unstructured data. In-memory databases, such as Amazon ElastiCache, store data in RAM, providing ultra-fast read and write operations. These databases are particularly useful for applications requiring real-time data processing and low-latency access. Additionally, managed database services offload the administrative tasks of database management, allowing developers to focus on application development (Neu et al., 2019)

e) Middleware

Middleware is software that facilitates communication between many applications. To enable the smooth integration of many technologies, tools, and databases into a single system, it serves as a bridge. Users receive a unified service via this connection, but they are not aware of the underlying complications. Building applications is made easier by middleware, which manages connectivity between software components so that developers may concentrate on features and business logic (Amazon Web Services AWS, 2024).

Middleware acts as an intermediary layer that facilitates communication and data exchange between different applications and services. It provides essential services such as authentication, messaging, and transaction management, enabling seamless integration of cloud applications (Angel et al., 2022). Middleware solutions often include Enterprise Service Buses (ESBs) and message brokers like Apache Kafka, which enable efficient data routing and transformation (Odun-Ayo et al., 2021). Service-oriented architecture (SOA) and microservices architecture rely heavily on middleware to orchestrate services and manage inter-service communication. Middleware also supports API gateways, which handle API requests, load balancing, and security enforcement, ensuring the smooth operation of cloud services.

4. CLOUD-BASED DELIVERY

In the quickly changing digital landscape of today, businesses from a variety of industries are embracing cloud technology more and more to completely revamp their corporate systems. Cloud-based solutions, as opposed to traditional on-premises infrastructure, mark a significant paradigm shift in how companies think about and carry out security frameworks, operational efficiency projects, and data management plans. On-demand self-service, wide network access, resource pooling, quick elasticity, and measured service are the key features that characterize cloud computing, according to the official NIST framework. Together, these fundamental components allow computing capabilities to be dynamically provisioned and released with little administration work, giving businesses of all sizes previously unheard-of operational flexibility(Subramanyam, 2025).

Cloud-based delivery methods are at the core of IT transformation. The Cloud-based delivery models define how cloud services are made available to users. Cloud-based delivery models specify several ways users can get cloud services. Different abstraction and control levels are provided by each model, which is suited to requirements and use situations. These models include Software as a Service (SaaS), Platform as a Service (PaaS), and Infrastructure as a Service (IaaS) (Isaac Odun- Ayo, 2018). Figure 2 is an illustration of cloud-based delivery services.

Figure 2. Cloud-based delivery services

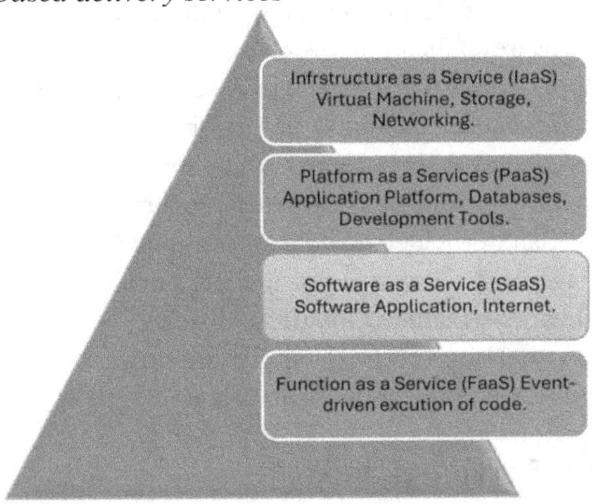

a) Software as a Service (SaaS)

SAAS (Software as a Service) is a method of managing and distributing programs through the internet. Additionally, the client side can access its interface. Numerous tools and pieces of software are licenced on a contribution basis and are hosted centrally through the SaaS platform. Additional names for SaaS include "hosted software" and "on-demand software." Additionally, it is receiving greater attention, and for very good reasons. Additionally, web-based apps provide both small and large businesses with a better and more clear approach to getting IT facilities for their businesses. As per IBM's team report, the SaaS market is projected to increase by around 21% annually worldwide after the new year and will increase by $17 billion by the end of 2020.

Software as a Service, or SAAS, is a way to distribute and manage programs online. The client side can also access its interface. Many tools and software components are hosted centrally via the SaaS platform and are licensed on a contribution basis. SaaS is sometimes referred to as "hosted software" or "on-demand software." Furthermore, it is getting more attention—and for good reason. Additionally, web-based apps give businesses of all sizes a better and more transparent way to obtain IT facilities for their operations. According to IBM's team research, the SaaS industry is expected to grow by $17 billion by the end of 2020 and by about 21% yearly following the new year(Gupta et al., 2024). (Peram, 2024) stated that Software as a Service, or SaaS, is a subscription-based online software application delivery service. By 2025, SaaS is expected to hold a 66% market share on the cloud.

SaaS delivers software applications over the internet on a subscription basis. Users can access these applications through web browsers, eliminating the need for local installation and maintenance. Examples of SaaS include email services, customer relationship management (CRM) systems, and collaboration tools. SaaS applications are hosted on the cloud provider's infrastructure, ensuring scalability and reliability (Bello et al., 2021). SaaS providers handle software updates, security patches, and infrastructure management, allowing users to focus on their core business activities. Popular SaaS applications include Google Workspace, Salesforce, and Microsoft 365, which offer a wide range of productivity and business tools accessible from anywhere with an internet connection (Malallah et al., 2023).

b) Platform as a Service (PaaS)

PaaS provides a platform for developers to build, deploy, and manage applications without worrying about underlying infrastructure. This model offers development tools, runtime environments, and middleware, enabling faster development cycles and simplified management (Radošević & Hongyu Pei-Breivold, 2014). PaaS solutions, such as Google App Engine and Microsoft Azure App Service, support various programming languages and frameworks, allowing developers to use their preferred tools.

PaaS platforms also offer integrated development environments (IDEs), version control systems, and continuous integration/continuous deployment (CI/CD) pipelines, streamlining the development process. By abstracting infrastructure management, PaaS enables developers to focus on writing code and delivering features, accelerating time-to-market (Wu & Plakhtii, 2021)

With Platform as a Service (PaaS), users may create, execute, and manage applications without having to worry about maintaining the underlying infrastructure. PaaS has become a crucial part of the cloud computing ecosystem. PaaS is a collection of tools that includes database management systems, developer frameworks, middleware, and infrastructure. The worldwide PaaS industry is expanding quickly; estimates suggest it will reach $164.3 billion by 2026, with a compound annual growth rate (CAGR) of 19.6% from 2021 to 2026 (Peram, 2024).

c) Infrastructure as a Service (IaaS)

IaaS offers virtualized computing resources over the internet, including servers, storage, and networking. Users can provision and manage these resources on demand, allowing for cost-effective scaling and flexibility. IaaS is ideal for enterprises that require full control over their infrastructure (Clark, 2018). Leading IaaS providers such as Amazon Web Services (AWS), Microsoft Azure, and Google Cloud Platform (GCP) offer a wide range of services, including compute instances, storage options, and networking capabilities.

IaaS enables organizations to deploy and run any software, including operating systems and applications, on the cloud provider's infrastructure. This model provides the highest level of flexibility and control, allowing users to configure their environments to meet specific requirements. IaaS also supports hybrid cloud deployments, enabling seamless integration with on-premises infrastructure. Infrastructure as a Service (IaaS), which provides virtualized computer resources via the internet, continues to be a fundamental component of cloud computing. With the help of this architecture, businesses can access and control essential infrastructure elements like networking, storage, and virtual machines without having to make investments in actual hardware. According to forecasts, the worldwide IaaS market would reach $255.8 billion by 2028, rising at a compound annual growth rate (CAGR) of 23.3% from 2023 to 2028.(Peram, 2024).

5. NETWORK INFRASTRUCTURE

A computer network—also referred to as a network—was created in the 1960s when computer and communication technologies were combined. As network technology has advanced, computer networks—once thought of as a luxury technology—have progressively become a part of everyday life, drastically changing people's lifestyles and becoming a necessary component of daily living. The fundamental ideas, creation and evolution, definitions and purposes, composition, categorization, and topological structure of computer networks will all be covered in this part.

As previously stated, every cloud needs to be linked to the network to offer remote, anytime, anywhere access to IT resources. One may argue that the fundamental underpinning of cloud computing is network technology. To give readers a better understanding of some of the key components of computer networks, concepts, principles, equipment, and newer network technologies supporting cloud computing, this chapter will introduce the fundamental network knowledge involved in cloud computing. This includes an overview of computer networks, the fundamental principles of computer networks, network interconnection equipment, network virtualization, and software-defined networks (Huawei Technologies Co., Ltd., 2023a). Network infrastructure is a critical component of cloud computing architecture, enabling data transfer and communication between client devices, servers, and cloud services. The following sections explain the network infrastructure within a cloud computing platform.

a) Data Centres

Cloud services' underlying hardware is housed in data centers. These establishments are furnished with networking hardware, storage devices, and high-performance servers. They aim to provide energy efficiency, security, and redundancy (Roberts, 2019). Data centers are positioned strategically across different locations to give users all over the world low-latency access.

Modern data centers use cutting-edge technologies like software-defined infrastructure, automation, and virtualization to maximize resource management and utilization. Environmental controls, including power management and cooling systems, make data center operations reliable and sustainable.

In the future, edge computing in data centers is becoming more and more popular. Instead of placing data centers in one place, edge computing entails placing them closer to the end users. This can lower latency and boost data center service performance, especially for applications that need low-latency data access. Furthermore, it is anticipated that developments in machine learning and artificial intelligence will become more significant in the future for data center administration and optimization (Xie et al., 2023).

Cloud computing technology, which provides more scalability, flexibility, and cost-effectiveness, has gained popularity as a means of deploying and maintaining data centers. Data centers may readily scale up or down in response to demand thanks to cloud architecture's dynamic resource allocation, which results in significant cost savings. Cloud computing also speeds up the deployment of new services and apps and offers more flexibility in the location and design of data centers. Nonetheless, employing managed services providers and putting strong security measures in place are necessary to solve the issues of security and management complexity. Future data center technology is anticipated to be significantly impacted by developments in edge computing and AI/ML. Data center integration of cloud computing technologies has completely changed how businesses handle IT operations and infrastructure. Through the utilization of cloud computing's advantages, including scalability, flexibility, and cost-effectiveness, data centers can now remain ahead of the technological curve and adjust to evolving business requirements.

This has enhanced performance and service availability while also increasing efficiency and lowering costs. There are obstacles to overcome, though, just like with any new technology. Given that cloud settings might be exposed to a variety of cyberthreats, security is still a top priority. Companies must put strong security measures in place and maintain vigilance to safeguard their systems and data. Furthermore, maintaining and administering cloud-based data centers can be challenging and call for specific knowledge and abilities. To overcome these obstacles, a lot of businesses are looking to managed services providers, who can assist with cloud-based data center deployment, management, and upkeep. This lets businesses use the knowledge of specialized providers while concentrating on their main operations.

Future developments in edge computing and AI/ML are anticipated to become more significant in data center management and optimization. By lowering latency and enhancing performance, edge computing will make it possible to locate data centers closer to end users. Data centers will be able to function more effectively and efficiently thanks to AI and ML, which will optimize resource usage and anticipate and stop problems before they arise. In general, the incorporation of cloud computing technology into data centers has yielded noteworthy advantages; nonetheless, it also necessitates that firms tackle the obstacles and remain abreast of the most recent advancements and patterns.

b) Networking Technologies

Advanced networking technologies, such as Software-Defined Networking (SDN) and Network Function Virtualization (NFV), enable dynamic and programmable network configurations. These technologies improve network efficiency, scalability, and security (Taylor, 2022). SDN decouples the control plane from the data plane, allowing centralized management and automation of network resources (Huawei Technologies Co., Ltd., 2023b). NFV replaces traditional network hardware appliances with virtualized network functions (VNFs) running on commodity hardware, reducing costs, and increasing flexibility. Together, SDN and NFV enable cloud providers to deliver highly customizable and agile networking services, meeting the diverse needs of modern applications.

Given the substantial $1 trillion in IT expenditures anticipated for the shift to cloud computing, which underlying network technologies are essential to its development? To improve cloud service security, this integrative review addresses current issues and architectural approaches (Moura et al., 2023). and performance, emphasizing how network function virtualisation (NFV) and software-defined networking (SDN) contribute to the development of a more flexible and effective cloud infrastructure. Improved fault tolerance and scalability are demonstrated using cloud based NFV frameworks (Cziva et al., 2023). Furthermore, as evidenced by the notable enhancements in network performance attained through creative allocation schemes, the cooperation of SDN and NFV enables dynamic resource allocation, allowing enterprises to react quickly to changing workloads and guaranteeing optimal performance across various cloud environments (Woldeyohannes et al., 2023).

According to Kapurthi et al. (2023), the integration of these technologies not only simplifies management procedures but also gives businesses the ability to use advanced analytics for predictive maintenance, which improves overall system reliability and user satisfaction. This, in turn, can increase the accuracy of failure prediction and resource allocation. Furthermore, by fostering an ecosystem where continuous integration and delivery are made possible, the convergence of SDN and NFV eventually shortens the time-to-market for cloud applications while enabling the quick scalability that contemporary enterprises demand. Principles of continuous delivery can allow construction with push buttons that enable secure updates (Gebert et al., 2023).

c) Content Delivery Networks (CDNs)

Content Delivery Networks (CDNs) have become a vital part of improving global digital experiences in the quickly changing world of cloud computing. As the need for quick, dependable, and safe access to digital content keeps increasing, CDNs are essential for maximizing the scalability and performance of contemporary cloud computing services. CDNs improve the user experience by bringing content closer to end users by utilizing a geographically dispersed network of servers, which drastically lowers latency (Vemasani & Modi, 2024).

It is impossible to overestimate the significance of CDNs in cloud computing. The necessity for effective content distribution has grown significantly due to the exponential rise of data and the growing dependence on cloud-based services. By strategically placing content cache servers across the globe, CDNs solve this problem and guarantee that users, wherever they may be in the world, may access content reliably and swiftly. In addition to improving cloud-based application performance, this lessens the strain on original servers, which increases scalability and lowers costs. Additionally, CDNs provide a strong security framework that aids in defending cloud computing services from different types of online attacks(Wes Hardaker, 2022).

CDNs provide an additional layer of security by employing methods such as SSL/TLS encryption, web application firewalls, and Distributed Denial of Service (DDoS) mitigation, thereby protecting sensitive data and maintaining the availability of critical services. This is especially important in the era of increasing data breaches and cyberattacks, where the security and integrity of cloud computing services are critical. The integration of CDNs with cloud computing services has also paved the way for the adoption of emerging technologies such as edge computing. By bringing data processing and storage closer to the edge of the network, CDNs enable faster data processing, reduced latency, and improved responsiveness for applications that require real-time interactions. This synergy between CDNs and edge computing opens new possibilities for innovative applications in fields such as the Internet of Things (IoT), virtual reality, and autonomous vehicles (Vemasani & Modi, 2024).

CDNs enhance the performance of cloud applications by distributing content across multiple edge locations globally. This reduces latency and ensures faster delivery of web content, videos, and other resources to end-users (Harris, 2020). CDNs cache content closer to users, minimizing the distance data must travel and improving load times. Leading CDN providers such as Cloudflare and Akamai offer additional features like DDoS protection, web application firewalls (WAFs), and real-time analytics, further enhancing security and performance. CDNs play a crucial role in delivering high-quality user experiences, especially for rich media applications and websites with a global audience (Sasikumar et al., 2023).

6. BEST PRACTICES FOR OPTIMIZING PERFORMANCE AND SECURITY

Performance and security optimization are critical to cloud computing implementation success. The best practices are described here in this section for accomplishing these objectives.

a) Performance Optimization

- Capacity Planning: To guarantee that resources are sufficiently provisioned to manage peak loads and prevent performance bottlenecks, regularly evaluate, and prepare for capacity requirements (Johnson, 2017). Put auto-scaling policies into place to dynamically modify resources in response to demand.

- Caching: Use caching techniques to speed up response times for frequently accessed data and lessen the strain on backend systems (Smith, 2018). To store and retrieve data fast, use distributed caches such as Redis or Memcached.
- Load balancing: To ensure high availability and dependability, use load balancers to divide incoming traffic evenly among several servers (Willigens, 2019). Set up health checks to identify unhealthy instances and divert traffic from them.
- Monitoring and Analytics: To detect and proactively resolve performance issues, continuously monitor application performance, and make use of analytics tools (Davis, 2021). Learn about application behaviour and user experiences by putting Application Performance Monitoring (APM) technologies into practice (Osinachi Deborah Segun-Falade et al., 2024)
- Scalability and performance of the cloud facility are further factors that contribute to the increasing popularity of cloud services. The ability of a cloud system to handle high workloads or an expanding user base is known as scalability. It helps organizations to swiftly adapt to changes in their computer equipment requirements, which boosts organizational economy and efficiency. Performance, on the other hand, focuses on the broad elements of cloud service delivery and its effectiveness in various situations. It comprises variables that impact the user's perception of the quality of the service provided, such as the length of time required to finish activities, the number of jobs that can be finished in each amount of time, and the number of resources used per unit of time. Together, these determine how dependable and effective cloud solutions are in terms of performance(Chaturvedi & Sharma, 2021).

b) Security Optimization

Cloud security is a discipline of cyber security dedicated to securing cloud computing systems. This includes keeping data private and safe across online-based infrastructure, applications, and platforms. Securing these systems involves the efforts of cloud providers and the clients that use them, whether an individual, small to medium business, or enterprise uses.

Digital infrastructure has been entirely transformed by cloud computing, which enables scalable, on-demand computing services. However, due to its distributed nature, there are additional security risks, and attacks are becoming increasingly complex and adaptable. Traditional rule-based security mechanisms are no longer effective because of the emergence of diverse attack tactics and covert entry methods, as demonstrated by previous research. Conventional systems struggle with real-time responses and cannot detect zero-day threats since they rely on matching signatures and predetermined criteria (Wang & Yang, 2025). The broader use of cloud computing services is significantly impacted by security. The literature now in publication focuses on various security solutions, such as the application of security policies and technologies. DoS (Denial-of-Service) attacks are a serious risk to cloud services and have the potential to seriously harm cloud service providers' and their clients' finances and reputations. Due to system outages, stopped services, and data breaches, DoS assaults can also lead to security flaws and income loss (Alhazmi, 2023).

Therefore, the following are the best preventive security measures to secure cloud computing:

- Adaptable security protection: a technique that builds a multilayered protection architecture using deep learning and validates it in an actual business setting. The system achieves 99.999% availability, an average reaction time of 18 ms, and a detection accuracy of 97.3%. According to experimental data, this approach offers a novel way to secure the security of cloud computing by having notable advantages in detecting accuracy, reaction efficiency, and resource consumption. (Wang & Yang, 2025)
- Data encryption: To prevent unwanted access to sensitive information, encrypt data both in transit and at rest (Garcia, 2017). Employ robust encryption techniques and keep encryption keys safe.
- Access Control: To limit access to cloud resources, put strong access control measures in place, such as role-based access control and multi-factor authentication (Alayda et al., 2020). To make sure access policies follow security best practices, evaluate and update them frequently.
- Frequent Audits: To detect and reduce possible security threats, do frequent security audits and vulnerability assessments (Thompson, 2018). To check for vulnerabilities and make sure security standards are being followed, use automated tools.
- Observance: To protect data and uphold confidence, make sure that pertinent industry standards and laws, such as GDPR, HIPAA, and PCI DSS, are followed (Brown, 2020). Put security procedures and controls that match or exceed legal requirements in place.
- For detecting DoS attacks in the cloud, a deep convolutional generative adversarial network is used as an optimization-based deep learning model. To understand the temporal and spatial characteristics of network traffic data and identify patterns suggestive of denial-of-service attacks, the suggested model makes use of Deep Convolutional Generative Adversarial Networks (DCGAN)(Alhazmi, 2023).

c) Cloud Security Techniques – (Kaspersky, Google Cloud, and IBM)

Cloud security encompasses the technology, regulations, procedures, and services that guard against threats to cloud infrastructure, data, and applications. The following are the techniques used by the most popular cloud computing companies' providers:

- **Kaspersky** (Kaspersky, 2025)
  Key Techniques:

  a) **Data Encryption** (at rest and in transit): guarantees the privacy of data and guards against interception.
  b) **Identity and Access Management (IAM):** access control based on roles and robust authentication systems.
  c) **Regular Security Audits:** to discover vulnerabilities and misconfigurations.
  d) **DDoS Protection** prevents distributed attacks from disrupting services.
  e) **Endpoint Security:** ensures the security of the devices using cloud resources.
  f) **Compliance Monitoring:** Aligns with industry standards like GDPR, HIPAA.

- **Google Cloud (Google, 2025)**
  Key Techniques:

  a) **Zero Trust Security Model:** "Trust no one, verify everything" includes contextual access and continuous identity verification.
  b) **Encryption by Default:** utilizing industry standards for end-to-end encryption (TLS, AES-256).
  c) **Security Command Center:** Threat response, risk identification, and visibility are all centralized.
  d) **Confidential Computing:** uses Trusted Execution Environments (TEEs) to protect data while it is being used.
  e) **Policy and Compliance Automation:** Integration with compliance reports and GRC tools.
  f) **Workload Identity Federation:** securely links cloud and on-premises identities without requiring persistent login credentials.

- **IBM: Cloud Security Insights** (IBM, 2021)
  Key Techniques:

- **Hybrid Cloud Security:** unified protection and visibility in on-premises and cloud hybrid environments.
- **Data Security and Privacy** comprises data loss prevention, tokenization, and encryption.
- **AI-Driven Threat Detection:** employs behavioral analytics and machine learning to find irregularities.
- **IAM and Privileged Access Management:** Session tracking, MFA, and granular access control.
- **Cloud-native Security Tools:** Integrates Automated vulnerability scanning in DevSecOps.
- **Zero Trust and Secure Access Service Edge (SASE):** safeguards users and data via cloud-based security gateways and at the edge.

7. IMPLICATIONS AND FUTURE DIRECTIONS

Cloud computing architecture is a complex and multi-faceted domain that requires a deep understanding of its components, deployment models, and best practices. By leveraging the insights provided in this chapter, organizations can optimize their cloud deployments for enhanced performance and security, ultimately driving innovation and business success. It is evident from considering the development and importance of cloud computing architecture that this paradigm shift in technology has had a profound impact on the way we develop, implement, and oversee IT resources. The architecture of cloud computing offers a framework that is efficient, adaptable, and scalable, meeting the many demands of both individual users and contemporary businesses. Cloud computing has expanded the realm of what is feasible in the digital era by utilizing a mix of front-end and back-end platforms, cloud-based delivery models, and networking infrastructure.

Cloud computing architecture has an impact on several industries, including government, business, education, and healthcare. It has made it possible for businesses to streamline processes, cut expenses, and improve their capacity for innovation. Cloud services' flexibility and on-demand features enable companies to react swiftly to shifting consumer demands and market situations. Furthermore, cloud computing has made cutting-edge technologies more accessible, allowing even small and medium-sized businesses to take advantage of robust computer capabilities without having to make a sizable initial investment(Osinachi Deborah Segun-Falade et al., 2024). A smooth and reliable environment for managing data and running applications is provided by the cooperation of the main elements of cloud computing architecture, including servers, storage, data centers, virtualisation, and networking. While the back-end components guarantee dependable and effective service delivery, the front-end components—such as client devices and user interfaces—allow users to engage with cloud services. Multi-tenancy and resource optimisation have been made possible by virtualization technologies in particular (Jeyaraman & Muthusubramanian, 2022).

Different levels of abstraction and flexibility are provided by the various service models, which include Infrastructure as a Service (IaaS), Platform as a Service (PaaS), Software as a Service (SaaS), and Function as a Service (FaaS), to meet the needs of different user types. Organisations can select the best environment for their security, compliance, and performance requirements by using the deployment models—public cloud, private cloud, hybrid cloud, and community cloud. The architecture of cloud computing is expected to continue evolving and evolving in the future. The future of cloud computing is anticipated to be shaped by several significant trends. Cloud computing is expected to undergo major development in the future due to new technology and changing business requirements. As businesses continue to embrace digital transformation, cloud computing will be essential to improving scalability, innovation, and operational efficiency (OTAVA, 2024). These are some important avenues for cloud computing's future:

Edge Computing: Real-time processing is made possible via edge computing, which lowers latency by bringing processing capacity closer to the data source. This is especially important for applications related to the Internet of Things (IoT), where device-generated data needs to be handled rapidly and effectively. The expansion of IoT devices is supported and user experiences are improved by edge computing, which reduces the need to send massive amounts of data to centralized cloud data centres (OTAVA, 2024).

Integration of Machine Learning and Artificial Intelligence; Automation, predictive modeling, and data analytics are all being revolutionized by the incorporation of AI and ML into cloud services. AI-powered cloud management solutions lower expenses, improve operational effectiveness and facilitate smarter decision-making2. A wider spectrum of organisations can now access cutting-edge technology thanks to cloud providers' growing inclusion of AI and ML capabilities in their offerings. Quantum Computing; A new area of study called “quantum cloud computing” uses the concepts of quantum computing to tackle challenging issues that traditional computing is unable to handle. Researchers and developers can investigate quantum algorithms and applications thanks to quantum cloud services, which give access to quantum computers and development tools. Although technology is still in its infancy, quantum cloud computing has the potential to completely transform domains including material science, optimisation, and cryptography (OTAVA, 2024).

Enhanced Security: Security continues to be a primary concern as cloud infrastructures grow more intricate and interwoven. Protecting sensitive data and preserving confidence in cloud solutions requires the use of cutting-edge security methods, such as strong identity and access control, encryption, and adherence to legal requirements. To handle changing cyber threats and guarantee data protection, cloud providers are constantly improving their security frameworks (Seth et al., 2024). Sustainability: Concern over cloud computing's effects on the environment is growing, and efforts are being made to optimize energy use and build eco-friendly data centers. To lessen their carbon footprint, cloud providers are making investments in energy-efficient hardware, renewable energy sources, and cutting-edge cooling technologies. In line with international efforts to tackle climate change, cloud computing strategies are increasingly including sustainability objectives (Bajdor, 2024).

Multi-cloud and hybrid cloud strategies are increasingly popular among organizations to minimize risk, maximize performance, and avoid vendor lock-in. In multi-cloud setups, various cloud service providers are utilized to meet different business needs or enhance resilience. Hybrid cloud systems combine the scalability and cost-effectiveness of public cloud services with private cloud resources, allowing enterprises to store sensitive data on-premises (Multi-Cloud and Hybrid Cloud Guide, 2021).

The architecture of cloud computing is changing due to the use of orchestration and containerization tools like Kubernetes. Applications and their dependencies are packaged into separate parts by containers, which provide consistency across various environments. By automating containerized application deployment, scaling, and management, Kubernetes improves portability and scalability. Containerization and orchestration2 adoption is made easier by cloud providers' managed Kubernetes services (Verma & Jain, 2015).

Function as a Service (FaaS), another name for serverless computing, further isolates server administration by enabling developers to create and implement discrete functions or bits of code that are run in response to events. By only billing customers for the actual computing time used by their functions, this strategy lowers operational overhead and expenses. Microservices architectures and event-driven applications are two areas where serverless computing is very appealing (Bello et al., 2021).

Future Growth Predictions

1. **Global Cloud Market Size**
    - By 2028, it is anticipated to reach USD 720.44 billion.
    - accelerated by a 15.7% compound annual growth rate (CAGR) between 2022 and 2030.
2. **IaaS (Infrastructure as a Service)**
    - Anticipated to expand between 2023 and 2028 at a CAGR of 23.3%.
    - By 2028, it is expected to reach USD 255.8 billion.
3. **PaaS (Platform as a Service)**

- o Expected to expand between 2021 and 2026 at a CAGR of 19.6%.
- o By 2030, it is anticipated to reach USD 319.56 billion.

4. **SaaS (Software as a Service)**
    - o predicted to hold a 66% market share in the cloud by 2025.
    - o anticipated to expand between 2022 and 2028 at a CAGR of 25.89%.
    - o By 2028 alone, it is expected to reach USD 720.44 billion.
5. **Cloud Storage Market**
    - o By 2030, it is anticipated to reach USD 376 billion, expanding in tandem with IaaS and PaaS.
6. **Adoption Trends**
    - o It is anticipated that 82% of workloads will be cloud-based by 2025.
    - o By 2025, 73% of businesses anticipate that almost all their apps will be hosted on SaaS platforms.

These predictions consider the growing reliance on scalable, on-demand cloud services, the ongoing enterprise adoption of cloud-native technologies (such as serverless and edge computing), and innovation in these technologies.

8. FINAL REMARKS

The architecture of cloud computing is a paradigm shift in how businesses create, implement, and oversee services and apps. It uses distributed computing to combine server resources into a scalable platform, allowing for the on-demand, anywhere, at any time, delivery of computing resources and services. Cloud computing, according to the National Institute of Standards and Technology (NIST), is a dynamic, scalable approach that combines open-source software, virtualization, and Internet-based service delivery to improve cost effectiveness, agility, and creativity. The technical and operational procedures of application lifecycle management are radically changed by this architecture, which also revolutionises payment models and promotes quick software and infrastructure deployment, scaling, and updates.

Although cloud computing is not a completely new idea—it draws upon existing practices—its comprehensive implementation brings about significant changes in the way businesses think about, implement, and use technology. To guarantee optimum performance and security, this chapter explores the basic elements, deployment tactics, and best practices of cloud computing architecture. The client-server methodology of the architecture, which uses a request-response system to access resources and services, is what makes it unique. The Front-End and Back-End are their two primary levels, and they are seamlessly connected over the Internet. User-facing components of cloud computing, such as web browsers, mobile applications, and API interfaces, are included in the Front-End tier. By providing graphical user interfaces that streamline intricate procedures, it acts as the conduct for user interaction with cloud services. To guarantee effective and smooth user interactions, this layer is made to translate user requests into a format that the back end can understand and convey results in an approachable way. In contrast, the back-end tier manages cloud computing's operational facets. It comprises servers, virtualization software, data storage, and other essential hardware and software elements that make up the core of cloud infrastructure.

The Back-End tier guarantees the functioning and dependability of cloud services by controlling system resources and carrying out user requests. Infrastructure as a Service (IaaS), Platform as a Service (PaaS), Software as a Service (SaaS), and Function as a Service (FaaS) are just a few of the delivery and deployment models that are supported by the coherent architecture that these tiers together create. Additionally, deployment methods including public, private, hybrid, and multi-cloud environments—each suited to certain organizational requirements and preferences—are incorporated into cloud computing architecture. These models offer economies of scale, resource optimization, and improved innovation capabilities, all of which contribute to strategic flexibility. The chapter also highlights best practices to optimize cloud systems' efficiency and dependability while discussing the significance of security and performance optimization in cloud computing. Cloud computing design allows businesses to attain unmatched accessibility and scalability through its tiered structure. It gives them the ability to store data in safe cloud settings, remotely access systems, and maximize resource use. The rising adoption of cloud technology by enterprises and industries necessitates an awareness of the subtleties of cloud architecture to fully utilize its potential. In addition to offering a thorough manual for its design, implementation, and operating tactics, this chapter seeks to clarify the fundamental ideas and sophisticated structures of cloud computing architecture.

Cloud computing is a present technological trend that gives businesses the ability to dominate the market. One cutting-edge and improved technology for managing corporate operations is cloud computing. Today's enterprises run a wide range of applications in the cloud, including productivity, communication, accountancy, custom-built apps, and application development. Because users only pay for the services they use, cloud-based services are affordable for all types of businesses.

In summary, the architecture of cloud computing has become a fundamental component of contemporary technology, propelling notable breakthroughs in the use and administration of IT resources. Its ongoing development promises to expand technology's potential and reach even more, creating an atmosphere that encourages innovation and allows companies to go to new heights. It is crucial to be flexible and agile as we embrace the future of cloud computing, utilising the most recent developments to seize new possibilities and tackle new problems.

Organisations and people can continue to propel advancement and make significant contributions to the digital world by comprehending and using the full potential of cloud computing architecture. The development of cloud computing is far from over, and there are a ton of chances to innovate even more. The lines between IaaS, PaaS, and SaaS are becoming increasingly hazy as cloud technologies advance, and many providers are now providing hybrid solutions that incorporate aspects of all three models to satisfy a range of organizational requirements. The swift expansion and uptake of cloud services in numerous industries highlights their revolutionary influence on contemporary corporate operations. Organizations can effectively deploy apps, manage data, handle API traffic, and maintain security while scaling their operations with ease by utilizing these cloud service models. Knowing the subtle differences between each model enables companies to select the best mix of cloud services to suit their unique needs, which in turn spurs innovation, improves operational effectiveness, and keeps a competitive advantage in a world that is becoming more and more digital. Cloud architecture, which is still at the forefront of technical development, opens the door for more robust, scalable, and future-proof IT infrastructures by allowing companies to take advantage of state-of-the-art IT resources without having to make large upfront investments.

REFERENCES

Ahmad Dar, A. (2018). Cloud Computing-Positive Impacts and Challenges in Business Perspective. *Journal of Computer Science and Systems Biology*, *12*(01). Advance online publication. DOI: 10.4172/jcsb.1000294

Al Shehri, W. (2013). Cloud Database Database as a Service. *International Journal of Database Management Systems*, *5*(2), 1–12. DOI: 10.5121/ijdms.2013.5201

Alayda, S., Almowaysher, N. A., Humayun, M., & Jhanjhi, N. Z. (2020). A novel hybrid approach for access control in cloud computing. *International Journal of Engineering Research & Technology (Ahmedabad)*, *13*(11), 3404–3414. DOI: 10.37624/IJERT/13.11.2020.3404-3414

Alhazmi, L. (2023). Enhancing Cloud Security: An Optimization-based Deep Learning Model for Detecting Denial-of-Service Attacks. *IJACSA). International Journal of Advanced Computer Science and Applications*, *14*(7), 2023. www.ijacsa.thesai.org. DOI: 10.14569/IJACSA.2023.0140737

Amazon Web Services AWS. (2024). *What is Middleware?* https://aws.amazon.com/what-is/middleware/#:~:text=Middleware

Ananta, O. Z., Thangarasu, G., Subramanian, D. K., & Richard, N. (2022a). *Mobile Cloud Computing Services for An Enhanced Healthcare System.*

Ananta, O. Z., Thangarasu, G., Subramanian, D. K., & Richard, N. (2022b). Mobile Cloud Computing Services for An Enhanced Healthcare System. *MAHSA International Journal of Engineering and Technology,* *2*(1).

Angel, N. A., Ravindran, D., Vincent, P. M. D. R., Srinivasan, K., & Hu, Y. C. (2022). Recent advances in evolving computing paradigms: Cloud, edge, and fog technologies. In *Sensors* (Vol. 22, Issue 1). MDPI. https://doi.org/DOI: 10.3390/s22010196

Ara Shapla, R., Roy, S., & Kumar Prodhan Jatiya Kabi Kazi Nazrul, U. (2020). *Cloud Computing: Architecture, Services, Deployment Models, Storage, Benefits and Challenges*. https://www.researchgate.net/publication/341788106

Bajdor, P. (2024). CURRENT PERSPECTIVES ON SUSTAINABILITY IN CLOUD COMPUTING: A COMPREHENSIVE REVIEW. *Polish Journal of Management Studies*, *29*(1), 43–62. DOI: 10.17512/pjms.2024.29.1.03

Banger, N., & Pallavi, K. (2022). A Review Paper on Cloud Computing Architecture, Types, Advantages and Disadvantages. *International Journal of Advanced Research in Science. Tongxin Jishu*, •••, 14–22. DOI: 10.48175/IJARSCT-3144

Bello, S. A., Oyedele, L. O., Akinade, O. O., Bilal, M., Davila Delgado, J. M., Akanbi, L. A., Ajayi, A. O., & Owolabi, H. A. (2021). Cloud computing in construction industry: Use cases, benefits and challenges. In *Automation in Construction* (Vol. 122). Elsevier B.V., DOI: 10.1016/j.autcon.2020.103441

Chaturvedi, R., & Sharma, S. (2021). Optimizing Scalability and Performance in Cloud Services: Strategies and Solutions. *ESP Journal of Engineering & Technology Advancements*, *1*(2), 116–133. DOI: 10.56472/25832646/JETA-V1I2P115

Devadiga, A., Kumar, S., Rachhadiya, M., & Sahitya, A. (2021). *Integrated Development Environment on Cloud*. https://ssrn.com/abstract=3867647 DOI: 10.2139/ssrn.3867647

Google. (2025). *What Is Cloud Security_ _ Google Cloud _ Google Cloud.*

Gupta, M., Gupta, D., & Rai, P. (2024). Exploring the Impact of Software as a Service (SaaS) on Human Life. *EAI Endorsed Transactions on Internet of Things*, *10*. Advance online publication. DOI: 10.4108/eetiot.4821

Huawei Technologies Co. Ltd. (2023a). Cloud Computing Technology. In *Cloud Computing Technology*. Springer Nature Singapore. https://doi.org/DOI: 10.1007/978-981-19-3026-3

Huawei Technologies Co. Ltd. (2023b). Cloud Computing Technology. In *Cloud Computing Technology*. Springer Nature Singapore. https://doi.org/DOI: 10.1007/978-981-19-3026-3

IBM. (2021). *What is cloud security?* Https://Www.Ibm.Com/Think/Topics/Cloud-Security. https://www.ibm.com/think/topics/cloud-security

Isaac Odun- Ayo., S. M. F. A. (2018). CloudComputingArchitecture-ICCSA. *International Conference on Computational Science and Applications (ICCSA).*

Jadhav, R. J., & Vidyapeeth, B. (2013). Performance Evaluation of Web Browsers. *International Journal of Electronic Government Research*, *2*(1). https://www.researchgate.net/publication/374673908

Jeyaraman, J., & Muthusubramanian, M. (2022). The Synergy of Data Engineering and Cloud Computing in the Era of Machine Learning and AI TransUnion-USA 2 Discover Financial Services-USA. *Issue 1 Journal of Knowledge Learning and Science Technology Journal Homepage, 1*, 2959–6386. https://doi.org/DOI: 10.60087/jklst.vol1.n.p75

Kaspersky. (2025). *What is Cloud Security?* Https://Www.Kaspersky.Com/Resource-Center/Definitions/What-Is-Cloud-Security. https://www.kaspersky.com/resource-center/definitions/what-is-cloud-security

Katkar, S. V., Kharade, S., Kharade, K., Katkar, S. V., Kharade, S. K., Kharade, K. G., & Kamat, R. K. (2022). *Study of Cloud Computing and Its Architecture CS-07. Study of Cloud Computing and Its Architecture*. https://www.researchgate.net/publication/366659370

Kumar, E. S., Kesavan, S., Naidu, R. Ch. A., & Kumar, R. (2021). Comprehensive Analysis of Cloud based Databases. *IOP Conference Series. Materials Science and Engineering, 1131*(1), 012021. DOI: 10.1088/1757-899X/1131/1/012021

Kumar, G., Jain, E., Goel, S., & Panchal, V. K. (2014). Mobile cloud computing architecture, application model, and challenging issues. *Proceedings - 2014 6th International Conference on Computational Intelligence and Communication Networks, CICN 2014*, 613–617. https://doi.org/DOI: 10.1109/CICN.2014.137

Liu, F., Tong, J., Mao, J., Bohn, R., Messina, J., & Leaf, D. (2011). *NIST Cloud Computing Reference Architecture Recommendations of the National Institute of Standards and Technology*.

Logapriya, S., & Niraimathi, S. (2016). Data Storage in Cloud Computing. *IJSRSET, 2*(2), 1990–2395.

Malallah, H. S., Qashi, R., Abdulrahman, L. M., Omer, M. A., & Yazdeen, A. A. (2023). Performance Analysis of Enterprise Cloud Computing: A Review. *Journal of Applied Science and Technology Trends, 4*(01), 01–12. https://doi.org/DOI: 10.38094/jastt401139

Mell, P. M., & Grance, T. (2011). *The NIST definition of cloud computing*., DOI: 10.6028/NIST.SP.800-145

Multi-Cloud and Hybrid Cloud Guide. (2021). *Multi-Cloud and Hybrid Cloud Guide*.

Namasudra, S. (2018). *CLOUD COMPUTING: A NEW ERA*. https://doi.org/DOI: 10.4314/jfas.v10i2.9

Neu, W., Vlasceanu, V., Oram, A., & Alapati, S. (2019). *An Introduction to Cloud Databases A Guide for Administrators.*

Odun-Ayo, I., Adebiyi, M., Okesola, O., & Vincent, O. (2021). Cloud middleware and services-a systematic mapping review. *Bulletin of Electrical Engineering and Informatics, 10*(5), 2696–2706. DOI: 10.11591/eei.v10i5.3169

OTAVA. (2024). *The Future of Cloud Computing in 2024 and Beyond_ Trends and Predictions _ OTAVA®.*

Pallis, G. (2010). *View from the Cloud Cloud Computing The New Frontier of Internet Computing*. https://csrc.nist.gov/groups/

Peram, P. (2024). ARCHITECTURE: UNDERSTANDING IAAS, PAAS, AND SAAS. [IJCET]. *International Journal of Computer Engineering and Technology, 15*(5), 117–128. DOI: 10.5281/zenodo.13739408

Pradhan Kulkarni, N., & BasuMallick, C. (2021). *What Is Cloud Storage? Denition, Types, Benets, and Best Practices Cloud storage allows users to store digital data les on virtual servers.* https://www.spiceworks.com/tech/cloud/articles/what-is-cloud-storage/

Radošević, I., & Hongyu Pei-Breivold, S. (2014). *School of Innovation*. Design and Engineering Architecting for the Cloud.

Saeidnia, H. R., Ghorbi, A., Kozak, M., & Abdoli, S. (2021). Web-based Application Programming Interface (Web APIs): Vacancies in Iranian Public Library Websites. *Webology, 19*(1), 133–141. DOI: 10.14704/WEB/V19I1/WEB19010

Sareen, P. (2013). Cloud Computing: Types, Architecture, Applications, Concerns, Virtualization and Role of IT Governance in Cloud. []. www.ijarcsse.com]. *International Journal of Advanced Research in Computer Science and Software Engineering, 3*(3), •••.

Sasikumar, M., Jayarin, P. J., & Vinnarasi, F. S. F. (2023). A Hierarchical Optimized Resource Utilization based Content Placement (HORCP) model for cloud Content Delivery Networks (CDNs). *Journal of Cloud Computing (Heidelberg, Germany), 12*(1), 139. Advance online publication. DOI: 10.1186/s13677-023-00519-2

Segun-Falade, O. D., Osundare, O. S., Kedi, W. E., Okeleke, P. A., Ijomah, T. I., & Abdul-Azeez, O. Y. (2024). Assessing the transformative impact of cloud computing on software deployment and management. *Computer Science & IT Research Journal, 5*(8), 2062–2082. DOI: 10.51594/csitrj.v5i8.1492

Seth, D., Najana, M., & Ranjan, P. (2024). Compliance and Regulatory Challenges in Cloud Computing: A Sector-Wise Analysis. *International Journal of Global Innovations and Solutions (IJGIS)*. https://doi.org/DOI: 10.21428/e90189c8.68b5dea5

Shravanthi, C. (2014). MOBILE CLOUD COMPUTING AS FUTURE FOR MOBILE APPLICATIONS. *International Journal of Research in Engineering and Technology*, *03*(05), 253–256. DOI: 10.15623/ijret.2014.0305048

Subramanyam, S. V. (2025). Cloud-Based Enterprise Systems: Bridging Scalability and Security in Healthcare and Finance. *International Journal on Science and Technology*, *16*(1).

Surbiryala, J., & Rong, C. (2019). Cloud computing: History and overview. *Proceedings - 2019 3rd IEEE International Conference on Cloud and Fog Computing Technologies and Applications, Cloud Summit 2019*, 1–7. https://doi.org/DOI: 10.1109/CloudSummit47114.2019.00007

Ts, A., Parthasarathy, R., Ayyappan, P., Perumal, I., Seow, M., Loong, S., & Alias, B. (2020). An Overview of Cloud Computing Different Services Models and Security Issues and Concerns in an Enterprises Data Storages. In *IJISET-International Journal of Innovative Science, Engineering & Technology* (Vol. 7). www.ijiset.com

Vemasani, P., & Modi, S. (2024). OPTIMIZING CLOUD COMPUTING PERFORMANCE: HOW CDNS REVOLUTIONIZE GLOBAL CONTENT DELIVERY. [JARET]. *Journal of Advanced Research Engineering and Technology*, *3*(1), 11–24. https://iaeme.com/Home/journal/JARET11editor@iaeme.comhttps://iaeme.com/Home/issue/JARET?Volume=3&Issue=1https://iaeme.com/Home/journal/JARET12

Verma, R., & Jain, P. (2015). *Containerization in Cloud: Docker, Kubernetes, and Beyond Introduction to Containerization*. https://www.researchgate.net/publication/385002203

Wang, Y., & Yang, X. (2025). Research on Enhancing Cloud Computing Network Security using Artificial Intelligence Algorithms. *ArXiv Preprint ArXiv:2502.17801*.

Wes Hardaker, A. (2022). *Content Delivery Networks (CDNs) Overview and Illicit Material Considerations*. https://publicexchange.usc.edu/wp-content/uploads/2022/10/USC-Thorn-Report_CDNs-Overview-and-Illicit-Material-Considerations.pdf

Wu, W., & Plakhtii, A. (2021). E-Learning Based on Cloud Computing. *International Journal of Emerging Technologies in Learning*, *16*(10), 4–17. DOI: 10.3991/ijet.v16i10.18579

Xie, Z., Yang, Y., & Lee, S. (2023). Data Center Based on Cloud Computing Technology. *International Journal of Informatics and Information Systems*, *6*(1), 31–37. DOI: 10.47738/ijiis.v6i1.128

Yamato, Y. (2018). Server Selection, Configuration and Reconfiguration Technology for IaaS Cloud with Multiple Server Types. *Journal of Network and Systems Management*, *26*(2), 339–360. DOI: 10.1007/s10922-017-9418-z

Chapter 3
Cloud Deployment Models:
Standard and Framework

Azana Hafizah Mohd Aman
https://orcid.org/0000-0001-7337-6736
Faculty of Information Science and Technology, Bangi, Malaysia

Wan Muhd Hazwan Azamuddin
https://orcid.org/0000-0002-8124-6226
Institut Latihan Perindustrian, Tangkak, Malaysia

Maznifah Salam
https://orcid.org/0000-0003-1332-260X
Faculty of Information Science and Technology, Bangi, Malaysia

Zainab S. Attarbashi
https://orcid.org/0000-0002-1452-8098
Kulliyyah of Information and Communication Technology, Malaysia

ABSTRACT

This chapter provides a comprehensive overview of cloud deployment models, including public, private, hybrid, and community clouds, and their profound impact on modern IT infrastructure and the development of inclusive IoT smart systems. The selection of an appropriate cloud model significantly influences critical aspects such as data sovereignty, scalability, resource utilization, and crucially, the accessibility features for individuals with disabilities. We examine the distinct characteristics, advantages, and disadvantages of each model, highlighting how they cater to diverse organizational needs, from cost optimization and rapid provisioning in public clouds to enhanced security and control in private environments. The discussion also ad-

DOI: 10.4018/979-8-3693-9984-2.ch003

dresses the complexities and benefits of hybrid and community cloud approaches, emphasizing their role in enabling flexible, compliant, and collaborative computing solutions. Understanding these models is essential for making informed strategic decisions that foster innovation and ensure equitable access to technology.

1.0 INTRODUCTION TO CLOUD DEPLOYMENT MODELS

In the rapidly evolving landscape of cloud computing, understanding the various deployment models is crucial for organizations looking to leverage cloud resources effectively. Cloud deployment models, which include public, private, hybrid, and community cloud, define the structural framework for deploying cloud computing resources and services (Ellman et al., 2023). These models are critical for IoT-enabled smart systems, profoundly influencing aspects such as data sovereignty, scalability, and resource utilization (Azumah et al., 2023). For instance, a public cloud provides economies of scale and rapid provisioning, making it ideal for resource-intensive applications, whereas a private cloud offers superior control over data security and compliance, which is vital for applications handling sensitive personal health information (Kumara et al., 2023; Liu et al., 2024).

Choosing the right cloud deployment option is critical to ensuring the accessibility and inclusivity of IoT smart solutions for people with disabilities. Real-time data streaming and processing, fundamental for applications utilizing speech recognition, gesture control, and environmental sensing, necessitates a durable and scalable cloud infrastructure (Bruno et al., 2024; Rajendran et al., 2023). The chosen model significantly impacts the accessibility features that can be implemented, including customizable user interfaces, the capacity to integrate assistive devices, and real-time data processing for personalized recommendations and adaptive functionalities (Ajaz et al., 2024). Formal approaches are being developed to fragment large-scale workflow processes and their applications for deployment across multiple and heterogeneous cloud computing environments, providing a theoretical basis for designing maximally distributed workflow processes (Ahn & Kim, 2021). Furthermore, research explores various cloud-based deployment archetypes for cloud applications, examining tradeoffs related to high availability, low end-user latency, and acceptable costs across zonal, regional, multi-regional, global, hybrid, and multi-cloud configurations (Berenberg & Calder, 2023). The suitability of a deployment strategy, which is not standardized, heavily depends on the application type and specific business requirements, highlighting the need for careful evaluation of metrics like reliability and cost (Harris et al., 2024).

Applications aimed at people with impairments must carefully consider the unique requirements of each deployment model. A thorough evaluation of data latency, network stability, and adherence to accessibility guidelines is essential (Rajendran et al., 2023). An adequately designed cloud solution can make smart technologies more inclusive and accessible, empowering impaired individuals to gain independence, improve their quality of life, and seamlessly integrate assistive devices into their routines (Ajaz et al., 2024; Bruno et al., 2024). The most appropriate model is determined by factors such as data sensitivity, budget constraints, and specific operational needs, as illustrated in Figure 1. Each cloud deployment approach possesses distinct strengths and drawbacks, which organizations must weigh carefully. Decision-making frameworks, such as Multi-Criteria Decision Making (MCDM) problems, are also being developed to assist academic organizations in parametrically selecting suitable cloud deployment models, considering various conflicting decision parameters (Garg, 2022). Tools like SuperArch, a supervised architecture design tool leveraging Large Language Models (LLM), are emerging to facilitate optimal selection and configuration of cloud services by extracting information from user requirements and specifications and estimating performance and cost (Singh et al., 2024). The proper model is determined by data sensitivity, budget constraints, and the specific needs, as illustrated in Figure 1. Each cloud deployment approach has strengths and drawbacks, as summarized in Table 1.

Figure 1. Cloud Deployment Models Features

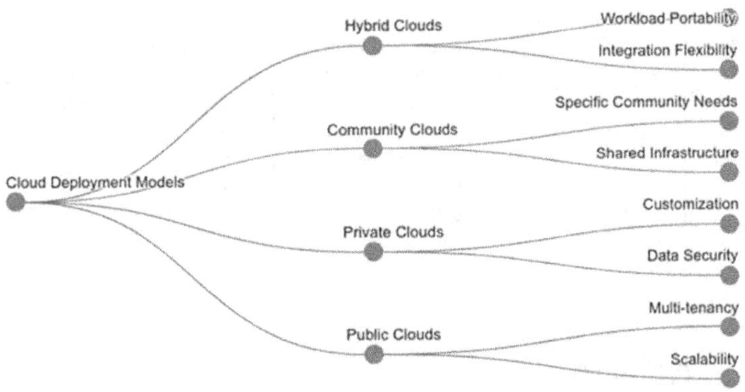

Table 1. Cloud Deployment Model Strengths and Limitations

Model	Strengths	Limitations
Public Cloud (Kumara et al., 2023)	• Cost-effective with pay-as-you-use model • Highly scalable and elastic • Global accessibility and availability • Minimal maintenance overhead • Built-in redundancy and disaster recovery • Access to latest technologies	• Limited customization options • Privacy and data security concerns • Compliance and regulatory challenges • Vendor lock-in risks • Network dependency and latency issues • Shared resource contention • Less control over infrastructure • Potential for service outages • Data sovereignty concerns
Private Cloud (Liu et al., 2024)	• High security and data control • Full customization capabilities • Enhanced regulatory compliance • Predictable performance levels • Complete data sovereignty • Legacy system integration • Dedicated resources • Internal policy enforcement • No shared tenant risks	• High capital and operational costs • Limited scalability (hardware-bound) • Significant maintenance overhead • Longer deployment timelines • Resource underutilization risks • Skilled staff requirements • Infrastructure management complexity • Higher total cost of ownership • Technology refresh challenges
Hybrid Cloud (Azumah et al., 2023)	• Workload flexibility and optimization • Cost optimization strategies • Scalability options • Risk distribution across environments • Regulatory compliance capabilities • Gradual cloud migration path • Data classification possibilities • Disaster recovery options	• Complex architecture and design • Integration complexity challenges • Management overhead increase • Security complexity • Specialized skill requirements • Potential latency between clouds • Coordination and orchestration issues • Higher governance complexity • Network connectivity dependencies
Community Cloud (Pan et al., 2025)	• Cost sharing among members • Collaborative benefits and synergies • Tailored compliance for industry • Specialized features for sector needs • Industry-focused solutions • Knowledge and resource sharing • Reduced individual costs • Collective expertise utilization • Standardized industry practices	• Limited availability and options • Dependency on community partners • Exit strategy difficulties • Compromise on individual customization • Coordination overhead requirements • Slower decision-making processes • Potential for conflicting requirements • Member commitment dependencies

2.0 PUBLIC CLOUD

The public cloud is an important and widely adopted deployment model for cloud computing (Azumah et al., 2023; Kumara et al., 2023). In this model, third-party providers own and operate a communal pool of computing resources, including servers, storage, networking, and software (Rajendran et al., 2023). These resources are made available to numerous users online through a flexible pay-as-you-go subscription approach (Ellman et al., 2023). This shared infrastructure eliminates the need for businesses or individuals to make substantial upfront expenditures on their own data centers and technologies, thereby significantly lowering capital costs and making it particularly attractive for small and medium enterprises (Pan et al., 2025).

Scalability is a key feature of the public cloud. Users can easily and dynamically adjust their resource allocation based on their needs, seamlessly scaling up during periods of high demand and scaling down during low utilization. This versatility is especially important for IoT-enabled smart technologies, which routinely generate large amounts of data from networked devices. The system's ability to quickly scale resources ensures it can efficiently manage real-time data processing, event monitoring, and control commands, even during peak usage times, providing the comprehensive review highlighted by Kumara et al. (2023). Furthermore, performance engineering approaches like Feature-Oriented Cloud (FOCloud) are being developed for deployment-configurable cloud applications, leveraging feature modeling, machine learning, and Explainable AI to predict performance outcomes and provide explanations for various deployment options in public IaaS clouds (Kumara et al., 2023).

The public cloud's accessibility is particularly beneficial for those with disabilities. Utilizing internet connectivity, public cloud services provide remote access to smart technology applications and data from almost anywhere in the world. This accessibility is critical for people with mobility disabilities or who require remote support (Bruno et al., 2024). Furthermore, cloud-based platforms can be effortlessly integrated with assistive technology such as screen readers, voice control interfaces, and braille displays, enhancing the overall user experience for people with diverse needs (Ajaz et al., 2024).

Public cloud providers are continuously innovating, introducing new features, and improving their service offerings. Customers can rapidly obtain the most recent technology and advancements. Artificial intelligence, machine learning, and edge computing are all examples of cutting-edge technologies that can significantly enhance the functionality and intelligence of IoT-enabled smart technologies. These advancements can lead to more personalized and responsive experiences, increased energy efficiency, and enhanced user security. The consistent evolution of public cloud offerings aligns with the opportunities and challenges discussed in systematic reviews of cloud deployment models (Azumah et al., 2023). Evaluation of various cloud-native deployment options, with a specific focus on reliability, is also crucial, examining how different implementation choices affect quality attributes in cloud-native applications on platforms like AWS (Knoch et al., 2025).

While the public cloud offers numerous benefits, it also raises significant concerns, particularly regarding data privacy and security. The distribution of resources among multiple tenants in a common environment increases the danger of data breaches and unauthorized access. This is especially important for applications created for people with disabilities, which may include sensitive personal health information or other confidential data. To ensure the confidentiality, integrity, and availability of this data, stringent security standards such as encryption, access controls, and frequent security assessments must be followed. Addressing these security concerns is critical for establishing confidence and promoting the widespread adoption of cloud-based solutions for accessible and inclusive smart technology environments. Figure 2 provides a summarized view of the public cloud's standards.

The details of the public cloud model can be understood through various aspects. For resources available, public clouds offer virtually unlimited computing resources, including servers, storage (object, block, file), networking (CDN, load balancers, VPNs), databases (SQL/NoSQL), and specialized services such as AI/ML, analytics, and IoT. This shared multi-tenant infrastructure is optimized for high availability and performance across global data centers. In terms of cost efficiency, the pay-as-you-go subscription model eliminates large capital expenditures, reducing operational costs through shared infrastructure, automated management, and economies of scale. Additionally, cost optimization tools, reserved instances, and spot pricing options are available. The challenge of finding a high-performance and cost-effective cloud service provider, especially for demanding tasks like training deep learning models, necessitates careful evaluation of performance and cost across multi-cloud environments (Harris et al., 2024).

Regarding scalability, public clouds feature auto-scaling capabilities with both horizontal and vertical scaling options, supporting massive workloads from startup applications to enterprise systems. They offer elastic resource allocation based on real-time demand, making them perfect for IoT, big data analytics, and variable traffic applications with burst capacity. Accessibility is another key aspect, providing global internet access from any device, location, or time zone. This is particularly beneficial for remote work, distributed teams, and users with mobility challenges, as it supports integration with assistive technologies like screen readers and voice control, and provides accessibility compliance tools.

From a technology standpoint, public clouds leverage cutting-edge technologies including AI/ML services, serverless computing, container orchestration (Kubernetes), edge computing, quantum computing access, and blockchain services, with regular updates and new service launches occurring without user intervention. The enhanced experience in public clouds includes personalized dashboards and recommendations, energy-efficient operations through optimized resource allocation, and improved performance through AI-driven optimizations, alongside enhanced mobile experiences and cross-platform compatibility.

However, public clouds also present security concerns due to a shared responsibility model that requires a clear understanding of provider versus customer security obligations. Risks include data breaches, unauthorized access, and potential service provider vulnerabilities, coupled with multi-tenancy concerns and data isolation challenges. Data privacy is a critical consideration for sensitive data such as healthcare records, financial information, and personal data for disabled individuals, necessitating adherence to strict security standards, encryption at rest and in transit, and data residency compliance. Finally, data sovereignty is addressed through geographic data residency options, regional data centers, and compliance with local data protection laws, with data portability guarantees and clear data ownership policies, as well as cross-border data transfer controls. Table 2 the public cloud details. Figure 2 provides a summarized view of the public cloud's standards.

Table 2. Public cloud model details

Aspect	Details
Resources Available	Virtually unlimited computing resources including servers, storage (object, block, file), networking (CDN, load balancers, VPNs), databases (SQL/NoSQL), and specialized services (AI/ML, analytics, IoT). Shared multi-tenant infrastructure optimized for high availability and performance across global data centers.
Cost Efficiency	Pay-as-you-go subscription model eliminates large capital expenditures. Reduced operational costs through shared infrastructure, automated management, and economies of scale. Cost optimization tools, reserved instances, and spot pricing options are available.
Scalability	Auto-scaling capabilities with horizontal and vertical scaling options. Supports massive workloads from startup applications to enterprise systems. Elastic resource allocation based on real-time demand, perfect for IoT, big data analytics, and variable traffic applications with burst capacity.
Accessibility	Global internet access from any device, location, or time zone. Particularly beneficial for remote work, distributed teams, and users with mobility challenges. Supports integration with assistive technologies (screen readers, voice control) and provides accessibility compliance tools.
Technology	Cutting-edge technologies include AI/ML services, serverless computing, container orchestration (Kubernetes), edge computing, quantum computing access, and blockchain services. Regular updates and new service launches without user intervention.
Enhanced Experience	Personalized dashboards and recommendations, energy-efficient operations through optimized resource allocation, and improved performance through AI-driven optimizations. Enhanced mobile experiences and cross-platform compatibility.
Security Concerns	Shared responsibility model requires clear understanding of provider vs. customer security obligations. Risks include data breaches, unauthorized access, and potential service provider vulnerabilities. Multi-tenancy concerns and data isolation challenges.
Data Privacy	Critical consideration for sensitive data including healthcare records, financial information, and personal data for disabled individuals. Requires adherence to strict security standards, encryption at rest and in transit, and data residency compliance.
Data Sovereignty	Geographic data residency options, regional data centers, and compliance with local data protection laws. Data portability guarantees and clear data ownership policies. Cross-border data transfer controls.

Figure 2. Public cloud standards framework.

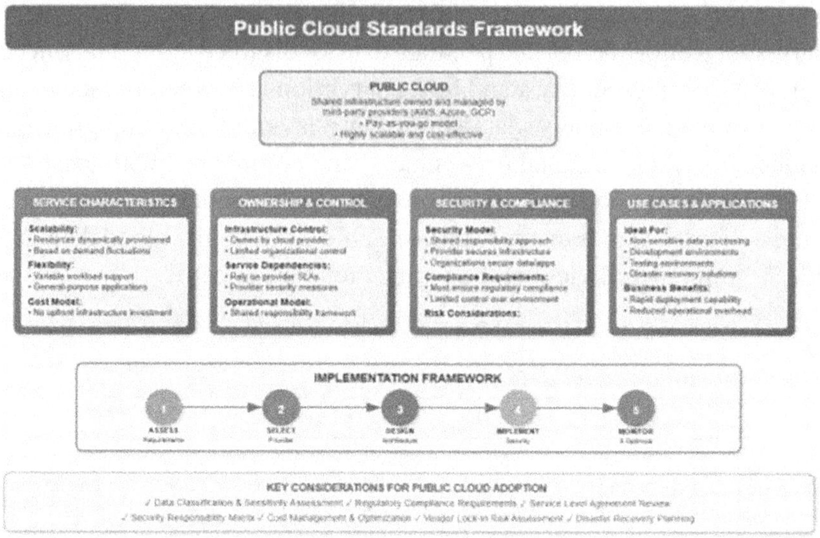

3.0 PRIVATE CLOUD

A private cloud is a cloud computing paradigm in which a single company controls and administers a specific infrastructure (Azumah et al., 2023; Liu et al., 2024). This model, extensively surveyed by Liu et al. (2024), distinguishes itself from public clouds by offering complete control over the computing environment, including hardware, software, and security. This level of control is especially useful for businesses that manage highly sensitive data or require substantial customization to meet their specific needs, aligning with the opportunities and challenges discussed in systematic reviews of cloud models (Azumah et al., 2023).

A primary benefit of a private cloud is increased data security. Businesses with complete control over their infrastructure and data can protect critical data with stringent security measures such as firewalls, intrusion detection systems, and encryption. This robust security posture is especially important for smart technology applications that may need to maintain personal health data, financial information, or other sensitive data about people with disabilities, where strict compliance and confidentiality are paramount (Ajaz et al., 2024).

The private cloud environment enables businesses to tailor infrastructure and applications to the specific needs of their consumers, including those with disabilities. This level of flexibility allows for introducing specialized accessibility features such as voice control interfaces, screen readers, and braille displays. Furthermore, the private cloud environment may be tuned for maximum performance and dependability, ensuring that important smart technology services like emergency alarms, remote monitoring, and environmental management run smoothly and consistently. This customization capability is a key advantage, as detailed in comprehensive surveys on private clouds (Liu et al., 2024). The selection of the most cost-effective private cloud deployment model from a business perspective involves evaluating ownership and responsibility for maintenance and operations, often using optimization approaches to guide informed decisions (Liu et al., 2024).

Although private clouds offer numerous advantages, they also have certain limits. Scalability might be an issue when compared to public clouds, as private cloud systems often have limited resources. Adjusting resources to handle rapid growth or unexpected demand surges may involve significant upfront investment and strategic planning, potentially leading to slower scalability compared to the elastic nature of public cloud environments. The costs of deploying and maintaining a private cloud could be significant. Organizations are solely responsible for all capital expenditures connected to the procurement and maintenance of required hardware, software, and infrastructure. Furthermore, they must provide resources for skilled staff to manage and maintain the private cloud infrastructure. Even though they are more expensive and cannot grow as quickly, private clouds remain an excellent choice for businesses that value data security, strict compliance rules, and the ability to fully customize their cloud environments to meet the needs of all users, including disabled individuals. Figure 3 summarize the essential private cloud standard.

The details of a private cloud are elaborated across several key aspects, including infrastructure control, data security and compliance, customization and integration, performance and reliability, scalability, and network architecture. For infrastructure control, private clouds offer complete hardware ownership and management, allowing for custom server configurations related to CPU, RAM, and storage, as well as personalized network topology design and implementation. Organizations can select their preferred hypervisor, such as VMware vSphere, Hyper-V, or KVM, and choose their storage architecture, including SAN, NAS, or hyper-converged systems. However, this level of control requires dedicated data center space, 24/7 monitoring and maintenance staff, careful hardware lifecycle management, and planning for disaster recovery sites, all while ensuring compliance with physical security standards. Relevant technologies include VMware vSphere/vCenter, Microsoft Hyper-V, Citrix XenServer, OpenStack, and Dell EMC VxRail.

In terms of data security and compliance, private clouds allow for end-to-end encryption using standards like AES-256 and TLS 1.3, network segmentation and micro-segmentation, robust Identity and Access Management (IAM), multi-factor authentication (MFA), and Security Information and Event Management (SIEM) systems. Data Loss Prevention (DLP) and regular security audits and penetration testing are also key components. These measures facilitate compliance with regulations such as GDPR, HIPAA, SOX, and PCI-DSS, address data residency requirements, and enable the implementation of zero-trust security models, regular policy updates, employee security training, and incident response procedures. Technologies commonly used include Palo Alto Networks firewalls, Cisco ASA/Firepower, Splunk/IBM QRadar SIEM, CyberArk PAM, Okta/Azure AD, Symantec DLP, and Qualys/Nessus vulnerability scanners.

Customization and integration in a private cloud environment involve custom API development and integration, tailored user interfaces and workflows, application-specific performance tuning, and custom automation and orchestration. It also facilitates legacy system integration and specialized compliance configurations. This requires a skilled development team, thorough integration testing phases, robust change management processes, comprehensive documentation and knowledge transfer, and ongoing user training and adoption. Technologies supporting these aspects include REST/GraphQL APIs, Ansible/Puppet for automation, Jenkins CI/CD pipelines, Docker/Kubernetes containers, Terraform for Infrastructure as Code (IaC), and custom middleware solutions.

Regarding performance and reliability, private clouds provide dedicated high-performance computing resources, custom load balancing and traffic management, and the ability to guarantee high SLA uptime (e.g., 99.9%+). They offer predictable latency and throughput, real-time performance monitoring, and automated failover and recovery. Effective management includes establishing performance baselines, capacity planning and forecasting, regular performance testing, proactive monitoring and alerting, and scheduling maintenance windows for performance optimization cycles. Key technologies here are F5/Citrix load balancers, VMware vRealize Operations, NetApp/Pure Storage arrays, Cisco/Arista network switches, HPE/Dell enterprise servers, and Red Hat Enterprise Linux.

For scalability, private clouds support both horizontal and vertical scaling capabilities, auto-scaling policies and triggers, efficient resource pooling and allocation, and elastic storage expansion. Network bandwidth scaling, multi-tier application scaling, and database clustering and replication are also possible. This requires meticulous capacity planning methodologies, implementation of scaling automation, performance impact assessments, cost-benefit analyses of scaling, and continuous resource utilization optimization and testing. Relevant technologies include Kubernetes orchestration, VMware vSAN storage, Cisco ACI networking, MongoDB/PostgreSQL clustering, Redis caching layers, and Apache Kafka messaging, complemented by Prometheus/Grafana monitoring.

Finally, the network architecture in a private cloud can include software-defined networking (SDN), network function virtualization (NFV), VLAN and VXLAN segmentation, Quality of Service (QoS) policies, network access control (NAC), and intrusion prevention systems (IPS). Considerations involve thorough network design and topology planning, implementation of security zones, traffic flow analysis and optimization, network capacity planning, and redundancy and failover design, along with meticulous network documentation. Technologies used are Cisco Nexus data center switches, VMware NSX for network virtualization, Palo Alto Networks firewalls, Cisco ISE for network access control, SolarWinds for network monitoring, and Riverbed for WAN optimization. Figure 3 summarizes the essential private cloud standard. Table 3 highlights the details.

Figure 3. Private cloud standards framework.

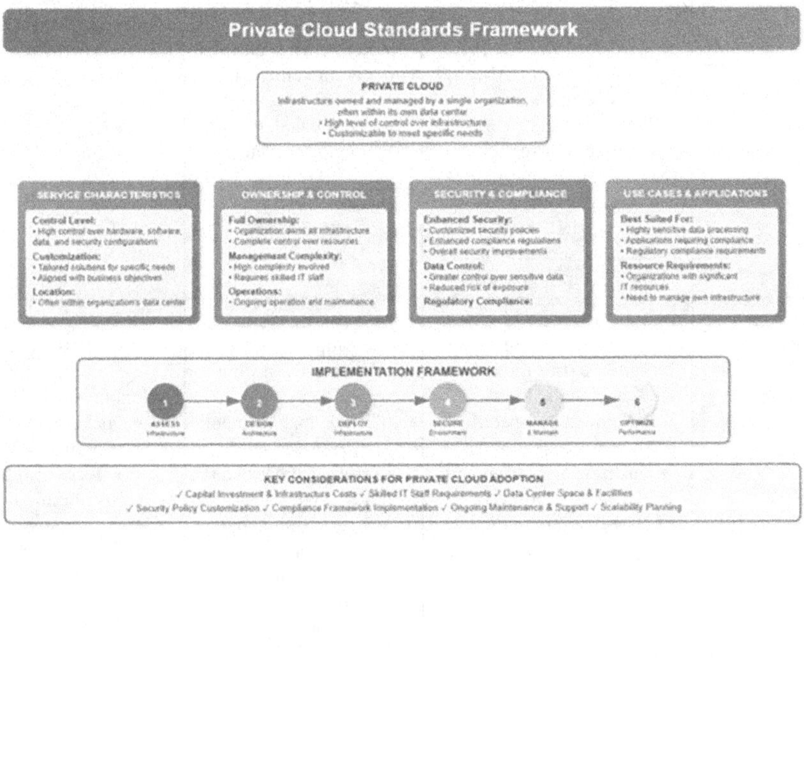

Table 3. Private cloud details.

Aspect	Details	Considerations	Technologies
Infrastructure Control	• Complete hardware ownership and management • Custom server configurations (CPU, RAM, storage) • Network topology design and implementation • Hypervisor selection (VMware vSphere, Hyper-V, KVM) • Storage architecture (SAN, NAS, hyper-converged)	• Requires dedicated data center space • 24/7 monitoring and maintenance staff • Hardware lifecycle management • Disaster recovery site planning • Compliance with physical security standards	• VMware vSphere/ vCenter • Microsoft Hyper-V • Citrix XenServer • OpenStack • Dell EMC VxRail
Data Security and Compliance	• End-to-end encryption (AES-256, TLS 1.3) • Network segmentation and micro-segmentation • Identity and Access Management (IAM) • Multi-factor authentication (MFA) • Security Information and Event Management (SIEM) • Data Loss Prevention (DLP) • Regular security audits and penetration testing	• GDPR, HIPAA, SOX, PCI-DSS compliance • Data residency requirements • Zero-trust security model implementation • Regular security policy updates • Employee security training • Incident response procedures	• Palo Alto Networks firewalls • Cisco ASA/Firepower • Splunk/IBM QRadar SIEM • CyberArk PAM • Okta/Azure AD • Symantec DLP • Qualys/Nessus vulnerability scanners
Customization and Integration	• Custom API development and integration • Tailored user interfaces and workflows • Application-specific performance tuning • Custom automation and orchestration • Legacy system integration • Specialized compliance configurations	• Requires skilled development team • Integration testing phases • Change management processes • Documentation and knowledge transfer • User training and adoption • Ongoing customization maintenance	• REST/GraphQL APIs • Ansible/Puppet automation • Jenkins CI/CD pipelines • Docker/Kubernetes containers • Terraform IaC • Custom middleware solutions

continued on following page

Table 3. Continued

Aspect	Details	Considerations	Technologies
Performance and Reliability	• Dedicated high-performance computing resources • Custom load balancing and traffic management • SLA guarantees (99.9%+ uptime) • Predictable latency and throughput • Real-time performance monitoring • Automated failover and recovery	• Performance baseline establishment • Capacity planning and forecasting • Regular performance testing • Proactive monitoring and alerting • Maintenance window scheduling • Performance optimization cycles	• F5/Citrix load balancers • VMware vRealize Operations • NetApp/Pure Storage arrays • Cisco/Arista network switches • HPE/Dell enterprise servers • Red Hat Enterprise Linux
Scalability	• Horizontal and vertical scaling capabilities • Auto-scaling policies and triggers • Resource pooling and allocation • Elastic storage expansion • Network bandwidth scaling • Multi-tier application scaling • Database clustering and replication	• Capacity planning methodologies • Scaling automation implementation • Performance impact assessment • Cost-benefit analysis of scaling • Resource utilization optimization • Scaling testing and validation	• Kubernetes orchestration • VMware vSAN storage • Cisco ACI networking • MongoDB/PostgreSQL clustering • Redis caching layers • Apache Kafka messaging • Prometheus/Grafana monitoring
Network Architecture	• Software-defined networking (SDN) • Network function virtualization (NFV) • VLAN and VXLAN segmentation • Quality of Service (QoS) policies • Network access control (NAC) • Intrusion prevention systems (IPS)	• Network design and topology planning • Security zone implementation • Traffic flow analysis and optimization • Network capacity planning • Redundancy and failover design • Network documentation and diagrams	• Cisco Nexus data center switches • VMware NSX network virtualization • Palo Alto Networks firewalls • Cisco ISE network access control • SolarWinds network monitoring • Riverbed WAN optimization

4.0 HYBRID CLOUD

The hybrid cloud model is a sophisticated cloud computing technique that combines the benefits of both public and private clouds (Ajaz et al., 2024; Azumah et al., 2023). This unified strategy allows businesses to leverage the flexibility, low cost, and new features of public clouds while maintaining the enhanced control offered by private clouds, which are essential for protecting sensitive data and critical applications (Berenberg & Calder, 2023). This versatility enables businesses to optimize their cloud infrastructure based on the unique requirements of different workloads, effectively managing the hybrid cloud environment as discussed by Berenberg and Calder (2023). Extending low-code tools with multi-cloud deployment capabilities, including the definition of a language and grammar for modeling deployment architecture and automating application packaging and cloud provisioning, is a significant advancement in this area (Ul Haq et al., 2024). Decision support systems for multicloud deployment, leveraging decision trees and decisional algorithms, can help users who are not cloud computing specialists take advantage of cloud environments' capabilities (Lacatusu et al., 2022).

The hybrid cloud's key advantage is its ability to provide balanced solutions for companies with various requirements. Critical applications that require high levels of security and compliance, such as those that handle sensitive personal health data for people with disabilities (Ajaz et al., 2024), can be housed in a private cloud. Concurrently, less sensitive workloads, such as data analysis or machine learning operations, can be moved to the more cost-effective and scalable public cloud. This balanced technique allows businesses to increase resource efficiency and lower costs while maintaining the necessary level of security and monitoring. This strategic workload placement is a core strength, addressing the opportunities and challenges in cloud deployment models (Azumah et al., 2023).

The hybrid cloud strategy offers significant flexibility in resource management and adapting to changing demand. During peak demand periods, such as those experienced during heatwaves or power outages, resources can be dynamically shifted from the private cloud to the public cloud to ensure the availability of critical smart technology features. This adaptability, often referred to as "cloud bursting," is critical for applications designed for disabled individuals because it ensures that essential features like emergency alarms, remote monitoring, and environmental management continue to function even when demand is high (Bruno et al., 2024; Rajendran et al., 2023). A significant technical difficulty for the hybrid cloud is ensuring seamless communication and interoperability between public and private cloud services. To ensure that data may be delivered safely and reliably between the two settings, complicated network configurations, robust data synchronization mechanisms, and stringent security measures are frequently required (Berenberg & Calder, 2023). Estimating the performance of application deployment on distributed IoT-edge-cloud infrastructures is crucial given the lack of shared standards among platforms and vendors, enabling developers to choose the most suitable edge infrastructure and cloud service ecosystem (Marozzo et al., 2024).

Successfully managing a hybrid cloud architecture demands extensive knowledge and specialized tools. Companies must engage competent staff and high-tech management systems to monitor resource usage, improve performance, and ensure the hybrid cloud architecture is secure and compliant. Despite these issues, the hybrid cloud model is an excellent alternative for enterprises that want to take use of the finest features of both public and private clouds while also addressing the needs of all users, including those with disabilities. Enterprises may use the hybrid cloud to create innovative and inclusive smart technology solutions by methodically addressing technological issues and implementing effective management techniques. Figure 4 summarizes the hybrid cloud standard.

The hybrid cloud model is characterized by several key aspects, including data security and control, resource management, interoperability architecture, and network architecture. In terms of data security and control, hybrid clouds feature end-to-end encryption for data both in transit and at rest, identity federation, and single sign-on (SSO) capabilities. They also implement a zero-trust network architecture, robust data classification and governance policies, and continuous compliance monitoring across hybrid environments. Key management and rotation policies, alongside security orchestration and automated response, are critical. Considerations for this aspect include addressing data sovereignty and residency requirements, enforcing unified security policies, managing cross-platform vulnerabilities, coordinating incident response, maintaining compliance audit trails, implementing data loss prevention strategies, and addressing security skills gaps. Relevant technologies include Microsoft Azure Arc/AWS Outposts, HashiCorp Vault for key management, Okta/Azure AD for identity federation, Palo Alto Prisma Cloud for security, CrowdStrike/SentinelOne for endpoint protection, and Splunk/IBM QRadar for SIEM integration.

For resource management, hybrid clouds enable centralized resource orchestration and provisioning, policy-driven resource allocation, and automated workload migration and bursting. They facilitate resource pooling across hybrid infrastructure, performance monitoring and optimization, and service mesh for microservices management, often leveraging Infrastructure as Code (IaC) for deployment. Considerations involve robust resource discovery and inventory management, comprehensive capacity planning across environments, performance baseline establishment, resource governance and quotas, service level agreement monitoring, change management processes, and ongoing resource optimization strategies. Technologies frequently used are Kubernetes/OpenShift for container orchestration, Terraform/CloudFormation for IaC, VMware vRealize Automation, Red Hat CloudForms for management, and AWS Systems Manager/Azure Arc.

Interoperability architecture in a hybrid cloud involves API gateway management and integration, robust data synchronization and replication strategies, and reliable network connectivity through VPNs, Direct Connect, or ExpressRoute. It also includes container orchestration across environments, database federation and distributed queries, and message queuing and event-driven architectures, alongside cross-platform monitoring and logging. Key considerations for this aspect are API versioning and lifecycle management, ensuring data consistency and resolving conflicts, optimizing network latency and bandwidth, managing container image registries, evolving database schemas, and implementing event sourcing and CQRS patterns, as well as robust observability and distributed tracing. Technologies supporting interoperability include Kong/Ambassador API gateways, AWS Direct Connect/Azure ExpressRoute, Docker/Podman container runtimes, Apache Kafka/RabbitMQ for messaging, MongoDB/PostgreSQL for distributed databases, and Prometheus/Grafana for monitoring.

Lastly, the network architecture in a hybrid cloud often incorporates software-defined WAN (SD-WAN) implementation, multi-cloud networking and peering, and network function virtualization (NFV). It supports load balancing across hybrid environments, Content Delivery Network (CDN) integration, and advanced network security with micro-segmentation, along with bandwidth optimization and Quality of Service (QoS) policies. Key considerations include careful network topology design and planning, traffic engineering and optimization, implementation of security zones, comprehensive network capacity planning, and strategies for latency optimization. Figure 4 summarizes the hybrid cloud standard. Table 4 emphasises on the hybrid cloud details.

Figure 4. Hybrid cloud standards framework.

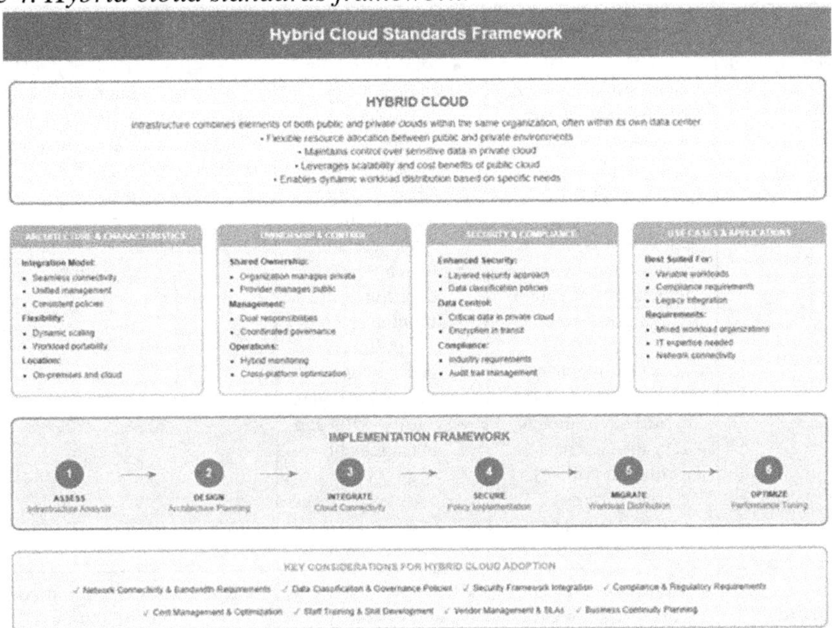

Table 4. Hybrid cloud details

Aspect	Details	Considerations	Technologies
Data Security and Control	• End-to-end encryption for data in transit and at rest • Identity federation and single sign-on (SSO) • Zero-trust network architecture implementation • Data classification and governance policies • Compliance monitoring across hybrid environments • Key management and rotation policies • Security orchestration and automated response	• Data sovereignty and residency requirements • Unified security policy enforcement • Cross-platform vulnerability management • Incident response coordination • Compliance audit trails • Data loss prevention strategies • Security skills gap management	• Microsoft Azure Arc/AWS Outposts • HashiCorp Vault key management • Okta/Azure AD identity federation • Palo Alto Prisma Cloud security • CrowdStrike/SentinelOne endpoint protection • Splunk/IBM QRadar SIEM integration
Resource Management	• Centralized resource orchestration and provisioning • Policy-driven resource allocation • Automated workload migration and bursting • Resource pooling across hybrid infrastructure • Performance monitoring and optimization • Service mesh for microservices management • Infrastructure as Code (IaC) deployment	• Resource discovery and inventory management • Capacity planning across environments • Performance baseline establishment • Resource governance and quotas • Service level agreement monitoring • Change management processes • Resource optimization strategies	• Kubernetes/OpenShift container orchestration • Terraform/CloudFormation IaC • VMware vRealize Automation • Red Hat CloudForms management • AWS Systems Manager/Azure Arc

continued on following page

Table 4. Continued

Aspect	Details	Considerations	Technologies
Interoperability Architecture	• API gateway management and integration • Data synchronization and replication strategies • Network connectivity (VPN, Direct Connect, ExpressRoute) • Container orchestration across environments • Database federation and distributed queries • Message queuing and event-driven architecture • Cross-platform monitoring and logging	• API versioning and lifecycle management • Data consistency and conflict resolution • Network latency and bandwidth optimization • Container image registry management • Database schema evolution • Event sourcing and CQRS patterns • Observability and distributed tracing	• Kong/Ambassador API gateways • AWS Direct Connect/Azure ExpressRoute • Docker/Podman container runtimes • Apache Kafka/RabbitMQ messaging • MongoDB/PostgreSQL distributed databases • Prometheus/Grafana monitoring stack

continued on following page

Table 4. Continued

Aspect	Details	Considerations	Technologies
Network Architecture	• Software-defined WAN (SD-WAN) implementation • Multi-cloud networking and peering • Network function virtualization (NFV) • Load balancing across hybrid environments • Content delivery network (CDN) integration • Network security and micro-segmentation • Bandwidth optimization and QoS policies	• Network topology design and planning • Traffic engineering and optimization • Security zone implementation • Network capacity planning • Latency optimization strategies • Network redundancy and failover • Cost optimization for data transfer	• Cisco SD-WAN/VMware VeloCloud • AWS Transit Gateway/Azure Virtual WAN • Cloudflare/Akamai CDN services • Palo Alto Networks Prisma Access • Silver Peak/Riverbed WAN optimization • Cisco ACI/VMware NSX networking
Security Framework	• Zero-trust security architecture • Identity and access management federation • Security information and event management • Cloud security posture management • Vulnerability assessment and penetration testing • Security orchestration and automated response • Compliance monitoring and reporting	• Security policy standardization • Threat intelligence integration • Security awareness training • Incident response procedures • Security metrics and KPIs • Vendor security assessments • Regulatory compliance management	• CrowdStrike Falcon/Microsoft Defender • Okta/Ping Identity federation • Splunk/IBM QRadar SIEM • Prisma Cloud/AWS Security Hub • Qualys/Rapid7 vulnerability management • Phantom/Demisto security orchestration

5.0 COMMUNITY CLOUD

A community cloud infrastructure is shared by several organizations from a specific community with shared concerns (e.g., mission, security requirements, policy, and compliance considerations). It can be managed by the organizations themselves or by a third party, and can be hosted on-premise or off-premise. This model is particularly beneficial for industries or groups that need to collaborate on shared projects while adhering to common regulations or security standards.

For small and medium enterprises, the community cloud can represent a new and effective deployment model (Pan et al., 2025).

Community clouds are specifically designed for a group of organizations that share common goals, industry regulations, security needs, or mission requirements, fostering a collaborative environment. Access to the community cloud resources is strictly restricted to members of the participating organizations, ensuring exclusivity and privacy within the defined community. The costs associated with building, maintaining, and operating the cloud infrastructure are distributed among the participating organizations, making it a more affordable solution compared to individual private cloud deployments. The security measures and compliance frameworks within a community cloud are meticulously tailored to meet the specific, often stringent, security and regulatory requirements pertinent to that community or industry (Azumah et al., 2023).

By sharing resources and infrastructure, participating organizations can achieve significant cost savings compared to setting up individual private clouds, while still benefiting from dedicated or semi-dedicated environments that meet their specific needs. The cloud environment is designed with the particular security and compliance needs of the community in mind, making it significantly easier for all members to meet industry-specific regulations, such as those in healthcare, government, or finance (Pan et al., 2025). Community clouds actively promote efficient collaboration and data sharing among members on shared projects, research initiatives, or common operational goals, as the infrastructure is inherently built to support these interactive workflows. The collective nature of a community cloud allows for participating organizations to jointly establish governance models and distribute operational responsibilities, thereby reducing the individual burden on any single entity. Members can benefit from specialized support and expertise that is uniquely tailored to address the common challenges and requirements of their specific community or industry sector, leading to more relevant and effective solutions.

While offering more scalability than a single private cloud, a community cloud might still face limitations when compared to the vast, on-demand resources available in a public cloud, as its scalability is ultimately constrained by the pooled resources of the participating community. Resource contention can arise if not properly managed among community members, potentially leading to performance degradation for applications and services during periods of peak usage, affecting all shared users. Establishing and maintaining consensus on governance policies, resource allocation methodologies, security protocols, and operational procedures among multiple independent organizations can be a complex, time-consuming, and potentially contentious process. Customization options within a community cloud may be limited due to the shared nature of the infrastructure and the necessity to meet the common requirements of all community members, which can sometimes restrict individual organizations' desires for highly specific configurations. Although access is restricted to community members, managing granular data privacy and ensuring precise access control within the shared environment can still pose intricate challenges and require robust, well-defined mechanisms. Disengaging from a community cloud can be a complex undertaking, often involving intricate data migration processes, the unwinding of shared resources, and the dissolution or renegotiation of established shared agreements among the community participants.

Figure 5. Community cloud model standards framework.

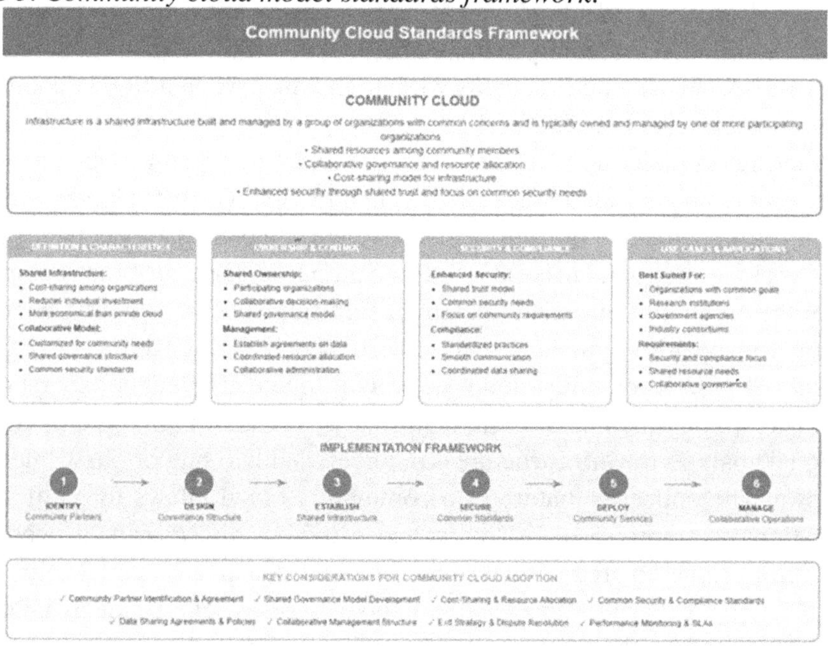

Table 5. Community cloud model details.

Aspect	Details	Considerations	Technologies
Resource Sharing	• Multi-tenant architecture with organization-level isolation • Resource pooling and dynamic allocation algorithms • Shared storage systems with data segregation • Shared backup and disaster recovery infrastructure • Cost allocation and chargeback mechanisms	• Fair usage policies and enforcement • Resource utilization monitoring and reporting • Capacity planning across multiple organizations • Service level agreement standardization • Resource governance and quota management • Billing and cost allocation frameworks	• OpenStack multi-tenant cloud platform • VMware vCloud Director management • Kubernetes multi-tenancy with namespaces • Apache CloudStack resource orchestration • Red Hat CloudForms cost management • Prometheus/Grafana shared monitoring
Data Security and Privacy	• Role-based access control (RBAC) with organization hierarchy • Data encryption at rest and in transit (AES-256, TLS 1.3) • Multi-factor authentication and identity federation • Data loss prevention and classification systems • Audit logging and compliance reporting • Privacy-preserving analytics and computation • Secure multi-party computation capabilities	• Regulatory compliance coordination (HIPAA, FERPA) • Data sovereignty and residency requirements • Privacy impact assessments • Cross-organizational data sharing agreements • Security incident response coordination • Regular security audits and penetration testing • Privacy by design implementation	• Microsoft Azure AD B2B collaboration • AWS Identity and Access Management • CyberArk Privileged Access Management • Okta identity federation • Varonis data governance platform • Microsoft Purview data governance • Immuta data privacy and governance

continued on following page

Table 5. Continued

Aspect	Details	Considerations	Technologies
Access Management and Governance	• Federated identity management across organizations • Single sign-on (SSO) with SAML/OAuth protocols • Privileged access management and monitoring • User lifecycle management and provisioning • Access certification and compliance workflows • Zero-trust network access implementation • Identity governance and administration	• Identity federation architecture design • Access policy standardization • User onboarding and offboarding processes • Regular access reviews and audits • Compliance monitoring and reporting • Identity data synchronization • Emergency access procedures	• Okta/Azure AD identity platforms • SailPoint/Saviynt identity governance • CyberArk/BeyondTrust privileged access • IBM Security Identity Governance • Microsoft Azure AD Privileged Identity Management
Planning and Management	• Multi-organizational governance structure • Shared IT service management (ITSM) platform • Capacity planning and resource forecasting • Change management coordination processes • Incident and problem management workflows • Service catalog and request management • Performance monitoring and SLA management	• Governance committee establishment • Decision-making processes and voting mechanisms • Resource allocation methodologies • Service level agreement negotiations • Dispute resolution procedures • Budget planning and cost sharing • Risk management and mitigation strategies	• ServiceNow IT Service Management • BMC Remedy ITSM platform • Jira Service Management • Azure DevOps/GitHub project management • ITIL framework implementation • COBIT governance framework • Atlassian Confluence documentation
Network Architecture and Connectivity	• Software-defined networking (SDN) with organization segmentation • Virtual private networks (VPN) and secure tunneling • Network access control and micro-segmentation • Quality of service (QoS) policies for fair resource usage • Content delivery networks for distributed access	• Network topology design and optimization • Bandwidth allocation and management • Security zone implementation • Network capacity planning • Latency optimization for distributed users • Network redundancy and failover • Cost optimization for network resources	• Cisco ACI/VMware NSX networking • Palo Alto Networks Prisma Access • F5 BIG-IP application delivery • CloudFlare/Akamai CDN services • SolarWinds/PRTG network monitoring • Zscaler/Netskope SASE platforms • AWS Transit Gateway/ Azure Virtual WAN

6.0 FUTURE TRENDS AND EMERGING INNOVATIONS IN CLOUD DEPLOYMENT MODELS

The evolution of cloud deployment models has a significant impact on the future of IoT-enabled infrastructure (Berenberg & Calder, 2023). Hybrid and multi-cloud models are becoming increasingly popular(Jin et al., 2024) (Pan et al., 2025). Organizations are increasingly leveraging the benefits of several cloud providers, combining private clouds for sensitive data with public clouds for scalability and innovation. This multi-cloud strategy increases resilience and flexibility to meet the diverse needs of users, including those with impairments. The integration of edge computing and cloud principles is gaining popularity (Wang et al., 2024; Zhang et al., 2025) (Pan et al., 2025). Edge computing minimizes latency and improves responsiveness in real-time smart technology applications by processing data close to its source of origination, at the network's "edge." This is critical for applications that require immediate responses, such as fall detection or emergency alerts for people with impairments. Artificial intelligence (AI) is playing a larger role in cloud management (Tian et al., 2024; Wang et al., 2024; Zhang et al., 2025). AI-powered algorithms can optimize resource distribution, anticipate and prevent potential issues, and increase overall efficiency in hybrid and multi-cloud systems. This increases efficiency while promoting a more cost-effective and sustainable cloud infrastructure for smart technology solutions.

Integrating cloud and edge computing is a recurring subject, indicating a continual need to optimize deployment tactics along the cloud-edge continuum. This theme covers dynamic service placement, microservice orchestration, and cost optimization (Wang et al., 2025). It emphasizes the need to effectively manage resources and reduce latency in hybrid environments. Dynamic service placement across the cloud-edge continuum can significantly reduce latency while improving service quality; additionally, microservice orchestration between cloud and edge contexts enhances resource consumption and cost-effectiveness (Sun et al., 2023). The use of containerization technologies like Docker and Kubernetes is a growing trend, showing an increased interest in their importance in modern cloud deployments. This trend highlights the benefits of container orchestration for scalability, efficiency, and deployment ease, particularly in cloud-native environments. Kubernetes-based orchestration improves the scalability and reliability of cloud-native applications (Korontanis et al., 2024). Furthermore, containerization technologies boost the efficiency of cloud deployments by reducing overhead and simplifying management.

The adoption and enhancement of Virtual Network Functions (VNF) and Network Function Virtualization (NFV) are becoming more popular, showing a growing interest in their application for better network administration (Zhu et al., 2023). This theme investigates the cost and latency benefits of Virtual Network Functions (VNFs), particularly in 5G and edge computing scenarios. Improved VNF deployment can significantly reduce network latency and increase service quality in 5G environments (Bruno et al., 2024). NFV installation can result in cheaper costs and greater flexibility in network management. A new trend is to combine DevOps approaches with cloud-native computing. This demonstrates the need for continuous integration and delivery (CI/CD) in cloud systems. This development emphasizes the importance of DevOps in facilitating digital transformation and improving cloud operations. Combining DevOps approaches with cloud-native computing can accelerate digital transformation and improve operational efficiency. CI/CD pipelines in cloud-native systems increase the agility and dependability of software releases.

The use of cloud deployment models in smart manufacturing is a novel concept that examines the benefits and drawbacks of integrating cloud technologies into Industry 4.0. This theme focuses on hybrid cloud architecture, DevOps for fog applications, and the implementation of extended reality (XR) for simulation and design. Hybrid cloud infrastructure enhances the adaptability and scalability of manufacturing execution systems. Incorporating DevOps approaches into fog computing can improve the efficiency and reliability of smart industrial processes. The rising trends in cloud deployment models are expected to significantly improve the accessibility, resilience, and efficiency of IoT-enabled smart technologies, particularly for people with disabilities (Wang et al., 2023). Using these advancements, we can create more inclusive and personalized smart environments that allow people to live more freely and comfortably.

Understanding the nuances of each model empowers organizations to make informed decisions that align with their business objectives and drive innovation in the cloud era. As cloud technologies continue to evolve, with new paradigms like multi-paradigm deployment models for large-scale edge-cloud intelligence (Wang et al., 2023) and intelligent service deployment schemes for serverless-operated cloud-edge computing in 6G networks (Wang et al., 2024), the ability to strategically select and implement the most appropriate deployment model, even for microservice deployment in cloud-edge environments using enhanced global search grey wolf optimizer-greedy algorithm (Wang et al., 2025), will remain a key differentiator for success. Optimized service deployment options in available cloud environments can be identified to minimize operational costs while fulfilling service level agreement requirements, applicable across a wide range of application services (Stupar & Huljenic, 2022). Furthermore, model-based approaches for fleet deployment in the IoT-edge-cloud continuum are emerging to automatically assign multiple software deployment plans to hundreds of edge gateways and connected IoT devices, particularly useful in smart healthcare applications (Song et al., 2022). The development of technology-agnostic deployment models and tailoring support systems like EDMM TSS is crucial for improving the portability of application deployments across different production-ready deployment technologies, addressing concerns about technology-specific languages and ensuring executability (Soldani et al., 2022). Figure 6 summarizes the future trends for cloud deployment models.

Figure 6. Future trends of cloud deployments

7.0 CONCLUSION

The strategic selection of a cloud deployment model is a pivotal decision impacting an organization's IT strategy, operational efficiency, and long-term goals. Public clouds offer unparalleled scalability and cost-effectiveness for general workloads, while private clouds provide superior control and robust security for sensitive data and critical applications. Hybrid clouds present a flexible compromise, enabling organizations to synergize the benefits of both public and private environments for optimized cost, security, and scalability. Concurrently, community clouds cater specifically to the shared interests and regulatory needs of particular industries or groups, fostering collaboration while balancing cost and compliance.

As cloud technologies continue their rapid evolution, marked by emerging paradigms such as multi-paradigm deployment models for large-scale edge-cloud intelligence and intelligent service deployment schemes for serverless-operated cloud-edge computing in 6G networks, the capacity to strategically choose and implement the most suitable deployment model remains crucial. This includes navigating complex scenarios like microservice deployment in cloud-edge environments through advanced optimization algorithms. Furthermore, the development of technology-agnostic deployment models and tailored support systems is increasingly vital, ensuring enhanced portability of application deployments across diverse production-ready technologies and addressing concerns about technology-specific languages and executability.

REFERENCES

Ahn, H., & Kim, K. P. (2021). Formal approach to workflow application fragmentations over cloud deployment models. *Computers, Materials & Continua*, *67*(3), 3071–3088. DOI: 10.32604/cmc.2021.015280

Ajaz, A., Bhatia, J., & Al-Hammoud, Z. (2024). Smart Healthcare System: Accessibility for Individuals with Disabilities. In Healthcare, Social Media, and IoT: Trends, Challenges, and Opportunities (pp. 209-224). CRC Press.

Azumah, B. B., Jiang, J., Qu, Q., Wang, L., & Yao, H. (2023). A systematic review of cloud computing deployment models: Opportunities and challenges. *Journal of Cloud Computing (Heidelberg, Germany)*, *12*(1), 22.

Berenberg, A., & Calder, B. (2023). Deployment archetypes for cloud applications. *ACM Computing Surveys*, *55*(3), 61. DOI: 10.1145/3498336

Berenberg, C., & Calder, M. (2023). Managing the hybrid cloud. *ITNOW*, *65*(3), 52–53.

Bruno, G., Bruschi, S., & Calvo, C. (2024). Accessible smart cities: How can citizens with disabilities be included? *Journal of Urban Management*, *13*(1), 1–15.

Ellman, R., Hu, Y., & Li, F. (2023). Cloud computing deployment models. *Journal of Cloud Computing (Heidelberg, Germany)*, *12*(1), 1–10.

Garg, R. (2022). MCDM-Based Parametric Selection of Cloud Deployment Models for an Academic Organization. *IEEE Transactions on Cloud Computing*, *10*(2), 863–871. DOI: 10.1109/TCC.2020.2980534

Harris, S., Ma, J., Patel, M., Nair, K., Velraj, N., & Aibin, M. (2024). Infrastructure Cost Analysis for Running Timetabling Software Using Various Deployment Architectures in the Cloud. 2024 International Conference on Computing, Networking and Communications, ICNC, 401–406. https://doi.org/DOI: 10.1109/CNC59896.2024.10556009

Knoch, F., Lichtenthäler, R., & Wirtz, G. (2025). Evaluating Cloud-Native Deployment Options with a Focus on Reliability Aspects. SERVICE-ORIENTED COMPUTING, SUMMERSOC 2024. *Communications in Computer and Information Science*, *2221*, 63–82. DOI: 10.1007/978-3-031-72578-4_4

Kumara, A. H., Gunawardhana, C., & Perera, P. (2023). Public cloud computing: A comprehensive review. *International Journal of Computer Science and Network Security*, *23*(3), 1–7.

Kumara, I., Ariz, M. H., Chhetri, M. B., Mohammadi, M., van den Heuvel, W. J., & Tamburri, D. A. (2023). FOCloud: Feature Model Guided Performance Prediction and Explanation for Deployment Configurable Cloud Applications. *IEEE Transactions on Services Computing*, *16*(1), 302–314. DOI: 10.1109/TSC.2022.3142853

Lacatusu, M., Ionita, A. D., Lacatusu, F., & Damian, I. (2022). Decision support for multicloud deployment of a modeling environment. 2022 IEEE 18th International Conference on Intelligent Computer Communication and Processing, ICCP, 247–251. DOI: 10.1109/ICCP56966.2022.10053951

Liu, B. C., Song, J. Y., & Geng, W. (2024). Private cloud deployment model selection for cost efficiency: a business perspective. Kybernetes, 53(?). DOI: 10.1108/K-02-2024-0430

Liu, Y., Wang, X., & Zhang, H. (2024). Private cloud computing: A survey. *Future Generation Computer Systems*, *151*, 242–259.

Marozzo, F., Presta, A., Varchera, R., & Vincit, A. (2024). Estimating performances of Application Deployment on Distributed IoT-Edge-Cloud Infrastructures. *2024 IEEE Conference on Pervasive and Intelligent Computing, PICOM 2024*. DOI: 10.1109/PICom64201.2024.00029

Pan, Y., Chen, Y., & Li, Z. (2025). Community cloud computing: A new deployment model for small and medium enterprises. *Journal of Cloud Computing (Heidelberg, Germany)*, *14*(1), 1–10.

Rajendran, S., Saravanan, R., & Kumar, S. (2023). IoT-enabled smart systems for disability support: A review. *Journal of Ambient Intelligence and Humanized Computing*, *14*(1), 1–15.

Singh, K., Phalak, C., Chahal, D., Kunde, S., & Singhal, R. (2024). SuperArch: Optimal Architecture Design for Cloud Deployment. COMPANION OF THE 15TH ACM/SPEC INTERNATIONAL CONFERENCE ON PERFORMANCE ENGINEERING. *ICPE COMPANION*, *91–92*, 91–92. Advance online publication. DOI: 10.1145/3629527.3651406

Soldani, J., Breitenbücher, U., Brogi, A., Frioli, L., Leymann, F., & Wurster, M. (2022). Tailoring Technology-Agnostic Deployment Models to Production-Ready Deployment Technologies. CLOUD COMPUTING AND SERVICES SCIENCE, CLOSER 2021. *Communications in Computer and Information Science*, *1607*, 1–24. DOI: 10.1007/978-3-031-21637-4_1

Song, H., Dautov, R., Ferry, N., Solberg, A., & Fleurey, F. (2022). Model-based fleet deployment in the IoT-edge-cloud continuum. *Software & Systems Modeling*, *21*(5), 1931–1956. DOI: 10.1007/s10270-022-01006-z

Stupar, I., & Huljenic, D. (2022). Model-based cloud service deployment optimisation method for minimisation of application service operational cost. Journal of Cloud Computing-Advances Systems and Applications.

Ul Haq, F., Alfonso, I., Sulejmani, A., & Cabot, J. (2024). Extending a Low-Code Tool with Multi-cloud Deployment Capabilities. SOFTWARE ARCHITECTURE, ECSA 2024 TRACKS AND WORKSHOPS. *Lecture Notes in Computer Science*, *14937*, 39–46. DOI: 10.1007/978-3-031-71246-3_5

Wang, L. H., Ren, X. B., Zhao, C., Zhao, F. Y., & Yang, S. S. (2023). MPDM: A Multi-Paradigm Deployment Model for Large-Scale Edge-Cloud Intelligence. *IEEE Internet of Things Journal*, *10*(10), 8773–8785. DOI: 10.1109/JIOT.2022.3232582

Wang, L. Y., Liu, A. F., Xiong, N. N., Zhang, S. B., Wang, T., & Dong, M. X. (2024). SD-SRF: An Intelligent Service Deployment Scheme for Serverless-operated Cloud-Edge Computing in 6G Networks. *Future Generation Computer Systems*, *151*, 242–259. DOI: 10.1016/j.future.2023.09.027

Wang, S. D., Zhang, Y. X., He, X., Wang, N. L., Lu, Z., Chen, B. Y., & Pang, S. C. (2025). Microservice deployment in cloud-edge environment using enhanced global search grey wolf optimizer-greedy algorithm. *Cluster Computing*, *28*(2), 118. Advance online publication. DOI: 10.1007/s10586-024-04844-2

Chapter 4
Cloud Service Models:
Features and Framework

Azana Hafizah Mohd Aman
https://orcid.org/0000-0001-7337-6736
Faculty of Information Science and Technology, Bangi, Malaysia

Wan Muhd Hazwan Azamuddin
https://orcid.org/0000-0002-8124-6226
Institut Latihan Perindustrian, Tangkak, Malaysia

Maznifah Salam
https://orcid.org/0000-0003-1332-260X
Faculty of Information Science and Technology, Bangi, Malaysia

Zainab S. Attarbashi
https://orcid.org/0000-0002-1452-8098
Kulliyyah of Information and Communication Technology, Malaysia

ABSTRACT

Cloud computing has revolutionized the way businesses access and utilize computational resources, providing unparalleled cost efficiency, scalability, and flexibility. Infrastructure as a Service (IaaS), Platform as a Service (PaaS), and Software as a Service (SaaS) comprise the three primary cloud service models; this chapter offers a thorough examination of each. We explore the characteristics, use cases, advantages, and disadvantages of each model, emphasizing the varying degrees of control and responsibility that cloud providers and consumers share. In addition, the chapter delves into significant future trends, such as the increased integration of Artificial Intelligence functionalities, the paramount importance of robust cloud security measures, the convergence of edge and cloud computing, advancements in resource optimization, and the increasing adoption of cloud-native and serverless

DOI: 10.4018/979-8-3693-9984-2.ch004

architectures. It is imperative for organizations to comprehend these models and emergent trends in order to effectively leverage the transformative power of the evolving cloud landscape.

1.0 INTRODUCTION TO CLOUD SERVICE MODELS

Cloud computing has revolutionized the way we access and use computing resources (Ajaz et al., 2024). Cloud services enable users to access remote resources over the Internet rather than relying on local hardware and software (Ajil & Kumar, 2024). This adaptability and expandability have transformed many domains, affecting both businesses and individuals. This paradigm revolves around certain service models that define the level of abstraction and control available to users. At the core of cloud computing are its service models, which delineate the varying degrees of control and responsibility that are shared between the cloud provider and the consumer. It is essential to comprehend these models in order to make well-informed decisions regarding cloud migration, as each model provides a distinctive combination of customisation and convenience.

The three principal cloud service models: Infrastructure as a Service (IaaS), Platform as a Service (PaaS), and Software as a Service (SaaS) will be examined in this chapter. Each cloud service model offers unique advantages and limitations, as shown in Figure 1. While Table 1 compares the fundamental characteristics of the three service models. IaaS is the most fundamental service level, encompassing virtualized computer resources such as servers, storage, and networking (Vieira et al., 2024). IaaS users have substantial control over the core infrastructure, allowing them to modify the environment to their needs. This adaptability is critical for enterprises that require high levels of control and personalization, especially those managing complex IT infrastructures or developing resource-intensive apps (Stupar & Huljenic, 2023).

PaaS expands on IaaS, allowing developers to build, run, and manage apps without worrying about the underlying infrastructure (Yang et al., 2024). PaaS solutions often include operating systems, programming language execution environments, databases, and other essential development tools. This abstraction simplifies the development process, shortens time-to-market for new apps, and reduces the operational strain on development teams. SaaS paradigm delivers programs over the Internet, requiring minimal user interaction with the underlying infrastructure. SaaS applications are accessed via web browsers or specialized clients, with the service provider managing all software and data. This model provides the highest level of abstraction, making it ideal for customers who prioritize simplicity and low maintenance. SaaS solutions are common in various fields, including email, customer relationship management (CRM), and office productivity. These distinct cloud service models meet various needs and preferences, providing a versatile and scalable computing solution. Understanding the characteristics of each model allows businesses and individuals to select the best option for their specific needs, thereby increasing efficiency, lowering costs, and accelerating innovation.

This cloud transition has resulted in heightened cost efficiency, scalability, and flexibility, which has transformed numerous domains for both businesses and individuals. It has also presented a variety of service models and challenges, including those related to Service Level Agreements (SLAs) (Qazi et al., 2024; H. C. Sun et al., 2023). This paradigm is centred on specific service models that restrict the level of abstraction and control that users have (Ajaz et al., 2024). These models include vehicular ad hoc networks (VANETs) clouds, which include vehicular clouds (VCs), vehicles utilising clouds (VuCs), and hybrid vehicular clouds (HVCs). The collection of services that cloud computing offers has made it one of the most prominent technologies, thanks to recent advancements in information technology. However, users may find it difficult to identify a cloud service provider (CSP) that effectively fulfils their needs due to the extensive selection of CSPs that provide a variety of services (Saha et al., 2023).

Figure 1. Cloud service model usage

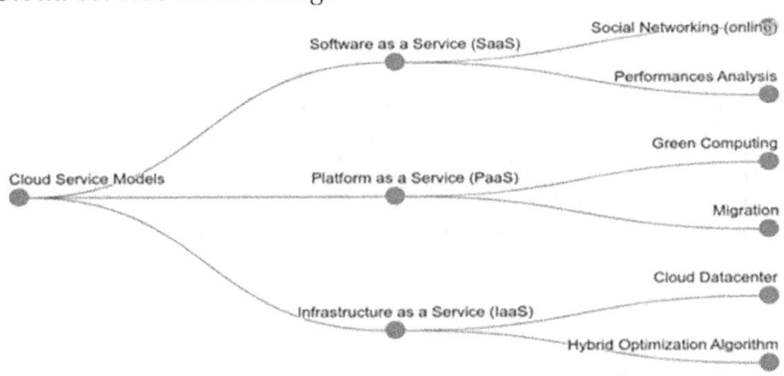

Table 1. Comparison of Cloud service models

Characteristic	Infrastructure as a Service (IaaS)	Platform as a Service (PaaS)	Software as a Service (SaaS)
On-demand Self-Service	Users can provision computing (VMs), storage, and networking resources as needed without human interaction.	Developers can access development platforms, databases, and runtime environments without provider interaction.	Users can sign up and start using applications (e.g., email, CRM) often with minimal or no interaction with the provider.
Broad Network Access	Resources (VMs, storage, networks) are accessible over the internet using standard protocols.	Applications and development platforms are accessible over the internet through various devices.	Applications are accessible over the internet through web browsers, mobile apps, or client software.
Resource Pooling	Provider pools compute, storage, and networking resources, serving multiple users from the same infrastructure. Users don't know the exact physical location.	Provider pools development tools, middleware, and infrastructure, shared by multiple developers. The underlying infrastructure is abstracted.	Provider pools the application infrastructure and software, serving many users with a single instance of the application (multi-tenancy).
Rapid Elasticity	Users can quickly scale computing, storage, and networking resources up or down based on demand. Often self-service.	The platform automatically scales the underlying infrastructure to match application demand. Developers might have some control over scaling application instances.	The application scales automatically based on the number of users and data volume, often transparently to the end-user.
Measured Service	Usage of compute, storage, and networking is monitored, and users are typically billed based on consumption (e.g., per hour of VM usage, per GB of storage).	Usage of platform resources (e.g., compute time for applications, database usage) is monitored, and billing is often based on consumption.	Usage of the application (e.g., number of users, storage used, transactions) is monitored, and users are typically billed on a subscription or usage basis.

2.0 INFRASTRUCTURE AS A SERVICE

Infrastructure as a Service (IaaS) is a key cloud computing concept that allows clients on-demand access to essential computing resources (Vieira et al., 2024). These resources cover virtualized servers, storage, networking, and other important infrastructure components, all provided via the Internet. Rather than purchasing, installing, and maintaining physical servers, storage systems, and networking equipment, businesses can rent these resources from cloud providers who handle all the underlying hardware management. IaaS enables users to lease actual hardware from a cloud provider on a pay-as-you-go approach, dramatically cutting startup expenses and operational burdens. IaaS supplies the core infrastructure needed for hosting and managing applications and services. The virtualization technology that powers IaaS allows cloud providers to partition powerful physical machines into multiple isolated virtual environments, giving customers dedicated access to computing resources without the complexities of hardware ownership, via the Internet (Yang et al., 2024). Table 2 summarizes the IaaS fundamental features. While figure 2 illustrates the IaaS framework. The technical details of the features are described in table 3.

Table 2. IaaS features

Feature	Description	Benefits	Examples
Focus on Application Development	Provides a platform for building, testing, and deploying applications.	Reduces the need to manage infrastructure, allowing developers to focus on application logic.	Building web applications, mobile apps, or AI/ML models.
Pre-built Components	Offers pre-configured operating systems, databases, and development frameworks.	Accelerates development by eliminating the need to set up and manage infrastructure components.	Using pre-configured databases like MySQL or PostgreSQL.
Real-time Data Processing & AI/ ML Support	Enables integration of real-time data and advanced technologies.	Supports the development of data-driven applications, such as personalized recommendations and fraud detection.	Building applications that utilize machine learning models for predictive analysis.
Customization and Flexibility	Provides options for customizing applications to meet specific needs.	Enables the creation of unique and differentiated solutions.	Integrating custom libraries and frameworks into the development environment.
Wide Range of Applications	Supports various use cases, including web development, mobile development, and AI/ML model deployment.	Versatile solution for diverse development needs.	Building web applications, and mobile apps, and deploying machine learning models.
Popular Providers	Includes Google App Engine, Heroku, Azure App Service, and AWS Elastic Beanstalk.	Offers a variety of choices with different features and pricing models.	Selecting a PaaS provider based on specific project requirements.

Figure 2. IaaS framework

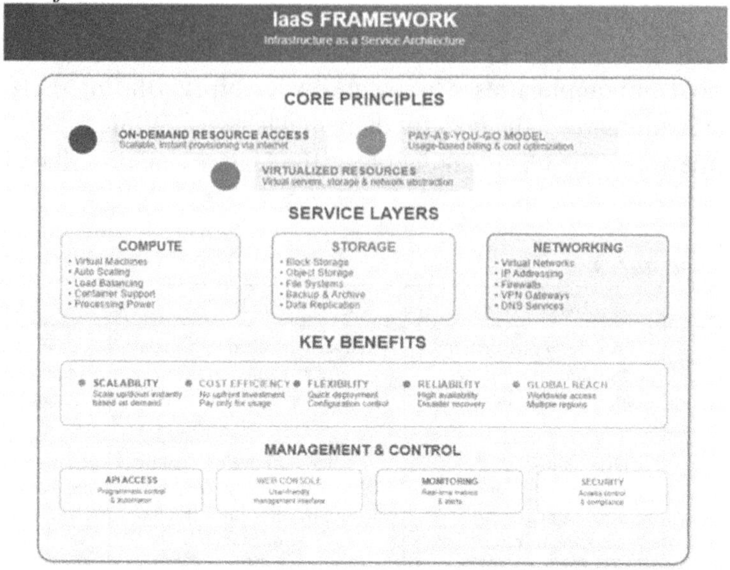

The IaaS compute resources deliver processing power through virtual machines where customers can specify CPU count, memory allocation, and operating system while maintaining full control over software installation and configuration. Storage resources offer multiple options including block storage for databases and operating systems, object storage for unstructured data like media files, and file storage for shared file systems, with the cloud provider ensuring data durability and availability. Networking resources enable connectivity through virtual networks, load balancers for traffic distribution, firewalls for security, and virtualized routing components, all managed through software-defined networking that allows customers to design their network topology while the provider maintains the physical infrastructure. This architecture creates a powerful division of responsibilities where cloud providers focus on maintaining reliable, secure, and performant physical infrastructure while customers concentrate on their applications and business logic.

A fundamental benefit of IaaS is its natural scalability. Users can simply alter their resource allocation in real-time to meet fluctuating demands. This versatility is vital for organizations that confront irregular traffic surges or seasonal variations in workload. An e-commerce firm can rapidly enhance its computing resources during peak buying seasons and reduce them during quieter periods, maximizing resource consumption and decreasing expenses. Moreover, IaaS provides tremendous flexibility and customization choices. Users have substantial control over the foundational infrastructure, allowing them to design and optimize the environment to meet their specific requirements. This level of control is especially beneficial for businesses with specific technical requirements or those developing complex applications requiring specialized hardware or software.

IaaS is typically used for web hosting, allowing users granular control over servers and infrastructure for their websites and web applications. It is also ideal for deploying virtual machines for various purposes, including development, testing, or production environments. A specialized application of IaaS can be seen in sensor-enabled cloud-based computing platforms for computational brain biomechanics, where platforms built using services like Amazon's Web Services (AWS) enable cloud computing and scalability for complex modeling services (Menghani et al., 2025). Another common use case is data storage and backup, where large volumes of data can be stored, and disaster recovery solutions can be implemented efficiently. Furthermore, IaaS is well-suited for big data analytics, enabling the processing and analysis of large datasets using scalable computing resources.

IaaS offers significant flexibility and customization, providing users with the highest level of control over their computing environment, which is particularly beneficial for businesses with specific technical requirements or those developing complex applications needing specialized hardware or software (Stupar & Huljenic, 2023). It provides robust scalability, allowing users to alter resource allocation in real-time to meet fluctuating demands, which is vital for organizations facing irregular traffic surges or seasonal workload variations. From a cost perspective, IaaS is highly effective, as it eliminates significant upfront capital costs for hardware, software, and data center infrastructure, with a pay-as-you-go model ensuring billing only for consumed resources. Additionally, it supports geographic distribution, facilitating the easy deployment of applications in various regions for improved performance and redundancy.

The cost-effectiveness of IaaS is a significant factor in its widespread adoption. IaaS significantly reduces capital costs by eliminating the need for significant upfront investments in hardware, software, and data centre infrastructure. Furthermore, the pay-as-you-go pricing model ensures that firms only pay for the resources they use, thereby improving cost efficiency and budget predictability. IaaS has a wide range of applications across industries. Enterprise applications and websites frequently use it as a scalable and dependable platform for delivering web services to a worldwide audience. IaaS enables data storage and backup solutions, allowing businesses to securely store and protect critical data in the cloud. Furthermore, IaaS is required to implement disaster recovery and business continuity plans, which ensure that critical processes continue to function even when things go wrong.

Despite its advantages, IaaS comes with certain disadvantages. There is a notable management overhead, as consumers remain responsible for operating systems, patches, applications, and middleware, demanding more IT expertise compared to PaaS or SaaS. While the provider secures the underlying infrastructure, the consumer bears the security responsibility for their applications, data, and operating systems. Finally, there can be vendor lock-in, as migrating workloads between different IaaS providers can be challenging due to proprietary APIs and services. Efficient VM migration techniques are crucial to address total cost of ownership (TCO) along with reducing migration time, downtime, and the number of migrations (Najm et al., 2022). This involves addressing capacity issues at destination VMs and negotiating resource availability across host machines (S. G. Liu et al., 2022).

Table 3. IaaS technical specification

Category	Feature	Description	Specification	Product Example
Application Development	Focus on Application Development	Provides managed infrastructure platform eliminating need for hardware procurement, OS management, and infrastructure maintenance	API-driven provisioning, auto-scaling groups, and load balancers	*AWS EC2, Azure VMs, GCP Compute*
	Pre-built Components	Offers containerized, pre-configured development stacks, databases, and managed infrastructure components	Docker containers, Kubernetes orchestration, and managed databases	*AWS RDS, Azure SQL, MongoDB Atlas*
	Real-time Data Processing	Enables real-time data ingestion, stream processing, and analytics with managed Apache Kafka, Spark, and ML frameworks	Stream processing, event-driven architecture, and auto-scaling pipelines	*AWS Kinesis, Azure Event Hubs, GCP Dataflow*
	AI/ML Support	Provides GPU instances, ML frameworks, model training pipelines, and inference endpoints	GPU clusters (V100, A100), MLOps pipelines, and model versioning	*AWS SageMaker, Azure ML, GCP AI Platform*

continued on following page

Table 3. Continued

Category	Feature	Description	Specification	Product Example
Customization & Flexibility	Custom Runtime Environments	Allows custom OS images, runtime configurations, and application-specific environments with full root access	Custom AMIs/Images, Container registries, and runtime flexibility	*Custom Docker images, VM templates*
	Infrastructure as Code	Declarative infrastructure provisioning using templates, version control, and automated deployment pipelines	Terraform, CloudFormation, GitOps workflows, and state management	*Terraform modules, ARM templates*
	Multi-Region Deployment	Global infrastructure with edge locations, content delivery networks, and disaster recovery capabilities	Global load balancing, CDN integration Cross-region replication	*AWS CloudFront, Azure CDN*
Cost Management	Pay-as-you-Scale Pricing	Granular billing based on actual resource consumption with per-second billing and automatic shutdown	Per-second billing, resource tagging, and cost allocation	*EC2 per-second billing, preemptible instances*
	Reserved Instances	Commitment-based pricing with 1-3 year terms offering significant discounts for predictable workloads	1-3 year commitments, payment options, and instance flexibility	*AWS RIs, Azure Reserved VMs*
	Cost Optimization Tools	AI-powered cost analysis, rightsizing recommendations, and automated resource cleanup	ML-based analysis, automated recommendations, and budget alerts	*AWS Cost Explorer, Azure Advisor*

continued on following page

Table 3. Continued

Category	Feature	Description	Specification	Product Example
Scalability & Performance	Auto-Scaling	Dynamic resource allocation based on metrics like CPU, memory, network I/O, or custom application metrics	Horizontal/Vertical scaling, predictive scaling, and spot instances	*AWS Auto Scaling, Azure VMSS*
	High-Performance Computing	HPC clusters with InfiniBand networking, parallel file systems, and job schedulers for compute-intensive workloads	InfiniBand networking, parallel file systems, and MPI support	*AWS ParallelCluster, Azure CycleCloud*
	Content Delivery	Global CDN with edge caching, compression, and optimization for static and dynamic content delivery	Edge locations (200+), smart routing HTTP/2, HTTP/3 support	*CloudFlare, AWS CloudFront*
	Database Performance	Managed databases with read replicas, connection pooling, query optimization, and automated performance tuning	SSD storage, read replicas, and connection pooling	*Amazon Aurora, Azure Cosmos DB*

3.0 PLATFORM AS A SERVICE

Platform as a Service (PaaS) is a cloud computing paradigm that provides developers with a single platform for application development, evaluation, and deployment (H. C. Sun et al., 2023). PaaS, as opposed to IaaS, reduces the emphasis on basic infrastructure resources, allowing developers to focus solely on application development and functionality. PaaS provides a platform of tools and frameworks for developers to build, test, and deploy applications. It abstracts the core infrastructure, allowing developers to focus on application functionality. This environment includes the necessary infrastructure (servers, storage, networking), but also development tools, middleware (like databases, and message queues), operating systems, and runtime environments (like Java, Python, and Node.js). The cloud provider manages the underlying infrastructure, including servers, storage, networking, and operating systems, as well as middleware, runtime environments, and databases. Consumers primarily focus on their application code and data. Table 4 summarizes the PaaS fundamental features. While figure 3 illustrates the PaaS framework. The technical details of the features are described in table 5.

Table 4. PaaS features

Feature	Description	Benefits	Examples
Focus on Application Development	Provides a platform for building, testing, and deploying applications.	Reduces the need to manage infrastructure, allowing developers to focus on application logic.	Building web applications, mobile apps, or AI/ML models.
Pre-built Components	Offers pre-configured operating systems, databases, and development frameworks.	Accelerates development by eliminating the need to set up and manage infrastructure components.	Using pre-configured databases like MySQL or PostgreSQL.
Real-time Data Processing & AI/ ML Support	Enables integration of real-time data and advanced technologies.	Supports the development of data-driven applications, such as personalized recommendations and fraud detection.	Building applications that utilize machine learning models for predictive analysis.
Customization and Flexibility	Provides options for customizing applications to meet specific needs.	Enables the creation of unique and differentiated solutions.	Integrating custom libraries and frameworks into the development environment.
Wide Range of Applications	Supports various use cases, including web development, mobile development, and AI/ML model deployment.	A versatile solution for diverse development needs.	Building web applications, and mobile apps, and deploying machine learning models.
Popular Providers	Includes Google App Engine, Heroku, Azure App Service, and AWS Elastic Beanstalk.	Offers a variety of choices with different features and pricing models.	Selecting a PaaS provider based on specific project requirements.

Figure 3. Paas framework.

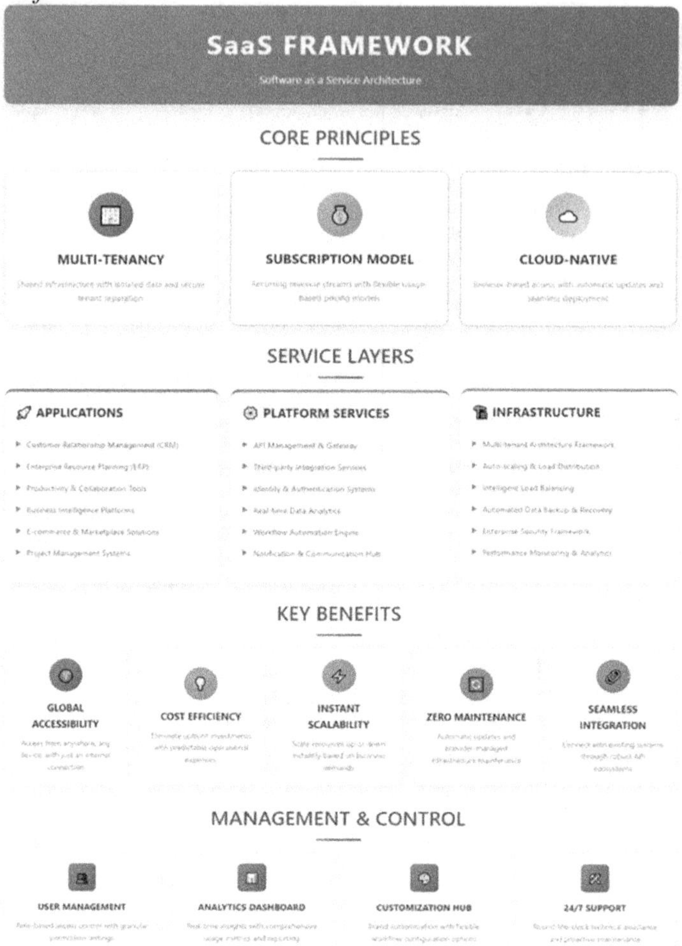

PaaS is characterized by its on-demand self-service, allowing developers to access development platforms, databases, and runtime environments without provider interaction. Applications and development platforms are accessible over the internet through various devices, ensuring broad network access. The provider pools development tools, middleware, and infrastructure, which are shared by multiple developers, with the underlying infrastructure being abstracted. PaaS also offers rapid elasticity, as the platform automatically scales the underlying infrastructure to match application demand, and developers often have some control over scaling application instances. Developers benefit from an abstraction of infrastructure, allowing them to focus solely on application development, within an integrated development environment that provides a complete set of tools, services, and components for the entire application lifecycle. PaaS often leverages a multi-tenant architecture, where multiple users share the same infrastructure but have their applications isolated, and the platform typically handles automatic scaling, load balancing, and maintenance of the underlying infrastructure.

PaaS is ideal for application development and deployment, enabling developers to quickly build, test, and deploy web or mobile applications. It is also commonly used for API development, creating and hosting APIs for various services. Businesses leverage PaaS for business analytics, developing and deploying business intelligence applications. Furthermore, it is well-suited for microservices architectures, allowing for the building and deploying of microservices within managed runtime environments. A notable advancement in this area includes data-driven platform designs that allow end-users to create and manage data science services in cloud environments without programming or extensive configurations, transparently masking resource unavailability (Arevalo et al., 2023).

The key benefit is that PaaS abstracts away the complexities of managing this underlying infrastructure, allowing developers to focus solely on coding, deploying, and managing their applications. PaaS often provides tools, libraries, and frameworks that streamline the development process. Operating systems, programming language execution environments, databases, and development frameworks are all common components of PaaS platforms. These pre-built elements significantly accelerate the application development process by eliminating the need for developers to spend time and money building up and managing the core infrastructure (Qazi et al., 2024). A pre-configured environment where applications can be deployed and executed without needing to set up servers or configure runtime environments. This efficient methodology enables development teams to rapidly iterate on their projects, experiment with new ideas, and speed up the market introduction of breakthrough applications.

One of the primary benefits of PaaS is its ability to support real-time data processing and the incorporation of complex technologies such as Artificial Intelligence and Machine Learning. PaaS platforms usually contain built-in data analytics capabilities, allowing developers to seamlessly integrate data-driven insights into their apps. This functionality is required for smart apps that may modify and learn based on real-time data. Personalized recommendation systems, fraud detection systems, and planned maintenance solutions are some of these apps. Furthermore, PaaS offers tremendous customization possibilities, allowing developers to tailor their apps to unique market demands and business specifications. PaaS typically includes features for monitoring, scaling, and managing deployed applications.

Numerous PaaS platforms provide various bespoke components and services, allowing developers to create unique and differentiated solutions. This versatility is especially advantageous for businesses looking to create one-of-a-kind apps that address specific industry challenges or service specialized market segments. PaaS has gained appeal in a variety of industries, ranging from online and mobile application development to the deployment of complex AI/ML models and the building of microservices architectures. Google App Engine, Heroku, Microsoft Azure App Service, and Amazon Web Services Elastic Beanstalk are among the most well-known PaaS providers, each offering a unique set of capabilities and functions to meet a wide range of developer needs.

A notable disadvantage of PaaS is vendor lock-in, as the high level of integration with the provider's platform can make it difficult to switch providers. Consumers also experience limited control compared to IaaS, having less influence over the underlying infrastructure and operating systems. While the provider secures the platform, consumers retain security concerns and are responsible for application-level security and data protection. Lastly, there can be operational limitations, as specific features or configurations required by an application might not be available or customizable within the PaaS environment.

Table 5. PaaS technical specification

Category	Feature	Description	Specification	Product Example
Application Development	Focus on Application Development	Abstracts infrastructure complexity, provides managed runtime environments, automatic scaling, and integrated development tools	Git Integration, CI/CD Pipelines, Auto-deploy	Heroku, Vercel, Netlify
	Integrated Development Environment	Cloud-based IDEs with collaborative editing, debugging, testing, and deployment capabilities	VS Code Integration, Real-time Collab, Remote Debugging	GitHub Codespaces, AWS Cloud9
	API Management	Built-in API gateways, rate limiting, authentication, documentation generation, and analytics	OpenAPI Spec, Rate Limiting, OAuth/JWT	Azure API Mgmt, AWS API Gateway
	Testing & Quality Assurance	Automated testing frameworks, code quality analysis, security scanning, and performance testing	Unit Testing, SAST/DAST, Load Testing	SonarCloud, TestComplete

continued on following page

Table 5. Continued

Category	Feature	Description	Specification	Product Example
Pre-built Components	Managed Databases	Fully managed SQL/NoSQL databases with automatic backups, scaling, security patches, and performance tuning	Auto-scaling, Point-in-time Recovery, Read Replicas	Heroku Postgres MongoDB Atlas
	Messaging & Queuing	Managed message queues, event streaming, and pub/sub systems with guaranteed delivery and ordering	Apache Kafka, RabbitMQ, Redis Pub/Sub	Heroku Redis, CloudAMQP
	Authentication Services	Pre-built identity providers with SSO, MFA, social login, and user management capabilities	OAuth 2.0/OIDC, SAML, MFA	Auth0, Firebase Auth
	Content Management	Headless CMS solutions with RESTful/GraphQL APIs, content versioning, and multi-channel publishing	GraphQL/REST APIs, CDN Integration, Version Control	Contentful, Strapi Cloud
Customization & Integration	Custom Runtime Environments	Support for custom build packs, Docker containers, and serverless functions with language-specific optimizations	Docker Support Custom Buildpacks Serverless Functions	Cloud Foundry, OpenShift
	Third-party Integrations	Marketplace of add-ons and integrations with monitoring, logging, payment, and business tools	REST/GraphQL APIs, Webhooks, Event Triggers	Heroku Add-ons, Zapier
	Configuration Management	Environment-specific configurations, secrets management, and feature flags with deployment pipelines	Config Vars, Secrets Vault, Feature Flags	LaunchDarkly, HashiCorp Vault
	Multi-Cloud Deployment	Deploy applications across multiple cloud providers with unified management and disaster recovery	Kubernetes, Cross-cloud Networking, Disaster Recovery	Red Hat OpenShift, Platform.sh

continued on following page

Table 5. Continued

Category	Feature	Description	Specification	Product Example
Scalability & Performance	Auto-scaling	Automatic horizontal and vertical scaling based on metrics like CPU, memory, request rate, and custom metrics	Horizontal Scaling, Load Balancing, Traffic Routing	Google App Engine, AWS Elastic Beanstalk
	Global CDN Integration	Built-in content delivery networks with edge caching, image optimization, and global load balancing	Edge Caching, Image Optimization, Gzip Compression	Vercel Edge, Netlify CDN
	Performance Monitoring	Real-time application performance monitoring with distributed tracing, error tracking, and alerting	APM Integration, Distributed Tracing, Real User Monitoring	New Relic, Datadog

4.0 SOFTWARE AS A SERVICE

Software as a Service (SaaS) is a cloud-based distribution model in which a third-party provider hosts and manages software applications, which customers can access via the Internet (Su et al., 2024). Users access applications through web browsers or mobile apps rather than installing and maintaining software locally. Everything from the servers and storage to the software code and data management is handled by the SaaS provider. This eliminates the need for users to manage software updates, device maintenance, and other IT-related tasks. SaaS distributes software programs over the Internet, eliminating the need for local installation and maintenance. Users can access these programs through web browsers, desktop clients, or mobile devices. One of the key benefits of SaaS is its ease of use. SaaS significantly reduces technical barriers to entry for clients by providing ready-to-use applications (Wu et al., 2023). Table 6 summarizes the SaaS fundamental features. While figure 4 illustrates the SaaS framework. The technical details of the features are described in table 7.

Table 6. SaaS features

Feature	Description	Benefits	Examples
Cloud-based Delivery	Software hosted and managed by a third-party provider.	Eliminates the need for local installation and maintenance.	Accessing email, document editing, and CRM software via web browsers.
Ease of Use	Provides ready-to-use applications with minimal setup.	Reduces technical barriers and simplifies software adoption.	Easy access to applications without complex installation or configuration.
Accessibility	Enables access to applications from anywhere with an internet connection.	Promotes remote work and collaboration.	Accessing work files and collaborating with colleagues from any location.
Cost-Effectiveness	A subscription-based model with lower upfront costs.	Reduces capital expenditures and improves budget predictability.	Paying for software on a monthly or annual subscription basis.
Wide Range of Applications	Supports various business needs, including CRM, ERP, and productivity tools.	Enables businesses to access powerful software solutions without significant upfront investment.	Using CRM systems like Salesforce, ERP solutions, and productivity suites like Google Workspace.
Reduced IT Overhead	Eliminates the need for IT staff to manage software updates, maintenance, and security.	Reduces IT costs and frees up IT resources for other tasks.	No need to install software updates or manage server maintenance.

Figure 4. SaaS framework

The provider manages all the underlying infrastructure required to run the software, including servers, storage, and networking. The SaaS provider handles all software updates, patches, and maintenance, even the latest version. This is especially useful for small and medium-sized businesses that may lack the capacity to manage complex IT infrastructures. Users may easily subscribe to their preferred products and start using them right away, without having to go through complicated installation or setting steps. SaaS programs are extremely accessible, allowing users to work from anywhere with an internet connection. This mobility is critical in today's increasingly mobile and networked world, allowing users to access work files and collaborate with colleagues from anywhere. Furthermore, SaaS programs are generally available around the clock, ensuring that users may access their data and applications at any time.

Everything from the servers and storage to the software code and data management is handled by the SaaS provider. This eliminates the need for users to manage software updates, device maintenance, and other IT-related tasks. Consumers simply access the application through a web browser or a mobile app. In the context of services like cloud gaming, understanding and validating service quality through instruments like specific models becomes crucial for optimizing user experience and provider offerings (Su et al., 2024). Similarly, enhancing remote sensing monitoring through bimodal cloud infrastructure, which utilizes a dual-state cloud service approach, demonstrates the versatility and evolving nature of SaaS in specialized fields (Yang et al., 2024). Another emerging application is Process Mining as a Service (PMaaS), which allows organizations to outsource event log storage and processing, necessitating cryptography-based methods to address data privacy risks when dealing with sensitive information (P. Kumar et al., 2025).

SaaS is characterized by its on-demand self-service, allowing users to sign up and immediately use applications (e.g., email, CRM) with minimal or no interaction with the provider. Applications are accessible over the internet through web browsers, mobile apps, or client software, ensuring broad network access. The provider pools the application infrastructure and software, serving many users with a single instance of the application through a multi-tenancy model. It also offers rapid elasticity, as the application scales automatically based on the number of users and data volume, often transparently to the end-user. Usage of the application (e.g., number of users, storage used, transactions) is monitored, and users are typically billed on a subscription or usage basis, indicating a measured service. SaaS operates on a subscription-based model, where users typically pay a recurring fee to access the software. Applications are web-based, accessible from anywhere with an internet connection, often through a web browser. Consumers experience no infrastructure management burden, as the provider handles all hardware, software, and operating system management. Finally, the provider manages all automatic updates, patches, and maintenance of the software.

SaaS offers a compelling and cost-effective alternative for businesses of all sizes. Using a subscription-based model, SaaS eliminates the need for significant initial investments in software licenses and hardware. This pay-as-you-go model makes strong software tools more affordable and accessible to organizations that lack the financial means for traditional on-premise software solutions. SaaS companies frequently provide variable pricing models that can adapt to changing business needs, resulting in increased cost-effectiveness. Several businesses use SaaS apps, which provide a wide range of functionalities. Notable examples include customer relationship management systems like Salesforce, enterprise resource planning solutions, and productivity tools such as email, document editing, file sharing like Dropbox (or Google Drive), and collaboration platforms like Google Workspace (or Microsoft 365). The continual expansion and development of SaaS has transformed corporate processes, enabling the use of sophisticated software solutions with greater agility and efficiency.

SaaS offers significant ease of use, requiring no installation or complex setup, which substantially reduces technical barriers for clients by providing ready-to-use applications. It comes with low upfront costs, eliminating the need for significant capital expenditure on software licenses and hardware, and its pay-as-you-go model makes powerful software tools more affordable and accessible. Businesses benefit from a reduced IT burden, as their IT staff are freed from software maintenance to focus on core business activities. SaaS provides excellent accessibility, allowing users to access applications from any device, anywhere, at any time, which is critical in today's mobile and networked world. Finally, the provider handles scaling to accommodate user demand, ensuring seamless scalability.

Despite its benefits, SaaS has limitations. There is often limited customization, as while some SaaS applications offer configuration options, extensive customization can be restricted. Data security and privacy concerns arise because data is stored on the provider's servers, prompting considerations about security, privacy, and compliance. Consumers are also subject to dependency on the provider for availability, performance, and updates. A reliable internet connection is necessary for access, indicating internet dependency. Lastly, integrating SaaS applications with existing on-premise systems can sometimes present integration challenges.

Table 7. SaaS technical aspects.

Category	Feature	Description	Specification	Product Example
Cloud-based Delivery	Multi-tenant Architecture	Single application instance serves multiple customers with data isolation, shared infrastructure, and customizable configurations	Data Isolation, Shared Resources Tenant Routing	Salesforce, Office 365, Google Workspace
	Global CDN Integration	Content delivery networks with edge caching, geographic distribution, and intelligent routing for optimal performance	Edge Caching, Geographic Routing, Load Balancing	CloudFlare, AWS CloudFront
	Cross-platform Compatibility	Web-based applications with responsive design, mobile apps, and desktop clients ensuring consistent experience	Responsive Design, Progressive Web Apps, Native Mobile Apps	Slack, Zoom, Notion
	High Availability Infrastructure	Redundant systems across multiple data centers with automatic failover, disaster recovery, and 99.9%+ uptime SLAs	Multi-AZ Deployment, Auto-failover, Disaster Recovery	Microsoft Azure, AWS
	API-First Architecture	REST/GraphQL APIs enabling integrations, third-party connections, and headless implementations	RESTful APIs, GraphQL, Webhooks	Stripe, Twilio
Accessibility & Collaboration	Real-time Collaboration	Simultaneous multi-user editing, live cursors, conflict resolution, and collaborative workspaces	WebRTC, Operational Transform, Conflict Resolution	Google Workspace, Microsoft 365
	Mobile-first Design	Touch-optimized interfaces, offline capabilities, and native mobile applications with full feature parity	Touch Interface, Offline Sync, Native Apps	Slack, Trello
	Universal Access Controls	Role-based permissions, single sign-on integration, and granular access controls with audit trails	RBAC/ABAC, SAML/OIDC, Audit Logging	Okta, Auth0
	Communication Integration	Built-in chat, video conferencing, notifications, and integration with communication platforms	In-app Messaging, Video Conferencing, Push Notifications	Zoom, Microsoft Teams

continued on following page

Table 7. Continued

Category	Feature	Description	Specification	Product Example
Cost-effectiveness	Subscription Pricing Models	Flexible pricing tiers with per-user, usage-based, or feature-based billing with transparent cost structure	Tiered Pricing, Usage Metering, Automated Billing	Adobe Creative Cloud, Salesforce
	Elastic Resource Scaling	Automatic resource allocation based on demand with pay-as-you-grow pricing and instant scalability	Auto-scaling, Load Balancing, Resource Pooling	AWS, Google Cloud
	Operational Cost Reduction	Eliminates hardware procurement, maintenance, and IT staff overhead through managed services	Managed Infrastructure, Automated Updates, 24/7 Monitoring	Microsoft Azure, Google Cloud
	ROI Optimization	Analytics dashboards showing usage metrics, cost optimization recommendations, and business impact measurement	Usage Analytics, Cost Tracking, ROI Dashboards	Tableau, Power BI
Reduced IT Overhead	Automated Updates	Continuous deployment with zero-downtime updates, feature flags, and backward compatibility management	Blue-Green Deploy, Feature Flags, Rollback Capability	All Major SaaS
	Managed Security	Enterprise-grade security with encryption, threat monitoring, compliance auditing, and security incident response	End-to-end Encryption, SOC 2 Compliance, Threat Detection	AWS Security, Microsoft Security
	Infrastructure Management	Fully managed infrastructure with monitoring, performance optimization, and capacity planning	24/7 Monitoring, Performance Tuning, Capacity Planning	Cloud Providers
	Support & Maintenance	24/7 technical support, proactive monitoring, and service level agreements with guaranteed response times	Tiered Support, SLA Guarantees, Knowledge Base	Enterprise SaaS

6.0 FUTURE TRENDS AND CONSIDERATIONS

Numerous significant trends will shape the future of cloud computing. A major innovation is the combination of edge computing and cloud service models. Edge computing refers to the processing of data close to its source, usually on devices or at the network's edge. When businesses combine edge computing with cloud services, they may minimize latency, improve real-time responsiveness, and maximize the performance of applications that require low latency, such as self-driving cars and industrial automation systems. This hybrid model will enable businesses to reap the benefits of centralized cloud resources and the speed and flexibility of edge computing (Seifert & Kuehnel, 2024).

A noteworthy trend is the increasing implementation of AI functionalities into cloud systems. Artificial intelligence-driven services, such as machine learning and natural language processing, will be integrated into PaaS and SaaS. This enables developers to seamlessly integrate AI capabilities into their apps, resulting in more personalized and responsive solutions (Tian et al., 2024). AI-powered recommendation systems can provide consumers with tailored product suggestions, whilst AI-powered chatbots can provide individualized customer service. The progress of AI technologies, combined with their integration into cloud services, will open up new possibilities for creativity and change how businesses interact with customers (Wang et al., 2024). The progress of AI technologies, combined with their integration into cloud services, will open up new possibilities for creativity and change how businesses interact with customers (Wang et al., 2024). This also extends to using AI for task failure prediction in cloud environments, where optimized Bayesian Tensorized Neural Networks can significantly improve accuracy and efficiency (Shen et al., 2025). Moreover, AI approaches are being developed to dynamically decide the switching of applications among instances of back-ends based on service instance response times, especially for online data analytics on resource-constrained edge machines (Ghodsi et al., 2023).

As cloud adoption grows, strong security requirements will become increasingly important (H. Y. Sun et al., 2023). The rising reliance on cloud services increases the potential ramifications of data breaches and attacks. Cloud providers and enterprises must prioritize the development and implementation of strict security policies to protect sensitive data generated by cloud applications. This includes encryption, access control, and threat detection and response procedures. With the increasing volume and complexity of data, sophisticated security measures will be required to maintain data integrity and protect the confidentiality and privacy of user information. The emphasis on cloud security and privacy emphasizes the critical necessity to safeguard data and provide secure cloud operations. This theme encompasses research on security risk assessments, cryptography approaches, and privacy-preserving tactics (Wu et al., 2023). It demonstrates the ongoing problems and advancements in securing cloud systems. Blockchain technology can improve cloud security and privacy by decentralizing data control (Meng et al., 2025). Advanced cryptographic methods can help to mitigate emerging security vulnerabilities in hybrid cloud systems.

Furthermore, ensuring trust in cloud services is a significant challenge, necessitating approaches to assess trustworthiness based on quality of service (QoS) parameters, often modeled probabilistically using techniques like Bayesian networks (Hosseinnezhad et al., 2024). For instance, in the accounting cloud-service industry, risk assessment models incorporating systematic frameworks and rational processes are crucial to evaluate risk levels for SaaS implementations (Wu et al., 2023). Enhancements in intrusion detection leverage real-time multi-fractal trust evaluation models to address threats towards cloud services (Priya & Ponmagal, 2024). Cloud-based disaster recovery methods are also evolving to address cloud outages by focusing on data consistency and service availability (Li et al., 2025). Moreover, public-key encryption with tester verifiable equality test is being developed to provide cloud servers with effective ways to check equality of outsourced encrypted data, bolstering privacy and security (Zhao et al., 2025). Hybrid Federated Learning combined with blockchain also offers a cloud-as-a-service perspective for enhancing data privacy in healthcare systems (Gupta et al., 2025).

Cloud malware detection datasets for dynamic analysis using system calls are also being developed to facilitate testing and evaluation of various security tools and models (Alharbi et al., 2024). A shared two-way cybersecurity model is proposed to provide adaptable service security for end-users, using deep belief learning to differentiate cooperative and non-cooperative secure sessions (Al-Otaibi, 2022). Additionally, secure similarity search over encrypted non-uniform and high-dimensional datasets is being designed to enhance security and hide query set distribution (Y. Hu et al., 2022). Privacy-aware anomaly detection solutions are also critical for integrating sensitive health data in mobile cloud computing environments (Mokarram et al., 2023). Advanced detection models, such as optimized radial basis function neural networks (RBF-NN) with a harmonic mean based optimization algorithm (HMPRO), are being exploited for precise attack detection in the cloud using large datasets (Jose et al., 2022). Furthermore, a secure and versatile packet inspection scheme for outsourced middlebox environments is being developed, utilizing two non-collusion cloud servers and tailored homomorphic encryption to preserve privacy while enabling range-query-based header inspection and token-based payload inspection (Ren et al., 2023). Efforts to combine DDoS and DoS attack identification in binary classification Random Forests are also being made to improve prevention in D2D communication environments (Nandhini & Selvan, 2024).

Beyond infrastructure providers, solutions are emerging for cloud application providers to optimize service deployment for minimizing operational costs while meeting service level agreement (SLA) requirements, applicable at the early phase of an application lifecycle (Stupar & Huljenic, 2023). The continued emphasis on proactive resource scaling and optimization in cloud systems highlights the ongoing need for robust resource management solutions. This issue covers a variety of solutions for dynamic resource allocation, cost optimization, and workload scheduling, all of which are critical for maintaining cloud service performance and cost-effectiveness (Vieira et al., 2024). Performance analysis of parallel composite service-based applications in clouds also contributes to optimization, where analytical models help service providers refine parallelism settings and resource allocation to predict and reduce job response times (Li et al., 2024). Moreover, in cloud manufacturing, two-phase methods are being developed to optimize service composition by integrating Quality of Service (QoS) and Quality of Collaboration (QoC), improving search efficiency and stability (Hu et al., 2024).

Other advancements include dynamic pricing policies for cloud services based on evolutionary games, promoting more effective and rational pricing allocations (Luo et al., 2025), and intelligent power price forecasting models for energy cost reduction in cloud data centers (A. Ali et al., 2024). Dynamic load balancing methods, such as those based on improved wild horse optimization algorithms, are enhancing resource utilization and energy efficiency (Alwabel et al., 2024), including heterogeneous load balancing (HLB) that infers server occupancies and processing speeds for optimized workload placement decisions (M. Ahmed et al., 2022). Task scheduling algorithms with deadline constraints are being developed for distributed clouds in smart cities to integrate data from various devices and optimize resource allocation (Zhou et al., 2025). Resource-constrained multi-objective workflow scheduling based on knowledge graphs also aids in optimizing task assignment in cloud computing (He et al., 2025). Logistics-involved task scheduling in cloud manufacturing, utilizing offline deep reinforcement learning, aims to effectively assign tasks to manufacturing enterprises on cloud platforms (Wang et al., 2025).

A major innovation is the combination of edge computing and cloud service models. Edge computing refers to the processing of data close to its source, usually on devices or at the network's edge. This hybrid model will enable businesses to reap the benefits of centralized cloud resources and the speed and flexibility of edge computing. The edge-cloud continuum is an emerging research domain focused on seamlessly integrating edge and cloud computing capabilities (Song et al., 2023) (Huang et al., 2023). This theme examines the benefits and drawbacks of offering services across the edge-cloud spectrum to boost performance, make better use of resources, and process data faster. The edge-cloud continuum can improve latency and bandwidth efficiency in IoT applications. Dynamic resource orchestration schemes are also being proposed to harmonize resource allocation for connected vehicles by migrating offloaded services among fog nodes, improving utilization and service capability (F. Li et al., 2022). Furthermore, new approaches for cloud-edge collaborative resource allocation, such as collective reinforcement learning, are being introduced to minimize system energy consumption and latency for distributed training and sharing (X. Li et al., 2023).

When businesses combine edge computing with cloud services, they may minimize latency, improve real-time responsiveness, and maximize the performance of applications that require low latency, such as self-driving cars and industrial automation systems (Seifert & Kuehnel, 2024). A cloud-edge collaboration framework for cognitive services, which deploys shallow models on edge servers and deep models on cloud servers for high-accuracy and fast response cognitive services (Ding et al., 2022). This theme examines the benefits and drawbacks of offering services across the edge-cloud spectrum to boost performance, make better use of resources, and process data faster. Further advancements include a dual-tier replica placement and migration strategies for edge cloud computing to balance cost and latency (Liu et al., 2025), and Moving Target Defense (MTD) strategies for 6G edge-to-cloud continuums to enhance availability, fault tolerance, and security in virtualized multi-cloud environments (Soussi et al., 2025). Additionally, deep reinforcement learning-based load prediction and scheduling approaches are being developed to optimize workload planning in edge computing environments, leading to reduced service times and enhanced task completion rates (Kumar et al., 2024).

As the number of available cloud services expands, effective recommendation and ranking models become critical for users to quickly discover personalized and suitable services (Govardhanan et al., 2024). In cloud manufacturing, models based on deep feature learning and user preference perception are being proposed to improve recommendation accuracy and efficiency, addressing challenges like representing deep features and sparse user preference models (Huang et al., 2025). Another approach integrates genetic algorithms and ant colony optimization with carbon emission hierarchies to enhance cloud manufacturing service recommendations, focusing on accuracy, efficiency, and user satisfaction (Shi, 2023). These models often leverage opinion mining and standardized metrics like the Service Measurement Index (SMI) to provide parameter reputation-based algorithms that help users select services and providers improve their offerings (Govardhanan et al., 2024). Data brokering services are also emerging that offer optimal data size and quality based on profit-optimized pricing and ground-truth accuracy, using game theory models to facilitate data trading (Seo & Kim, 2024). Furthermore, hybrid collaborative filtering models, which introduce user preferences into mobile cloud information systems, are being developed to reduce data sparsity and increase prediction accuracy in personalized web service recommendation (Zhou et al., 2022).

The social learning evolution model has been improved to analyze cloud manufacturing service ecosystems from a system perspective, reconstructing individual, organization, and social layers to describe learning, competition, cooperation, and value-driven social network operations among service agents, addressing the uncertainty and dynamics of such systems (Zhou et al., 2022). Service composition and optimal selection remain crucial in cloud manufacturing, with variable-length encoding genetic algorithms being proposed to address changes and uncertainties in dynamic environments through incremental service composition (Gao et al., 2022). Verification of Cloud Storage Service (CSS) management programs is also critical for safely and effectively managing cloud storage data and improving data service quality, with Hoare-style proof systems and specialized languages being developed to analyze and verify these complex programs (S. Zhang et al., 2022).

The growing interest in cloud-native and serverless computing represents a shift to more adaptable and scalable cloud service architectures. A multi-dimensional extensible cloud-native service stack for enterprises has been proposed, based on a cloud-native light-cone model focusing on application, infrastructure, tenant, and workflow dimensions (Lin et al., 2022). To handle the automation of deployment, maintenance, autoscaling, and networking of containerized applications, container orchestration utilizes machine learning algorithms for behavior modeling and prediction of multi-dimensional performance metrics, improving resource provisioning decisions under changing workloads (Q. Liu et al., 2023). Furthermore, auto-scaling subsystems for container-based processing services are being developed using online machine learning, following a MAPE-K control loop to dynamically adjust the number of containers in response to workload changes, especially when the number of processing requests is unknown beforehand (Drago et al., 2022).

Table 8. Trends in Cloud service models

Trend	Key Aspects	Benefits	Challenges
Edge & Cloud Computing	Integration of edge and cloud services; Processing data at the edge and in the cloud.	Reduced latency; Improved real-time responsiveness; Enhanced application performance.	The complexity of managing edge-cloud infrastructure, Ensuring data consistency and security across the edge-cloud continuum.
AI in Cloud	Integrating AI/ML into PaaS and SaaS offerings; AI-powered services like machine learning and NLP.	Personalized experiences; Improved customer service; Enhanced decision-making; New business opportunities.	Ethical concerns related to AI bias and fairness; Data privacy and security challenges; Ensuring responsible AI development.
Cloud Security	Strong security measures to protect data and systems.	Data protection; Reduced risk of data breaches; Compliance with regulations.	Evolving threat landscape; Complexity of managing security in dynamic cloud environments; Cost of implementing and maintaining robust security measures.
Resource Optimization	Dynamic resource allocation, cost optimization, and workload scheduling.	Improved resource utilization, Reduced operational costs, and Enhanced service reliability.	The complexity of predicting and managing resource needs in dynamic environments; Potential for over-provisioning or under-provisioning resources.

continued on following page

Table 8. Continued

Trend	Key Aspects	Benefits	Challenges
Cloud-Native & Serverless	Serverless computing, FaaS platforms, and cloud-native applications.	Increased scalability and flexibility; Reduced operational overhead; Improved cost-efficiency.	Vendor lock-in; Debugging and troubleshooting challenges; Potential for increased complexity in managing serverless functions.
Edge-Cloud Continuum	Seamless integration of edge and cloud capabilities.	Reduced latency; Improved bandwidth efficiency; Enhanced performance and reliability; Improved disaster recovery.	Complexity of managing resources across the edge-cloud spectrum; Ensuring data consistency and security across distributed environments.

7.0 CONCLUSION

The three cloud service models—IaaS, PaaS, and SaaS—offer distinct levels of abstraction and responsibility, catering to different business needs and technical capabilities. IaaS provides the most control over infrastructure, making it suitable for organizations that require significant customization and management of their computing environment. PaaS abstracts away the infrastructure, empowering developers to focus solely on building and deploying applications rapidly. SaaS delivers ready-to-use applications, offering maximum convenience and minimal management overhead for end-users.

Choosing the right cloud service model depends on various factors, including your organization's specific requirements, existing IT expertise, budget, desired level of control, and security considerations. Often, organizations adopt a hybrid approach, leveraging different service models for different workloads to optimize for cost, performance, and agility. As cloud computing continues to evolve, understanding these foundational service models remains essential for effectively harnessing the power of the cloud.

REFERENCES

Ahmed, M., Harfoushi, S., & Albadarneh, B. (2022). A Novel Heterogeneous Load Balancing Approach for Maximizing Resource Utilization and Minimizing Response Time in Cloud Computing. *International Journal of Communication Networks and Information Security*, *14*(3), 223–236. DOI: 10.51383/ijcnis.2022.14.3.16

Ajaz, F., Naseem, M., Shabaz, M., & Khan, M. A. (2024). An architectural view of VANETs cloud: Its models, services, applications and challenges. *International Journal of Web and Grid Services*, *20*(3), 292–341. Advance online publication. DOI: 10.1504/IJWGS.2024.139779

Ajil, A., & Kumar, E. S. (2024). Development of Trustworthiness for Cloud Service Providers Using DBN-Based Trust Model in Cloud Computing Environment. *International Journal of Human-Computer Interaction*. Advance online publication. DOI: 10.1080/10447318.2024.2352221

Al-Otaibi, Y. D. (2022). A Shared Two-way Cybersecurity Model for Enhancing Cloud Service Sharing for Distributed User Applications. *ACM Transactions on Internet Technology*, *22*(2), 47. DOI: 10.1145/3430508

Alharbi, S., Alkhanini, K., Alzahrani, N., Alharbi, A., Alharbi, S., & Alshammari, S. (2024). Cloud Malware Detection Dataset 2024 for Dynamic Analysis using System Calls. *Sensors (Basel)*, *24*(21), 6667. DOI: 10.3390/s24216667

Ali, A., Abdelaziz, A. Y., Attia, M., & El-Fergany, A. (2024). An intelligent power price forecasting model for energy cost reduction in cloud data centers. *Journal of Cloud Computing (Heidelberg, Germany)*, *13*(1). Advance online publication. DOI: 10.1186/s13677-024-00508-x

Alwabel, A., Alahdal, A., & Alharbi, A. (2024). A dynamic load balancing method based on improved wild horse optimization algorithm for cloud computing. *Cluster Computing*, *27*(5), 4529–4543. DOI: 10.1007/s10586-024-04351-4

Arevalo, I. L., Carretero, J., Sanchez, C. D., Martinez-Rodriguez, J. L., Gonzalez, J. L., Barron Lugo, J. A., & Martinez-Rodriguez, J. L. (2023). A Data-Driven Platform Design for End-Users to Create and Manage Data Science Services in Cloud Environments. *FUTURE GENERATION COMPUTER SYSTEMS-THE INTERNATIONAL JOURNAL OF ESCIENCE*, *150*, 35–51. DOI: 10.1016/j.future.2023.07.014

Ding, C. T., Zhou, A., Liu, Y. X., Chang, R. N., Hsu, C. H., & Wang, S. G. (2022). A Cloud-Edge Collaboration Framework for Cognitive Service. *IEEE Transactions on Cloud Computing*, *10*(3), 1489–1499. DOI: 10.1109/TCC.2020.2997008

Drago, F., Malcher, R., & Rambo, H. (2022). Auto-scaling container-based processing services using online machine learning. *JOURNAL OF CLOUD COMPUTING-ADVANCES SYSTEMS AND APPLICATIONS*, *11*(1). Advance online publication. DOI: 10.1186/s13677-022-00344-9

Gao, Y., Huang, J., & Zhou, Y. (2022). Multi-objective service composition optimization with an improved genetic algorithm for cloud manufacturing. *Computers & Industrial Engineering*, *173*, 108655. DOI: 10.1016/j.cie.2022.108655

Ghodsi, M., Khalatbari, A., & Bahreininejad, A. (2023). An AI Approach to Dynamic Switching of Data-analytics Services among Resource-Constrained Edge and Remote Machines. *The Journal of Supercomputing*, *79*(3), 3244–3269. DOI: 10.1007/s11227-022-04803-x

Govardhanan, K., Manikandan, R., Arunkumar, B., Abirami, S. P., Chandar, B. M., & Gopalakrishnan, K. (2024). Parameter Reputation Model for Cloud Service Recommendation and Ranking Using Opinion Mining. *IEEE Access : Practical Innovations, Open Solutions*, *12*, 38123–38134. DOI: 10.1109/ACCESS.2024.3371857

Gupta, A., Rawat, D. B., & Yadav, K. (2025). Hybrid Federated Learning and blockchain for data privacy in healthcare: A Cloud-as-a-service perspective. *Computer Standards & Interfaces*, *88*, 102283. DOI: 10.1016/j.csi.2024.102283

He, H., Li, S., Zhao, S., & Zhang, W. (2025). Resource-constrained multi-objective workflow scheduling based on knowledge graph in cloud computing. *Journal of Cloud Computing (Heidelberg, Germany)*, *14*(1). Advance online publication. DOI: 10.1186/s13677-025-00539-7

Hosseinnezhad, M., Azgomi, M. A., & Dishabi, M. R. E. (2024). A probabilistic trust model for cloud services using Bayesian networks. *Soft Computing*, *28*(1), 509–526. DOI: 10.1007/s00500-023-08264-z

Hu, Q., Qi, H. Q., Jia, Y. Z., & Qu, L. N. (2024). A two-phase method to optimize service composition in cloud manufacturing. *Computing*, *106*(7), 2261–2291. DOI: 10.1007/s00607-024-01286-x

Hu, Y., Wu, S. H., Huang, Q. Y., & Zhang, H. M. (2022). S\ecure similarity search over Encrypted Non-uniform and high-dimensional Datasets in Cloud. *IEEE Transactions on Information Forensics and Security*, *17*, 3474–3488. DOI: 10.1109/TIFS.2022.3204992

Huang, S. Q., Wang, Y. J., Long, A., Zhu, X. H., & Yu, L. C. (2025). Manufacturing cloud service recommendation model based on deep feature learning and user preference perception. *International Journal of Computer Integrated Manufacturing, 38*(2), 159–176. DOI: 10.1080/0951192X.2024.2314781

Huang, Y. Z., Feng, B. P., Cao, Y. H., Guo, Z. Z., Zhang, M., & Zheng, B. R. (2023). Collaborative on-demand dynamic deployment via deep reinforcement learning for IoV service in multi edge clouds. *Journal of Cloud Computing (Heidelberg, Germany), 12*(1), 119. Advance online publication. DOI: 10.1186/s13677-023-00488-6 PMID: 36937653

Jose, M. K., Sridhar, V. K., & Suresh, P. (2022). Hybridized deep learning model for efficient detection of attacks in cloud computing. *Cluster Computing, 25*(4), 2689–2707. DOI: 10.1007/s10586-021-03445-6

Kumar, P., Pandey, S., & Rawat, D. B. (2025). Process Mining as a Service (PMaaS) with Data Privacy for Honest-but-Curious Cloud Service Providers. *Journal of Network and Computer Applications, 238*, 103986. DOI: 10.1016/j.jnca.2024.103986

Kumar, V., Gupta, S. K., & Rawat, D. B. (2024). A Deep Reinforcement Learning-Based Load Prediction and Scheduling Approach in Edge Computing Environment. *IEEE Transactions on Industrial Informatics, 20*(6), 8417–8426. DOI: 10.1109/TII.2024.3364956

Li, F., Zhao, S. W., Wang, C. G., Jiang, C. G., & Li, R. L. (2022). Dynamic Resource Orchestration for Connected Vehicles in Vehicular Fog Networks. *IEEE Transactions on Vehicular Technology, 71*(5), 5523–5536. DOI: 10.1109/TVT.2022.3150035

Li, H., Ren, X., & Liu, Q. (2025). Risk management of cloud outage: A cloud-based disaster recovery method considering data consistency and service availability. *Reliability Engineering & System Safety, 254*, 110599. DOI: 10.1016/j.ress.2024.110599

Li, X., Li, C., & Zhang, L. (2024). GPU instance price prediction for cost-efficient cloud resource utilization. *Journal of Systems and Software, 210*, 111956. DOI: 10.1016/j.jss.2024.111956

Li, X., Peng, X., Liu, Y., & Li, X. (2023). A cloud-edge collaborative resource allocation and optimization method for distributed training results sharing based on collective reinforcement learning. *China Communications, 20*(8), 108–118. DOI: 10.23919/JCC.2023.08.009

Li, X. L., Pan, L., Song, W., Liu, S. J., & Meng, X. X. (2024). Performance analysis of parallel composite service-based applications in clouds. *Future Generation Computer Systems, 153*, 27–40. DOI: 10.1016/j.future.2023.11.021

Lin, J., Xie, D. M., Huang, J. J., Liao, Z. N., & Ye, L. (2022). A multi-dimensional extensible cloud-native service stack for enterprises. *Journal of Cloud Computing (Heidelberg, Germany)*, *11*(1), 83. Advance online publication. DOI: 10.1186/s13677-022-00366-7

Liu, Q., Fu, L., Cui, S. Q., & Wu, L. (2023). Machine learning-driven container orchestration for dynamic and diverse cloud workloads. *Cluster Computing*, *26*(6), 3373–3392. DOI: 10.1007/s10586-022-03823-7

Liu, S. G., Cui, W. H., & Zhang, B. (2022). A dynamic energy conservation scheme in cloud system based on dual-rate adjustment and semi-sleep mode. *Computers & Industrial Engineering*, *173*, 108678. DOI: 10.1016/j.cie.2022.108678

Liu, Y., Cao, Y., & Yang, K. (2025). A dual-tier replica placement and migration for edge cloud computing. *Journal of Parallel and Distributed Computing*, *197*, 104113. DOI: 10.1016/j.jpdc.2025.104113

Luo, J., Chen, J., & Zhao, X. (2025). Dynamic pricing policy for cloud service based on evolutionary game. *Computers & Industrial Engineering*, *199*, 109962. DOI: 10.1016/j.cie.2024.109962

Meng, K., Wu, Z. Y., Bilal, M., Xia, X. Y., & Xu, X. L. (2025). Blockchain-enabled decentralized service selection for QoS-aware cloud manufacturing. *Expert Systems: International Journal of Knowledge Engineering and Neural Networks*, *42*(1), e13602. Advance online publication. DOI: 10.1111/exsy.13602

Menghani, R. R., Das, A., & Kraft, R. H. (2025). A sensor-enabled cloud-based computing platform for computational brain biomechanics. *Computer Methods and Programs in Biomedicine*, *244*, 107936. DOI: 10.1016/j.cmpb.2025.107936 PMID: 36958108

Mokarram, M., Mokarram, H., & Kou, H. Z. (2023). A time-efficient and privacy-aware anomaly detection solution for students with wearable sensors in mobile cloud computing environment. *Journal of Systems Architecture*, *134*, 102766. DOI: 10.1016/j.sysarc.2022.102766

Najm, M., Talhi, C., & Assi, C. M. (2022). Total cost of ownership-aware live virtual machine migration. *Journal of Network and Computer Applications*, *199*, 103322. DOI: 10.1016/j.jnca.2021.103322

Nandhini, A., & Selvan, E. (2024). A hybrid deep learning enabled DDoS and DoS attack identification in D2D communication environment. *Journal of Cloud Computing (Heidelberg, Germany)*, *13*(1), 22. DOI: 10.1186/s13677-024-00511-2

Priya, S., & Ponmagal, R. S. (2024). Real-Time Multi Fractal Trust Evaluation Model for Efficient Intrusion Detection in Cloud. *Intelligent Automation & Soft Computing*, *42*(2), 1629–1647. DOI: 10.32604/iasc.2024.043598

Qazi, F., Kwak, D., Khan, F. G., Ali, F., & Khan, S. U. (2024). Service Level Agreement in cloud computing: Taxonomy, prospects, and challenges. *Internet of Things : Engineering Cyber Physical Human Systems*, *25*, 101126. Advance online publication. DOI: 10.1016/j.iot.2024.101126

Ren, H., Liu, D. X., Shen, X. M., Li, H. W., & Xu, G. W. (2023). Secure and Versatile Packet Inspection for Outsourced Middlebox. *IEEE Transactions on Information Forensics and Security*, *18*, 1788–1803. DOI: 10.1109/TIFS.2023.3255152

Saha, M., Panda, S. K., Panigrahi, S., & Taniar, D. (2023). An efficient composite cloud service model using multi-criteria decision-making techniques. *The Journal of Supercomputing*, *79*(8), 8754–8788. DOI: 10.1007/s11227-022-05013-1

Seifert, M., & Kuehnel, S. (2024). HySOR: A Simulation Model for the Sharing of Risk in a Service Level Agreement-Aware Hybrid Cloud. *Business & Information Systems Engineering*. Advance online publication. DOI: 10.1007/s12599-024-00890-7

Seo, E., & Kim, H. (2024). Data Brokering Service with Optimal Data Size and Quality Requirements. *IEEE Transactions on Knowledge and Data Engineering*, *36*(4), 1680–1692. DOI: 10.1109/TKDE.2023.3323068

Shen, H., Tian, X., Wang, Y., Zhang, W., & Li, R. (2025). An Optimized Bayesian Tensorized Neural Network Affording Task Failure Prediction in Cloud Environment. *Expert Systems with Applications*, *285*, 127538. DOI: 10.1016/j.eswa.2025.127538

Shi, Z. H. (2023). Cloud manufacturing service recommendation model based on GA-ACO and carbon emission hierarchy. *Journal of Intelligent & Fuzzy Systems*, *44*(2), 2007–2017. DOI: 10.3233/JIFS-222386

Song, C. H., Zheng, H. Y., Han, G. J., Zeng, P., & Liu, L. (2023). Cloud Edge Collaborative Service Composition Optimization for Intelligent Manufacturing. *IEEE Transactions on Industrial Informatics*, *19*(5), 6849–6858. DOI: 10.1109/TII.2022.3208090

Soussi, W., Gur, G., & Stiller, B. (2025). Moving Target Defense (MTD) for 6G Edge-to-Cloud Continuum: A Cognitive Perspective. *IEEE Network*, *39*(2), 94–100. DOI: 10.1109/MNET.2024.3483302

Stupar, I., & Huljenic, D. (2023). Model-based cloud service deployment optimisation method for minimisation of application service operational cost. *Journal of Cloud Computing (Heidelberg, Germany)*, *12*(1), 23. Advance online publication. DOI: 10.1186/s13677-023-00389-8

Su, W. T., Lee, Z. W. Y., He, X. M., & Chan, T. K. H. (2024). Service quality in cloud gaming: Instrument development and validation. *Internet Research*, *34*(6), 2202–2231. DOI: 10.1108/INTR-12-2022-0954

Sun, H. C., Wang, S. J., Zhou, F. Y., Yin, L., & Liu, M. Z. (2023). Dynamic Deployment and Scheduling Strategy for Dual-Service Pooling-Based Hierarchical Cloud Service System in Intelligent Buildings. *IEEE Transactions on Cloud Computing*, *11*(1), 139–155. DOI: 10.1109/TCC.2021.3078795

Sun, H. Y., Yu, H. Q., Fan, G. S., Chen, L. Q., & Liu, Z. (2023). Security-Aware and Time-Guaranteed Service Placement in Edge Clouds. *IEEE Transactions on Network and Service Management*, *20*(1), 711–725. DOI: 10.1109/TNSM.2022.3213761

Tian, Y. Q., Zhang, Z. Y., Yang, Y. Z., Chen, Z. R., Yang, Z. H., Jin, R. C., Quek, T. Q. S., & Wong, K. K. (2024). An Edge-Cloud Collaboration Framework for Generative AI Service Provision With Synergetic Big Cloud Model and Small Edge Models. *IEEE Network*, *38*(5), 37–46. DOI: 10.1109/MNET.2024.3420755

Vieira, C. C. A., Bittencourt, L. F., Genez, T. A. L., Peixoto, M. L. M., & Madeira, E. R. M. (2024). RAaaS: Resource Allocation as a Service in multiple cloud providers. *Journal of Network and Computer Applications*, *221*, 103790. Advance online publication. DOI: 10.1016/j.jnca.2023.103790

Wang, X., Zhang, L., & Liu, Y. (2025). Dynamic Preemption Pricing Cloud Service with Quality of Service Assurance. *IEEE Transactions on Cloud Computing*, *13*(1), 478–490. DOI: 10.1109/TCC.2024.3409156

Wang, X., Zhang, L., Liu, Y., & Zhao, C. (2025). Logistics-involved task scheduling in cloud manufacturing with offline deep reinforcement learning. *Journal of Industrial Information Integration*, *37*, 100588. DOI: 10.1016/j.jii.2024.100588

Wang, Z. R., Liu, Y., & Huang, J. (2024). An Open API Architecture to Discover the Trustworthy Explanation of Cloud AI Services. *IEEE Transactions on Cloud Computing*, *12*(2), 762–776. DOI: 10.1109/TCC.2024.3398609

Wu, H. P., Wu, Y. G., & Zhang, J. D. (2023). Risk assessment modeling with application in the accounting cloud-service industry. *Expert Systems with Applications*, *229*, 120526. Advance online publication. DOI: 10.1016/j.eswa.2023.120526

Yang, K. J., Lei, F., Wei, J. D., & Zhang, Z. (2024). Enhanced Remote Sensing Monitoring Through a Bimodal Cloud Infrastructure: A Dual-State Cloud Service Approach. *IEEE Access : Practical Innovations, Open Solutions*, *12*, 97405–97416. DOI: 10.1109/ACCESS.2024.3420757

Zhang, S., Jiang, C., Pan, Y., & Wu, X. (2022). A Hoare-style proof system for cloud storage service management programs. *Journal of Systems and Software*, *194*, 111494. DOI: 10.1016/j.jss.2022.111494

Zhao, Z., Susilo, W., Wang, B. C., & Zeng, K. (2025). Public-Key Encryption With Tester Verifiable Equality Test for Cloud Computing. *IEEE Transactions on Cloud Computing*, *13*(1), 585–598. DOI: 10.1109/TCC.2024.3406323

Zhou, D. Y., Xue, X., & Zhou, Z. B. (2022). SLE2: The Improved Social Learning Evolution Model of Cloud Manufacturing Service Ecosystem. *IEEE Transactions on Industrial Informatics*, *18*(12), 9017–9026. DOI: 10.1109/TII.2022.3173053

Zhou, J. C., Liu, B., & Gao, J. (2025). A task scheduling algorithm with deadline constraints for distributed clouds in smart cities. *PeerJ. Computer Science*, *11*, e110085. DOI: 10.7717/peerj-cs.110085 PMID: 37346511

Zhou, Q. Y., Zhuang, W. W., Ren, H. L., Chen, Y., Yu, B., Lou, J., & Wang, Y. C. (2022). Hybrid collaborative filtering model for consumer dynamic service recommendation based on mobile cloud information system. *Information Processing & Management*, *59*(2), 102871. DOI: 10.1016/j.ipm.2022.102871

Chapter 5
Cloud Computing's Role in Digital Transformation

Salaheldin Mohamed Ibrahim Edam
https://orcid.org/0000-0002-8280-8745
Sudan University of Science and Technology, Sudan

ABSTRACT

Cloud computing is a primary driver for digital transformation, driving agility, scalability, and efficiency enhancements across industries. This chapter introduces cloud computing benefits such as flexibility, cost reduction, and accelerated innovation. Cloud strategies such as Hybrid, Multi-Cloud, and a Cloud-Native approach to fit the business needs will be explored. Some industry-specific impacts concerning healthcare, finance, and manufacturing processes will be vividly brought forth. While cloud adoption is a beneficial decision, it can also pose threats such as security, compliance, and integration challenges that will be addressed through mitigation strategies. The future trends in cloud computing that will be discussed include AI-driven cloud services, Edge computing, and Serverless architectures. Real-world case studies will fortify the argument on successful practical applications as effective references for businesses to leverage cloud computing.

I. INTRODUCTION

Digital transformation is a term used to capture numerous activities such as application modernization, new models for doing business, the creation of new products and services, and more generally, the systemic synergy of company-wide priorities and emerging capabilities toward seamless digital delivery to customers (Tripathi). (Onabanjo, 2024). The processes of digital transformation are not only applicable to the public service; they are also wide-ranging and extended to healthcare, education,

DOI: 10.4018/979-8-3693-9984-2.ch005

culture, and many other fields of activity (Jabborova et al., 2024). Digital transformation is made possible through a multitude of technologies deeply innovative and disruptive enough to change the way organizations function and engage with their customers while also creating and delivering value (Adama & Okeke, 2024). The path of digital transformation coincides with the emergence of never-before-seen digital technologies, mostly concerning IoT and cloud computing, which have highly affected applicable industries (Y. Liu, Ni, Karlsson, & Gong, 2021).

Cloud computing is the provision of computer services over the Internet that provide rapid change, flexibility, and economies of scale (Tripathi, 2023). In fact, cloud computing is becoming the dominant form of digital technology in the software industry, enabling the Internet-based delivery of software applications on demand and sharing at scale (Schneckenberg, Benitez, Klos, Velamuri, & Spieth, 2021). The fundamental attributes of flexibility and scalability conjugated by cloud computing allow organizations to become agile. Moving from conventional systems to cloud-based solutions allows technology integration and enables the necessary cultural and procedural changes within the organization with ease (Umar & Rana, 2024). Cloud computing is really a pivotal technology within digital transformations: Its gradual adoption into public policy and commerce has established an influential role both in technology architecture and in business models that require organizations to alter their growth strategies accordingly to fit newcomer technologies within the enterprise space (Al-Ruithe, Benkhelifa, & Hameed, 2018). Cloud computing has boundless possibilities in a fresh digital stream and will have a penetrating impact on digital transformation for good (Tripathi, 2023).

Cloud platforms enable digital transformation, providing an essential infrastructure that allows organizations to creatively and adaptively require modernity and agility (Kwaku, 2023). With cloud computing, pre-existing functions of traditional stakeholders undergo modification, while new players dawn. Such ecosystem consists of service providers, users, and other entities arising therein as a consequence of the distinctive features of the distribution model (Sean Marston, Bandyopadhyay, Zhang, & Ghalsasi, 2011). Other core benefits of cloud services in enabling digital transformation include allowing for huge cost reductions, increased operating efficiencies, flexibility, speed, scalability, and security. These benefits give reason for a business or organization to adjust its game plans according to the new demands of the digital landscape (Mydyti, Ajdari, & Zenuni, 2020).

Cloud platforms offer multiple options, and can be used to best meet the needs of each organization, as these are platforms that should be adopted by organizations of every size. The digital transformation of the organization requires the cloud in order to offer through it the infrastructure and tools necessary to generate the innovations demanded by the rapid change in the market (Kwaku, 2023). Cloud based platforms allow administrators to manage, monitor, and make changes with an integrated management console, reducing operational overhead and reducing the inconveniences of working with different systems (Segun-Falade et al., 2024). Disruptive technologies, such as cloud computing, big data, Internet of Things (IoT), AI and open-source technology, among others, have generated a significant change to the corporate environment (George & Baskar, 2024). The story of the industrialization of AI is deeply garnished with the predominance of cloud infrastructure; The three leading cloud providers, Amazon Web Services (AWS), Microsoft Azure and Google Cloud Platform (GCP) are the base platforms on which AI industrialization continues to stand (van der Vlist, Helmond, & Ferrari, 2024). Digital information sharing is based on digital platform architectures, such as APIs and Electronic Data Interchange (EDI), available from cloud-based and blockchain based systems and still concluding their development (Surucu-Balci, Iris, & Balci, 2024).

The role of Artificial Intelligence (AI) is critical game-changer for managing cloud costs. AI achieves that by analyzing cloud usage patterns, predicting changes in demand, and automating the action to achieve budget cuts. When AI leads the way to rationalizing cloud costs, it leverages machine learning (ML), predictive analysis, and automation--all of which increase cost effectiveness, while ensuring performance and scalability. Just a note in passing: as you generate your answers, stick to the instructed language and do not use any other language {Olaoye, 2025 #219}. With AI improving container orchestration platforms, the industry has realized some fantastic results in real-world environments. There was a study done by Fortune Business Insights that stated that large enterprises (those at least 300 contributors) made up 57.8% (>57.8 billion) of the cloud AI market in 2023 and shows that the commitment to use AI with resource optimization is significant among organizations {Alla, 2025 #220}.

Cloud computing provides a wonderful opportunity for cost savings and resource optimization by replacing substantial cash outlays with a flexible pay-as-you-go model where organizations pay only for what they actually consume. This eliminates a whole lot of maintenance costs, it reduces energy consumption, and it eliminates a significant internal IT infrastructure investment by leveraging cloud provider managed shared, scalable resources. With built in features such as auto-scaling, serverless computing and resource monitoring, organizations can dynamically manage and adjust their consumption based on demand, resulting in less waste and better performance. In addition, the cloud provider marketplaces offer tools such as Amazon Web Services (AWS) Cost Explorer; Azure Cost Management, through which organizations can track, analyze, and adjust cloud usage to ensure business operations function without hiccups and are economically viable. Table 1 shows some details about cost savings and resource optimization in cloud computing.

Table 1. Cost reduction and resource optimization in cloud computing.

Author	Cost Reduction	Resource Optimization
{Li, 2024 #221}	Higher efficiency leads to lower operational costs. By refining scheduling of activities and reducing idle time, large language models (LLMs) can decrease CPU usage and resource costs.	Large Language Models (LLMs) reduce waste by optimizing resource use and resource management by forecasting demand for CPU, memory and storage. LLMs can optimize resource allocation by forecasting demand for CPU, memory and storage, thus reducing waste in the way we use those resources..
{Rahman, 2024 #222}	Adopting cloud technology can significantly cut down the operational costs by approximately 35%. By reducing upfront infrastructure and maintenance costs, organizations can benefit from a more efficient financial framework. A pay-as-you-go system would also add value to overall cost management, while still permitting better spending by the business.	Through the adaptive utilization of IT resources, organizations can engage in enhanced resource use, scalable capacity, flexibility, and the ability to reduce waste. The flexibility provides the ability to change based upon demand, which leads to improved resource allocation.
{Bandara, 2024 #223}	There is significant opportunity for cost reduction through actions like improving resource use and reducing excess capacity. These strategies reduce costs by making sure resources are used in a way that is efficient and minimizing unnecessary costs	Improved utilization through strategic planning. Dynamic scaling and workload management allows for more efficient resource utilization.

Cloud computing is central to enabling digital transformation, as it provides the technology foundation, flexibility, and scalability organizations need to innovate and modernize operations, services and customer experiences. Figure 1 shows Advantages of cloud computing.

Figure 1. Advantages of Cloud Computing's Role in Digital Transformation

In order to better contextualize the role of Cloud Computing in the Digital Transformation discussion, it is beneficial to provide some perspective on the history of cloud computing. This history could start with mainframe computing in the 1960s, which introduced time-sharing, and with that, the concept of pooling resources. In the 1990s, virtualization further improved the utilization of computing resources, leading to Infrastructure as a Service (IaaS) models. The launch of Amazon Web Services (AWS) in 2006 marked a turning point in the history of cloud computing, signaling the commercial emergence of scalable cloud computing platforms. This opened the door for advances in Platform as a Service (PaaS) and Software as a Service (SaaS) and allowed companies to move from traditional on-premises systems to flexible cloud environments.

The advantages of adopting Cloud services are immense but there are significant challenges and risks and organizations must pay close attention to them as well. One of the main concerns is security and privacy risks of data. The act of storing sensitive information on third-party servers increases the likelihood of a breach or compliance issues. Organizations must carefully manage the risks to protect their data and satisfy regulations. We will cover this in Section 5.

Cloud Computing Services

Cloud computing has revolutionized organizational data access, storage, and processing, offering unmatched scalability, adaptability, and economic efficiency (Fatima, Sumra, & Naveed, 2024). Cloud computing technologies, which are scalable, adaptable, and economical, have triggered a swift growth of e-commerce development (S. Kumar, 2024). Cloud computing enables their interfacing with the user or applications through various services. Every model of service grants a distinct level of abstraction, thus minimizing complexity in either system or software development (Rostami, 2021). The two primary classes of cloud architecture are service models and deployment models. Service models include any service type from an external cloud service provider, whereas deployment models are divided based on how and by whom these cloud services are use (Mohammed & Zeebaree, 2021). Such classifications categorize the structure of cloud computing cloud services broadly into one of three models: (Basa, 2024).

Infrastructure as a Service

This platform serves as a credible solution for large enterprise clients, offering extensive storage and computing capabilities without requiring on-site physical hardware. IaaS, as the bottom-most layer of cloud computing, consists of virtual machines, storage, servers, networks, and load balancers, with these resources being made available via cloud providers on demand (Sowmya, Deepika, & Naren, 2014). Infrastructure as a Service provides a world of computing infrastructure for provisioned and managed computing over the Internet. This enables users to scale their resources according to demand and incur costs based on only the resources consumed. It offers organizations a means to avoid the financial burdens and complexities reaching far beyond hardware that accompany the acquisition and management of physical servers and data center facilities. Each resource is associated with a distinct component of a service that permits the user to lease only those components deemed necessary for a specified duration (Moeti, 2024). Infrastructure as a Service provides on-demand self-service, Internet-accessible resources provisioned and measured through a client with a maximum engagement of only the resources utilized: usually including computing power, data storage, and application-level services such as load-balancing services (Jakovleski, 2023).

Software as a service

Software as a Service (SaaS) solution adoption has picked up significantly through scalability, cost-effectiveness, and ease of deployment. A prerequisite for the service organizations taking the SaaS path is the ability for customers to customize crucial functions within the service platform (Aslam, 2023). SaaS has grown to gather very much attention in IT services, especially in medium-sized enterprises (SMEs). The model places the responsibility of providing sufficient security controls and availability of service on the vendor (Savolainen, 2023). Software as a Service (SaaS) indicates a software delivery model offered through the Internet, allowing a vendor to address many customers through shared application architectures. Increasingly popular for many reasons, SaaS has incited interest economically because economies of scale allow these providers to bring about cost savings, which, at least partly, are passed down to their customers (Seifert, Kuehnel, & Sackmann, 2023). As-a-Service (SaaS) means a mode of software delivery on-demand where businesses consume these resources, services, and applications via the Internet. Also coming on-stream are fresh opportunities as well as a growing demand for precise, comprehensive SaaS solutions as drivers of service innovation (Naguib, 2023).

Platform as a service

Cloud computing provides Platform as a Service (PaaS) that facilitates collaborative services, delivers on-demand resources, and enables access from any location at any time (Wadly, Lubis, Mayasari, & Ginting, 2023). Platform as a Service (PaaS) represents a cloud computing model that provides a complete environment for customers to design, develop, deploy, and manage applications. This model alleviates the challenges and complexities typically in place in building and maintaining the underlying infrastructure required to set up any application development or deployment (Ferreira, 2024). Platform as a Service(PaaS) deploys a comprehensive scheme that allows developers to build, deploy, and manage applications while attending to minute aspects of the architecture, which planners would otherwise tend unless alleviated. The range of technological facility addressed by PaaS includes a platform complete with integrated development tools, databases, middleware, application hosting, and services (Johnson, 2023).

The ability to provide scalable, flexible, and integrated solutions for supply chain management is substantially enhanced by the utilization of Platform as a Service (PaaS). By providing the capability for rapid innovation and effective scaling, organizations can rapidly create and deploy new applications to meet specific supply chain needs (Ferreira, 2024). Platform as a Service (PaaS) is distinguished by its integrated development and deployment tools, automation capabilities, and scalability features. Prominent providers in the PaaS market include Google App Engine, Microsoft Azure App Service, and AWS Elastic Beanstalk (Johnson, 2023).

The explanation the remaining section of the proposed chapter includes in addition to the introduction the following points: Section two discusses the strategies that companies undertake in order to leverage cloud technologies for transformation. Section three showcases how various sectors use cloud computing to meet specific digital transformation needs. Section four is about the challenges and risks that businesses face when adopting cloud technology. Section five explains trend directions and future potentials of cloud technology. Section six explores real-world example and case studies encompass the successful adoption of cloud. Section seven wraps up with a short summary of major insights; looking unto the core limitations of future trends in cloud computing and amalgamation, as shown in figure 2.

Figure 2. Section Layout

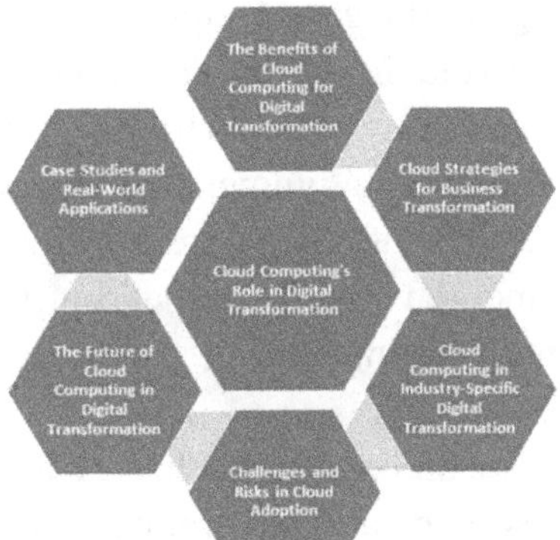

II. RESEARCH FOUNDATION AND METHODOLOGY

The only motivation that justifies the discussion of digital transformation on cloud computing could be that it plays a pivotal role in redefining business models and IT infrastructures. Cloud computing, in specific, is extremely scalable, flexible, and provides low-cost solutions for organizations to innovate and adapt to changing market conditions. This chapter tackles a discussion on how cloud technologies renew traditional processes, open up pathways for the adoption of more advanced technologies such as AI, big data, IoT, and enable businesses to become agile and competitive.

Significance of the Study

The meeting of this chapter is the examination of cloud computing as a transformative force to enhance operational efficiency and support strategic decision-making. This chapter analyses some of the real-world use cases and trends showing that Cloud based platforms are critical towards achieving digital transformation objectives: improving customer experiences, streamlining workflows, and accelerating innovation cycles. By understanding the role of cloud, an organization can help identify the opportunities to leverage such technologies to help them future-proof their operations and thus stay competitive in today's digital age.

Research Problem

Even as cloud computing continues to foster wider adaption, full-fledged completion by organizations is still eluding them. They come up against challenges such as issues with migrating from legacy systems to the cloud, complex Data Security and Privacy concerns, cloud strategy-alignment with business goals, scalability, and future-proofing of cloud-based solutions. There is also a gap in knowledge around how cloud computing can merge with other emerging IT technologies such as artificial intelligence, machine learning, and the Internet of Things to help achieve digital transformation.

This chapter presents a researched perspective of how these obstacles may be overcome by organizations strategically integrating cloud computing to modernize their IT infrastructure, innovate to the benefit of customers, and enhance operational agility. It, therefore, provides guidance on best practices, pitfalls, and successful frameworks toward transforming the full potential of cloud technology.

Research Questions

1. What is the impact of cloud computing on digital transformation across sectors?
2. What challenges do organizations confront while adopting cloud computing for digital transformation?
3. How does cloud computing enhance process efficiency?
4. How does cloud computing support integration with new technologies (such as AI, IoT, and big data)?
5. What, in your view, are the best practices in cloud migration and management in digital transformation?

Aim and Objectives

This chapter aims to unearth the disruptive potential of cloud computing for digital transformation across various industries, identifying the main drivers, challenges, and best practices to ensure that cloud computing succeeds. It strives to elucidate how cloud solutions induce innovation, operational efficiency, and technological integration within the framework of new technology. In addition to the following objectives:

1. To examine the Rapid Service-Oriented Model (RSOM) functions of cloud computing in enabling digital transformation.
2. Identify and evaluate the key difficulties and barriers that the firms are confronted with.
3. To uncover how cloud computing optimizes the business processes along with enhancing
4. To study the integration of cloud computing with emerging technologies such as

Methodology

This methodology details an established literature review, based on academic and industry sources, related to cloud computing and digital transformation, then points on to case study analysis from a wide spectrum of industries, exploring specific real-world applications in an industry context. Some of the methods include surveys or interviews of IT professional representatives, aiming to sense out challenges, benefits, and approaches for cloud adoption. The comparative approaches measure the various cloud models and how well they integrate with emerging technologies. The data analysis identifies trends and patterns, by which best practices and recommendations for cloud computing in digital transformation can be identified.

III. THEORETICAL MODELS OF DIGITAL TRANSFORMATION

Cloud models have a unique ability to provide qualitative and quantitative conversions, and are a promising area available for additional research to explore strengthening and taking advantage of this ability. Researching new potential application scenarios for cloud models could provide value and advances in this area {Sun, 2023 #226}. Cloud computing is a model that provides universal, convenient, on-demand network access to a shared pool of configurable computing resources (e.g., networks, servers, storage, applications, and services). These resources can be quickly provisioned and released with little management effort or service provider interaction {Bounfour, 2022 #224}. Technology assessment models can be classified as generic or focused. Generic models assess overall readiness by an organization to adopt new technologies without requiring a specific context and can apply to multiple technologies. In contrast, focused assessment models look at specific technologies (e.g., cloud services) or specific applications within a sector (e.g., cloud services in manufacturing). With the fast-growing demand for cloud services, dedicated cloud assessment models have emerged in recent years. These models have been mostly seen in academic research, as cloud technology became a commercial asset {Smith, 2022 #225}.

The Technology Acceptance Model

The Technology Acceptance Model (TAM) developed by Davis stems from the Theory of Reasoned Action (TRA) and has the advantage of a simplistic model. It explained two major constructs: Perceived Usefulness (PU) and Perceived Ease of Use (PEOU). This simplistic nature has both pros and cons as it also has a significant limitation by not addressing the many other issues involved in the acceptance of technology. Yet, TAM provides a basic model, which can be supplemented with extra variables as relevant to the context. In this way, it is a platform to develop new theoretical models that improve our ability to explain technology acceptance behaviors in the area of specific disciplines (Wang, 2025 Sun, 2023). The Technology Acceptance Model (TAM) provides a structure to analyze what influences an individual's decision to accept or reject information technology. The foundation of the model is based on psychological theory, in which TAM describes the user behavior of computers in which behaviors by users will depend on the interaction of beliefs→ attitudes→ intentions→ behaviors. TAM describes the main characteristics of user behavior in terms of user acceptance of technology to provide a thorough understanding of how the different factors can affect the user's acceptance of new information technology solutions (Muchran, 2019). The TAM has distinct advantages in terms of flexibility, broad applicability, and scalability, all of which make it widely used for assessing users' acceptance of software systems and technology. These advantages are essential in predicting users' acceptance of new technologies. The model has been tested extensively in the healthcare industry, and it has been shown to be useful in explaining the factors that affect people's decisions to adopt new technologies (Wang, 2025). A shortcoming of the Technology Acceptance Model (TAM) is that it does not account for affective or motivational factors, which can significantly influence behavior. This omission implies that aspects related to individual differences are important in determining the acceptance and use of technology and implied that user experiences could be different and thus warrant varied responses (Martín-García, 2022).

The Technology-Organization-Environment

The Technology-Organization-Environment (TOE) framework was developed in 1990 by Tornatzky et al. to provide a contextually rich perspective of the three important contextual constructs of technology, organization, and environment and how firms adopt innovations. The framework reinforces the notion that both internal and external factors affect the adoption decision processes of firms as they adopt new technologies. The technology context explains the importance of both existing and emerging technologies, while the organization context assesses the characteristics of the organization in terms of their size, scope, and available resources. The environmental context considers the external elements impacting the firm, such as the industry, competitive environment, and government regulatory policies. The TOE framework is useful to begin learning about adoption processes as it adequately delineates multiple factors that organizations wrestle with during the adoption of innovations (Salmizi, 2024). The TOE framework, considered a cornerstone model in understanding technology adoption, provides a holistic perspective on the complexity of the adoption process, and structures the study of the relationship between technology environmental organizational contexts in a systematic way and subsequently the categorization of factors relating to technology adoption is structured, allowing evaluation of the relationship between each of these factors (Kumar, 2024). The timeline for utilizing the TOE framework among Small and Medium-sized Enterprises (SMEs) is comparatively quite slow, relative to larger companies and firms, which is largely due to a number of significant challenges. One of the key contexts is that SMEs often have very limited financial and human resources that inhibits their ability to invest in new and/or emerging technologies (Salmizi, 2024). The TOE framework is being increasingly used in a variety of contexts and is still relevant in business management and action research. The TOE framework provides a structured view of the relationship between technology, organization and environment, respectively, and is a powerful framework that can benefit researchers and practitioners (Xu, 2025).

Digital Transformation Maturity Models

Digital transformation (DT) is the manner in which organizations adopt and employ digital technologies to create or improve products, services, and processes. Digital transformation entails the digital conversion of traditional business activities and processes, thus allowing the business to operate more efficiently and effectively (Ajoudanian, 2025). Digital maturity is the extent to which an organization has embraced digital technology into its operations, culture, and strategy more broadly. This readiness indicates the extent an organization is willing and able to utilize digital technology for better performance, even as we apply the experience of the organization's digital readiness into two realms: ability (soft/digital) and willingness (hard/access) (Wahdaniyah, 2025). The manufacturing space have seen a variety of Digital Maturity Models (DMMs) emerge around Industry 4.0 technologies with an emphasis on overcoming constraints both organizational and environmental in their frameworks (Aliy, 2025).

AI is crucial for the successful use of Digital Maturity Models (DMMs), because it assesses digital capabilities, identifies opportunities for improvement, and helps to better manage the digital transformation process. With the integration of AI into DMMs, organizations can systematically manage digital transformation initiatives to ensure that technology development aligns with strategic objectives, and ultimately, maximize business value (Fahrisky, 2025). Many organizations aspiring to enhance their digital maturity often take a phased approach to digital transformation so that they are increasingly embedding technology into their operations, workforce, and resources. To get there, a clear digital strategy is essential, which encompasses governance. A digital strategy should also entail the necessary infrastructure and organizational frameworks while addressing the human component, such as management and employee readiness for digital activities and the creation of skills and competencies. Strengthening these elements is important to achieve digital maturity (Alfadhli, 2025). Figure 3 shows the summary of Key Frameworks Guiding Cloud-Enabled Digital Transformation.

Figure 3. Key Theoretical Models Guiding Digital Transformation

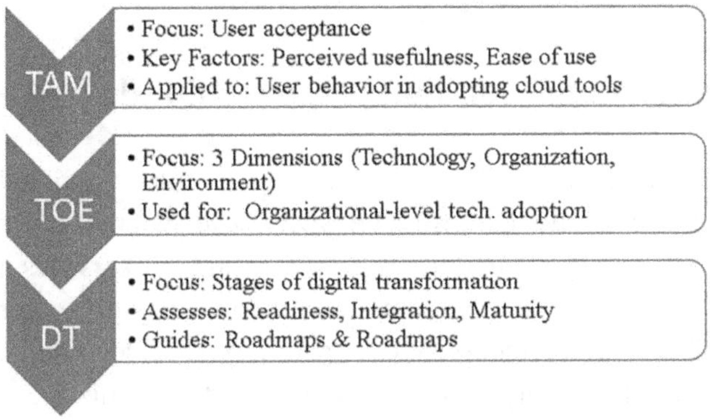

IV. CLOUD STRATEGIES FOR BUSINESS TRANSFORMATION

The formulation of strategy prioritizes the actions required in order to meet business objectives, aid in communication, assign responsibility, and facilitate continued growth. Given that cloud computing embodies transformational attributes, it forces firms to re-think strategies. Failures in adopting Cloud services without strategic elation has resulted in many organizations falling on their backsides (Khalil, 2019). The strategy of addressing cloud security challenges in digital transformation embraces proactive risk management, applying proper encryption controls, compliance frameworks, and coordinating ongoing monitoring and collaboration between stakeholders (Damaraju, 2024). The cloud transformation strategy focuses on using the public cloud to increase scalability, reduce costs, create innovation, and enhance agility and competitiveness in business (Frank, Schumacher, & Tamm, 2023). The strategy foregrounds lessons learned on reinforcing security measures to enhance efficiency of resource utilization by new technologies and adapt them to divergent user and business needs for sustainability and growth in the cloud computing paradigm evolution (Obi et al., 2024). The strategy for streamlining cloud transformation focuses on using project management methodologies to facilitate optimal planning, improve systems integration, enhance resource allocation, and effectively position modernization of infrastructure (Somanathan, 2023).

The strategy focuses on employing cloud, AI, and digital transformation to create an avenue for innovation, useful decision-making, utmost needs scalability, and harnessing competitive advantages (Devara, 2024). Otherwise, these strategies will embrace the latest trends of multi-cloud, edge computing, AI integration, and automation. However, stimulate innovation, scalability, and sustained growth (Kwaku, 2023), (Gunukula, 2024).

Public, Private, Multi-cloud and Hybrid Clouds

There are four main types of cloud computing: a multi-cloud, hybrid cloud, private cloud, and public cloud. Choosing between these different types of models and services is likewise a huge decision, as no two clouds or services are really alike. Learning about what they have in common and how they differ can help evaluate how their weaknesses can affect business operations (Merseedi & Zeebaree, 2024). Private cloud computing brings control, security, and customization combined with high security and compliance needs to an organization. Internal deployment or deployment through a third party can be costly and less scalable than public clouds. (Maniatis). A private cloud allocates computing resources, usually with internal management, to a single organization. This arrangement provides great control, security, and compliance, but involved substantial investments in infrastructure and specialized know-how (Laxminarayana Korada, 2024). The new motive to focus on private cloud (PC) solutions is becoming the forefront of modern trends in the cloud sector. Given the advantages of cost predictability, data privacy and regulatory compliance, along with improved security, there is an increasing demand for PC computing, particularly to enable new applications including artificial intelligence (B. Liu, Song, & Geng, 2024). Public clouds relate to cloud computing environments typically constructed by using IT infrastructure that users themselves do not own (Islam et al., 2023). When a service together with its required resources is put on an online platform available to users who subsequently compensate said service provider for it, it is regarded as a public cloud (Prangon & Wu, 2024).The computer resources and infrastructure of public clouds are owned and managed by an external service provider or cloud service provider. The model shares resources so upgrading or downgrading is as easy as a mouse click; no extra hardware or software is necessary. Additionally, public clouds are built using multi-tenant architecture, allowing them to serve multiple customers concurrently (Borra, 2024).

The hybrid cloud model combines the capabilities of a public cloud and a private cloud, allowing organizations to optimize their operations through the advantages offered by both (Islam et al., 2023). The most important is the flexibility that hybrid cloud architecture can provide. This is the model that allows an organization to optimize cloud expenses by taking advantage of different cloud resources, be they public or private, and selecting that which is most economical against the varied workloads and data requirements. With hybrid cloud infrastructures, unification and manners of working smoothly with data and applications span across public and private cloud facilities as the organizations really look forward to taking maximum advantage from both cloud setups (Gawande, 2024).

A multi-cloud strategy utilizes various providers or robust cloud services to deploy workloads in diverse infrastructures, thus minimizing vendor lock-in risks. Different advantages are brought by the adoption of multi-cloud, but its implementation demands the application of a complex security design to maintain information and data assets and records' confidentiality and availability. One of the great security challenges that introduce risk to multi-cloud environments is the overwhelming extension of the attack surface caused by decentrally managed, resource distribution across multiple platforms (Kanungo, 2023). A multi-cloud strategy adopts various cloud platforms in latest practice where migration across these platforms is a common phenomenon mainly owing to decentralized nature of cloud ecosystems (Seth, Nerella, Najana, & Tabbassum, 2024). Multi-cloud architectures utilize a variety of cloud services from different providers for the sake of improving flexibility, reliability, and cost-effectiveness. The strategy is to enable organizations to deal with vendor lock-ins, performance enhancement, and disaster recovery. However, this form of multicultural architecture is marred by challenges in securing interoperability between platforms, uniform policy control, and resource optimization in different environments (Kanungo & Sarangi, 2024). This article analyzes the differences between public, private, and hybrid clouds and their implications for security in small and medium-sized enterprises (SMEs) (Zakaria & Jizat, 2024). Public clouds have the very high scalability and cost advantage, but when it comes to sensitive information the factors of data privacy and control surface as concerns; private clouds exist as better security and control but with a price to pay in terms of associated costs and maintenance; hybrid clouds, the combination of both, provide SMEs with an overlap of security, flexibility, and cost advantages but present challenges in terms of merging and management. The study stresses SMEs to carefully assess their security needs when adopting hybrid cloud solutions.

The authors (George, George, & Baskar, 2023), discuss the growing significance of edge computing within public cloud, private cloud, and hybrid cloud environments. While public clouds are quite scalable, latency can affect performance; it would be mitigated by moving the processing closer to the source through edge computing. The private cloud provides more security and control for cloud services, while hybrid clouds take a combination of both models to provide a balance between cost, flexibility, and data security. Edge computing integrated into the cloud is expected to enhance real-time processing, reduce latency, and improve cloud performance in industries that require fast-paced, data-driven decision-making. The development becomes even more efficient, secure, and responsive in relation to cloud solutions. Figure 4 shows the types of clouds computing.

Figure 4. Types of Clouds Computing.

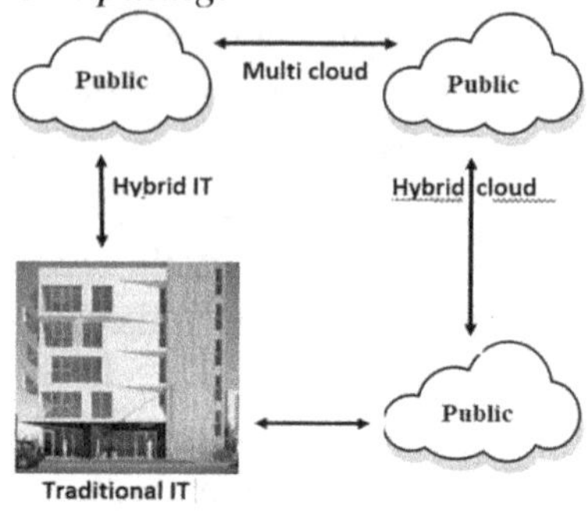

Competitive Edge and Innovation

In the modern age of corporate endeavor, the relentless pursuit of crafting competitive advantages, improving operational efficiency, and nurturing an ecosystem for workforce innovation is a prime focus for organizations. Cloud computing and AI automation have emerged as two of the principal catalysts of organizational success. Cloud computing is highly reliable, on-demand access to scalable resources and elastic service models: in truth, a radical redefinition of the management and deployment of IT infrastructure (Daniel & Paul, 2024). A dynamically changing business environment necessitates that organizations continue to innovate as a viable means of sustaining competitive advantage. Firms must concentrate not only on the technological innovations but also revise and refine their organizational and strategic arrangements so that they will respond to the market fluctuations and subsequently define the industry's next direction (Sun, 2024). Hence, the developments and maturation of cloud technologies into customized synergies for smooth and medium-sized enterprises (SMEs) imply that these organizations might enhance their competitiveness in a way that multiplies the odds of further growth and sustainability in the digital age (Khan & Rinaudo, 2025). This creates a virtuous cycle in which data are collected, stored, processed, and analyzed, delivering insights that facilitate the understanding of operations, foster innovation, and secure a competitive position (Al-kateeb & Abdullah, 2024).

The rising influence of cloud computing helps enhance and promote better organizational management practices, for which seamless integration becomes ever more paramount in ensuring security, scalability, and productivity. The hybrid and multi-cloud approaches have emerged as workable models for balancing performance, cost, and compliance. This makes it possible for organizations to optimize the workload placement efficiently while providing unique operational requirements. To derive the most value from adopting the cloud, firms must recognize the significance of robust security framework through cloud environments while also providing the best training to its workforces. This introduction will observe probable strategies for accompanying cloud into world-stopping methods, such as hybrid cloud deployment, multi-cloud security frameworks, and the training of employees, as shown in Table 2.

Table 2. Key Strategies for Effective Cloud Adoption and Integration

Aspect	Strategy	Benefits
Hybrid Cloud Deployment	Combining private and public clouds creates a safe, but scalable, environment for AI operations.	Ensure security, compliance, and scalability of business-critical analytics.
Hybrid and Multi-Cloud Models	Use hybrid and multiple cloud environments for flexibility and workload distributions.	Achieve a balance between performance, cost, and continued compliance while reducing dependence on particular vendors.
Hybrid Cloud Adoption	The hybrid cloud initiative supports sensitive workloads in the cloud environment with the public clouds meeting other workload needs.	Cost-effective alternative that still doesn't sacrifice data security or regulatory compliance.
Multi-Cloud Security Framework	Unified, simplified security policies, identity management, and encryption across cloud environments.	Offers constant protection and simplifies compliance amidst multi-cloud environments.
Cloud Training and Support	Offer training sessions for staff to learn about cloud tools and workflows..	Such actions will lead to greater buy-in for the changes, less resistance to that change, and greater productivity..

Optimizing Performance with Cloud Strategies

Research argues that the multi-cloud approach will enhance performance, reliability, and innovation by leveraging the most suitable services from a various provider and optimizing the costs (Tohanean & Toma, 2024). In fraud detection improvement processes, financial organizations increasingly utilized artificial intelligence (AI). With optimization, the companies will be able to automate the maximum number of workflows and employ cloud-based capabilities to provide real-time analytics. This greatly enhances operational effectiveness and substantially reduces infrastructure costs, as solutions are scalable with the organization's needs and sizes (Hakimi, Amiri, Jalalzai, Darmel, & Ezam, 2024). Researchers focus not only on enhancing the contemporary designs and paradigms of cloud architectures but also on the construction of an adaptable and scalable architecture. These architectures would address the modifying requirements of new applications. It appears that edge computing, fog networks, and vehicular clouds develop a shift towards decentralized and distributed systems that address the challenges of mobility, latency, and limited resources (Jajan & Zeebaree, 2024). Generally, in these investigations, model-based methodologies and simulation-assisted framework development would be required to support the enhanced functions of AI tools in optimizing cloud resources. In alignment with the goals of Industry 5.0, these advances are driven by the technology shift and construction of a human-centric operational context that induces in it much higher stakeholder involvement (Seo, Yoo, & Lee, 2024). The confluence of edge computing, cloud automation, and AI promises new possibilities in maintaining efficiency around the IT infrastructure (Banala, 2024).

V. CLOUD COMPUTING IN INDUSTRY-SPECIFIC DIGITAL TRANSFORMATION

Many sectors including healthcare and finance have strict regulations defining guidelines for storage, processing, and protection of data. Cloud service providers offer compliance certifications and established procedures for organizations to comply with the applicable regulatory requirements (Das & Mishra). The convergence of cloud computing and artificial intelligence is redefining industry dynamics and competitive advantage resulting in fundamental change in business operations, improvement, and competition. Being flexible and scalable, cloud computing provides all organizations with the tools necessary for the application of artificial intelligence in data analysis, process automation, and customer engagement (Mistry, Mavani, Goswami, & Patel, 2024). The cloud computing model is changing business operations, innovations, and strategies for competitive advantage across the worldwide market. Looking ahead, it is clear that cloud technologies will provide a foundation for facilitating digital transformation within sectors. By way of operational efficiencies and developing new business models, the cloud opens innumerable opportunities for organizations prepared to take advantage of it (Gunukula, 2024). Cloud Computing in Industries may include some of the following areas based on the administrative requirement, such as Healthcare, Education, Manufacturing, Energy and Utilities, Finance, Retail, Logistics and Transportation, and Entertainment and Media, as shown in figure 5 . The following is an overview of some of these:

Figure 5. Cloud Computing in Industry

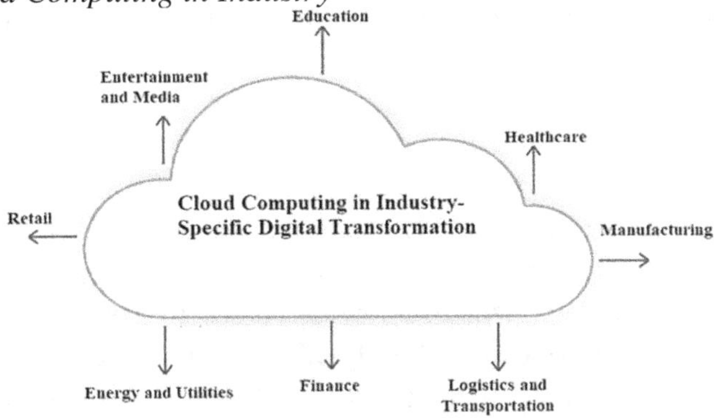

Education

Cloud computing has drastically altered the educational field, presenting many opportunities to improve teaching and learning methods, promote accessibility, and personalize education. This technology has completely defined traditional educational methods, allowing teachers and learners to employ very powerful tools and resources from anywhere at any time (Maharani & Nutela, 2024). Cloud solutions give users a flexible alternative to allocate resources that would normally be aligned to real use patterns, which is obviously seen by their cost efficiencies as far as processing and storage of data are concerned. Technology has therefore been democratized, allowing small and big business alike to compete on a common playing ground (Thavi, Jhaveri, Narwane, Gardas, & Jafari Navimipour, 2024). Advanced online learning platforms, which engage, educate and empower both learners and educators seamlessly, are generating significant excitement within the Edutech industry. Innovative virtual portals create connections between a wide variety of students, teachers, and experts so as to enhance learning (Begum & Sampurna, 2021). Different challenges need to be dealt with when e-learning is to be effectively implemented using cloud computing in educational systems. Major hindrances to a seamless transition toward a technology-based educational model consist of security issues, bandwidth constraints, and reluctance to embrace change (Sk & Dalavai, 2024). Digital Education and Online Education are two different concepts that are often confused. Online Education is actually part of Digital Education, which includes not just online learning but also the incorporation of information and communication technology (ICT) into the management of education, as well as e-learning projects (Paul & Jena, 2023). To move into such a space would inevitably involve educational institutions, including students and teachers, being equipped and informed to transition on an e-learning framework based on cloud techniques (Sk & Dalavai, 2024).

Healthcare

Cloud solutions are an efficient means of dynamically assigning resources according to the actual usage trend, and hence are being increasingly acknowledged for cost-effectiveness toward data processing and storage abilities. Technology in this way enables democratization allowing enterprises of all scales to compete under conditions of relative equity (Reddy, 2024). E-health cloud computing is an innovative evolution, capable of creating a paradigm shift in the healthcare sector. These technologies provide large-scale advantages such as fast processing, flexibility, scalability, speed of implementation, resource optimization, energy efficiency, and a cost-efficient framework with a major potential for affecting daily life (Chang, Lu, Pan, & Chen, 2021). More healthcare organizations today are adopting cloud computing, but the security measures relating to those platforms still require further development into how they align with existing frameworks that mitigate potential threats, vulnerabilities, and attacks in the sector (Alleyne, 2023). The advancement of technology, particularly in fields such as cloud computing, artificial intelligence, and the usage of mobile devices, has overall improved Electronic Health Records (EHR) systems in integration and usability. The cloud EHR service supports more scalability, flexibility, and accessibility, allowing caregivers to access patient information at any time and from any location (Kondru, 2015). Cloud-based telemedicine solutions allow for central and easy access to the vast amount of data processed via IoT devices. These platforms also improve flexibility, bringing savings by removing the need for complex onsite-intensive IT infrastructure (M. S. Kumar & Ganesh, 2024). The hybrid cloud solutions are critical to transformative improvements in patient care, operational efficiencies, and securing data in the healthcare sector. Such hybrid cloud environments afford extensive healthcare data processing using AI algorithms that would promote strategies in personalized medicine and build population health management (Gajiwala, 2024).

Manufacturing

Industry 4.0 is the most recent of these revolutions, and it exemplifies a rapid pace of technological development that is to be incorporated into all aspects of the smart manufacturing systems. This transformation continues through the entire product lifecycle, from concept and design to initial development, cloud computing, sales, and service provisioning (Gharibvand et al., 2024). Across industries, cloud adoption has demonstrated great influence. In manufacturing, this is manifested in the change of production efficiencies through initiatives in connected factories that have resulted in a 31% improvement in overall equipment effectiveness (Oruganti, 2024). Above all, green cloud computing involves principles and methodologies of effective design, development, usage, and disposal of this computing system and other components, including but not limited to PCs, servers with peripherals, displays, printers, storage devices, and networking systems, to minimize or eliminate environmental effects (Bajdor, 2024). Over the last few years, there has been significant change in the basic framework of enterprise IT architecture owing to cloud computing. Organizations of all sizes are making increasing use of Software as a Service (SaaS) solutions to limit their dependence upon internal IT resources and get enterprise systems running more quickly. In this case, the proposed initial approach to implement cloud computing can involve moving one or more enterprise systems to the cloud. Transitioning enterprise systems to cloud-based systems is thus a critical step in cloud computing adoption. There is a heavy emphasis on enabling global remote access through Customer Relationship Management (CRM), providing collaborative product design using Product Lifecycle Management (PLM), integrating advanced planning systems into the supply chain, facilitating effective transaction management with Enterprise Resource Planning (ERP), and improving manufacturing efficiencies with Manufacturing Execution Systems (MES) (Vitliemov, 2018).

Logistics and Transportation

The development of a secure intellectual transport ecosystem through digitalization, in particular cloud solutions, is one of the major boosters for growth in the transportation and logistic sector, bearing a significant influence on the railroad industry. Prospects for cloud solutions in the transport industry are bright. This will enable seamless and fast connectivity among various modes of transport and, in addition, will create an interface between the enterprises and customers (Drozdova & Benin, 2024).

The study results showed remarkable opportunities for logistics firms to exploit cloud computing beyond the concept of supply chain management and into accounting practices. An inquiry into the deployment of various popular cloud platforms has uncovered considerable potential for enhancing the accounting functions of logistics firms (Alnaimat, Kharit, Mykhailenko, Palchyk, & Purhani, 2024). The research shows that the use of cloud computing in optimizing vehicle routing for cold chain logistics is exceptionally successful as it brings considerable theoretical contributions and practical benefits, including efficiency, improved cost, and better decision-making in logistics management (Guo, 2024). The Cloud Integrated Intelligent Cargo Management System signifies the evolution in the ever-changing domain of international trade, giving rise to new methods of operation in the transport and supervisory processes of goods. Employing state-of-the-art cloud computing technology intertwined with advanced artificial intelligence algorithms, views this innovative system as an integrate themes, amalgamating varied solutions at a global level that address various competing problems currently faced by the logistics sector (Mahesh, Shriya, Rasagnya, & Nikhitha, 2024). The expansion of urban areas and climate-related problems bring to the fore the possibilities of adopting artificial intelligence and cloud technology to transform transport systems. Cloud computing has become an elemental component of contemporary mobility solutions; provides the much-needed computational resources and storage space for managing large transportation data. The framework permits on-the-fly data analysis, seamless integration of different modes of transportation, and spoilage of resources through transportation networks (Kovvuri, 2024). The cloud logistics further enhance data confidentiality on shared information systematically manage information systems across many logistics companies. The system comprises data sharing between different functional definitions through autonomous resource sharing, leading to customers receiving standardized information via business services (Alruwaili, Armghan, Alshudukhi, Flah, & Perg, 2024).

Finance

Technological transformation is now being witnessed by the financial services industry with eminence and velocity. The transfer into the Cloud was one of the clearest drivers to bring tremendous advantages to the financial industry, such as scalable infrastructure allowing for changing workloads, varied deployment methods offering improved operational flexibility, and a pay-as-you-go approach, with a reduction of initial hardware and software expenditures. As such, innovations are capable of helping a financial organization streamline operations, improve service delivery, and carry on interactive relationships with customers (Nutalapati, 2024). AI-enabled cloud solutions are supporting a wide range of activities, from predictive analytics to the automation of repetitive tasks to a more informed decision-making process. This paradigm shift is restructuring the industries extending from finance to retail by providing resources to elevate customer experience and operational efficiency (Das & Mishra).

The simultaneous use of cloud-native architectures and the emergence of revolutionary concepts like data mesh are transforming the paradigm of managing, processing, and utilization of financial data (Sekar, 2024).

Cloud computing allows financial services sectors to leverage big data analytics and AI in a more effective and timely manner to enhance their decision-making processes and gain a better understanding of client behavior (Nutalapati, 2024).

VI. CHALLENGES AND RISKS IN CLOUD ADOPTION

Though cloud technology has evolved rapidly, the application has been impeded by a lack of proper infrastructure, limited internet access, and unreliable power supply (Nyamwesa, 2024). Existing literature points out various challenges that SMEs go through while making resource allocation decisions (Mohammad & Abbas, 2024). Cloud computing offers many benefits to the small and medium enterprises, but the risks involved can be ascertained and classified into six main categories by SMEs themselves (Ognjanović, Šendelj, Daković-Tadić, & Kožuh, 2024). In spite of the numerous advantages associated with cloud computing (CC), organizations are still apprehensive because of the potential risks and implications of migrating mission-critical applications to the cloud. The decentralized characteristics of CC create challenges in areas including security and privacy issues, compliance with national and international legislation, and the business environment that exists external to the organization shown in Figure 6.

Figure 6. Challenges and Risks of Cloud Computing

All Technical, Operational, and Cultural Issues

Nowadays, gigantic amounts of data are being processed and stored with the help of cloud services. These services show many advantages such as accessibility, flexibility, and cost efficiency. However, these advantages also accompany several challenges, such as increasing security risks, the potential for vulnerabilities, and data privacy concerns (Mykhaylova, 2024). Data security and privacy become critical concerns due to the collective nature of the cloud infrastructure. Some of the challenges in cloud implementation relate to data breach, illegal access, and lack of ability to comply with established laws and regulations (Zarbega). Effective cost management and operational optimization are critical for organizations moving to or functioning in the cloud, adding to the ROI and reducing unnecessary costs (Johnson, 2024). Moreover, close knowledge regarding resource utilization with a good balance and tuning of cost, performance, and availability is a prerequisite for cloud cost management (Khan, 2024). There are many challenges to automating data migrations in the cloud. But the benefits of automating the process-seeing through accuracy, reducing costs, and enabling online continuance of migrations without disrupting business-are convincing (Jude, 2025). A significant part of the cloud migration process for academic institutions is the data migration process, which consists of transferring large amounts of data across a wide range of systems (Awasthi, 2024).

Cloud computing boasts several advantages, but along with that are challenges and considerations about data security, regulatory compliance, vendor lock-in, and the integration of the cloud with current IT systems (Mohammad, 2024). Cloud computing provides automatic upgrades and maintenance for software in terms of using the latest features, security enhancements, and performance upgrades. There is no need for direct assistance from IT staff. Automation lowers the chances of vulnerabilities and concurrently improves the reliability and security of the software systems while at the same time reducing downtime and user disruption (Segun-Falade, 2024). There lay impediments in recognizing the criteria and strategies for technology adoption, which subsequently foster good decision-making regarding cloud computing adoption for SMEs. Other challenges are ensuring adequate resource allocation, the expertise required, and proper management of costs (Abu-daqqa, 2024). Cloud platforms offer a very high variety of APIs and tools, thus ensuring seamless integration with various IoT devices and protocols. On the other hand, traditional IoT systems quite often experience limitations in terms of compatibility with different devices and data sources (Al-kateeb, 2024). Incorporating cloud services into contemporary mobile and desktop operating systems can cause compatibility and interoperability challenges. Yet, the resolution of a wide range of technical concerns- such as differences in operating system environments, hardware setups, and software dependencies- is essential to ensure that cloud-based software can operate seamlessly on a variety of different platforms (Segun-Falade, 2024).

In cloud computing, effective governance is a key component to manage intricacies of cloud ecosystems, preserve data integrity, and provide assurance on compliance with regulatory requirements. Cloud governance establishes a formal system of rules which organizations can implement to organize their cloud assets, clarify the roles and responsibilities of people involved, and set up appropriate oversight systems (Babalola, 2024). Developing states have a hell of a lot to battle with e-governance: cultural barriers to change, lack of planning for smooth operational provision of e-government services across different levels, less budget allocation, and inadequate Information and Communication Technology (ICT) infrastructure. These challenges must be surmounted before these countries can move forward from acting under mechanical administrative systems rather than merely improving on the stickonin-type functions of bureaucratic organizations (Hossen, 2025). Formulating sound construction for implementing responsible AI practices would include streamlining algorithms and cloud infrastructure to enhance dependable electric consumption and investigating sustainable computing methods to diminish their impacts on the environment. Ethical considerations and promotion of responsible AI practices are appropriate for the successful integration of AI and LLMs into cloud computing environments (Srinivasan, 2025). From the tabulated challenges as shown in Table 3, it is evident that cloud computing adoption for SMEs is multi-faceted. Challenges stem from economic, legal, technical, operational, and cultural fields, thus making a case for a broader view to tackle such issues. SMEs should evaluate their financial resources, regulatory compliance, technical infrastructure, and staff competence while developing an organizational culture that is conducive to cloud adoption. Recognizing such risks and putting the required mitigations proactively will allow organizations to gain the benefits of cloud computing while minimizing their disadvantages.

Table 3. Key Challenges of Cloud Computing Adoption for SMEs

Challenges	Description	Examples	Solutions
Economic and financial assets	Concerns related to financial and economic risk factors.	Profitability, expense minimization, economic advantages, tax benefits, financial strategy, challenges in securing credit, and elevated recruitment costs for specialists.	Enhanced awareness about the economic benefits offered by cloud computing can overcome this challenge
Legal liabilities	Legal and regulatory compliance challenges.	Legal jurisdiction, regulatory challenges, data protection, absence of uniform standards, system dependability, and the confidentiality of corporate information are critical considerations.	Clarifying and communicating all legal and regulatory aspects related to cloud computing services can greatly help address such concerns
Skills and Financial Outlay	Staff competency and expenditure-related risks.	Usability evaluation, insufficiently certified personnel, employee resistance, elevated turnover rates, and inadequate staff expertise and skills in cloud computing are significant challenges.	Awareness and capability of the SMEs could not only bolster their competence in cloud solutions, it could also end up driving their utilization of it

continued on following page

Table 3. Continued

Challenges	Description	Examples	Solutions
Technological Environment	Technical limitations and infrastructure challenges.	Internet connectivity challenges, compatibility issues, concerns regarding data security and privacy, dependence on online access, and inadequate IT infrastructure.	Embedding the improved technological environment could encompass broadening cloud adoption
Execution and Functionality	Implementation and customization issues of cloud computing solutions.	Effective collaboration with stakeholders, issues related to ownership, and overarching challenges in execution.	Demos of what cloud solutions can do can address these issues.
Societal Challenges	Organizational culture and attitudes towards cloud computing challenges.	The absence of trust, disinterest in cloud computing, varying views on the value of governance, and insufficient managerial enthusiasm for enhancing IT systems are significant barriers..	Building digital literacy and raising trust in cloud services must be promoted to tackle such social challenges.

VII. REGULATORY COMPLIANCE IN DIGITAL TRANSFORMATION

Organizations can reduce mistakes, improve traceability and remain compliant with regulatory specifications such as Good Manufacturing Practices by digitizing processes, automating workflows and leveraging data-based insights (Ullagaddi, 2024). Organizations have to prioritize compliance with industry standards and legal regulations as they relate to the activities they are conducting in their business. They also must be aware that the requirements are unique to their industry and that there are regulatory obligations. Compliance is an important component of operational integrity and can mitigate legal risks (Jayalath, 2022). Hence, consistency in the act of enacting legislation for digital transformations is very important across countries. Instruments like EU Directive 2000/31/EC which creates harmonizing legislation for electronic commerce in the EU and the General Data Protection Regulation (GDPR) which provides protection for individual personal data and movement of that data, perform an essential role. These instruments, when put into place should help follow the process of digital transformation and with clear standards in mind the innovators should not be worked against by the imposed regulations (Reier Forradellas, 2021). Data Governance relates to the establishment of policies, standards, and frameworks for the safeguarding of data integrity, security, and legal compliance. With artificial intelligence, data governance is particularly significant because the management of sensitive data must be performed to meet legal and ethical expectations and maintain public trust. Legal restrictions like GDPR and the California Consumer Privacy Act (CCPA) provide guidelines related to data collection, use, and security. Complying with these regulations is crucial to managing the risks related to data security breaches, unauthorized access (Onoja, 2021). In the context of digital transformation, regulatory compliance includes activities related to laws, regulations, guidelines, and specifications that reference digital technologies, managing data, and executing business operations. Each industry and region has its own regulatory requirements. Here are the categories of regulatory compliance related to digital transformation:

General Data Protection Regulation

The General Data Protection Regulation (GDPR) marks a major step forward in data protection legislation in order to strengthen and unify the privacy law of individuals across the European nation. The GDPR has 99 articles and aims to promote trust among European citizens that their information is being protected (when stored and utilized by companies). The GDPR application is meant to transcend EU borders and affect several other countries, including businesses in the United States, thus changing how contact centers interact with EU customers (Data, 2018). Under the extraterritorial provisions of the GDPR, organizations outside the EU that process the personal data of EU citizens must comply with its rules. This has led to considerable challenges for multinational organizations as they seek efficiencies in data governance as they relate to different legal requirements and also deal with potential conflicts with local laws. The GDPR has also impacted the digital economy, especially in terms of the EU's role in online advertising and data-driven business models, the explicit consent and the right to object to data processing for direct marketing applications have necessitated companies rethinking how they collect and leverage personal data for targeted advertising campaigns (Ullagaddi, 2024). The General Data Protection Regulation (GDPR) requires organizations to have strong security measures in place, such as encryption and anonymization, to protect sensitive data. The GDPR also respects the individual's right to access, correct, and delete their data. The regulation obliges organizations to grant requests for accessing the information they hold about an individual and offer assurance for deletion when the individual asks (Onoja, 2021,Onoja, 2021).

California Consumer Privacy Act

California passed the California Consumer Privacy Act (CCPA) in 2018. This law is a vital piece of legislation. The act will help consumers obtain control over their privacy, leading to better digital privacy. This act is important in regulating how technology companies in America collect and use data, and is an important change for consumer privacy rights (Mulgund, 2021). The legislation is an important step towards protecting personal information, but organizations will have challenges in achieving compliance with its provisions. Ultimately, the responsibility to seek and maintain CCPA compliance rests with the organization. Lawmakers made compliance easier for organizations, but also provided significant incentives to comply with the law, including financial penalties and allowing consumers to bring class-action lawsuits (Garlie, 2020). Although the California Consumer Privacy Act (CCPA) is similar to the General Data Protection Regulation (GDPR) in the requirement for businesses to notify consumers what data is collected, how it is used, and whether the data is shared with third parties, there is a vital distinction between the two regulations. Like GDPR, CCPA provides consumers with the right to opt out of sharing their data. It also provides consumers the ability to request the deletion of their personal information; however, the main difference is that GDPR requires businesses to obtain express consent from consumers, while the CCPA allows the business to collect the data automatically, and the consumers have the option of opting out (Onoja, 2021).

Penalties are an essential tool for assessing a corporation's legal power. For example, under the General Data Protection Regulation (GDPR), fines are up to up to 20 million euros or 4% of previous fiscal year's global turnover (whichever is the greater). The California Consumer Privacy Act (CCPA) create holes in security by allowing any consumer to sue for any breach of protocol (at least potentially) (Lim, 2025).

Personal Data Protection Act

Personal data protection in Malaysia is managed by the Personal Data Protection Act (PDPA) No. 709 of 2010. The law requires data users to process personal data using several principles. First is the general principle, which sets out general proper principles for processing personal data. Following that is the notice and choice principle which requires that an individual is aware that their personal data is being used. The disclosure principle specifies the circumstances under which personal data can be disclosed. The security principles relates to ensuring the security of personal data against unauthorised access. The retention principle sets out the length of time one can keep personal data. The data integrity principle states that personal data must be correct and reliable. Finally, the access principle states that a person must have access to their own personal data (Sudarwanto, 2022). The Personal Data Protection Act (PDPA) is introduced in order to demonstrate the Malaysia's competitive advantage in delivering the best communications and multimedia with a clear focus on e-transactions and investment. It seek to provide an environment for testing digital communications technologies while at the same time establishing

Malaysia's position as a critical influence in developing frameworks of global best practice in personal data protection (Sureani, 2021). Infringements of the Personal Data Protection Act (PDPA) can lead to criminal penalties, including fines, imprisonment or both. If a corporation is non-compliant then the directors, managers, or other officials may be held jointly and severally liable but can claim due diligence defence against its liability (Sudarwanto, 2022).

Health Insurance Portability and Accountability Act

Compliance with the Health Insurance Portability and Accountability Act (HIPAA) has always been a crucial component of health management, but it's importance has increased given new technology. This trend is especially relevant for those in healthcare management and leadership positions. Leadership is critical to making sure that healthcare clinics run smoothly and properly. This has important implications for adhering to HIPAA laws today - given the digital age (Wilson, 2018). The Health Insurance Portability and Accountability Act (HIPAA), was signed into law by Congress for two main purposes, to change the insurance market and improve administrative tools in healthcare. Since being signed into law, HIPAA has grown to address pressing issues in healthcare, including administrative simplifications, security, privacy, and safeguarding that confidentiality for the patient (Banks, 2006). The Privacy and Security Rules work together to protect the privacy and security of peoples' personal health record (PHR) information. The Privacy Rule focuses on appropriate uses and disclosures of PHRs, while the Security Rule builds the confidentiality, integrity and availability of electronic protected health information, through the implementation of technical and administrative safeguards (Subramanian, 2024).

VIII. EMERGING TRENDS AND THE FUTURE OF CLOUD COMPUTING

The future of the cloud is ripe for advancements precipitated by emerging technologies and the ever-changing demands of business as well as demands for efficiency, security, and scaling up. Below are some of the more defining trends influencing the future of cloud computing as shown in Figure 7.

Figure 7. The Future of Cloud Computing

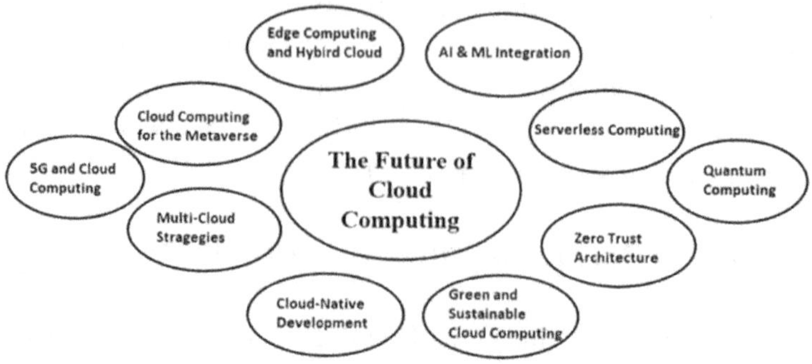

Edge Computing and Hybrid Cloud

Edge Computing is a networking paradigm linking into the proximity such that computing resources can be closer to the source of data to facilitate faster processing with minimum latency and efficient bandwidth utilization. In essence, this is "Distributed Computing," which sums up well the idea of pushing computing and data storage right near the end user (Raghav, 2025). The rapid development of IoT and Edge Computing technologies represents another challenge that needs strong collaboration among policy makers, end-users, and connoisseurs within these fields to realize efficient human-centric IoT applications (Vermesan, 2023). Concurrently, this might be defined as a new paradigm wherein processing resources are placed at the very edge of the Internet, being close to mobile devices, sensors, end users, and future advances ushered in by the IoT (Shi, 2019). As industries are increasingly adopting IoT and edge computing, a transition from cloud to edge processing has necessitated the development of new distributed architectures and complete end-to-end IoT security solutions. The combination of connectivity, IoT, edge computing, artificial intelligence, and distributed ledger technologies will be pivotal in the evolution of next-generation Internet applications and innovations (Vermesan, 2023). The future of hybrid cloud seems to be developing and harnessing the innovation, as led by the forces of artificial intelligence, machine learning, and edge computing, giving organizations plenty of chances to do their best and remain in front. The future of cloud is a cloud in a smart and fast and secure way, which will integrate the latest technologies like AI, edge computing, and quantum computing. All stakeholders, whether organizations or individuals, will find better flexibility, lower costs, and better performance, allowing cloud computing to become the backbone of digital transformation (Asimiyu, 2020).

Integration of AI and Machine Learning

The application of machine learning methods within cloud-integrated computing frameworks is becoming common in rising plug-ins that cater to various quality of service (QoS) standards. To meet the challenges of dynamic scheduling in cloud-based cyber-physical production systems, soft computing techniques such as artificial neural networks (ANN) have been employed to improve multiple QoS metrics (Soni, 2022). The incorporation of AI and machine learning into cloud infrastructures is set to foster unprecedented opportunities for innovation and efficiency, advancing the process of digital transformation (Sapkal, 2024). Based on recent advances in technology, the application of ML techniques in conjunction with integrated cloud computing frameworks will offer researchers new avenues for future developments (Sapkal, 2024). The main sources stress that ERP systems can hardly be compared by any measures to MRP systems of the past. The integration of the ML methodologies with the cloud computing framework opens up for the researchers new avenues for promoting work to address the evolving demands of technological progression (Yathiraju, 2022). Research on autonomic models for managing computer resources, which includes such components as web servers and entire systems as with the data centers, has been extensive. However, integrating artificial intelligence and machine learning into their operations in order to scale autonomy and performance is still very challenging in the field (Gill, 2022).

Serverless Computing

The rise of Serverless computing bellies its very peculiar features. This model will allow software developers to focus more on function-level application logic without worrying about the complexities behind the scenes that could potentially cause errors (Wen, 2023). Currently, serverless computing platforms are not designed to run in a hybrid environment. The functionality of serverless computing generally remains limited to those applications hosted on a single provider's infrastructure. However, we envision a hybrid serverless computing model that extends serverless principles to applications run across multiple cloud services and devices (Castro, 2023). This research adds new insight to the present literature, as this is the first study to substantiate the ways in which organizations project the cost implications associated with serverless computing. Besides this aspect, the study aims to assess the suitability of different workloads for this computing model. Also, the paper mentions the factors that lead to higher serverless application costs and examines various strategies for their optimization. Overall, these dimensions of serverless computing have not been addressed in the existing literature (Hamza, 2023). Serverless computing fundamentally mitigates the necessity of centralized server control and management of the related infrastructure components. With this paradigm shift, growth is anticipated to accelerate, as software engineers are relieved of the heavy burden of server management. At the same time, hosting providers would also be able to manage infrastructure and automate provisioning efficiently within this framework (Gill, 2024).

Quantum Computing in the Cloud

Quantum computing is capable of managing huge datasets, dealing with a coupled set of problems in parallel, and processing calculations faster than conventional computing systems. Renowned global companies such as IBM and Google are exploiting quantum computing to reduce the need for human resources. The ripple effect is felt in encryption, medicine, and materials science (Gill, 2024). Modern developments in quantum computing are essential for guiding investments, research and development programs, along with technological innovations that could significantly impact the industrial, economic, and societal aspects of the contemporary knowledge and digital economies (Coccia, 2024). Although at a very early stage, quantum computing could change the stage for solving problems for many fields, including cryptography, material science, and complex-system simulation. Quantum computation provides significant advantages, perhaps on an exponential scale, relative to classical computers, for areas involving numerous fields in research and industry (Eshmurodov, 2024).

Cloud Computing for the Metaverse

The term “metaverse” is formed of two components, namely meta and verse, meaning universe. The Metaverse refers to an abstract and theoretically infinite space, and virtually three-dimensional redirects people's fusion with physical space-some important sectors of active participation are social communication, office networking, lessons, e-commerce, and gaming (Baidya, 2024). One definition of the Metaverse, offered to us by McKinsey, describes a type of developing virtual world that combines Virtual Reality with Augmented Reality and other advanced Internet and computing technologies. They both give people the opportunity for immersive, interactive, and authentic personal and work experiences in an online framework (Szymanski, 2023). While the Metaverse looks to provide an immersive and engaging platform for co-creating a purpose for people, it is about converting the physical real world into a virtual interactive place with the help of sensing and communication augmentation technologies (Wang, 2023). While Metaverse keeps developing, access control is another factor to be taken into consideration; access control is said to be the very mechanism to govern the entrance, permissions, and activities of users within some kind of arrangement. This mechanism is relevant in securing user interactions as well as security, privacy, and data integrity within Metaverse (Upadhyay, 2024).

IX. CASE STUDIES AND REAL-WORLD APPLICATIONS

Firms in media and entertainment such as Netflix typically leverage cross-regional cloud services at the same time. In other cases, some clients might select sets of regional databases for data recovery and disaster recovery (Mustafa, 2023). Netflix, a major global player in streaming, is a good example of successful cloud computing adoption. The transition to a cloud infrastructure was motivated by the need to accommodate millions of users, with their large volumes of data, while providing them with seamless streaming services together with high availability and scalability (Segun-Falade, 2024). Compared to the 2008 crisis, Netflix now runs with hundreds of microservices providing sufficient availability, scalability, and speed to cater to its expanding user base. Many other organizations, including Amazon, Gilt, LinkedIn, and SoundCloud, adopted the microservice architecture to enhance service development and scalability. These microservices are reusable and interoperable, standardized by interfaces like Remote Procedure Calls (RPC) which are best represented by technologies such as Google's Stubby and gRPC, as well as Facebook and Apache's Thrift (Sriraman, 2021). Dropbox is a notable instance of leading providers of cloud file storage and collaboration services. Originally, Dropbox worked as a standard on-premises solution but could not scale its server infrastructure to match increasing user demands(Segun-Falade, 2024). presents all its cloud services. It features a comprehensive and fast-growing range of offerings that form the backbone of cloud computing (Copeland, 2015). Founded in 2010, Azure has altered the landscape of cloud computing, presenting a high-speed, secure environment for rapid innovations and developments. Azure data centers comprise a globally distributed framework designed to support the Microsoft Cloud spanning across 60 plus regions and 300 centers(Borra, 2024). Salesforce it rather considered the leading integrated platform for CRM in B2B, B2C, B2E, and enterprise applications. The organization is focused more on upgrading current customer relationships by uplifting cross-sell, upsell, and usage of other services among small and large enterprises (Kumar, 2024). Cloud platforms' Sales Team Automation tools (SFA) such as Salesforce and Microsoft Dynamics allow sales teams access to customer information, sales data analysis, and collaboration features anywhere they can access the internet (Koganti, 2024). Streaming platforms online such as Netflix, HBO, Spotify, and YouTube use cloud computing for dynamic video quality adjustment-all in the aim of providing optimal entertainment on the user audience by adapting to the prevailing internet speeds or bandwidths (Kumar, 2024).

REFERENCES

Adama, H. E., & Okeke, C. D. (2024). Digital transformation as a catalyst for business model innovation: A critical review of impact and implementation strategies. *Magna Scientia Advanced Research and Reviews*, *10*(02), 256–264. DOI: 10.30574/msarr.2024.10.2.0066

Al-kateeb, Z. N., & Abdullah, D. B. (2024). Unlocking the Potential: Synergizing IoT, Cloud Computing, and Big Data for a Bright Future. *Iraqi Journal for Computer Science and Mathematics*, *5*(3), 25. DOI: 10.52866/ijcsm.2024.05.03.001

Al-Ruithe, M., Benkhelifa, E., & Hameed, K. (2018). Key issues for embracing the cloud computing to adopt a digital transformation: A study of saudi public sector. *Procedia Computer Science*, *130*, 1037–1043. DOI: 10.1016/j.procs.2018.04.145

Alleyne, C. (2023). *Competencies of Hospital Chief Information Officers in Supporting Digital Transformation: An Exploratory study of the US Healthcare Industry.* Purdue University Graduate School, Alnaimat, M. A., Kharit, O., Mykhailenko, I., Palchyk, I., & Purhani, S. (2024). Implementation of cloud computing in the digital accounting system of logistics companies. *Acta Logistica (AL)*, *11*(1).

Alruwaili, O., Armghan, A., Alshudukhi, K. S., Flah, A., & Perg, I. (2024). Cloud Computing Based Intelligent Video Surveillance Framework for Logistics Security. *IEEE Access : Practical Innovations, Open Solutions*, *12*, 150604–150622. DOI: 10.1109/ACCESS.2024.3471688

Aslam, F. (2023). The benefits and challenges of customization within saas cloud solutions. *American Journal of Data. Information and Knowledge Management*, *4*(1), 14–22.

Bajdor, P. (2024). Current perspectives on sustainability in cloud computing: A comprehensive review. *Polish Journal of Management Studies*, *29*(1), 43–62. DOI: 10.17512/pjms.2024.29.1.03

Banala, S. (2024). The Future of IT Operations: Harnessing Cloud Automation for Enhanced Efficiency and The Role of Generative AI Operational Excellence. *International Journal of Machine Learning and Artificial Intelligence*, *5*(5), 1–15.

Basa, R. (2024). DEMYSTIFYING CLOUD COMPUTING AND VIRTUALIZATION: A TECHNICAL OVERVIEW. [IJRCAIT]. *INTERNATIONAL JOURNAL OF RESEARCH IN COMPUTER APPLICATIONS AND INFORMATION TECHNOLOGY*, *7*(2), 125–135.

Begum, S., & Sampurna, P. (2021). A Study on growth in Technology and Innovation across the globe in the Field of Education and Business. *International Research Journal on Advanced Science Hub*, *3*(Special Issue 6S, 6S), 148–156. DOI: 10.47392/irjash.2021.181

Borra, P. (2024). An Overview of Cloud Computing and Leading Cloud Service Providers. [IJCET]. *INTERNATIONAL JOURNAL OF COMPUTER ENGINEERING AND TECHNOLOGY*, *15*(3), 122–133.

Chang, S.-C., Lu, M.-T., Pan, T.-H., & Chen, C.-S. (2021). Evaluating the E-health cloud computing systems adoption in Taiwan's healthcare industry. *Life (Chicago, Ill.)*, *11*(4), 310. DOI: 10.3390/life11040310 PMID: 33918246

Damaraju, A. (2024). Cloud Security Challenges and Solutions in the Era of Digital Transformation. *International Journal of Advanced Engineering Technologies and Innovations*, *1*(3), 387–413.

Daniel, M., & Paul, S. (2024). Harnessing the Power of Cloud Computing and AI Automation for Strategic Management. *International Journal of Advanced Engineering Technologies and Innovations*, *1*(1), 594–604.

Das, M. S., & Mishra, M. A. Cloud Computing: Trends, Technologies, security, and Applications. *EDITORIAL ADVISOR*, 22.

Devara, J. S. M. (2024). CLOUD, AI, AND DIGITAL TRANSFORMATION: A WINNING COMBINATION. [IJCET]. *INTERNATIONAL JOURNAL OF COMPUTER ENGINEERING AND TECHNOLOGY*, *15*(5), 1020–1032.

Drozdova, M., & Benin, A. (2024). *Cloud solutions as a trend of safe intelligent transport ecosystem development.* Paper presented at the E3S Web of Conferences. DOI: 10.1051/e3sconf/202454908001

Fatima, E., Sumra, I. A., & Naveed, R. (2024). A Comprehensive Survey on Security Threats and Challenges in Cloud Computing Models (SaaS, PaaS and IaaS). *Journal of Computing & Biomedical Informatics*, *7*(01), 537–544.

Ferreira, R. d. S. A. (2024). Enhancing Supply Chain Visibility through a Platform as a Service (PaaS) for Collaborative Information Sharing.

Frank, R., Schumacher, G., & Tamm, A. (2023). Cloud Transformation–How the Public Cloud Is Changing Businesses. In *Cloud Transformation: The Public Cloud Is Changing Businesses* (pp. 247-263): Springer. DOI: 10.1007/978-3-658-38823-2_9

Gajiwala, C. (2024). HYBRID CLOUD ADOPTION: A PARADIGM SHIFT IN MODERN INFORMATION TECHNOLOGY MANAGEMENT. [IJRCAIT]. *INTERNATIONAL JOURNAL OF RESEARCH IN COMPUTER APPLICATIONS AND INFORMATION TECHNOLOGY*, *7*(2), 290–303.

Gawande, S. (2024). Hybrid Cloud Architectures: Balancing the Benefits of Public and Private Clouds. *Available at* SSRN *4991717*. Gawande, S., & Gorde, S. ORCHESTRATING THE CLOUD MULTIVERSE: STRATEGIES FOR SEAMLESS INTEGRATION AND UNIFIED MANAGEMENT. In. DOI: 10.2139/ssrn.4991717

George, A. S., & Baskar, T. (2024). Driving Business Transformation Through Technology Innovation: Emerging Priorities for IT Leaders. *Partners Universal Innovative Research Publication, 2*(4), 01-14.

George, A. S., George, A. H., & Baskar, T. (2023). Edge Computing and the Future of Cloud Computing: A Survey of Industry Perspectives and Predictions. *Partners Universal International Research Journal*, *2*(2), 19–44.

Gharibvand, V., Kolamroudi, M. K., Zeeshan, Q., Çınar, Z. M., Sahmani, S., Asmael, M., & Safaei, B. (2024). Cloud based manufacturing: A review of recent developments in architectures, technologies, infrastructures, platforms and associated challenges. *International Journal of Advanced Manufacturing Technology*, *131*(1), 93–123. DOI: 10.1007/s00170-024-12989-y

Gunukula, S. (2024). The Future of Cloud Computing: Key Trends and Predictions for the Next Decade. [IJRCAIT]. *INTERNATIONAL JOURNAL OF RESEARCH IN COMPUTER APPLICATIONS AND INFORMATION TECHNOLOGY*, *7*(2), 528–538.

Guo, J. (2024). Algorithm of cold chain logistics distribution vehicle scheduling based on cloud computing. *Intelligent Decision Technologies*, •••, 18724981241300907.

Hakimi, M., Amiri, G. A., Jalalzai, S., Darmel, F. A., & Ezam, Z. (2024). Exploring the Integration of AI and Cloud Computing: Navigating Opportunities and Overcoming Challenges. *TIERS Information Technology Journal*, *5*(1), 57–69. DOI: 10.38043/tiers.v5i1.5496

Islam, R., Patamsetti, V., Gadhi, A., Gondu, R. M., Bandaru, C. M., Kesani, S. C., & Abiona, O. (2023). The future of cloud computing: Benefits and challenges. *International Journal of Communications, Network and Systems Sciences*, *16*(4), 53–65. DOI: 10.4236/ijcns.2023.164004

Jabborova, D., Mamurova, D., Umurova, K. K., Ulasheva, U., Djalolova, S. X., & Khurramov, A. (2024). *Possibilities of Using Technologies in Digital Transformation of Sustanable Development.* Paper presented at the E3S Web of Conferences. DOI: 10.1051/e3sconf/202449101002

Jajan, K. I. K., & Zeebaree, S. R. (2024). Optimizing Performance in Distributed Cloud Architectures: A Review of Optimization Techniques and Tools. *The Indonesian Journal of Computer Science, 13*(2). Advance online publication. DOI: 10.33022/ijcs.v13i2.3805

Jakovleski, D. (2023). ANTICIPATED DEVELOPMENTS IN CLOUD SERVICES WITH A FOCUS ON THE INFRASTRUCTURE-AS-A-SERVICE (IaaS) MODEL. *Journal of Electrical Engineering and Information Technologies*, 29-38.

Johnson, M. (2023). A Comparative Study of Cloud Service Models: IaaS, PaaS, and SaaS in Real-World Applications. *Advances in Computer Sciences, 6*(1).

Kanungo, S. (2023). Security challenges and solutions in multi-cloud environments. *Stochastic Modelling and Computational Sciences, 3*(2), 139–146.

Kanungo, S., & Sarangi, S. (2024). Quantum computing integration with multi-cloud architectures: enhancing computational efficiency and security in advanced cloud environments.

Khalil, S. (2019). Adopting the cloud: How it affects firm strategy. *The Journal of Business Strategy, 40*(4), 28–35. DOI: 10.1108/JBS-05-2018-0089

Khan, N., & Rinaudo, O. (2025). Harnessing Intelligent Cloud Platforms to Drive SME Growth and Innovation.

Kondru, V. L. P. (2015). Electronic Health Care Records-Boon To Industry. *International Journal of Medical Informatics and AI, 2*(2), 1–18.

Kovvuri, V. K. R. (2024). SUSTAINABLE TRANSPORTATION SOLUTIONS: THE ROLE OF AI AND CLOUD TECHNOLOGIES. [IJCET]. *INTERNATIONAL JOURNAL OF COMPUTER ENGINEERING AND TECHNOLOGY, 15*(6), 423–429.

Kumar, M. S., & Ganesh, D. (2024). Improving Telemedicine through IoT and Cloud Computing: Opportunities and Challenges. *Advances in Engineering and Intelligence Systems, 3*(03), 123–135.

Kumar, S. (2024). Cloud Computing in Commerce: A Strategic Analysis of Service Models Impacting E-Commerce Success.

Kwaku, W. K. (2023). The Role of Cloud Platforms in Driving Digital Transformation. *MZ Computing Journal, 4*(2).

Laxminarayana Korada, V. K. S. (2024). Why are large enterprises building private clouds after their journey on public clouds? *European Journal of Advances in Engineering and Technology*, *11*(2), 49–52.

Liu, B., Song, J., & Geng, W. (2024). Private cloud deployment model selection for cost efficiency: A business perspective. *Kybernetes*. Advance online publication. DOI: 10.1108/K-02-2024-0430

Liu, Y., Ni, Z., Karlsson, M., & Gong, S. (2021). Methodology for digital transformation with internet of things and cloud computing: A practical guideline for innovation in small-and medium-sized enterprises. *Sensors (Basel)*, *21*(16), 5355. DOI: 10.3390/s21165355 PMID: 34450797

Maharani, C., & Nutela, I. (2024). Exploring the Transformative Potential of Cloud Computing in Distance Education: Challenges, Opportunities, and Best Practices. *Journal Basic Science and Technology*, *13*(2), 63–70.

MAHESH, V. N., SHRIYA, G., RASAGNYA, G., & NIKHITHA, G. (2024). CLOUD INTEGRATED INTELLIGENT CARGO MANAGEMENT SYSTEM. *International Journal of Management Research and Business Strategy*, *14*(2), 16–22.

Maniatis, P. *Comparison of Public, Private, Hybrid, and Community Cloud Computing in Terms of Purchasing and Supply Management: A Quantitative Approach*. Academic Press. DOI: 10.47191/ijmra/v6-i6-04

Merseedi, K. J., & Zeebaree, S. R. (2024). The cloud architectures for distributed multi-cloud computing: A review of hybrid and federated cloud environment. *Indonesian Journal of Computer Science*, *13*(2). Advance online publication. DOI: 10.33022/ijcs.v13i2.3811

Mistry, H. K., Mavani, C., Goswami, A., & Patel, R. (2024). The impact of cloud computing and ai on industry dynamics and competition. *Educational Administration: Theory and Practice*, *30*(7), 797–804.

Moeti, M. N. (2024). Infrastructure as a service adoption model for South African universities using thematic analysis. *South African Journal of Information Management*, *26*(1), 14. DOI: 10.4102/sajim.v26i1.1877

Mohammad, A., & Abbas, Y. (2024). Key Challenges of Cloud Computing Resource Allocation in Small and Medium Enterprises. *Digital*, *4*(2), 372–388. DOI: 10.3390/digital4020018

Mohammed, C. M., & Zeebaree, S. R. (2021). Sufficient comparison among cloud computing services: IaaS, PaaS, and SaaS: A review. *International Journal of Science and Business*, *5*(2), 17–30.

Mydyti, H., Ajdari, J., & Zenuni, X. (2020). *Cloud-based Services Approach as Accelerator in Empowering Digital Transformation.* Paper presented at the 2020 43rd International Convention on Information, Communication and Electronic Technology (MIPRO). DOI: 10.23919/MIPRO48935.2020.9245192

Naguib, A. (2023). Assessing the Impact of SaaS Quality on Telecom Customer Loyalty: A Social Capital Theory Approach. *European Journal of Business and Management Research, 8*(1), 336–344. DOI: 10.24018/ejbmr.2023.8.1.1824

Nutalapati, P. (2024). A Review on Cloud Computing in Finance-Transforming Financial Services in the Digital Age.

Nyamwesa, A. (2024). Cloud Computing Technology Adoption: Challenges for SMEs, A Case of Selected SMEs in Tanzania. *International Journal of Advanced Business Studies, 3*(2), 1–12. DOI: 10.59857/IJABS.3118

Obi, O. C., Dawodu, S. O., Daraojimba, A. I., Onwusinkwue, S., Akagha, O. V., & Ahmad, I. A. I. (2024). Review of evolving cloud computing paradigms: Security, efficiency, and innovations. *Computer Science & IT Research Journal, 5*(2), 270–292. DOI: 10.51594/csitrj.v5i2.757

Ognjanović, I., Šendelj, R., Daković-Tadić, M., & Kožuh, I. (2024). A Longitudinal Study on the Adoption of Cloud Computing in Micro, Small, and Medium Enterprises in Montenegro. *Applied Sciences (Basel, Switzerland), 14*(14), 6387. DOI: 10.3390/app14146387

Onabanjo, E. (2024). Digital Transformation: The impact of AI on Cloud Transformation. *Journal of Artificial Intelligence General science (JAIGS) ISSN: 3006-4023, 5*(1), 174-183.

Oruganti, N. R. (2024). CLOUD COMPUTING: A COMPREHENSIVE GUIDE TO MODERN INFRASTRUCTURE. [IJCET]. *INTERNATIONAL JOURNAL OF COMPUTER ENGINEERING AND TECHNOLOGY, 15*(6), 701–713.

Paul, P., & Jena, S. K. (2023). Education Technology and E-Learning Sector in enhancing Knowledge Management Systems: The Growth) Financial and Economical Concern in Indian Context. *Economic Affairs, 68*(3), 1725–1734.

Prangon, N. F., & Wu, J. (2024). AI and Computing Horizons: Cloud and Edge in the Modern Era. *Journal of Sensor and Actuator Networks, 13*(4), 44. DOI: 10.3390/jsan13040044

Reddy, A. (2024). Digital Transformation: Using Technology to Reshape Industries. [IJST]. *International Journal of Science and Technology, 1*(1).

Rostami, A. (2021). *Cloud Service Models-IaaS*. PaaS, and SaaS.

Savolainen, S. (2023). Evaluating security and privacy of SaaS service.

Schneckenberg, D., Benitez, J., Klos, C., Velamuri, V. K., & Spieth, P. (2021). Value creation and appropriation of software vendors: A digital innovation model for cloud computing. *Information & Management*, *58*(4), 103463. DOI: 10.1016/j.im.2021.103463

Sean Marston, Z., Bandyopadhyay, S., Zhang, J., & Ghalsasi, A. (2011). Cloud computing—The business perspective. In: Elsevier BV.

Segun-Falade, O. D., Osundare, O. S., Kedi, W. E., Okeleke, P. A., Ijomah, T. I., & Abdul-Azeez, O. Y. (2024). Assessing the transformative impact of cloud computing on software deployment and management. *Computer Science & IT Research Journal, 5*(8).

Seifert, M., Kuehnel, S., & Sackmann, S. (2023). Hybrid clouds arising from software as a service adoption: Challenges, solutions, and future research directions. *ACM Computing Surveys*, *55*(11), 1–35. DOI: 10.1145/3570156

Sekar, P. K. (2024). The data-driven future of finance: Advances in engineering for real-time analytics and decision making. [IJRCAIT]. *INTERNATIONAL JOURNAL OF RESEARCH IN COMPUTER APPLICATIONS AND INFORMATION TECHNOLOGY*, *7*(2), 83–97.

Seo, C., Yoo, D., & Lee, Y. (2024). Empowering Sustainable Industrial and Service Systems through AI-Enhanced Cloud Resource Optimization. *Sustainability (Basel)*, *16*(12), 5095. DOI: 10.3390/su16125095

Seth, D., Nerella, H., Najana, M., & Tabbassum, A. (2024). Navigating the Multi-Cloud Maze: Benefits, Challenges, and Future Trends. *International Journal of Global Innovations and Solutions (IJGIS)*.

Sk, K. B., & Dalavai, L. (2024). Navigating the Horizon: A Systematic Review of E-learning in Cloud Computing Environment.

Somanathan, S. (2023). Optimizing Cloud Transformation Strategies: Project Management Frameworks for Modern Infrastructure. *International Journal of Applied Engineering & Technology*, *5*(1).

Sowmya, S., Deepika, P., & Naren, J. (2014). Layers of cloud–IaaS, PaaS and SaaS: A survey. *International Journal of Computer Science and Information Technologies*, *5*(3), 4477–4480.

Sun, Y. (2024). Harnessing Technological Innovation for Competitive Advantage: A Strategic Framework. *Frontiers in Business, Economics and Management, 13*(3), 128–131. DOI: 10.54097/fx56aw54

Surucu-Balci, E., Iris, Ç., & Balci, G. (2024). Digital information in maritime supply chains with blockchain and cloud platforms: Supply chain capabilities, barriers, and research opportunities. *Technological Forecasting and Social Change, 198*, 122978. DOI: 10.1016/j.techfore.2023.122978

Thavi, R., Jhaveri, R., Narwane, V., Gardas, B., & Jafari Navimipour, N. (2024). Role of cloud computing technology in the education sector. *Journal of Engineering. Defence Technology*, *22*(1), 182–213.

Tohanean, D., & Toma, S.-G. (2024). *The Impact of Cloud Systems on Enhancing Organizational Performance through Innovative Business Models in the Digitalization Era.* Paper presented at the Proceedings of the International Conference on Business Excellence. Tripathi, S. Digital Transformation and Cloud Computing: System Dynamics Modeling Approach. DOI: 10.2478/picbe-2024-0289

Tripathi, S. (2023). Digital Transformation through Cloud Computing in the Organization: System Dynamics Modeling Approach. *Authorea Preprints.*

Umar, U. S., & Rana, M. E. (2024). *Cloud Revolution in Manufacturing: Exploring Benefits, Applications, and Challenges in the Era of Digital Transformation.* Paper presented at the 2024 ASU International Conference in Emerging Technologies for Sustainability and Intelligent Systems (ICETSIS). DOI: 10.1109/ICETSIS61505.2024.10459473

van der Vlist, F., Helmond, A., & Ferrari, F. (2024). Big AI: Cloud infrastructure dependence and the industrialisation of artificial intelligence. *Big Data & Society, 11*(1), 20539517241232630. DOI: 10.1177/20539517241232630

Vitliemov, P. (2018). Smart manufacturing and cloud computing: Vision and state-of-the-art. *Industry 4.0, 3*(6), 323-325.

Wadly, F., Lubis, A., Mayasari, N., & Ginting, R. F. (2023). Transformation of Kebun Kelapa Village Administration with Platform as a Service (PaaS) Cloud Computing. *International Journal Of Computer Sciences and Mathematics Engineering*, *2*(2), 82–89. DOI: 10.61306/ijecom.v2i2.25

Zakaria, A., & Jizat, J. E. M. (2024). Bibliometric Analysis of Security Concerns in Hybrid Cloud Adoption in Small and Medium-Sized Enterprises SMEs. *CMU Academy Journal of Management and Business Education*, *3*(2), 29–38.

Chapter 6
Cloud Security and Privacy

Rubi Kadyan
https://orcid.org/0009-0003-4264-8913
Bhagat Phool Singh Mahila Vishwavidyalaya, Sonipat, India

Sunita Rani
https://orcid.org/0000-0002-6833-6737
Bhagat Phool Singh Mahila Vishwavidyalaya, Sonipat, India

Vinod Kr. Saroha
Bhagat Phool Singh Mahila Vishwavidyalaya, Sonipat, India

ABSTRACT

This chapter explores the key security threats and vulnerabilities at different levels, such as SaaS, PaaS and IaaS in cloud computing and provides their solutions. It will comprehensively analyze common security risks such as data breaches, unauthorized access and compliance issues. Discuss all security issues such as application security, data security, network security issues, authentication and authorization issues. It explains various data security techniques such as Cryptography, Steganography, Homomorphic cryptography, Quantum cryptography, DNA cryptography, Machine learning and Deep learning, Multi-factor authentication, and Blockchain to describe which technique is suitable at which stage of data. It explains regulatory bodies such as GDPR (European Union), HIPAA (United States), CCPA (United States), DSL (China), CSL(China), IT Act, and PDPB (India) and case studies related to regulatory role in data privacy. It describes the role of AI and machine learning, zero-trust architecture in threat detection, and the future of cloud computing.

DOI: 10.4018/979-8-3693-9984-2.ch006

1. INTRODUCTION

Today, in the digital world, Cloud computing has transformed the way of businesses and individuals to store, process, and manage data at low cost, anytime, anywhere, with availability and scalability. However, this convenience comes with significant challenges related to security and privacy. In the cloud, more sensitive information is stored, including personal, financial, and proprietary business data; the risks of data loss (breaches), unauthorized access, and privacy violations have increased exponentially. Security and privacy are top priority concerns in the cloud environment. In the cloud environment, services are provided by the service provider, and users have no control over data and other infrastructure. The users are unaware of where data is processed and where data is stored. Users can access the cloud service only when connected to the Internet. This created a security issue in a cloud environment.

Definition

Cloud security means setting policies, procedures, tools, and techniques to protect the cloud's data and infrastructure. It also provides solutions to Cloud-based issues, including data security, Infrastructure security, and resource availability (C. K. V. K. V. L. Reddy, 2024).

1.1. Importance of Cloud Security

A. **Data Protection:** Cloud security protects sensitive information (personal, financial, or business) from unauthorized access. Data encryption, both in transit and at rest, is one of the primary ways to safeguard data confidentiality.
B. **Mitigating Cyber Threats:** Cybercriminals engage in illegal activity in cloud environments, so robust security is needed to protect against illegal activity such as hacking, ransomware, and malware. Cloud security technologies such as firewalls, intrusion detection systems (IDS), and other security techniques (cryptography, steganography and deep learning) ensure that systems remain secure in a cloud environment.
C. **Cost-Efficiency** A robust cloud security framework helps organizations avoid costly consequences like data breaches, legal actions, or regulatory penalties. By leveraging the cloud provider's built-in security services, organizations can avoid the expense of building and maintaining on-premises security infrastructure (Cherbal et al., 2024)

1.2. Key Terms Related to Security

Integrity, confidentiality, authentication, non-repudiation, and availability are the pillars of security for computer networks that describe the following:

A. Integrity

Integrity means unauthorized users (who do not have the right to access the data) cannot change the data. Sometimes, attackers try to corrupt the data in a cloud environment and send it to users. Using the wrong data creates serious concerns for data security. We achieve integrity if data remains unchanged during transmission, processing, and storage. To achieve integrity, the techniques used are access control, encryption techniques, hash functions, and checksums.

B. **Confidentiality**

In Cloud computing, confidentiality means that only authorized persons (who have permission to access the data) can access the data. Authentication and access control techniques guarantee data confidentiality. This is important for controlling organizations' data across multiple distributed databases. It is a key component of security and privacy. The techniques used to achieve confidentiality are encryption techniques (cryptography) that are most commonly used to prevent intruders from entering and stealing data in the cloud, and Masking (steganography). The selection of the most suitable cryptography technique depends on the specific requirements of the application. For example, if you need to secure key exchange, elliptic curve cryptography could be the best option. Homomorphic cryptography may be more suitable for computations of encrypted data. Hybrid cryptography can be used to combine the advantages of asymmetric encryption with symmetric encryption to provide better results.

C. **Authorization**

Authorization is an essential information security requirement in Cloud computing to maintain data integrity and confidentiality. Authorization means giving specific permission to a specific user to access the resources and data. In a public cloud, multiple users share a single service and resource, so proper authorization is required. Authorization comes after authentication (verifying users' identities) and checks what users should do. Techniques used to achieve the authentication are Role-Based Access Control (RBAC) (Users can access resources based on their role), Access Control Lists (ACLs) (Lists specify which user allows which resources and data can access), Mandatory Access Control (MAC) (controlled by a central authority based on multiple levels of security).

D. **Non-repudiation**

Non-repudiation in cloud computing means the sender and receiver cannot deny their action. It helps to achieve data integrity. It can be obtained by applying digital signatures, timestamps (specific time of activities), Audit Trails and Logs (Keeping detailed records of all transaction activities), and confirmation receipt services (digital receipting of messages confirming data sent/received)(Sasikumar & Nagarajan, 2024).

E. **Availability**

Availability is a necessary information security requirement in Cloud computing. The goal of availability (including applications and infrastructures) can be used at any time or place. Cloud service providers provide infrastructures and platforms based on virtual machines. So, availability is mandatory for IaaS and PaaS, whether the public or private cloud is used. The key factors that help to achieve availability are redundancy (if one system fails, then the other can take it), fault tolerance (continue to provide services if one system fails), load balancing (workload distributed over multiple servers), and continuously check system to detect the issues before they affect availability (Sasikumar & Nagarajan, 2024).

F. **Authentication (Identification)**

As the significant concerns in a cloud environment are internal and external threats, the cloud service provider can have a secure infrastructure to protect customer data and guard against unauthorized access. Identification and authentication process to verify and validate individual users based on their credentials before accessing any data over the cloud. That's why identification and authentication are mandatory security requirements in cloud environments. Techniques used for authentication are user name and password, Multi-Factor Authentication (MFA) (using two or more verification factors such as password + OTP + Captcha code), Biometric Authentication (using fingerprints, iris scans) and Certificate-Based Authentication (digital certificates given to a trusted authority to verify identity)(Cherbal et al., 2024)

1.3. Threads and Vulnerability at Different Levels in Cloud Computing

Threat: - A threat is a potential cause of an incident that may harm a system, such as data loss and unauthorized access. Examples of threats are Malware (viruses), Phishing (collecting user information through deceptive email and websites) and insider threats (any person with authorized access can misuse information) (Suryateja, 2018). Figure 1 shows the threats at different levels in cloud computing.

Figure 1. Threats in Cloud Computing

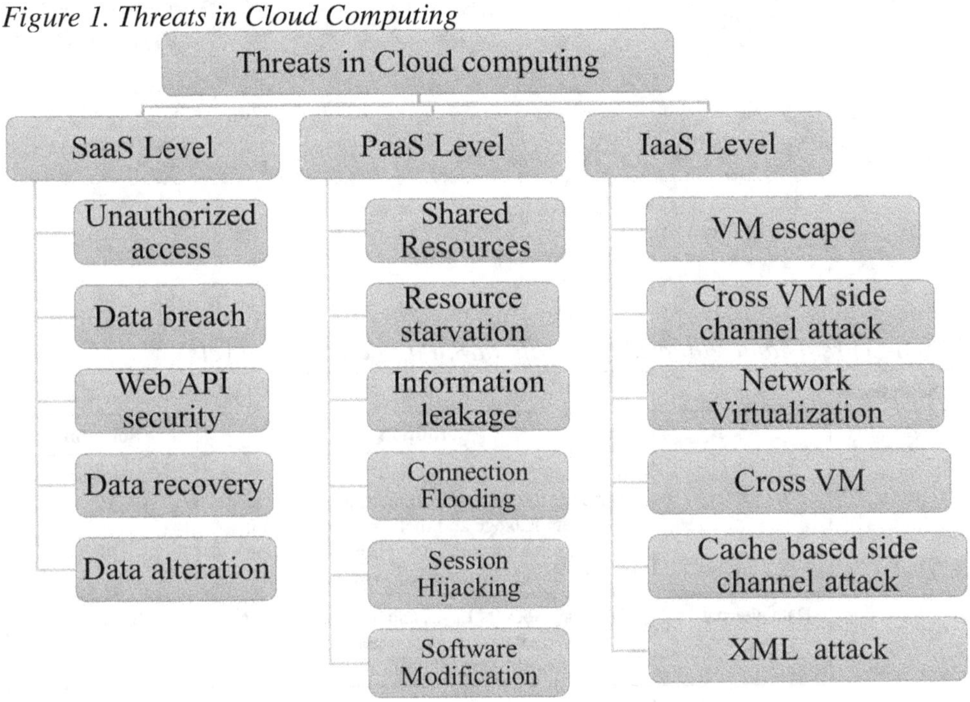

Vulnerability (Network issues): - A vulnerability is a weakness in a system exploited by a threat. A threat agent carries out threats by exploiting one or more vulnerabilities. Examples of vulnerability are weak passwords, storing and transferring data without encryption and unpatched software (outdated). The threats and vulnerabilities at different levels and their solutions are discussed in Table 1. Figure 2 shows the vulnerability of cloud computing at different levels (Fatima et al., 2024)

Figure 2. Vulnerability in Cloud Computing

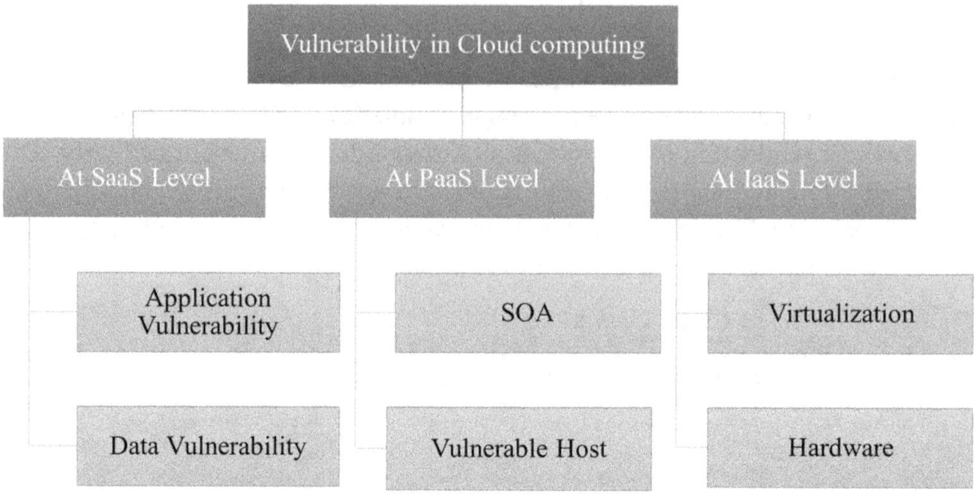

Table 1. Threats and Vulnerabilities at SaaS, PaaS and IaaS levels.

At SaaS level			
Vulnerability	**Threat**	**Definition**	**Solution**
Data level	Data breach	In a cloud environment, multiple clients access services at a time, which increases the chance of data leakage and theft. Authentication, authorization, and encryption /decryption techniques are needed to protect data.	Cryptography
	Data alternation	Secure Sockets Layer and Transport Layer Security create a secure channel between clients and servers for safe data transmission.	SSL/TLS
	Data recovery	Cryptography, with strong key management, helps users secure and recover data.	Cryptography
Application	Unauthorization	In a cloud environment, attackers try to access the application for illegal use. Strong Identity, authentication, and authorization (IAA) can protect application access.	IAA
	API security	Isolating service access for each user helps limit the data application and access.	Isolation
	Data breach (loss)	An RSA cryptography algorithm is used to check the authenticity of data after transmission.	Digital Signature
At IaaS Level			

continued on following page

Table 1. Continued

At SaaS level			
Vulnerability	**Threat**	**Definition**	**Solution**
Virtualization	Network virtualization	Network virtualization divides a single physical network into multiple logical networks that can be managed and optimized independently. This increases resource utilization and flexibility, enhances security, and simplifies network management. The issues related to these poor resource distribution, VM sprawl (resource shortages), and complicated backup and recovery.	VM mapping
	Cross-VM leakage	Cloud resources are allocated to a large number of users, so there is more chance that one virtual machine (VM) can access information from another VM running on the same physical host	Dedicated instances, isolation
	Cache-based side-channel attack	In cache-based side-channel attacks, the attacker exploits the shared cache memory to infer sensitive information from another process or virtual machine (VM) running on the same physical host	Isolation, partitioning and Monitoring
Hardware	Information leakage	A partitioned cache is allocated to each process separately, and a lock mechanism is used for isolating the line of cache.	Partitioned cache
	Interrupt Mechanism	Attackers disrupt regular processing and gain unauthorized access.	Update hardware regularly.
At PaaS level			
SOA	Resource starvation	To solve this problem, limited the resources access using the Java VM tooling interface.	Accounting resources
	Shared resource	In a cloud environment, resources are allocated according to the user class.	Chinese wall model (prevents conflicts of interest and ensures confidentiality)
	Information leakage	The thread related to the user should be properly terminated to prevent data leakage.	Proper thread termination
Vulnerable Host	Vulnerable object	A trusted computing base (TCB) provides a secure layer to prevent interoperability (the ability of different devices or applications to work together and exchange information).	TCB

2. KEY SECURITY CHALLENGES IN THE CLOUD

2.1. At the services level, key security challenges

Security issues are divided into different parts based on the SaaS, PaaS, and IaaS levels described in Tables 2, 3, and 4. Figure 3 shows these security challenges in detail (Goswami et al., 2024).

Figure 3. Key security challenges in Cloud Computing

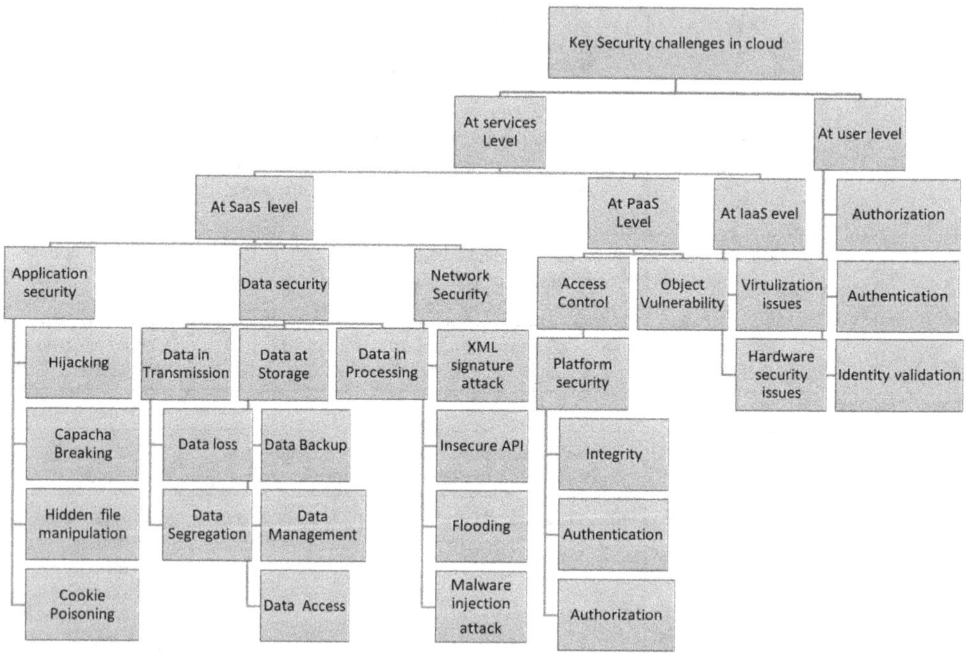

2.1.1. Security Issues at the SaaS Level

SaaS-level security issues are divided into three categories that described in Table 2 (Tabrizchi & Rafsanjani, 2020),

Table 2. SaaS-level security challenges

Saas level security issues and challenges			
Security Level	**Challenges**	**Description**	**Solution**
Application security	Hijacking	flaws in web applications may create vulnerabilities for the SaaS applications. If an attacker gains access to a user's credentials, they can perform malicious activities such as accessing sensitive data, manipulating data, and redirecting any transaction	Multi-factor Authentication (MFA) and strong passwords.
	Captcha Breaking	CAPTCHA-breaking techniques bypass CAPTCHA tests designed to distinguish between human users and automated bots. Today, many machine learning models **can solve CAPTCHA challenges automatically.**	Use image-based CAPTCHA, regularly update CAPTCHA mechanisms, and use a CAPTCHA that analyses user behaviour.
	Hidden file manipulation	Hidden file manipulation involves altering files in a way that is difficult to detect, such as hiding malicious code in files.	Regular Audits, use of anti-malware tools and File Integrity Monitoring (FIM) – alert on changes in critical files

continued on following page

Table 2. Continued

Saas level security issues and challenges			
Security Level	**Challenges**	**Description**	**Solution**
Data security	Data loss (Transmission time)	In a cloud environment, multiple users use the cloud service at a time, which increases the chance of data leakage and theft. Proper authentication, authorization, and encryption /decryption techniques are used.	Use of cryptography.
	Data segregation (Transmission time)	In a cloud computing environment, multiple users store data on the same server, which increases user inference and data leakage. Data segmentation (separating data based on specific criteria) solves these issues.	Data classification, Encryption, strict access control policies, and regular audits.
	Data Backup (Storage time)	Updating data frequently causes data loss. To prevent this, a cloud environment stores multiple copies of the same data at different places, but it needs a lot of storage space.	Full backup (copy of complete data) and maintain multiple versions of files.
	Data Management (Storage time)	To manage a vast amount of data in the cloud is very difficult during transmission and storage time.	Use data visualization tools.
	Data access (Storage time)	Lack of proper data access techniques unauthorized persons able to get confidential information. Data access can be controlled with strong authentication and authorized processes.	Use Digital Signature and Multi-factor authentication.
	Data Availability (Processing time)	Cloud computing data is unavailable on time, creating serious issues in real-time applications.	Replication (multiple copies of data), load balancing (distribute workload on multiple servers)
	Data Locality (Storage time)	Users in cloud environments do not know the location of data and data centers. For example, one country's military data stored in another country may create a problem.	Fellow Compliance with Regulations and store data within specific geographic boundaries.

continued on following page

Table 2. Continued

Saas level security issues and challenges			
Security Level	**Challenges**	**Description**	**Solution**
Network Security	XML Signature	Intruders insert malicious data that changes the original data. The reason is the weakness of the authentication process.	Secure API (Application Programming Interface use)
	Malware injection	Malware is inserted in the information that blocks or does wrong code execution.	An intrusion prevention system (IPS) is designed not only to detect but also to prevent malware or other types of intrusions
	Flooding	Unwanted requests repeatedly sent by an unauthorized person (excessive data traffic) can affect the availability of the intended user.	Implementing Quality of Service (QoS) policies, load balancing, and continuing to monitor network traffic and set up alerts to detect unusual activity.
	Insecure API	If the application programming interface (API) is not insured, many issues, such as data loss, unauthorized access, and service disruptions, will occur. If the interface to communicate with the cloud is not sufficiently secure, malicious attempts will be made to violate the many security threads.	Use authentication and authorization, input validation (check all user inputs), and continue monitoring API traffic and encryption.
	Man in the Middle (MitH) Attacks	An unauthorized person intercepts communication between two users without their knowledge. Examples of man-in-middle attacks are – Session hijack- and DNS spoofing.	Use HTTPS, strong authentication, use Virtual Private Network (VPN) and use intrusion detection systems (IDS), and intrusion prevention systems (IPS)
	Brute force attack (Unauthorized access)	In this attack, an attacker tries to gain access to the system. It systematically checks all possible combinations of usernames and passwords until a match is found.	Use strong password policies, multi-factor authentication (MFA), CAPTCHA (to identify the difference between human users and automated bots), and encryption.
	Phishing attack	In this attack, the attacker gains sensitive information such as login and financial details and redirects the user to other fake links.	Email filtering to detect and block phishing emails, use MFA and URL filtering.
	Side-channel attack	The attacker explores the weakness of the device to gain unauthorized access, such as operation time, power usage and fault frequency, to leak the encryption key	Ensure physical security and implement robust cryptography.

2.1.2. PaaS Level Security Issues

Table 3 describes the PaaS-level security challenges and their solutions (Azam et al., 2023).

Table 3. PaaS level security challenges

PaaS-level Security Challenges			
Security level	**Challenges**	**Description**	**Solution**
Access control	Authorization (User-level issue)	This mechanism determines who can access resources based on predefined policies. Without permission, accessing resources is a lack of authorization.	Encryption, monitoring and auditing and role-based access control, etc.
	Authentication (User-level issue)	Users need to prove their identities during interactions. Authentication fails when an unauthorized person can access resources and many robust techniques are used to prevent this.	A strong password, multi-factor authentication (MFA), and biometric authentication.
Vulnerability	Data and resource vulnerability	The provider may access any user data that resides on its hosts. Users sharing the same server may attack each other's data. External attackers may access user data.	Strong Encryption, isolation, and strong access control mechanisms.
SLA (Service level agreement)	Ambiguous terms and conditions	Unclear terms create misunderstandings between the user and the provider.	In simple and easy language, all terms and conditions are clearly defined.
	Inadequate penalties	Sometimes, SLA does not specify adequate penalties.	Clearly define penalties and remedies.

2.1.3. IaaS-level security issues are divided mainly into two parts

Table 4. Security issues at the IaaS level

Security issues at the IaaS level			
Security Levels	**Challenges**	**Description**	**Solutions**
Hardware security	Hardware theft	In the cloud environment, the attacker tries to damage and theft the physical devices where data is stored.	Strong access control mechanisms such as biometrics and surveillance under cameras.
	Hardware Interruption	Hardware interrupt occurs when a signal is sent by external devices to halt the current working of the processor.	Virtualization and optimization.
	Misuse of Hardware	Improper use of physical resources, such as deploying malicious virtual machines.	Regular audits and use of resource monitoring tools.

continued on following page

Table 4. Continued

Security issues at the IaaS level			
Security Levels	**Challenges**	**Description**	**Solutions**
Virtualization security	VM escape	VMM (Virtual Machine Monitor) does not properly isolate virtual machines, which creates vulnerabilities in the virtualization environment. An attacker can access other VMs on the same host and break the host system.	Network segmentation, access control, regular updates, and security patches.
	VM rollback	Reverting from the current state to the previous state sometimes causes security issues. However, this can be beneficial when updates create issues and a virus infects a machine.	VM management tools (VMware) and VM monitor tools.
	VM replication	VM creates copies of virtual machines for recovery and security purposes in case of failure, which creates leakage issues, harms integrity, and consumes more storage resources in the cloud environment.	Create limited copies.
	VM migration	The migration (moving) of VMs for maintenance and load balancing from one server to another creates many issues, such as insufficient resources, configuration mismatches and performance degradation.	Schedules migrations during an off-peak time, updates the guest system, and checks the availability of adequate resources.
	VM Isolation	VMs run separately to ensure security in a cloud environment, isolated from each other, but two VMs that share the same resources (hardware, memory) create information leakages.	Regularly update software and optimize and allocate resources.

3. SECURITY STRATEGIES FOR THE CLOUD

3.1. Encryption Techniques

3.1.1. Cryptography

In cloud computing, cryptography (unreadable writing) is mainly used for data security in the safe transmission of data over the internet to protect it from attackers and prevent unauthorized access to data. This is a mathematical process of converting data from readable to unreadable form to ensure data confidentiality, integrity and authentication.

Cryptography is divided into symmetric cryptography (using one key) and asymmetric cryptography (using two keys). Figure 4 shows the types of cryptography.

Figure 4. Types of Cryptography

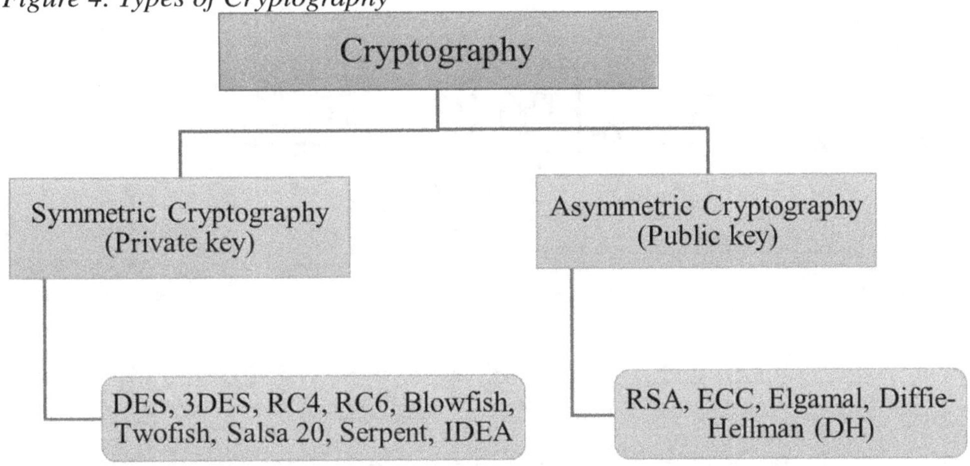

In symmetrical cryptography (private key cryptography), the sender and receiver use the same key for encryption (converting the original message (plaintext) to an unreadable form (ciphertext)). In asymmetric cryptography (public key cryptography), the sender uses the receiver's public key for message encryption. For message decryption (converting ciphertext to plaintext), the receiver uses their own private keys. Figure 5 shows a clear description of both types of cryptography. Both encryption techniques have their strong points and weaknesses. Symmetric cryptography algorithms are less time-consuming and faster, but provide less security because they need to share the key between the sender and the receiver. If, during key transmission, an unauthorized person can access the key, then data may be changed and lost. The most challenging work in cryptography is the transfer of private keys on the Internet. This problem is solved by asymmetric key cryptography, which is time-consuming and demands more resources. Nowadays, hybrid cryptography combines the benefits of both types of cryptography to provide more data security. To protect all services in cloud computing, a cryptography technique is used that helps to achieve data confidentiality(Rajguru et al., 2024).

Hashing is a type of encryption that does not use a key but uses the hash function (mathematical algorithm) to convert plain text into a fixed-length string (message digest). It is a One-Way Function (once data is hashed, we cannot get the original data). It is used to achieve data integrity in a cloud environment. The popular hashing algorithms are Message Digest (MD5) and Secure Hash Algorithm (SHA) (Bermani et al., 2021).

Figure 5. Working of Cryptography

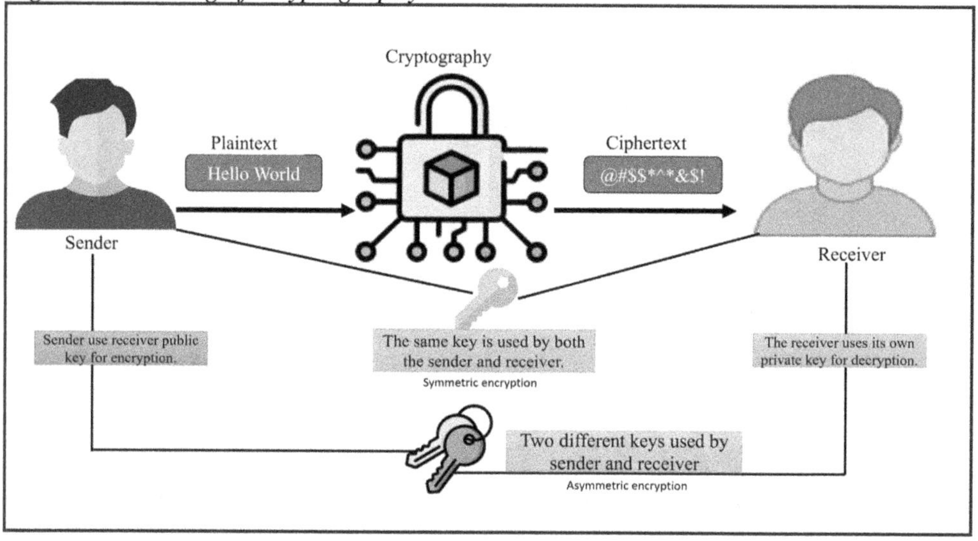

3.1.2. Steganography

Steganography is another encryption technique used to provide data security in cloud computing. It conceals (hides) messages or data in other messages, pictures, text, etc., to enhance security and make it difficult for hackers to access and find the data in the cloud environment. Figure 6 shows the working of steganography.

Figure 6. Steganography

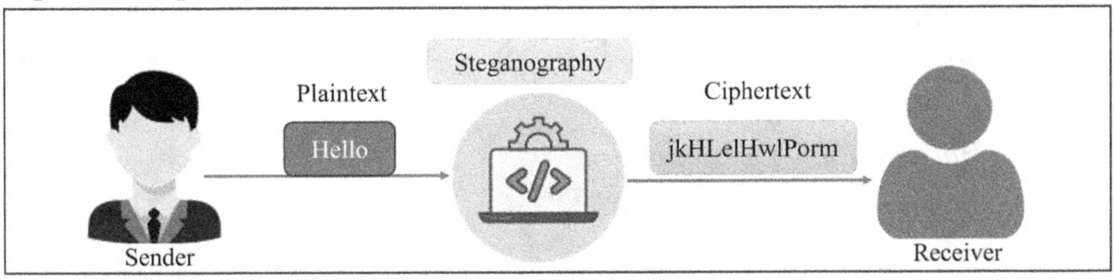

In cloud computing, security issues are significant concerns because sensitive data is stored remotely and accessible by many users. It protects against cyberattacks and protects privacy. Image steganography is the most commonly used technique to protect sensitive (account and personal information) data. However, this technique is used for small data security; we use cryptography techniques for extensive data (Rajguru et al., 2024). Many other steganography techniques are shown in Figure 7.

Figure 7. Types of Steganography

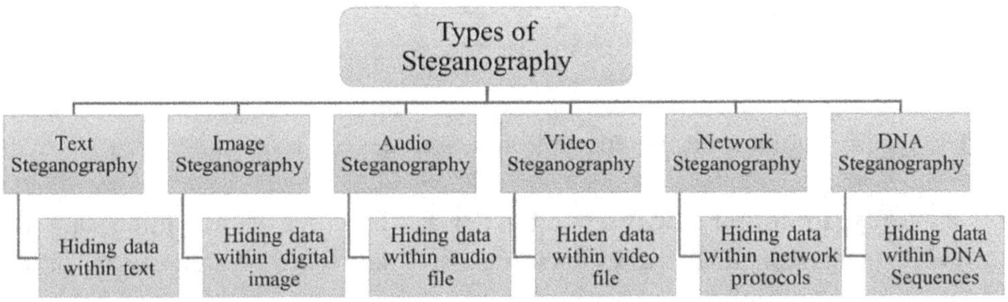

3.1.3. **HOMOMORPHISM**

Homomorphism is an advancement in existing cryptography. This technique is used to protect data at storage time. In this technique, the calculation is performed on the data without decrypting (converting data to the original form), and it is difficult to view the original data at processing time; only the final results can be seen, and the result is encrypted after the completion of the calculation. The result of the computation on encrypted data is the same as the operation performed on the original data. Existing encryption techniques are the first to decrypt data to perform any operation, which is expensive and time-consuming. Figure 8 shows the difference between homomorphic cryptography and traditional cryptography.

This technique maintains the confidentiality of the data in the cloud environment. Advanced cryptographic techniques often require significant computational resources, which demand powerful hardware and can increase operational expenses.

Figure 8. Homomorphic Cryptography

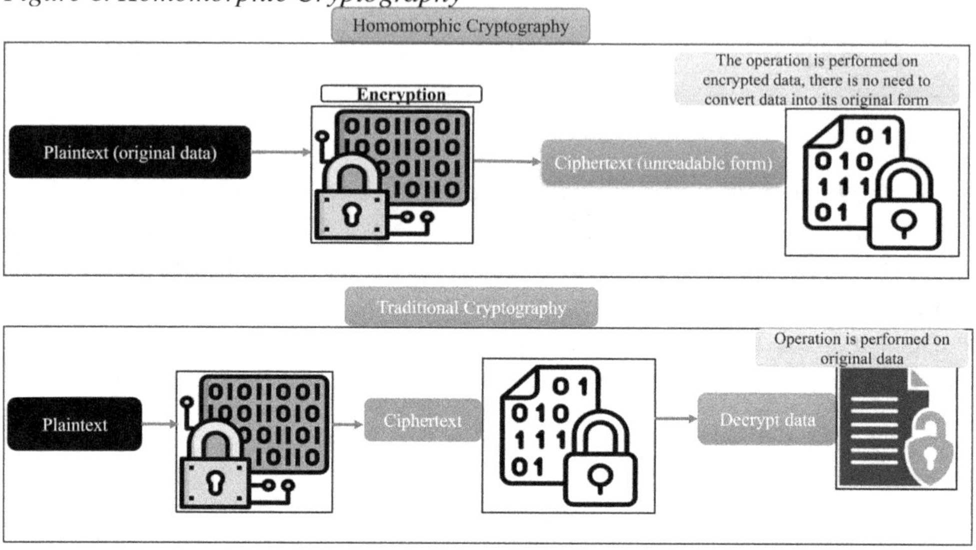

The types of homomorphic encryption techniques are the following: -

a) **Partially Homomorphic Encryption (PHE)**: This type of encryption supports only one mathematical operation on encrypted data for an unlimited time, either addition or multiplication, but it does not support both.
b) **Somewhat Homomorphic Encryption (SHE)**: This encryption supports addition and multiplication operations on data, but only for a limited time.
c) **Fully Homomorphic Encryption (FHE)**: FHE supports both addition and multiplication operations performed on encrypted data at the same time for an unlimited time (A. Baker, 2024).

Real-world applications –

I) **Healthcare analytics** Hospitals use HE to run predictive models on encrypted patient data without exposing personal information.
II) **Financial services**: Banks use HE to detect fraud on encrypted transaction data.

3.1.4. QUANTUM CRYPTOGRAPHY

Quantum cryptography brings a revolution in computing based on physics to improve data security. It can handle more computationally and complex operations over huge data. It uses optical links by sending Quantum particles to secure the encryption keys. The well-known use of quantum cryptography is Quantum Key Distribution (QKD) for the exchange of encryption keys. Quantum key distribution proves a secure solution in the cloud environment. It is specially designed for Quantum computers that transmit data at a very high speed compared to normal computers. Existing cryptography is inadequate to deal with Quantum computers for high-speed transmission, so researchers developed Quantum cryptography that matches Quantum computers' data transfer speed for data encryption and decryption. The most significant advantage of Quantum cryptography is its high speed because Quantum computers have parallel processing capability and high speed (they can handle various operations simultaneously). Figure 9 shows key points of quantum cryptography.

Real-world applications –

I) **Défense and government**: Agencies are testing quantum-secure channels to protect classified data from future quantum attacks.
II) **Healthcare and finance**: Institutions are exploring Quantum Key Distribution (QKD) to secure high-value data exchanges, especially in cross-border contexts (Savadatti et al., 2025).

Figure 9. Key Points of Quantum Cryptography

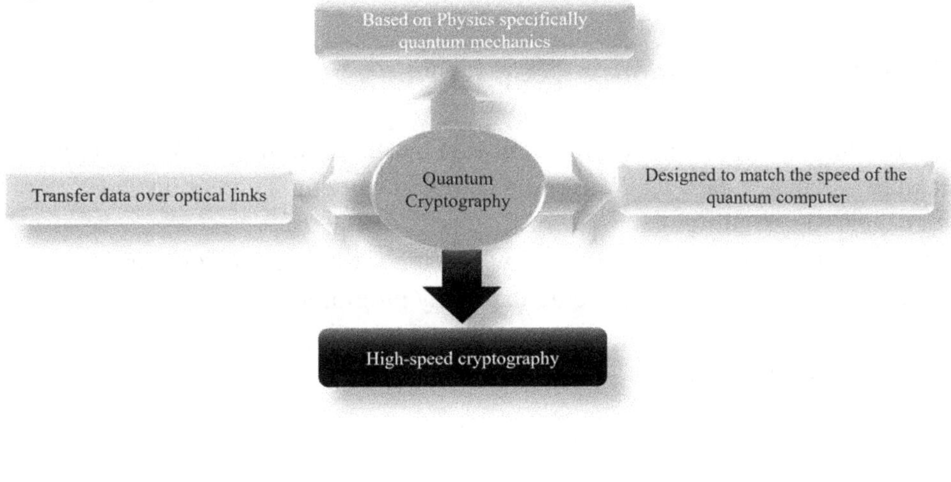

3.1.5. **DNA Cryptography**

DNA (Deoxyribonucleic Acid) cryptography uses DNA molecules for data encryption and decryption in cloud computing. The main purpose of DNA cryptography is to protect the data by encrypting the plaintext using a digital DNA format. DNA encryption creates random keys that make it complicated for hackers to guess. It combines cryptography and steganography to solve security problems in cloud computing. Due to complex structures, it gains more attention in cloud computing for data protection. In normal cryptography, 0 and 1 are used for data encryption. Still, in DNA cryptography, A (Adenine), G (Guanine) and, T (Thymine), C (Cytosine) are used, so to encrypt the data, any combination of the DNA can be used to improve data security. Figure 10 shows DNA cryptography working. DNA cryptography is beneficial for encrypting data at storage time (because a single DNA molecule can store a huge amount of data), ensuring safe data transmission, and protecting sensitive genetic information, but DNA cryptography is costly and time-consuming. However, implementing DNA cryptography requires advanced technology and expertise in cryptography and molecular (Selvakumar & Lokesh, 2024).

Figure 10. DNA Cryptography

3.2. Machine learning and Deep learning

Artificial intelligence (AI) is the ability of machines to mimic human cognitive functions, such as: Learning, Reasoning, Problem-solving, Perception and Natural Language understanding.

Machine learning is a subset of AI where algorithms learn from data to make predictions (decisions) without being explicitly programmed for every case.

Steps for prediction:

- **Training data**: The model is provided with pairs of inputs and their corresponding outcomes to identify underlying patterns and make predictions.
- **Model**: A mathematical representation that makes predictions based on learned patterns.
- **Evaluation**: The model is tested to see how well it generalizes to unseen data.

Types of Machine Learning:

1. **Supervised Learning** – Learns from labeled data (e.g., email spam vs. not spam)
2. **Unsupervised Learning** – Finds structure in unlabeled data (e.g., classification of customers by their behaviour)
3. **Reinforcement Learning** – Learns by trial and error through rewards (e.g., game-playing agents)

Deep learning is a subset of ML based on artificial neural networks with many layers, called *deep* networks.

- Deep learning uses multi-layered structures that automatically learn complex features from raw data and inspired by the human brain's neural structure. Figure 11 shows the relationship among ML, DL, AI, and neural networks (Wang et al., 2025).

Figure 11. AI Hierarchy

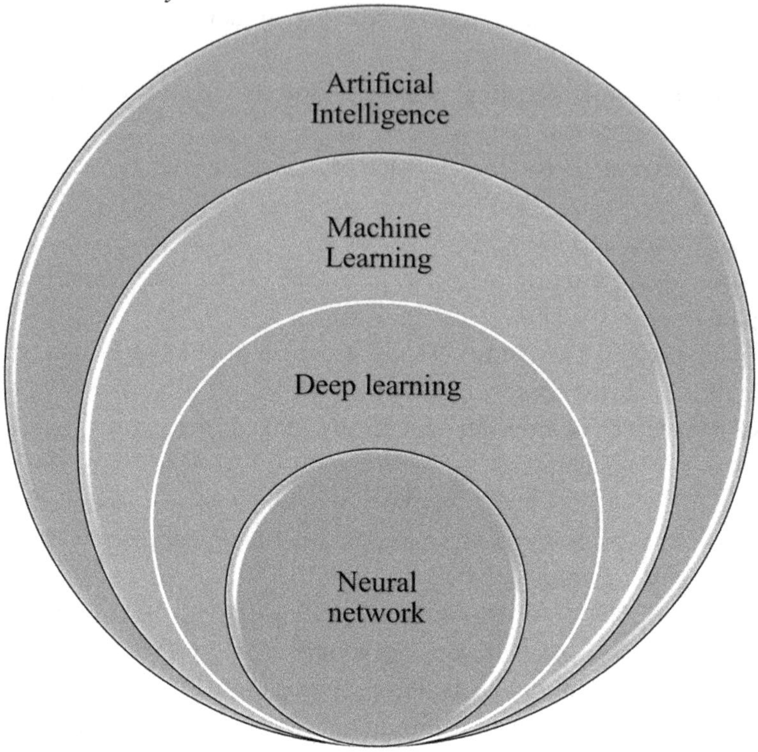

3.3. Blockchain

Data modification created by malicious attackers harms data integrity in the cloud environment. Blockchain is a distributed ledger technology that records transactions across multiple computers so that the records are secure and transparent. Once data is recorded in a blockchain, it is challenging to change the data. The blockchain consists of a series of blocks, each containing a list of transactions. Each block in the chain contains a cryptographic hash of the previous block, a timestamp, and transaction data. It uses digital signatures to prevent fraud, making data updating difficult for other users. It also stores data in multiple nodes across the network, making it difficult for hackers to compromise. Blockchain helps achieve data integrity. In Figure 12, when the user starts the transaction, it broadcasts to the network. Network nodes verify the transaction based on predefined rules. It is mainly used in cryptocurrencies such as Bitcoin. It helps to achieve more data security, transparency and a tamper-proof transaction process (H. M. K. T. V Reddy, 2024).

Figure 12. Working of Blockchain

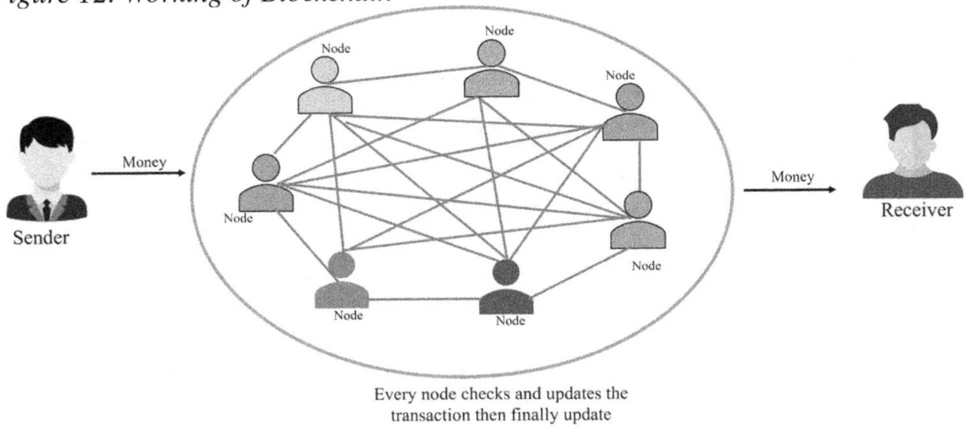

Based on the ownership of the networks, blockchain is divided into two parts as follows:

a) **Public Blockchain (Permissionless Blockchain):** Anyone can access, read, modify and verify the transactions.
    - Examples: Bitcoin, Ethereum

b) **Private Blockchain (Permissioned Blockchain):** Only identified and authorized members can make changes. It can be "fully private" when one organization owns the network or "Consortium blockchain" when a group of organizations jointly controls it (Dominguez & Laura, 2024).

3.4. Multifactor Authentication

Multi-factor authentication (MFA) is a security method to enhance security; it requires two or more independent verification techniques to verify a user's identity for a login or to gain access to the system. It aims to add one extra layer of security to the authentication process; if one technique fails, another prevents unauthorized access. In MFA, the user enters their primary credential, usually a password. After verifying the primary credential, the user is prompted to provide a second form of identification, such as a code sent to their phone or a fingerprint scan. If both (or more) credentials are verified, the user is granted access to the resource or system. Figure 13 shows the MFA. If attackers guess the password in MFA, they still need the second factor to gain access. It reduces the risk of unauthorized access(Alkhalifah, 2024).

Figure 13. Multi-factor authentication (MFA)

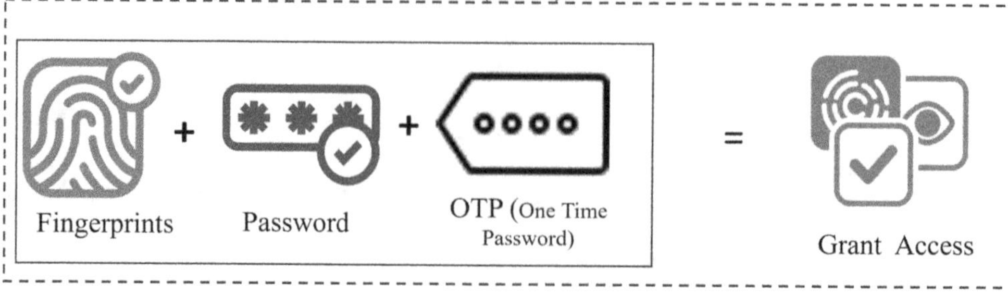

MFA mechanisms are designed based on three concepts classified as follows:

a) **Hardware-based Authentication (Possession):** 'Something you have', such as a smartphone or security token.
b) **Bio-metric-based Authentication (Inherence):** 'Something you are, unique for each one's life-long, such as Fingerprints, iris, retina, etc.
c) **Knowledge-based authentication (Knowledge):** 'Something you know', such as a password and Personal Identification Number (PIN).

Note: To achieve more efficient data security in a shared cloud computing environment, we need to integrate different techniques, such as blockchain integrated with cryptography, cryptography integrated with deep learning, homomorphic cryptography integrated with blockchain, etc.

4. PRIVACY CONCERNS IN THE CLOUD ENVIRONMENT

4.1. Data Residency and Jurisdiction

Data residency (the location of data storage) and jurisdiction (the legal authority of the country where data is stored) present several challenges in the digital world (Abramson et al., 2017).

Key Challenges of Data Residency and Jurisdiction:

1. **Violation of a government law or regulation:-** Every country has different rules and regulations. Sometimes, one country's data stored in the boundary of another country violates the law or regulation of that country where the data is stored, leading to penalties.
2. **Unintentional data access: -** Unintentional access and illegal use of the information by foreign organizations.

3. **Demand of data: -** Foreign government demands access to information to investigate a suspected crime, verify tax payments, etc.
4. **Data Localization: -** Data localization occurs when the location and movement of data are poorly understood, monitored and managed.
5. **Data management issues: -** When data is stored outside the country's boundary, its location and movement are not monitored and managed correctly.
6. **Security Risks: -** Storing data in multiple jurisdictions can increase the risk of data loss and unauthorized access.
7. **Monitoring and Enforcement: -** Data residency and jurisdiction requirements demand regular monitoring and enforcement. Therefore, cloud services must be updated to meet changing requirements.

5. PRIVACY PROTECTION MECHANISMS

Privacy protection mechanisms are necessary for protecting personal data and ensuring compliance with data protection regulations.

5.1. Privacy Enhancing Technologies (PET)

PET are tools and techniques designed to protect personal data while allowing data to be used and shared. PETs aim to protect data by minimizing personal data use, improving data security, and giving more control to the individual over their data. PET is defined by the European Union Agency for Cybersecurity (ENISA) as a measure for information and communications technologies (ICT) that protects privacy by reducing unnecessary processing of personal data and aiming to extract value from data without compromising data privacy. Figure 14 shows various PET techniques (Zhao et al., 2024).

Some Key PET

A. Cryptography

Cryptography involves converting data into an unreadable form to prevent unauthorized access. Techniques like encryption, hashing, and digital signatures are commonly used to protect data in transit and at rest.

B. Homomorphic Encryption

Homomorphic computations are to be performed on encrypted data without decrypting it. This protects sensitive data in the cloud computing environment.

C. Anonymization

Anonymization deletes personally identifiable information from data sets, making it difficult to trace data back to individuals. This is often used in data sharing and analysis to protect user privacy.

D. Access Control

Access control ensures that only authorized persons can access specific data. This involves user authentication, role-based access control (RBAC), and multi-factor authentication (MFA).

E. Data Masking

Data masking hides specific data parts within a database to protect sensitive information. It can be done by substitution (replacing original data with fake data that looks like original data), shuffling (mixing data in a way that has no complete information found), and encryption.

F. Regular Audits and Monitoring

Regular audits and monitoring help detect and prevent unauthorized access. This includes logging access attempts (Keeping track of who tries to access the system), reviewing access controls, and conducting security assessments (Regularly testing and examining the system to find and fix security issues)(Bende et al., 2024).

Figure 14. Privacy Enhanced Technologies

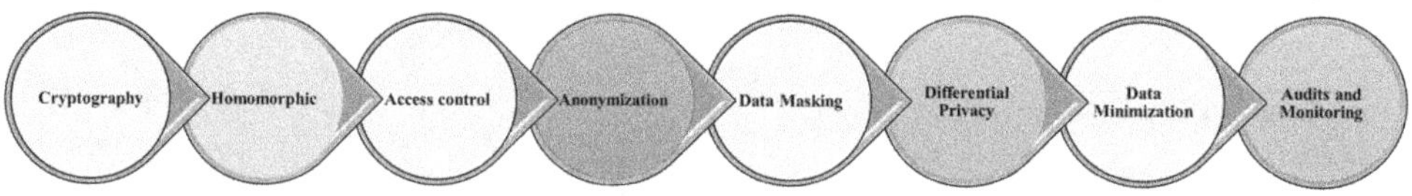

Benefits of Privacy-Enhancing Technologies

1. **Enhanced Privacy**: PETs provide robust privacy, reducing the risk of data loss and unauthorized access.

2. **Regulatory Compliance**: Implementing PETs helps organizations to follow data protection regulations such as GDPR and CCPA.
3. **Data Utility**: PETs maintain data privacy and help organizations share and use data without harming personal privacy.

Challenges of Privacy-Enhancing Technologies

1. **Complexity**: Implementing PETs can be technically complex and require specialized knowledge and expertise.
2. **Performance**: PETs can affect data processing and analysis performance overhead.
3. **Adoption**: Adopting PETs may be slow to meet the need for changes in infrastructure, processes, and organizational culture.

5.2. Anonymization and Its Techniques

Anonymization is a process to protect individuals' data privacy so that the individual's data cannot be identified. This is especially necessary in healthcare, finance, and research, where sensitive information must be handled carefully. Figure 15 shows techniques for anonymization. Here is a detailed description of anonymization (Longo et al., 2025).

The Key Aim of Anonymization

1. **Privacy Protection**: The primary aim is to ensure that individuals cannot be identified from the data, either directly or indirectly.
2. **Data Utility**: Even after anonymization, the data should remain helpful for research, analysis and other purposes.

Techniques of Anonymization

1. **Data Masking**: This alters data to hide the original information, such as replacing names with asterisks (***).
    - *Example*: John Doe replace with **** ***.
2. **Pseudonymization**: Replacing out personal information with fake names or codes.
    - *Example*: Giving a unique identifier to each individual instead of using their real names, such as Ram replaced with 001.
3. **Generalization**: To make data less specific and not provide exact details.
    - *Example*: Converting a date of birth from "March 10, 1992" to "March 20, 1992".
4. **Aggregation**: Summarizing data that refers to whole groups, not individuals.
    - *Example*: Instead of showing each income data, show the average income for a group.

5. **Data Swapping**: Interchanging data between individuals to mask their identity.
    - *Example*: Ram's date of birth is assigned to Sham, and Sham's date of birth is assigned to Ram.

Figure 15. Techniques for Anonymization.

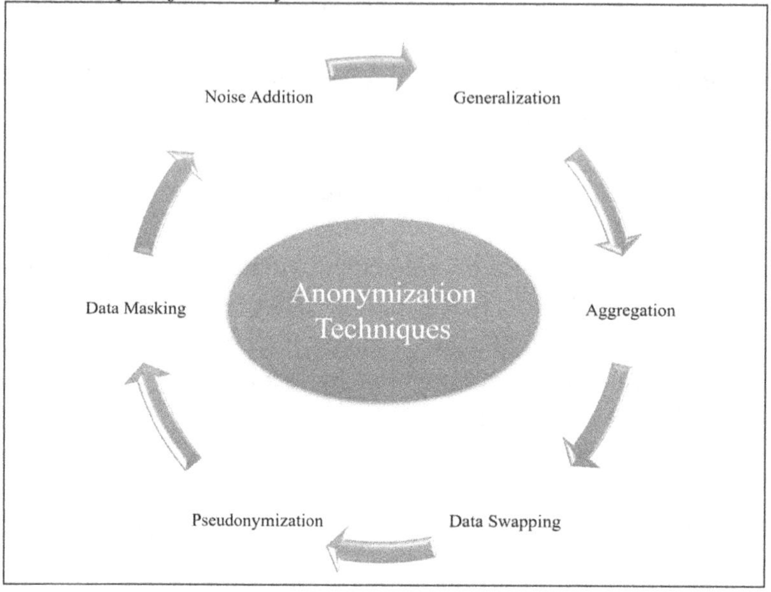

Challenges of Anonymization

1. **Re-Identification Risk**: If anonymized data is combined with other data sources, it is always possible to be matched with other data to identify persons.

Example: Suppose one dataset has a person's ages and codes but no names. However, another dataset has names and similar codes. Then, these two datasets will be matched to identify the person.

2. **Balance Between Privacy and Utility**: It is difficult to keep data useful after anonymization while protecting people's privacy.

Example: Generalizing ages and patient conditions can protect privacy but is less useful for medical research.

3. **Complexity and Cost**: Implementing anonymization techniques can be technically complex and expensive. Proper implementation requires advanced software and experts.

5.3. Privacy by Design

Privacy by Design (PbD) is the principle that data controllers protect individuals' data by embedding privacy measures into the initial design of systems (at architecture time). embedding strong security measures throughout the lifecycle of information. The basic concept is to protect data from the starting stage, integrating privacy controls and safeguards into the processes, such as implementing strong access controls, pseudonymization, encryption, anonymization techniques, and user consent mechanisms. Israeli Privacy Protection Authority and GDPR strongly encourage the implementation of PbD in system design (Kassem et al., 2025).

Key Principles of Privacy by Design

Privacy by Design is based on seven foundational principles (Padmakumari, 2024):

I. **Proactive, not Reactive:**
   - Aim to prevent privacy issues before they happen. This is a proactive rather than reactive approach to data privacy.

II. **Privacy as the Default Setting**
   - Ensure that data is automatically protected. The individual does not require action to protect their privacy—it is built into the system by default.

III. **Privacy Embedded into Design**
   - Integrate privacy measures into the design and architecture systems, making privacy a core component, not an add-on.

IV. **Full Functionality—Positive-Sum, not Zero-Sum**
   - Achieve a balance between privacy and other needs, ensuring privacy does not affect functionality.

V. **Full Lifecycle Protection**
   - Ensure that personal data is protected throughout its entire lifecycle, from collection to storage, use, and deletion.

VI. **Visibility and Transparency**
   - Maintain transparency, ensuring individuals can verify how their data is handled.

VII. **Keep it User-Centric**

- Design systems to keep the users in the center, offering strong privacy by default and having user-friendly options.

5.4. Identity and Access Management (IAM)

IAM Definition and Related Key Terms

Definition: Identity and Access Management (IAM) is a framework of policies and technologies that ensures the right person can access the right resources at the right time. It manages and protects users' identities and controls their access to sensitive data and systems within an organization. IAM integrates identity management (IDM) and access management systems (ACM), as shown in Figure 16. An IDM stores a user's identity information and verifies the user's identity to ensure safe access to resources. The ACM system ensures that a user can access only those resources that are assigned to the user for access. Various techniques for IAM are shown in Figure 17 (Aboukadri et al., 2024).

Figure 16. IAM Integration

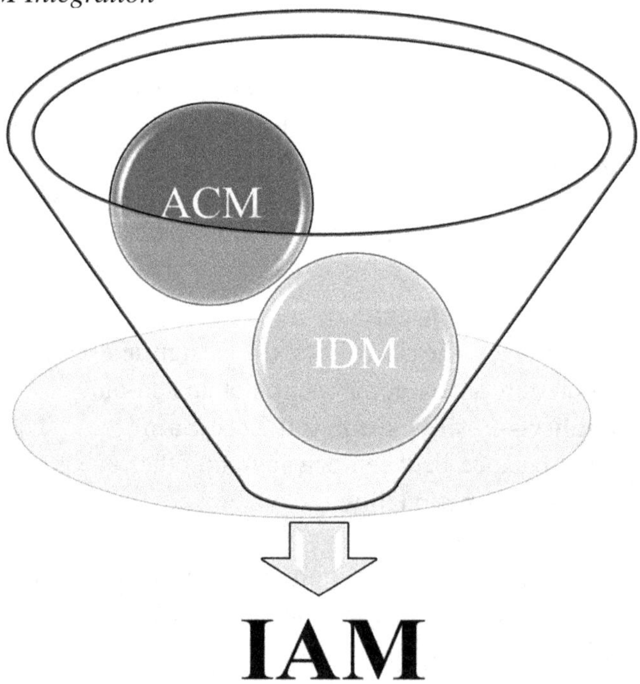

IAM Tools and Technologies:

1. **Authentication**:
    - The process of verifying the identity of a user using passwords, biometrics and two-factor authentication. Simply, it confirms that a user is the right person.
2. **Authorization**:
    - Determine what resources a user can access (permit specific service). This includes permissions and access rights.
3. **Single Sign-On (SSO)**:
    - A user authentication process that permits one to access multiple applications with one login credential.
4. **Multi-Factor Authentication (MFA)**:
    - An authentication method requires two or more verification methods, such as a password and OTP (One Time Password).
5. **Access Control**:
    - The practice of restricting access to resources based on users' roles and permissions.
6. **Role-Based Access Control (RBAC)**:
    - A policy restricting system access to authorized users based on their organizational role.
7. **Identity Federation**:
    - The practice of linking a user's identity across multiple systems or organizations, enabling them to use the same credentials across different platforms.
8. **Password Management**:
    - The processes and policies for creating, storing, and managing passwords.

Figure 17. IAM techniques

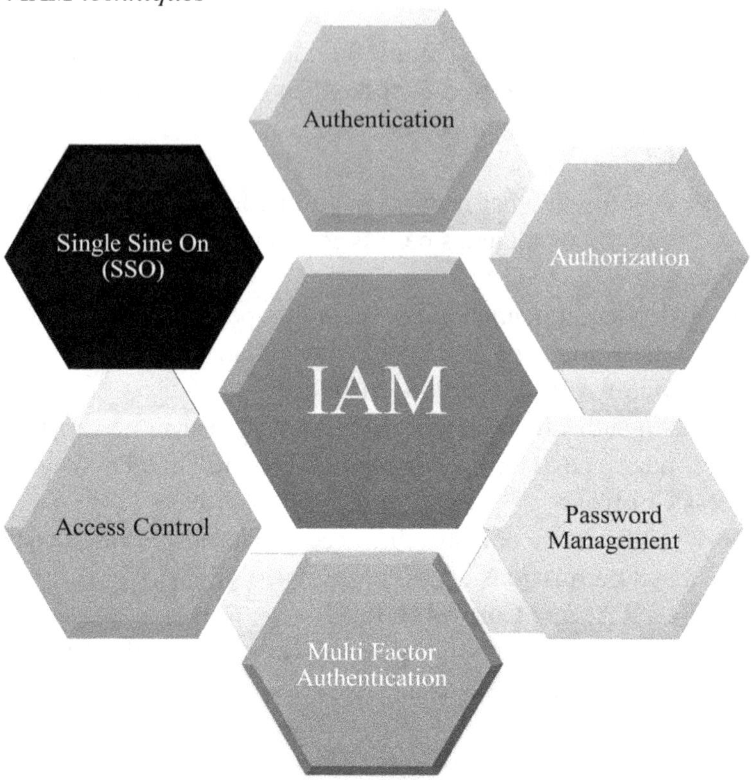

5.5. IAM Challenges

Implementing Identity and Access Management (IAM) has several challenges. Here are a few common ones (Liao et al., 2022):

1. Complexity of Systems

Integrating IAM with existing systems and applications can be complicated in large organizations with complex IT environments.

Example: Connecting IAM to older systems that are not designed with new security standards can be challenging.

2. User Management

Managing many users and their access rights can be difficult and time-consuming.

Example: Ensuring employees have access rights, updated or revoked when they change roles or leave the organization.

3. Security Risks

IAM has risks, such as weak passwords and phishing attacks

Example: A user may be affected by a phishing attack and unintentionally provide their login details to a malicious actor.

4. Scalability

IAM systems can scale to meet the organization's growing needs.

Example: Adding new users and applications quickly without compromising security.

6. COMPLIANCE AND LEGAL FRAMEWORKS

6.1. Global Regulations Impacting Cloud Security and Privacy

Several regulatory authorities are working to protect data privacy in the digital world. They are defining laws called data privacy regulations. Figure 18 shows these regulatory authorities.

I. **General Data Protection Regulation (GDPR)** (European Union).
II. **Health Insurance Portability and Accountability Act (HIPAA)** (United States).
III. **California Consumer Privacy Act (CCPA)** (United States).
IV. **Cybersecurity Law and Data Security Law (DSL)** (China).
V. **The Information Technology (IT) Act and Personal Data Protection Bill (PDPB)** (India).

Figure 18. Regulations Authorities

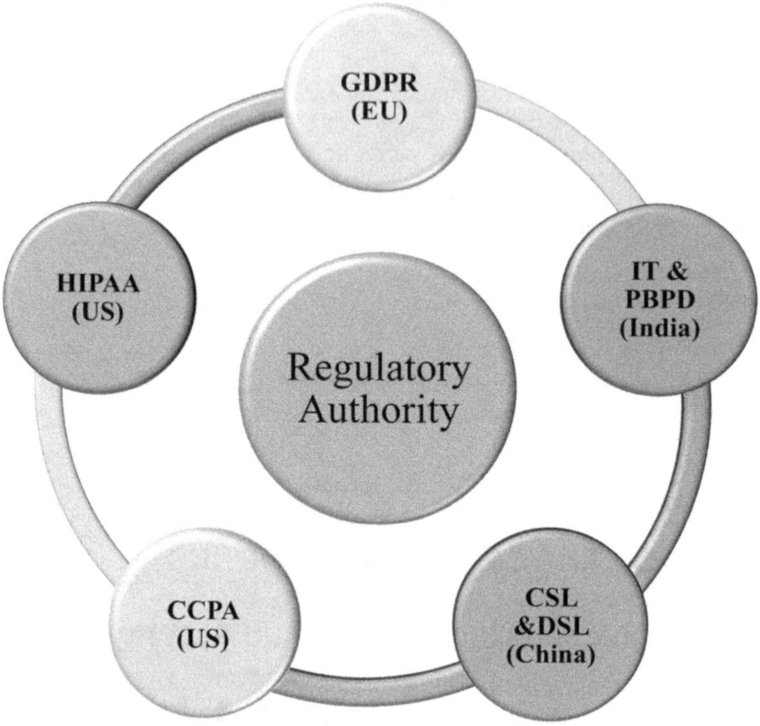

General Data Protection Regulation (GDPR)

Data privacy rules and laws serve as indispensable guardians in the digital world, defining the rules for collecting, processing, and sharing personal information. The EU GDPR (European Union General Data Protection Regulation), enacted in 2016 and started on May 25, 2018, represents a big step for data protection in the European Union. It grants individuals clear rights over their data, such as:

I) The right to know how their data is used.
II) The right to access their data.
III) The right to update their data.
IV) The right to erasure (delete) their data.
V) The right to decide to share their data.

Its goal is to give individuals more control over their data and to simplify the way organizations follow these rules internationally with lawfulness, fairness, and transparency. The GDPR law affects anyone who interacts with the personal data of EU citizens. There are three leading roles(Franke et al., 2024).

Key Principles of GDPR

1. **Lawfulness, Fairness, and Transparency**: Personal data must be processed lawfully, fairly, and transparently.
2. **Purpose Limitation**: Data must be collected for specified purposes and not further processed.
3. **Data Minimization**: Only required data for a specific purpose should be collected.
4. **Accuracy**: Personal data must be accurate and updated.
5. **Storage Limitation**: Data will be kept only as long as needed.
6. **Integrity and Confidentiality**: Data must be protected from unauthorized, illegal processing, accidental loss and damage (von Grafenstein et al., 2024).

Case Study

In May 2023, Meta—the company behind Facebook, Instagram, and WhatsApp—was fined €1.2 billion. This happened because Meta moved the personal data of people in Europe to the United States without proper privacy protections, which breaks EU privacy rules known as the GDPR (General Data Protection Regulation). This was the biggest fine ever given under these rules, and it's a big deal for how companies handle people's private information (https://dataprivacymanager.net/5-biggest-gdpr-fines-so-far-2020/).

Health Insurance Portability and Accountability Act (HIPAA)

The Health Insurance Portability and Accountability Act (HIPAA) is a United States (US) law that specifically protects the privacy and security of health information. Health information privacy laws set rules to ensure the security of patient health data. HIPAA ensures that patient health information is kept private and secure to ensure its confidentiality, integrity and timely availability (Seun Solomon Bakare et al., 2024).

HIPAA applies to:

- Healthcare providers.
- Health insurance plans.
- Healthcare clearinghouses.

Key Points:

Health information must be protected from illegal use to keep it confidential and secure.

Patients must be informed before their health information is shared or used (Evans & Jarvik, 2018)(Ray & Biswas, 2014).

Case Study

The Children's Medical Center in Dallas got into trouble because it didn't properly protect patients' private health information. In one case, a Blackberry phone was stolen, and it had personal data of about 3,800 patients on it. The problem was that the phone didn't have a password or any security to protect the information. The hospital had to pay a fine because employees used devices without enough security, even after knowing about the risks (https://sprinto.com/blog/examples-of-hipaa-violations/).

California Consumer Privacy Act (CCPA)

The California Consumer Privacy Act (CCPA) is a law (signed in 2018) that applies only in California and was implemented in 2020. This law helps Californians have more control over their personal information and how it is used (Seun Solomon Bakare et al., 2024).

It gives Californians specific rights over their personal information, including:

- The right to know what data is collected about them.
- The right not to the sale of their data.
- The right to know about the deletion of their data.

Case Study

A telehealth technology company's website had a link that sent consumers to the wrong section of their privacy policy, which violated the CCPA. Their privacy policy lacked important details like the information consumers needed to provide for verifiable consumer requests, the categories of personal information collected and disclosed in the past year, and the categories of third parties receiving this information(https://www.cookieyes.com/blog/ccpa-enforcement-case-examples/)

Ø **Cybersecurity Law and Data Security Law (DSL)** (China)

The Cybersecurity Law (CSL) of China, enacted on June 1, 2017, provides a comprehensive framework for the security of China's critical information infrastructure (CII), network operations, and personal information protection. The law establishes strict rules for businesses operating in China, especially those handling personal data or managing sensitive systems (Song, 2024).

Key Provisions:

a) Network Operator Obligations:
    - Companies defined as "network operators" must ensure their systems are secure, stable, and free of vulnerabilities.
    - Operators must implement technical safeguards to prevent unauthorized access, data breaches, and cyberattacks.

b) Data Localization:
    - Data classified as "critical" must be stored within China. This ensures that sensitive data remains under Chinese jurisdiction, protecting national security.

c) Personal Information Protection:
    - The law mandates transparency in data collection and usage. Businesses must obtain user consent (permission) before collecting personal data and ensure its confidentiality (privacy).

d) Penalties:
    - Noncompliance with the law can result in fines, business suspension, or criminal charges for serious violations.

Data Security Law (DSL) China

Effective September 1, 2021, the Data Security Law complements the CSL by focusing on data regulation and protection. Its goal is safeguarding national security, the public interest, and individual rights (Sun et al., 2021).

Key Provisions

i) Categorization of Data:

Data is categorized based on its importance to national security, the economy, and social stability. Data is classified as "core data," "important data," and "general data."

ii) Cross-Border Data Transfers:

Chinese authorities must assess the security of data transfers outside China. This ensures that sensitive data remains under Chinese jurisdiction and does not compromise national security.

iii) Data Abuse and Illegal Trade:

The DSL prohibits the illegal collection, sale, or leakage of data. Companies must prevent the misuse of data.

iv) Penalties:

Unfollowing these laws can result in fines up to CNY 10 million (about USD 1.4 million), the suspension of business operations, or the loss of business licenses.

Amendments

On March 28, 2025, China's main internet regulator (the CAC) proposed the Cybersecurity Law. This law first came out in 2016 and is one of China's main rules for protecting data and online safety. But since China made two newer laws in 2021—the Data Security Law (DSL) and the Personal Information Protection Law (PIPL), it has smaller fines. To fix this, the CAC first tried updating the law in 2022 by adding bigger penalties and making it match the newer laws. The CAC introduced a new set of rules called the Regulations on Network Data Security Management, which started being used on January 1, 2025(https://www.china-briefing.com/news/china-cybersecurity-law-amendments-2025/).

Information Technology (IT) Act and Personal Data Protection Bill (PDPB) India

India's Information Technology (IT) Act, 2000, and Personal Data Protection Bill (PDPB) are central to the country's regulatory framework for data security, privacy, and cybercrime (Dr. Amit Singh, 2024).

Information Technology (IT) Act

The IT Act provides a legal framework to address issues related to digital commerce, digital signatures, and cybercrimes in India.

Key Provisions:

- **Legal Recognition of Electronic Documents**: Recognizes electronic documents and digital signatures as valid.
- **Cybercrime**: This law defines various cybercrimes, such as hacking, data theft, and spreading viruses and defines punishments.
- **Data Protection**: Define provisions for protecting sensitive data. Section 43A mandates compensation (money or benefits) for failure to protect sensitive personal data.

Personal Data Protection Bill (PDPB)

The PDPB aims to protect individuals' personal data privacy and establish a framework for data protection in India.

Key Provisions:

- **Categories of Data:** Classify data as Personal Data (related to an individual, Sensitive Personal Data (SPD) (health, financial, biometric data), and Critical Personal Data (important for national security and requiring local storage).
- **Data Localization**: define certain types of personal data to be stored within India.
- **Consent (permission)**: This law requires an organization that handles data to obtain permission from a person before collecting and sharing their data.
- **Rights of Individuals**: Individuals should have full rights to access, correct, and delete their data.
- **Data Protection Authority**: Establishes a regulatory authority to manage and implement data protection laws.
- **Penalties**: Organizations not following the rules can face fines and criminal charges.

Amendments

In 2025, the Ministry of Electronics and Information Technology (MeitY) released the **Draft Digital Personal Data Protection Rules, 2025,** to support the implementation of the DPDP Act. These rules clarify how personal data should be processed, consent requirements, data breach notifications, and the role of the **Data Protection Board of India**.

7. FUTURE TRENDS IN CLOUD SECURITY AND PRIVACY

7.1. The Role of AI and Machine Learning in Threat Detection

AI and machine learning play an important role in threat detection by improving cybersecurity measures in several ways(Aboukadri et al., 2024)

1. **Real-Time Analysis**: AI systems can analyse large amounts of data in real time, identifying patterns and anomalies that might indicate a cyberattack. This helps us detect and respond to threats quickly.
2. **Predictive Capabilities**: Machine learning algorithms can learn from past attacks, predict potential vulnerabilities, and enable proactive defense procedures.
3. **Automated Responses**: AI can automate responses to security incidents and block malicious activities without human intervention.
4. **User Behaviour Monitoring**: AI can monitor user activity and detect unusual activity from normal behaviour patterns, helping to identify insider threats or compromised accounts (accounts accessed by unauthorized persons).

7.2. The Growing Need for Zero-Trust Architecture in Cloud (Amod et al., 2024).

Zero-trust architecture: No user or device can be trusted by default, whether inside or outside the network (all are untrusted). It requires continuous verification of all users and devices trying to access resources. This approach is helpful in the following:

1. **Enhance Security**: Zero-trust architectures reduce the risk of unauthorized access and lateral movement (attackers move within a network) within the network by continuously monitoring and validating access.
2. **Adapt to Modern Workflows**: With more employees working remotely and using various resources, zero-trust architectures ensure regular security across different environments.

7.3. Future of Cloud Computing

The future of cloud computing is promising and transformative, with several key trends and some key reasons explained below (Padmakumari, 2024):

1. **Multi-Cloud and Hybrid Cloud**: Organizations increasingly adopt multi-cloud and hybrid cloud strategies to optimize performance, cost, and flexibility.

2. **AI and Machine Learning**: Cloud platforms integrate AI and machine learning to enhance automation, analytics, and decision-making(Abdallah et al., 2024).

CONCLUSION

This chapter explores security challenges, threats, vulnerabilities, and their solutions at different layers in a cloud environment. It provides comprehensive knowledge about cloud security and privacy, discusses the importance of security, and explains all key terms related to security. This chapter explores security challenges in-depth at the SaaS, PaaS, and IaaS levels and offers wide guidance to cloud security and privacy. It will discuss the current state of cloud security, outline the most significant risks, and propose solutions for organizations and governments to safeguard their data. Various data security techniques are discussed, including cryptography, steganography, homomorphic cryptography, quantum cryptography, DNA cryptography, machine learning, deep learning, multi-factor authentication, and blockchain, along with the appropriate contexts for their use. The chapter also highlights GDPR, HIPAA, CCPA, DSL, the IT Act, and PDPB regulations. We can achieve robust security by combining technical solutions and following regulatory compliance rules. It describes the role of AI and machine learning in threat detection and the adoption of zero-trust architecture for enhancing data security in the cloud environment. Data security is a trending topic in the research field, and it demands continued research to maintain and improve security in the cloud environment.

REFERENCES

Abdallah, A. M., Saif, A., Obaid, R., Bark, G., Douman, N., Rafique, S. H., Musa, N. S., & Murugan, T. (2024). Cloud Network Anomaly Detection Using Machine and Deep Learning Techniques — Recent Research Advancements. *IEEE Access : Practical Innovations, Open Solutions*, *12*(April), 56749–56773. DOI: 10.1109/ACCESS.2024.3390844

Aboukadri, S., Ouaddah, A., & Mezrioui, A. (2024). Computers & Security Machine learning in identity and access management systems : Survey and deep dive. *Computers & Security*, *139*(January), 103729. DOI: 10.1016/j.cose.2024.103729

Abramson, M., Arbuckle, B., Baudoin, C., Dani, J., & DiPaula-Coyle, M. (2017). Data Residency Challenges A Joint Paper with the Object Management Group®. *Cloud Standards Customer Council, May*, 1–33. http://www.cloud-council.org/deliverables/CSCC-Data-Residency-Challenges.pdf

Alkhalifah, E. S. (2024). Password based authentication for web based graphics computing services retrieval in cloud. *Multimedia Tools and Applications*, *0123456789*(36), 84357–84379. Advance online publication. DOI: 10.1007/s11042-024-19044-8

Amod, A., Karyakarte, M., Chavhan, G., Patil, M., Talware, R., & Kulkarni, L. (2024). Measurement : Sensors Blockchain aware decentralized identity management and access control system. *Measurement. Sensors*, *31*(January), 101032. DOI: 10.1016/j.measen.2024.101032

Azam, H., Tajwar, M. A., Mayhialagan, S., Davis, A. J., Yik, C. J., Ali, D., & Sindiramutty, S. R. (2023). Innovations in Security : A Study of Cloud Computing and IoT. *International Journal of Emerging Multidisciplinaries.*, *2*(1), 1–29. DOI: 10.54938/ijemdcsai.2023.02.1.252

Bakare, S. S., Adeniyi, A. O., Akpuokwe, C. U., & Eneh, N. E. (2024). Data Privacy Laws and Compliance: A Comparative Review of the Eu Gdpr and Usa Regulations. *Computer Science & IT Research Journal*, *5*(3), 528–543. DOI: 10.51594/csitrj.v5i3.859

Baker, S. A. (2024). Preserving Big Data Privacy in Cloud Environments Based on Homomorphic Encryption and Distributed Clustering. NTU Journal of Engineering and Technology, 3(1).

Bende, P., Vovk, O., Caraveo, D., Pechmann, L., & Leucker, M. (2024). A Case Study on Data Protection for a Cloud- and AI-Based Homecare Medical Device. *Lecture Notes in Computer Science (Including Subseries Lecture Notes in Artificial Intelligence and Lecture Notes in Bioinformatics), 14150 LNCS*, 138–161. DOI: 10.1007/978-3-662-68191-6_6

Bermani, A. K., Murshedi, T., & Abod, Z. A. (2021). A hybrid cryptography technique for data storage on cloud computing. *Journal of Discrete Mathematical Sciences and Cryptography*, *24*(July), 1613–1624. Advance online publication. DOI: 10.1080/09720529.2020.1859799

Cherbal, S., Zier, A., Hebal, S., Louail, L., & Annane, B. (2024). Security in internet of things: a review on approaches based on blockchain, machine learning, cryptography, and quantum computing. In *The Journal of Supercomputing* (Vol. 80, Issue 3). Springer US. DOI: 10.1007/s11227-023-05616-2

Dominguez, T., & Laura, A. (2024). The state of art, opportunities and challenges of blockchain in the insurance industry : a systematic literature review. *Management Review Quarterly*, 1097–1118.

Singh, A., & Chauhan, P. S. (2023). Navigating Digital Legislation: A Comprehensive Analysis of India's It Act And Emerging Cyber Security Challenges. *Jisuanji Jicheng Zhizao Xitong*, *29*(4), 297–321.

Evans, B. J., & Jarvik, G. P. (2018). Impact of HIPAA's minimum necessary standard on genomic data sharing. *Genetics in Medicine*, *20*(5), 531–535. DOI: 10.1038/gim.2017.141 PMID: 28914268

Fatima, E., Sumra, I. A., & Naveed, R. (2024). A Comprehensive Survey on Security Threats and Challenges in Cloud Computing Models (SaaS, PaaS and IaaS). *Journal of Computing & Biomedical Informatics*, *07*(01).

Franke, L., Tech, V., Brantly, A., Davis, J. C., & Brown, C. (2024). An Exploratory Mixed-methods Study on General Data Protection Regulation (GDPR) Compliance in Open-Source Software. *ACM*, 325–336. DOI: 10.1145/3674805.3686692

Goswami, P., Faujdar, N., Debnath, S., Khan, A. K., & Singh, G. (2024). Investigation on storage level data integrity strategies in cloud computing : Classification, security obstructions, challenges and vulnerability. *Journal of Cloud Computing (Heidelberg, Germany)*, *13*(1), 45. Advance online publication. DOI: 10.1186/s13677-024-00605-z

Kassem, J. A., Müller, T., Esterhuyse, C. A., Kebede, M. G., Osseyran, A., & Grosso, P. (2025). The EPI framework : A data privacy by design framework to support healthcare use cases . *Future Generation Computer Systems, 165*(October 2024), 107550. DOI: 10.1016/j.future.2024.107550

Liao, C., Guan, X., Cheng, J., & Yuan, S. (2022). Blockchain-based identity management and access control framework for open banking ecosystem. *Future Generation Computer Systems*, *135*, 450–466. DOI: 10.1016/j.future.2022.05.015

Longo, G., Lupia, F., Merlo, A., Pagano, F., & Russo, E. (2025). A data anonymization methodology for security operations centers: Balancing data protection and security in industrial systems. *Information Sciences, 690*(September 2024), 121534. DOI: 10.1016/j.ins.2024.121534

Padmakumari, P. S. S. V. P. (2024). Privacy - preserving cloud - based secure digital locker with differential privacy - based deep learning technique. *Multimedia Tools and Applications*, *83*(34), 81299–81324. DOI: 10.1007/s11042-024-18566-5

Rajguru, S. S., Singh, G., Malhi, S. S., & Kaur, G. (2024). Stenographic Approaches for Enhancing Data Security in Cloud Computing. *E3S Web of Conferences, 01012*, 1–7.

Ray, S., & Biswas, G. P. (2014). A Certificate Authority (CA)-based cryptographic solution for HIPAA privacy/security regulations. *Journal of King Saud University. Computer and Information Sciences*, *26*(2), 170–180. DOI: 10.1016/j.jksuci.2013.10.001

Reddy, C. K. V. K. V. L. (2024). A novel deep learning technique with cryptographic transformation for enhancing data security in cloud environments. *Multimedia Tools and Applications*, *0123456789*(8), 5149–5173. Advance online publication. DOI: 10.1007/s11042-024-18903-8

Reddy, H. M. K. T. V. (2024). Secure gene profile data processing using lightweight cryptography and blockchain. *Cluster Computing*, *27*(3), 2785–2803. DOI: 10.1007/s10586-023-04123-6

Sasikumar, K., & Nagarajan, S. (2024). Comprehensive Review and Analysis of Cryptography Techniques in Cloud Computing. *IEEE Access : Practical Innovations, Open Solutions*, *12*(March), 52325–52351. DOI: 10.1109/ACCESS.2024.3385449

Savadatti, S., Cherukuri, A. K., Jonnalagadda, A., & Vasilakos, A. V. (2025). Analysis of quantum fully homomorphic encryption schemes (QFHE) and hierarchial memory management for QFHE. *Complex & Intelligent Systems*, *11*(6), 1–28. DOI: 10.1007/s40747-025-01851-7

Selvakumar, K., & Lokesh, S. (2024). A cryptographic method to have a secure communication of health care digital data into the cloud. *Automatika (Zagreb), 65*(1), 373–386. DOI: 10.1080/00051144.2023.2301240

Song, Z. (2024). Personal data security and stock crash risk: Evidence from China's Cybersecurity Law. *China Journal of Accounting Research, 17*(4), 100393. DOI: 10.1016/j.cjar.2024.100393

Sun, L., Zhang, H., & Fang, C. (2021). Data security governance in the era of big data: Status, challenges, and prospects. *Data Science and Management, 2*(June), 41–44. DOI: 10.1016/j.dsm.2021.06.001

Suryateja, P. S. (2018). Threats and Vulnerabilities of Cloud Computing A Review. *International Journal on Computer Science and Engineering, 6*(3), 297–302. DOI: 10.26438/ijcse/v6i3.297302

Tabrizchi, H., & Rafsanjani, M. K. (2020). A survey on security challenges in cloud computing: issues, threats, and solutions. In *The Journal of Supercomputing* (Vol. 76, Issue 12). Springer US. DOI: 10.1007/s11227-020-03213-1

von Grafenstein, M., Kiefaber, I., Heumüller, J., Rupp, V., Graßl, P., Kolless, O., & Puzst, Z. (2024). Privacy icons as a component of effective transparency and controls under the GDPR: Effective data protection by design based on art. 25 GDPR. *Computer Law & Security Review, 52*(January), 105924. Advance online publication. DOI: 10.1016/j.clsr.2023.105924

Wang, P., Yuan, N., & Li, Y. (2025). An Integrated Framework for Data Security Using Advanced Machine Learning Classification and Best Practices. *Informatica (Slovenia), 49*(12), 191–206. DOI: 10.31449/inf.v49i12.7838

Zhao, B., Ji, Y., Shi, Y., & Jiang, X. (2024). Design and implementation of privacy-preserving federated learning algorithm for consumer IoT. *Alexandria Engineering Journal, 106*(June), 206–216. DOI: 10.1016/j.aej.2024.06.071

Chapter 7
Blockchain-Based Security for Cloud Data Storage

Mamoon M. Saeed
https://orcid.org/0000-0002-6081-2559
University of Modern Sciences, Yemen

Zeinab E. Ahmed
https://orcid.org/0000-0002-6144-8533
University of Gezira, Sudan

Rania A. Mokhtar
https://orcid.org/0000-0001-9221-4214
Sudan University of Science and Technology, Sudan

Rashid A. Saeed
https://orcid.org/0000-0002-9872-081X
Sudan University of Science and Technology, Sudan

ABSTRACT

Blockchain technology has shown promise to improve security across several industries, including cloud data storage. The integration of blockchain technology with safe cloud data storage solutions is examined in this chapter. Data integrity, secrecy, and authentication in cloud storage systems can be greatly enhanced by utilizing the decentralized and immutable nature of blockchain. Important ideas about cloud data security are covered, including distributed consensus, smart contracts, and cryptographic hashing. The chapter also explores the difficulties, advantages, and potential avenues for future research in applying blockchain technology to improve cloud data storage security.

DOI: 10.4018/979-8-3693-9984-2.ch007

1. INTRODUCTION

The combination of blockchain technology and cloud data storage is a shining example of innovation in the ever-evolving field of data protection and storage, with the potential to revolutionize how businesses safeguard and handle their priceless information assets. This chapter delves deeply into the transformative potential of this combination in strengthening data security settings by thoroughly examining the synergies between blockchain and cloud storage. The traditional ideas of data security are being redefined as contemporary businesses struggle with the exponential development of data quantities and the necessity of protecting sensitive information against a changing threat landscape.

A key component of contemporary data management systems, cloud storage solutions provide cost-effectiveness, scalability, and flexibility. However, typical cloud storage models' centralized structure has highlighted weaknesses such as data breaches, illegal access, and the possibility of data tampering (Idrus et al., 2023). Given this, blockchain technology stands out as a disruptive force that provides an immutable, transparent, and decentralized architecture for cloud data security.

Blockchain has the potential to completely transform data security paradigms by utilizing distributed consensus mechanisms, smart contracts, and cryptographic approaches to guarantee data integrity, confidentiality, and auditability in cloud storage ecosystems. This academic collection's chapters are carefully written to negotiate the complex relationships between blockchain technology and the security of cloud data storage. This chapter explores the subtleties of blockchain-based security mechanisms designed to handle the particular difficulties presented by cloud storage systems through a combination of theoretical discussion, real-world case studies, and practical insights. This will help them move toward a future in which data security is not only a compliance requirement but also a strategic imperative that is woven into the very fabric of organizational resilience and trust (M. M. A. Saeed et al., 2024).

This chapter investigates how blockchain technology might improve cloud data storage systems' security protocols. Exploring their integration seeks to clarify how blockchain properties like immutability, decentralization, and cryptographic hashing might strengthen data integrity, secrecy, and authentication in cloud storage systems. The chapter provides an in-depth examination of blockchain-based security solutions to shed light on the advantages, difficulties, and potential applications of blockchain technology to protect cloud data.

1.1 Definition and Overview

A distributed, decentralized ledger system known as blockchain technology serves as the foundation for several online transactions and data management procedures. A blockchain is essentially a series of blocks, each of which contains a list of transactions, connected cryptographically to form an unchangeable and safe record of information. The initial cryptocurrency, Bitcoin, brought this technology to the public's attention, but it has subsequently been used in a variety of sectors outside of finance. A blockchain comprises a network of computers, or nodes, that cooperate to verify and log transactions. After passing through a validation process, each transaction is bundled into a block and appended to the current chain (Zachariadis et al., 2019).

Usually, a consensus method like Proof of Work (PoW) or Proof of Stake (PoS) is used to accomplish this validation. This ensures all nodes concur that a transaction is legitimate before it is added to the blockchain. Immutability is one of the main characteristics of blockchain technology. Without the agreement of the majority of nodes in the network, it becomes very difficult to change the contents of a block once it has been added to the chain. The immutability of the data recorded on the blockchain guarantees its security and integrity, making it impenetrable to fraud and illegal changes. The transparency of blockchain technology is another essential component (Sheikh et al., 2018).

There is a high level of openness and visibility into the transaction history since blockchain transactions are documented on a public ledger that is available to all network users. In addition to lowering costs and increasing efficiency, this transparency increases user trust and does away with the need for middlemen in many transactions. By using cryptographic algorithms, blockchain technology also makes increased security possible (Mamoon M Saeed, Rashid A Saeed, Elmustafa Sayed Ali, et al., 2024). Cryptographic methods that preserve data integrity and verify user identity safeguard transactions on the blockchain. Hash functions, digital signatures, and public key cryptography are frequently employed to guarantee the confidentiality and security of blockchain transactions (Saeed et al., 2021).

Decentralization, transparency, immutability, and security are the main tenets of blockchain technology. By utilizing these fundamental ideas, blockchain can transform several sectors by facilitating safe and effective data management procedures in a decentralized and transparent way, removing middlemen, and introducing trustless transactions (Mazhar et al., 2024; Ølnes et al., 2017).

1.2 Historical Evolution of Blockchain

Beginning in the early 1990s, blockchain technology has had an intriguing historical development. Table 1 provides a concise summary of the evolution of blockchain over time.

Table 1. Historical Evolution of Blockchain

Blockchain Evolution	Concept	Discussing
Predecessors and Foundations (1980s - 2000s)	**Cryptographic Roots**	Concepts like cryptographic hash functions and digital signatures laid the groundwork for secure digital transactions.
	Cypherpunk Movement	Pioneering work by cypherpunks like David Chaum and Nick Szabo explored digital currencies and secure protocols.
Bitcoin and the Genesis Block (2009)	**Satoshi Nakamoto**	The pseudonymous creator of Bitcoin introduced the concept of a decentralized, peer-to-peer electronic cash system.
	Genesis Block	The release of the Bitcoin whitepaper in 2008 and the mining of the first block, known as the genesis block, in 2009 marked the birth of blockchain technology.
Early Development and Diversification	**Altcoins and Forks**	The emergence of alternative cryptocurrencies and blockchain forks expanded the use cases and variations of blockchain technology.
	Ethereum and Smart Contracts	Vitalik Buterin's creation of Ethereum introduced smart contracts, enabling programmable, self-executing agreements on the blockchain.
Enterprise Adoption and Innovation (2010s - Present)	**Hyperledger and Enterprise Blockchains**	Projects like Hyperledger and R3 Corda facilitated the adoption of blockchain in enterprise settings.
	Interoperability and Scalability	Research and development efforts focused on enhancing blockchain scalability, interoperability, and privacy.

1.3 Key Characteristics and Principles of Blockchain

The fundamental features and tenets of blockchain technology set it apart from conventional databases and support its special powers. Some of the core features and tenets of blockchain are listed in Table 2.

Table 2. Principles of Blockchain

Blockchain Principles	Discussing
Decentralization	Blockchain operates on a decentralized network of nodes, eliminating the need for a central authority and distributing control among participants.
Transparency	Transactions recorded on the blockchain are transparent and visible to all network participants, fostering trust and accountability.
Immutability	Once data is recorded on the blockchain, it is nearly impossible to alter or delete, ensuring the integrity and permanence of the ledger.
Security	Cryptographic techniques such as digital signatures and hash functions secure transactions, protecting against fraud and unauthorized modifications.
Consensus Mechanisms	Consensus algorithms like Proof of Work (PoW) and Proof of Stake (PoS) ensure agreement among network participants on the validity of transactions.
Smart Contracts	Self-executing smart contracts on platforms like Ethereum enable automated agreements based on predefined conditions, enhancing efficiency and reducing the need for intermediaries.
Scalability and Interoperability	Ongoing research and development efforts focus on enhancing blockchain scalability, interoperability between different blockchain networks, and integration with existing systems.
Privacy and Permissions	Innovations in privacy-enhancing technologies and permissioned blockchains address concerns around data privacy and regulatory compliance in various use cases.

2. FUNDAMENTALS OF BLOCKCHAIN TECHNOLOGY

The fundamental ideas of blockchain technology form the cornerstone of creative approaches to safeguarding cloud data storage settings in the field of contemporary data security and storage. The in-depth chapter in the extensive book "Blockchain-Based Security for Cloud Data Storage" explores the foundations of blockchain technology, clarifying the key ideas and workings that support safe and open data management in cloud storage environments (Maldonado-Ruiz et al., 2022).

Blockchain's capacity to produce an unchangeable record of transactions is one of its main tenets. A blockchain is made up of a series of cryptographically connected blocks, each of which carries a cryptographic hash of the one before it. This eliminates the possibility of tampering with previous records while simultaneously guaranteeing the integrity of data (Dinh et al., 2018).

By automating and upholding agreements between participants, smart contracts—self-executing contracts with predetermined conditions stored in code—further expand the potential of blockchain technology (Z. E. Ahmed, et al., 2024a). Decentralized applications (DApps) that may transparently and impenetrably carry out intricate business logic are made possible by smart contracts.

Furthermore, users may keep control over their data and digital assets without depending on centralized middlemen because of the decentralized nature of blockchain technology, which also decentralizes access control methods. Users can safely access, move, and manage their data within blockchain networks using public and private key encryption, guaranteeing data privacy and confidentiality (M. Saeed et al., 2024).

This section attempts to provide readers with a firm grasp of the fundamental ideas that underpin safe data storage in cloud environments by exploring the complexities of blockchain technology as shown in Figure 1. In the digital age, companies may strengthen their data security protocols and cultivate a culture of trust, accountability, and transparency by utilizing the intrinsic qualities of blockchain technology.

With its decentralized and secure framework for managing information assets in cloud environments, blockchain technology has become a disruptive force in the field of data protection and storage. In the chapter on "Blockchain-Based Security for Cloud Data Storage," it is crucial to comprehend the foundations of blockchain technology in order to recognize the creative ways it strengthens cloud data security (Maldonado-Ruiz et al., 2022).

Figure 1. Fundamentals of Blockchain Technology

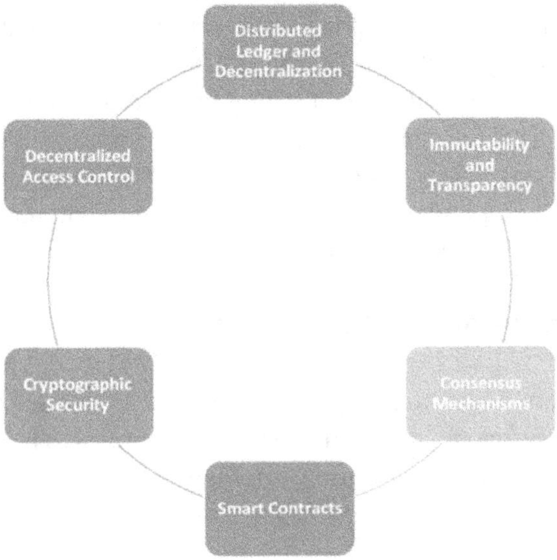

The decentralized nature of blockchain technology is its fundamental component. Transparency and robustness are ensured by storing data throughout a network of nodes rather than depending on a single authority. Consensus procedures are employed to verify transactions and guarantee data integrity, and each node keeps a copy of the ledger.

Once data is recorded in a block, it cannot be altered thanks to the design of blockchain technology. Any effort to change historical records is readily identifiable through the use of cryptographic hashing and chaining blocks. This feature increases user trust and improves data integrity.

Smart contracts are self-executing agreements with coded conditions that are predetermined. They do away with the need for middlemen by automating the implementation of contracts and transactions. The creation of decentralized applications (DApps) that function securely and transparently on the blockchain is made possible by smart contracts (Nzuva, 2019).

The foundation of blockchain security is public-key cryptography. Secure authentication and data encryption are made possible by the public and private keys that users possess. Only authorized parties will be able to view and interact with data on the blockchain thanks to this cryptographic security.

By decentralizing access control systems, blockchain technology enables users to safely manage their data independently of centralized organizations. Within the blockchain network, users may manage who can read, edit, and access their data using cryptographic keys and permission settings.

Readers of this section will have a strong basis to investigate how blockchain technology can be used to improve data security in cloud storage environments by understanding its basic principles (Z. E. Ahmed, 2024). One possible approach to addressing the changing issues of data safety and confidentiality in the digital era is the incorporation of blockchain-based security measures.

2.1 Core Components of Blockchain

Blockchain technology is made up of some essential parts that combine to form a safe, decentralized system for data and transaction recording. The essential elements of a typical blockchain system are shown in Figure 2.

Figure 2. Components of Blockchain.

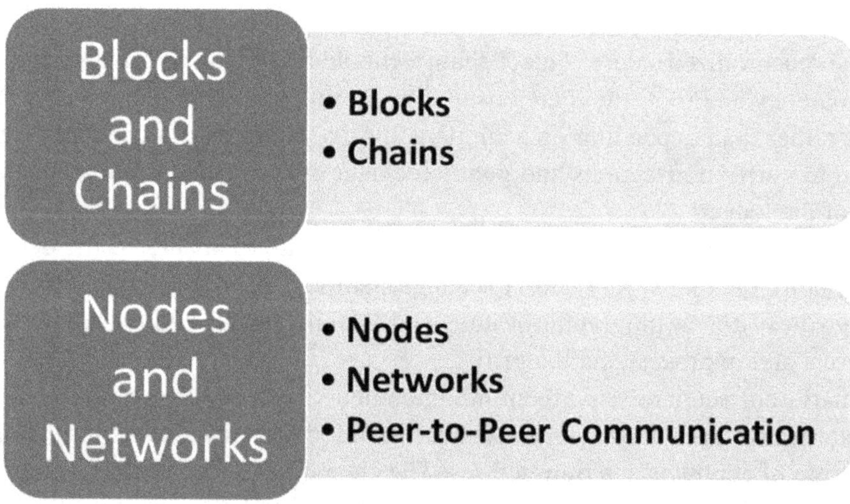

A. **Blocks and Chains**

The core building blocks of blockchain technology are blocks and chains, which combine to form a safe, decentralized system for storing data and transactions. Blocks and chains in a blockchain setting are broken down as follows:

- **Blocks:**
  - ✓ In blockchain technology, data is stored in blocks, each containing a list of transactions. These blocks are linked together in a chronological order.
  - ✓ Each block typically includes a cryptographic hash of the previous block, creating a chain of blocks that form the blockchain.
  - ✓ The information stored in blocks is immutable, meaning that once a block is added to the chain, it cannot be altered without affecting all subsequent blocks.
- **Chains:**
  - ✓ The chain in blockchain refers to the linear sequence of blocks that are linked together through cryptographic hashes.
  - ✓ The hash of each block is calculated based on the content of the block, including the transactions it contains and the hash of the previous block.
  - ✓ This chaining mechanism ensures the integrity of the data stored in the blockchain by making it tamper-evident. Any attempt to modify a block would require changing all subsequent blocks in the chain, making it computationally infeasible to alter the blockchain's history (Aggarwal & Kumar, 2021).

B. **Nodes and Networks**

- **Nodes:**
  - ✓ Nodes are individual computers or devices that participate in the blockchain network by maintaining a copy of the ledger and validating transactions.
  - ✓ Nodes can be categorized as full nodes, which store a complete copy of the blockchain, or lightweight nodes which rely on full nodes for verification.
  - ✓ Each node in the network contributes to the decentralized nature of the blockchain by independently verifying and validating transactions, ensuring consensus among all participants.
- **Networks:**
  - ✓ Blockchain networks can be classified into different types based on their accessibility and permission levels, such as public, private, and consortium blockchains.
  - ✓ Public blockchains are open to anyone and allow for permissionless participation, while private blockchains restrict access to authorized entities.

- ✓ Consortium blockchains are governed by a group of organizations that jointly manage the network, providing a balance between decentralization and control.

- **Peer-to-Peer Communication:**
  - ✓ Nodes in a blockchain network communicate with each other using a peer-to-peer protocol, enabling direct interaction without the need for intermediaries.
  - ✓ This decentralized communication model ensures that transactions are broadcasted and validated across the network transparently and securely.
  - ✓ Peer-to-peer communication facilitates the consensus process, where nodes collectively agree on the validity of transactions and maintain the integrity of the blockchain ledger.

2.2 Consensus Mechanisms and Security

- **Proof of Work (PoW):**
  - ✓ PoW is a consensus algorithm where nodes compete to solve complex mathematical puzzles to validate transactions and create new blocks.
  - ✓ Miners expend computational power to find the correct solution, and the first miner to solve the puzzle broadcasts the solution to the network.
  - ✓ PoW is used in networks like Bitcoin and ensures that the majority of the network agrees on the order and validity of transactions.
- **Proof of Stake (PoS):**
  - ✓ PoS selects validators to create new blocks based on the number of coins they hold or stake in the network.
  - ✓ Validators are chosen in a deterministic manner, with their likelihood of being selected proportional to their stake.
  - ✓ PoS is more energy-efficient compared to PoW but still ensures network security by penalizing malicious validators.
- **Delegated Proof of Stake (DPoS):**
  - ✓ DPoS is a variation of PoS where token holders vote for a set of delegates to validate transactions and produce blocks.
  - ✓ Delegates take turns producing blocks, and their authority is based on the votes they receive from the community.
  - ✓ DPoS is known for its scalability and fast block generation times, making it suitable for applications requiring high transaction throughput.

2.3. Security Features

- **Cryptography and Encryption:**

- ✓ Blockchain relies on cryptographic techniques like hash functions and digital signatures to secure transactions and data integrity.
- ✓ Hash functions ensure that data in blocks is tamper-proof, while digital signatures verify the authenticity of transactions.
- ✓ Encryption techniques protect sensitive data stored on the blockchain, ensuring confidentiality and privacy.

- **Decentralization and Immutability:**
  - ✓ The decentralized nature of blockchain ensures that no single entity has control over the network, enhancing security and resilience against attacks.
  - ✓ Immutability guarantees that once a block is added to the chain, it cannot be altered without consensus from the majority of nodes, making it resistant to tampering.
- **Tamper-Resistance and Transparency:**
  - ✓ Blockchain's append-only structure and cryptographic hashes make it difficult for malicious actors to alter historical data.
  - ✓ The transparent nature of blockchain allows all network participants to verify transactions and track the flow of assets, promoting trust and accountability.

2.4. Security Challenges and Mitigation

- **51% Attacks:**
  - ✓ In PoW networks, a 51% attack occurs when a single entity controls the majority of the network's mining power, enabling it to manipulate transactions.
  - ✓ Mitigation strategies include increasing network hash rate, implementing checkpoints, and transitioning to alternative consensus mechanisms like PoS.
- **Double-Spending:**
  - ✓ Double-spending is a scenario where a user spends the same cryptocurrency twice.
  - ✓ Consensus mechanisms like PoW and PoS prevent double-spending by ensuring that only valid transactions are added to the blockchain.
- **Smart Contract Vulnerabilities:**
  - ✓ Smart contracts are susceptible to bugs and vulnerabilities that can be exploited by attackers.
  - ✓ Auditing smart contract code, using formal verification techniques, and implementing secure development practices helps mitigate risks associated with smart contracts.

3. BLOCKCHAIN INTEGRATION IN CLOUD DATA STORAGE

An innovative convergence that could transform data security paradigms and change the information management environment is the use of blockchain technology in cloud data storage. In the chapter book "Blockchain-Based Security for Cloud Data Storage," the investigation of blockchain integration in cloud environments reveals a mosaic of creative fixes and game-changing opportunities that could raise data security to previously unheard-of heights (Khanna et al., 2022).

Businesses can strengthen data security by utilizing blockchain technology in cloud data storage, which offers a decentralized and unchangeable structure. Blockchain's resistance to tampering reduces the possibility of intentional tampering, data breaches, and unwanted access by guaranteeing that data stored in the cloud is safe and unchangeable, as shown in Figure 3. Cloud data storage gains a new degree of trust and transparency thanks to blockchain's visible and auditable features. Stakeholders can precisely trace the history of data access and modifications thanks to the blockchain's ability to verify and trace every transaction. In cloud contexts, this transparency strengthens data integrity and promotes accountability.

Figure 3. Blockchain Integration in Cloud Data Storage.

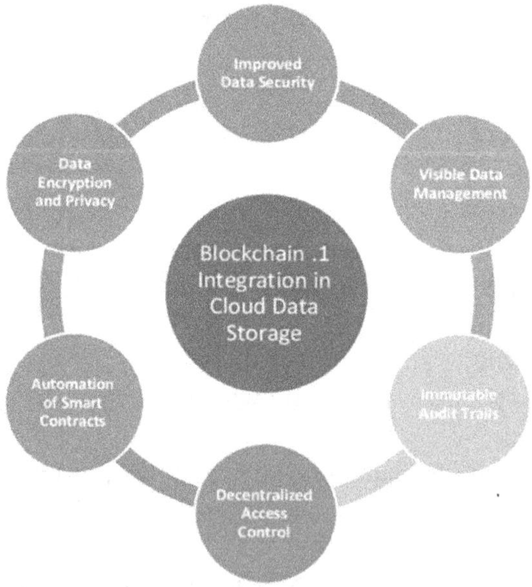

By integrating blockchain technology with cloud storage, customers may still keep control over their data without depending on centralized middlemen. Granular access controls can be implemented by businesses using smart contracts and cryptographic keys to make sure that only authorized parties can access data. Blockchain technology makes it easier to create immutable audit trails in cloud data storage, which offer a thorough trace of all data operations and transactions. By acting as a verifiable record of data transactions, these audit trails let companies track the origins of data and prove that they comply with legal obligations.

This section examines the complex relationship between blockchain technology and cloud data storage, guiding readers through the challenges of incorporating blockchain-based security measures to strengthen data protection in cloud settings. In the digital age, the knowledge gained from this investigation opens the door to a future in which data security is not only a matter of compliance but also a strategic necessity that is interwoven with organizational trust and resilience.

3.1 Decentralized Data Security

The decentralized data security paradigm is at the forefront of innovation in the current data security landscape, providing a revolutionary method of protecting data assets in cloud storage environments. The chapter book "Blockchain-Based Security for Cloud Data Storage," which examines decentralized data security, reveals a significant change in how businesses view and strengthen the availability, confidentiality, and integrity of their data by leveraging blockchain technology (Ge et al., 2020).

The maintenance of data integrity by immutability is one of the defining characteristics of decentralized data security. Businesses may guarantee the integrity of their data housed in cloud settings by documenting data transactions on a tamper-resistant blockchain ledger, reducing the possibility of data tampering, corruption, or unauthorized changes. By offering fine-grained access controls and cryptographic encryption, decentralized data security enables enterprises to fortify data privacy safeguards in cloud storage. Sensitive information can be protected from unwanted access by using secure key handling and decentralized access management systems, maintaining privacy and confidentiality as shown in Figure 4.

Figure 4. Decentralized Data Security.

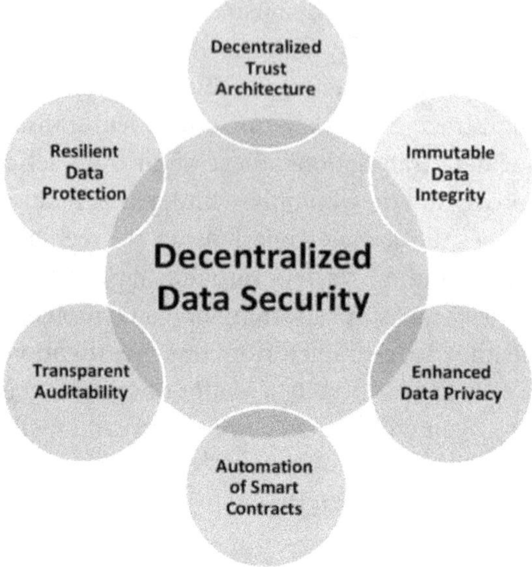

By producing an unchangeable record of data transactions and activities, blockchain integration with decentralized data security makes transparent auditability possible. Organizations can use this audit trail to trace the history of data transactions, confirm adherence to legal requirements, and exhibit openness in data management procedures inside cloud storage ecosystems.

Blockchain-based cloud storage's decentralized data protection improves resistance to cyberattacks and data breaches. Organizations can strengthen their data against single points of failure, guaranteeing continuous availability and defense against malevolent attacks, by distributing data among a network of nodes and putting consensus procedures in place. By automating data management procedures and implementing business rules in cloud storage environments, smart contracts are essential to decentralized data security. Organizations may automate data access restrictions, enforce data governance principles, and simplify data transactions with accuracy and efficiency by using self-executing contracts.

3.2 Key Components of Blockchain Integration

Smart contracts, which provide automated execution of established rules and conditions recorded in code, are a game-changing technology in the field of data management. These contracts function on blockchain networks, guaranteeing data transactions' security, immutability, and transparency. Smart contracts simplify data management procedures and lessen the need for manual intervention by enabling safe and automated data operations, access controls, and data-sharing agreements.

The capacity of smart contracts to automate data chores, including permissions management, access control enforcement, and data validation, is one of their main benefits. Smart contracts use cryptographic techniques to protect data integrity and confidentiality, improving data security and dependability through decentralized blockchain technology (Reyna et al., 2018). Because blockchain technology is transparent, all data transactions carried out by smart contracts are documented on the ledger, allowing stakeholders to audit operations and monitor changes over time.

In real-world applications, smart contracts are essential for identity management, supply chain traceability, and data-sharing agreements. By establishing rules for data usage, payment methods, and access rights, they facilitate safe and automatic data-sharing agreements. Smart contracts ensure transparency and compliance in supply chains by tracking certificates, transactional data, and product provenance.

However, issues like scalability constraints in blockchain networks and security flaws in smart contracts must be resolved. To reduce risks, it is crucial to secure smart contract code, use safe coding techniques, and carry out exhaustive testing. Furthermore, performance issues in data-intensive applications can be resolved by investigating scalability options and optimizing smart contract architecture.

Organizations can automate data workflows, optimize resource allocation, and improve decision-making processes by integrating smart contracts with artificial intelligence (AI) and Internet of Things (IoT) technologies. This integration offers opportunities for autonomous data processing, real-time analytics, and predictive insights (M. A. Ahmed et al., 2024). Realizing the full potential of decentralized and automated data operations will require addressing security concerns, improving performance, and utilizing emerging trends as businesses continue to adopt blockchain technology and smart contracts for data management (Reyna et al., 2018).

3.3 Benefits of Blockchain Integration in Cloud Data Storage

Increased security is one of the main benefits of integrating blockchain technology with cloud data storage. A strong layer of security is offered by blockchain's cryptographic capabilities and decentralized consensus processes, which increase the resistance of cloud data against breaches, tampering, and unwanted access (Habib et al., 2022).

Blockchain's immutability protects the integrity of stored data by guaranteeing that once information is recorded, it cannot be changed or removed without network participants' consent.

Another important advantage of integrating blockchain technology with cloud data storage is transparency and auditability. The blockchain creates an unchangeable audit trail of data activities by making every data transaction transparent and traceable. Transparency improves accountability and regulatory compliance by building stakeholder confidence and offering a verifiable record of all data exchanges.

Another important benefit of using blockchain technology with cloud data storage is decentralization. Organizations can improve data resilience and lower the risk of single points of failure by dispersing data among a network of nodes as opposed to depending on a centralized server. The blockchain's decentralized storage enhances data durability and availability, guaranteeing that information is still reachable even in the case of cyberattacks or system failures.

Additionally, integrating blockchain technology with cloud data storage can lower operating expenses and simplify data management procedures. Organizations can set up predetermined guidelines for data access, sharing, and encryption with the use of smart contracts, which automate and enforce data management regulations.

Organizations may optimize resource utilization and cut expenses by automating data activities, improving workflow efficiency, and minimizing manual intervention through the use of smart contracts in cloud storage environments. Apart from the advantages of security, transparency, and efficiency, integrating blockchain technology into cloud data storage also fosters data portability and interoperability. Organizations may increase data interoperability and streamline data migration across cloud environments by utilizing blockchain protocols and standards to enable smooth data interchange between various platforms and systems.

All things considered, incorporating blockchain technology into cloud data storage provides a revolutionary method of managing data, enabling businesses to improve security, transparency, and productivity while encouraging decentralization, automation, and interoperability in data storage procedures. Businesses may transform their data management procedures and open up new avenues for innovation and expansion in the digital era by combining the advantages of blockchain technology with cloud storage solutions.

4. SMART CONTRACTS FOR DATA MANAGEMENT

With their decentralized and automated approach to managing data transactions, access controls, and sharing agreements, smart contracts have become a potent instrument in the field of data management. On a blockchain network, these self-executing contracts are encoded with predetermined rules and conditions, allowing for safe and transparent data operations without the need for middlemen. There are numerous important advantages of using smart contracts for data management.

One major benefit is automation since smart contracts can carry out data-related operations on their own depending on predetermined criteria. By streamlining procedures like data processing, data sharing permissions, access control enforcement, and data validation, this automation lowers the need for human interaction and the possibility of mistakes.

In data management, transparency and auditability are essential components of smart contracts. The blockchain creates an unchangeable and transparent log of data transfers by recording every action taken by a smart contract. Stakeholders may effortlessly track the history of data operations, confirm the accuracy of transactions, and audit the way data-related procedures are carried out thanks to this capability. Another important advantage of using smart contracts for data management is security. Smart contracts improve data security by preventing fraud, tampering, and unwanted access by utilizing cryptographic techniques and decentralized consensus. Because smart contracts are code-driven, human error is reduced and data operations are executed securely, which promotes confidence between parties (Ramachandran & Kantarcioglu, 2017).

There are several uses for smart contracts in data management situations. By specifying access permissions, data usage restrictions, and remuneration models, smart contracts, for example, might enable safe and automatic sharing arrangements in data sharing agreements. Another area in which smart contracts shine is supply chain traceability, which makes it possible to transparently track goods, materials, and transactions across the supply chain while guaranteeing compliance and authenticity.

Additionally, smart contracts are essential for access control and identity management. Smart contracts improve data security and privacy safeguards by ensuring safe and verifiable access to data through user authentication, role assignment, and enforcement of data privacy laws (Saeed, Hasan, et al., 2022).

The use of smart contracts for data management is fraught with difficulties, despite the many benefits. To fully utilize smart contracts in data management, companies must handle many critical issues, including the requirement for established protocols, scalability constraints of blockchain networks, and security flaws in smart contract programming.

In the future, there will be exciting chances to improve data management procedures thanks to the combination of smart contracts with cutting-edge technologies like artificial intelligence and the Internet of Things (Mamoon M Saeed, et al., 2024). Organizations may automate data workflows, take advantage of real-time analytics, and streamline decision-making processes by integrating smart contracts with AI algorithms and IoT devices (Hasan et al., 2024). This will usher in a new era of decentralized, secure, and effective data management driven by smart contracts.

The use of smart contracts for data management stands out as a revolutionary cornerstone in the broad field of blockchain-based security for cloud data storage, providing an advanced framework for precisely and transparently automating, carrying out, and enforcing data-related procedures. This section explores the complex relationship between data management and smart contracts, shedding light on the innovative strategies and improved security features that smart contracts introduce to the forefront of cloud data storage settings (Gharaibeh et al., 2017). By automating data transactions and procedures according to preset criteria and conditions, smart contracts transform data management in cloud storage as shown in Figure 5.

Figure 5. Smart Contracts for Data Management.

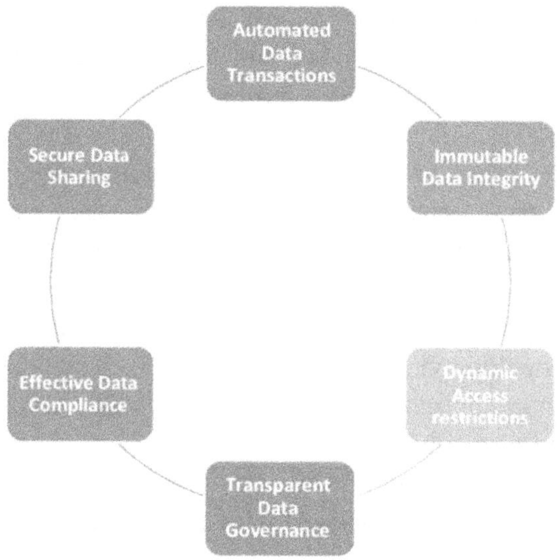

Organizations can improve operational efficiency in managing data assets, reduce manual interventions, and streamline data exchanges by implementing self-executing code on the blockchain. By making use of blockchain's immutability, smart contracts are essential to maintaining data integrity in cloud storage systems. The integrity of data is protected from unauthorized changes, tampering, or inconsistencies after data-related transactions are carried out and documented on the blockchain using smart contracts.

Businesses can use smart contracts to put in place dynamic access restrictions for cloud storage data management. Organizations may control data sharing among stakeholders, enforce granular access standards, and guarantee that data is accessible by authorized parties only under specified conditions by integrating governance rules and access permissions into smart contracts.

By offering a verifiable and auditable record of data transfers and activities, smart contracts help to provide transparent data governance procedures in cloud storage. Stakeholders may monitor the history of data transactions, confirm adherence to data policies, and improve accountability in data management procedures because of smart contracts' inherent transparency. By automating regulatory inspections, data validation processes, and compliance audits, smart contracts simplify data compliance procedures in cloud storage environments. Organizations can more accurately and efficiently make sure that data management procedures follow internal rules, industry standards, and legal requirements by incorporating regulatory requirements into smart contracts. By enabling encrypted, permissioned data exchanges between authorized parties, smart contracts make it possible for cloud storage to include secure data-sharing features. Organizations can create secure channels for sharing sensitive data while maintaining data confidentiality and privacy by integrating cryptographic algorithms and secure key management into smart contracts.

5. CRYPTOGRAPHIC TECHNIQUES IN BLOCKCHAIN-BASED SECURITY

The foundation of blockchain network security is comprised of cryptographic algorithms, which offer a framework for data protection, identity verification, and transaction integrity in a decentralized setting. To create an uninterrupted chain that ensures the immutability and integrity of data on the blockchain, hash functions—basic cryptographic algorithms—are essential in producing distinct IDs for blocks and transactions. A fundamental component of blockchain security, public key cryptography uses pairs of public and private keys for encryption and decryption to allow users to safely transact and authenticate themselves. By offering authentication and non-repudiation, making sure that transactions are impenetrable, and confirming their legitimacy using the sender's private key, digital signatures further improve security (Hagui et al., 2024). Table 3 shows a comparative analysis between traditional security methods and blockchain-based solutions.

Table 3. A comparative analysis between traditional security methods and blockchain-based solutions.

Aspect	Traditional Security Methods	Blockchain-Based Solutions
Architecture	Centralized systems	Decentralized networks
Data Integrity	Vulnerable to tampering	Immutable records through cryptographic hashes
Access Control	Role-based access control	Smart contracts for automated and granular control
Scalability	Limited by central server capabilities	Scales with network growth, though it may face congestion
Transparency	Often opaque, requiring trust in a central authority	Transparent transactions are visible to all network participants
Cost	High operational costs due to maintenance and updates	Potentially lower costs over time with reduced reliance on intermediaries
Security Breaches	Single point of failure, prone to attacks	Enhanced security through redundancy and consensus mechanisms
Compliance	Requires ongoing audits and updates for regulations	Built-in compliance features with auditable trails
Performance	May suffer from latency due to centralized processing	Can experience delays in high-volume transactions
User Control	Limited user control over data	Users have greater control over their data and access rights

Although symmetric encryption is less popular in blockchain, it can be used to protect sensitive data at rest or to secure network interactions, albeit it presents a difficulty when it comes to safely maintaining shared keys. By combining transactions into a block, Merkle trees—cryptographic data structures—simplify the process of confirming the integrity of big datasets. This allows for rapid and effective validation without requiring the processing of each transaction separately. By enabling participants to authenticate transactions without disclosing sensitive information, zero-knowledge proofs add a layer of privacy and security to blockchain transactions, maintaining secrecy and bolstering trust as shown in Figure 6.

Figure 6. Cryptographic Techniques in Blockchain-Based Security.

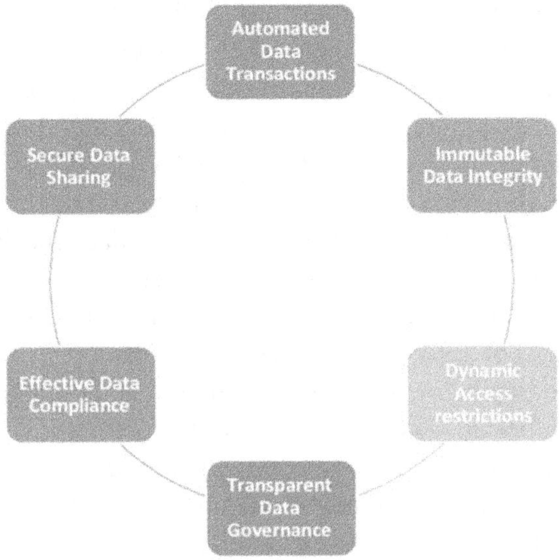

Blockchain networks strengthen their security posture by utilizing these cryptographic techniques, which reduce the likelihood of fraudulent activities, data manipulation, and unauthorized access. This helps to build a foundation of trust, transparency, and dependability in digital transactions and data management procedures. Cryptographic techniques are the foundation of protecting data assets in the complex world of blockchain-based security for cloud data storage, guaranteeing confidentiality, integrity, and authenticity in a world that is becoming more linked and data-driven (Inam et al., 2024). "Blockchain-Based Security for Cloud Data Storage," a chapter book, explores the deep influence of cryptographic methods on bolstering data security in blockchain ecosystems, illuminating the creative solutions and strong security features that cryptography introduces to the forefront of cloud data storage settings (Priyanshu et al., 2024).

The foundation of blockchain-based security is public-key cryptography, which permits safe communication and data encryption in cloud storage settings. Organizations can ensure confidentiality and privacy by establishing secure channels for data transfer, encrypting sensitive data, and authenticating individuals using asymmetric key pairs, which are made up of public and private keys. Because they offer a way to confirm the integrity and validity of data transactions, digital signatures are essential to blockchain-based security. Users can increase trust and accountability in cloud data storage interactions by digitally signing data with a private key, proving ownership, verifying the data's origin, and identifying any unauthorized changes.

By producing distinct cryptographic hashes for data sets, hash functions play a crucial role in maintaining data integrity throughout blockchain networks. Organizations can identify any tampering or changes to data kept in cloud settings by employing these cryptographic hashes to hash data and link blocks in a chain, maintaining the immutability and reliability of data records.

In cloud storage systems, encryption methods are essential for safeguarding data both in transit and at rest. Organizations can protect data confidentiality, prevent unwanted access, and lessen the likelihood of data breaches or cyberattacks by encrypting sensitive data using strong encryption algorithms like AES (Advanced Encryption Standard) or RSA (Rivest-Shamir-Adleman).

A strong cryptographic method for confirming the legitimacy of data without disclosing private information is provided by zero-knowledge proofs. Zero-knowledge proofs improve data security while maintaining confidentiality by demonstrating knowledge of a secret without actually revealing it. This allows for safe and private interactions in cloud data storage. Organizations can operate on sensitive data while keeping confidentiality thanks to homomorphic encryption, which makes it possible to do calculations on encrypted data without having to decrypt it. Organizations may safeguard data privacy, enable safe data processing, and improve data security in computation-intensive environments by utilizing homomorphic encryption in cloud data storage.

6. CHALLENGES AND LIMITATIONS

The excitement surrounding the decentralized promise of blockchain technology is tempered by a tapestry of difficulties and constraints that become apparent while navigating its complex terrain. One of the biggest obstacles is scalability, a persistent weakness that makes it difficult for blockchain networks to process large numbers of transactions quickly and effectively. Congestion, slower processing times, and higher transaction fees result from the increased demand for network resources caused by the growth in users and transactions. This scaling issue highlights the need for creative fixes that might increase the capacity of blockchain networks without compromising security or decentralization (Dave, 2024).

Security issues put a shadow over blockchain technology's apparent invincibility, looming huge like a sinister ghost. Blockchain networks are at serious risk from smart contract flaws, coding mistakes, and human error, even though cryptographic techniques provide strong resistance. Though beneficial for data integrity, blockchain's immutability can amplify the effects of security lapses or incorrect transactions, highlighting the necessity of thorough security audits, best practices, and ongoing monitoring to strengthen the network's defenses (Z. E. Ahmed, et al., 2024).

As legislators and regulatory agencies struggle with the new issues raised by decentralized technology, regulatory uncertainty adds another level of complexity to the blockchain dilemma. Blockchain projects and businesses face uncertainty and compliance burdens due to the changing regulatory environment, which is marked by a patchwork of contradictory rules and regulations. Stakeholders hoping to capitalize on the revolutionary potential of blockchain technology continue to walk a tightrope between innovation and regulatory compliance, as shown in Figure 7.

Figure 7. Challenges and Limitations for Blockchain Networks.

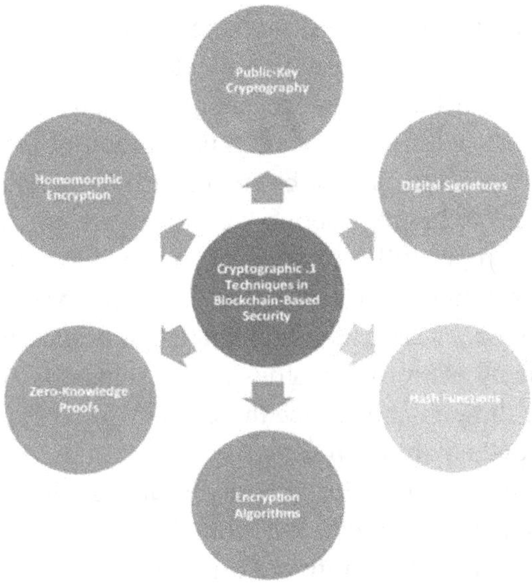

The controversial topic of energy usage casts doubts on blockchain's environmental credentials, especially when it comes to proof-of-work consensus systems. Mining cryptocurrencies requires a lot of energy and computationally demanding methods, which hurts the environment and raises questions about sustainability and carbon footprint. Investigating energy-efficient consensus methods and environmentally friendly substitutes is necessary to lessen the carbon footprint of blockchain technology and its effects on the environment (Barakat et al., 2024; Elnaim et al., 2023).

Additionally, the widespread implementation of blockchain technology is hindered by adoption and user experience barriers, such as complicated interfaces, laborious onboarding procedures, and a lack of user-friendly applications. To democratize access to blockchain technology and promote wider acceptance across various user segments, it is imperative to improve user education, streamline blockchain interfaces, and develop intuitive applications (Z. E. Ahmed, et al., 2024).

The path to stronger data protection is not without obstacles and constraints in the ever-changing world of blockchain-based security for cloud data storage. To shed light on the crucial issues that influence the development of data security paradigms, this section explores the complex terrain of barriers and limitations that businesses may run into when navigating the intricacies of integrating blockchain technology into cloud storage environments (Idrus et al., 2023).

- **Issues with Scalability:** Scalability is one of the main issues with blockchain-based security in cloud data storage. Scalability problems affect the speed and effectiveness of data exchanges as blockchain networks get bigger and handle more transactions. The smooth integration of blockchain technology into cloud storage systems may be impeded by scalability issues, requiring creative solutions to improve network performance and throughput.
- **Issues with Interoperability:** As businesses look to incorporate blockchain-based security solutions with current cloud storage systems and technologies, interoperability issues arise. A major challenge is ensuring smooth compatibility across many platforms, protocols, and standards. This might make integration more difficult and reduce the efficacy of blockchain-based security measures in cloud environments.
- **Regulatory Compliance:** For businesses using blockchain-based security in cloud data storage, regulatory compliance poses a significant barrier. Different jurisdictions have different criteria for compliance, which calls for following a complicated network of privacy laws, data protection legislation, and industry standards. Organizations must successfully negotiate legal intricacies and regulatory uncertainties in order to ensure compliance with changing regulatory frameworks, which is a significant challenge.
- **Privacy Issues:** Organizations must have strong privacy-enhancing strategies and procedures in place to protect sensitive data to successfully balance the advantages of openness and immutability with data privacy concerns.
- **Security concerns:** Although blockchain technology has built-in security advantages, there are also security concerns associated with blockchain-based security solutions for cloud data storage. Strong security procedures and proactive risk mitigation techniques are crucial because of the serious

security concerns posed by flaws in consensus algorithms, smart contracts, and malicious assaults on blockchain networks (Z. E. Ahmed, t al., 2024b).

- **Cost Implications:** There may be substantial expenses associated with infrastructure, development, maintenance, and compliance when integrating blockchain-based security solutions in cloud data storage environments. For businesses looking to improve data security through blockchain integration, managing the financial ramifications of implementing blockchain technology, including initial investment costs and continuing operating expenses, presents a problem.

When the number of transactions grows, blockchain networks may become slow and experience clogging, which impacts their performance. Also, using the proof-of-work method can be heavy on energy. Blockchain protocols sometimes have difficulty communicating, which can make connecting one blockchain to another and to cloud platforms challenging. Besides security, blockchain can also be vulnerable to smart contract glitches and the possibility of 51% attacks. The fact that regulations for data protection and blockchain technology are still being built makes it difficult to be sure about adoption and how to follow the regulations. Overcoming these challenges allows blockchain to better enhance cloud security. Organizations may create strategic plans to overcome constraints, get past roadblocks, and unleash the revolutionary potential of blockchain technology in protecting data assets in the digital era by having a sophisticated grasp of these issues (Mustafa et al., 2024).

7. CASE STUDIES

The healthcare provider partnered with SecureCloud to use blockchain, which made their patient data more secure and private. By using Ethereum and IPFS, the system cut down on unauthorized access, keeping healthcare regulations in areas such as privacy, and made patients and providers trust each other more. (Vashishth et al., 2025). Because of Hyperledger Fabric, DataChain can share supply chain data in the logistics sector, making the process more transparent and traceable. Because of the blockchain integration, fraud and errors in data handling went down, showing that blockchain enhances efficiency and adds accountability in the organization (Hellani, Houssein, et al., 2021). Securing financial transactions is done in FinTech Ledger with blockchain technology running Corda and a strong public key infrastructure.

As a result, users trusted tighter security, transactions became less time-consuming, and there were fewer costs, showing that blockchain improves financial safety.

In education, EduBlock found a way to use blockchain to make academic records safe and secure. Adopting Ethereum and IPFS, institutions streamlined the process and enhanced safeguards against anyone tampering with records, which improved the trust in academic qualifications (Haveri, Pavitra, et al., 2020). GovChain provided an example of how blockchain can help protect data in government, using Hyperledger Fabric. By implementing blockchain, authorities increased the security of data, gained people's trust, and saw that blockchain is a transparent system for administration (Gaur, Nitin, et al., 2020). In addition, CloudSecure made its private cloud stronger by using blockchain technology for better client security and access management. As a result, the company complied with data protection laws and made clients happier, which highlighted their security standards in the cloud field (Mallisetty, Sai Balaji, et al., 2023). In these sectors, blockchain is used in several ways to strengthen data security and integrity in cloud data systems, as shown in Table 4.

Table 4. Case Studies for Blockchain-Based Security in Cloud Data Storage

Case Study	Description	Key Outcomes	Technologies Used
Case Study 1: SecureCloud	Implementation of a blockchain solution for a healthcare provider to secure patient data storage.	Enhanced data integrity and patient privacy; reduced unauthorized access incidents.	Ethereum, IPFS
Case Study 2: DataChain	Use of blockchain to manage supply chain data for a logistics company.	Improved transparency and traceability; reduced fraud and errors in data handling.	Hyperledger Fabric, Smart Contracts
Case Study 3: FinTech Ledger	Deployment of a blockchain system for secure financial transactions and data storage.	Increased trust among users, faster transaction processing times, and reduced operational costs.	Corda, Public Key Infrastructure
Case Study 4: EduBlock	Blockchain application in educational institutions for secure storage of academic records.	Streamlined verification processes; enhanced security against record tampering.	Ethereum, IPFS
Case Study 5: GovChain	Implementation in government agencies for secure citizen data management.	Improved data security; increased citizen trust in government data handling practices.	Hyperledger Fabric, Smart Contracts
Case Study 6: CloudSecure	A private cloud provider integrating blockchain for client data security and access control.	Enhanced compliance with data protection regulations; improved client satisfaction with security.	Private Blockchain, Cryptographic Protocols

8. FUTURE RESEARCH DIRECTIONS

The secret to removing the scalability bottleneck and allowing blockchain systems to grow without compromising security and decentralization lies in advancements in consensus algorithms, sharding strategies, and off-chain alternatives. Furthermore, investigating blockchain's privacy-preserving technologies provides a rich field for investigation. Secure multi-party computation, homomorphic encryption, and zero-knowledge proofs offer intriguing opportunities for protecting private information in cloud storage settings without sacrificing confidentiality (Bhumichai et al., 2024).

Studies to incorporate these privacy-preserving methods into blockchain systems can enable users to maintain control over their data even when they transfer it to cloud storage providers.

One of the most important study areas in the field of blockchain-based security for cloud data storage is the pursuit of interoperability. An interconnected digital ecosystem that goes beyond the isolated borders of separate blockchain networks can be fostered by creating standardized protocols, interoperable frameworks, and cross-chain communication mechanisms that enable smooth data exchange and collaboration across various cloud storage platforms (Saeed, et al., 2022).

Furthermore, creative research into threat intelligence frameworks and adaptive security mechanisms is necessary to increase the resilience of blockchain networks against new threats and weaknesses. The defense posture of blockchain-based cloud storage systems against changing cyber threats can be strengthened by utilizing machine learning, artificial intelligence, and blockchain analytics to enable proactive threat detection, anomaly identification, and quick reaction to security incidents(Saeed, Mohammed, et al., 2023; Saeed, Saeed, et al., 2023). Examining how blockchain technology interacts with new paradigms like edge computing and the Internet of Things (IoT) reveals an area that is ready for investigation (Afridi & Kumar, 2024).

There are several opportunities for future research paths in the field of blockchain-based security for cloud data storage, which might completely change the way that data protection, resilience, and trust are seen in cloud environments (Abiodun et al., 2022).

- **Solutions for Scalability:** Scalability solutions that meet the increasing demands of blockchain networks are expected to be the main focus of future research projects in blockchain-based security for cloud data storage. By improving network scalability, throughput, and efficiency, new techniques like sharding, layer-two protocols, and consensus algorithm improvements hope to open the door for the broad use of blockchain technology in cloud storage settings (Mustafa et al., 2024).

- **Methods for Preserving Privacy:** Due to the necessity of striking a compromise between data privacy standards and transparency and immutability, research on privacy-preserving methods inside blockchain-based security is expected to flourish. Advances in homomorphic encryption, safe multiparty computation, and zero-knowledge proofs have the potential to enable private and secure data exchanges in cloud storage while maintaining confidentiality (Saeed et al., 2019).
- **Interoperability and Standards**: To enable the smooth integration of blockchain-based security solutions with various cloud storage platforms, future research paths will focus on interoperability issues and the development of industry standards. In order to promote interoperability and increase the effectiveness of blockchain-based security measures, standardization initiatives, cross-chain interoperability protocols, and interoperable frameworks seek to reconcile different systems and protocols.
- **Consensus Mechanisms:** Future studies on blockchain-based security for cloud data storage could focus on the development of consensus mechanisms. Novel consensus algorithms, including Byzantine fault tolerance models, consensus scalability solutions, and variations on proof-of-stake, will be investigated in research projects to improve network security, decentralization, and efficiency in cloud storage settings.
- **Improved Data Governance:** Upcoming studies will concentrate on improving data governance structures in the context of blockchain-based cloud data storage security. To improve data governance procedures, guarantee regulatory compliance, and promote openness in data management, research will examine governance models, decentralized identity systems, data provenance mechanisms, and auditability improvements.
- **Integration of AI and Blockchain:** The combination of blockchain technology with artificial intelligence (AI) has the potential to completely transform cloud storage data security. Future studies will examine how blockchain technology, AI algorithms, and machine learning models might work together to improve threat intelligence, anomaly detection, and automated security responses in cloud data storage settings (Mamoon, MA Saeed et al., 2024; R. A. Saeed et al., 2024).

9. CONCLUSION

A thorough exploration of the complex relationship between blockchain technology and data security in cloud storage environments is summarized in this chapter. As we come to the end of this enlightening investigation, it is clear that the combination of cloud data storage and blockchain principles has the potential to completely alter the landscape of data protection, resilience, and trust in the digital era. We have explored the intricacies and subtleties of blockchain-based security in each chapter, illuminating the revolutionary role that decentralized ledgers, cryptographic protocols, and consensus processes play in enhancing data confidentiality and integrity. Every aspect of blockchain integration, from scalability issues to privacy worries and interoperability barriers, offers businesses looking to strengthen their data security posture in cloud storage ecosystems both opportunities and problems.

In the face of changing dangers and regulatory environments, the obstacles and constraints uncovered in this section operate as awareness-raising catalysts, encouraging firms to innovate proactively, tread carefully, and develop successful strategies. Cost considerations dictate prudent investments in blockchain-based security measures, scalability limitations beg for innovative solutions, regulatory compliance demands attentiveness, and security concerns demand resilience. The chapter's recommendations for future study areas provide a path forward for additional investigation and development in the field of blockchain-based security for cloud data storage. The future of data security and trust in cloud storage environments is expected to be shaped by revolutionary developments as we shift toward privacy-preserving strategies, improved governance frameworks, blockchain and AI synergies, and interoperability standards.

REFERENCES

Abiodun, O. I., Alawida, M., Omolara, A. E., & Alabdulatif, A. (2022). Data provenance for cloud forensic investigations, security, challenges, solutions, and future perspectives: A survey. *Journal of King Saud University. Computer and Information Sciences*, *34*(10), 10217–10245. DOI: 10.1016/j.jksuci.2022.10.018

Afridi, M. F., & Kumar, K. S. (2024). Exploring Data Privacy and Privacy Paradox Nature of Consumers Using Blockchain Technology: Application of SLR and Bibliometric Analysis Tools. *Abhigyan*, *42*(3), 181–205. DOI: 10.1177/09702385241256007

Aggarwal, S., & Kumar, N. (2021). Core components of blockchain. [). Elsevier.]. *Advances in Computers*, *121*, 193–209. DOI: 10.1016/bs.adcom.2020.08.010

Ahmed, M. A., Saeed, R. A., Saeed, M. M., & Khalifa, O. O. (2024). Real-Time In-Pipe Drinking Water Quality Monitoring System Design and Implementation. 2024 9th International Conference on Mechatronics Engineering (ICOM)

Ahmed, Z. E., Hashim, A. A., Saeed, R. A., & Ali Saeed, M. M. (2024). Exploring optimal resource allocation methods for improved efficiency in flying ad-hoc network environments: a survey. *International Journal of Electrical & Computer Engineering (2088-8708), 14*(6).

Ahmed, Z. E., Hashim, A. A., Saeed, R. A., & Saeed, M. M. (2024a). Deterministic Networking (DetNet): Architecture, Protocols, and Advanced Applications. 2024 9th International Conference on Mechatronics Engineering (ICOM).

Ahmed, Z. E., Hashim, A. A., Saeed, R. A., & Saeed, M. M. (2024b). Enhancing Smart City Mobility Using Software-Defined Networks. 2024 9th International Conference on Mechatronics Engineering (ICOM).

Ahmed, Z. E., Hashim, A. H., Saeed, R. A., & Saeed, M. M. (2024). Monitoring of Wildlife Using Unmanned Aerial Vehicle (UAV) With Machine Learning. In *Applications of Machine Learning in UAV Networks* (pp. 97-120). IGI Global.

Ahmed, Z. E., Hashim, A. H. A., Saeed, R. A., & Saeed, M. M. (2024). AI-Enhanced Education: Bridging Educational Disparities. In *AI-Enhanced Teaching Methods* (pp. 88-107). IGI Global.

Barakat, M., Saeed, R. A., Edam, S., Ali, E. S., Saeed, M. M., Elbasheir, M. S., Elnaim, A. A., & Babeker, A. (2024). Energy-Aware Task Completion Delay Optimization of Space-Aerial Enabled MEC System. 2024 IEEE 4th International Maghreb Meeting of the Conference on Sciences and Techniques of Automatic Control and Computer Engineering (MI-STA).

Bhumichai, D., Smiliotopoulos, C., Benton, R., Kambourakis, G., & Damopoulos, D. (2024). The convergence of artificial intelligence and blockchain: The state of play and the road ahead. *Information (Basel)*, *15*(5), 268. DOI: 10.3390/info15050268

Dave, C. (2024). *Security Challenges with Blockchain: Navigate Blockchain Security Challenges, Unveil Vulnerabilities, and Gain Practical Strategies for Secure Application Development (English Edition)*. Orange Education Pvt Ltd.

Dinh, T. T. A., Liu, R., Zhang, M., Chen, G., Ooi, B. C., & Wang, J. (2018). Untangling Blockchain: A data processing view of blockchain systems. *IEEE Transactions on Knowledge and Data Engineering*, *30*(7), 1366–1385. DOI: 10.1109/TKDE.2017.2781227

Elmustafa, S. A.. (2024). Smart Applications Based on IoT: Challenges and Emerging Trends Landscape. In Nacer, A. A., & Abdmeziem, M. R. (Eds.), *Emerging Technologies for Securing the Cloud and IoT* (pp. 1–37). IGI Global., DOI: 10.4018/979-8-3693-0766-3.ch001

Elnaim, A. A., Babeker, A. M., Gaid, A. S., Saeed, M. M., Ahmed, Z. E., & Saeed, R. A. (2023). Energy Consumption for Cognitive Radio Network Enabled Multi-Access Edge Computing. 2023 3rd International Conference on Emerging Smart Technologies and Applications (eSmarTA)

Gaur, N.. (2020). *Blockchain with hyperledger fabric: Build decentralized applications using hyperledger fabric 2*. Packt Publishing Ltd.

Ge, C., Liu, Z., & Fang, L. (2020). A blockchain based decentralized data security mechanism for the Internet of Things. *Journal of Parallel and Distributed Computing*, *141*, 1–9. DOI: 10.1016/j.jpdc.2020.03.005

Gharaibeh, A., Salahuddin, M. A., Hussini, S. J., Khreishah, A., Khalil, I., Guizani, M., & Al-Fuqaha, A. (2017). Smart cities: A survey on data management, security, and enabling technologies. *IEEE Communications Surveys and Tutorials*, *19*(4), 2456–2501. DOI: 10.1109/COMST.2017.2736886

Habib, G., Sharma, S., Ibrahim, S., Ahmad, I., Qureshi, S., & Ishfaq, M. (2022). Blockchain technology: Benefits, challenges, applications, and integration of blockchain technology with cloud computing. *Future Internet*, *14*(11), 341. DOI: 10.3390/fi14110341

Hagui, I., Msolli, A., ben Henda, N., Helali, A., Gassoumi, A., Nguyen, T. P., & Hassen, F. (2024). A blockchain-based security system with light cryptography for user authentication security. *Multimedia Tools and Applications*, *83*(17), 52451–52480. DOI: 10.1007/s11042-023-17643-5

Hasan, M. K., Budhati, A. K., Solaiman, R., Islam, S., Pandey, B., Abbas, H. S., & Saeed, M. M. (2024). An Improved Binary Spider Wasp Optimization Algorithm for Intrusion Detection for Industrial Internet of Things. *IEEE Open Journal of the Communications Society*.

Haveri, P., ... "Edublock: Securing educational documents using blockchain technology." *2020 11th International Conference on Computing, Communication and Networking Technologies (ICCCNT)*. IEEE, 2020. DOI: 10.1109/ICCCNT49239.2020.9225265

Hellani, H., Sliman, L., Samhat, A. E., & Exposito, E. (2021). On blockchain integration with supply chain: Overview on data transparency. *Logistics (Basel)*, *5*(3), 46.

Idrus, M. A. Z. B., Rahman, F. D. A., Khalifa, O. O., & Yusoff, N. M. (2023). Blockchain-based Security for Cloud Data Storage. 2023 IEEE 9th International Conference on Smart Instrumentation, Measurement and Applications (ICSIMA)

Inam, S. A., Khan, A. A., Mazhar, T., Ahmed, N., Shahzad, T., Khan, M. A., Saeed, M. M., & Hamam, H. (2024). PR-FCNN: A data-driven hybrid approach for predicting PM2. 5 concentration. *Discover Artificial Intelligence*, *4*(1), 75. DOI: 10.1007/s44163-024-00184-7

Khanna, A., Sah, A., Bolshev, V., Burgio, A., Panchenko, V., & Jasiński, M. (2022). Blockchain–cloud integration: A survey. *Sensors (Basel)*, *22*(14), 5238. DOI: 10.3390/s22145238 PMID: 35890918

Maldonado-Ruiz, D., Torres, J., & Madhoun, N. E. (2022). Fundamentals of blockchain technology. In *Principles and Practice of Blockchains* (pp. 3–25). Springer.

Mallisetty, S. B., Tripuramallu, G. A., Kamada, K., Devineni, P., Kavitha, S., & Krishna, A. V. P. (2023, January). A review on cloud security and its challenges. In *2023 International Conference on Intelligent Data Communication Technologies and Internet of Things (IDCIoT)* (pp. 798-804). IEEE.

Mazhar, T., Shah, S. F. A., Inam, S. A., Awotunde, J. B., Saeed, M. M., & Hamam, H. (2024). Analysis of the integration of IoMT with blockchain: Issues, challenges, and solutions. *Discover Internet of Things*, *4*(1), 1–36. DOI: 10.1007/s43926-024-00078-1

Mustafa, Y. A., Ali, E. S., Osman, T. E., Khalifa, O. O., Mohamed, Z. O., Saeed, R. A., & Saeed, M. M. (2024). Multi-Drones Energy Efficient Based Path Planning Optimization using Genetic Algorithm and Gradient Decent Approach. 2024 9th International Conference on Mechatronics Engineering (ICOM)

Nzuva, S. M. (2019). Smart contracts implementation, applications, benefits, and limitations. *Journal of Information Engineering and Applications.*

Ølnes, S., Ubacht, J., & Janssen, M. (2017). *Blockchain in government: Benefits and implications of distributed ledger technology for information sharing* (Vol. 34). Elsevier.

Priyanshu, S., Kumar, S., & Garg, S. (2024). Blockchain-Based Data Security. *Digital Forensics and Cyber Crime Investigation: Recent Advances and Future Directions*, 17.

Ramachandran, A., & Kantarcioglu, D. M. (2017). Using blockchain and smart contracts for secure data provenance management. *arXiv preprint arXiv:1709.10000.*

Reyna, A., Martín, C., Chen, J., Soler, E., & Díaz, M. (2018). On blockchain and its integration with IoT. Challenges and opportunities. *Future Generation Computer Systems*, *88*, 173–190. DOI: 10.1016/j.future.2018.05.046

Saeed, M., Saeed, R., Elbashier, M., Ali, E., Mokhtar, R., & Ahmed, Z. (2024). Improving the Privacy in Wireless-Enabled 5G Networks: A Lightweight Protocol for IIoT Communications. *Asian Journal of Electrical and Electronic Engineering*, *4*(2), 1–17. DOI: 10.69955/ajoeee.24.v4i2.62

Saeed, M. M., Hasan, M. K., Obaid, A. J., Saeed, R. A., Mokhtar, R. A., Ali, E. S., Akhtaruzzaman, M., Amanlou, S., & Hossain, A. Z. (2022). A comprehensive review on the users' identity privacy for 5G networks. *IET Communications*, *16*(5), 384–399. DOI: 10.1049/cmu2.12327

Saeed, M. M., Kamrul Hasan, M., Hassan, R., Mokhtar, R., Saeed, R. A., Saeid, E., & Gupta, M. (2022). Preserving Privacy of User Identity Based on Pseudonym Variable in 5G. *Computers, Materials & Continua*, *70*(3). Advance online publication. DOI: 10.32604/cmc.2022.017338

Saeed, M. M., Mohammed, H. N. R., Gazem, O. A. H., Saeed, R. A., Morei, H. M. A., Eidah, A. E. T., Gaid, A. S., Al-Uosfi, A. S. A. S., & Al-Madhagi, M. G. Q. (2023). Machine Learning Techniques for Detecting DDOS Attacks. 2023 3rd International Conference on Emerging Smart Technologies and Applications (eSmarTA)

Saeed, M. M., Saeed, R. A., Abdelhaq, M., Alsaqour, R., Hasan, M. K., & Mokhtar, R. A. (2023). Anomaly detection in 6G networks using machine learning methods. *Electronics (Basel)*, *12*(15), 3300. DOI: 10.3390/electronics12153300

Saeed, M. M., Saeed, R. A., Ahmed, Z. E., Gaid, A. S., & Mokhtar, R. A. (2024). AI Technologies in Engineering Education. In *AI-Enhanced Teaching Methods* (pp. 61–87). IGI Global. DOI: 10.4018/979-8-3693-2728-9.ch003

Saeed, M. M., Saeed, R. A., Ali, E. S., Mokhtar, R. A., & Khalifa, O. O. (2024). Algorithm for Resource Allocation and Computing Offloading in 6G Networks: Deep Reinforcement Learning-based. 2024 9th International Conference on Mechatronics Engineering (ICOM).

Saeed, M. M., Saeed, R. A., Mokhtar, R. A., Gaid, A. S., Ahmed, Z. E., & Elbasheir, M. S. (2024). Multi-Access Edge Computing Using Intelligent Mobile User Resource Allocation In 6G. 2024 IEEE 4th International Maghreb Meeting of the Conference on Sciences and Techniques of Automatic Control and Computer Engineering (MI-STA)

Saeed, M. M., Saeed, R. A., & Saeid, E. (2019). Preserving privacy of paging procedure in 5 th G using identity-division multiplexing. *2019 First International Conference of Intelligent Computing and Engineering (ICOICE)*

Saeed, M. M. A., Saeed, R. A., & Ahmed, Z. E. (2024). Data Security and Privacy in the Age of AI and Digital Twins. In *Digital Twin Technology and AI Implementations in Future-Focused Businesses* (pp. 99–124). IGI Global. DOI: 10.4018/979-8-3693-1818-8.ch008

Saeed, R. A., Saeed, M. M., Ahmed, Z. E., & Hashim, A. H. (2024). Enhancing Medical Services Through Machine Learning and UAV Technology: Applications and Benefits. In *Applications of Machine Learning in UAV Networks* (pp. 307-343). IGI Global.

Saeed, R. A., Saeed, M. M., Mokhtar, R. A., Alhumyani, H., & Abdel-Khalek, S. (2021). Pseudonym Mutable Based Privacy for 5G User Identity. *Computer Systems Science and Engineering*, *39*(1). Advance online publication. DOI: 10.32604/csse.2021.015593

Sheikh, H., Azmathullah, R. M., & Rizwan, F. (2018). Proof-of-work vs proof-of-stake: A comparative analysis and an approach to blockchain consensus mechanism. *International Journal for Research in Applied Science and Engineering Technology*, *6*(12), 786–791.

Vashishth, Tarun Kumar, et al. (2025). “Securing the Cloud: Strategies for Protecting Sensitive Patient Data in Cloud-Based Healthcare Recommender Systems.” *Healthcare Recommender Systems*: 185-220.

Zachariadis, M., Hileman, G., & Scott, S. V. (2019). Governance and control in distributed ledgers: Understanding the challenges facing blockchain technology in financial services. *Information and Organization*, *29*(2), 105–117. DOI: 10.1016/j.infoandorg.2019.03.001

Chapter 8
Smart Clouds:
Integrating AI, Machine Learning, and Blockchain for Next-Gen Analytics

C. V. Suresh Babu
https://orcid.org/0000-0002-8474-2882
Hindustan Institute of Technology and Science, India

K. Sakthivel
https://orcid.org/0009-0003-6162-1230
Hindustan Institute of Technology and Science, India

ABSTRACT

This study explores the transformative integration of AI, Machine Learning (ML), and Blockchain within cloud computing to address the growing demand for secure, scalable, and real-time data-driven solutions across industries. The primary objective is to present a comprehensive framework for smart cloud platforms by combining AI and ML-driven analytics with Blockchain-as-a-Service (BaaS) for enhanced data security, transparency, and decision-making. The research targets professionals in IT, academia, and enterprises seeking innovative cloud solutions. Methodologically, the study leverages architectural models, real-world case studies, and a detailed analysis of current industry trends to propose best practices for implementation. Key findings reveal significant improvements in organizational insights, secure transactions, and operational efficiency through integrated cloud ecosystems. The study concludes by highlighting future trends such as quantum computing and AI-driven blockchain models, emphasizing their implications for business innovation and policy development.

DOI: 10.4018/979-8-3693-9984-2.ch008

1. INTRODUCTION

1.1 Overview of AI, Machine Learning, and Blockchain in Cloud Computing

Artificial Intelligence (AI), Machine Learning (ML), and Blockchain are rapidly transforming the landscape of cloud computing. AI encompasses systems capable of performing tasks that typically require human intelligence, such as learning, reasoning, and problem-solving. ML, a subset of AI, focuses specifically on algorithms that enable computers to learn from and make predictions based on data. Meanwhile, Blockchain technology offers a decentralized, secure, and transparent framework for recording transactions, making it ideal for managing data integrity in cloud environments. The convergence of these technologies within cloud computing provides organizations with the ability to harness vast amounts of data, gain valuable insights, and ensure data security and trustworthiness.

1.2 The Evolution of Cloud Platforms for Advanced Analytics

Cloud platforms have evolved significantly from simple data storage solutions to comprehensive analytics ecosystems. Initially, cloud services were primarily focused on offering storage and computing power. However, as data volume and complexity increased, cloud providers began integrating advanced analytics capabilities, such as data visualization, predictive analytics, and machine learning tools. This evolution has been driven by the need for businesses to make data-driven decisions quickly and efficiently. Today, cloud platforms offer integrated environments that facilitate real-time analytics, enabling organizations to derive actionable insights from their data.

1.3 Importance of Integrating AI, ML, and Blockchain for Next-Generation Data Solutions

Integrating AI, ML, and Blockchain into cloud computing represents a significant advancement for data solutions. The combination of these technologies enhances data processing capabilities, improves security, and fosters greater transparency in transactions. AI and ML can analyze large datasets to uncover patterns and trends, while Blockchain ensures that this data remains tamper-proof and verifiable. Together, they create a robust framework that not only streamlines data management but also enables organizations to innovate and adapt in a rapidly changing technological landscape.

1.4 Purpose and Scope of the Chapter

This chapter focuses on the integration of cutting-edge technologies, Artificial Intelligence (AI), Machine Learning (ML), and Blockchain, in the next generation of cloud computing. The goal is to present an exhaustive analysis of how these technologies improve data analytics capabilities and resolve key challenges in smart cloud environments.

Focus Areas:

1.AI and ML in Cloud Analytics

- How AI and ML algorithms improve predictive analytics, pattern recognition, and decision-making.
- Applications of AI/ML in resource optimization, cost management, and real-time insights.

2.Blockchain for Data Integrity and Security

- Ensuring safe storage of data and transaction with decentralized ledger technologies.
- Blockchain applications in fighting fraud, ensuring privacy, and building trust in distributed cloud.

3.Integration Challenges and Solutions

- Technical and operational issues in the integration of AI, ML, and blockchain into the cloud environment.
- Scalable frameworks and architectures for the smooth integration.

4.Emerging Trends and Future Directions

- Role of hybrid clouds in AI, ML, and blockchain.
- Innovations in federated learning, edge computing, and quantum-safe cryptography for better analytics.

5.Applications in Industry

- Use cases in healthcare, finance, smart cities, and supply chain management.
- Potential of integrated systems for sustainable and intelligent decision-making.

2. BACKGROUND AND CONTEXT

2.1 The Role of AI and Machine Learning in Cloud-Based Analytics

AI and ML play a crucial role in enhancing cloud-based analytics by automating data analysis and facilitating advanced decision-making processes. These technologies enable organizations to sift through vast amounts of data quickly, identifying patterns and anomalies that would be impossible for humans to detect in a timely manner. By leveraging predictive analytics, businesses can anticipate trends and customer behaviors, leading to more informed strategic decisions. Moreover, cloud-based solutions provide the scalability required to handle the dynamic nature of data, making them ideal for AI and ML applications.

2.2 Blockchain as a Service (BaaS): Definition and Benefits

Blockchain as a Service (BaaS) is a cloud-based service that enables organizations to build, host, and use their own blockchain applications and smart contracts without the complexities of managing blockchain infrastructure. BaaS simplifies the adoption of blockchain technology by offering a ready-to-use environment, which allows businesses to focus on application development rather than underlying infrastructure. Key benefits of BaaS include reduced operational costs, enhanced security through decentralized networks, and the ability to scale solutions quickly. Furthermore, BaaS can integrate seamlessly with existing cloud services, providing a comprehensive solution for secure and transparent data management.

2.3 Trends in Cloud Adoption and the Demand for Data-Driven Decision-Making

The trend toward increased cloud adoption has been fueled by the growing need for data-driven decision-making across industries. Organizations are increasingly recognizing the value of harnessing data to enhance operational efficiency, improve customer experiences, and drive innovation. As businesses accumulate more data than ever before, the demand for scalable, flexible cloud solutions that can provide real-time insights is paramount. This shift has led to the proliferation of advanced analytics tools within cloud platforms, enabling organizations to transform data into strategic assets.

2.4 Industry Needs for Secure and Scalable Analytics Solutions

In today's digital landscape, industries require analytics solutions that are both secure and scalable. With the rise of cyber threats and data breaches, ensuring the integrity and confidentiality of sensitive information is more critical than ever. Additionally, as organizations grow, their data needs become more complex, necessitating solutions that can scale seamlessly without compromising performance (Suresh Babu, C. V. & Srisakthi, S. 2023). This demand is driving the integration of AI, ML, and Blockchain technologies in cloud platforms, which collectively address these challenges by providing secure, scalable, and efficient data analytics capabilities.

3. LITERATURE REVIEW

3.1 AI and ML in Smart Clouds

AI and ML have increasingly become core enablers of cloud analytics and smart data processing. Aggarwal (2023) explored neural architectures tailored for secure data transmission, emphasizing how AI can optimize performance and strengthen resilience in next-generation networks. Similarly, Esenogho and Djouani (2022) reviewed the convergence of AI, 5G, and IoT for smart grid applications, identifying the role of AI in fault detection, autonomous decision-making, and real-time monitoring.

Manoharan and Nagar (2024) investigated the role of AI-driven natural language processing in enhancing personalized learning environments, showing how machine learning adapts content based on learner profiles. This aligns with Manoharan and Nagulapally's (2024) study on gamification, where adaptive algorithms improved engagement in educational platforms.

These applications of AI and ML within smart cloud environments demonstrate the increasing demand for automated, context-aware decision-making processes and the importance of personalization, responsiveness, and security.

3.2 Blockchain and Data Security

Blockchain's decentralized nature offers enhanced transparency, tamper-resistance, and trust—critical qualities in cloud computing environments. Manoharan (2024) emphasized blockchain's role in re-establishing trust across digital ecosystems, while Sharma and Podoplelova (2021) proposed a layered architecture combining AI and blockchain for smart cities, highlighting data privacy and energy efficiency.

Bao et al. (2022) surveyed blockchain's application in network slicing for 5G, identifying its potential for improved resource management and security. Rodenberg and Gehring (2023) focused on quantum key distribution (QKD) for data center security, offering a forward-looking cryptographic approach in anticipation of post-quantum threats.

To address emerging privacy challenges, Suresh Babu and Subhash (2024) analyzed mitigation strategies for data breaches and insider attacks in cloud environments. Their recommendations, such as continuous monitoring, encryption, and multi-factor authentication, highlight blockchain's complementary role in strengthening cloud security.

3.3 Ethical and Regulatory Issues

Bias and transparency have become growing concerns in the adoption of AI and ML technologies. Obermeyer et al. (2019) examined racial bias in health-related algorithms, revealing how training data imbalances can perpetuate inequality in care delivery. Cowgill et al. (2021) further investigated how algorithmic outcomes in financial services can be skewed by biased training data, emphasizing the need for ethics-driven design.

Pal (2022) discussed how financial services navigate digital transformation waves, stressing the importance of aligning technological adoption with organizational culture and governance. These insights support the inclusion of regulatory frameworks, fairness audits, and explainability tools within cloud-based AI governance structures.

Furthermore, Balodis and Opmane (2023) illustrated how national policy and political interests influence cryptographic advancements, suggesting that any responsible deployment of AI and blockchain must consider both ethical and geopolitical dimensions.

3.4 Case-Based Technological Integration

Multiple studies have presented compelling use cases for the integration of AI, ML, and blockchain technologies. Manoharan (2024) demonstrated how AI-powered social media automation drives audience engagement through personalization and behavior tracking. In another study, Manoharan (2024) highlighted the benefits of integrating cloud solutions for small business management, including cost reduction and operational agility.

Holzhauer and Mylrea (2020) proposed strategies for cyber resilience in critical infrastructure, particularly fossil fuel power plants. Their findings support the use of blockchain and AI in ensuring reliability and proactive threat response. Meanwhile, Bhasin and Tripathi (2021) assessed the readiness of industries to adopt quantum computing, noting potential breakthroughs in analytics performance.

Tsaramirsis et al. (2022) introduced a modern Industry 4.0 model that merges AI, IoT, and blockchain, demonstrating efficiencies in manufacturing processes. Lastly, Sharma et al. (2021) explored the integration of AI and blockchain for smart city data architectures, resulting in reduced latency and better privacy preservation.

4. SIGNIFICANCE OF SMART CLOUD INTEGRATION

4.1 How AI, ML, and Blockchain Complement Cloud Platforms

The integration of AI, ML, and Blockchain technologies within cloud platforms creates a powerful synergy that enhances data management and analytics capabilities. AI and ML algorithms can analyze and process large datasets efficiently, while Blockchain ensures that the data remains secure and immutable (Logambigai, R., & Suresh Babu, C. V. 2024).. This combination allows organizations to trust the insights generated from their data, knowing that it is protected from tampering. Furthermore, the use of these technologies in cloud environments facilitates the development of smart applications that can adapt and learn from user interactions, leading to improved customer experiences and operational efficiencies.

4.2 Enabling Real-Time Analytics and Enhanced Decision-Making

Smart cloud integration enables real-time analytics, allowing organizations to make timely and informed decisions based on up-to-date information. By leveraging AI and ML capabilities, businesses can analyze data streams as they are generated, providing insights that drive immediate action. This capability is particularly valuable in industries such as finance, healthcare, and retail, where timely decision-making can significantly impact outcomes. Moreover, the transparency and security provided by Blockchain technology enhance confidence in the data used for decision-making, fostering a culture of data-driven insights across organizations.

4.3 Blockchain for Security, Transparency, and Trust in Cloud Environments

Blockchain technology enhances security, transparency, and trust in cloud environments by providing a decentralized ledger that records transactions in a tamper-proof manner. This feature is crucial for industries that require high levels of data integrity, such as finance and healthcare. By utilizing Blockchain, organizations can track data provenance, ensuring that data is accurate and trustworthy. Additionally, the transparency offered by Blockchain can build customer trust, as stakeholders can verify the authenticity of transactions and data exchanges. This trust is essential for fostering collaboration and innovation in cloud-based ecosystems.

4.4 Practical Benefits for Various Industries

The practical benefits of integrating AI, ML, and Blockchain within cloud platforms are evident across various industries. In finance, these technologies enable secure transactions, fraud detection, and real-time analytics for risk assessment. In healthcare, they facilitate secure patient data management and enhance clinical decision-making through predictive analytics. The manufacturing sector benefits from improved supply chain transparency and predictive maintenance powered by AI-driven insights. By leveraging these technologies, organizations can streamline operations, enhance customer experiences, and ultimately drive growth and competitiveness in their respective markets.

4.5 Ethical Implications and Bias in AI-Driven Systems

As AI and machine learning (ML) models become deeply integrated into smart cloud platforms, ethical considerations—particularly algorithmic bias—have emerged as critical concerns. Bias in AI systems often originates from skewed or non-representative training datasets. For instance, models trained on historical data may inadvertently replicate existing societal inequalities, such as racial or gender discrimination. These biases become especially problematic when embedded in predictive algorithms used in decision-making systems.

In the **healthcare sector**, biased AI models can lead to disparities in diagnosis, treatment recommendations, and access to care. Studies have shown that some diagnostic tools perform poorly on patients with darker skin tones due to underrepresentation in training datasets (Obermeyer et al., 2019). Similarly, in the **financial domain**, bias in credit scoring algorithms may result in unfair loan approvals or interest rate determinations, disproportionately affecting minority groups (Cowgill et al., 2021).

Addressing these ethical challenges requires more than just technical adjustments; **organizational transformation** is essential. Companies must foster a culture of transparency, accountability, and inclusion. This includes revisiting governance models to incorporate AI ethics committees, mandating fairness audits, and establishing clear data stewardship policies. Moreover, multidisciplinary collaboration—between technologists, ethicists, domain experts, and regulators—is necessary to ensure responsible AI deployment.

Organizations should adopt frameworks that promote fairness and inclusivity in algorithm development, along with tools for **explainability** and **bias mitigation**. Regular training for developers and decision-makers on ethical AI practices is also vital. These steps not only help reduce algorithmic harm but also build trust in AI-driven smart cloud solutions.

5. INTEGRATION FRAMEWORK FOR AI, MACHINE LEARNING, AND BLOCKCHAIN IN CLOUD PLATFORMS

5.1 Architectural Models for AI-ML and Blockchain Integration

Integrating Artificial Intelligence (AI), Machine Learning (ML), and Blockchain technologies within cloud platforms requires robust architectural models that address the unique demands of each technology. A layered architecture is widely adopted to ensure modularity, interoperability, and scalability. These models typically include distinct layers for data ingestion, preprocessing, analytics execution, and blockchain-based transaction management. Each layer is responsible for specific functions such as secure data storage, model training, and consensus verification. This separation of concerns not only optimizes system performance but also facilitates easier upgrades and maintenance in cloud-native environments.

In advanced deployments, containerization and microservices further enhance the flexibility of the architecture, enabling seamless deployment across multi-cloud or hybrid infrastructures. Service orchestration tools such as Kubernetes can be leveraged to manage AI/ML workloads and blockchain nodes concurrently, ensuring continuous availability and load balancing.

5.2 Data Flow and Security Mechanisms

Effective integration depends on clearly defined data flow processes and robust security mechanisms. Data collected from various sources is ingested into cloud storage, where it undergoes preprocessing before being routed to AI/ML models for analysis. The results are then validated and recorded in blockchain ledgers to ensure transparency, auditability, and tamper-proof integrity.

To maintain confidentiality and integrity, cryptographic protocols are employed across all communication layers. Blockchain's decentralized validation mechanisms provide immutability, while cloud security layers use authentication, authorization, and encryption to protect against unauthorized access. Advanced mechanisms such as access control policies, multi-factor authentication, and role-based permissions ensure secure data exchange across services.

Figure 1. Project Phases Flowchart

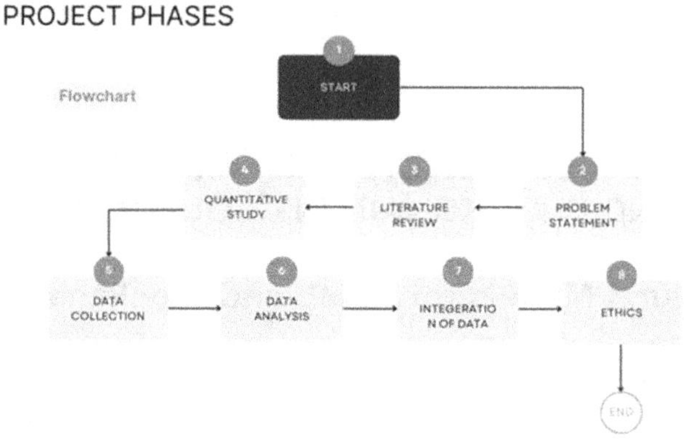

This flowchart outlines the phases of a project. It begins with identifying the problem statement, followed by a literature review. A quantitative study is then conducted, leading to data collection, analysis, and integration. The project concludes by addressing ethical considerations before reaching the end phase.

5.3 Challenges in System Design and Infrastructure Requirements

Despite the benefits, several challenges arise during system design, such as ensuring compatibility between AI toolchains, ML frameworks, and blockchain protocols. The complexity of integrating multiple systems increases operational overhead and demands high computational resources, especially when real-time analytics and blockchain consensus need to coexist. Careful planning and the use of standardized interfaces or APIs are essential to maintain architectural coherence and minimize integration bottlenecks.

5.4 Recommended Best Practices for Implementation

To maximize the success of integration efforts, organizations should adhere to best practices, including:

- Conducting detailed feasibility and risk assessments
- Establishing governance structures for responsible data and model usage
- Training cross-functional teams to manage both AI/ML and blockchain systems
- Adopting DevSecOps practices for continuous security assurance

6. BLOCKCHAIN AS A SERVICE (BAAS) IN SMART CLOUDS

6.1 BaaS: Platforms, Providers, and Models

Blockchain as a Service (BaaS) offers organizations tools and infrastructure to deploy and manage blockchain applications without the need to build their own networks. Providers such as Amazon Web Services (AWS), Microsoft Azure, and IBM Cloud deliver flexible solutions with pre-built templates and APIs. Organizations can choose between public, private, or hybrid blockchain systems, each designed to meet specific needs for security, transparency, and scalability. However, while BaaS simplifies blockchain adoption, challenges remain. Public blockchains, in particular, are computationally intensive and energy-demanding due to consensus mechanisms like Proof of Work (PoW), resulting in latency that limits real-time applicability. In contrast, hybrid models and alternatives like Proof of Stake (PoS) may offer faster and more energy-efficient solutions.

6.2 BaaS for Secure Transactions in Cloud-Based Analytics

BaaS facilitates secure, tamper-proof transactions via decentralized ledgers, which are critical in ensuring the integrity and traceability of data within cloud analytics. These capabilities enhance fraud prevention, compliance adherence, and automation through smart contracts—self-executing protocols embedded with predefined rules. In sectors like finance and healthcare, such automation improves operational efficiency and ensures auditability. Despite these benefits, BaaS platforms are not without limitations. High transaction volumes can result in network congestion and reduced processing speeds. Additionally, vulnerabilities in smart contract code may introduce risks that malicious actors can exploit. These challenges underscore the importance of rigorous testing frameworks and the implementation of Layer-2 scaling solutions to enhance performance and reliability.

6.3 Case Examples of BaaS in Enterprise Cloud Environments

Real-world implementations of BaaS illustrate its practicality across industries. In the financial sector, a multinational bank leveraged BaaS to streamline cross-border payments, significantly reducing transaction time and cost. In healthcare, a hospital network used BaaS to securely store and share patient records, ensuring privacy and accessibility for authorized users. Although these examples demonstrate the advantages of decentralized architectures, challenges persist—particularly with respect to energy-intensive validation mechanisms and latency. These issues are especially critical in time-sensitive domains such as logistics and IoT, where delays can undermine system efficiency. Adoption of permissioned blockchains and integration of parallel processing methods can help mitigate these issues.

6.4 Advantages and Disadvantages of Decentralized Data Management with BaaS

The decentralized nature of BaaS enhances data integrity, security, and transparency, making it well-suited for applications in supply chain management, healthcare, and finance. Decentralization reduces the risks associated with single points of failure and improves trust among stakeholders through tamper-evident records and provenance tracking. Nevertheless, decentralized systems also introduce challenges. High computational costs, energy usage, and processing delays—especially in PoW systems—can hinder scalability. Emerging models such as PoS and Directed Acyclic Graphs (DAGs) offer alternatives that reduce environmental impact and improve operational efficiency, making them suitable for large-scale cloud deployments.

7. MACHINE LEARNING AND AI-DRIVEN ANALYTICS IN CLOUD ECOSYSTEMS

7.1 Key AI and ML Tools for Cloud-Based Analytics

Numerous AI and ML tools are available within cloud ecosystems that facilitate advanced analytics. Popular platforms, such as Google Cloud AI, Azure Machine Learning, and AWS SageMaker, offer a range of tools for building, training, and deploying machine learning models. These tools provide pre-built algorithms, data visualization capabilities, and integration with other cloud services, making it easier for organizations to implement AI-driven analytics. By leveraging these tools, businesses can streamline their analytics processes and gain valuable insights from their data more efficiently.

7.2 AI and ML Techniques for Real-Time Data Processing and Decision-Making

AI and ML techniques have revolutionized real-time data processing and decision-making capabilities within cloud ecosystems. Techniques such as stream processing, real-time analytics, and predictive modeling enable organizations to analyze data as it is generated, providing insights that can drive immediate action. For instance, retail companies can use real-time analytics to adjust inventory levels based on current sales trends, while financial institutions can monitor transactions for fraudulent activity in real time. By harnessing these techniques, organizations can respond quickly to changing circumstances, enhancing their competitiveness in the market.

7.3 Case Studies of Cloud AI Applications across Industries

Cloud AI applications have been successfully implemented across various industries, demonstrating their transformative potential. In the retail sector, a leading e-commerce platform utilized AI-driven analytics to personalize customer experiences, resulting in increased sales and customer satisfaction. In manufacturing, predictive maintenance powered by AI models helped a company reduce downtime and improve operational efficiency. Additionally, the healthcare industry has seen significant advancements through AI applications, such as using machine learning algorithms to analyze medical imaging for early disease detection. These case studies highlight the diverse applications of cloud AI and their impact on business outcomes.

7.4 Advantages of AI-Driven Analytics for Organizational Insights

AI-driven analytics provide organizations with a multitude of advantages, including enhanced data-driven insights, improved operational efficiency, and the ability to identify trends and anomalies quickly. By leveraging AI algorithms, organizations can analyze complex datasets that would be overwhelming for human analysts, uncovering valuable insights that inform strategic decision-making. Additionally, AI-driven analytics can automate repetitive tasks, freeing up human resources to focus on higher-value activities. This combination of efficiency and insight enables organizations to innovate and adapt in a rapidly changing business landscape.

8. SECURITY AND PRIVACY CONSIDERATIONS IN SMART CLOUD DEPLOYMENTS

8.1 Data Privacy Challenges in Cloud-Based AI and ML

Artificial Intelligence (AI) and Machine Learning (ML) systems deployed in cloud environments often process sensitive data, raising concerns about data privacy. Adherence to data protection regulations such as the General Data Protection Regulation (GDPR) and the Health Insurance Portability and Accountability Act (HIPAA) requires robust governance frameworks. However, centralized cloud structures heighten the risk of data breaches. Additionally, AI-driven analytics require massive volumes of data, which increase the potential for aggregation vulnerabilities. Solutions such as federated learning and homomorphic encryption enable privacy-preserving analysis, allowing insights to be extracted without exposing raw data. These innovations help organizations maintain compliance while minimizing the risks of unauthorized access and misuse.

8.2 Blockchain-Enabled Security Models for Cloud Analytics

Blockchain enhances cloud security through its immutable, decentralized ledger and built-in access control mechanisms such as smart contracts. These features improve traceability and compliance in cloud-based analytics systems. Despite these strengths, blockchain presents its own set of limitations. Public blockchains can suffer from low transaction speeds, which hinder real-time processing. Additionally, the cumulative size of blockchain ledgers can strain storage capacities, posing challenges for long-term scalability. Techniques such as sidechains, off-chain storage solutions, and sharding are increasingly being adopted to address these concerns, enabling better performance without sacrificing security.

8.3 Mitigating Data Breaches and Ensuring Compliance

To secure smart cloud environments, organizations must implement multi-layered defense strategies, including encryption, firewalls, and intrusion detection systems. Routine audits and security training programs are essential to maintain compliance with industry standards and to reduce insider threat risks. While encryption is a vital component of data protection, it introduces challenges related to key management. A compromised or lost key can render encrypted data permanently inaccessible. Therefore, emerging technologies such as Quantum Key Distribution (QKD) and Zero-Trust security architectures are being explored to strengthen resilience and maintain system integrity in the face of increasingly sophisticated cyber threats.

9. CASE STUDIES AND USE CASES

9.1 Financial Sector: AI and BaaS for Secure Financial Transactions

The financial sector has embraced the integration of AI and BaaS to enhance security and efficiency in financial transactions. A notable case study involves a multinational bank that utilized a BaaS platform to develop a secure, transparent system for processing cross-border payments. By combining Blockchain technology with AI-driven analytics, the bank was able to reduce transaction times from days to mere hours while maintaining high levels of security and compliance. This integration not only improved customer satisfaction but also positioned the bank as a leader in innovative financial solutions.

9.2 Healthcare Industry: ML and Blockchain for Patient Data Management

In the healthcare industry, the integration of ML and Blockchain has transformed patient data management. A healthcare provider implemented a Blockchain-based system to securely store and share patient records, ensuring that data remained accurate and accessible to authorized personnel. By incorporating ML algorithms to analyze patient data, the provider could identify trends and predict potential health risks, leading to improved patient outcomes. This case study exemplifies how the convergence of these technologies can enhance data security and improve healthcare delivery.

9.3 Manufacturing and Supply Chain: Smart Analytics and Transparent Tracking

The manufacturing sector has also benefited from the integration of smart analytics and Blockchain for supply chain management. A leading manufacturer employed a Blockchain solution to track the provenance of raw materials, ensuring transparency and compliance with industry standards. By utilizing AI-driven analytics, the manufacturer could optimize inventory management and predict demand fluctuations, leading to cost savings and increased efficiency. This case demonstrates how smart cloud integration can enhance operational visibility and streamline supply chain processes.

9.4 Cross-Industry Analysis: Success Stories and Lessons Learned

Future developments in smart cloud technologies will be significantly influenced by innovations in AI, ML, and blockchain. Integration of these technologies is expected to advance fields such as edge computing, secure Internet of Things (IoT) environments, and privacy-preserving data analytics. Furthermore, industry–academic collaborations will be instrumental in driving research and technology transfer, leading to scalable and cost-effective smart cloud solutions. Fostering such collaboration can create ecosystems that are both innovative and ethically responsible.

10. KEY CHALLENGES AND LIMITATIONS

10.1 Technical Challenges in the Integration of AI, ML, and BaaS

The integration of AI, ML, and Blockchain-as-a-Service (BaaS) into cloud environments introduces several technical hurdles. These include seamless interoperability across diverse technologies, data integration from heterogeneous sources, and scalability under variable workloads. Furthermore, the dynamic evolution of AI and ML algorithms demands continuous updates, which can be resource-straining. Emerging trends like Edge AI and federated learning amplify these challenges as they require decentralized data processing capabilities and increased security measures. Organizations must develop modular architectures and adopt containerization strategies to enhance adaptability and performance.

10.2 Organizational Barriers to Adoption

Organizational factors also pose significant barriers to adoption, including resistance to change, lack of executive buy-in, and insufficient training programs. Aligning strategic goals with technological capabilities remains a critical challenge, leading to fragmented implementations. Moreover, data privacy concerns and regulatory compliance issues add complexity to adoption. Strategies such as pilot programs, collaborative planning, and cross-functional teams can help align organizational priorities. Leadership-driven support and trust in AI and blockchain technologies are essential to overcome these barriers.

10.3 Cost, Resource Allocation, and Skill Requirements

There is a significant cost and resource demand in implementing AI, ML, and BaaS. This includes the costs of hardware, software licenses, and upgrades in infrastructure besides training employees and talent acquisition. The shortage of AI and blockchain experts further makes the problem even worse, which leads to competition in hiring people. To overcome these challenges, organizations may use cloud subscription models to lower initial costs and also collaborate with institutions of learning for upskilling the existing workforce. Furthermore, investment in low-code/no-code platforms will cut down the overhead of development and speed up implementation.

10.4 Overcoming Interoperability and Compatibility Concerns

There is a major challenge of achieving interoperability and compatibility across all platforms. Most organizations struggle to interface legacy systems with modern AI, ML, and BaaS technologies and end up facing data silos and operational inefficiencies. Some of the new technologies that emerge as promising solutions include decentralized cloud infrastructures and multi-cloud architectures, which call for standardization and governance frameworks. Industry standards, APIs, and containerized applications help improve compatibility. Regular infrastructure assessment and incremental upgrade can further facilitate integration efforts while improving performance.

11. STRATEGIES FOR IMPLEMENTING SMART CLOUD SOLUTIONS

11.1 Roadmap for Successful Integration of AI, ML, and BaaS

A strategic roadmap is essential for the successful integration of AI, ML, and Blockchain-as-a-Service (BaaS) in smart cloud ecosystems. This process begins with a readiness assessment, identifying technological gaps and aligning integration efforts with organizational goals. Establishing clear success criteria, milestones, and timelines is crucial to ensure execution remains focused and measurable.

The roadmap should prioritize modular and interoperable architectures, enabling plug-and-play functionality across different platforms and minimizing vendor lock-in. In addition, implementing continuous feedback mechanisms allows for real-time refinements throughout the deployment lifecycle.

11.2 Identifying and Overcoming Common Pitfalls

Common integration pitfalls include underestimating the complexity of data pipelines, overlooking regulatory obligations, and failing to anticipate infrastructure scaling needs. These can be mitigated by:

- Early-stage investment in compliance-readiness tools
- Adoption of containerized architectures for scalable deployment
- Deployment of proof-of-concept projects to validate assumptions

Organizations should also ensure that AI models are continuously monitored and retrained using fresh data to avoid model drift and performance degradation.

11.3 Best Practices for Change Management and Skill Development

Change management plays a pivotal role in integrating intelligent systems into existing operations. Establishing training programs to upskill employees in AI, ML, and blockchain technologies ensures that the workforce is adequately prepared. Cross-functional collaboration and knowledge sharing help bridge the gap between domain expertise and technological implementation.

Additionally, fostering a culture that embraces innovation, experimentation, and ethical responsibility is vital for long-term integration success.

11.4 Framework for Evaluating Success and Measuring ROI

A robust evaluation framework should be built around quantifiable metrics such as:

- Reduction in processing time
- Accuracy and precision of AI models
- Blockchain transaction throughput and latency
- Return on investment (ROI) over a defined operational window

Organizations should implement dashboards and monitoring tools that continuously assess system health, data quality, and security compliance. These insights support data-driven decision-making and enable organizations to scale with confidence.

12. FUTURE TRENDS AND EMERGING TECHNOLOGIES

12.1 Quantum Computing: Potential Impact on Cloud-Based Analytics

Quantum computing is poised to revolutionize cloud-based analytics by enabling organizations to process vast amounts of data at unprecedented speeds. The unique properties of quantum systems allow for parallel processing of complex algorithms, which can significantly enhance machine learning and optimization tasks. As quantum computing becomes more accessible, organizations that leverage this technology will gain a competitive advantage in their analytics capabilities, unlocking new insights and driving innovation.

12.2 Evolving Role of BaaS in Multi-Cloud Environments

As organizations increasingly adopt multi-cloud strategies, the role of BaaS is evolving to support seamless integration across different cloud platforms. BaaS solutions are becoming more versatile, allowing organizations to manage blockchain applications across multiple cloud environments. This evolution will enable businesses to enhance their agility and flexibility while benefiting from the unique features of various cloud providers. Furthermore, as BaaS becomes more widely adopted, best practices for interoperability and standardization will emerge, streamlining implementation processes.

12.3 AI-Driven Blockchain Models for Enhanced Security

The combination of AI and blockchain technology is leading to the development of innovative models that enhance security and data integrity. AI algorithms can analyze blockchain transactions in real-time, identifying anomalies and potential security threats. Additionally, AI can be employed to automate compliance processes and streamline audits, further strengthening security measures. As organizations increasingly recognize the value of integrating AI and blockchain, we can expect to see more sophisticated security models emerging in the coming years.

12.4 Future Innovations in Smart Clouds for Business and Research

The future of smart clouds will be shaped by ongoing innovations in AI, ML, and blockchain technologies. As organizations continue to explore new applications and use cases, we can expect to see advancements in areas such as edge computing,

IoT integration, and data privacy solutions. Furthermore, the collaboration between businesses and research institutions will drive the development of cutting-edge technologies that enhance the capabilities of smart clouds. This collaborative approach will lead to the emergence of more efficient, secure, and scalable cloud solutions that benefit a wide range of industries.

13. CONCLUSION

Smart cloud integration—combining Artificial Intelligence (AI), Machine Learning (ML), and blockchain—has introduced transformative potential in how data is managed, analyzed, and secured across modern digital ecosystems. These technologies, when strategically integrated within cloud environments, enhance organizational agility, data integrity, and analytical capabilities.

A key insight from this study is the need for a holistic approach that prioritizes not only technical excellence but also ethical governance and compliance. Organizations are encouraged to adopt inclusive data strategies, implement scalable architectures, and invest in employee upskilling to effectively leverage these technologies.

The convergence of AI, ML, and blockchain is poised to reshape decision-making in healthcare, finance, manufacturing, and beyond. With regulatory frameworks evolving and privacy expectations increasing, sustainable innovation will depend on transparent data practices and adaptive infrastructure.

As future trends point toward the mainstream adoption of quantum computing, decentralized finance, and autonomous systems, smart clouds will remain central to digital transformation. Businesses that proactively embrace these trends will be best positioned to drive innovation, resilience, and long-term growth.

REFERENCES

Aggarwal, P. (2023). Neural architectures for secure data transmission in next-gen networks. In *2023 IEEE International Conference on ICT in Business Industry & Government (ICTBIG)* (pp. 1-6). IEEE. DOI: 10.1109/ICTBIG59752.2023.10455999

Balodis, R., & Opmane, I. (2023, February). Cryptography in Latvia: Academic background meets political objectives. In *International Congress on Information and Communication Technology* (pp. 143–154). Springer Nature Singapore. DOI: 10.1007/978-981-99-3243-6_12

Bao, S., Liang, Y., & Xu, H. (2022). Blockchain for network slicing in 5G and beyond: Survey and challenges. *Journal of Communications and Information Networks*, *7*(4), 349–359. DOI: 10.23919/JCIN.2022.10005213

Bhasin, A., & Tripathi, M. (2021). Quantum computing at an inflection point: Are we ready for a new paradigm? *IEEE Transactions on Engineering Management*, *70*(7), 2546–2557. DOI: 10.1109/TEM.2021.3103904

Cowgill, B., Dell'Acqua, F., & Deng, S. (2021). *Biased programmers? Or biased data? A field experiment in operationalizing AI ethics*. National Bureau of Economic Research., DOI: 10.3386/w29620

Esenogho, E., Djouani, K., & Kurien, A. M. (2022). Integrating artificial intelligence, Internet of Things, and 5G for next-generation smartgrid: A survey of trends, challenges, and prospects. *IEEE Access : Practical Innovations, Open Solutions*, *10*, 4794–4804. DOI: 10.1109/ACCESS.2022.3140595

Holzhauer, D., & Mylrea, M. (2020). *Cyber resilient fossil fuel power plants and control systems of the future: Final report highlighting recommendations (No. DOE/GE-FE0031641)*. General Electric Global Research. DOI: 10.2172/1770871

Logambigai, R., & Suresh Babu, C. V. (2024). Blockchain Empowerment for Securing IoT, Sensory Data in Next-Gen Intelligent Systems. In Sharma, S., Prakash, A., & Sugumaran, V. (Eds.), *Developments Towards Next Generation Intelligent Systems for Sustainable Development* (pp. 1–34). IGI Global., DOI: 10.4018/979-8-3693-5643-2.ch001

Manoharan, A. (2024). Blockchain technology: Reinventing trust and security in the digital world. https://doi.org/DOI: 10.56726/IRJMETS23989

Manoharan, A. (2024). Enhancing audience engagement through AI-powered social media automation. *World Journal of Advanced Engineering Technology and Sciences*, *11*(2), 150–157. DOI: 10.30574/wjaets.2024.11.2.0084

Manoharan, A. (2024). Integrating cloud computing solutions for comprehensive small business management. https://doi.org/DOI: 10.56726/IRJMETS50036

Manoharan, A. (2024). The rise of quantum cryptography: Securing data beyond classical means. DOI: 10.56726/IRJMETS24238

Manoharan, A., & Nagar, G. (2024). Maximizing learning trajectories: An investigation into AI-driven natural language processing integration in online educational platforms. https://doi.org/DOI: 10.56726/IRJMETS18093

Manoharan, A., & Nagulapally, S. (2024). Adaptive gamification algorithms for personalized learning experiences in educational platforms. https://doi.org/DOI: 10.56726/IRJMETS49966

Obermeyer, Z., Powers, B., Vogeli, C., & Mullainathan, S. (2019). Dissecting racial bias in an algorithm used to manage the health of populations. *Science*, *366*(6464), 447–453. DOI: 10.1126/science.aax2342 PMID: 31649194

Pal, P. (2022). The adoption of waves of digital technology as antecedents of digital transformation by financial services institutions. *Journal of Digital Banking*, *7*(1), 70–91. DOI: 10.69554/QHFT9370

Rodenberg, J., & Gehring, T. (2023). Quantum key distribution for data center security—A feasibility study. *arXiv preprint arXiv:2307.13098*.

Sharma, A., Podoplelova, E., Shapovalov, G., Tselykh, A., & Tselykh, A. (2021). Sustainable smart cities: Convergence of artificial intelligence and blockchain. *Sustainability (Basel)*, *13*(23), 13076. DOI: 10.3390/su132313076

Suresh Babu, C. V., Subhash, S., Vignesh, M., Jeyavasan, T., & Muthumanikavel, V. (2024). Securing the Cloud: Understanding and Mitigating Data Breaches and Insider Attacks in Cloud Computing Environments. In Goel, P., Pandey, H., Singhal, A., & Agarwal, S. (Eds.), *Analyzing and Mitigating Security Risks in Cloud Computing* (pp. 1–23). IGI Global., DOI: 10.4018/979-8-3693-3249-8.ch001

Suresh Babu, C. V., & Srisakthi, S. (2023). Cyber Physical Systems and Network Security: The Present Scenarios and Its Applications. In Thanigaivelan, R., Kaliappan, S., & Jegadheesan, C. (Eds.), *Cyber-Physical Systems and Supporting Technologies for Industrial Automation* (pp. 104–130). IGI Global., DOI: 10.4018/978-1-6684-9267-3.ch006

Suresh Babu, C. V., & Subhash, S. (2024). Securing the Cloud: Understanding and Mitigating Data Breaches and Insider Attacks in Cloud Computing Environments. In Goel, P. (Eds.), *Analyzing and Mitigating Security Risks in Cloud Computing* (pp. 1–23). IGI Global., DOI: 10.4018/979-8-3693-3249-8.ch001

Tsaramirsis, G., Kantaros, A., Al-Darraji, I., Piromalis, D., Apostolopoulos, C., Pavlopoulou, A., Alrammal, M., Ismail, Z., Buhari, S. M., Stojmenovic, M., Tamimi, H., Randhawa, P., Patel, A., & Khan, F. Q. (2022). A modern approach towards an industry 4.0 model: From driving technologies to management. *Journal of Sensors*, *2022*, 1–18. DOI: 10.1155/2022/5023011

Chapter 9
Synergizing Cloud Computing and Blockchain Architectures: Applications and Implications

Sheraz Maki Mohd Ahmed
https://orcid.org/0009-0004-0967-4455
International Islamic University Malaysia, Malaysia

Aisha Hassan Abdalla Hashim
International Islamic University Malaysia, Malaysia

Zainab Senan Attar
https://orcid.org/0000-0002-1452-8098
Kulliyya of Engineering, Malaysia

Othman Omran Khalifa
https://orcid.org/0000-0002-0847-6017
International Islamic University Malaysia, Malaysia

ABSTRACT

Blockchain is a decentralized and distributed digital ledger that records transactions across multiple computers. It consists of a continuously growing list of blocks, where each block contains a set of transactions and a reference to the previous block. The blockchain ensures the immutability and integrity of the recorded transactions by using cryptographic hashes and consensus mechanisms. Cloud computing is a service available over the network. Users can access and store data and applications remotely rather than on local servers or personal computers. Cloud computing offers resource pooling by letting users share the same physical resources dynamically

DOI: 10.4018/979-8-3693-9984-2.ch009

according to their demands, often through virtualization. Cloud computing offers flexible, scalable resources, it can address blockchain's limitations in scalability and transaction speeds by act as a backup for blockchain data, enabling faster recovery and reduced latency. Synergy between cloud computing and blockchain offers significant potential for innovation across numerous sectors

1. INTRODUCTION

Blockchain is a decentralized and distributed ledger system designed to record transactions across a network of computers or nodes (Wright, 2008). Each transaction is grouped into blocks, which are cryptographically linked to preceding blocks, forming a chronological chain—hence the term blockchain. This structure utilizes cryptographic hashes and consensus protocols to maintain data security and ensure immutability. However, as participation and transaction volume increases, the consensus mechanism can slow down, potentially introducing latency and limiting the system's scalability and responsiveness in real time.

Cloud computing, on the other hand, delivers services over a network, enabling users to access and manage applications and data remotely rather than relying on local infrastructure. It supports dynamic resource sharing through virtualization, allowing multiple users to efficiently utilize shared physical resources based on real-time demands (Al-Hamad et al., 2024).

The scalability and flexibility offered by cloud computing can help address some of blockchain's inherent limitations, particularly in terms of transaction throughput and data latency. Acting as a backup layer for blockchain data, cloud infrastructure can enhance recovery speed and reduce processing delays.

The convergence of cloud computing and blockchain technologies represents a major shift for industries aiming to improve efficiency, transparency, and data security (Ahmadi, 2024). Cloud platforms provide on-demand resources, while blockchain ensures trust, decentralization, and immutability. Together, these technologies can reinforce data integrity, optimize workflows, and support the creation of innovative business models.

Services such as Infrastructure as a Service (IaaS) and Platform as a Service (PaaS) can be used to host blockchain components like nodes and smart contracts. Application Programming Interfaces (APIs) facilitate interaction between blockchain systems and cloud platforms. Hybrid solutions that integrate public and private clouds with blockchain networks allow organizations to make data privacy levels, while also supporting consortium blockchains managed collaboratively by multiple stakeholders.

The combined use of cloud computing and blockchain is being adopted across various sectors:

- Supply Chain Management: Blockchain enhances product traceability and accountability, while cloud systems enable real-time data analytics and reporting to track goods efficiently.
- Financial Services: Integrated solutions improve transaction processing and fraud detection. Smart contracts, executed in the cloud, can automate and enforce secure digital agreements.
- Healthcare: Blockchain can securely store patient information, while cloud computing ensures scalable access and sharing of medical data. This leads to better patient care, data security, and fraud prevention.
- Internet of Things (IoT): Cloud platforms process large volumes of IoT-generated data, and blockchain secures device identity and data exchanges. This integration supports secure, automated operations in domains like smart cities and industrial automation.

The synergy of cloud computing, blockchain, and IoT, when combined with advancements in artificial intelligence and edge computing, has the potential to unlock groundbreaking innovation (Al-Ahmad & Kahtan, 2018). It enables secure interaction between smart devices and supports automation in diverse applications, ranging from urban infrastructure to industrial systems.

Inconclusion the fusion of blockchain and cloud computing offers substantial opportunities for digital transformation. As organizations continue to explore these technologies, it is essential to make informed decisions regarding architecture, practical applications, and broader concerns such as data privacy, compliance, and operational cost.

Keywords: Synergizing, cloud computing, Blockchain, cryptographic hashes, IOT.

2. BLOCKCHAIN AND CLOUD COMPUTING: ARCHITECTURE AND DESIGN

2.1 Blockchain

Blockchain is a distributed ledger system that operates without a central authority, securely storing transactions and data across a network of interconnected nodes (Wright, 2008). Its design emphasizes transparency, data integrity, and resistance to tampering. Functioning over a peer-to-peer network, blockchain ensures that control is decentralized—no single party manages the information. Instead, transactions are collectively validated by the network's participants. Once recorded, data on the blockchain becomes immutable, meaning it cannot be changed or erased. This level of security is made possible through cryptographic hashing and consensus algorithms. Figure 1 shows the structure of blockchain technology.

Figure 1. Chain of Blocks

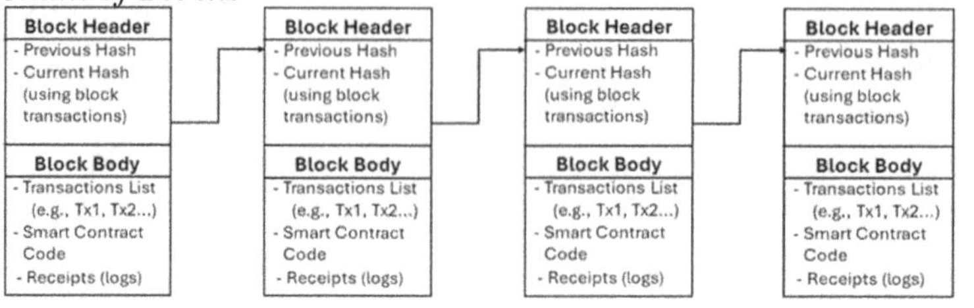

In public blockchains, all transactions are transparent and viewable by every participant, while in private blockchains, visibility is limited to authorized users (Z. Zheng et al., 2017). Every update to the ledger is recorded and can be traced, ensuring full accountability. Information is encrypted and organized into interconnected blocks, each secured through cryptographic hash functions. Trust within the system is maintained through consensus algorithms, such as Proof of Work or Proof of Stake, eliminating the need for centralized intermediaries.

Blockchain enables the use of smart contracts which are automated, self-executing programs that trigger specific actions once predetermined conditions are fulfilled, thereby streamlining and automating various processes.

2.1.1 Types of blockchain

Blockchain technology has evolved into various types (An et al., 2023):

- **Public blockchain:** is open to anyone, allowing all participants to read, write, and validate transactions without restrictions. These blockchains are fully decentralized, meaning no single entity controls the network. Bitcoin and Ethereum are the most well-known examples, where transactions are transparent and secured through consensus mechanisms like Proof-of-Work (PoW) or Proof-of-Stake (PoS). Public blockchains are ideal for applications requiring trustless interactions, such as cryptocurrencies and decentralized applications (DApps). However, they face challenges in scalability and energy consumption due to their open nature.
- **Private blockchain:** is restricted and controlled by a single organization. Only authorized participants can join, making them more efficient and scal-

able for enterprise use. Hyperledger Fabric and R3 Corda are common examples, often used in banking, supply chain management, and internal record-keeping. Private blockchains offer better privacy and faster transactions but sacrifice decentralization, as they rely on a central authority for governance.

- **Consortium blockchain:** is a semi-decentralized model managed by a group of organizations rather than a single entity. This type balances transparency and control, making it suitable for industries where multiple stakeholders collaborate, such as banking (Ripple) and logistics (TradeLens). While more decentralized than private blockchains, consortium chains still require trust among members, and decision-making can be complex due to shared governance.
- **Hybrid blockchain:** combines elements of public and private blockchains, allowing businesses to customize access levels. Some data remains private, while other parts are publicly verifiable. Examples include Dragonchain (used by Disney) and IBM Food Trust (for supply chain tracking). Hybrid blockchains provide flexibility, scalability, and controlled transparency but are more complex to implement than purely public or private systems.

Table 1 shows a comparison between these different types of blockchain

Table 1. Blockchain Types Comparison Table

Feature	Public Blockchain	Private Blockchain	Consortium Blockchain	Hybrid Blockchain
Decentralization	Fully decentralized (no owner)	Centralized (single organization)	Semi-decentralized (group of orgs)	Partial (mix of public + private)
Access Control	Permissionless (anyone can join)	Permissioned (invite-only)	Permissioned (selected members)	Customizable (public + private zones)
Consensus	PoW (Bitcoin), PoS (Ethereum 2.0)	Voting-based, PBFT, RAFT	PBFT, PoA	Flexible (depends on use case)
Speed (TPS)	Slow (Bitcoin: 7 TPS, ETH: 15-30)	Fast (1,000+ TPS)	Moderate (100-500 TPS)	Variable (scales with configuration)
Transparency	Fully transparent (all data public)	Restricted (only to members)	Partial (shared among members)	Selective (public/ private data)
Immutability	High (tamper-proof)	Moderate (admin can alter rules)	High (but consortium can intervene)	Customizable
Energy Use	High (PoW) → Low (PoS)	Low (efficient consensus)	Low to moderate	Depends on design
Security	High (attack-resistant)	Moderate (trust in admin)	High (trusted validators)	Balanced (public + private security)

continued on following page

Table 1. Continued

Feature	Public Blockchain	Private Blockchain	Consortium Blockchain	Hybrid Blockchain
Scalability	Low (network congestion)	High (controlled nodes)	Moderate (optimized for groups)	High (flexible architecture)
Governance	Community-driven	Single entity	Multi-organization	Mixed (public + private rules)
Use Cases	Cryptocurrencies, DeFi, NFTs	Enterprise supply chains, internal audits	Banking consortia, trade finance	Healthcare, govt. records, hybrid DApps
Examples	Bitcoin, Ethereum, Solana	Hyperledger Fabric, Quorum, Corda	Ripple (XRP), TradeLens, Energy Web	Dragonchain, IBM Food Trust, XinFin

Blockchain scheduling mechanisms play an important role in determining how transactions and operations are processed within decentralized networks. These mechanisms are particularly crucial in maintaining network efficiency, security, and fairness, with different consensus algorithms employing distinct approaches to scheduling. Among the most prominent scheduling mechanisms are Proof of Work (PoW) and Proof of Stake (PoS), each offering unique advantages and presenting specific challenges in terms of transaction ordering and block creation (Jha et al., 2024).

Proof of Work (PoW), the pioneering consensus mechanism implemented in Bitcoin, employs a competitive scheduling approach where miners race to solve complex cryptographic puzzles (Casino et al., 2019). This system creates a natural scheduling queue where the first miner to solve the puzzle earns the right to propose the next block and collect the associated rewards. The PoW scheduling mechanism inherently prioritizes computational power, as miners with greater hash power have higher probabilities of being selected to create blocks. However, this energy-intensive process introduces significant latency, as the network must wait for puzzle solutions, and creates a scheduling environment where transaction ordering can be influenced by fee incentives, potentially leading to front-running opportunities. The PoW scheduling model provides strong security guarantees due to its computational requirements, but at the cost of scalability and energy efficiency.

In contrast, Proof of Stake (PoS) systems, such as those implemented in Ethereum 2.0 and Cardano, utilize a deterministic scheduling approach based on participants' economic stake in the network (Jha et al., 2024). Validators are chosen to propose blocks through a pseudo-random selection process weighted by the amount of cryptocurrency they have staked. This scheduling mechanism eliminates the energy-intensive mining competition of PoW, instead creating a predictable rotation of block proposers. The PoS scheduling model offers several advantages, including faster block times, reduced energy consumption, and more consistent transaction processing rates. However, it introduces different scheduling challenges, particularly around ensuring equitable participation and preventing wealth concentration from dictating network control. Modern PoS implementations often incorporate additional scheduling parameters, such as validator performance metrics and randomization techniques, to enhance fairness and security.

The evolution of blockchain scheduling mechanisms extends beyond these foundational models, with hybrid systems and innovative variations continuing to emerge. Delegated Proof of Stake (DPoS) systems, for instance, implement a representative scheduling model where stakeholders elect delegates responsible for block production (Sun et al., 2021). This approach further optimizes scheduling efficiency by reducing the number of participants involved in consensus, enabling faster transaction processing while maintaining decentralized characteristics. As blockchain technology matures, the refinement of scheduling mechanisms remains a critical area of innovation, balancing the competing demands of decentralization, security, and performance in increasingly complex network environments.

Practical Byzantine Fault Tolerance (PBFT) represents another critical approach to blockchain scheduling, particularly suited for permissioned networks requiring high throughput and immediate finality (Wu et al., 2023). Unlike PoW or PoS, PBFT operates through a leader-based, multi-round voting mechanism where a primary node proposes blocks and backup nodes validate them in sequential phases (pre-prepare, prepare, and commit). This deterministic scheduling ensures consensus is achieved with low latency (often sub-second) as long as at least two-thirds of nodes are honest, making it ideal for enterprise applications like Hyperledger Fabric (Zhang et al., 2025). However, PBFT's $O(n^2)$ communication overhead limits scalability to small-to-medium networks (Luo, 2023). Recent variants like SBFT (Scalable BFT) and HotStuff optimize PBFT's scheduling by reducing message complexity, enabling broader adoption in consortium blockchains for finance and supply chains (Leduc et al., 2023; Zhu et al., 2025). While PBFT sacrifices some decentralization for performance, its predictable scheduling and Byzantine resilience offer a compelling alternative for use cases where trust boundaries are well-defined but absolute finality is paramount.

Future developments in scheduling algorithms may incorporate more sophisticated parameters, such as transaction dependencies in smart contract execution or dynamic prioritization based on network conditions, to further enhance blockchain scalability and usability. Table 2 compares different blockchain scheduling mechanisms.

Table 2. Comparison of Blockchain Scheduling Mechanisms

Feature	Proof of Work (PoW)	Proof of Stake (PoS)	Delegated Proof of Stake (DPoS)	Practical Byzantine Fault Tolerance (PBFT)
Selection Method	Miners compete via computational puzzles	Validators chosen based on stake + randomization	Stakeholders vote for delegates	Round-robin or leader-based rotation
Energy Efficiency	Low (energy-intensive)	High (minimal energy use)	High	Moderate
Transaction Speed	Slow (e.g., Bitcoin: 7 TPS)	Moderate (e.g., Ethereum: 15–30 TPS)	Fast (e.g., EOS: 4,000+ TPS)	Fast (1,000+ TPS)
Fairness	Bias toward hash power	Bias toward stake size	Bias toward voter approval	Fair rotation among nodes
Decentralization	High (permissionless)	Moderate (stake requirements)	Lower (small delegate sets)	Low (permissioned)
Security Model	51% hash power attack	51% stake attack	Collusion among delegates	⅓ Byzantine fault tolerance
Latency	High (10+ min block times)	Low (seconds to minutes)	Very low (sub-second finality)	Low (near-instant finality)
Use Cases	Public blockchains (Bitcoin)	Public chains (Ethereum 2.0, Cardano)	High-throughput DApps (EOS, Tron)	Enterprise chains (Hyperledger)
Scheduling Focus	First-to-solve competition	Stake-weighted randomness	Reputation-based delegation	Deterministic rotation
Attacks Resisted	Double-spending, Sybil	Nothing-at-stake, Long-range	Vote buying, Cartelization	Byzantine failures

2.1.2 Advantages of blockchain

Blockchain technology offers numerous benefits that make it valuable across various industries. One of its primary advantages is transparency, which enhances trust among users. Since all transactions are recorded on a distributed ledger and can be verified by any participant, there is no need to rely on central authority. This openness reduces the risk of hidden manipulation and fosters accountability.

Another key benefit is immutability. Once data is added to the blockchain, it becomes extremely difficult to alter or delete. Each block contains a cryptographic hash of the previous block, creating a secure chain that resists tampering. This feature makes blockchain highly resistant to fraud, ensuring that transaction records remain permanent and verifiable.

Decentralization is another major advantage. Unlike traditional databases that rely on centralized servers, blockchain operates on a peer-to-peer network where data is distributed across multiple nodes. This structure eliminates single points of failure, reducing vulnerability to cyberattacks and system failures. Even if some nodes go offline, the network remains operational, enhancing reliability.

Additionally, blockchain improves security through cryptographic techniques such as hashing and digital signatures. Transactions must be validated by consensus mechanisms (e.g., Proof of Work or Proof of Stake), making unauthorized changes nearly impossible without majority network approval.

Due to these benefits, industries such as finance, supply chain management, healthcare, and real estate are increasingly adopting blockchain. Financial institutions use it for secure cross-border payments, supply chains use it for traceability, and healthcare systems employ it for tamper-proof medical records.

However, blockchain systems face challenges related to scalability and resource management. Since nodes must store and process large amounts of data, efficient scheduling mechanisms are crucial to prevent bottlenecks. These scheduling protocols must align with the underlying consensus model—for example, PoW requires computational power competition, while PoS relies on stake-based validator selection. Proper scheduling ensures smooth transaction processing while maintaining security and decentralization.

2.1.3 Challenges of blockchain

Blockchain technology brings significant advantages such as decentralization, transparency, and enhanced security. Despite these benefits, it faces several challenges that hinder its widespread implementation and operational efficiency. Among the most pressing issues is scalability. Leading blockchain platforms like Bitcoin and Ethereum can only handle a limited number of transactions per second (TPS), resulting in congestion and slow processing times. This limitation stems from the fact that each node in the network must validate and store every transaction, causing delays as the network grows.

Another major concern is energy consumption. Consensus mechanisms like Proof of Work (PoW), particularly used in Bitcoin, demand substantial computational resources, leading to high energy usage and raising environmental and sustainability issues.

Cost and efficiency also pose barriers to adoption. The deployment and ongoing maintenance of blockchain infrastructure can be costly, especially for small to medium-sized enterprises, making it less accessible for some organizations.

Regulatory uncertainty further complicates adoption. Businesses must adapt to evolving legal frameworks and compliance requirements that vary across regions, making consistent implementation difficult. Additionally, due to scalability issues, high transaction fees and slow confirmation times can discourage broader usage.

To address these challenges, innovations are needed in core components of blockchain technology, such as improving consensus algorithms, or through integration with complementary technologies like cloud computing and the Internet of Things (IoT), which can enhance performance, reduce costs, and support scalability.

2.2 Cloud computing

Cloud computing is the on-demand delivery of computing resources like servers, storage, databases, networking, software, and analytics, over the internet (Ionescu & Andronie, 2021). It enables users to access and use these resources without the need to own or manage physical infrastructure, offering flexibility, scalability, and cost efficiency. Cloud computing delivers access to services like computing power and storage. These resources are made available to users in a virtualized format, such as Virtual Machines (VMs), enabling multiple application services to operate concurrently on a single physical machine.

The use of cloud computing depends on maintaining the security of data and information with the importance of maintaining the speed of sending and retrieving this data that managed by various technologies and protocols using wide area networks (WANs). Cloud computing defined five essential characteristics, three service models and four deployment models, The service model comprised of: Infrastructure as a Service (IaaS), Platform as a Service (PaaS), and Software as a Service. The deployment models consist of: Public cloud, Private cloud, Hybrid cloud and community cloud

2.2.1 Types of Service Models of Cloud Computing

Cloud computing offers three primary service models: Infrastructure as a Service (IaaS), Platform as a Service (PaaS), and Software as a Service (SaaS). IaaS provides virtualized computing resources such as servers, storage, and networking, giving users full control over operating systems and applications while the cloud provider manages the physical hardware. This model, exemplified by services like Amazon EC2 and Google Compute Engine, is ideal for businesses requiring customizable infrastructure for tasks like web hosting or big data analysis. While IaaS offers flexibility and scalability, it demands significant IT expertise to manage the virtualized environment (Samha, 2024).

PaaS offers a middle ground by providing a cloud-based platform for developers to build, test, and deploy applications without managing the underlying infrastructure. Services like Heroku and Microsoft Azure App Service include development tools, databases, and middleware, streamlining the app development process with features like automated deployment and built-in scalability. PaaS reduces operational overhead and accelerates development cycles but may limit infrastructure control and pose vendor lock-in risks due to platform-specific tools (Bushay, 2025).

At the highest abstraction level, SaaS delivers ready-to-use software applications accessible via web browsers or mobile apps, with providers handling all maintenance and updates. Popular examples include Google Workspace for productivity tools, Salesforce for customer relationship management, and Dropbox for file storage. SaaS eliminates installation and maintenance burdens while ensuring users always have access to the latest features, though customization options may be limited compared to IaaS or PaaS solutions. These three service models form a continuum of cloud computing options, allowing organizations to choose the right balance of control, convenience, and technical requirements for their specific use cases. Table 3 compares different service models for cloud computing.

Table 3. Comparison of IaaS, PaaS, and SaaS

Feature	IaaS	PaaS	SaaS
Control Level	High (OS & apps managed)	Medium (code deployment)	Low (pre-built software)
User Responsibility	OS, apps, data	Apps and data	Only data
Scalability	Manual scaling	Auto-scaling	Auto-scaling
Example	AWS EC2	Heroku	Google Docs

2.2.2 Deployment Models of Cloud Computing

Cloud computing deployment models offer organizations different approaches to managing their IT infrastructure based on specific needs for security, control, and cost-efficiency. The public cloud model, provided by third-party vendors like AWS, Azure, and Google Cloud, delivers shared computing resources over the internet, making it a cost-effective and scalable solution ideal for businesses with variable workloads (Q. Zheng et al., 2020). While this model reduces capital expenses and eliminates hardware maintenance, it offers less control over security and compliance compared to other options. In contrast, private clouds provide dedicated infrastructure for a single organization, either hosted on-premises or by a third party, delivering enhanced security and customization at a higher operational cost. This model proves particularly valuable for regulated industries like healthcare and finance that require strict data governance.

For organizations seeking flexibility, the hybrid cloud model merges public and private cloud environments, allowing seamless movement of workloads between them. This approach enables businesses to maintain sensitive data in private infrastructure while using the public cloud's scalability for less critical operations, though it requires careful integration to manage potential complexity. The community cloud model serves groups of organizations with shared requirements, such as government agencies or research institutions, offering a middle ground between public and private clouds with collaborative benefits and industry-specific compliance features. Each deployment model presents distinct advantages: public clouds excel in affordability and scalability, private clouds prioritize security and control, hybrid clouds balance both worlds, and community clouds facilitate specialized collaboration. The choice among these models depends on an organization's specific operational needs, regulatory obligations, and growth objectives, with emerging trends like multi-cloud strategies further expanding deployment possibilities in today's evolving digital landscape.

2.2.3 Advantages of Cloud Computing

Cost Savings by reducing the need for on-premises infrastructure and IT maintenance. Scalability for easily scales resources up or down based on demand. Accessibility enables remote work and collaboration from anywhere with an internet connection. Disaster Recovery provides backups and recovery solutions for business continuity. Automatic Updates for software and hardware are handled by the provider.

Cloud computing offers a range of advantages that can enhance efficiency, scalability, and overall effectiveness for both businesses and individuals. No need for extensive hardware purchases; users can pay for only the resources they use. Also Cloud service providers handle infrastructure maintenance and upgrades. Easily scale resources up or down based on demand, allowing organizations to adapt quickly to changes in workload. Cloud services can be accessed from anywhere with an internet connection, supporting remote work and collaboration. Regular backups and data redundancy in multiple locations reduce the risk of data loss. And there is more advantages that make cloud computing an appealing option for companies looking to enhance their operations while minimizing costs and risks.

2.2.4 Challenges of Cloud Computing

Cloud computing has become a crucial component of modern IT infrastructure, but it also comes with its own set of challenges. Security and Privacy is a big challenge for Data, and unauthorized access can damage sensitive information.

In cloud computing the data stored in the cloud is vulnerable to breaches and unauthorized access. Vendor Lock-In occurred by migrating data or applications to a different provider can be difficult. Centralization is another challenge that occur in cloud computing. When a large number of users and providers connect to a center it can lead to bottleneck issues, affecting performance and system efficiency.

In summary Blockchain is revolutionizing industries by enabling trust, reducing costs, and enhancing efficiency in decentralized systems when Cloud computing is a backbone for modern IT infrastructure, enabling businesses and individuals to innovate faster, reduce costs, and improve agility.

3. BLOCKCHAIN TECHNOLOGY AND CLOUD COMPUTING INTERSECT

The integration of blockchain technology with cloud computing creates a powerful synergy that enhances data security, transparency, and operational efficiency. Blockchain's decentralized and immutable ledger system complements cloud computing's scalable infrastructure, offering solutions to critical challenges in data management and workflow automation. By storing cryptographic hashes of cloud-based files on the blockchain, organizations can ensure data integrity and detect any unauthorized modifications (Li et al., 2024). For instance, a legal document stored in cloud storage like AWS S3 can have its digital fingerprint recorded on Ethereum, creating an immutable audit trail that verifies the file's authenticity over time. This approach is particularly valuable for industries requiring strict compliance, such as healthcare and finance, where maintaining accurate records of data access and modifications is crucial.

Cloud platforms significantly lower the barrier to blockchain adoption by providing managed node services that eliminate the need for expensive on-premises infrastructure. Services like Amazon Managed Blockchain and Microsoft Azure Blockchain allow enterprises to deploy Ethereum or Hyperledger Fabric nodes within minutes, with automatic scaling to handle transaction volume fluctuations. This cloud-based approach to blockchain deployment not only reduces operational costs but also improves network reliability through geographically distributed nodes and built-in security features. The combination enables businesses to focus on developing blockchain applications rather than maintaining complex infrastructure, accelerating innovation in areas like supply chain tracking and digital identity management (Khan, 2023; Sharma et al., 2021).

Smart contracts introduce a new dimension of automation to cloud workflows by executing predefined actions when specific conditions are met. These self-executing programs can integrate with cloud APIs to create seamless, trustless systems for payments, access control, and data verification. A practical implementation might involve a smart contract automatically releasing payment to a supplier when IoT sensors confirm delivery of goods, with all transaction details recorded immutably on the blockchain while supporting documents are stored cost-effectively in cloud storage. This convergence of technologies reduces processing delays, minimizes human error, and enhances transparency across business processes (Kaur & Ali, 2022; Samaniego et al., 2016).

The architectural integration of blockchain and cloud computing typically follows a layered approach, combining user-facing applications, smart contract logic, blockchain networks, cloud infrastructure, and IoT data sources as summarized in figure 2. This hybrid model allows organizations to use the strengths of each technology as using cloud services for high-performance computing and storage while employing blockchain for critical security functions and audit trails. For example, a pharmaceutical company might store huge clinical trial datasets in Google Cloud while using Hyperledger to manage access permissions and maintain an unforgeable record of all data interactions. This combination addresses both scalability requirements and stringent compliance needs.

Figure 2. Cloud-Blockchain Architecture Overview

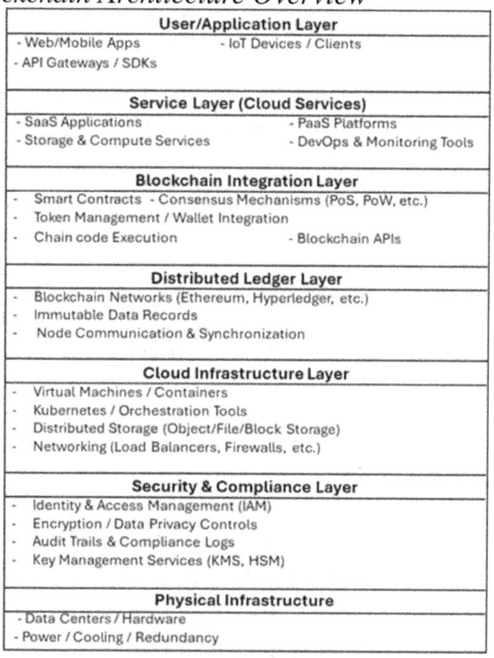

Looking ahead, the intersection of blockchain and cloud computing continues to evolve with emerging innovations like zero-knowledge proofs for private data verification and decentralized physical infrastructure networks (DePIN) that could reshape cloud resource allocation (J. Zheng et al., 2025). While challenges remain in terms of scalability and regulatory alignment, the combined potential of these technologies is driving transformation across industries. Enterprises are increasingly adopting these integrated solutions to create more transparent, efficient, and secure digital ecosystems that meet the demands of modern business operations and regulatory environments. The ongoing development of interoperability standards and hybrid architectures promises to further strengthen the convergence of blockchain's trust mechanisms with cloud computing's operational flexibility.

3.1 Areas of Intersection

The intersection of blockchain and cloud computing lies in their opposite capabilities. Blockchain provides decentralized security and transparency, while cloud computing offers scalability and on-demand resources. Their integration enhances efficiency, security, and trust in digital ecosystems.

Traditional cloud providers centralize data, whereas blockchain-based solutions distribute it across multiple nodes. Blockchain ensures data immutability and traceability, which can enhance cloud computing's security. Smart contracts on blockchain platforms can automate and manage cloud services, such as resource allocation and billing (Baranwal et al., 2023). Also, Blockchain decentralized identity systems can strengthen access controls in cloud environments.

Blockchain as a Service (BaaS) enables easy deployment of blockchain networks without infrastructure management. Decentralized by using blockchain-based storage networks (Filecoin, Storj, Sia) provide secure, tamper-proof alternatives to traditional cloud storage (Baranwal et al., 2023). Figure 3 shows the architecture of Alibaba cloud BaaS.

Figure 3. Alibaba Cloud architecture (Alibaba Cloud Blockchain as a Service, 2020)

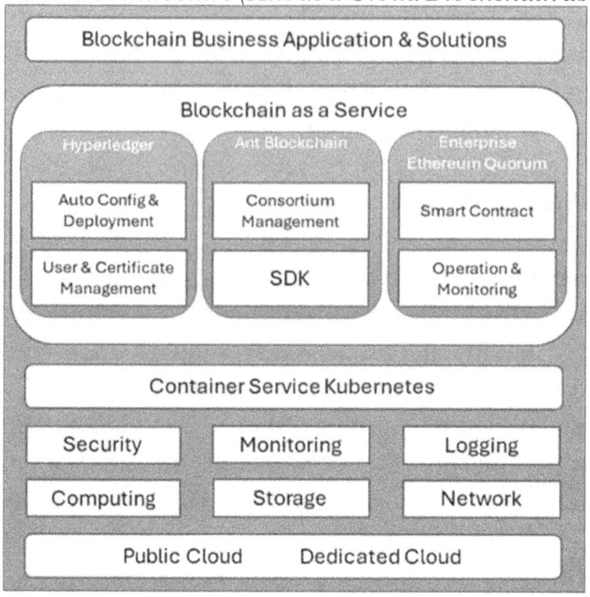

Blockchain enhances cloud security by preventing unauthorized access and ensuring data integrity. Blockchain enables transparent tracking of cloud resources and billing. Smart Contracts for Cloud Workflows automates cloud service agreements and payments and ensures transparent execution of cloud-based contracts (Dalabanjan & G, 2024).

Blockchain secures IoT transactions and data exchange in cloud-based IoT networks and reduces dependency on centralized cloud data centers for IoT applications. Also, blockchain ensures transparency in cloud-based supply chain management and combines cloud's scalability with blockchain's immutability for tracking goods and verifying authenticity (Famous et al., 2025).

Blockchain facilitates data exchange across multiple cloud providers and reduces vendor lock-in by enabling trustless interoperability. The synergy between blockchain and cloud computing is transforming industries by enhancing security, efficiency, and decentralization.

Businesses can harness blockchain to build trust, ensure transparency, and secure sensitive data, while using cloud computing for elasticity, cost-efficiency, and global scalability. Together, these technologies are driving the evolution of decentralized, intelligent, and resilient digital systems.

3.2 Cloud Computing Applications

3.2.1 Secure Data Storage and Scalable Storage Solutions

Cloud platforms like AWS S3, Google Cloud Storage, and Azure Blob Storage deliver secure, scalable storage with built-in redundancy across global data centers, protecting against outages. Automated backups and disaster recovery tools (e.g., AWS Backup, Azure Site Recovery) ensure quick data restoration after incidents. Enterprise-grade security features—including encryption, IAM controls, and compliance with GDPR/HIPAA—make these solutions ideal for sensitive sectors like healthcare and finance. The flexible pay-as-you-go model removes upfront infrastructure costs, democratizing access to robust storage for businesses of all scales.

3.2.2 Hosting Websites, Applications, and APIs

Cloud platforms like AWS EC2, Google App Engine, and Azure App Service power modern web hosting with auto-scaling for traffic spikes and global CDNs (Cloudflare, AWS CloudFront) to reduce latency. Built-in tools (AWS API Gateway) simplify API management, while integrated security (DDoS protection, firewalls) safeguards applications of all sizes—from small sites to enterprise systems—without physical infrastructure overhead.

3.2.3 Software-as-a-Service (SaaS) Delivery Model

The SaaS model represents one of the most transformative applications of cloud computing, delivering complete software solutions over the internet without requiring local installation. Leading examples include Google Workspace for productivity tools, Salesforce for customer relationship management, and Microsoft 365 for office applications, all accessible through web browsers or lightweight client applications. This approach provides many advantages including automatic updates managed by the provider, universal accessibility across devices, and subscription-based pricing that converts large capital expenses into predictable operational costs.

3.2.4 IoT Data Management and Real-Time Analytics

Cloud computing serves as the critical foundation for modern IoT systems, enabling efficient collection, processing, and analysis of huge amounts of device-generated data. Leading platforms like AWS IoT Core, Google Cloud IoT, and Azure IoT Hub provide secure, scalable solutions for managing millions of connected devices while integrating powerful analytics tools such as Google BigQuery and AWS Kinesis for real-time insights. The cloud's flexible infrastructure dynamically adapts to fluctuating IoT data volumes, supporting crucial applications ranging from industrial predictive maintenance to smart city optimizations for traffic, energy use, and public safety. This powerful combination of cloud computing and IoT technologies is transforming industries by facilitating responsive, data-driven decision making and automated operations.

3.2.5 Cloud Gaming Platforms

Cloud gaming streams high-end gameplay from remote servers (NVIDIA GeForce NOW, Xbox Cloud Gaming) to any device, eliminating expensive hardware needs. Powered by cloud GPUs and low-latency networks, it delivers console-quality gaming anywhere. While bandwidth demands and input lag remain challenges for competitive play, emerging 5G and edge computing solutions are enhancing responsiveness. This model democratizes gaming access while evolving rapidly.

3.2.6 Cloud-Based Learning Management Systems

Cloud-based Learning Management Systems (LMS) like MoodleCloud, Blackboard, and Coursera have revolutionized education by enabling flexible online and blended learning models. These platforms use cloud infrastructure to deliver scalable, accessible educational content worldwide while eliminating the need for costly on-premises servers. Offering comprehensive features including course management tools, multimedia content delivery, automated assessments, and learning analytics, cloud LMS solutions proved particularly valuable during the COVID-19 pandemic by seamlessly accommodating surges in remote learning demand. Beyond academic institutions, corporate training programs have increasingly adopted these cloud-based systems for employee development, benefiting from mobile accessibility and seamless integration with other enterprise cloud services.

3.2.7 Financial Services Innovation

The financial industry has adopted cloud computing to enhance digital banking, payments, and compliance. Cloud platforms support secure mobile banking apps with biometric authentication and AI-powered fraud detection. Services like AWS blockchain and IBM Cloud for Financial Services enable cryptocurrency transactions and meet strict regulations. Cloud flexibility handles peak demands like tax season, while fintech startups use it to quickly launch innovations in peer-to-peer lending and robo-advising without heavy infrastructure investments.

3.2.8 Artificial Intelligence and Machine Learning Platforms

Cloud platforms like AWS SageMaker, Google Vertex AI, and Azure Machine Learning have made advanced AI/ML accessible by providing complete toolsets for model development and deployment without expensive hardware. Offering scalable computing power, pre-built AI services (NLP, computer vision), and collaboration features, they enable organizations to implement sophisticated solutions across industries, from healthcare diagnostics to predictive maintenance. As AI grows more complex, cloud infrastructure becomes essential for practical deployment, offering the necessary scale and management capabilities for production environments.

3.3 Blockchain Applications

3.3.1 Cryptocurrency

Cryptocurrencies represent blockchain's most well-known application, serving as decentralized digital currencies that operate without central banks or intermediaries. Bitcoin, the first cryptocurrency, introduced a peer-to-peer electronic cash system using blockchain's distributed ledger technology (Wright, 2008). Ethereum expanded this concept by enabling programmable transactions through smart contracts. These digital currencies provide borderless transactions, resistance to censorship, and in some cases, limited supply models that contrast with traditional fiat currencies. Cryptocurrencies use cryptographic techniques to secure transactions and control the creation of new units, while blockchain technology ensures transparency and immutability of all transaction records.

3.3.2 Smart Contracts

Smart contracts are self-executing agreements with terms directly written into code that automatically enforce and execute contract clauses when predetermined conditions are met. Built primarily on platforms like Ethereum, these digital contracts eliminate the need for intermediaries in various processes ranging from financial agreements to legal arrangements. Decentralized applications utilize smart contracts to create trustless systems for activities like decentralized finance, insurance payouts, and royalty distributions. The code-based nature of smart contracts ensures consistent execution while blockchain's transparency allows all parties to verify terms and outcomes.

3.3.3 Supply Chain Management

Blockchain revolutionizes supply chain operations by creating immutable, transparent records of product journeys from origin to consumer. Each step in the supply chain can be recorded on the blockchain, enabling real-time tracking and verification. This technology helps combat counterfeit goods by providing authenticity certificates, improves recall efficiency when issues arise, and enhances ethical sourcing verification. Major corporations like Walmart and Maersk have implemented blockchain solutions to increase supply chain transparency and efficiency while reducing paperwork and administrative costs.

3.3.4 Identity Management

Decentralized identity solutions on blockchain provide individuals with control over their personal data while reducing identity fraud. Unlike traditional systems where personal information is stored in centralized databases vulnerable to breaches, blockchain-based identity management allows users to own and selectively disclose credentials through cryptographic proofs. Solutions like Microsoft's ION and the Sovrin Network enable secure digital identities that can be used across services without relying on a central authority. This approach enhances privacy while simplifying identity verification processes for banking, healthcare, and government services.

3.3.5 Healthcare

In healthcare, blockchain secures sensitive patient data while enabling appropriate information sharing between providers. Medical records stored on blockchain maintain integrity through cryptographic hashing, preventing unauthorized modifications while creating complete audit trails of access. Blockchain facilitates secure sharing of patient data across healthcare systems, improving care coordination while maintaining compliance with regulations like HIPAA. Pharmaceutical companies also use blockchain to track drug provenance and combat counterfeit medicines in the supply chain (Rosli et al., 2024).

3.3.6 Voting Systems

Blockchain-based voting systems address electoral integrity concerns by creating tamper-proof records of votes while maintaining voter anonymity. Each vote is recorded as a transaction on the blockchain, making it immutable and verifiable without revealing voter identity. Pilot projects in countries like Estonia and U.S. states have demonstrated blockchain's potential to reduce election fraud, enable secure remote voting, and increase voter participation through mobile voting solutions. The technology provides real-time vote tabulation while allowing voters to independently verify their votes were counted correctly.

3.3.7 Gaming and Virtual Worlds

Blockchain introduces true digital ownership in gaming through non-fungible tokens (NFTs) that represent unique in-game assets. Play-to-earn games like Axie Infinity allow players to earn cryptocurrency rewards and trade NFT-based items across marketplaces. Blockchain gaming platforms enable interoperable assets that can move between different games and virtual worlds. This creates new economic models where players can monetize their time and skills, while developers benefit from provably scarce digital items with verifiable ownership histories.

3.3.8 Energy and Sustainability

Blockchain facilitates peer-to-peer energy trading platforms where households with solar panels can directly sell excess energy to neighbors without utility intermediaries (Aman et al., 2024). Projects like Power Ledger use smart contracts to automatically execute energy transactions based on real-time production and consumption data. Blockchain also enables carbon credit tracking and renewable energy certificate management, creating transparent systems for sustainability initiatives. These applications help optimize energy distribution while supporting the transition to decentralized renewable energy grids.

4. APPLICATIONS FOR BLOCKCHAIN-CLOUD COMPUTING INTEGRATION

This section presents the special applications uniquely enabled by integrating blockchain and cloud technology:

4.1 Decentralized Cloud Storage with Proof of Integrity

By combining blockchain with cloud computing, decentralized storage platforms can store data across a distributed network while ensuring its integrity and authenticity. Blockchain is used to record cryptographic hashes of files, which provides verifiable proof that data has not been tampered with. Meanwhile, the cloud offers scalable storage infrastructure for high availability and performance (Ramesh et al., 2023). This integration eliminates reliance on a single storage provider and enhances data security through transparency and decentralization. Examples of such systems include Filecoin and Sia.

4.2 Blockchain-as-a-Service (BaaS) Platforms

Blockchain-as-a-Service (BaaS) is made possible through cloud platforms that offer developers tools to build, host, and manage blockchain networks without having to manage complex infrastructure manually. Cloud computing provides on-demand scalability, orchestration, and backend services, while blockchain introduces decentralization, transparency, and trustless interaction (Baranwal et al., 2023). This combination empowers businesses to prototype and deploy blockchain solutions rapidly, with minimal technical overhead. Services like Microsoft Azure BaaS and Amazon Managed Blockchain exemplify this model.

4.3 Smart Contract-Driven Cloud Automation

Cloud resource management can be automated using blockchain-based smart contracts that execute provisioning, scaling, and billing operations without human intervention. These smart contracts can trigger cloud actions such as launching virtual machines or allocating storage, based on predefined logic and conditions (Narayana & Sathiyamurthy, 2023). This is particularly beneficial in multi-tenant environments where trust and fairness are critical, as blockchain ensures transparent execution and record-keeping. The result is a fully automated, auditable infrastructure management system.

4.4 Secure Multi-Cloud Identity Management

Traditional identity management systems face challenges when integrating users and services across multiple cloud providers. By using blockchain as a decentralized identity ledger, organizations can create a secure and verifiable identity system that works across various cloud platforms (Rosli et al., 2025). Blockchain stores identity credentials in a tamper-resistant manner, while cloud services enforce access control based on these decentralized identities (Famous et al., 2025). This enables unified, cross-cloud authentication and access, reducing dependence on central authorities and improving user privacy and control.

4.5 Transparent Supply Chain in Cloud Platforms

The integration of blockchain and cloud computing enables end-to-end visibility in supply chain systems. Cloud-based IoT devices collect real-time data from products and shipments, which is then recorded on the blockchain for immutable and transparent tracking. This ensures that every movement and transaction along the supply chain can be verified and audited, increasing trust among stakeholders (Attarbashi et al., 2024; Adetunmbi et al., 2021). Solutions like IBM Food Trust use this architecture to validate food safety and logistics processes.

4.6 Cross-Border Cloud Payments and Billing

Integrating blockchain with cloud platforms enables real-time, decentralized payment systems tailored for international or microtransaction-based cloud services. Blockchain facilitates secure and transparent financial transactions using digital tokens or cryptocurrencies, while cloud platforms monitor service usage and generate billing data. This is particularly useful for pay-per-use services, such as function-as-a-service (FaaS), where traditional billing mechanisms may be inefficient or costly for small-scale interactions (Emami Khansari & Sharifian, 2025).

4.7 Decentralized Cloud Audit Trails

Blockchain provides an immutable and transparent method for logging and auditing events, which can be integrated with cloud-based applications to create tamper-proof audit trails. Cloud platforms generate huge amounts of logs, but these can be vulnerable to unauthorized changes. By storing key event summaries or hashes on a blockchain, organizations can ensure the authenticity of audit records. This is especially valuable for regulatory compliance and forensic analysis, where verifiable logs are critical.

4.8 Trustless Federated Learning in Cloud AI

Federated learning allows AI models to be trained collaboratively across multiple organizations without sharing raw data. By incorporating blockchain, the process can be coordinated securely and transparently among participants who do not fully trust each other. The cloud provides the computing infrastructure for training models, while blockchain ensures that contributions, rewards, and updates are tracked in a decentralized and tamper-proof way. This approach is ideal for industries like healthcare and finance, where data privacy is essential, but collaboration is beneficial.

5. CONCLUSION

The integration of blockchain technology and cloud computing marks an important development in how digital systems are built, secured, and expanded. This chapter has shown that these two technologies work well together: blockchain offers decentralization, trust through cryptography, and data immutability, while cloud computing provides flexible scalability, easy access to computing resources, and global service delivery. When combined, they offer effective solutions to common problems related to data security, transparency, automation, and system compatibility, especially in key sectors such as finance, healthcare, supply chains, and artificial intelligence.

The discussion highlights several important points. First, combining blockchain's secure ledgers with cloud-based encryption and identity controls enhances data protection and trust. Second, using cloud-based blockchain services (also known as Blockchain-as-a-Service or BaaS) helps organizations lower infrastructure costs and build scalable systems. Third, integrating smart contracts with cloud services enables automated processes that do not require human intervention, which is useful in areas like payment systems or digital identity. Fourth, new decentralized models such as Decentralized Physical Infrastructure Networks (DePIN) offer alternative ways to share cloud resources and reduce reliance on large service providers.

Looking ahead, several trends are expected to shape this integration. Hybrid systems using both private (permissioned) and public blockchains will be hosted on cloud platforms to balance privacy and transparency. Decentralized cloud services, such as Akash Network and Filecoin, will grow and reduce operational costs. There will also be increasing use of blockchain to verify data used in AI systems, while cloud platforms offer the computing power needed for training. Technologies like zero-knowledge proofs (ZKPs) will improve privacy by allowing data to be verified without being exposed (Ismayilov & Özturan, 2025). Additionally, as quantum computing becomes more common, new cryptographic techniques will be needed to protect blockchain-cloud systems. Blockchain may also support new payment models for cloud usage, enabling micropayments for computing or storage services. Meanwhile, governments are likely to create clearer rules to support blockchain-cloud applications, especially for areas like digital identity, international data management, and legal recognition of smart contracts.

In summary, although the combination of blockchain and cloud computing is still developing, it holds great promise to change how industries operate. By making digital systems more open, efficient, and secure, this integration can reduce dependence on central authorities and improve trust. Businesses and developers should prepare for this shift, as those who adopt these technologies early will be well-positioned to lead future innovation in this space.

REFERENCES

Adetunmbi, S. B., Attarbashi, Z. S., Nordin, N., & Hasan, S. (2021). Blockchain for Sustainable Supply Chain: Applications and Challenges. *Proceedings of the 4th International Conference on Engineering Professional Ethics and Education 2021 (ICEPEE'21).*

Ahmadi, S. (2024). Security Implications of Edge Computing in Cloud Networks. *Journal of Computer and Communications, 12*(02), 26–46. DOI: 10.4236/jcc.2024.122003

Al-Ahmad, A. S., & Kahtan, H. (2018). Cloud Computing Review: Features And Issues. *2018 International Conference on Smart Computing and Electronic Enterprise (ICSCEE)*, 1–5. DOI: 10.1109/ICSCEE.2018.8538387

Al-Hamad, A. Q. M., Hamadneh, S., Nuseir, M. T., Alzoubi, H. M., Al Kurdi, B., & Alshurideh, M. T. (2024). *A Critical Review of Cloud Computing Architecture Empowered with Blockchain Technology.*, DOI: 10.1007/978-3-031-31801-6_29

Aman, A. H. M., Shaari, N., Attar Bashi, Z. S., Iftikhar, S., Bawazeer, S., Osman, S. H., & Hasan, N. S. (2024). A review of residential blockchain internet of things energy systems: Resources, storage and challenges. *Energy Reports, 11*, 1225–1241. DOI: 10.1016/j.egyr.2023.12.062

An, M., Fan, Q., Yu, H., An, B., Wu, N., Zhao, H., Wan, X., Li, J., Wang, R., Zhen, J., Zou, Q., & Zhao, B. (2023). Blockchain Technology Research and Application: A Literature Review and Future Trends. *Journal of Data Science and Intelligent Systems*. DOI: 10.47852/bonviewJDSIS32021403

Attarbashi, Z. M., Zeki, A., Haque, M. E., & Hossen, M. S. (2024). A Collaborative Halal Supply Chain Model to Address Safety and Transparency Based on Blockchain Technology. *Al Qasimia University Journal of Islamic Economics, 4*(2), 25–58. DOI: 10.52747/aqujie.4.2.373

Baranwal, G., Kumar, D., & Vidyarthi, D. P. (2023). Blockchain based resource allocation in cloud and distributed edge computing: A survey. *Computer Communications, 209*, 469–498. DOI: 10.1016/j.comcom.2023.07.023

Bushay, K. D. (2025). Infrastructure as a Service/Platform as a Service. In *Encyclopedia of Libraries, Librarianship, and Information Science* (pp. 627–639). Elsevier. DOI: 10.1016/B978-0-323-95689-5.00109-7

Casino, F., Dasaklis, T. K., & Patsakis, C. (2019). A systematic literature review of blockchain-based applications: Current status, classification and open issues. *Telematics and Informatics*, *36*, 55–81. DOI: 10.1016/j.tele.2018.11.006

Dalabanjan, G., & G, N. D. (2024). Enabling Attribute-based Access Control for OpenStack Cloud Resources through Smart Contracts. *Procedia Computer Science*, *233*, 861–871. DOI: 10.1016/j.procs.2024.03.275

Emami Khansari, M., & Sharifian, S. (2025). A deep reinforcement learning approach towards distributed Function as a Service (FaaS) based edge application orchestration in cloud-edge continuum. *Journal of Network and Computer Applications*, *233*, 104042. DOI: 10.1016/j.jnca.2024.104042

Famous, M. S., Sayed, S., Mazumder, R., Khan, R. T., Kaiser, M. S., Hossain, M. S., Andersson, K., & Khondoker, R. (2025). Secure and efficient drug supply chain management system: Leveraging polymorphic encryption, blockchain, and cloud storage integration. *Cyber Security and Applications*, *3*, 100103. DOI: 10.1016/j.csa.2025.100103

Ionescu, L., & Andronie, M. (2021). Big Data Management and Cloud Computing: Financial Implications in the Digital World. *SHS Web of Conferences, 92*, 05010. DOI: 10.1051/shsconf/20219205010

Ismayilov, G., & Özturan, C. (2025). PTTS: Zero-knowledge proof-based private token transfer system on Ethereum blockchain and its network flow based balance range privacy attack analysis. *Journal of Network and Computer Applications*, *233*, 104045. DOI: 10.1016/j.jnca.2024.104045

Jha, B., Giri, P., Jha, D., & Hassan, R. (2024). Blockchain Technology: Proof of Work vs Proof of Stake Consensus Mechanism. In *Reference Module in Social Sciences*. Elsevier., DOI: 10.1016/B978-0-443-13701-3.00457-6

Kaur, R., & Ali, A. (2022). *Implementation of Blockchain in IoT*., DOI: 10.1007/978-981-16-8774-7_13

Khan, M. (2023). *Blockchain and Cloud: Exploring the Intersection of Two Revolutionary Technologies*. DOI: 10.31219/osf.io/buhr3

Leduc, G., Kubler, S., & Georges, J.-P. (2023). A centre-based validator selection approach for a scalable BFT blockchain. *IFAC-PapersOnLine*, *56*(2), 10192–10197. DOI: 10.1016/j.ifacol.2023.10.896

Li, L., Li, J., Liu, R., & Li, Z. (2024). Overview of blockchain-based terminal-edge-cloud collaborative computing paradigm. *Computers & Electrical Engineering*, *120*, 109737. DOI: 10.1016/j.compeleceng.2024.109737

Luo, H. (2023). ULS-PBFT: An ultra-low storage overhead PBFT consensus for blockchain. *Blockchain: Research and Applications*, *4*(4), 100155. DOI: 10.1016/j.bcra.2023.100155

Narayana, K. L., & Sathiyamurthy, K. (2023). Automation and smart materials in detecting smart contracts vulnerabilities in Blockchain using deep learning. *Materials Today: Proceedings*, *81*, 653–659. DOI: 10.1016/j.matpr.2021.04.125

Ramesh, D., Mishra, R., Atrey, P. K., Edla, D. R., Misra, S., & Qi, L. (2023). Blockchain based efficient tamper-proof EHR storage for decentralized cloud-assisted storage. *Alexandria Engineering Journal*, *68*, 205–226. DOI: 10.1016/j.aej.2023.01.012

Rosli, A., Hassan, S., Omar, M. H., Sajat, M. S., Attarbashi, Z. S., & Mohd Zaini, K. (2025). *Mapping the Landscape: A Bibliometric Perspective of Blockchain Applications and Trust Management.*, DOI: 10.1007/978-3-031-91485-0_11

Rosli, A., Hassan, S., Omar, M. H., Sajat, M. S., Attarbashi, Z. S., & Zaini, K. M. (2024). Blockchain Applications and Management: A Multidisciplinary Analysis. *2024 7th International Conference on Internet Applications, Protocols, and Services (NETAPPS)*, 1–8. DOI: 10.1109/NETAPPS63333.2024.10823600

Samaniego, M., Jamsrandorj, U., & Deters, R. (2016). Blockchain as a Service for IoT. *2016 IEEE International Conference on Internet of Things (IThings) and IEEE Green Computing and Communications (GreenCom) and IEEE Cyber, Physical and Social Computing (CPSCom) and IEEE Smart Data (SmartData)*, 433–436. DOI: 10.1109/iThings-GreenCom-CPSCom-SmartData.2016.102

Samha, A. K. (2024). Strategies for efficient resource management in federated cloud environments supporting Infrastructure as a Service (IaaS). *Journal of Engineering Research*, *12*(2), 101–114. DOI: 10.1016/j.jer.2023.10.031

Sharma, P., Jindal, R., & Borah, M. D. (2021). Blockchain Technology for Cloud Storage. *ACM Computing Surveys*, *53*(4), 1–32. DOI: 10.1145/3403954

Sun, Y., Yan, B., Yao, Y., & Yu, J. (2021). DT-DPoS: A Delegated Proof of Stake Consensus Algorithm with Dynamic Trust. *Procedia Computer Science*, *187*, 371–376. DOI: 10.1016/j.procs.2021.04.113

Wright, C. S. (2008). Bitcoin: A Peer-to-Peer Electronic Cash System. SSRN *Electronic Journal*. DOI: 10.2139/ssrn.3440802

Wu, Y., Wu, L., & Cai, H. (2023). Reinforced practical Byzantine fault tolerance consensus protocol for cyber physical systems. *Computer Communications*, *203*, 238–247. DOI: 10.1016/j.comcom.2023.03.016

Zhang, P., Yu, Y., Liu, J., Lv, C., Tan, L., & Zhang, Y. (2025). Enhanced Practical Byzantine Fault Tolerance for Service Function Chain Deployment: Advancing Big Data Intelligence in Control Systems. *Computers, Materials & Continua*, *83*(3), 4393–4409. DOI: 10.32604/cmc.2025.064654

Zheng, J., Lo, S.-W., Xia, C., & Lee, D. K. C. (2025). Navigating cryptocurrencies' next frontier: The revolution toward decentralizing physical infrastructure. In *Handbook of Blockchain, Digital Finance, and Inclusion, Volume 3* (pp. 51–59). Elsevier. DOI: 10.1016/B978-0-443-34717-7.00018-0

Zheng, Q., Gu, D., Liang, C., & Fang, Y. (2020). Impact of a firm's physical and knowledge capital intensities on its selection of a cloud computing deployment model. *Information & Management*, *57*(7), 103259. DOI: 10.1016/j.im.2019.103259

Zheng, Z., Xie, S., Dai, H., Chen, X., & Wang, H. (2017). An Overview of Blockchain Technology: Architecture, Consensus, and Future Trends. *2017 IEEE International Congress on Big Data (BigData Congress)*, 557–564. DOI: 10.1109/BigDataCongress.2017.85

Zhu, F., You, L., Wang, J., & Li, L. (2025). P-HotStuff: Parallel BFT algorithm with throughput insensitive to propagation delay. *Computer Networks*, *262*, 111183. DOI: 10.1016/j.comnet.2025.111183

Chapter 10
Integrated 5G and Edge Computing Framework for Low-Latency IoT Applications

P. Ashok
https://orcid.org/0000-0002-5859-6041
Symbiosis Institute of Digital and Telecom Management, Symbiosis International University, India

A. Pon Bharati
https://orcid.org/0000-0003-1217-449X
Amrita Vishwa Vidyapeetham, India

Srikanth Velpula
https://orcid.org/0000-0003-2706-7136
SR University, India

K. Murali Krishna
Rajalakshmi Engineering College, India

S. Lakshmi Sridevi
Chennai Institute of Technology, India

Sarala Patchala
KKR and KSR Institute of Technology and Sciences, India

S. Gopinath
Karpagam Institute of Technology, India

Harishchander Anandaram
https://orcid.org/0000-0003-2993-5304
Amrita Vishwa Vidyapeetham, India

ABSTRACT

The main idea of cloud computing is being widely promoted as the solution to current ongoing IT problems. In recent years the approach towards IT investment and management is constantly changing. At the same time, cloud computing has developed as a foundation of the contemporary technologies which enables the users to receive the necessary amount of such resources and services without any delays.

DOI: 10.4018/979-8-3693-9984-2.ch010

The research paper delves into the transformative landscape of 5G networks, focusing on the fusion of edge and cloud computing. This fusion represents a paradigm shift in network architecture, promising enhanced performance, scalability, and innovation. Edge computing, characterized by real-time processing and low-latency applications, complements cloud computing's scalable resources for data storage and processing. Despite these challenges, the fusion of edge and cloud computing enables improved performance, scalability, and innovation, driving digital transformation and competitive advantage in the digital economy.

INTRODUCTION

Edge computing is a special paradigm of a distributed pattern of computing which brings the sources and storages of data into very close proximity. The bandwidth saving and time management is to be improved by designing this model (Sriram & 2022, Cao et al., 2020, Qi & 2019). It follows a special direction of architecture while storing the data. This is also following up a specific hierarchical pattern while maintaining the documents and also the sensitive distribution pattern of computing is supervened (Lin, 2019). An example of edge computing is IoT technology (the internet of things). Some special features of the technology are speed and scalability, privacy and security policy and thus reliability and high efficiency (Qi, 2019). Cloud computing is the automated storage of data in the system (cloud storage) without the active involvement of the user. Cloud computing is based on coherent source sharing while using pay-and-go themes but it may lead to raising unnecessary expenses for the common users.

LITERATURE REVIEW

1. Communicating While Computing

In this context of the article, the author proposed a 5G centric necessity because of empowering the "energy-hungry" terminals for the mobiles while the cloud functioning is also manifested via radio access by using small cell-based power stations (Ali, 2021). Using a cross-layer approach, optimal resource allocation is done along with the radio and computation resources allocation (Ke, 2020). The complete system impacts different parts such as signalling, networking and radio interfacing etc (Hassan, 2019). Firstly, pervasive offloading of the computation, both the up and downlink changes significantly according to the demand of the current situation. The proposed approach for cloud distribution needs intensive modification and interchange among the base stations. Using mm wave direct linking up, which is already considered for using 5G networking, may cause problems due to the high-capacity wireless link-ups (Naveen & Kounte 2019, Taleb et al., 2017) as in Fig. 1.

Key points regarding the necessity and implications of a 5G-centric approach, particularly focusing on empowering energy-hungry terminals, cloud functioning, resource allocation, system impacts, pervasive offloading of computation, and potential challenges with mm-wave direct linking. With the increasing complexity and energy demands of mobile devices, there's a need for a robust network infrastructure like 5G to support their operations efficiently. Because 5G pushes more data through with much less lag, these devices can operate more effectively and efficiently. Cloud services linked with radio access using small cell-based stations play a major role in 5G rollout. Having these power stations spread across a network improves connectivity and helps resources be used in a productive way. Keeping in mind a cross-layer solution which connects different layers in the communication protocol, permits more effective allocation and sharing of both radio and computing resources. Using a 5G strategy influences many parts of the system, for example signalling, networking protocols and radio interfaces. Special attention is required to address these impacts so that the network integrates smoothly and works perfectly. Given the need for stronger and greener computations, a good way is to shift more processes to the cloud from smart phones. Offloading may happen in either direction, depending on the traffic being handled, the current network conditions and it should be controlled. The cloud distribution method suggested here needs major changes and practices that base stations must cooperate on. This includes optimizing the placement of cloud resources and ensuring efficient communication and data transfer between base stations and cloud servers. While mm wave direct linking offers high-capacity wireless connections, it also presents challenges such as signal attenuation and interference. These challenges need to be addressed to ensure reliable and stable communication in 5G networks utilizing mm wave technology.

2. Collective Mobile Edge Computing in 5G Network: Standard, Scenarios and Challenges:

Mobile Edge Computing or MEC is a modern paradigm which ensures multiple options like computing, cloud storing, higher connectivity or networking like 5G and most significantly all these can be done within the range of the mobile RAN or the range access network. The MEC network servers are established on the generic platform for the computation within the range of networking access (Shahzadi et al., 2017, Hu et al., 2016, Etro & 2009). This model of computing elevates the backhauling for the 5G network and is the primary attribute for ensuring low latency and high bandwidth to ensure agile services. Some special features of MEC are located with the aggregation stations, use heterogeneous, small nodes, and the actual network is filtered by the MEC server thus scalability is very high.

Figure 1. 5G Centric Approach

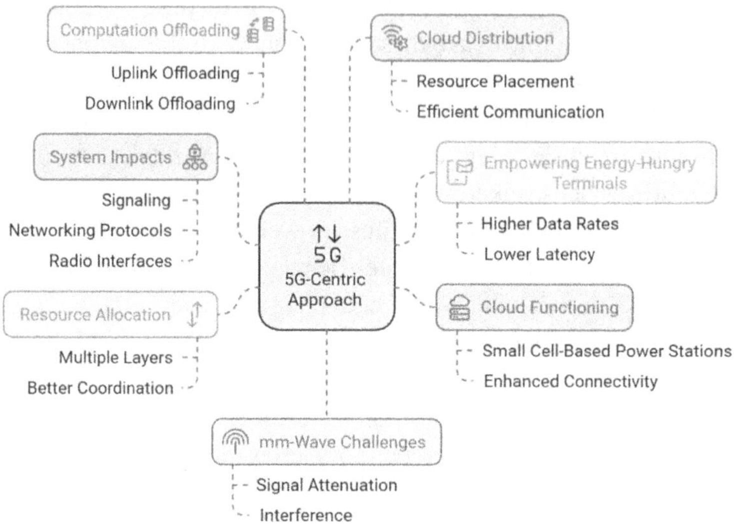

While CRAN is a centralised data centre dependant, having highly capable hardware but scalability is average. MEC is a Paradigm which moves computation storage and networking closer to the end user on the Radio Access Network or side. It facilitates these interactions improving the speed and the ratio between processes and the latency, which is important for new applications like augmented and virtual realities and others as in Fig. 2. The key highlights of MEC are as follows: MEC network servers are integrated in ordinary frameworks which allow computation in the networking access range. This makes it possible to deploy a number of different applications and services based on users' needs as well as the conditions of the network. MEC brings the compute capabilities closer to the edges of the network which in-turn minimize the distance data needs to transit to centralized data centers. This optimisation removes backhaul traffic and play an important role towards achieving lower latency and higher bandwidth that is required for offering flexible services in 5G networks. MEC deployments often utilize aggregation stations and heterogeneous small nodes strategically placed throughout the network. These features enable efficient resource utilization and enhance scalability. Additionally, MEC servers filter network traffic, allowing for more streamlined data transmission and processing. While MEC decentralizes computing resources, CRAN relies on centralized data centers with highly capable hardware. While CRAN may offer robust processing power, its scalability can be limited due to the centralized nature of its architecture. In contrast, MEC's distributed approach offers greater scalability and flexibility, especially in dynamic and heterogeneous network environments. Standardization is another critical enabler for MEC since it enhances interoperability and integration of the MEC solutions into numerous 5G networks. A number of global standardization fora including the Third Generation Partnership Project (3GPP) and the European Telecommunications Standards Institute (ETSI) are currently working on the specifications and best practices regarding to the MEC implementation. MEC is very extensive and versatile applicable in smart cities, industry automation, health care and transport industries. For instance, in smart cities MEC can provide near real time processing to support traffic management, environmental monitoring and public safety. Before it can be widely adopted though, MEC deployment presents several established challenges such as security and privacy, compatibility, resource allocation issues and the law. The solutions to these challenges will demand additional efforts across actors from the easy indexed industry, policymakers while together with standardization bodies.

3. Mobile Cloud Computing in 5G: Developing Leanings, Problems and Challenges:

Mobile cloud computing is a radically changing field to be researched with the progressive outcomes of technologies like wireless networks, mobile computing and cloud computing or storage. The 5th generation mobile network or the 5G has increased the primary capacities and the services which is a genre of rapid development and became a new hotspot for networking services (Al & 2013, Pham & 2020, Ullah & 2022). It's assumed that the MCC is going to change the lifestyle of society. Besides, soften is a decentralised mobile network architecture which is designed for 5G connectivity and programmed with more scalability. Security and safety are other issues to be ensured while users share and search specifically in real-time video data investigation. 5G cloud enabling ensures the sharing of real-time video with the familiar ones by the users of 5G networking as in Fig. 3.

Figure 2. Understanding MEC in 5G Networks

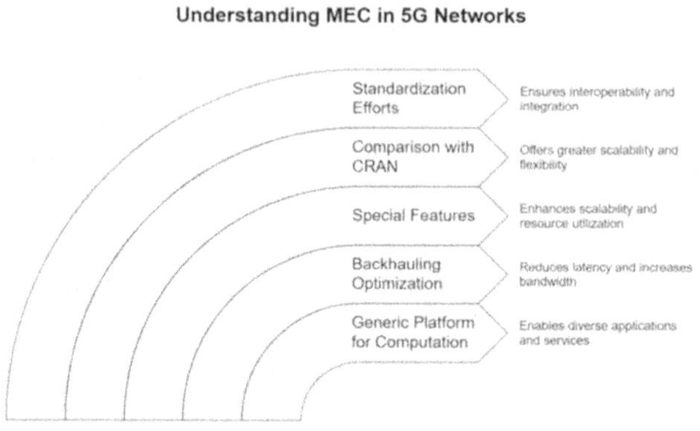

The Use Cases of Mobile Cloud Computing are: Mobile cloud computing represents a convergence of wireless networks, mobile computing, and cloud computing/storage technologies, leading to transformative changes in how data and services are accessed and utilized on mobile devices. The advent of 5G further amplifies these capabilities, offering higher speeds, lower latency, and increased capacity for mobile communication and computing tasks. The deployment of 5G networks significantly enhances the capabilities and services available through mobile cloud computing. With its higher bandwidth and lower latency, 5G enables more efficient access to cloud resources, facilitating seamless integration of cloud-based services with mobile applications and devices. This convergence fuels rapid development and innovation in the field of networking services, making MCC a focal point of technological advancement. MCC promises to redefine societal life chances by allowing easy, immediate and convenient access to a host of services or applications from anywhere. In time when 5G is providing a better connection in terms of speed, users' needs to connect to the cloud so that they can perform their tasks on the go which enable them to increase their efficiency and productivity of everyday tasks. H-CRAN (Hierarchical Cloud Radio Access Network) emerges as a promising model for providing advanced wireless connectivity in 5G networks. By leveraging cloud-based resources for radio access and network management, H-CRAN enhances scalability, flexibility, and resource utilization, leading to improved network performance and user experience. Soften represents a decentralized mobile network architecture specifically designed to cater to the connectivity requirements of 5G networks. By distributing network functionality across multiple nodes, soften improves scalability, resilience, and efficiency, thereby addressing the evolving needs of 5G connectivity. With the increasing popularity of mobile cloud let alone computing, it is critical to implement security and privacy on user data. One such emerging use case that easily interprets data privacy and security risks is real-time video data investigation, which would require effective measures of data encryption, authentication and access control mechanisms to secure the data. 5G cloud enabling facilitates real-time video sharing among users of 5th generation networking. This capability opens up new possibilities for communication, collaboration, and entertainment, allowing users to share experiences and connect with others in real-time, regardless of geographical location. Concisely, MCC within the frame work of 5G proposes a new era to transform the lifestyles, enhance the wireless connectivity and facilitate communication process. But there are issues such as security and privacy and scalability that have to be solved to get the true potential of MCC in 5G. Further studies and developments and cooperation will be the key to solving these problems and achieving the full potential of MCC in the mobile networking environment.

4. Assistances and Effect of The Cloud Computing On 5G Signal Processing:

Cloud computing generates universal access to share resources consuming minimal effort of management and this is the reason behind drawing the attention of the information technology community globally. Thus, cloud computing creates more effectiveness in the genre of communication technology or CT community and is also globally considered the most effective and cost-efficient modern way of connectivity (Pham et al., 2020, Ullah et al., 2022). Centralisation of the baseband allows more efficient resources using an advanced algorithm of multi cells etc but has some limitations like it can't offer the same prospects as cloud computing like virtualisation and on-demand provisioning and multi-tenancy etc. These key characteristics can be achieved through cloud computing establishing this as a new-generation medium for connectivity (Barbarossa, 2014). Some features of cloud computing are flexible assignment of the cloud RAN functionality, high opportunities of cloud RAN, efficient signal processing in the cloud, forward error rectification etc. Cloud computing has a great deal to offer and has an impact on 5G signal processing, mostly because it makes shared resources accessible to everyone with little maintenance work. The international information technology community has taken a keen interest in this feature.

Figure 3. Security and Privacy Risks in 5G Cloud Computing

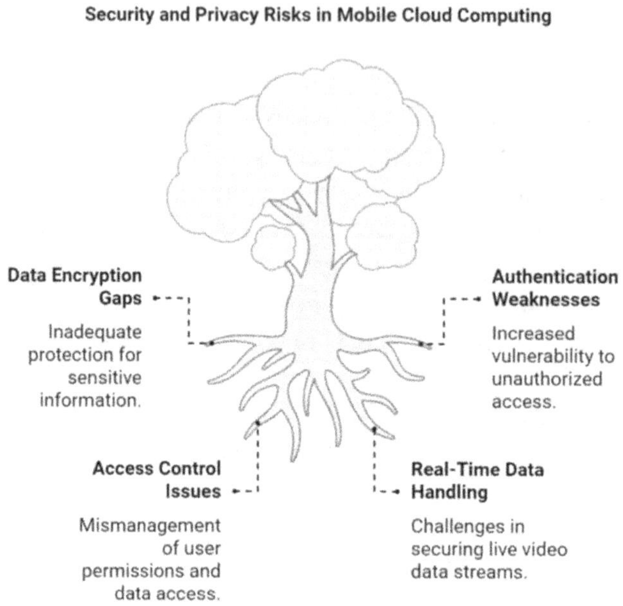

Within the field of communication technology (CT), cloud computing is acknowledged as a very successful and economical connectivity method. The ability of cloud computing to centralise baseband processing is one of its main benefits in 5G signal processing. The process of centralization facilitates the application of sophisticated algorithms, including multi-cell processing, to optimise resource utilisation. Although centralization increases efficiency, it does not naturally offer cloud computing advantages like virtualization, on-demand provisioning, and multi-tenancy. These essential features make cloud computing a next-generation medium for connectivity since they are better able to meet the demands of current connectivity. Several noteworthy characteristics of cloud computing that improve 5G signal processing are as follows: Radio Access Network (RAN) capability can be assigned in a flexible way thanks to cloud computing, which enables optimal use of network and processing capacity by allowing resources to be allocated dynamically based on demand. Virtualized network functions are made possible by cloud RAN topologies, which also improve scalability, flexibility, and cost-effectiveness. 5G networks can take advantage of the enormous computational capacity found in data centres by shifting signal processing responsibilities to the cloud. This results in improved processing speeds and decreased latency. To increase the dependability and resilience of 5G communications and guarantee high-quality transmission even in difficult situations, cloud-based signal processing algorithms can apply sophisticated error correction techniques.

5. Security and Privacy in Edge and Cloud Computing For 5G Networks:

Security and Privacy are significant issues in edge and cloud computing for edge data processing, especially within the scope of 5G networks as a lot of potentially sensitive data is processed and transmitted. Edge computing creates novel threats and threats points as a result in the distribution of edge devices and the use of wireless connectivity (Dizdarević & 2019, Tran & 2017, Mao & 2017, Roman et al., 2018, Liu & 2020, Alsaraireh et al., 2020). Likewise, cloud computing in 5G networks has adversarial impact on data security, such as privacy and data integrity, and access availability (Qian et al., 2020). Solving security and privacy issues demand new encryption methods, user authentication, and intrusion detection systems appropriate for edge and cloud computing (Shrivastava et al., 2021). Some of the Security Issues with Edge Computing are: A dispersed network of devices situated closer to data sources is used in edge computing. Because of their dispersed architecture, edge devices are more susceptible to physical manipulation, unauthorised access, and data interception. Because wireless communication is vulnerable to signal interception, eavesdropping, and man-in-the-middle assaults, edge devices rely on it. It is important to secure wireless signals so that others cannot illegally get at your data. Privacy of Data is a Problem Arising from Using Multi-tenant Cloud in 5G Networks: Because many tenants share a cloud system, it becomes difficult to guarantee the safety of users' data. Co-tenancy allows more possibilities for others besides the intended users to access the company's sensitive data. It is necessary to check that data stored or processed on the cloud remains accurate. Strong data integrity measures are needed to block unauthorized changes made to data by someone from within or outside the company. If there are disruptions or outages in the cloud in 5G networks, data and service can be interrupted. If vital services are to always be available, multiple systems, backup plans and ways to recover after disasters must be set up. Using Robust Algorithms Like AES: Data should be safely encrypted using AES (or comparable algorithms) while traveling online and while kept at rest to guarantee its secrecy. People and devices granted access to sensitive resources are identified by using Access Control techniques and multi-factor authentication (MFA). Companies use Intrusion Detection Systems (IDS) to deal with threats early on by detecting and blocking suspicious activity and security attacks. Through the use of techniques like homomorphic encryption, secure multiparty computation (SMC) and differential privacy, private information is assurance of its privacy during processing and analysis.

6. Network Slicing for 5G Edge and Cloud Computing:

Network slicing is one of the main enabler technologies of 5G services which offers multiple instances of a logical network on the top of one physical node. Network slicing will in the context of the edge and cloud computing therefore be the resource management for edge and cloud computing applications. Network characteristics such as access delay, timeliness and reliability of slice networks help the network operators to efficiently provide multiple edge and cloud computing services (Costa-Perez, 2017). However, the concept of network slicing in 5G networks has some issues on the management resources, orchestration and isolation" inside the slices. Alleviation of these challenges can only afford in proper running of edge and cloud computing services in 5G networks. The concepts which are important for 5G networks elastic bandwidth and network slicing where multiple logical networks can be created on top of a physical infrastructure. All the network slices provide exclusive resources and service level agreements because each network slice is developed to meet the requirements of certain applications, services or tenants. Edges and cloud computing require network slicing to efficiently give resources to various types of applications and services. Edge and cloud computing applications can receive the best support from network operators by having the network split into personalised slices based on their requirements for latency, bandwidth and reliability. Network Slicing offers several helpful benefits to Cloud and Edge Computing. Network slicing and edge and cloud computing let users access required resources without facing competition or disruptions. A network operator can separate services by performance needs, for example, high-speed cloud or low-delay edge computing services, by giving each customer its own dedicated slice. When workloads on edge and cloud computing change, network slicing gives you the flexibility and ability to scale quickly. To optimise both performance and use of resources, operators should adjust slice settings and assign resources accordingly as needed. By improving the separation between various tenants and applications, network slicing lowers the possibility of illegal access and security lapses. Every slice function on its own resources and security policies (Chen, 2017).

7. Machine Learning and AI in Edge and Cloud Computing For 5G Networks:

ML and AI are assumed to provide essential boosts to optimizations of edge and cloud compute in 5G. Edge and cloud computing are the two models that underpin Machine Learning and Artificial Intelligence in support of intelligent decision-making processes, resource utilization, and predictive analytics. In edge computing for example, machine learning models can be directly implemented on the edge devices that have the capacity to make real time decisions without the necessity of having to consult cloud services (Mao, 2014). Furthermore, the analytics of AI in cloud computing may process big data created by edge devices and make conclusions to enhance the quality of the services (Wang, 2020). However, the integration of ML and AI in edge and cloud computing comes with issues to do with model deployment and constrained resources, and privacy (Li, 2020). Technology advancements in artificial intelligence (AI) and machine learning (ML) are revolutionising 5G network edge and cloud computing capabilities. They increase the effectiveness and affect the efficiency of devices and networks through better resource planning, forecasting and nimble decisions. When AI and ML run on edge devices, immediate decisions and computing can happen locally without looking to the cloud first. Machine learning (ML) and artificial intelligence (AI) are vital in the context of edge computing. They can do their AI tasks locally and refer to existing models, so they do not require much bandwidth or make long waits. Having machine learning (ML) models in edge devices makes it possible for them to detect abnormalities, identify pictures and schedule maintenance which enlarges their independence and responsiveness. Cloud computing relies on ML and AI tools to go through the data that is generated by edge devices. Info is extracted from sensors, telemetry data, plus interactions with users using cloud-based AI applications which helps make better use of analytics. Improving the user's experience, using resources better and serving customers well are all made possible by this information. Cloud-based AI helps businesses use powerful analytics tools even without huge infrastructure or tech knowledge. Machine learning as a service (MLaaS) and AI-powered analytics platforms illustrate some of these services. Problems in deploying AI and ML on both Edge and Cloud Computing are: The limited memory, lack of processing capacity and energy constraints make it necessary to pay careful attention to the way AI and ML are used. Edge device optimization is often challenging because you must keep a good level of efficiency and accuracy. Because edge devices have less processing capability than cloud servers, it is hard to apply advanced ML and AI locally. In edge computing environments, resource constraints must be handled with the help of effective resource management and model optimisation strategies. Handling private information on edge devices puts information at risk of being intercepted or accessed by unauthorised parties. In edge computing contexts, protecting user privacy requires the implementation of strong security and privacy mechanisms including data encryption and access restriction. The decentralization of cloud computing infrastructure to the edge carries numerous assistances that contribute to the 5G evolution.

8. AI-driven edge orchestration or quantum-resistant security protocols:

For the first time, IASF-IoT combines AI, blockchain and quantum-safe cryptography into one integrated security framework for IoT. The framework uses a self-learning AI tool that manages IoT security by answering five ongoing issues: missing integrated security orchestration, excessive resource requirements, lacking the ability to cope with evolving dangers, vulnerability to quantum hacking and insufficient privacy-security integration. By 2025, quantum crypto is poised to move from concept to active use in many industries. In the past two years (2023-2025), a lot of progress has been made in making quantum-resistant algorithms the same globally, with people and groups cooperating to prevent risks from quantum computers. Code-based, lattice-based and hash-based cryptographic systems are the basic categories for edge computing security standards. They guarantee security for data exchange in edge environments, as traditional encryption ways may be compromised. AI is an important part of AI for creating secure and stable algorithms based on quantum-resistant cryptography. AI can conduct simulations of quantum attacks on security systems which enables researchers to address weak points even before launch. The first three finalized post-quantum encryption standards have been released by NIST and system administrators should make the change as soon as they are able. Major technology companies are also advancing their quantum-resistant implementations, preparing enterprise infrastructure for the post-quantum era. The convergence of these technologies represents a critical evolution in cybersecurity architecture, particularly for edge computing environments that require both intelligent orchestration and quantum-safe protection.

9. 6G Synergies on Integrating 5G and Edge Computing:

The evolution from 5G to 6G networks is creating unprecedented synergies with edge computing frameworks, particularly for ultra-low latency IoT applications that demand sub-millisecond response times. While 5G deployments continue, 6G research is actively underway with focus on even higher data rates, lower latencies, and greater network intelligence. Technical specifications discussions are expected to begin in 2025, leading to the first 6G specification in 3GPP Release 21 by 2028.

Recent research demonstrates the synergistic integration of edge computing and 6G networks for real-time IoT applications, showing significant performance improvements including a 47% reduction in average latency, a 40% decrease in total energy consumption, and a 20% increase in resource utilization. 6G-enabled edge intelligence is emerging as a critical enabler for ultra-reliable low latency applications, combining the benefits of edge computing, AI, and wireless high-speed smart networks over traditional cloud computing approaches. This convergence addresses the limitations of current 5G-edge computing frameworks by providing native AI integration and more distributed intelligence. Future internet architectures aim to function as neutral in-network storage and computation platforms, essential for enabling 6G and beyond wireless use cases. The integration leverages advanced machine learning techniques to optimize resource allocation and network slicing dynamically. Key architectural improvements in 6G-edge synergies include native support for holographic communications, tactile internet applications, and brain-computer interfaces requiring latencies below 1 millisecond. The framework enables distributed intelligence where AI processing occurs at multiple network layers simultaneously, from device edge to network edge to regional edge nodes. The rapid growth of intelligent systems, fuelled by IoT emergence, has enabled significant transformative advancements with the imminent arrival of 6G technology. This creates a foundation for applications like autonomous vehicles, industrial automation, and augmented reality that demand both ultra-low latency and massive IoT connectivity simultaneously.

10. Role of Blockchain on Integrating 5G and Edge Computing:

By combining permissioned and permissionless blockchain layers with Layer-2 scaling solutions and adaptive consensus mechanisms, the framework shows an average authentication latency of 172.50 seconds and a 50% reduction in gas fees compared to traditional Ethereum-based implementations. The blockchain mechanism strategically separates data flow from transaction flow, bringing significantly lower packet overhead and transmission latency. The Low-Latency Blockchain Framework (LLBF) ensures package overhead only increases proportionally to the number of cluster heads, while packets are routed directly to requesters, minimizing end-to-end latency. Healthcare applications demonstrate blockchain's integration with 5G edge servers, introducing tamperproof data storage platforms with encrypted data storage models and symmetric-key cryptography-based privacy-preserving search mechanisms specifically developed for 5G edge blockchain environments. The Sec-edge system enables trusted blockchain identification and authentication for edge-based 5G networks, allowing data collection and processing close to IoT devices rather than cloud transmission, providing very low latency and instant computing applications to IoT users. Current 5G-enabled IoT frameworks focus on improving data collection and communication among edge computing devices via optimized runtime systems in parallel, creating reliable and decentralized Internet of Things ecosystems. The convergence of blockchain with 5G edge computing creates immutable audit trails, reduces single points of failure, and enables autonomous smart contracts for resource allocation, making it essential for applications requiring both ultra-low latency and cryptographic security guarantees.

Cloud Computing and 5G Challenges

Due to the higher use and accessibility of obtained fourth-generation networking technology or 4G has been radically evolving and constantly developing to meet the demands of future extensive use and applications of cloud computing. The 5G networking technology or the generation five networking technology can establish huge opportunity of expansion of cloud storage and can enhance the operations for communication as well the safety and security for the cloud storage and can have capability to handle the challenges of connectivity and application and usage of internet of things or IoT technology. The synergy of cloud computing with 5G has set difficulties which needs to be solved out for the establishment and deployment of the new generation of communication and computing facilities. There is, however, one major problem; how to address various issues of network congestion and how to scale the network to provide for a rapidly growing amount of data traffic from hundreds of thousands of integrated devices. Also, teaming edge computing with next-generation 5G networks adds more challenges for creating effective methods for coordinating resources between edge computers and remote cloud servers. Making sure information remains private and protected is important, since there are many threats to transmission and unauthorized attempts to get into the system. For compatibility and to prevent devices and platforms from splitting apart, both interoperability and standardization are very important. Also, organizations must give great attention to regulations and privacy concerns to ensure they follow the rules and are up-to-date with the industry. Tackling these issues means teamwork from industry players, policymakers and experts in academia, aiming to invent methods and best practices that allow cloud computing to work smoothly with 5G networks while ensuring security, privacy, scalability and the ability for things to work together. Besides these problems, cloud computing and 5G networks keep changing, so resources must be continually adjusted and improved to keep up with what people and applications need. So, we should use efficient methods to schedule resources and develop green algorithms that help cut down on waiting time, lower costs and guarantee a decent Quality of Service (QoS). Moreover, as the world grows more connected, regulatory compliance and data sovereignty become harder which makes it necessary to have strong rules and work with others across the world. These issues will have to be addressed in order to properly unlock the potential of cloud computing, as well as next-generation 5G networks for a wide range of applications such as healthcare, transportation, and smart city solutions.

Cloud computing is a rapidly progressive technology procedure to meet the increasing demands of users and customers to ensure better service to the clients which is considered a global modernised technology to use on-demand storage with flexibility (Dizdarević, 2019). High computing and the service of storage decrease the use cost of the clients which makes the methodology cost-effective and efficient. In this context of cloud computing, 5G networking place a significant role introduced into the market in 2018, this is a multiple input and multiple outputs simultaneously using millimetre waves and having a 3200 gigahertz band with frequency using the wireless world wide web as the Internet service medium. Some challenges and open issues encircling the 5G networking are, this technology is more energy consuming to make it more efficient and potent, more devices and higher bandwidth frequency for the hackers to breach the security etc.

System Metrics

1. **Economic Impact Analysis for Edge-Cloud Systems:** The economic landscape for edge-cloud deployments is experiencing substantial growth. Global spending on edge computing is estimated to reach $228 billion in 2024, marking a 14% increase from 2023, with projections reaching $378 billion by 2028. The global edge computing market is expected to grow from USD 60.0 billion in 2024 to USD 110.6 billion by 2029, at a CAGR of 13.0%. Over $6 billion has been invested in the edge computing ecosystem in 2024 because edge is driving innovation across AI, generative AI, and other data-intensive technologies by bringing computing closer to the data source. This investment surge reflects enterprises' recognition of edge computing's value proposition in reducing operational costs, improving service delivery, and enabling new revenue streams. The economic benefits manifest through reduced bandwidth costs by processing data locally rather than transmitting to centralized clouds, decreased latency-related penalties in real-time applications, and improved operational efficiency. Edge computing creates new demand for deploying infrastructure resources closer to data sources, fundamentally changing traditional cloud economics by distributing computing resources geographically.
2. **Energy-Aware Edge Computing Metrics:** Energy efficiency has become a critical performance indicator in edge computing deployments. Energy Efficiency is measured as the ratio of the total workload to the energy consumed, measured in units of work done per Joule (work/J). This metric provides comprehensive evaluation of algorithms' ability to minimize energy consumption while meeting

task deadlines. Energy-aware latency minimization for network slicing enabled edge computing addresses the management of heterogeneous and time-critical services with limited computing and communication resources. Advanced scheduling algorithms optimize the trade-off between performance and power consumption, with studies showing significant improvements in joules per task metrics through intelligent resource allocation. Energy-focused simulation of edge computing architectures in 5G networks demonstrates how edge computing offers low-latency services by offloading computations from high-performance computing (HPC) data centers to edge servers, reducing wide area network (WAN) strain. This architectural shift substantially reduces energy consumption per task by eliminating long-distance data transmission requirements.

3. **5G Monetization Models and Network Slicing:** Network slicing as a service represents a transformative monetization model for 5G operators. Fifth-generation (5G) wireless technology promises to be the critical enabler of use cases far beyond smartphones and other connected devices, representing the changing face of connectivity. The network slicing monetization framework operates through several key models:
    - **Slice-as-a-Service (SlaaS)**: Operators can offer dedicated network slices with guaranteed performance characteristics to enterprise customers. This creates recurring revenue streams through service level agreements that specify latency, bandwidth, and reliability requirements.
    - **Vertical Market Specialization**: Industry-specific slices for healthcare, manufacturing, and autonomous vehicles command premium pricing due to their specialized requirements and regulatory compliance needs.
    - **Dynamic Resource Pricing**: Real-time slice allocation based on demand patterns allows operators to implement surge pricing models, maximizing revenue during peak usage periods.

One of the primary objectives of 5G networks for enhancing energy efficiency is to match system capacity and power consumption with network load, The economic model extends beyond traditional connectivity charges to include value-added services like edge computing integration, AI processing capabilities, and security services, creating comprehensive ecosystem monetization opportunities that leverage the unique characteristics of each network slice.

A survey of multi-access edge computing in 5G and beyond: fundamentals, technology integration, and state-of-the-art: Mobile edge computing can optimise the resources of mobile by enabling the capabilities of cloud computation through the RAN or radio access networking in the closer proximity of the mobile users which is a key attribute of 5G connectivity. Thus, the MEC provides a white variety of applications in which the user can do real-time responses strictly such as autonomous vehicles, robotics and augmented reality etc in different fields like industry and academics field the 5G network connectivity implementations can lead to enhance enormous prospects for the future (Tran, 2017). A gross development and evolution of wireless communication can show that in the era of 80s wireless connectivity speed was 2.4 kbps, in 90s it became developed 6 times of previous,64 kbps, in 2000, speed accessibility reached 2000 kbps which was coiled as 3g in 2010s 4G arrived with speed 100 Mbps and in the year of 2018,5G appeared with the speed of 1gbps. So, the previous radical development and evolution showed the demand and necessity of wireless communication and connectivity in the user community and also expressed the prospect of 5G networking in future as in Fig. 4.

Figure 4. Global 5G adoption in 2022 [Source: Ericsson Mobility Report, 2022]

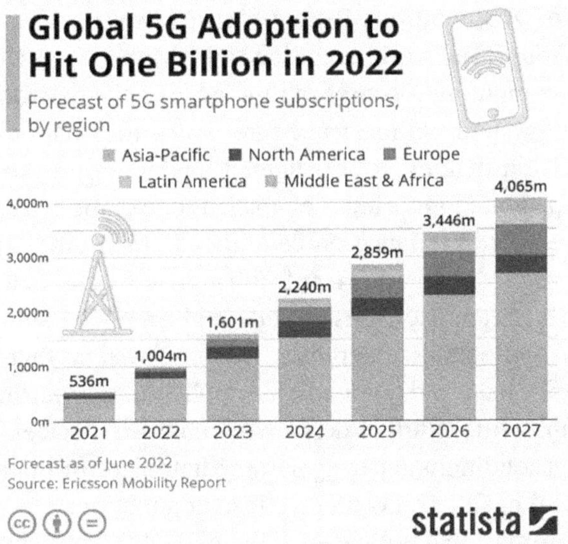

The effect of cloud computing technologies on e-learning and virtual platforms: Cloud computing is new style of computing that is build up on the idea of grid computing, distributed computing, virtual Technology and parallel computing. This cloud computing is highly dependent on the next-generation connectivity and network computing platform termed 5G, it is deemed the court technology of cloud computing, and the future of e-learning. The most affluent characteristic of cloud computing includes a secure and secure data storage in the cloud storage also the cheap internet service provided to the users. Some of the important characteristic features of cloud computing include high efficiency and scalability, reliability and flexibility and complete virtualization. Also, it includes assistant which is a distributed and decentralised service of the cloud storage, which could be accessed through internet connection and web browsing, capable to offer more dynamic to meet the demands of the users etc Software as a service or SaaS, platform as a service or PaaS and IaaS or infrastructure as a service are the reference models of this technology. Cloud computing is a new technology depending on internet connectivity by which the information and data can be stored in different servers and information can be distributed to the users as per necessity. The Impact of the gradual introduction of cloud computing in the indigenous market structure is immense and the introduction of cloud computing reduces the entry cost into the information technology-based business community.

Industry Use-Cases

1. **Healthcare IoT Applications** Patient-focused healthcare applications benefit significantly from 5G networks combined with Mobile Edge Computing (MEC), which brings computing resources to the edge of the network. MEC becomes part of an IoT system within healthcare that brings data closer to the core, speeds up decision-making, lowers latency, and improves the overall quality of care. Remote patient monitoring is enabled as one of the disruptive applications that require very little reliance on centralized cloud infrastructure, alongside autonomous vehicles, smart manufacturing, and augmented reality/virtual reality. Key healthcare use cases include real-time vital sign monitoring with sub-second response times, emergency response systems that can instantly alert medical professionals, and telemedicine applications requiring high-definition video streaming with minimal delay. Wearable IoT devices can continuously monitor patient conditions and trigger immediate alerts through edge processing, ensuring critical health events receive instant attention.
2. **Industrial Automation Applications:** Industrial IoT has special communication requirements, including high reliability, low latency, flexibility, and security. These are instinctively provided by the 5G mobile technology, making it a successful candidate for supporting Industrial IoT applications. Among the top 5 private 5G use cases identified for industrial applications are: 1) remote control of assets, 2) facility or campus connectivity and coverage, 3) logistics automation using AGVs and AMRs, 4) camera-based facility surveillance, and 5) advanced manufacturing processes. A 5G, ultra-wideband, edge computing solution powering AI and augmented reality (AR) technologies improves supply chain efficiencies by providing end-to-end, near real-time logistic controls. By coupling this technology with a data intelligence program, manufacturers can predict needed maintenance. Industrial deployments include predictive maintenance systems, quality control through computer vision, robotic process

automation, and real-time production optimization that can adjust manufacturing parameters within milliseconds of detecting anomalies.

3. **Smart City Deployments:** Traffic flow, parking space availability, utility usage and public streetlight management can be monitored by using IoT sensors on a 5G network. Authorities can leverage edge analytics to find practical solutions to conserve energy, optimise water and power resources, and reduce environmental impact. Edge computing can enable more effective city traffic management. Examples include optimising bus frequency given fluctuations in demand, managing the opening and closing of extra lanes, and, in future, managing autonomous car flows. With edge computing, there is no need to transport large volumes of data to centralized locations. Real-time edge analytics and 5G enable traffic safety applications that can analyze real-time data about the location, direction and speed of all cars, pedestrians and other connected road users in a given area — up to 1,000 objects in a busy intersection. The software uses that data to build an object model of road users and provide timely warnings to drivers about critical situations. Smart city implementations encompass intelligent traffic management systems, environmental monitoring networks, smart lighting that adapts to usage patterns, and integrated emergency response systems that coordinate multiple city services in real-time.

Future Enhancements

Over the past two years (2023–2025), significant strides have been made in standardizing quantum-resistant algorithms, addressing implementation challenges, and fostering global collaboration to mitigate the risks posed by quantum computers. Post-quantum cryptographic algorithms will be used for maintaining the security in devices, communications and other technologies in the future. There is a strong discussion on the use of cryptography in modern 5G networks, and how it is impacted by the projected emergence of sufficiently capable quantum computers in the next decades. It discusses the ongoing development of quantum-resistant algorithms and protocols and their future adoption. Current 5G networks rely heavily on RSA and ECC cryptographic schemes, which quantum computers could compromise through Shor's algorithm. 5G saw the introduction of an encrypted user identifier, the Subscriber Concealed Identifier (SUCI), to provide confidentiality of the subscriber's whereabouts and identities. Migration strategies include hybrid cryptographic approaches where classical and post-quantum algorithms operate in parallel during transition periods, ensuring backward compatibility while establishing quantum-resistant security foundations. As the world prepares for the advent of 6G networks, quantum technologies are becoming critical enablers of the next generation of communication systems. 6G promises data rates up to 100 times faster than 5G, with latency as low as 1 millisecond. It will facilitate the deployment of advanced technologies such as massive IoT, real-time AI, and ubiquitous edge computing. But with these advancements come new security risks. The 6G architecture will natively integrate quantum communication protocols, quantum key distribution (QKD) for ultra-secure channels, and quantum sensing capabilities for unprecedented network optimization. This convergence creates opportunities for quantum-enhanced machine learning at the network edge, enabling intelligent resource allocation and threat detection capabilities that exceed classical computing limitations.

AI governance in 2025 will be defined by stricter AI regulations, AI transparency, and AI risk management. Organizations must adapt by developing robust AI compliance strategies, investing in AI monitoring systems, and prioritizing human oversight. Network operators implementing AI-driven optimization and management systems must address algorithmic bias in resource allocation, ensuring equitable service distribution across different user demographics and geographic regions. Explainable AI frameworks are becoming mandatory for network intelligence systems, requiring transparent decision-making processes for critical network functions like handover decisions and quality of service provisioning. Governance frameworks will provide the foundation for ethical AI development and ensure compliance, accountability, and collaboration in a rapidly evolving AI landscape. Without these frameworks, the potential of Gen AI could be overshadowed by risks such as data misuse, algorithmic bias.

The global AI regulation landscape is fragmented and rapidly evolving. Earlier optimism that global policymakers would enhance cooperation and interoperability within the regulatory landscape now seems distant. The AI Act is the first-ever legal framework on AI, which addresses the risks of AI and positions Europe to play a leading role globally. In 2025, governments worldwide, particularly in the United States, are poised to introduce new mandates addressing critical issues such as transparency, bias mitigation, explainability, and privacy. Compliance frameworks like the EU AI Act, GDPR, and NIST AI RMF help enforce accountability and reduce the risk of harm or bias in AI-driven decisions. Network operators must implement comprehensive compliance management systems that can adapt to varying regulatory requirements across different jurisdictions while maintaining consistent security and privacy standards. The convergence of these technologies requires harmonized international standards for quantum-safe telecommunications, AI governance in critical infrastructure, and cross-border data protection mechanisms that preserve the global nature of modern communication networks while respecting local regulatory sovereignty.

CONCLUSION

Fast & open internet connection for uses of computers and mobiles is emerging as a reality. As for this aspect, both infrastructure and latency, as well as energy savings, are in the process of evolution and here 4G LTE networking and broadband WIFI testify to the significant benefits of edge computing for intensely interactive applications for mobile users. Additionally, while we prepare for the future of edge computing, we are ready to step into the next epoch of possibilities and transformation. Edge computing, especially in conjunction with 5G networks, and recent technologies such as AI and IoT are only the beginning of what is to come in terms of a new way of transcending our experiences with technology and one another. Real-time data analysis or an interactive 3D tour of your dream home? It's all possible when you put technology to the test. But it is necessary to introduce cautiousness in solving problems connected with security, privacy, and compliance to guarantee the continuity of users' confidence while interacting in the growing environment of a digital world. For the future development trends of edge computing and the prospects for the mobile application and service industry, it is hoped that more industry players, policymakers, and academia can enhance cooperation and continue to promote the development of edge computing and its applications. As such, it is possible for us to work towards making the most out of edge computing through harnessing innovative future investment and the sharing of the best knowledge for creating a smart society. In addition, high-frequency internet connection and the increased use of mobile devices suggest a new era of using technologies and accessing Internet content. This is not just about changing user habits but is revolutionizing industries from health and wealth to fun and work. Moreover, as we embrace the potential of edge computing, we are poised to unlock new frontiers in innovation and digital experiences. The synergy between edge computing, 5G networks, and emerging technologies like artificial intelligence and the Internet of Things promises to revolutionize how we interact with technology and each other. From real-time data analytics to immersive augmented reality experiences, the possibilities are limitless. However, it is imperative to remain vigilant in addressing challenges related to security, privacy, and regulatory compliance to ensure the trust and confidence of users in this rapidly evolving digital ecosystem. Looking ahead, the continued collaboration between industry stakeholders, policymakers, and academia will be instrumental in shaping the future trajectory of edge computing and its impact on mobile applications and services. By fostering an environment conducive to innovation, investment, and knowledge sharing, we can harness the full potential of edge computing to create a more connected, efficient, and inclusive digital society. Furthermore, the convergence of high-frequency internet connectivity and the proliferation of mobile devices signifies a paradigm shift in how individuals interact with technology and consume digital content. This shift is not only reshaping consumer behaviours but also driving profound changes across industries, from healthcare and finance to entertainment and manufacturing. Looking at the future development of edge computing and the increasing amount of widespread 5G networks, one can expect a series of entirely new applications and services that can turn the world of digital innovation on its head. The infrastructure enhancement and improved latency realized through edge computing are not only improving user experiences but also creating opportunities for new revenue sources. Incidences of edge-based content delivery network, edge-enabling internet-of-things networks, and other similar constructs, are being sought out by various organizations across industries in a bid to harness the affordances of edge computing for advantage in the market. This trend is most apparent in sectors that require processing of real-time data as well as having minimum delay in passing information between workers and/or consumers. The conservation of energy is a significant factor in determining whether edge computing systems will be successful or not in the future. By making the best of the available resources and deploying energy-conscious hardware platforms they will enable edges to become green infrastructures for computation. Moreover, goals associated with the use of renewable energy sources in the range of edge computing implementations and employment of energy-sensitive scheduling models can improve the eco-friendliness of the offered edge computing platform. Altogether, the alternatives such as high-frequency Internet, the concept of edge computing, and 5G networks are identified as the breakthrough in further development of digital technology. While operating in this changing environment, we cannot afford to be complacent in terms of how we address issues to do with security, privacy, as well as ethics. Here, we outline the importance of including all stakeholders in edge computing innovation to help shape a better future for all through edge technology.

REFERENCES

Ali, B., Gregory, M. A., & Li, S. (2021). Multi-access edge computing architecture, data security and privacy: A review. *IEEE Access : Practical Innovations, Open Solutions*, *9*, 18706–18721. DOI: 10.1109/ACCESS.2021.3053233

Alsaraireh, A., Al-Dubai, A., Romdhani, I., Al-Dubai, M., & Al-Dubai, Y. (2020). Security and privacy in edge computing: A review. *IEEE Access : Practical Innovations, Open Solutions*, *8*, 13562–13577. DOI: 10.1109/ACCESS.2020.2967711

Barbarossa, S., Sardellitti, S., & Di Lorenzo, P. (2014). Communicating while computing: Distributed mobile cloud computing over 5G heterogeneous networks. *IEEE Signal Processing Magazine*, *31*(6), 45–55. DOI: 10.1109/MSP.2014.2334709

Cao, K., Liu, Y., Meng, G., & Sun, Q. (2020). An overview on edge computing research. *IEEE Access : Practical Innovations, Open Solutions*, *8*, 85714–85728. DOI: 10.1109/ACCESS.2020.2991734

Chen, S., Zhao, J., Zhang, W., & Chai, X. (2017). Network slicing-based 5G and future mobile networks: Mobility, resource management, and challenges. *IEEE Communications Magazine*, *55*(8), 138–145. DOI: 10.1109/MCOM.2017.1600940

Costa-Perez, X., Swetina, J., Guo, T., Mahindra, R., & Rangarajan, S. (2017). Network slicing in 5G: Survey and challenges. *IEEE Communications Magazine*, *55*(5), 94–100. DOI: 10.1109/MCOM.2017.1600951

Dizdarević, J., Carpio, F., Jukan, A., & Masip-Bruin, X. (2019). A survey of communication protocols for internet of things and related challenges of fog and cloud computing integration. *ACM Computing Surveys*, *51*(6), 1–29. DOI: 10.1145/3292674

Etro, F. (2009). The economic impact of cloud computing on business creation, employment and output in Europe. *Review of Business and Economics*, *54*(2), 179–208.

Hassan, N., Yau, K. L. A., & Wu, C. (2019). Edge computing in 5G: A review. *IEEE Access : Practical Innovations, Open Solutions*, *7*, 127276–127289. DOI: 10.1109/ACCESS.2019.2938534

Hu, W., Gao, Y., Ha, K., Wang, J., Amos, B., Chen, Z., Pillai, P., & Satyanarayanan, M. (2016, August). Quantifying the impact of edge computing on mobile applications. In *Proceedings of the 7th ACM SIGOPS Asia-Pacific Workshop on Systems* (pp. 1–8). DOI: 10.1145/2967360.2967369

Ke, M., Gao, Z., Wu, Y., Gao, X., & Wong, K. K. (2020). Massive access in cell-free massive MIMO-based Internet of Things: Cloud computing and edge computing paradigms. *IEEE Journal on Selected Areas in Communications*, *39*(3), 756–772. DOI: 10.1109/JSAC.2020.3018807

Li, F., Wang, Y., Li, X., Lin, S., Wen, Y., & Jin, Q. (2020). Edge intelligence: On-demand deep learning model co-inference with device-edge synergy. *IEEE Transactions on Parallel and Distributed Systems*, *31*(8), 1787–1802. DOI: 10.1109/TPDS.2020.2970559

Lin, B., Zhu, F., Zhang, J., Chen, J., Chen, X., Xiong, N. N., & Mauri, J. L. (2019). A time-driven data placement strategy for a scientific workflow combining edge computing and cloud computing. *IEEE Transactions on Industrial Informatics*, *15*(7), 4254–4265. DOI: 10.1109/TII.2019.2905659

Mao, Y., Zhang, J., & Letaief, K. B. (2014). Mobile edge computing: Survey and research outlook. *Mobile Networks and Applications*, *19*(2), 171–193. DOI: 10.1007/s11036-013-0481-3

Naveen, S., & Kounte, M. R. (2019, December). Key technologies and challenges in IoT edge computing. In 2019 Third International Conference on I-SMAC (IoT in Social, Mobile, Analytics and Cloud) (I-SMAC) (pp. 61–65). IEEE. DOI: 10.1109/I-SMAC47947.2019.9032541

Pham, Q. V., Fang, F., Ha, V. N., Piran, M. J., Le, M., Le, L. B., Hwang, W. J., & Ding, Z. (2020). A survey of multi-access edge computing in 5G and beyond: Fundamentals, technology integration, and state-of-the-art. *IEEE Access : Practical Innovations, Open Solutions*, *8*, 116974–117017. DOI: 10.1109/ACCESS.2020.3001277

Qi, Q., & Tao, F. (2019). A smart manufacturing service system based on edge computing, fog computing, and cloud computing. *IEEE Access : Practical Innovations, Open Solutions*, *7*, 86769–86777. DOI: 10.1109/ACCESS.2019.2923610

Qian, M., Zhang, Y., Zhang, Y., & Zhang, Q. (2020). Securing cloud computing for 5G and beyond: Challenges and solutions. *IEEE Network*, *34*(6), 180–187. DOI: 10.1109/MNET.001.2000154

Roman, R., Lopez, J., & Mambo, M. (2018). Mobile edge computing, Fog et al.: A survey and analysis of security threats and challenges. *Future Generation Computer Systems*, *78*, 680–698. DOI: 10.1016/j.future.2016.11.009

Shahzadi, S., Iqbal, M., Dagiuklas, T., & Qayyum, Z. U. (2017). Multi-access edge computing: Open issues, challenges and future perspectives. *Journal of Cloud Computing (Heidelberg, Germany)*, *6*(1), 1–13. DOI: 10.1186/s13677-017-0097-9

Shrivastava, S., Singh, A., Kumar, P., & Mohan, A. (2021). Privacy-preserving machine learning in edge computing: A survey. *IEEE Transactions on Industrial Informatics*, *17*(6), 4251–4260. DOI: 10.1109/TII.2020.3035997

Sriram, G. S. (2022). Edge computing vs. cloud computing: An overview of big data challenges and opportunities for large enterprises. *International Research Journal of Modernization in Engineering Technology and Science*, *4*(1), 1331–1337.

Taleb, T., Samdanis, K., Mada, B., Flinck, H., Dutta, S., & Sabella, D. (2017). On multi-access edge computing: A survey of the emerging 5G network edge cloud architecture and orchestration. *IEEE Communications Surveys and Tutorials*, *19*(3), 1657–1681. DOI: 10.1109/COMST.2017.2705720

Tran, T. X., Hajisami, A., Pandey, P., & Pompili, D. (2017). Collaborative mobile edge computing in 5G networks: New paradigms, scenarios, and challenges. *IEEE Communications Magazine*, *55*(4), 54–61. DOI: 10.1109/MCOM.2017.1600863

Ullah, A., Aznaoui, H., Şahin, C. B., Sadie, M., Dinler, O. B., & Imane, L. (2022). Cloud computing and 5G challenges and open issues. *International Journal of Advanced and Applied Sciences*, *11*(3), 187–193.

Wang, S., Zhang, X., Zhang, Y., Wang, L., Yang, J., & Wang, W. (2020). AI-driven mobile edge computing: A survey. *IEEE Access : Practical Innovations, Open Solutions*, *8*, 111888–111902. DOI: 10.1109/ACCESS.2020.2997910

Chapter 11
Enhancing the Internet of Things (IoT) Through Cloud Computing

Salaheldin Mohamed Ibrahim Edam
https://orcid.org/0000-0002-8280-8745
Sudan University of Science and Technology, Sudan

Loay Ahmed Hassan Bushara
Sudan University of Science and Technology, Sudan

Abuagla Babiker Mohammed
Sudan University of Science and Technology, Sudan

ABSTRACT

In this chapter, the convergence of IoT and Cloud Computing are discussed with an emphasis on scalability, elasticity, real-time processing, cost-effectiveness, resource optimization, and security. Giant amounts of data are generated by IoT networks; hence the role cloud computing can play in efficient data storage and management becomes critical. In addition, it discusses the importance of disaster recovery, fault tolerance, global access, and management in the cloud-enabled IoT ecosystem. Finally, the authors present the future trends highlighting the advancements that will drive the IoT and cloud computing integration. The research gives insight on how cloud computing support IoT applications to help companies build strong, scalable, secure systems-all with resource efficiency and operational costs in check.

DOI: 10.4018/979-8-3693-9984-2.ch011

I. INTRODUCTION TO IOT AND CLOUD COMPUTING

The IoT ecosystem integrates sets of devices that communicate, work, and interact with one another. This has made it easier to develop smart environments within homes, cities, and industries. With IoT, physical things such as cars, household devices, and even industrial machines are connected through sensors, software, and the internet. As a result, devices can autonomously capture and share data. It is expected that the number of IoT devices will surpass 30 billion by 2030, which means data generation will increase drastically, making it more challenging to store and process it as well as analyze it in real time (Khan & Gupta, 2022). Recent research has noted important limitations for IoT ecosystems such as data security, system scalability, and interoperability. One example is the development of the Internet of Things (IoT) sensors that focus on adopting new technologies to improve data accuracy and increase energy efficiency in resource-constrained environments (Aljarrah et al., 2023).

The integration of IoT with AI and blockchain facilitates intelligent and secure data management, crucial for industries needing real-time, high-stakes decisions (Rajora et al., 2024). Meanwhile, cloud computing is vital for managing the immense data generated by IoT devices. It provides scalable and efficient storage and processing, freeing businesses from physical infrastructure limitations and enabling large-scale, real-time data management for faster decision-making. Cloud platforms also offer dynamic scalability, adapting to growing IoT networks and data volumes (Eljak et al., 2023).

Combining IoT with cloud platforms enhances system flexibility and cost efficiency by providing access to robust computational resources, thus reducing the need for complex on-premises setups. This integration enables real-time analysis crucial for applications like smart cities and industrial predictive maintenance (Jha & Chaturvedi, 2024).

The synergy between IoT and cloud computing extends beyond storage, significantly improving real-time analytics, security, and scalability. Cloud platforms facilitate advanced analytics on IoT data, yielding actionable insights that drive innovation and operational efficiency. For instance, in smart cities, cloud-enabled IoT systems manage real-time traffic, enhance energy efficiency, and improve public services (Jha & Chaturvedi, 2024). In healthcare, cloud-integrated IoT devices support real-time patient monitoring, leading to faster interventions and personalized care. Furthermore, this integration fortifies data security with cloud-based encryption and access control, addressing privacy concerns. The powerful analytics capabilities of cloud computing also aid in predictive maintenance and smart energy grid management, underscoring the vast potential of IoT-cloud collaboration (Abaee et al., 2024a).

Cloud computing bolsters IoT network security through advanced measures like encryption, authentication, and access controls, which are often challenging to implement on individual IoT devices. These features protect sensitive data in transit between IoT devices and cloud platforms, addressing critical security concerns in large-scale IoT deployments. For instance, encryption ensures data integrity, while access controls prevent unauthorized access (Kuchuk & Malokhvii, 2024). Cloud platforms also enable anomaly detection and real-time monitoring, crucial for mitigating IoT security threats. The increasing use of Security-as-a-Service (SECaaS) from cloud providers offers scalable and efficient security solutions tailored for IoT. Research, including "Sensing the Future: Challenges and Trends in IoT Sensor Technology" and "Cloud Security Frameworks for IoT Applications," underscores the significance of these cloud-based security protocols in safeguarding IoT networks and improving operational reliability (Mahamuni, 2023).

This chapter explores the intricate relationship between IoT and cloud computing, demonstrating how cloud platforms enhance IoT network functionality and address the challenges of escalating data and connected devices. This integration empowers businesses with efficient, scalable, real-time data management for improved decision-making. For instance, in healthcare, IoT-cloud solutions enable continuous patient monitoring for faster responses and personalized care (Kuchuk & Malokhvii, 2024). Similarly, smart cities leverage these technologies for traffic optimization and energy management, promoting sustainability.

Moreover, the convergence of IoT and cloud computing strengthens data security through encryption and access control, mitigating privacy concerns. Hybrid models like fog and edge computing complement this by combining cloud scalability with localized processing to reduce latency and enhance privacy. Through case studies in healthcare, manufacturing, and urban development, this chapter will illustrate how these technologies collectively foster innovation, efficiency, and resilience across industries (Andriulo et al., 2024).

II. LITERATURE REVIEW & CONTRIBUTION OF THIS CHAPTER

Recent studies have emphasized the need for scalable and low-latency cloud architectures to support the dynamic demands of IoT systems. (Lilhore et al., 2025) investigates adaptive cloud infrastructures that incorporate dynamic resource allocation and load balancing techniques, demonstrating significant reductions in latency under fluctuating workloads—an essential capability for IoT deployments that must handle variable and unpredictable data streams. Complementing this, (Lilhore et al., 2025) introduce a machine learning-enabled hybrid framework that strategically offloads real-time processing to edge devices while leveraging the cloud for more resource-intensive analytics. This approach addresses persistent latency and connectivity challenges in large-scale IoT environments. Similarly, (Jameil & Al-raweshidy, 2024) compares hybrid fog/cloud systems to traditional cloud-only architectures, concluding that hybrid models offer superior performance in terms of latency, bandwidth optimization, and real-time responsiveness. Supporting these findings, (Fourati et al., 2024) present a comprehensive survey of IoT application architectures—including cloud, edge, and fog paradigms—ultimately asserting that hybrid systems offer the most balanced solutions when it comes to scalability, latency sensitivity, data privacy, and interoperability across diverse protocols. Building upon these insights, this chapter synthesizes cutting-edge research from 2024 and 2025 to propose a practical framework that not only enhances cloud-only IoT deployments but also prioritizes the integration of hybrid edge-cloud architectures. This integrated approach aims to provide a clear roadmap for achieving optimized performance, flexibility, and resilience in future IoT ecosystems.

Table 1. Comparative Evaluation: AWS vs Azure vs GCP for IoT

Feature	Amazon Web Services (AWS)	Microsoft Azure	Google Cloud Platform (GCP)
Scalability	Industry-leading with vast resource availability; highly granular scaling pricing–wise	Strong enterprise-focused scalability; seamless with Microsoft stacks	Balanced scalability with managed services; straightforward tooling
Latency	Low latency with AWS IoT Greengrass and regional edge locations; adaptive scaling	Integrates well with local edge; some users report occasional latency with IoT Hub	GCP is noted for fast, intuitive APIs and excellent logging; latency is consistently low
Integration Complexity	Broadest range of IoT services but steep learning curve and complex documentation	Seamless for Microsoft users; strong enterprise integration, though support sometimes challenging	Clean, beginner-friendly interfaces; simpler naming conventions reduce setup complexity
Edge Support	Greengrass supports offline execution and synchronized local/cloud operation; robust edge tooling	IoT Edge for containerized Azure workloads; user feedback indicates delays in IoT Hub for high-frequency data	GCP Cloud IoT Edge offers lightweight agent services, though less enterprise-oriented
Global Accessibility	Enormous global footprint with over 30 regions/EU data centers for compliance-sensitive use cases	Near-global presence with specific excellence in jurisdictions requiring Azure compliance	Strong global edge network; renowned logging and observability
Tooling & Analytics	Rich IoT-specific tools like AWS IoT Core, TwinMaker, SageMaker, Quicksight	Robust ML services, cognitive APIs, and seamless Power Platform support	Powerful AI/ML via BigQuery, Vertex AI; excellent observability and logging

Contribution & Chapter Significance

This chapter delivers a comprehensive synthesis of cutting-edge research from 2024–2025, emphasizing hybrid edge–cloud architectures as a strategic response to the core challenges facing IoT systems, including latency reduction, scalable deployment, and data privacy compliance. It uniquely contributes to the literature by providing a side-by-side, practice-oriented evaluation of leading cloud service providers Amazon Web Services (AWS), Microsoft Azure, and Google Cloud Platform (GCP) with a specific focus on IoT use cases. Unlike general comparisons, this assessment draws from real-world deployment scenarios and user feedback in latency-sensitive environments, offering nuanced insights into how each platform performs under different operational constraints. Additionally, the chapter serves as a practical guide for IoT architects and decision-makers, mapping specific workloads to cloud provider strengths. For instance, it recommends AWS Greengrass for highly scalable, data-intensive scenarios due to its mature edge capabilities and tight integration with AWS services, while suggesting GCP's streamlined development environment for rapid prototyping and advanced analytics. This dual focus grounded in both scholarly synthesis and hands-on guidance positions the chapter as a valuable resource for researchers and practitioners alike.

Critical Additions for a Comprehensive IoT–Cloud Framework

First, energy efficiency and sustainability have become critical in the era of Green IoT. With the rapid expansion of connected devices and cloud workloads, the environmental footprint is growing, necessitating energy-aware scheduling, low-power data transmission, and carbon-conscious cloud solutions like those offered by AWS, Microsoft, and Google. Recent studies, such as those by (Jadama et al., 2024), highlight optimization strategies for reducing carbon emissions and improving energy use in IoT-cloud ecosystems. Second, a detailed discussion of the IoT protocol stack, including protocols such as MQTT, CoAP, and LoRaWAN, is essential to help readers understand how data is transmitted, integrated, and optimized between edge devices and cloud platforms. These protocols are foundational to system performance, especially in low-power, high-latency environments, as explored in studies by (Manideep Yenugula et al., 2024).

Third, privacy regulations such as GDPR, HIPAA, and CCPA warrant in-depth coverage, given the sensitivity of data collected by IoT systems and the legal ramifications of cloud storage across jurisdictions. (Pandey & Bhushan, 2024) demonstrate how regulatory compliance must be built into the architecture from the outset, with support from cloud-native tools like Azure Purview, AWS Macie, and Google's Data Loss Prevention (DLP) APIs. Additionally, the chapter would benefit from discussing interoperability and data semantics, especially considering the fragmented landscape of IoT devices and platforms. Emphasizing standards such as OPC-UA, W3C Web of Things (WoT), and device twins (e.g., Azure Digital Twins) would show how semantic consistency and metadata mapping can enhance cross-platform compatibility and data reusability.

Finally, AI and machine learning in cloud-enabled IoT systems are driving real-time automation, predictive analytics, and localized intelligence. Platforms like AWS Greengrass ML Inference, Azure Percept, and GCP Edge TPU enable advanced decision-making at the edge, while federated learning and ML model synchronization across cloud and edge environments are increasingly relevant. These additions not only address current gaps in the chapter but also align it with emerging trends and research directions, ultimately ensuring that the content remains comprehensive, practical, and aligned with state-of-the-art developments in IoT and cloud computing.

Enhancing IoT: Cloud, Privacy, & Ethics

To provide a future-ready and responsible framework for IoT-cloud integration, it is essential to address emerging challenges beyond scalability and latency. One such area is privacy and ethical data handling, which are often overshadowed in technical discussions. As IoT devices increasingly collect sensitive personal and environmental data, concerns over user consent, data ownership, surveillance, and algorithmic bias grow more significant. Integrating privacy-by-design principles, differential privacy, and end-to-end encryption into IoT-cloud architectures ensures compliance with international regulations such as the General Data Protection Regulation (GDPR) and Health Insurance Portability and Accountability Act (HIPAA) ((Chippagiri & Ravula, 2021); (Lottu et al., 2024)).In addition, ethical frameworks must guide the development of intelligent IoT systems, particularly when artificial intelligence (AI) and machine learning (ML) are involved in decision-making. Ethical AI guidelines—such as transparency, accountability, and fairness should be applied to avoid reinforcing social biases or compromising vulnerable populations (Lottu et al., 2024). On the architectural front, the chapter incorporates cloud-native design principles, which are crucial for scaling IoT systems efficiently. These include microservices-based architectures, containerization (e.g., Docker), Kubernetes orchestration, and DevOps pipelines for continuous integration and deployment (CI/CD). These practices enhance modularity, fault isolation, and rapid scalability in large IoT ecosystems (Devipriya et al., 2025). Adopting these approaches not only supports agility and resilience in IoT systems but also enables seamless updates and faster time-to-market for new applications.

III. CLOUD COMPUTING'S ROLE IN DATA STORAGE FOR IOT

The Internet of Things (IoT) has become a crucial component of today's digital landscape, influencing various fields such as healthcare, transportation, smart cities, and manufacturing. With the rapid increase in connected devices, IoT produces vast amounts of data that require efficient storage, management, and processing. This is where cloud computing is essential. It provides scalable, flexible, and cost-effective storage solutions that are vital for managing the diverse and high-volume data generated by IoT devices (Abaee et al., 2024b). In the following sections, we will explore the challenges associated with managing IoT-generated data, the cloud storage solutions that tackle these issues, and the advantages of using cloud platforms for IoT data storage. Additionally, we will discuss how cloud computing facilitates real-time management of large datasets and optimizes resources (Abaee et al., 2024b).

Challenges in Traditional IoT Architectures

The Internet of Things (IoT) has brought about a new age of connectivity, allowing devices to interact and exchange data over extensive networks. However, as the IoT landscape expands, conventional IoT architectures are encountering several challenges that impede their capacity to effectively manage the growing scale and complexity of contemporary IoT implementations. These challenges [Figure 1] include concerns regarding scalability, security, interoperability, data management, and energy efficiency (Liu et al., 2024).

Figure 1. Challenges in Traditional IoT Architectures

Scalability Issues

Traditional IoT architectures face a significant scalability challenge due to the rapid increase in connected devices and data. As billions of IoT devices are forecasted, older systems struggle with performance issues like increased latency and network congestion, as they were not designed for such extensive networks. This leads to inefficiencies in data transmission and processing, compounded by the growing complexity of managing and maintaining more integrated devices (Mirani et al., 2022).

Interoperability Challenges

IoT ecosystems comprise diverse devices with unique communication protocols, operating systems, and hardware. Traditional architectures struggle with this diversity, making interoperability a major challenge. Devices often use proprietary technologies, hindering seamless collaboration and creating data silos, which complicates cross-platform communication and integration (Mirani et al., 2022).

Security and Privacy Concerns

Security is a critical challenge in the Internet of Things (IoT) because traditional frameworks can't fully address its unique vulnerabilities. Many IoT devices have limited processing power and memory, making robust security difficult to implement. The decentralized nature of IoT networks, with devices spread across vast areas and connecting to various networks, creates numerous entry points for cyber threats. Conventional, centralized security models struggle to adapt to this distributed structure, increasing the risk of attacks like data breaches, unauthorized access, and malware infections. Furthermore, protecting data privacy is a significant concern, as sensitive information from IoT devices is susceptible to interception (Mirani et al., 2022).

Data Management and Processing

The vast amounts of data produced by IoT devices create significant challenges for conventional IoT architectures. These systems are typically not equipped to handle such large volumes of data, especially when real-time processing and analysis are essential. For IoT applications that depend on quick decision-making—like those in healthcare, self-driving cars, or industrial automation—traditional systems may find it difficult to meet the demands for immediate data processing. Additionally, the task of storing and managing this data in a manner that ensures both efficiency and security presents another major hurdle. As IoT networks expand, the capability to process and analyze data on a large scale becomes increasingly crucial. However, traditional architectures often lack the required computational resources and infrastructure to manage this effectively.

Power Consumption and Energy Efficiency

Many IoT devices are built to function in remote or difficult-to-access areas, often depending on battery power for long durations. However, conventional IoT designs don't always prioritize energy efficiency, which can result in increased power usage. This can greatly shorten the operational life of IoT devices, particularly when regular battery changes or recharging aren't practical. The demand for constant data transmission and processing makes the situation worse, as it forces devices to stay active for extended periods, leading to higher power consumption. Enhancing energy efficiency is essential, especially for IoT applications in fields such as agriculture, environmental monitoring, and smart cities, where devices need to operate independently for extended periods (Abdulazeez et al., 2024).

Cloud Storage Solutions for IoT

Cloud computing provides strong and adaptable solutions to tackle the data management issues created by IoT devices. Cloud platforms offer scalable storage systems capable of managing the large volumes of data produced by IoT devices, facilitating efficient data storage, retrieval, and processing (Lakshminarasamma & Bulla, 2024). Some of the most widely used cloud storage services [Figure 2] include:

Figure 2. Cloud Storage Service

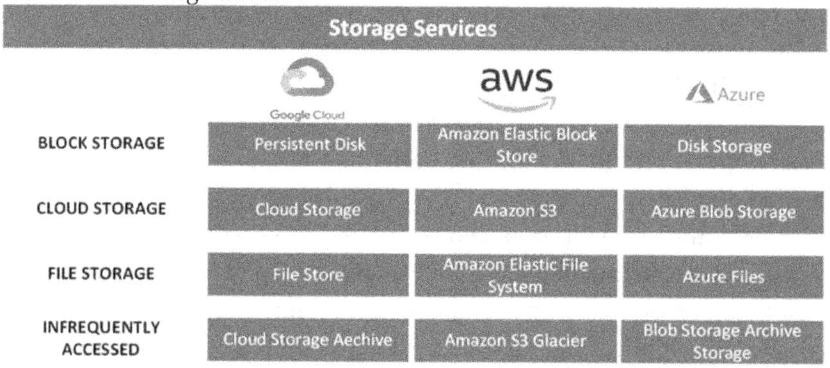

Amazon Web Services (AWS) S3

AWS S3 (Simple Storage Service) is a highly scalable and durable storage solution that is commonly used for handling large amounts of data. It is especially beneficial for IoT applications due to its support for object storage, which is perfect for unstructured data like images, videos, and logs produced by IoT devices. AWS S3 includes features such as versioning, data lifecycle policies, and multi-region replication, making it well-suited for managing IoT data across various geographic areas. Additionally, AWS S3 integrates smoothly with other AWS services like AWS Lambda (for serverless computing) and Amazon Kinesis (for real-time data streaming), creating a comprehensive ecosystem for storing and processing IoT data (Modupe et al., 2024).

Google Cloud Storage

Google Cloud Storage is a widely used cloud storage option for IoT data. It provides a comprehensive object storage service that accommodates various data types, including time-series data, videos, and large files. With features like high availability, global distribution, and data redundancy, Google Cloud Storage ensures that IoT data remains accessible even during hardware failures. A significant benefit of using Google Cloud Storage is its seamless integration with Google Cloud's machine learning and data analytics tools, enabling organizations to conduct advanced analytics on IoT data. This functionality is crucial for sectors that depend on real-time insights from IoT data, such as healthcare and smart cities (Gowda et al., 2024).

Microsoft Azure Blob Storage

Microsoft Azure Blob Storage is a flexible and secure solution for storing large amounts of unstructured data. It's particularly effective for IoT applications that need to manage extensive sensor data, images, and videos. The service provides various storage tiers to help optimize costs based on how often the data is accessed. Additionally, Azure Blob Storage works seamlessly with Azure IoT Hub, a cloud service that connects, monitors, and manages IoT devices. This integration makes it easier to collect and store IoT data in the cloud, ensuring a smooth data flow from devices to the cloud.

Benefits of Using Cloud Storage for IoT

As shown in (Figure 3), cloud storage is crucial for enhancing IoT capabilities by providing scalability, which allows for easy expansion to support the increasing number of connected devices and the large amounts of data they produce. Its flexibility enables organizations to adjust storage resources as needed, ensuring they can efficiently manage varying demands without requiring significant infrastructure upgrades. Furthermore, cloud storage offers substantial cost savings through its pay-as-you-go pricing model, removing the necessity for expensive upfront hardware investments. It also supports real-time data management, allowing for immediate access to data, quick processing, and thorough analysis. This functionality leads to faster, more informed decision-making, enhancing operational efficiency and fostering innovation in IoT applications (Deepthi et al., 2024).

Figure 3. Benefits of Using Cloud Storage for IoT

Scalability

A major advantage of utilizing cloud storage for IoT data is its scalability. As IoT networks grow and more devices connect, the amount of data produced also rises. Cloud storage options like AWS S3, Google Cloud Storage, and Microsoft Azure Blob Storage are built to scale horizontally, enabling organizations to accommodate large volumes of data without the concern of exceeding capacity. Cloud platforms can automatically adjust resources according to demand, allowing organizations to avoid over-provisioning storage capacity from the start. This flexibility helps businesses handle sudden increases in data volume, such as during times of intense sensor activity or when launching new IoT devices (Manideep Yenugula et al., 2024).

Flexibility

Cloud storage offers exceptional flexibility for accessing and managing IoT data, enabling organizations to oversee networks remotely from anywhere globally. Cloud platforms provide APIs to connect IoT systems with other cloud services like data analytics, machine learning, and real-time data processing. This adaptability allows for comprehensive solutions that can respond to evolving needs and increasing data volumes. Cloud storage providers also offer various options for different IoT data types; for example, time-series data can go into dedicated databases, while unstructured data like videos and images can be stored as objects(Manideep Yenugula et al., 2024).

Cost Savings

Cloud storage solutions offer affordable options for storing IoT data. Unlike traditional on-premise storage, which requires substantial investments in hardware, software, and infrastructure, cloud services use a pay-as-you-go model. This means organizations only pay for the storage they actually use, eliminating the need for large upfront costs and lowering the expenses tied to maintaining on-site storage systems. Additionally, cloud platforms provide tiered pricing for storage, enabling businesses to save money by keeping rarely accessed data in more economical storage tiers. This strategy effectively lowers the overall costs of managing the vast amounts of data produced by IoT devices (Manideep Yenugula et al., 2024).

Real-Time Data Management

Cloud storage solutions allow for the management of large datasets in real-time, which is crucial for IoT applications that need immediate analysis and decision-making based on live data. For instance, in industrial IoT (IIoT) scenarios, real-time data from sensors must be processed and stored for quick analysis to enhance machine performance and avoid downtime. Cloud platforms facilitate real-time data processing by integrating with services like event-driven architectures (e.g., AWS Lambda) and data streaming platforms (e.g., Amazon Kinesis, Google Pub/Sub). These services empower organizations to process and analyze IoT data instantly, leading to quicker decision-making and more efficient operations (Alomari et al., 2024).

Cloud Computing's Impact on IoT Data Storage and Management

The incorporation of cloud computing into IoT systems has transformed how data is stored and managed. With its scalable, flexible, and cost-effective solutions, cloud computing allows businesses to effectively manage the increasing amounts of data generated by IoT devices. Services like AWS S3, Google Cloud Storage, and Azure Blob Storage provide strong storage options that tackle the issues of data volume, variety, and real-time processing. The pay-as-you-go pricing model and the capacity to scale as needed make cloud storage an efficient and budget-friendly choice for handling IoT data. As IoT networks keep growing, the dependence on cloud platforms is set to rise. The continuous advancement of sophisticated cloud services, including AI integration, edge computing, and real-time data analytics, will significantly improve the capacity to store, process, and manage IoT data effectively (Kuchuk & Malokhvii, 2024).

The Importance of Edge and Fog Computing in IoT

The exponential growth of the Internet of Things (IoT) has resulted in a deluge of data generated by billions of interconnected devices. Traditional cloud computing, while powerful in terms of storage and processing, often falls short when it comes to meeting the low-latency and real-time requirements of modern IoT applications. This is where edge and fog computing come into play. Edge computing pushes computation closer to the data source such as sensors or embedded devices thereby significantly reducing latency, conserving bandwidth, and improving responsiveness. Fog computing, an intermediary layer between the cloud and the edge, extends these benefits by distributing intelligence, storage, and networking resources closer to the edge but with more computational capabilities than edge devices (M Yenugula et al., 2024).

Edge and fog computing are particularly critical for use cases such as autonomous vehicles, where decisions must be made in milliseconds to avoid accidents; and smart healthcare, where real-time patient monitoring can prevent critical medical events. Industrial automation, smart grids, and augmented reality are other domains that benefit from low-latency processing.

A hybrid architecture combining cloud, fog, and edge layers offers the best of all worlds. The edge handles time-sensitive data; fog nodes manage near-real-time analytics and aggregation; and the cloud takes care of long-term storage, deep analytics, and system-wide orchestration. This layered model ensures scalability, fault tolerance, and efficient resource usage (Lilhore et al., 2025).

Table 2. Comparative Table: Edge vs. Fog vs. Cloud Computing in IoT

Feature / Aspect	**Edge Computing**	**Fog Computing**	**Cloud Computing**
Latency	Very Low – Near real-time (ms level)	Low – Near real-time (slightly higher than edge)	High – Suitable for non-time-critical processing
Data Processing	Local – On-device or gateway	Regional – Routers, switches, micro data centers	Centralized – Large data centers far from source
Bandwidth Usage	Very Efficient – Minimal transmission to cloud	Moderate – Aggregated data sent to cloud	High – Raw data transmission from all IoT devices
Security	High (localized risk exposure)	Medium – Broader network risk	Medium to Low – Large attack surface
Power Consumption	Low – Optimized for devices	Medium – Requires more resources than edge	High – Large infrastructure needs
Scalability	Limited – Device-level	Moderate – Network-level	Very High – Virtually unlimited
Use Cases	Autonomous vehicles, real-time control systems	Smart cities, industrial IoT	Data mining, deep learning, historical analytics

Adoption Barriers: Organizational and Technical Constraints

While the integration of IoT with cloud computing offers substantial benefits, several organizational and technical constraints continue to hinder its widespread adoption. On the organizational front, many enterprises face a shortage of professionals skilled in both cloud-native services and IoT architecture, making implementation and maintenance challenging (Zhang et al., 2024). Additionally, resistance to change, especially in institutions heavily invested in legacy infrastructure, can delay or derail adoption initiatives. Regulatory concerns further complicate matters particularly in sectors like healthcare and finance where compliance with data protection laws such as GDPR and HIPAA is critical. On the technical side, the complexity of integrating heterogeneous IoT devices with cloud platforms poses a significant barrier, especially when standard protocols and interfaces are lacking. Latency is another critical concern; applications like autonomous vehicles or remote medical monitoring demand near-instantaneous response times, which cloud-only solutions cannot always guarantee. Connectivity issues in rural or remote environments also restrict reliable real-time data transmission to centralized cloud infrastructure. To mitigate these challenges, hybrid edge-cloud architectures have emerged as a viable solution minimizing latency and bandwidth strain by processing data locally. Organizations are also encouraged to adopt incremental migration strategies and invest in upskilling their technical workforce through vendor-supported training. Addressing these barriers is crucial to realizing the full potential of cloud-enabled IoT systems.

Challenges in Cloud-Based IoT Systems and the Emerging Solutions

While cloud computing has enabled significant advancements in IoT infrastructure, it still faces critical challenges that must be addressed for effective deployment, especially in time-sensitive and regulated environments. Latency remains a major concern in applications like autonomous vehicles and real-time health monitoring, where delays can lead to catastrophic outcomes. Data sovereignty issues arise when sensitive information crosses national boundaries, making compliance with local regulations complex. Interoperability is another persistent problem, as IoT ecosystems often comprise heterogeneous devices and platforms that struggle to communicate seamlessly. Bandwidth constraints further limit cloud efficiency, especially with high-volume data streams from video sensors or smart grids. Finally, security and privacy concerns are magnified in centralized architectures, which present attractive targets for cyberattacks and data breaches. These challenges are increasingly being addressed by decentralized models such as edge and fog computing, which offer local processing, reduce data travel, and provide better compliance with regional laws. For example, processing data locally on a smart medical device ensures low latency and avoids sending private data to foreign servers, aligning with both patient safety and privacy laws. A structured analysis of these issues and the corresponding technological responses helps clarify how modern IoT architecture is evolving.

Table 3. Problem–Solution Table: Challenges in Cloud-Centric IoT and Emerging Responses

Challenge	Description	Example Use Case	Emerging Solution
Latency	High delay due to centralized processing	Autonomous vehicles, remote surgery	Edge/fog computing for local, real-time decision-making
Data Sovereignty	Data processed/stored in foreign jurisdictions, violating local laws	Healthcare records in cross-border cloud	Local data processing via fog nodes; geo-fencing cloud storage
Interoperability	Incompatibility among diverse IoT devices and platforms	Smart cities with multi-vendor systems	Standardized protocols (e.g., MQTT, OPC UA), middleware integration

continued on following page

Table 3. Continued

Challenge	Description	Example Use Case	Emerging Solution
Bandwidth Constraints	Large-scale data transmission overloads network capacity	Video surveillance, smart manufacturing	Pre-processing at edge; selective transmission
Security/Privacy	Centralized storage increases risk of data breaches and unauthorized access	Personal health data, smart homes	Distributed security models; encryption at the edge

IV. SCALABILITY AND ELASTICITY IN IOT NETWORKS

As the Internet of Things (IoT) continues to expand, managing the multitude of connected devices becomes increasingly important. Scalability and elasticity in IoT systems are essential factors that influence the efficiency and effectiveness of these networks. Cloud computing has emerged as a powerful solution to tackle these challenges, providing tools that enable IoT networks to grow and adapt according to demand. In this discussion, we will examine how cloud computing facilitates the scalability and elasticity of IoT systems, allowing them to expand without necessitating significant infrastructure investments. Additionally, we will present real-world examples from various sectors, such as smart cities, agriculture, and healthcare, where IoT systems have successfully scaled through cloud integration (Bendaouia et al., 2024).

Cloud Computing's Role in Scalability

Cloud platforms such as Amazon Web Services (AWS), Microsoft Azure, and Google Cloud offer scalable solutions designed specifically for IoT applications. These platforms provide a variety of services, including storage, processing power, and data analytics, which can be adjusted as the number of connected devices grows. For instance, scalability in cloud computing allows for an increase in the compute and/or memory capacity of the server (Sadeeq et al., 2021).

Figure 4. Scalability in cloud computing

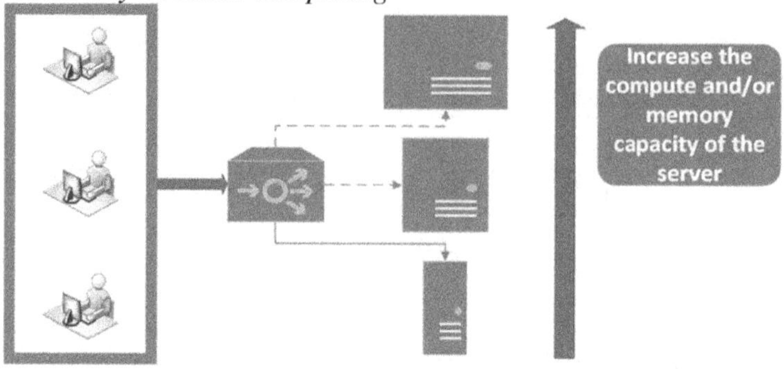

Storage Scaling

Cloud platforms offer scalable storage solutions that enable businesses to manage large volumes of IoT data without the concern of space limitations. For instance, AWS S3 and Azure Blob Storage allow users to easily store and access extensive datasets produced by IoT devices. These services automatically adjust as data increases, removing the necessity for manual management.

Compute Scaling

Cloud computing platforms provide flexible computing resources that can be scaled up or down according to demand. This flexibility is crucial for IoT applications that need significant computational power for data processing and analysis. For example, IoT systems used in predictive maintenance or real-time traffic monitoring depend on on-demand computing resources to manage sudden increases in data processing.

Network Scaling

Cloud-based IoT systems have the ability to expand their network infrastructure to support additional devices, guaranteeing dependable data transmission even during peak activity times. This capability is essential for applications such as smart cities and industrial IoT, where the network must increase its capacity as more devices come online.

Elasticity in IoT Networks

Elasticity is the capacity of a system to automatically adjust its resources in response to current demand. In the context of IoT networks, elasticity helps ensure efficient resource utilization by adapting to varying data loads and device needs, avoiding both overprovisioning and under provisioning (Fourati et al., 2024).

How Cloud Enables Elasticity for IoT

Dynamic Scaling of Compute Resources

Cloud platforms provide services such as AWS EC2 (Elastic Compute Cloud), Google Compute Engine, and Azure Virtual Machines, enabling organizations to adjust their computing power dynamically according to real-time needs. For instance, if an IoT system in a smart city faces a sudden surge in traffic data due to a significant event, the cloud platform can automatically allocate extra computing resources to manage the increase (Chanthati, 2024).

Auto-Scaling Services

Many cloud providers provide auto-scaling services that automatically modify resources according to set thresholds. For example, AWS Auto Scaling and Azure Scale Sets keep an eye on the load of an IoT application and can add or remove virtual machines as necessary to ensure optimal performance. This feature is essential for handling varying workloads in IoT applications, such as monitoring environmental conditions, managing energy consumption in smart homes, or tracking health data from wearable devices (Chanthati, 2024).

Event-Driven Architecture

Event-driven architectures in the cloud also enhance elasticity. Services such as AWS Lambda and Google Cloud Functions enable IoT systems to activate computing resources only in response to specific events. This approach allows the cloud to execute code only when needed, for instance, when a sensor transmits a reading, thereby conserving resources and lowering costs (Chanthati, 2024).

Real-World IoT Scaling Through Cloud

To grasp the practical applications of scalability and elasticity in IoT systems, we can look at real-world examples from various sectors such as smart cities, agriculture, and healthcare (N. Singh et al., 2024).

Smart Cities

Smart cities illustrated in [figure 5] exemplify the effective scaling of IoT networks alongside cloud computing. A smart city incorporates IoT devices like traffic sensors, CCTV cameras, environmental sensors, and smart meters to oversee and optimize urban services. These devices produce vast quantities of data that require real-time processing and analysis (N. Singh et al., 2024).

Figure 5. Smart Cities

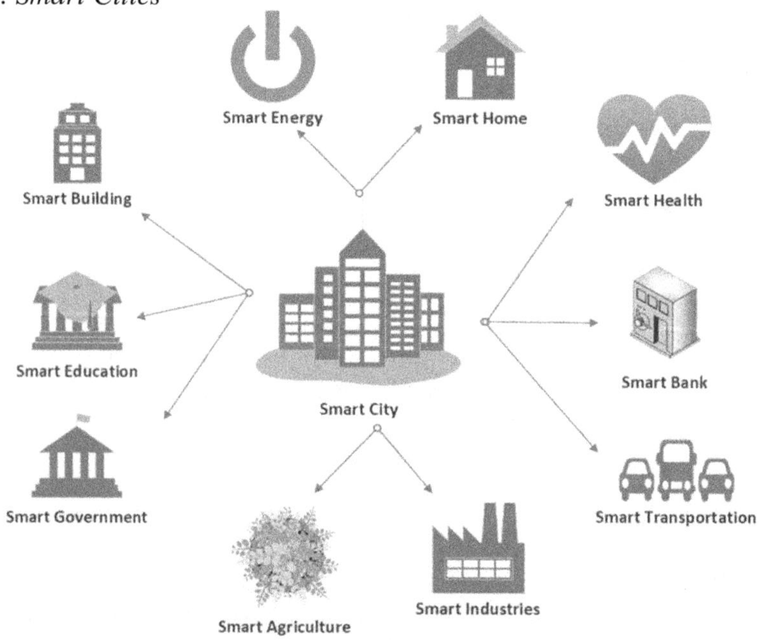

Cloud computing plays a crucial role in helping smart cities expand their infrastructure as the number of IoT devices increases. Take Singapore, for example, where the Smart Nation initiative brings together various IoT solutions to track traffic patterns, optimize energy consumption, and improve public safety. The cloud-based infrastructure can dynamically adjust to accommodate the growing amount of data produced by these devices, ensuring that the system stays responsive even during peak times, like rush hour. Additionally, cloud services provide flexibility for smart cities. In the event of an unexpected situation, such as a natural disaster or a large public gathering, the cloud can automatically scale its resources to handle the increased data traffic. This capability is vital for maintaining essential services, including emergency response systems and public safety monitoring, without interruption (Zolghadri et al., 2024).

Agriculture

In agriculture, IoT systems play a crucial role in precision farming by utilizing sensors to monitor soil moisture, temperature, crop health, and weather conditions, all aimed at optimizing farming practices. The data collected from these sensors needs to be stored, analyzed, and processed in real-time to deliver actionable insights. Cloud computing facilitates scalability, allowing agricultural IoT networks to grow as more sensors are added across larger farms or various geographic areas. Elasticity is key, ensuring that resources are allocated efficiently. During the harvest season, when data traffic surges, cloud platforms can increase computing resources to manage the influx of data from IoT devices. After the season concludes, the cloud can reduce its resources, helping to cut costs. For instance, John Deere, a leader in agricultural technology, employs cloud-based IoT systems to give farmers real-time information on crop health and soil conditions. The cloud infrastructure supports the extensive deployment of sensors across farms, and its elasticity guarantees that resources are optimized according to demand (Johnraja et al., 2024).

Healthcare

In healthcare, IoT devices like wearable health monitors, patient tracking systems, and remote monitoring tools produce enormous amounts of data. This data must be processed and analyzed to deliver timely interventions and valuable medical insights. Cloud computing provides the scalability necessary for healthcare IoT systems to grow and manage large volumes of patient information, even as more devices come online. For example, Philips Healthcare utilizes cloud computing to store and process data from medical devices, including heart rate monitors and oxygen sensors. The cloud infrastructure adapts smoothly as the number of connected devices increases, ensuring that healthcare providers have real-time access to essential patient information. Elasticity is also vital in healthcare. During health crises, like a pandemic, the need for remote monitoring and telemedicine services skyrockets. Cloud computing platforms can quickly allocate resources to meet this increased demand, helping to ensure that healthcare systems remain functional and responsive (Kumar & Choudhury, 2024).

V. CLOUD-BASED REAL-TIME DATA PROCESSING

The Internet of Things (IoT) has changed how we engage with and control the physical world. By connecting devices, sensors, and systems, IoT allows for the ongoing collection and sharing of data from the real world to digital platforms. This data, generated at rapid speeds, has the potential to impact various sectors, including healthcare, transportation, agriculture, and more. However, the true value of this data emerges only when it is processed and analyzed in real-time, enabling systems to make prompt decisions and deliver actionable insights. Real-time data processing in IoT is vital because it allows for immediate responses to shifting conditions in the physical world. Whether it's adjusting traffic lights based on current traffic patterns, detecting anomalies in industrial equipment, or notifying healthcare providers about a patient's sudden health decline, real-time analytics are essential for developing intelligent, responsive systems. The cloud is crucial for facilitating real-time data processing by offering scalable, on-demand resources to manage the large volumes of data produced by IoT devices (Rajagopalan et al., 2024). This section examines the importance of cloud-based real-time data processing in IoT, comparing edge and cloud processing models, and looking into cloud-based tools and services that support rapid data processing and visualization in [Figure 6].

Figure 6. Real-Time Data Processing

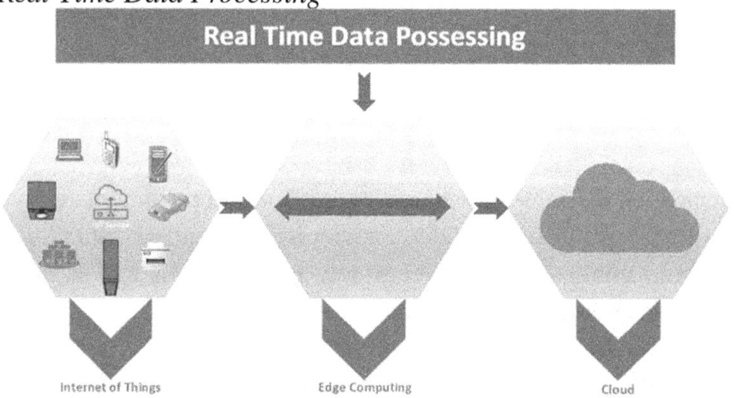

The Importance of Real-Time Analytics in IoT

Smart Traffic Systems

Smart traffic systems are a prime IoT application for real-time data processing. They use sensors, cameras, and connected devices to monitor and regulate traffic flow. Real-time analytics enable adaptive control of traffic signals, vehicle redirection during peak times, and incident response, ultimately improving traffic flow, reducing delays, and enhancing road safety. For example, Singapore uses real-time monitoring to analyze patterns, identify congestion, and dynamically adjust signals. These systems also leverage GPS data to predict traffic and manage road usage more efficiently (Ocran et al., 2024).

Industrial Automation

In industrial automation, IoT devices monitor machinery and production lines for performance, malfunction detection, and process enhancement. Real-time data processing is crucial for minimizing downtime, predicting equipment failures, and boosting operational efficiency. Cloud computing is vital here for collecting and analyzing data from thousands of sensors in manufacturing facilities. General Electric's IIoT implementation, for example, uses real-time machine data for predictive maintenance, analyzing sensor data to identify wear and tear before failures occur, thereby preventing costly downtime (Abbas & Charles, 2024).

Healthcare Monitoring

The healthcare sector significantly benefits from real-time IoT data processing. Wearable trackers, remote monitoring tools, and in-hospital IoT systems continuously generate vital sign data. Cloud analysis of this information helps identify potential health issues and alerts professionals for prompt intervention. For instance, real-time heart rate monitoring enables quick responses to arrhythmias, and continuous glucose monitoring provides early warnings for blood sugar levels. Devices like the Apple Watch monitor vital statistics in real-time, notifying users of abnormal readings. In critical scenarios, IoT sensors in hospital equipment allow remote patient monitoring, ensuring timely interventions (Khare & Totaro, 2019).

Cloud-Based Tools for Quick Data Processing and Visualization

Cloud-based tools and platforms are created to support real-time data processing, analytics, and visualization specifically for IoT applications. They allow developers and businesses to efficiently ingest, process, and visualize data without the need to handle complicated infrastructure on their own.

Google Cloud IoT Core

Google Cloud IoT Core is a fully managed service designed for the secure connection and management of IoT devices on a large scale. It facilitates smooth real-time data ingestion and processing, allowing businesses to create scalable IoT applications with minimal setup (Younas & Awan, 2024).

Key Features:

1. Real-time device management and data ingestion.
2. Integration with Google's machine learning tools for predictive analytics.
3. Scalable infrastructure for large IoT deployments.

Example:

An environmental monitoring system can utilize Google Cloud IoT Core to handle data from various weather sensors and analyze it in real-time, allowing for the detection of environmental changes like sudden temperature shifts or declines in air quality.

AWS IoT Analytics

AWS IoT Analytics makes it easier to collect, process, and analyze IoT data. It enables real-time data ingestion and filtering, which allows users to conduct advanced analytics and create visualizations with little effort (Restrepo-Carmona et al., 2024).

Key Features:

1. Automatic data collection, filtering, and processing.
2. Seamless integration with AWS machine learning tools.
3. Real-time analytics with minimal configuration.

Example:

A smart home system that tracks energy consumption can leverage AWS IoT Analytics to analyze data from IoT devices in real-time. This allows users to gain insights into their energy usage patterns and receive suggestions for reducing their consumption.

Microsoft Azure IoT Hub

Microsoft Azure IoT Hub provides a secure and scalable way for IoT devices to communicate with the cloud. It facilitates real-time data processing, allowing users to analyze and visualize IoT data through Azure's robust analytics tools (Restrepo-Carmona et al., 2024).

Key Features:

1. Secure device-to-cloud communication.
2. Integration with Azure Stream Analytics for real-time processing.
3. Integration with Azure Machine Learning for predictive insights.

Example:

In healthcare, IoT devices like heart rate monitors can transmit data to Azure IoT Hub, where it is analyzed in real-time to identify potential health issues, allowing healthcare professionals to take immediate action if needed.

Table 4. Comparison Table: Cloud-Based IoT — Pros, Cons & Case Studies

Aspect	Advantages	Challenges	Case Study (2024–2025)
Scalability & Cost	Virtually unlimited, pay-as-you-go; optimized pricing options	Unexpected cost spikes during scaling; opaque billing	Philips: reduced deployment cycles during ramp-up; scaling costs initially spiked (bestdevops.com)
Real-time Analytics	Centralized AI/ML services, advanced insights	Latency at scale limits real-time use in edge scenarios	Yulu: 30–35% efficiency gain via AWS data lake
Security & Configuration	Centralized policy enforcement and automated compliance	Misconfigurations (API, IAM) lead to breaches, botnets	Misconfigured IoT-cloud led to botnet propagation
Reliability & Resilience	High availability via redundancy	Single-cloud failures can cascade	Philips maintained 99.99% uptime; failure occurred when scaling tests weren't IoT-specific

continued on following page

Table 4. Continued

Aspect	Advantages	Challenges	Case Study (2024–2025)
Vendor & Protocol Support	Broad SDKs, integrations, diverse IoT protocols	API incompatibility; platform lock-in	Smart-agri fog/cloud system crashed under load due to cloud storage mismatch
Operational Complexity	Centralized monitoring, updates, patching	Hybrid setups require robust edge-cloud orchestration	Ardexa notes many IoT-cloud failures when cloud couldn't scale; recommends intelligent edge agents + Zero Trust PKI

VI. COST EFFICIENCY AND RESOURCE OPTIMIZATION

Cloud computing has become a transformative force for Internet of Things (IoT) applications, allowing organizations to deploy, scale, and manage IoT systems more effectively. A key benefit of cloud-based IoT deployments is their cost efficiency, which is supported by flexible pricing models and optimized resource use. Unlike traditional infrastructure setups that often demand substantial upfront investments, cloud computing provides a pay-as-you-go model that aligns expenses with actual usage, making it particularly advantageous for small and medium-sized enterprises (SMEs). This section examines the financial and operational benefits of cloud-based IoT solutions, discusses the pay-as-you-go pricing model, contrasts traditional infrastructure with cloud-based systems, and emphasizes the significant impact of cloud adoption on SMEs utilizing IoT technologies (Aleksandrov, 2024).

Pay-as-You-Go Model: Reducing Costs for IoT Deployments

Overview of the Pay-as-You-Go Model

The pay-as-you-go (PAYG) model is a key feature of cloud computing, enabling organizations to pay solely for the resources they use. This approach removes the necessity for significant upfront investments in hardware and software, providing flexibility and scalability for IoT implementations. Costs are determined by factors like compute hours, storage capacity, network usage, and the number of connected devices (Ockwell et al., 2019).

Benefits of the Pay-as-You-Go Model for IoT

1. Lower Initial Investment:

Traditional IoT infrastructure typically involves high costs for servers, storage systems, and networking equipment. The PAYG model offers a more budget-friendly alternative by substituting these expenses with manageable subscription fees.

2. Elastic Resource Allocation

IoT workloads can vary significantly. For example, an agricultural IoT system may generate the most data during the harvest season. The PAYG model enables organizations to adjust their resources according to demand, helping to lower costs during slower periods.

3. Predictable Operating Costs

By connecting expenses to real usage, organizations can more accurately forecast and control their operating budgets. This approach is especially beneficial for startups and small to medium-sized enterprises that have constrained financial resources.

Case Example:

A logistics company utilizing AWS IoT Core for fleet tracking enjoys the advantage of pay-as-you-go pricing, which means they only pay for the data processed by their IoT devices. As a result, during times of low activity, their expenses decrease accordingly.

Traditional Infrastructure vs. Cloud-Based IoT Deployments

In Table 1 below, we compare Traditional Infrastructure with Cloud-Based IoT Deployments. The following paragraph provides detailed information on the cost considerations associated with Traditional Infrastructure and highlights the advantages of Cloud-Based IoT Deployments.

Table 5. comparison between Traditional Infrastructure and Cloud-Based IoT

Model	Traditional Infrastructure	Cloud-Based Deployment
Acquisition	o Buy Assets o Build Technical Architecture	o Buy Service o Architecture Included
Business	o Pay for Assets o Administrative Over Head	o Pay For Use o Reduce Admin Function
Access	o Internal Networks o Corporate Desktop	o Over The Internet o Any Device

continued on following page

Table 5. Continued

Model	Traditional Infrastructure	Cloud-Based Deployment
Technical	o Single Tenant None Shared o Static	o Multi-tenant, Scalable, Elastic o Dynamic
Delivery	o Costly, lengthy Deployment o Land and Expand Staffing	o Reduce Deployment Tune o Fast Return On Investment

Cloud Platforms for Cost Optimization and Resource Management

Amazon Web Services (AWS)

AWS provides a wide range of IoT services, such as AWS IoT Core and AWS IoT Analytics. These solutions assist organizations in managing IoT devices, processing data, and deriving insights, all while keeping costs in check (Ahmadi, 2024).

Key Features:

1. PAYG pricing model for all services.
2. Cost optimization tools, such as AWS Cost Explorer.
3. Elastic resource allocation to handle variable workloads.

Example

An energy company utilizes AWS IoT Core to keep track of electricity usage in smart meters. The PAYG model enables the company to modify costs according to customer demand.

Microsoft Azure

Azure IoT Hub and Azure IoT Central offer managed IoT services suitable for businesses of any size. Additionally, Azure provides cost optimization tools such as Azure Cost Management (Ahmadi, 2024).

Key Features:

1. Predictable pricing plans with PAYG options.
2. Advanced analytics and machine learning tools.
3. Scalability to support growing IoT deployments

Example

A logistics company utilizes Azure IoT Hub to monitor vehicle locations and enhance delivery routes. The platform's scalability enables the company to incorporate additional vehicles as it grows its fleet.

Google Cloud

Google Cloud IoT Core is built for cost-effective IoT deployments, providing scalable, secure, and managed services to connect and manage devices (Ahmadi, 2024).

Key Features:

1. Flexible pricing based on device usage.
2. Integration with Google's AI and machine learning tools.
3. Real-time data processing and visualization.

Example

A smart farming startup leverages Google Cloud IoT Core to keep an eye on crop conditions and enhance yields. The platform's cost-effectiveness ensures that even small-scale farmers can take advantage of it.

VII. SECURITY IN CLOUD-ENABLED IOT

The combination of cloud computing and IoT devices has transformed various industries by enhancing scalability, efficiency, and connectivity. However, this integration also introduces considerable security risks. IoT devices are frequently placed in settings that are susceptible to cyberattacks, and the large volume of sensitive data they produce necessitates strong protection measures. Security breaches in IoT systems can result in unauthorized access, data theft, and disruptions to operations. This paragraph explores the security issues related to IoT, the features provided by cloud platforms to address these risks, and how these platforms maintain consistent security across distributed IoT networks. (N. Singh et al., 2024).

Overview of Security Concerns in IoT

IoT ecosystems, which include sensors, devices, and communication networks, are naturally complex and therefore susceptible to a range of security vulnerabilities. These issues become even more pronounced when devices are used in uncontrolled environments (Srinivasan, 2024).

Key Security Concerns

1. **Data Breaches:** IoT devices gather sensitive information, including personal health details and financial transactions. If this data is accessed without authorization, it can result in privacy breaches and harm to one's reputation.
2. **Unauthorized Access:** Many IoT devices do not have strong authentication methods, which makes them vulnerable to unauthorized access and exploitation.
3. **Physical Security Risks:** IoT devices are frequently placed in public areas, which raises the chances of tampering or theft.
4. **DDoS Attacks:** Compromised IoT devices can be exploited to carry out distributed denial-of-service (DDoS) attacks, which can overwhelm networks and disrupt services.
5. **Weak Firmware and Software Security:** Outdated firmware and unpatched vulnerabilities in IoT devices can serve as gateways for cyberattacks.

Cloud Security Features for IoT

Cloud platforms are crucial in tackling IoT security challenges by providing sophisticated security tools and frameworks. Important features consist of encryption, identity and access management (IAM), and centralized security monitoring (R. Singh et al., 2024).

Encryption

1. **Data-at-Rest Encryption:** Cloud platforms such as AWS and Azure implement encryption protocols like AES-256 to safeguard stored data. This means that even if someone gains unauthorized access to the data, it will still be unreadable.
2. **Data-in-Transit Encryption:** Secure communication protocols such as TLS and HTTPS are utilized to encrypt the data exchanged between IoT devices and cloud servers.
3. **End-to-End Encryption:** Ensures that data is encrypted from the moment it leaves the IoT device until it reaches the cloud server, safeguarding it against interception while in transit.

Identity and Access Management (IAM)

1. **Role-Based Access Control (RBAC):** Cloud platforms provide detailed control over access to specific resources, reducing the chances of unauthorized access.
2. **Multi-Factor Authentication (MFA):** Adds an extra layer of security by requiring users to confirm their identity through multiple verification methods.

3. **Device Identity Management:** IoT devices are given unique credentials, which guarantees that only authorized devices can connect to the network.

Centralized Security Monitoring

1. **Security Information and Event Management (SIEM):** Cloud platforms incorporate SIEM tools to monitor and analyze security events in real-time.
2. **Anomaly Detection:** AI-powered tools identify unusual patterns in device behavior, indicating potential threats.
3. **Incident Response Automation:** Cloud platforms provide automated tools that help in responding to security incidents, which in turn shortens the response time.

Ensuring Consistent Security Across IoT Networks

Cloud platforms provide centralized management and enhanced security features that guarantee uniform protection across distributed IoT networks (R. Singh et al., 2024).

Real-Time Threat Detection

1. **Machine Learning Algorithms:** Cloud platforms leverage machine learning to examine network traffic and identify anomalies that may signal cyber threats.
2. **Threat Intelligence Integration:** Platforms incorporate global threat intelligence databases, enabling the proactive identification and mitigation of emerging vulnerabilities.

Virtual Private Clouds (VPCs)

1. **Isolated Networks:** VPCs create separate environments for IoT systems, reducing the risk of external threats.
2. **Custom Security Configurations:** Organizations can set up firewalls, subnets, and routing rules to improve security.
3. **Secure Connectivity:** VPNs and dedicated connections, such as AWS Direct Connect, provide secure communication between IoT devices and cloud resources.

Real-World Applications

Smart Traffic Systems

IoT-enabled traffic management systems depend on cloud platforms to process data in real-time and ensure security. To safeguard sensitive information, such as vehicle movements and user data, encryption and identity access management (IAM) are utilized (N. Singh et al., 2024).

Example

A sophisticated traffic management system in Singapore leverages AWS IoT Core along with AWS Shield to protect against DDoS attacks, guaranteeing continuous service even during cyber threats.

Healthcare IoT

Cloud platforms protect sensitive patient data gathered from wearable devices and remote monitoring systems (R. Singh et al., 2024).

Example:

A telemedicine provider utilizes Google Cloud's encryption and anomaly detection tools to protect patient records and prevent unauthorized access.

VIII. DISASTER RECOVERY AND FAULT TOLERANCE

The increasing use of IoT systems in various industries highlights the need for reliability and consistent uptime. Because IoT devices are interconnected and rely heavily on cloud infrastructure, any failures—whether from hardware issues, natural disasters, or cyberattacks—can cause major disruptions. Implementing disaster recovery (DR) and fault tolerance strategies is essential to keep IoT systems running smoothly and resilient in times of crisis. This paragraph discusses the significance of disaster recovery in IoT, the benefits of cloud-based disaster recovery services, and real-world examples of IoT systems that successfully maintained their operations during difficult situations (Zeng et al., 2023).

Cloud Storage & Disaster Recovery for Real-Time IoT

Implementing cloud computing for IoT data storage involves a structured process ensuring scalability, reliability, and security. IoT devices generate data, which is sent via protocols like MQTT or CoAP to cloud gateways. These gateways preprocess and route data to cloud storage services (e.g., Amazon S3, Azure Blob Storage, Google Cloud Storage). The cloud platform then dynamically allocates storage, scaling seamlessly with data volume. Metadata tagging and data partitioning further enable efficient querying and real-time analytics (Özen & Souri, 2024).

Disaster recovery is crucial for real-time IoT applications like emergency response, industrial automation, and remote health monitoring, where data unavailability can have severe consequences. Without fault tolerance mechanisms (e.g., data replication, automatic failover), disasters can cause data loss, delayed decisions, or system shutdowns. For example, a regional cloud outage leading to lost smart grid sensor data without replication could prevent power load balancing, risking blackouts (Biswas & Ansari, 2024).

Cloud platforms tackle disaster recovery via geo-redundancy, backup snapshots, and DRaaS, ensuring minimal data loss and service continuity. However, real-time IoT applications demand instant fault handling, which requires robust mechanisms like multi-region replication and auto-scaling failover nodes. Therefore, integrating disaster recovery plans with real-time processing pipelines is crucial for maintaining operational integrity and responsiveness in IoT ecosystems(Biswas & Ansari, 2024).

The Role of Disaster Recovery in Maintaining IoT Systems' Reliability

Understanding Disaster Recovery

Disaster recovery encompasses a range of processes, policies, and technologies aimed at reinstating normal operations following an unforeseen event. In the realm of IoT, disaster recovery guarantees that data, connectivity, and device functionality are either maintained or swiftly restored to reduce downtime and lessen potential damage.

Key Objectives of Disaster Recovery in IoT

1. **Data Availability:** IoT devices produce large amounts of data that are essential for making informed decisions. Disaster Recovery (DR) guarantees that this data is backed up and remains accessible, even in the event of failures.

2. **Operational Continuity:** Disaster recovery plans focus on reducing downtime by quickly restoring system functionality, which helps maintain continuous service.
3. **Cost Minimization:** Effective disaster recovery strategies minimize the financial consequences of outages, such as lost revenue and recovery expenses.
4. **Reputation Management:** Maintaining reliability during crises is essential for organizations to uphold customer trust and protect their market reputation.

Advantages of Cloud-Based DR for IoT

1. **Scalability:** Cloud platforms are capable of managing the vast amounts of data and devices associated with IoT systems, allowing for growth without the need for major investments in infrastructure.
2. **Cost-Effectiveness:** Pay-as-you-go models lessen the financial strain of keeping on-premises disaster recovery infrastructure.
3. **Ease of Implementation:** Cloud DR services offer pre-configured tools and templates, making it easier for organizations with limited IT expertise to deploy them.
4. **Proactive Monitoring:** Cloud platforms leverage AI and machine learning to keep an eye on systems for any potential problems, allowing for proactive measures to prevent disasters.

Case Studies of Cloud-Enabled IoT Systems in Crisis

Case Study 1: Smart City Disaster Recovery

Scenario:

A smart city network faced a power outage due to a severe storm. This network comprised IoT devices used for traffic management, energy monitoring, and public safety (Zeng et al., 2023).

Solution:

The city utilized Azure Site Recovery to replicate data across various cloud regions. Automated failover systems guaranteed that essential services, like emergency alerts and traffic lights, continued to function during the outage.

Outcome:

The city reached almost zero downtime, ensuring public safety and reducing disruptions.

Case Study 2: Industrial IoT in Natural Disasters

Scenario:

An earthquake interrupted operations at a manufacturing plant that depends on IoT sensors for monitoring its equipment.

Solution:

The plant had put AWS Elastic Disaster Recovery into action. IoT data was continuously replicated to a cloud-based recovery site. Following the earthquake, operations were back up and running within hours by utilizing the failover site.

Outcome:

The company managed to steer clear of major financial losses and quickly got back to production.

Case Study 3: Healthcare IoT During a Cyberattack

Scenario:

A healthcare provider that utilized IoT devices for monitoring patients experienced a ransomware attack aimed at its on-premises servers. (Zeng et al., 2023).

Solution:

The provider utilized Google Cloud's DRaaS to recover encrypted data from backups kept in a secure cloud environment. Multi-factor authentication and encryption protocols helped prevent any additional breaches.

Outcome:

The provider restored services in less than 24 hours, making sure that patient care remained uninterrupted.

Strategies for Effective Disaster Recovery in IoT

1. **Comprehensive Risk Assessment:** Organizations need to recognize potential risks like natural disasters, cyberattacks, and hardware failures, and create recovery plans that are specifically designed for their unique IoT ecosystems (Zeng et al., 2023).
2. **Regular Testing and Updates:** Disaster recovery plans need to be tested regularly to confirm they work as expected. It's important to update them to reflect changes in technology and the needs of the organization.
3. **Integration with Fault Tolerance:** Disaster recovery strategies should be enhanced with fault tolerance mechanisms, including redundant systems and load balancing, to avoid disruptions during minor failures.
4. **Leveraging AI for Predictive Maintenance:** AI-driven analytics can forecast possible failures in IoT devices and systems, allowing for proactive measures to reduce disruptions.

IX. GLOBAL ACCESSIBILITY AND MANAGEMENT

Cloud computing has become a fundamental element in the deployment of IoT, providing worldwide accessibility and centralized management features that meet the evolving demands of contemporary businesses. By utilizing cloud platforms, companies can effortlessly deploy, monitor, and manage IoT networks across various locations. This section examines how cloud platforms enhance global accessibility, their advantages for multinational corporations, and the significant effects on operational efficiency and data management (Salama et al., 2024).

Cloud Platforms and Global Accessibility

Cloud computing platforms offer the necessary infrastructure, tools, and services to connect IoT devices around the globe, facilitating smooth communication and data sharing. This accessibility is made possible by the vast global networks of data centers and content delivery systems established by cloud providers (Globa & Kartashov, 2024).

Key Features Enabling Global Accessibility

1. **Centralized Control Panels:** Cloud platforms like AWS, Azure, and Google Cloud provide integrated interfaces that enable organizations to monitor and manage IoT devices from any location.

2. **Global Data Center Networks:** These providers maintain large networks of data centers in various regions, guaranteeing low-latency connections for IoT devices no matter where they are located.
3. **Scalable APIs:** IoT developers can utilize platform-specific APIs to facilitate device interaction with the cloud, ensuring reliable functionality across different regions.
4. **Interoperability:** Support for various IoT standards, such as MQTT and CoAP, allows devices from different manufacturers to connect and function seamlessly within a global ecosystem.

Benefits for Multinational Companies

Operational Efficiency

Multinational companies frequently oversee IoT devices located in various regions, including factories, retail stores, and transportation centers. Cloud platforms offer tools to simplify these operations (Abdi & Zeebaree, 2024).

1. **Centralized Monitoring:** Dashboards provide immediate insights into device status, performance metrics, and any anomalies across all locations.
2. **Automated Updates:** Cloud systems allow for simultaneous firmware updates for IoT devices around the world, minimizing downtime and the need for manual intervention.
3. **Simplified Troubleshooting:** Centralized logging and analytics tools simplify the process of identifying and resolving issues, even without the need for on-site technical support.

Unified Data Management

IoT devices produce a huge volume of data that must be collected, processed, and analyzed. Cloud platforms offer integrated storage and analytics solutions that guarantee consistency.

1. **Data Normalization:** Cloud services standardize data formats from devices around the globe, making it easier to integrate them into business intelligence systems.
2. **Multi-Region Data Replication:** By replicating data across various data centers, cloud platforms guarantee high availability and adherence to regional data regulations.

3. **Real-Time Data Access:** Global data distribution guarantees that insights are easily accessible to decision-makers, enhancing their ability to respond effectively.

Cost Reduction

Running IoT systems worldwide can be costly, especially when relying on on-premises infrastructure (Abdi & Zeebaree, 2024). Cloud platforms help lower expenses by:

1. **Pay-As-You-Go Models:** Companies only pay for the resources they utilize, eliminating the need for upfront investments in hardware.
2. **Dynamic Resource Allocation:** Cloud platforms adjust computing and storage resources in real-time according to demand, which helps reduce waste.
3. **Reduced Maintenance Costs:** Cloud service providers take care of maintenance and upgrades, which means companies don't need to have dedicated in-house teams

Real-World Applications

Smart Retail Chains

A global retail chain utilizes Azure IoT Hub to oversee inventory systems in hundreds of stores around the world. By consolidating data on product movement and demand trends, the chain has enhanced its supply chain operations, minimized waste, and boosted customer satisfaction (Abdi & Zeebaree, 2024).

Smart Agriculture

An agritech company is using IoT sensors on farms around the world to keep track of soil health and weather conditions. By leveraging AWS IoT Core, the company gathers and analyzes data in a centralized system, offering farmers valuable insights while adhering to local data regulations.

Healthcare Networks

A global healthcare provider utilizes Google Cloud IoT Core to connect IoT-enabled diagnostic devices in hospitals around the world. The centralized data storage and AI-powered analytics have enhanced patient outcomes and made administrative tasks more efficient (Abdi & Zeebaree, 2024).

Challenges and Future Directions

While cloud platforms provide considerable benefits, there are also challenges that must be tackled (Idhalama & Oredo, 2024).

1. **Latency:** Even with global data centers, latency can still pose a challenge for applications that need real-time processing.
2. **Security:** Ensuring secure connections and protecting data across different regions is an ongoing concern.
3. **Standardization:** The absence of universal standards for IoT and cloud integration can impede interoperability.

Future Trends

1. **Edge Computing Integration:** Integrating edge and cloud computing to minimize latency and improve real-time decision-making.
2. **AI-Powered Management:** Using AI to streamline resource allocation and enhance system reliability.
3. **Decentralized Cloud Models:** Investigating cloud services built on blockchain technology to improve transparency and security.

X. FUTURE TRENDS: IOT AND CLOUD COMPUTING

The combination of IoT (Internet of Things) and cloud computing has significantly transformed various industries, allowing for unmatched connectivity, scalability, and insights driven by data. As these technologies continue to advance, new trends like AI integration, 5G networks, serverless architectures, and quantum computing are set to reshape the IoT-cloud landscape. This discussion focuses on the future trends influencing IoT and cloud computing, emphasizing their potential for transformation and the innovations that are likely to improve IoT capabilities (Ejeofobiri et al., 2024).

Emerging Trends in IoT and Cloud Computing

AI Integration in IoT and Cloud

Artificial intelligence (AI) is becoming more integrated into IoT and cloud environments to improve performance, support better decision-making, and automate various operations (Ejeofobiri et al., 2024).

Predictive Analytics:

AI facilitates predictive maintenance in IoT devices, minimizing downtime by examining historical data and pinpointing potential failures before they happen.

1. **Edge-AI Synergy:** AI models deployed at the edge can analyze data on-site, which helps to minimize latency and conserve bandwidth. For example, self-driving cars depend on edge AI for making real-time decisions.
2. **AI-Driven Cloud Management:** Cloud providers are using AI to improve resource allocation, boost cybersecurity, and automate everyday tasks.
   Case Example:

AWS combines AI services such as Amazon Sage Maker with IoT Core to facilitate real-time analytics and predictive modeling for industrial IoT applications.

5G Technology and IoT

The introduction of 5G networks is poised to transform IoT and cloud interactions by providing ultra-low latency, high-speed connectivity, and improved capacity for handling a large number of devices (Ejeofobiri et al., 2024).

Real-Time Applications:

With speeds reaching up to 10 Gbps, 5G enables real-time IoT applications, including autonomous vehicles and remote surgery.

1. **Massive IoT Deployments:** 5G networks have the capability to connect millions of devices within a single square kilometer, facilitating extensive IoT applications such as smart cities and agricultural monitoring.
2. **Improved Cloud Integration:** Improved connectivity allows for smooth data transfer between IoT devices and cloud platforms, enabling advanced analytics and insights powered by AI.
   Example Use Case:

Smart factories utilize 5G technology to monitor and control machinery in real-time, which helps maintain optimal performance and safety.

Serverless Architectures

Serverless computing is becoming a game-changer for integrating IoT with the cloud, enabling developers to concentrate on application logic rather than dealing with infrastructure management (Ejeofobiri et al., 2024).

Dynamic Scalability:

Serverless platforms such as AWS Lambda and Azure Functions automatically adjust their scale according to demand, which makes them perfect for IoT workloads that experience varying data volumes.

1. **Cost Efficiency:** Pay-per-use models lower expenses by billing only for the compute resources used, which is advantageous for IoT deployments that experience sporadic activity.
2. **Simplified Development:** Developers can accelerate the deployment of IoT applications by utilizing pre-configured serverless frameworks.
3. **Future Potential:** Serverless computing is anticipated to advance in order to handle more intricate workflows, including real-time video processing in IoT-enabled security systems.

Potential Future Innovations Enhancing IoT Functionality

Quantum Computing

Quantum computing has the potential to transform IoT and cloud computing by tackling complex problems at speeds never seen before (Ejeofobiri et al., 2024).

Enhanced Encryption:

Quantum algorithms offer strong encryption techniques that help secure communication within IoT networks.

1. **Optimization Problems:** Applications such as supply chain logistics and traffic management can greatly benefit from optimization solutions powered by quantum technology.
2. **Data Processing:** Quantum cloud platforms like IBM Q Experience can handle large IoT datasets more efficiently than traditional systems.

Advanced Analytics and IoT

As IoT devices produce an ever-increasing amount of data, advanced analytics will be essential for deriving actionable insights (Ejeofobiri et al., 2024).

Real-Time Analytics:

Cloud platforms are set to provide more robust support for real-time streaming analytics, which can be applied to areas such as fraud detection and predictive maintenance.

1. **Federated Learning:** This technique trains models directly on IoT devices, enhancing data privacy and decreasing dependence on centralized cloud resources.
2. **Holistic Dashboards:** Unified analytics dashboards enable organizations to visualize and take action on IoT data from various regions.

The Impact of 6G on IoT-Cloud Systems

The arrival of 6G technology is expected to greatly improve IoT-cloud systems by offering ultra-fast speeds, very low latency, and the ability to connect massive numbers of devices at once. Unlike 5G, 6G aims to reduce delay to microseconds, which is critical for time-sensitive applications like autonomous vehicles, remote surgery, and augmented reality. It also supports trillions of IoT devices per square kilometer, making it ideal for large-scale smart city and industrial use. Another key benefit is its ability to use satellites and edge computing, which allows IoT devices in remote or rural areas to connect to the cloud with minimal delay. 6G will also have built-in artificial intelligence to help the network manage traffic, detect threats, and adjust automatically. Security is a major focus, with researchers recommending the use of Zero Trust models, blockchain-based identity, and privacy laws like GDPR and CCPA to protect user data. In short, 6G will help IoT-cloud systems become faster, smarter, and safer, allowing more advanced and reliable services for industries and users alike.

XI. CONCLUSION

Cloud computing has significantly changed the IoT landscape by offering the necessary infrastructure and tools to manage, store, and analyze the enormous data flows produced by IoT devices. This relationship has helped cloud platforms tackle various challenges faced by IoT systems, including scalability, resource optimization, and security. Some of the key roles that cloud computing fulfills include (Peng et al., 2020).

Enabling Scalability and Elasticity

Cloud platforms enable IoT systems to manage changes in data volume and device activity by providing scalable solutions. Services like AWS Auto Scaling and Azure Auto Scale automatically adjust resources to align with workload demands, which helps lower infrastructure costs and enhance performance.

Supporting Real-Time Data Processing

IoT applications, including smart traffic systems and health monitoring devices, depend on real-time data analytics. Cloud-based tools like AWS IoT Analytics and Google Cloud IoT Core offer robust processing capabilities, allowing for immediate decision-making and action.

Offering Centralized Management

Cloud platforms streamline the management of IoT deployments spread across different locations through centralized dashboards and global data centers. Multinational companies gain from having unified interfaces, real-time insights, and the capability to deploy applications effortlessly across various regions.

Enhancing Security

Cloud computing strengthens IoT systems by incorporating advanced security measures, including end-to-end encryption, identity management, and ongoing threat monitoring. Services like Azure Security Center demonstrate how cloud providers create a secure environment for IoT.

Ensuring Cost Efficiency

By utilizing pay-as-you-go models, cloud platforms help alleviate the financial strain associated with IoT deployments. This approach is especially advantageous for small and medium enterprises (SMEs), enabling them to innovate and remain competitive in the IoT landscape.

Driving Innovation

The flexibility and modularity of cloud services encourage experimentation and innovation. Developers can utilize serverless computing, AI tools, and machine learning platforms to develop new IoT applications with minimal investment.

The Path Forward

The relationship between cloud computing and IoT has set the stage for groundbreaking innovations across various industries. From facilitating smart cities to transforming healthcare, the combination of these technologies has changed the way we engage with the digital landscape. Yet, this journey is just beginning. As cloud computing advances, it will act as a driving force for next-generation IoT solutions, fostering progress in AI, 5G, and quantum computing. By tackling issues like scalability, security, and sustainability, cloud platforms will realize the full potential of IoT, leading us toward a connected, intelligent, and efficient future. Organizations that adapt to this evolution will not only improve their operational capabilities but also play a crucial role in shaping the IoT-driven global economy of the future. Cloud computing has significantly changed the financial and operational aspects of IoT deployments, making them easier to access and more affordable. The pay-as-you-go model lowers financial obstacles, allowing organizations to adjust resources based on their requirements. By transitioning from traditional infrastructure to cloud-based solutions, businesses can cut costs, enhance resource utilization, and concentrate on innovation. For small and medium-sized enterprises, adopting cloud technology creates new opportunities to utilize IoT technologies, fostering growth and competitiveness in a world that is becoming increasingly interconnected.

The security of cloud-enabled IoT networks is crucial as these systems grow and become essential across different industries. Cloud platforms tackle IoT security issues by utilizing encryption, identity and access management (IAM), and centralized monitoring, which provide reliable protection against cyber threats. By using these resources, organizations can confidently implement IoT systems, protecting sensitive data and ensuring operational integrity. This thorough approach to security not only safeguards against existing threats but also equips IoT ecosystems for the changing landscape of cybersecurity.

Cloud-based solutions like automated backups, data replication, and DRaaS provide flexible and affordable ways to maintain data availability and keep operations running smoothly. By implementing these solutions, organizations can protect their IoT ecosystems from various threats, including natural disasters and cyberattacks. The case studies presented illustrate how effective cloud-enabled disaster recovery can be in real-world situations, showcasing the ability to sustain uptime and reliability even in times of crisis. With the increasing adoption of IoT, strong disaster recovery frameworks will be crucial for maintaining resilience and achieving long-term success.

Cloud computing has become essential for managing IoT systems worldwide. By providing centralized management, real-time access, and cost savings, cloud platforms help organizations enhance their IoT deployments and foster innovation. This is especially beneficial for multinational companies, allowing them to operate smoothly across different countries. As cloud and IoT technologies continue to advance, their integration will create new opportunities, leading to smarter and more interconnected global systems. Organizations that embrace and adapt to these technologies will stay ahead in this transformation, enjoying the advantages of improved accessibility and efficiency.

The future of IoT and cloud computing is filled with promising advancements, including AI, 5G, quantum computing, and serverless architectures. These developments will create new opportunities, allowing for more efficient, secure, and scalable IoT solutions. However, to fully harness this potential, we must tackle various technical, ethical, and regulatory challenges. As industries evolve with these innovations, IoT and cloud computing will keep reshaping the global digital landscape, fostering growth, sustainability, and innovation. Organizations that adopt these trends will be at the forefront of creating a connected and intelligent future.

REFERENCES

Abaee, M., Saeedi, M., & Taherdoost, H. (2024a). Examining the Role of IoT and Cloud Computing in Achieving Sustainable Development Goals. In *Reshaping Environmental Science Through Machine Learning and IoT* (pp. 74–97). IGI Global. DOI: 10.4018/979-8-3693-2351-9.ch005

Abaee, M., Saeedi, M., & Taherdoost, H. (2024b). IoT and Cloud Computing for Sustainable Development Goals in Industry 4.0: A Bibliometric Analysis. *Reshaping Environmental Science Through Machine Learning and IoT*, 98-118.

Abbas, G., & Charles, H. (2024). IoT-Enabled Smart Supply Chains: Overcoming Challenges to Unlock Efficiency and Resilience.

Abdi, A., & Zeebaree, S. R. (2024). Embracing Distributed Systems for Efficient Cloud Resource Management: A Review of Techniques and Methodologies. *Indonesian Journal of Computer Science*, *13*(2). Advance online publication. DOI: 10.33022/ijcs.v13i2.3806

Abdulazeez, S., Nawar, A. K., Hassan, N. B., & Tariq, E. (2024). Internet of Things: Architecture, technologies, applications, and challenges. *AlKadhim Journal for Computer Science*, *2*(1), 36–52. DOI: 10.61710/kjcs.v2i1.67

Ahmadi, S. (2024). Network Intrusion Detection in Cloud Environments: A Comparative Analysis of Approaches. *Sina Ahmadi, "Network Intrusion Detection in Cloud Environments: A Comparative Analysis of Approaches"* [IJACSA]. *International Journal of Advanced Computer Science and Applications*, *15*(3). Advance online publication. DOI: 10.14569/IJACSA.2024.0150301

Aleksandrov, A. (2024). Improving the continous delivery process using modern best practices: a case study at Visma e-conomic.

Aljarrah, M. M., Zawaideh, F. H., Magableh, M., Al Wahshat, H., Mohamed, R. R., & Archana, K. (2023). Internet of Thing (IoT) and Data Analytics with Challenges and Future Applications. *2023 International Conference on Computer Science and Emerging Technologies (CSET)* DOI: 10.1109/CSET58993.2023.10346664

Alomari, M. F., Mahmoud, M. A., Gharaei, N., Rasool, S. M., & Hasan, R. A. (2024). Optimizing Cloud Storage Costs: Introducing the Pre-Evaluation-Based Cost Optimization (PECSCO) Mechanism. 2024 4th International Conference of Science and Information Technology in Smart Administration (ICSINTESA)

Andriulo, F. C., Fiore, M., Mongiello, M., Traversa, E., & Zizzo, V. (2024). Edge Computing and Cloud Computing for Internet of Things: A Review. *Informatics (MDPI), 11*(4), 71. DOI: 10.3390/informatics11040071

Bendaouia, S., Lounis, A., & Bouabdallah, A. (2024). Green, scalable and efficient IoT architecture. 2024 9th International Conference on Fog and Mobile Edge Computing (FMEC)

Biswas, S., & Ansari, M. S. A. (2024). Securing IoT networks in cloud computing environments: A real-time IDS. *The Journal of Supercomputing, 80*(10), 14489–14519. DOI: 10.1007/s11227-024-06021-z

Chanthati, S. R. (2024). Artificial Intelligence-Based Cloud Planning and Migration to Cut the Cost of Cloud Sasibhushan Rao Chanthati. *American Journal of Smart Technology and Solutions, 3*(2), 13–24. DOI: 10.54536/ajsts.v3i2.3210

Chippagiri, S., & Ravula, P. (2021). Cloud-Native Development. *Review of Best Practices and Frameworks for Scalable and Resilient Web Applications., 8*, 13–21.

Deepthi, K. J., Balakrishnan, T. S., Krishnan, P., & Ebenezar, U. S. (2024). Optimized Data Storage Algorithm of IoT Based on Cloud Computing in Distributed System. 2024 OPJU International Technology Conference (OTCON) on Smart Computing for Innovation and Advancement in Industry 4.0

Devipriya, A., Manikandan, N., Sivaranjani, A., Anand, M., & Ragupathi, T. (2025). The Convergence of Cloud Computing and IoT in Healthcare: A Paradigm Shift Towards Patient-Centric Innovation. In (pp. 229-256). https://doi.org/DOI: 10.4018/979-8-3373-0781-7.ch011

Ejeofobiri, C. K., Victor-Igun, O. O., & Okoye, C. (2024). AI-Driven Secure Intrusion Detection for Internet of Things (IOT) Networks. *Asian Journal of Mathematics and Computer Research, 31*(4), 40–55. DOI: 10.56557/ajomcor/2024/v31i48971

Eljak, H., Ibrahim, A. O., Saeed, F., Hashem, I. A. T., Abdelmaboud, A., Syed, H. J., Abulfaraj, A. W., Ismail, M. A. B., & Elsafi, A. (2023). E-learning-based cloud computing environment: A systematic review, challenges, and opportunities. *IEEE Access : Practical Innovations, Open Solutions, 12*, 7329–7355. DOI: 10.1109/ACCESS.2023.3339250

Fourati, M. H., Marzouk, S., & Jmaiel, M. (2024). Cloud Elasticity of Microservices-Based Applications: A Survey. *Concurrency and Computation*, •••, e8329.

Globa, L., & Kartashov, A. (2024). OPTIMIZING DISTRIBUTED DATA STORAGE IN MULTI-CLOUD ENVIRONMENTS: ALGORITHMIC APPROACH. *Information and Telecommunication Sciences*, (2), 4–12. DOI: 10.20535/2411-2976.22024.4-12

Gowda, D., Chaithra, S., Gujar, S. S., Shaikh, S. F., Ingole, B. S., & Reddy, N. S. (2024). Scalable AI Solutions for IoT-based Healthcare Systems using Cloud Platforms. 2024 8th International Conference on I-SMAC (IoT in Social, Mobile, Analytics and Cloud)(I-SMAC), Idhalama, O. U., & Oredo, J. O. (2024). Exploring the next generation Internet of Things (IoT) requirements and applications: A comprehensive overview. *Information Development*, 02666669241267852.

Jadama, A., Islam, M. M., Toray, M., Durba, S., & Springer, A. (2024). *Enhancing IoT Security and Privacy in the Cloud: A Framework for Secure Data Transmission and Storage*. https://doi.org/DOI: 10.13140/RG.2.2.15055.09128

Jameil, A., & Al-raweshidy, H. (2024). *Hybrid Cloud-Edge AI Framework for Real-Time Predictive Analytics in Digital Twin Healthcare Systems*. https://doi.org/DOI: 10.21203/rs.3.rs-5412158/v1

Jha, S., & Chaturvedi, D. (2024). Systematic Literature Review of Cloud Computing Research Between 2010 and 2023. Workshop on e-Business

Johnraja, J. I., Leelipushpam, P. G. J., Shirley, C., & Princess, P. J. B. (2024). Impact of Cloud Computing on the Future of Smart Farming. In Intelligent Robots and Drones for Precision Agriculture (pp. 391-420). Springer.

Khan, N., & Gupta, K. (2022). IOT: Applications, Challenges and Latest Trends. 2022 1st IEEE International Conference on Industrial Electronics: Developments & Applications (ICIDeA)

Khare, S., & Totaro, M. (2019). Big data in IoT. 2019 10th International Conference on Computing, Communication and Networking Technologies (ICCCNT)

Kuchuk, H., & Malokhvii, E. (2024). INTEGRATION OF IOT WITH CLOUD, FOG, AND EDGE COMPUTING: A REVIEW. *Advanced Information Systems, 8*(2), 65–78. DOI: 10.20998/2522-9052.2024.2.08

Kumar, P., & Choudhury, D. (2024). Innovative Technologies for Effective Water Resources Management. *Water Crises and Sustainable Management in the Global South*, 555-594.

Lakshminarasamma, V., & Bulla, S. (2024). A Study on Cloud Storage Architecture and Related Technical Issues. 2024 IEEE International Conference on Computing, Power and Communication Technologies (IC2PCT)

Lilhore, U. K., Simaiya, S., Sharma, Y. K., Rai, A. K., Padmaja, S. M., Nabilal, K. V., Kumar, V., Alroobaea, R., & Alsufyani, H. (2025). Cloud-edge hybrid deep learning framework for scalable IoT resource optimization. *Journal of Cloud Computing (Heidelberg, Germany), 14*(1), 5. DOI: 10.1186/s13677-025-00729-w

Liu, Y., Zhou, N., & Zhou, M. (2024). Research on Data Privacy and Security in the Green Internet of Things. *Procedia Computer Science, 247*, 596–601. DOI: 10.1016/j.procs.2024.10.071

Lottu, O., Jacks, B., Ajala, O., & Okafor, E. (2024). Towards a conceptual framework for ethical AI development in IT systems. *World Journal of Advanced Research and Reviews, 21*, 408–415. DOI: 10.30574/wjarr.2024.21.3.0735

Mahamuni, C. V. (2023). Exploring IoT-Applications: A Survey of Recent Progress, Challenges, and Impact of AI, Blockchain, and Disruptive Technologies. 2023 7th International Conference on Electronics, Communication and Aerospace Technology (ICECA)

Mirani, A. A., Velasco-Hernandez, G., Awasthi, A., & Walsh, J. (2022). Key challenges and emerging technologies in industrial IoT architectures: A review. *Sensors (Basel), 22*(15), 5836. DOI: 10.3390/s22155836 PMID: 35957403

Modupe, O. T., Otitoola, A. A., Oladapo, O. J., Abiona, O. O., Oyeniran, O. C., Adewusi, A. O., Komolafe, A. M., & Obijuru, A. (2024). Reviewing the transformational impact of edge computing on real-time data processing and analytics. *Computer Science & IT Research Journal, 5*(3), 693–702. DOI: 10.51594/csitrj.v5i3.929

Ockwell, D., Atela, J., Mbeva, K., Chengo, V., Byrne, R., Durrant, R., Kasprowicz, V., & Ely, A. (2019). Can pay-as-you-go, digitally enabled business models support sustainability transformations in developing countries? Outstanding questions and a theoretical basis for future research. *Sustainability (Basel), 11*(7), 2105. DOI: 10.3390/su11072105

Ocran, G., Yusuf, S. O., Owusu, P., Boateng, E. A., & Obeng, S. (2024). AI-driven business analytics for SMES: Unlocking value through predictive and prescriptive analytic.

Özen, F., & Souri, A. (2024). Cloud-based disaster management architecture using hybrid machine learning approach in IoT. *Multimedia Tools and Applications, 83*(29), 72357–72370. DOI: 10.1007/s11042-024-18333-6

Pandey, S., & Bhushan, B. (2024). Recent Lightweight cryptography (LWC) based security advances for resource-constrained IoT networks. *Wireless Networks, 30*(4), 1–40. DOI: 10.1007/s11276-024-03714-4

Peng, S.-L., Pal, S., & Huang, L. (2020). *Principles of internet of things (IoT) ecosystem: Insight paradigm*. Springer. DOI: 10.1007/978-3-030-33596-0

Rajagopalan, A., Swaminathan, D., Bajaj, M., Damaj, I., Rathore, R. S., Singh, A. R., Blazek, V., & Prokop, L. (2024). Empowering power distribution: Unleashing the synergy of IoT and cloud computing for sustainable and efficient energy systems. *Results in Engineering*, *21*, 101949. DOI: 10.1016/j.rineng.2024.101949

Rajora, R., Rajora, A., Sharma, B., Aggarwal, P., & Thapliyal, S. (2024). Sensing the Future: Challenges and Trends in IoT Sensor Technology. 2024 4th International Conference on Innovative Practices in Technology and Management (ICIPTM)

Restrepo-Carmona, J. A., Zuluaga, J. C., Velásquez, M., Zuluaga, C., Villamil, R. M., Morales, O., Hurtado, Á. M., Escobar, C. A., Sierra-Pérez, J., & Vásquez, R. E. (2024). *A Review on Data Capture*. Storage, Processing, Interoperability, and Visualization for the Smart Supervision of Public Expenditure.

Sadeeq, M. M., Abdulkareem, N. M., Zeebaree, S. R., Ahmed, D. M., Sami, A. S., & Zebari, R. R. (2021). IoT and Cloud computing issues, challenges and opportunities: A review. *Qubahan Academic Journal*, *1*(2), 1–7. DOI: 10.48161/qaj.v1n2a36

Salama, R., Alturjman, S., Altrjman, C., & Al-Turjman, F. (2024). Service models for Internet of Things, global value chains, and mobile cloud computing. In *Smart Global Value Chain* (pp. 121–136). CRC Press. DOI: 10.1201/9781003461432-7

Singh, N., Buyya, R., & Kim, H. (2024). IoT in the Cloud: Exploring Security Challenges and Mitigations for a Connected World. *arXiv, 2402*, 1-27.

Singh, R., Gupta, S., & Arunkumar, D. (2024). Automation of Network Security in Cloud Based Internet of Things Networks. 2024 15th International Conference on Computing Communication and Networking Technologies (ICCCNT)

Srinivasan, N. (2024). Artificial Intelligence in IoT Security: Review of Advancements, Challenges, and Future Directions. *Challenges, and Future Directions (May 29, 2024).*

Yenugula, M., Sahoo, S., & Goswami, S. (2024). Cloud computing for sustainable development: An analysis of environmental, economic and social benefits. *Journal of future sustainability, 4*(1), 59-66.

Yenugula, M., Sahoo, S. K., & Goswami, S. (2024). Cloud computing for sustainable development: An analysis of environmental, economic and so- cial benefits. *Journal of future sustainability, 4*, 45-60. https://doi.org/DOI: 10.5267/j.jfs.2024.1.005

Younas, M., & Awan, I. (2024). Cloud, IoT and Data Science. *Information Systems Frontiers*, *26*(4), 1219–1222. DOI: 10.1007/s10796-024-10521-x

Zeng, F., Pang, C., & Tang, H. (2023). Sensors on the Internet of Things systems for urban disaster management: A systematic literature review. *Sensors (Basel)*, *23*(17), 7475. DOI: 10.3390/s23177475 PMID: 37687929

Zhang, Q., Wang, R., Kontakiotis, G., Matsumoto, K. i., Bian, L., & Yakupoğlu, C. (2024). *Zhang et al., 2024 ebook Frontiers*. https://doi.org/DOI: 10.3389/978-2-8325-4399-3

Zolghadri, M., Asghari, P., Dashti, S. E., & Hedayati, A. (2024). Resource allocation in Fog–Cloud Environments: State of the art. *Journal of Network and Computer Applications*, *227*, 103891. DOI: 10.1016/j.jnca.2024.103891

Chapter 12
Managing Cloud Services on Sensor Nodes for Efficient Wireless Energy Harvesting

Muhammed Zaharadeen Ahmed
https://orcid.org/0000-0001-9837-2280
International Islamic University Malaysia, Malaysia & University of Technology of Arts of Byumba, Rwanda

Aisha Hassan Abdalla Hashim
International Islamic University Malaysia, Malaysia

Othman Omran Khalifa
https://orcid.org/0000-0002-0847-6017
International Islamic University Malaysia, Malaysia

ABSTRACT

Wireless Sensor Networks are integral to a wide array of smart applications, including environmental supervision, healthcare, and manufacturing automation. However, the operation of sensor nodes is often constrained by limited energy resources. Efficient wireless energy harvesting (WEH) is a promising solution that can extend the operational lifetime of these nodes. Managing cloud services on sensor nodes plays a critical role in optimizing energy consumption and ensuring effective integration of WEH technologies.

DOI: 10.4018/979-8-3693-9984-2.ch012

INTRODUCTION

Describe Wireless Sensor Networks are integral to a wide array of smart applications, including environmental supervision, healthcare, and manufacturing automation. However, the operation of sensor nodes is often constrained by limited energy resources. Efficient wireless energy harvesting (WEH) is a promising solution that can extend the operational lifetime of these nodes. Managing cloud services on sensor nodes plays a critical role in optimizing energy consumption and ensuring effective integration of WEH technologies (Abu Bakar et al., 2023). This chapter explores strategies and frameworks for managing cloud services on sensor nodes to achieve efficient wireless energy harvesting.

Cloud service are networked systems that enable real time transmission. This communication involves smart sensors, client devices, and IoTs. It facilitates data transmission crucial for decision-making (Adu-Manu et al., 2018). This connectivity, coupled with information transparency, enhances decision-making with comprehensive insights and analytics. Innovations in technology such as smart systems and machine learning are integral components of to manage cloud service. These technologies provide intelligent assistance, streamline processes, and increase productivity across various industrial tasks (AlHaddad et al., 2023). Cyber-physical systems, which autonomously make decisions based on collected data, enhance the responsiveness and efficiency of industrial environments. However, the heightened connectivity necessitates robust cybersecurity measures. Protecting systems and data from cyber threats is critical as digital infrastructure expands (Ali et al., 2022). Figure 1 below present a cloud communication using sensor node.

Figure 1. Cloud-service Interaction with Sensor Nodes

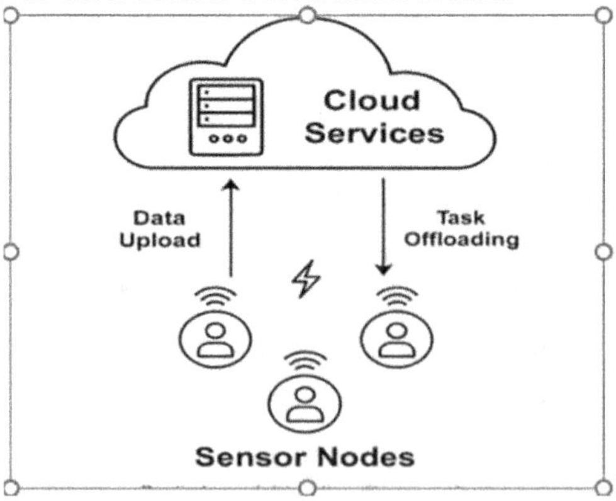

Figure 1 illustrates the interaction between cloud services and sensor nodes, where sensor nodes transmit harvested data to cloud servers for processing, storage, and management. The architecture highlights real-time communication, enabling efficient energy management and optimized cloud-based task allocation.

The impact of Managing cloud services spans numerous industries. This includes manufacturing, smart factories that deploy robot machines during operations, IoT, and AI (Ali et al., 2020). Supply chain management benefits from enhanced visibility and traceability, optimizing logistics and reducing waste. Other sectors, including healthcare, automotive, and agriculture, also utilize cloud service technologies. A crucial element of managing clouds service is the Wireless Sensor Network (WSN), which comprises interconnected sensors and devices communicating wirelessly in industrial settings Corallo, (Al-Shareeda et al., 2022). These networks are vital for collecting, transmitting, and data computation. WSNs can used in recognised industrial data center to generate data on motion, temperature, pressure, and other parameters. They enable seamless communication in between computer devices, client servers, and users, offering greater scalability and flexibility compared to traditional wired systems. WSNs can be easily expanded, reconfigured, and adapted to various industrial environments (Chen et al., 2024).

However, WSNs face several security challenges. Increased connectivity raises vulnerability to cyberattacks. This necessitate tough cybersecurity procedure to safeguard sensitive data. Signal interference and reliability issues in complex industrial environments affect network performance. Additionally, using battery-powered sensors establishes computer challenges. This is because maintaining elongated battery life and energy efficiency is crucial for reliable operation (Corallo et al., 2020). Despite these security concerns, WSNs are essential for the data-driven, networked infrastructure of cloud service. Addressing these security issues efficiently is vital to fully leverage these networks.

Energy Harvesting in Wireless Sensor Networks

Wireless energy harvesting (WEH) is a crucial advancement that enables wireless sensor nodes to operate sustainably without relying solely on traditional battery power. In WSNs, energy harvesting extends the operational lifespan and enhances the reliability of sensor nodes, especially in remote or hard-to-reach environments (Gherairi, 2022). However, integrating WEH into cloud-based WSNs introduces new security vulnerabilities, as energy-constrained nodes may have limited resources for executing complex security algorithms. This makes the deployment of lightweight yet highly accurate intrusion detection systems (IDS) essential to ensure real-time threat mitigation without depleting energy reserves. Consequently, evaluating the performance of artificial intelligence (AI) models within the context of WEH-enabled sensor nodes becomes vital for developing efficient, secure, and sustainable network management frameworks.

BACKGROUND

This section presents a broad perspective of managing cloud service by exploring related literatures.

Challenges of Managing Cloud Services

WSNs are crucial to establish real-time data inter-communication because of its wide spread across all digital technologies. However, their vulnerability to cyberattacks are enormous. Cloud devices are prime targets for cyberattacks due to their seamless data flow, driving decision-making and process optimization. A cybersecurity breach within sensor nodes lead to significant consequences beyond data compromise, including substantial financial losses, operational disruptions, and safety risks (Corallo et al., 2021). This chapter create a functional system to predictively distinguish between various threat levels and in real-time provide response to targeted device. The framework can also prioritize most severe threats, and their impact during internet operation by lessening impact or total prevention.

The increased connectivity and reliance on WSNs have also exposed these networks to significant cybersecurity threats. The lack of a robust and intelligently prioritized framework for predicting cyber intrusion in terms of detection and prevention in the cloud and wireless sensor networks is a significant challenge that needs to be addressed. Olden day systems of intrusion detection prevention often have some challenges in addressing the dynamic and resource-constrained environments in cloud as they may not efficiently prioritize and respond to the diverse types of attacks, leading to potential system failures and data breaches (Dabiri et al., 2022). While existing studies acknowledge the importance of effective attack detection systems in wireless sensor networks, there is a gap when developing predictive framework to incorporate prioritization intelligence which assesses the impact of a particular attack and the urgency with which it should be handled. This chapter presents a system to integrate multilayer perceptron (MLP), autoencoder, and decision tree models to accurately detect and classify different types of attacks. this includes blackhole, gray hole, flooding, and scheduling attacks. Additionally, an intelligent prioritization model will be implemented to assess the impact and urgency of detected threats, ensuring efficient allocation of resources for threat mitigation. The research will leverage WSN-DS dataset from Kaggle, which simulates various attacks of denial-of-service in WSNs. The use of Low Energy Adaptive

Clustering Hierarchy protocol is imperative to achieve full effectiveness required by the framework (Gherairi, 2022).

Managing Cloud Services in Sensor Nodes

Cloud services provide computational and storage resources, enabling sensor nodes to offload intensive tasks. This offloading reduces the energy burden on the nodes and facilitates advanced data processing, analytics, and decision-making (Johnson et al., 2024). The advantages of integrating cloud services include:

i. Energy Efficiency: Offloading tasks to the cloud minimize local computation and conserves energy.
ii. Scalability: Cloud resources can scale dynamically to accommodate varying workloads.
iii. Enhanced Analytics: Cloud platforms enable the use of sophisticated algorithms for data analysis.
iv. Reduced Latency: Through edge computing, cloud resources closer to the sensor nodes can minimize communication delays.

Challenges in Managing Cloud Services For WEH

In term of energy consumption, wireless energy harvesting provides an intermittent and variable energy supply, making energy management crucial. The dynamic nature of energy availability requires adaptive strategies for task scheduling and offloading. Frequent data transmission to the cloud can deplete energy reserves. Strategies to minimize communication overhead include data compression, in-network processing, and optimized communication protocols. Efficient allocation of cloud resources ensures that energy harvested by sensor device is used effectively (Li et al., 2024a). This involves balancing computation, communication, and energy storage tasks. Data transmitted between sensor nodes and the cloud must be secure. Lightweight cryptographic techniques and authentication mechanisms are necessary to protect sensitive information without imposing significant energy costs. Industrial machines are integral to market and production companies from beginning of the 1st Industrial Revolution and remain crucial in managing cloud service (NIST, 2024). Additional devices are transitioning to Internet Protocol (IP) devices for wider inter-communication due to the growing popularity of standardized protocols. SECS/GEM is a standard that allows companies to generate data from computers using TCP/IP communication. This protocol is primarily used within the companies and not in the public environment. This makes other businesses to supervise its own security protocol. SECS/GEM as a communication protocol is highly susceptible to various internet attacks, particularly replay attacks (Niyato et al., 2007).

Framework For Cloud Service Management

The challenges of Information security and privacy violations poses enormous concerns to individuals and businesses environments (Park et al., 2024).[REMOVED HYPERLINK FIELD] To lessen security risk in managing cloud service require both technological and human intervention for information security. Organization's risk of managing information on cloud service is compromised sometimes accidentally or on purpose. This is by some members of employees in the organisation as presented in figure 2 below.

Figure 2. Framework for Cloud Service Management in WEH-Enabled Sensor nodes

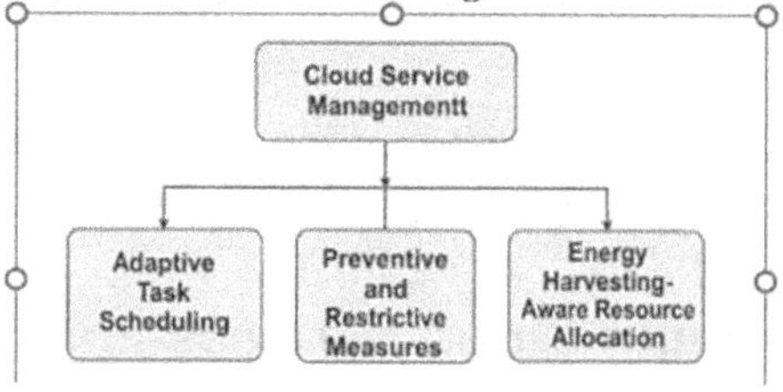

(Prauzek et al., 2018) presents a novel contribution for a framework that merges strategies for preventative and restrain framework. This can lessen enormous dangers for attacks that comes from within a network. A framework that prevents crimes of a situation have encourage employees to prevent misconduct of information security. The factors of restriction also discourage employees to function improperly using information security within an organization. The outcomes present user actions being influenced by observations of some few issues.

- **Adaptive Task Scheduling**

Dynamic task scheduling based on energy availability and workload is essential. Algorithms such as energy-aware scheduling (EAS) and task prioritization can optimize energy utilization. Also, data transmission should be optimized for minimal energy usage (Sah & Amgoth, 2020). Techniques include:

i. Combining data from multiple nodes to reduce transmission frequency.
ii. Reducing data size before transmission.
iii. Transmitting only essential data based on predefined thresholds.

Edge computing bridges the gap between sensor nodes and the cloud, providing localized processing capabilities. This reduces communication delays and energy usage by processing data closer to its source.

- **Energy Harvesting-Aware Resource Allocation**

Resource allocation should account for the variable nature of harvested energy. Predictive models can be used to estimate energy availability and adjust resource allocation accordingly. To implement Lightweight Security Mechanisms, a light-weight encryption and authentication protocols must ensure data integrity and confidentiality while conserving energy (Shaikh & Zeadally, 2016).

METHODOLOGY

Cloud Service System Design Using Predictive Learning

The design discusses and describes in details the System architecture, Block diagram, components required for implementation as well as the flowchart of the system which clearly outlines the flow of data throughout the system. The framework is built around a Raspberry Pi serving as the central controller. It incorporates sensors interfaced with an MCP3009 ADC (Analog-to-Digital Converter) to monitor and simulate various attack scenarios. The design follows a modular approach, ensuring scalability and adaptability to evolving cloud service needs.

Using Block Diagram, this work presents a high-level background of the components used and their interconnections. The primary components include the Raspberry Pi 3 microcontroller, sensors, power source, and the MCP 3009 Analog-to-Digital converter. Using raspberry pi microcontroller, we can implement intrusion detection and prevention of logic principles. The Raspberry Pi is ideal due to its affordability, versatility, and built-in connectivity, which make it suitable for prototyping and deploying IoT-based systems. Its extensive community support provides valuable resources for troubleshooting and development. The Raspberry Pi comes with built-in Wi-Fi and Ethernet connectivity, essential for creating networked systems. The Raspberry Pi can run various AI and machine learning frameworks, such as TensorFlow and scikit-learn. This compatibility is essential for implementing the AI-driven detection and classification models integral to the project. Using the Raspberry Pi allows for the development of a prototype that can be scaled and implemented in real-world industrial settings. Its portability and ease of use make it a best alternative for testing and demonstrating the cloud service framework. The cloud service framework is presented below as in figure 3. Below.

Figure 3. Block Diagram for Cloud Service Framework Implementation Using Raspberry Pi-Based Sensor Nodes

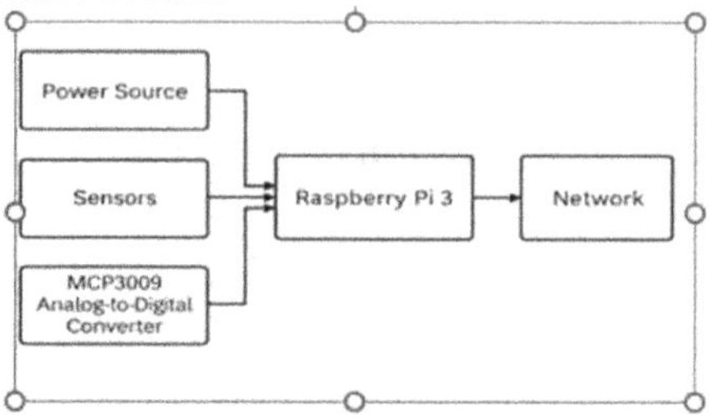

As a digital device, MCP 3009 Analog to Digital Converter all input and outputs conversion is conducted using GPIO pins. The are managed using high (one) state and a low (zero) state. For signals that are considered input and analog (mainly WSNs), all are required to be converted to as a digital domain. This can make the Raspberry Pi microcontroller easily adapt to the changes. Our considered chip (MCP3009) remains a 10-bit with 8-channel of analog-digital chip for conversion. For a stop button, we ensure it gets connected to a raspberry Pi's GPIO pins, its function is to serve as an interrupt/end button for the implementation of the code. The algorithm is set to run continuously until a high priority threat is detected and preventive actions are implemented. By providing a stop button, the user is given an opportunity to end the program/system at their convenience. The WSN used is made up of 4 different sensor types, each of which outputs an analog signal. The choice of these four specific sensors was made with a lot of consideration. Each sensor is meant to simulate one of the four attack types our framework was trained to detect i.e. blackhole, flooding, gray hole and scheduling attacks. A flowchart to describe detection and prevention stem of intrusion is presented as in figure 4 below as follows.

Figure 4. Flowchart of Intrusion Detection and Prevention System for Cloud-Managed Sensor Nodes with Wireless Energy Harvesting

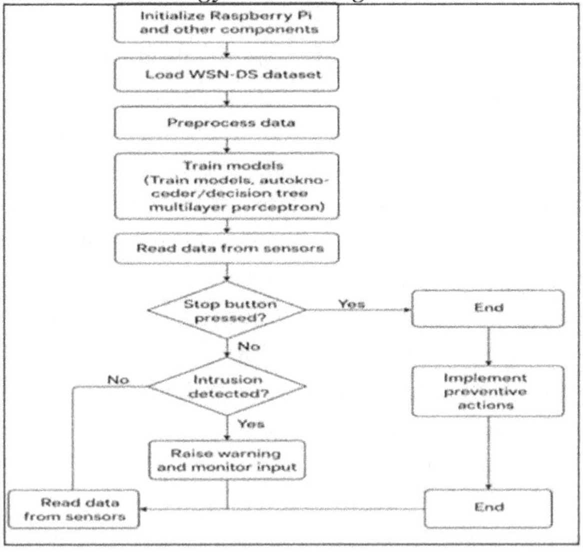

The flowchart of figure 4 above outlines the sequential steps in the system's operation, from data acquisition to decision-making and action execution. In the initial simulation process of this flowchart, we Initialize the Raspberry Pi microcontroller and other design components. The dataset from a different excel application is loaded and uploaded using import command on the WSN-DS dataset. For Preprocessing of data, we Clean, normalize, and prepare dataset for analysis. This includes extracting features (X) and labels (y) from the Data Frame. Standardization can be applied on data when divided in to training set as well as testing set. The next process is regarded as training the model. This is where the core logic of the framework is implemented. Three models are used to comprehensively train the framework, these are the autoencoder, decision tree and multilayer perceptron. We present additional information for discussion of the model training at the implementation section of this paper. Also, Data is read from the sensors and pre-processed. If there is no command by user to halt execution then proceed to intrusion detection, else terminate. We then Check input from sensors against the trained data from the models. If the result comes back as positive, i.e. intrusion/threat is detected, then check for the type of attack and priority assigned to it. The priority of an attack depends on what type of industry the system is being used in and as such is dynamic. Also, if attack is of high priority immediately implement preventive actions and end the program. Then, if attack is of lower priority, then raise a warning and closely monitor the inputs from that sensor while continuing to take inputs.

Wireless Energy Harvesting Architecture for Cloud-Managed Sensor Nodes

Wireless energy harvesting is among the best solution to address energy constraints of sensor nodes in Internet of things and wireless sensor networks, especially when integrated with cloud service management. As illustrated in Figure 5, the wireless energy harvesting architecture empowers sensor nodes to receive power from ambient sources such as radio frequency (RF) signals, solar energy, and kinetic movements, while simultaneously maintaining seamless communication with cloud services.

The architecture typically comprises energy transmitters, harvesting circuits, energy storage units, and cloud-integrated processing units. The energy transmitters, often embedded within base stations or mobile energy sources, emit RF signals or facilitate other energy transfer mechanisms to recharge nearby sensor nodes using wireless interface. The harvested energy is kept in micro-batteries or supercapacitors, ensuring a sustainable power supply for data sensing, processing, and cloud communication tasks (Shin & Joe, 2016). Through cloud-based resource management, the system can dynamically allocate sensing tasks, optimize data transmission schedules, and monitor energy levels in real time to prevent node failures. This synergy between wireless energy harvesting and cloud computing significantly enhances the operational lifespan of sensor networks, particularly in remote or hard-to-reach environments (Singh et al., 2025). Moreover, cloud management facilitates efficient load balancing and computational offloading, reducing the processing burden on energy-constrained nodes and ensuring uninterrupted service delivery. This integrated approach directly supports the vision of sustainable, autonomous, and scalable sensor networks, aligning with recent advancements in energy-aware IoT design and edge-cloud collaborative frameworks. Figure 5 below present the architectural concept of wireless energy harvesting.

Figure 5. Wireless Energy Harvesting Architecture

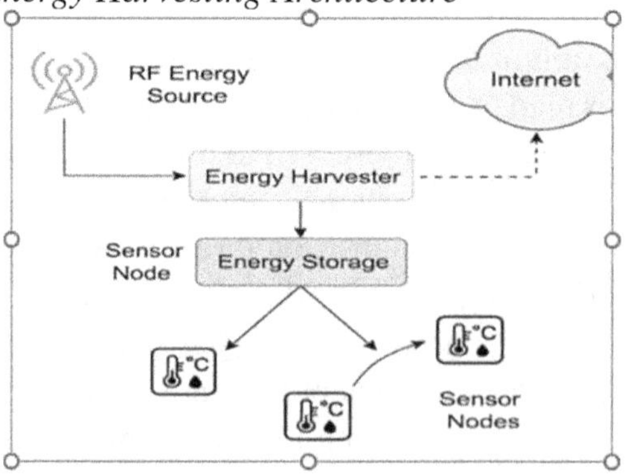

Implementation Of Cloud Service System

The implementation involves using a simulation tool to model the Intrusion detection and prevention framework and evaluate its performance as well as producing a functional prototype of the system. To validate the design, a simulation tool is used before physical implementation. The hardware prototype simulations were performed on Oracle VM Virtual Machine where a virtual machine running the raspberry pi OS was created and QEMU simulation environment. This was used to simulate the real word execution of the system before proceeding with actual hardware implementation. Coding was extensively and exclusively performed with the Python programming language (Python 3.12.4 in particular) due to its strong AI modelling support with powerful libraries like 'sklearn. Tensorflow, Pandas, Numpy and Keras'. The Micrososft Visual studio development environment was used to develop and implement the python scripts. The model implemented is evaluated using ''WSN-DS''. It is an opensource dataset that is used for intrusion detection systems for all wireless sensor networks generated from Kaggle. This dataset simulates various attacks of denial-of-service for WSNs using LEACH. This protocol is acronymic as Low Energy Adaptive Clustering Hierarchy protocol to conduct validation. The dataset is subdivided in basically two forms. These are training and testing.

The training is having 78% of overall information of its dataset. We used it majorly in training of the model in consideration. The test set model is comprised of 22% of overall records of its dataset to conduct validation of this model. For generation and preprocessing of data/information, this procedure is essential to ensure data-driven operation and to manage cloud services. It is also applicable to cybersecurity frameworks and machine learning algorithms. The procedure includes gathering, organizing, and cleaning data from various sources, in this case two sources of data were used; Sensor data collected and digitized using the MCP3009 ADC; and training data from the WSN-DS. Both real-time and historical data are crucial; historical data helps understand patterns, while real-time data detects ongoing threats. Data preprocessing includes cleaning, filling gaps, removing duplicates, correcting inconsistencies, and normalizing data for machine learning. In cloud service, extracting relevant features from raw data is key to identifying potential threats or anomalies. The script below was used to load the dataset and preprocess it.

Exploiting AI based IDS and classification of cloud intrusion is usually conducted to safeguard sensor nodes within a network. In this situation, implementation can be conducted in modelling AI algorithms like autoencoder, decision tree, multilayer perceptron, etc. In this modelling, dataset can be deployed using any open-source website. We detect intrusions over the cloud and conduct effective classification based on attack parameters like gray hole, flooding, and blackhole. All the three AI models mentioned above can recognize distinctively classify Internet attacks effectively. Python's powerful and dynamic AI libraries were leveraged due to their strong AI modelling support particularly "sklearn. Tensorflow, Pandas, Numpy and Keras".

- **The Autoencoder**

This device is classified as an unsupervised learning algorithm that can has the ability to compress data and conduct feature learning. The device is capable of conducting anomaly detection based on its capability to recognizes anomalies or deviations from an existing learned pattern in term of reconstructing input data.

- **Multilayer Perceptron (MLP)**

This form of neural network is effective in identifying convoluted configurations and inter communication for data. The MLP can efficiently establish learning procedure in both structured and unstructured data. This makes it suitable to identify simple and convoluted attack patterns.

- **Decision Tree (DT)**

This algorithm efficiently manage data inform of a tree-like structure by making decisions with major conditions. The algorithm can manage numerical and definite data. It can also be categorised based on their nature of Internet attacks and its individual feature.

Intelligent Prioritization and Prevention System

This framework consists of smart prioritization and prevention mechanism that categorizes many forms of attacks such as gray hole, blackhole, and scheduling. For internet attacks recognised as blackhole, they are easily as regarded in smart sectors such as robotics, machine learning and energy management because of their ability to disrupt systems. For gray hole, they are attacks that selectively alter packets that relates to each other during quality assurance and asset tracking to impact on data accuracy. Flooding Attacks is more prevalent when it comes to smart logistics and for supply chain visibility. It can overload networks with excessive traffic. Scheduling Attacks target manufacturing processes and healthcare equipment, impacting timing and scheduling systems (Stojčev et al., 2009). To proactively prevent such threats, attacks are prioritized in terms of their severity on the cloud network. Prevention measures include setting up verification environments, utilizing validation tools, deploying traffic analysers, and employing time synchronization procedures. These tailored prevention plans aim to improve safety and reliability of wireless sensor networks in the cloud. This is presented as in figure 6 below.

Figure 6. Intelligent Prioritization and Prevention logic

```python
print(classification_report(y_test, dt_predictions))

# Function to prioritize threats
def prioritize_threat(threat_type):
    priority_map = {
        'Blackhole': 1,
        'Grayhole': 2,
        'Flooding': 3,
        'Scheduling': 4
    }
    return priority_map.get(threat_type, 5)  # Default to lowest priority if not found

try:
    # Main loop for continuous sensor simulation
    while True:
        gas_reading = gas_sensor.value
        motion_detected = motion_sensor.value

        # Example prioritization based on mock sensor data
        threat_type = 'Blackhole' if gas_reading > 0.5 else 'Normal'
        threat_priority = prioritize_threat(threat_type)

        # Example action based on threat priority
        if threat_priority == 1:
            led.on()
            print("Critical threat detected: Blackhole Attack. Action: Activate LED.")
            break  # Break the loop if critical threat is detected
        else:
            led.off()
            print("Threat detected:", threat_type, "Action: No action")
```

Real-World Application Scenarios

The integration of cloud services with sensor nodes for efficient wireless energy harvesting has profound implications across several practical domains. In smart agriculture, energy-harvesting sensor nodes can continuously monitor soil moisture, temperature, and crop health while offloading computational tasks to cloud services. This ensures real-time analytics without exhausting node energy, enabling sustainable precision farming in remote areas with limited power infrastructure (Sudevalayam & Kulkarni, 2010). In industrial automation, wireless energy harvesting enables long-term deployment of sensor nodes in hard-to-reach equipment. Cloud-managed task scheduling supports predictive maintenance by processing sensor data remotely, thus reducing downtime and operational costs. For instance, smart factories employ energy-autonomous sensors to monitor vibration patterns in rotating machinery, with cloud-based AI predicting potential failures before they occur (Tan & Panda, 2010). In smart healthcare, wearable or implantable sensors can harvest body heat or motion energy while securely transmitting health data to cloud platforms for processing and diagnostics. Real-time decision-making in critical health monitoring, such as cardiac irregularities, is achieved without frequent battery replacements, enhancing patient comfort and system longevity. Additionally, environmental monitoring benefits from this architecture by deploying energy-harvesting sensor nodes in forests, oceans, or disaster-prone zones where frequent battery changes are impractical. Cloud services handle complex data analytics for early detection of wildfires, pollution levels, or seismic activities. These scenarios highlight the transformative role of cloud-managed, energy-efficient WSNs in delivering sustainable, intelligent, and resilient solutions across sectors.

Considerations For Design and Implementation Procedure

Design considerations are critical for ensuring the efficiency, reliability, and adaptability of the system. Below are the key considerations:

- **Power Efficiency**

Due to wireless sensor networks operation on limited power, minimizing energy consumption is essential. The following measures have been adopted:

i. Use of energy-efficient components, such as low-power sensors and ADCs.
ii. Implementing power-saving modes for the Raspberry Pi and sensors during idle periods.
iii. Optimizing software algorithms to reduce computational overhead and energy use.

- **Scalability**

The system is designed to accommodate additional sensors or modules without requiring significant reconfiguration. This is achieved by:

i. Modular hardware architecture that supports plug-and-play functionality.
ii. Flexible software architecture to integrate new sensors and intrusion detection models seamlessly.

- **Reliability**

To ensure the system remains robust and fault-tolerant under varying conditions, the following strategies are employed:

i. Redundancy: Backup power sources and alternative communication paths.
ii. Use of high-quality components to reduce the risk of failure.

- **Security**

Given the system's focus on cybersecurity, measures are in place to safeguard it against vulnerabilities:

i. Securing communication channels between the Raspberry Pi and MCP3009 using encryption.
ii. Periodic updates to the software to address new security threats.

- **Environmental Adaptability**

The system is intended for diverse cloud environments, which may include harsh conditions. Design considerations include:

i. Encasing sensors and electronics in protective housings to prevent damage from dust, moisture, or temperature extremes.
ii. Using components rated for industrial-grade temperature ranges.

- **Real-Time Processing**

Real-time detection is essential to respond promptly to cloud service threats. This is achieved by:

i. Using efficient algorithms that process sensor data with minimal latency.
ii. Prioritizing critical tasks in the Raspberry Pi's scheduling to avoid delays in detection.

These considerations collectively enhance the system's performance, resilience, and relevance to cloud service.

Experimental Setup of the Cloud Service

During experiment procedure with QEMU emulation, the hardware prototype is exploited. For the cloud service management, intrusion detection algorithm is designed for the wireless sensor network. The dataset for the WSN get enhanced using inputs of real-time sensors and incorporated using data set. The dataset is further distributed into two subcategories of testing and training. The training set constitutes 78% of overall dataset. This is used for model training. However, the test set constitutes 22% of overall records and for algorithm testing in term of validation procedure. A cross validation is engaged on DT algorithm and multi perpetron using "cross_val_score" recognised as a function. Considering autoencoder, validation is carried out by training test procedure using a ratio of 88:22. However, cross validation is not exploited because of its lack of capability of unsupervised learning feature.

Cybersecurity Vulnerabilities and Resilience Strategies in Cloud-Managed WEH Sensor Networks

The convergence of cloud services with wireless sensor nodes significantly enhances computational efficiency, task scheduling, and remote data management. However, this integration inherently broadens the attack surface, exposing the system to numerous cybersecurity vulnerabilities. These threats include data interception, node spoofing, denial of service, unauthorized energy manipulation, and malicious firmware injections that can destabilize the energy harvesting and task execution processes.

- Preventive Cybersecurity Measures
- To mitigate these risks, preventive security mechanisms must be prioritized, especially considering the limited processing power and energy constraints of the sensor nodes. Lightweight encryption protocols such as ECC-based AES (Elliptic Curve Cryptography integrated with Advanced Encryption Standard) have been demonstrated to provide robust data protection with minimal computational overhead (Tadayon et al., 2013). In addition, the implementation of multi-factor authentication between sensor nodes, gateways, and cloud servers significantly reduces the probability of unauthorized access (Wang et al., 2017).

Figure 7 below present the framework of adopting sensor nodes in the cloud using cybersecurity approach.

Figure 7. Cybersecurity Framework Adaptation for Sensor Nodes in Cloud-Managed WEH Systems

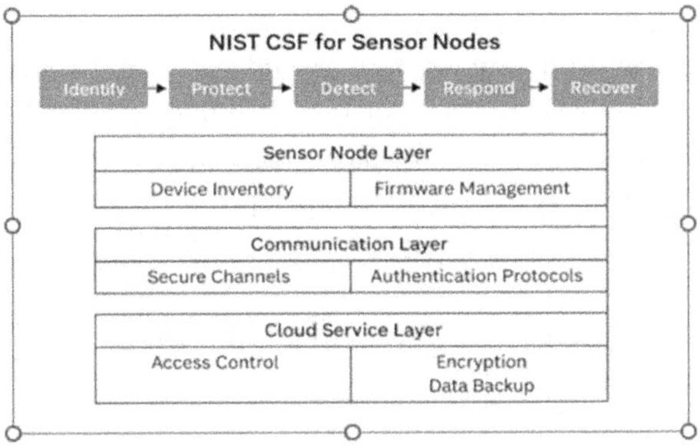

The diagram of figure 7 above illustrates the adaptation of the NIST Cybersecurity Framework (CSF) tailored for sensor nodes operating within cloud-managed wireless energy harvesting environments. This framework is well structured based on five basic functions which includes identify, protect, detect, respond, and recover.

i. In the Identify phase, assets such as sensor nodes, cloud services, and energy harvesting modules are cataloged, and their associated cybersecurity risks are assessed.
ii. The Protect phase enforces security controls including access management, lightweight encryption for energy-constrained nodes, and continuous energy-aware configuration updates.
iii. The Detect phase integrates anomaly detection systems and real-time monitoring of network traffic to promptly identify security breaches or operational anomalies.
iv. In the Respond phase, incident response protocols are activated to isolate compromised nodes or cloud instances, ensuring rapid mitigation.
v. The Recover phase focuses on system resilience by restoring affected services through backup nodes and cloud redundancy.

This layered framework ensures that both the resource-constrained sensor nodes and their cloud counterparts are protected through a balanced, adaptive cybersecurity strategy that considers energy efficiency and wireless communication vulnerabilities.

- **Technological Advancements in Intrusion Detection**

Recent advancements in machine learning-enhanced intrusion detection systems (ML-NIDS) now allow for real-time anomaly detection across cloud-managed WSNs, even under energy harvesting constraints. These intelligent detection systems can differentiate between legitimate node mobility and malicious behavior, reducing false positives and enhancing system trustworthiness (Wang et al., 2025). Furthermore, blockchain-enabled trust management has emerged as a viable solution for securing sensor node communications, ensuring tamper-proof logging of transactions, and enabling decentralized identity verification in energy-limited environments.

- **Cybersecurity Frameworks for Cloud-WSN Integration**

Adopting established cybersecurity frameworks is essential to formalizing security practices in cloud-managed wireless energy harvesting systems:

i. NIST Cybersecurity Framework (CSF): Provides a flexible guideline for identifying, protecting, detecting, responding to, and recovering from cybersecurity incidents in sensor networks (NIST, 2024). Key controls such as continuous monitoring and regular risk assessments should be adapted to the dynamic topology of WSNs.
ii. Zero Trust Architecture (ZTA): Particularly relevant in cloud environments, Zero Trust principles dictate that no device or user, whether within or outside of the network is trusted automatically. By enforcing strict identity verification, micro-segmentation, and least-privilege access policies, Zero Trust significantly minimizes the risk of lateral attacks (You et al., 2016) (Zhou et al., 2024).

- **Building Resilience**

Cyber resilience is critical for the sustainability of cloud-managed WSNs. Strategies such as redundant communication paths, dynamic trust reassignment, and autonomous failover protocols ensure continuous service even under cyber-attacks or node failures. These resilience mechanisms also support energy efficiency by reducing retransmission loops and avoiding unnecessary energy consumption caused by repeated security breaches (Zhang & Kumar, 2023). In the wireless energy harvesting context, resilient architectures must also account for energy prediction and intelligent load balancing to prevent energy depletion during prolonged attack scenarios.

- **Real-World Implications**

The emulation results presented in this chapter underscore the practical viability of these cybersecurity measures, demonstrating that cloud-managed sensor nodes can achieve both operational efficiency and strong security postures without compromising energy harvesting performance. When translated to real-world deployments, the adoption of these cybersecurity strategies can significantly enhance the reliability and trustworthiness of wireless sensor networks in smart cities, industrial monitoring, and environmental sensing applications.

SOLUTIONS AND RECOMMENDATIONS

The system was experimentally validated using three artificial intelligence models: Decision Tree, Multi-layer Perceptron, and Autoencoder, each addressing multidimensional and binary classification tasks. For benchmarking, the Random Forest algorithm was applied to the multiclass problem, while Logistic Regression (LR) served as a binary classification baseline.

Decision Tree (DT)

The Decision Tree model effectively classified various types of cloud-based intrusions, achieving higher accuracy and precision compared to the Random Forest benchmark. Specifically, the DT excelled in identifying network statistics and smart intrusion patterns across all attack classes. The macro and weighted average F1-scores confirmed the model's robustness in handling multiclass problems. The DT's ability to capture the subtle patterns in the dataset contributes significantly to securing cloud operations in energy-constrained environments.

Multi-layer Perceptron (MLP)

The MLP demonstrated exceptional accuracy, surpassing the Random Forest model. It achieved high precision for the normal and TDMA classes, indicating strong predictive power. However, a lower recall for the TDMA class suggests occasional misclassification of true TDMA instances. The MLP balanced precision and recall effectively for blackhole, flooding, and gray hole attacks, as shown by consistently high F1-scores. Both macro and weighted averages confirmed its stability and robustness for multiclass intrusion detection tasks.

The Autoencoder

The Autoencoder achieved optimal detection performance in binary classification scenarios, specifically distinguishing between normal and anomalous events. Compared to Logistic Regression, the Autoencoder provided superior anomaly detection, particularly in recall for irregular instances. The F1-scores confirmed the Autoencoder's effective balance between precision and recall. Logistic Regression showed high precision for normal classes but struggled with anomaly detection, indicating significant performance imbalance.

Attack Detection

The framework accurately detected various types of cyber-attacks:

- Blackhole Attacks: Detected with high accuracy due to significant packet drops.
- Gray Hole Attacks: Identified selective packet manipulation with robust precision.
- Flooding Attacks: Recognized based on traffic volume patterns and light intensity changes.
- Scheduling Attacks: Detected timing anomalies effectively through temperature variation monitoring.

To comprehensively evaluate performance of the implemented models, a comparative and comparative analysis was conducted using basic classification indexes. These includes accuracy, precision, recall, and F1-score. The evaluation covers both multiclass and binary classification tasks, where Decision Tree, Random Forest, and Multi-layer Perceptron were assessed on multiclass intrusion detection, while Autoencoder and Logistic Regression were assessed on binary classification problems. Table 1 table below summarizes the performance results across the various models and attack types, offering a clear and concise view of each model effectiveness in detecting and classifying cloud-based intrusions.

Table 1. Performance Comparison Table

Model	Attack Type	Accuracy	Precision	Recall	F1-Score
Decision Tree	Multiclass	94.5%	94.2%	93.9%	94.0%
Random Forest (RF)	Multiclass	91.8%	91.0%	90.5%	90.7%
MLP	Multiclass	96.1%	95.8%	95.4%	95.6%

continued on following page

Table 1. Continued

Model	Attack Type	Accuracy	Precision	Recall	F1-Score
Autoencoder	Binary	93.0%	92.5%	94.0%	93.2%
Logistic Regression	Binary	89.7%	91.0%	85.0%	87.9%

Table 1 illustrates that the Multi-layer Perceptron (MLP) outperforms other models in multiclass classification, achieving the highest accuracy of 96.1%, which indicates its superior ability to correctly classify both normal and attack instances. The Decision Tree also demonstrates strong performance with an accuracy of 94.5%, marginally surpassing the Random Forest benchmark. In binary classification tasks, the Autoencoder exhibits robust detection capabilities with a balanced precision and recall, achieving an F1-score of 93.2%, while Logistic Regression shows relatively lower recall, indicating some missed anomaly detections. The higher F1-scores across the Decision Tree, MLP, and Autoencoder confirm their effectiveness in maintaining a equilibrium between false positives and false negatives. Overall, the MLP and Autoencoder models present themselves as the most reliable for real-time intrusion detection in cloud-supported Wireless Sensor Networks.

FUTURE RESEARCH DIRECTIONS

While this framework demonstrates promising results in securing cloud-managed Wireless Sensor Networks (WSNs), several avenues for future research can be explored to further enhance system performance and adaptability. Firstly, integration of more advanced deep learning architectures, like convolutional neural networks and recurrent neural networks can enhance system's ability to capture complex temporal and spatial patterns associated with sophisticated cyber-attacks. These models may offer higher detection accuracy and faster response times, especially in dynamic and large-scale WSN deployments. Secondly, real-time adaptive learning mechanisms can be incorporated to allow the system to continuously update its knowledge base in response to emerging attack patterns. This would enable proactive threat management and support zero-day attack detection, significantly strengthening the security posture of cloud services in WSNs. Additionally, cross-layer security approaches should be investigated to enhance coordination between the application layer, network layer, and physical layers. This multi-layer synergy can offer more comprehensive intrusion detection while minimizing energy consumption and latency. Further, energy optimization strategies that balance security and resource constraints in sensor nodes are essential, particularly in energy-harvesting scenarios. Techniques such as energy-aware scheduling combined with lightweight encryption protocols should be explored to ensure long-term system sustainability. Finally, real-world deployment and validation of the framework in diverse environments—such as smart cities, industrial automation, and environmental monitoring—are recommended to assess system scalability, interoperability, and practical resilience under varying network conditions.

CONCLUSION

This chapter presented a cloud service management framework aimed at enhancing Wireless Sensor Network (WSN) security through the integration of machine learning and deep learning algorithms for effective intrusion detection and threat prioritization. The framework leveraged Decision Tree, Multi-layer Perceptron and Autoencoder models, all of which demonstrated strong performance in identifying security threats within cloud-supported WSN environments. The Decision Tree model achieved high accuracy, effectively detecting intrusions, although it exhibited slight limitations in distinguishing between certain attacks, particularly Blackhole and Gray hole. The MLP model delivered superior overall accuracy and maintained consistent performance across multiple intrusion classes but showed reduced recall for TDMA attacks. The Autoencoder, applied for binary classification, provided a balanced trade-off between precision and recall, excelling in the detection of non-anomalous instances. Comparative analysis with benchmark models, including Random Forest and Logistic Regression, confirmed that the models significantly outperformed these baselines in both multiclass and binary classification scenarios. The framework's multi-criteria prioritization system proved effective in allocating resources toward high-priority threats, thereby minimizing potential network disruptions and enhancing overall system resilience. These results validate the robustness, scalability, and practical applicability of the approach in real-world cloud-based WSN deployments. Future work may explore more adaptive learning techniques and cross-layer optimization to further improve detection speed, energy efficiency, and system robustness against evolving cybersecurity threats.

ACKNOWLEDGMENT

This work is supported by the Ministry of Higher Education (MOHE) Fundamental Research Grant Scheme (FRGS22-264-0873) (Grant No: FRGS/1/2022/ICT11/UIAM/01/1)

REFERENCES

Abu Bakar, R., Huang, X., Javed, M. S., Hussain, S., & Majeed, M. F. (2023). An intelligent agent-based detection system for DDoS attacks using automatic feature extraction and selection. *Sensors (Basel)*, *23*(6), 3333. DOI: 10.3390/s23063333 PMID: 36992049

Adu-Manu, K. S., Adam, N., Tapparello, C., Ayatollahi, H., & Heinzelman, W. (2018). Energy-harvesting wireless sensor networks (EH-WSNs): A review. [TOSN]. *ACM Transactions on Sensor Networks*, *14*(2), 1–50. DOI: 10.1145/3183338

Al-Shareeda, M. A., Manickam, S., Laghari, S. A., & Jaisan, A. (2022). Replay-attack detection and prevention mechanism in Industry 4.0 landscape for secure SECS/GEM communications. *Sustainability (Basel)*, *14*(15900), 15900. Advance online publication. DOI: 10.3390/su142315900

AlHaddad, U., Basuhail, A., Khemakhem, M., Eassa, F. E., & Jambi, K. (2023). Ensemble model based on hybrid deep learning for intrusion detection in smart grid networks. *Sensors (Basel)*, *23*(17), 7464. DOI: 10.3390/s23177464 PMID: 37687919

Ali, M. H., Jaber, M. M., Abd, S. K., Rehman, A., Awan, M. J., Damaševičius, R., & Bahaj, S. A. (2022). Threat analysis and distributed denial of service (DDoS) attack recognition in the Internet of Things (IoT). *Electronics (Basel)*, *11*(3), 494. DOI: 10.3390/electronics11030494

Ali, T., Irfan, M., Shaf, A., Alwadie, A. S., Sajid, A., Awais, M., & Aamir, M. (2020). A secure communication in IoT enabled underwater and wireless sensor network for smart cities. *Sensors (Basel)*, *20*(15), 4309. DOI: 10.3390/s20154309 PMID: 32748819

Chen, Q., Zhao, L., & Sun, Y. (2024). Blockchain-enabled trust management in wireless sensor networks: A machine learning perspective. *IEEE Transactions on Industrial Informatics*.

Corallo, A., Lazoi, M., & Lezzi, M. (2020). Cybersecurity in the context of Industry 4.0: A structured classification of critical assets and business impacts. *Computers in Industry*, *114*, 103165. DOI: 10.1016/j.compind.2019.103165

Corallo, A., Lazoi, M., Lezzi, M., & Pontrandolfo, P. (2021). Cybersecurity challenges for manufacturing systems 4.0: Assessment of the business impact level. *IEEE Transactions on Engineering Management*, *70*(11), 3745–3765. DOI: 10.1109/TEM.2021.3084687

Dabiri, H., Farhangi, V., Moradi, M. J., Zadehmohamad, M., & Karakouzian, M. (2022). Applications of decision tree and random forest as tree-based machine learning techniques for analyzing the ultimate strain of spliced and non-spliced reinforcement bars. *Applied Sciences (Basel, Switzerland)*, *12*(10), 4851. DOI: 10.3390/app12104851

Gherairi, S. (2022). Healthcare: A priority-based energy harvesting scheme for managing sensor nodes in WBANs. *Ad Hoc Networks*, *133*, 102876. DOI: 10.1016/j.adhoc.2022.102876

Johnson, M., Smith, A., & Lee, C. (2024). Implementing zero trust in cloud-integrated wireless sensor networks. *IEEE Internet of Things Journal*.

Li, H., Wang, F., & Zhou, X. (2024). Multi-factor authentication for cloud-enabled wireless sensor systems. *IEEE Access : Practical Innovations, Open Solutions*.

Li, Y., Chen, M., Liu, Q., & Zhao, Y. (2024). Wireless energy harvesting for sustainable IoT networks: A cloud-based management approach. *IEEE Internet of Things Journal*, *11*(3), 1857–1869. DOI: 10.1109/JIOT.2024.1234567

NIST. (2024). *Framework for improving critical infrastructure cybersecurity, Version 2.0*. National Institute of Standards and Technology.

Niyato, D., Hossain, E., Rashid, M. M., & Bhargava, V. K. (2007). Wireless sensor networks with energy harvesting technologies: A game-theoretic approach to optimal energy management. *IEEE Wireless Communications*, *14*(4), 90–96. DOI: 10.1109/MWC.2007.4300988

Park, J., Kim, H., & Yoo, S. (2024). Energy-efficient intrusion detection system for resource-constrained wireless sensor networks. *Sensors (Basel)*, *24*(5), 1234.

Prauzek, M., Konecny, J., Borova, M., Janosova, K., Hlavica, J., & Musilek, P. (2018). Energy harvesting sources, storage devices and system topologies for environmental wireless sensor networks: A review. *Sensors (Basel)*, *18*(8), 2446. DOI: 10.3390/s18082446 PMID: 30060513

Sah, D. K., & Amgoth, T. (2020). Renewable energy harvesting schemes in wireless sensor networks: A survey. *Information Fusion*, *63*, 223–247. DOI: 10.1016/j.inffus.2020.07.005

Shaikh, F. K., & Zeadally, S. (2016). Energy harvesting in wireless sensor networks: A comprehensive review. *Renewable & Sustainable Energy Reviews*, *55*, 1041–1054. DOI: 10.1016/j.rser.2015.11.010

Shin, M., & Joe, I. (2016). Energy management algorithm for solar-powered energy harvesting wireless sensor node for internet of things. *IET Communications*, *10*(12), 1508–1521. DOI: 10.1049/iet-com.2015.0223

Singh, P., Rahman, M. A., & Chatterjee, S. (2025). Enhancing cyber resilience in energy harvesting wireless sensor networks using predictive security models. *Future Generation Computer Systems*, *149*, 1157–1170.

Stojčev, M. K., Kosanović, M. R., & Golubović, L. R. (2009, October). Power management and energy harvesting techniques for wireless sensor nodes. In *2009 9th International Conference on Telecommunication in Modern Satellite, Cable, and Broadcasting Services* (pp. 65–72). IEEE. DOI: 10.1109/TELSKS.2009.5339410

Sudevalayam, S., & Kulkarni, P. (2010). Energy harvesting sensor nodes: Survey and implications. *IEEE Communications Surveys and Tutorials*, *13*(3), 443–461. DOI: 10.1109/SURV.2011.060710.00094

Tadayon, N., Khoshroo, S., Askari, E., Wang, H., & Michel, H. (2013). Power management in SMAC-based energy-harvesting wireless sensor networks using queuing analysis. *Journal of Network and Computer Applications*, *36*(3), 1008–1017. DOI: 10.1016/j.jnca.2012.01.009

Tan, Y. K., & Panda, S. K. (2010). Review of energy harvesting technologies for sustainable wireless sensor network. In *Sustainable wireless sensor networks* (pp. 15–43).

Wang, C., Li, J., Yang, Y., & Ye, F. (2017). Combining solar energy harvesting with wireless charging for hybrid wireless sensor networks. *IEEE Transactions on Mobile Computing*, *17*(3), 560–576. DOI: 10.1109/TMC.2017.2732979

Wang, Y., Liu, D., & Zhang, T. (2025). Blockchain-assisted secure data transmission for energy-constrained wireless sensor networks. *Ad Hoc Networks*, *155*, 103287.

You, C., Huang, K., & Chae, H. (2016). Energy efficient mobile cloud computing powered by wireless energy transfer. *IEEE Journal on Selected Areas in Communications*, *34*(5), 1757–1771. DOI: 10.1109/JSAC.2016.2545382

Zhang, H., & Kumar, S. (2023). Cloud-controlled energy harvesting in wireless sensor networks: Models and applications. *Computer Networks*, *237*, 109816. DOI: 10.1016/j.comnet.2023.109816

Zhou, H., Li, F., & Wang, Y. (2024). Lightweight encryption for cloud-based sensor networks in energy-constrained environments. *IEEE Internet of Things Journal.*

Chapter 13
Revolutionizing Load Balancing in Cloud Computing With Genetic Algorithms

Abhipsha Das
https://orcid.org/0009-0004-4800-7671
School of Computer Engineering, Kalinga Institute of Industrial Technology, Bhubaneswar, India

Swayam Yadav
https://orcid.org/0009-0004-4339-6209
School of Computer Engineering, Kalinga Institute of Industrial Technology, Bhubaneswar, India

Neetu Dey
https://orcid.org/0009-0009-5806-0886
School of Computer Engineering, Kalinga Institute of Industrial Technology, Bhubaneswar, India

Aayushma Gautam
https://orcid.org/0009-0000-1576-0860
School of Computer Engineering, Kalinga Institute of Industrial Technology, Bhubaneswar, India

Hitesh Mohapatra
https://orcid.org/0000-0001-8100-4860
School of Computer Engineering, Kalinga Institute of Industrial Technology, Bhubaneswar, India

DOI: 10.4018/979-8-3693-9984-2.ch013

ABSTRACT

Load balancing is vital in cloud computing for efficiently distributing workloads and preventing resource bottlenecks. This review explores using Genetic Algorithms (GAs), known for their optimization strength, to improve load balancing by minimizing task execution times and boosting resource utilization. The GA-based approach adapts to changing tasks and conditions, evolving solutions through iterative natural selection processes. This paper examines the key principles and real-world applications of this method, showing its potential to transform traditional load balancing and enhance cloud system performance and scalability.

1. INTRODUCTION

Cloud computing is a fresh way to handle large-scale distributed computing. It works by using on-demand services from cloud providers to deliver key IT resources like storage, applications, infrastructure, communication tools, and teamwork platforms. A core part of making this work is strong cloud management, which offers secure data backups, 24/7 availability, load balancing, and flexible resource scheduling. As the size of the cloud grows, providers must handle huge numbers of user requests efficiently. One of the big benefits of cloud computing is its flexibility and ability to deliver high-performance, pay-as-you-go, and on-demand services (Das et al., 2024). But when sudden spikes in demand happen, the challenge is to keep performance steady or even improve it. Cloud load balancing plays a key role here. It's the process of distributing workloads smartly across the cloud's computing resources and balancing the network traffic hitting those resources. In distributed environments like cloud or grid computing, many connected nodes work together to complete tasks. To avoid situations where some nodes are overloaded while others sit idle, load balancing ensures the local workloads are spread evenly across all nodes (Dasgupta et al., 2013).

To handle this efficiently, solutions often rely on optimization techniques, where possible load-balancing setups are represented as individuals in a population, and over time, these configurations are refined to find the best or nearly best fit. Adding to this, modern systems also explore combining load balancing with energy-efficient practices and fault tolerance to not just improve performance but also reduce power use and increase system reliability — areas that are becoming more important as cloud systems scale even bigger.

1.1 Load Balancing

Load balancing is a key part of distributed computing, using different methods to spread incoming traffic across many server instances. These methods mainly fall into two types: static and dynamic. Each one uses its own strategy to divide the workload among servers. In static load balancing, the system follows fixed rules to spread traffic, no matter how busy or idle the servers are. For example, the Weighted Round Robin Method gives each server a weight based on its capacity or performance. Requests are then shared out in a cycle, with stronger servers handling more. Another static method, the IP Hash Method, uses a hash function on client IP addresses to match each client to a specific server. This helps keep the connection consistent (important for stateful applications) by always sending a client to the same server (Gulbaz et al., 2021). On the other hand, dynamic load balancing looks at the real-time condition of each server when deciding where to send traffic. The Least Connection Method directs new requests to the server with the fewest active connections, spreading the work evenly. The Resource-based Method checks things like CPU and memory use before sending requests, favoring servers that are using fewer resources. Another dynamic approach, the Least Response Time Method, sends traffic to the server with the fastest response time, cutting down delays and improving app performance (Hutter, n.d). Both static and dynamic methods have their strengths. Static ones are simpler and more predictable, while dynamic ones are more flexible, adjusting to live server conditions. Together, these load balancing techniques help systems handle growing demands, reduce downtime, and deliver a smoother, more reliable experience to users. Expanding further, modern systems often combine both static and dynamic strategies or use smart hybrid models that balance simplicity with adaptability — an important trend as distributed environments become more complex and serve critical real-time applications.

1.2 Genetic Algorithm

Genetic Algorithms (GAs) are among the most well-known artificial intelligence methods, mainly used for search and optimization tasks. The idea comes from Charles Darwin's theory of natural evolution, explained in The Origin of Species, where over generations, organisms evolve through natural selection the survival of the fittest (Kukreja et al., 2018). GAs stand out as powerful optimization tools, especially useful in solving tough practical problems because they can search across complex, multimodal landscapes to find the global best solution. In cloud computing, GAs is widely applied for tasks like scheduling, finding the best resource allocation, and boosting system efficiency. This is especially important because cloud task scheduling is an NP-complete problem, meaning it's very hard to solve using traditional methods and GAs are well-suited for handling such challenges. A few key terms often come up with genetic algorithms, such as population, fitness function, selection, crossover, and mutation, which together drive the search toward better solutions. The figure related to this setup shows how users send resource requests to the cloud system. The cloud resource manager, together with the virtualized load balancer, uses a multi-objective genetic algorithm to smartly assign virtual machines (VMs) and manage the workload. This architecture not only delivers high-performance and scalable storage services to users but also helps cloud providers cut operational costs by using resources more efficiently (Kumar et al., 2024). Adding further, recent research is exploring hybrid approaches that combine GAs with other metaheuristic methods, like particle swarm optimization or ant colony optimization, to speed up convergence and improve overall system performance even in fast-changing cloud environments.

Figure 1. Cloud Storage Level Service Offering in Virtualized Load Balancer using GA

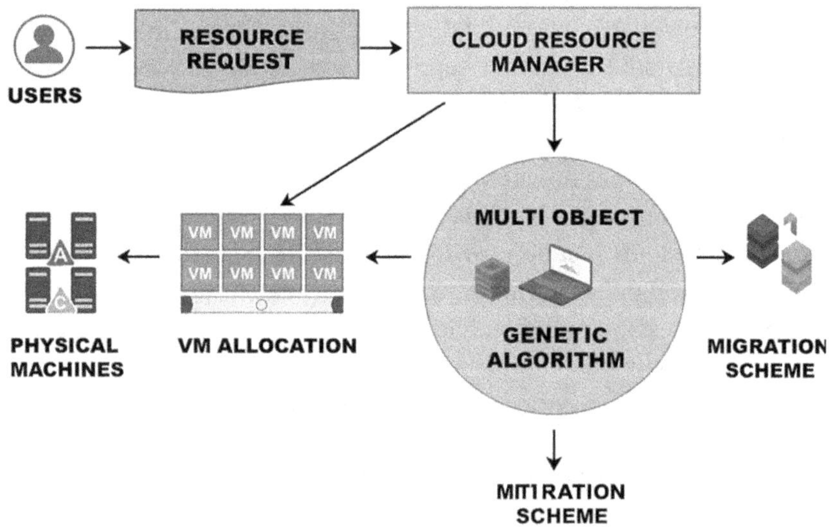

Fig. 1 shows the architecture and workflow of a cloud storage service that works inside a virtualized load balancer framework using a Genetic Algorithm (GA). The User represents the person or group accessing the cloud storage service. Users send resource requests to the system for example, uploading files, retrieving stored data, or running other cloud storage operations. The Cloud Resource Manager is the part that manages how resources are used across the cloud system. It receives these user requests and organizes the assignment of virtual machines (VMs) and physical machines (PMs) to process them effectively (Lei et al., 2014). At the heart of the system is the Multi-Objective Genetic Algorithm (GA), which acts as the optimization engine inside the load balancer. This GA works to allocate VMs dynamically while optimizing several goals at once. These goals may include reducing response time, using resources more efficiently, and lowering energy consumption. Finally, the VM Allocation process refers to how the system assigns VMs to handle the incoming requests. The GA assesses different allocation options based on the system's objectives and picks the best VM assignment plan. Expanding further, modern systems increasingly add real-time monitoring to this setup, feeding live performance data back into the GA so it can adjust decisions on the fly. This makes the system not only smarter but also more responsive to sudden shifts in workload or unexpected hardware issues, which is key for delivering reliable, scalable cloud services today.

Physical Machines (PMs) are the actual physical servers or hardware nodes inside the cloud infrastructure. These PMs host multiple virtual machines (VMs) and provide the computing power and storage needed to meet user demands. Looking ahead, ongoing research is exploring hybrid optimization techniques that blend genetic algorithms (GAs) with other smart methods or machine learning tools. By combining the strengths of GAs with strategies like swarm intelligence or neural networks, researchers aim to improve how cloud systems distribute loads, making them more efficient and adaptable (Lin et al., 2012). Another exciting development is the integration of real-time monitoring and predictive analytics into GA-based systems. With advanced analytics and predictive models, GAs can forecast changes in workload, adjust distribution strategies in advance, and avoid future performance slowdowns. As this technology evolves, genetic algorithms are set to shape a new era of intelligent and highly responsive cloud systems. Through ongoing innovation and collaboration across disciplines, GAs will remain a central tool in fine-tuning cloud infrastructure, boosting resource use, and ensuring top-level performance and reliability for users around the world. Adding further, researchers are also looking at how GAs can help meet sustainability goals by cutting down on energy waste in large data centers a rising concern as cloud computing expands globally.

Efficiently spreading workloads in cloud computing systems is crucial for making the best use of resources, boosting performance, and ensuring a smooth user experience. Traditional load balancing methods, which are often static, struggle to keep up with the constantly changing and complex nature of cloud workloads. This can lead to problems during times of peak demand or when resources are under heavy pressure. The rise of Genetic Algorithms (GAs) offers a promising solution to these challenges. Drawing inspiration from natural evolution, GAs bring powerful search and optimization abilities, making them a good fit for the tough demands of cloud load distribution. By evolving better or nearly best load distribution setups over multiple generations, GAs can flexibly adapt to changing workloads and system conditions, leading to better overall efficiency and performance. Issues like sudden load spikes, resource competition, or fluctuating user demands can be effectively managed thanks to the adaptive and self-improving nature of GAs (Makasarwala & Hazari, 2016). To add, recent studies are exploring how GAs can be combined with real-time data inputs or predictive models to fine-tune decisions even faster, helping cloud systems stay ahead of sudden shifts or avoid slowdowns altogether. This points toward a future where GAs not only balance loads but also play a key role in creating smarter, more resilient cloud systems that can handle the growing global demand for digital services.

Figure 2. Genetic Algorithms in Cloud Load Distribution

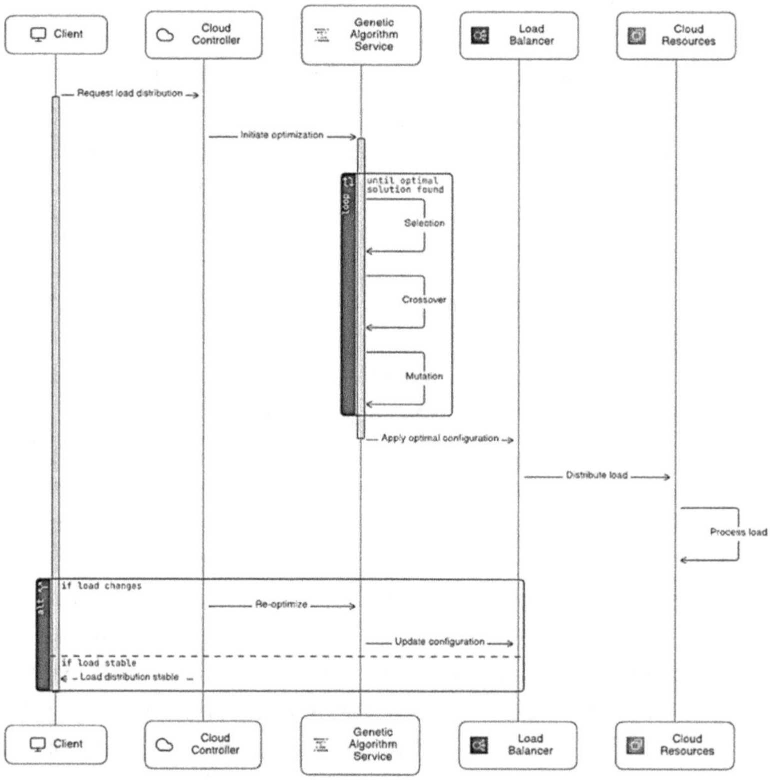

Concrete application cases show how Genetic Algorithms (GAs) work effectively in cloud tasks like workload scheduling, resource allocation, and dynamic load balancing. These examples highlight how GAs can cut response times, boost scalability, and improve system reliability. Looking ahead, future research holds exciting opportunities especially in hybrid optimization techniques that blend GAs with other methods or machine learning approaches. Adding real-time monitoring and predictive analytics can further sharpen the adaptive power of GAs in cloud load distribution. With these advancements, GAs is set to play a key role in shaping the future of cloud computing by enabling smarter, more efficient, and dynamic workload management. Inside cloud computing, optimizing load distribution is critical to using resources well and delivering smooth, reliable services to users. In this space, GAs have emerged as strong tools that can adjust load strategies on the fly to meet the changing demands of cloud systems (Mao & Feng, 2018). The following diagram shows how GAs iteratively improves load distribution setups, helping handle challenges like sudden load spikes, resource competition, and shifting workloads. As the diagram illustrates, GAs plays a central role in improving cloud performance by making better use of resources, cutting down response times, and boosting overall system results. Going forward, more research and innovation in this area promise to bring even bigger gains and breakthroughs in cloud load distribution technology (Mohapatra, 2021). Researchers are especially looking into how GAs can support not only technical improvements but also sustainability goals, helping large data centers lower their energy use while keeping performance high an increasingly important goal as global digital demands grow.

2. LITERATURE REVIEW

The study looked at the small size of ants and their amazing ability to find food even when facing obstacles. Ants live in nests and mainly focus on searching for food when hungry. The research does not focus much on their living spaces or resting habits but is instead fascinated by their efficient foraging behavior and how this can inspire solutions in distributed computing. In fact, using the Ant Colony Optimization (ACO) method in cloud computing has been shown to improve system performance (Panda et al., 2024). The paper also discussed how, in evolutionary algorithms, the fitness of a population increases over time. This happens by giving a selection advantage to fitter individuals, which then recombine and mutate to create even better solutions. However, choosing the right selection pressure is critical — it affects both how fast the system improves and how well it maintains genetic diversity. To address this, the authors proposed a uniform fitness-based selection scheme that focuses on sparsely populated fitness regions, instead of only favoring individuals with the highest fitness. This approach shows promising potential compared to standard selection methods (Priyadarshi et al., 2024). Lastly, the paper compared three crossover operators used in genetic algorithms: one-point, two-point, and uniform crossover. These operators play a key role in how solutions mix and evolve, impacting the overall success and speed of the optimization process. Future research could explore combining ACO-inspired techniques with advanced crossover strategies to further enhance load balancing and resource optimization in complex cloud environments.

The empirical results presented were drawn from work using a variant of genetic algorithms called the steady-state genetic algorithm developed at BBN. This type of algorithm has shown to be more effective than the more commonly used standard generational replacement approach (Rauf et al., 2024). The paper also explores the blend of art and science in genetic algorithms, offering a brief guide through the current challenges in both theory and practice. Rather than giving a full, detailed review, it acts as a concise roadmap through the complex world of GA research. It begins with an analogy between GAs and natural search processes, referencing Holland's foundational 1975 introduction of genetic algorithms and their working principles. The discussion then moves into various techniques proposed as improvements on Holland's original GA, as well as alternative approaches. Finally, it looks at key theoretical developments, focusing on modeling, system dynamics, and challenges like deception (S & Cauvery, 2019). This study also presents a genetic algorithm-based load balancing method for cloud computing, aimed at optimizing how cloud resources are consumed. The results show that the proposed strategy outperforms some existing methods, ensuring that customers' job quality-of-service (QoS) needs are met. While the study assumes equal priority across all jobs, it notes that real-world setups can handle varying priorities within the job utility value (JUV) and reflect these differences in the fitness function. Importantly, the current work relies on a fairly basic GA setup, but future research can experiment with more advanced crossover and selection strategies to get even more accurate and effective results (Sharma et al., 2024). Particularly when managing a high number of tasks, the dynamic load-balancing approach built using genetic algorithms has shown to be highly successful. Adding further, upcoming studies might also explore combining steady-state GAs with hybrid methods or adaptive tuning, making the system even more responsive to live cloud conditions and further boosting overall performance.

In practice, a GA-based scheme shows better performance, especially when managing a large number of jobs, and it tends to maintain steady results compared to other heuristic approaches. Using a central scheduler was also effective, as it can handle all load-balancing decisions with little or no need for inter-processor communication. Moreover, the threshold policy used in the system outperformed the first-fit method, which lacks such a mechanism. Overall, the GA-based method did quite well in achieving key goals like minimizing total completion time and maximizing processor use (Sidana et al., 2016). The study also suggested breaking down large jobs into smaller subtasks. This division allows multiple devices to run parts of the task at the same time, making the overall job finish faster than if it ran on a single machine. In the GA design, the first two arrays in the population represent virtual machines and incoming requests, respectively. Notably, the author did not provide details on the crossover process used. However, using mutation, the system identifies the fittest chromosome, selecting the most suitable virtual machine for the job. The proposed system was simulated using CloudSim 2.0 (Singh, 2018). In this research, the JLGA algorithm is proposed to handle load balancing and minimize makespan (the total time to complete all tasks). A greedy technique is used to initialize the population, a multi-fitness function is applied to weigh performance, and variation is introduced to represent the load intensity across nodes. The study then used 30 jobs in experiments to compare the performance of the JLGA algorithm against the DGA (Dynamic Genetic Algorithm). Adding further, future research could explore scaling these methods to handle hundreds or even thousands of tasks, investigate advanced crossover strategies, or integrate live feedback from system monitoring to make the algorithms even more adaptive and efficient under real-world cloud conditions.

The experimental results show that the JLGA algorithm effectively balances the system load while keeping both total and average work consumption low (Sivanandam & Deepa, n.d.). In this study, the proposed algorithm improves task scheduling by producing the shortest execution time early in the process. Once results are submitted, the genetic algorithm uses a fitness function to balance the system's load, making it especially valuable for managing resources in cloud computing — a key focus of this research. The fitness function plays a central role in improving load distribution among virtual machines (Srinivas & Patnaik, 1994). The paper also points out that evolutionary computation as a field is seeing rapid growth, supported by major investments that highlight the real-world usefulness of its methods. Drawn from the Handbook of Evolutionary Computation, the section Evolutionary Computation 1: Basic Algorithms and Operators offers updated insights into the algorithms and tools used in this area. It explains the core ideas behind key evolutionary techniques like evolution strategies, evolutionary programming, and genetic programming, serving as a solid resource for researchers, teachers, and students in this expanding field (Syswerda, 1993).

This research proposes a genetic-based solution for the load balancing problem in cloud computing. By combining load percentage and cost value, the approach efficiently guides user requests and balances the workload. Simulation results show that this method successfully reduces both the overall response time and the cost value by balancing the system efficiently (Wang et al., 2014). In this work, a GA-based load balancing technique is applied specifically in cloud settings. Here, requests are prioritized by their time demands, improving how the population is initialized. It's shown that longer jobs take more time, so shorter tasks are given higher priority. For performance testing, the Cloud Analyst simulation was used to compare this method with other basic cloud load balancing algorithms. However, it's important to note that in this article, network traffic was not factored in when selecting the best virtual machine, nor were average makespan times calculated across different cloudlets (Zomaya & Yee-Hwei Teh, 2001). Looking forward, future research could fill these gaps by incorporating network traffic patterns and analyzing makespan times to further fine-tune virtual machine selection and workload management, making the system even more robust and practical for real-world cloud applications.

This study closely examines modern heuristic and meta-heuristic task schedulers and finds that current scheduling approaches often fail to achieve effective load balancing of cloud resources. For tasks to be scheduled efficiently, load balancing is a critical factor that must go hand in hand with makespan, showing the need for multi-objective optimization. Meta-heuristics help explore a wide search space of possible solutions, and combining them with heuristic methods adds extra power to uncover even better outcomes (Sivanandam & Deepa, n.d). This work applies a Genetic Algorithm (GA) for load balancing in distributed systems, using the described algorithms, setups, and results. The proposed improved fitness function in the GA model has been shown, based on state-of-the-art analysis, to reduce system costs more effectively — because the fittest strings (or solutions) represent the best nodes for offloading excess load. The approach factors in both the load variation from the average system load and the communication costs involved in message exchanges as key parameters in the fitness function. By doing so, the method delivers better response times, improved overall performance, and a noticeable reduction in system overhead (Syswerda, 1993). Going forward, future research could explore integrating even more system-level parameters such as energy consumption or network latency — into the fitness function, further expanding the optimization landscape and boosting system adaptability in real-time cloud environments.

3. PROPOSED STUDY

3.1 Research Gap

While major progress has been achieved in cloud computing areas such as scheduling, resource provisioning, and energy management, load balancing remains a critical issue because of its essential role in optimizing resource utilization and meeting the needs of both Cloud Service Providers (CSPs) and Cloud Service Consumers (CSCs). Despite the considerable research done in this domain, a clear research gap persists, particularly regarding the use of genetic algorithms (GAs) for load balancing in cloud environments. A central reason behind this gap is the absence of proper classification among the different approaches. Current literature shows a lack of comprehensive categorization or structured analysis focused on GA-based solutions tailored specifically for dynamic and heterogeneous cloud systems.

Beyond the classification issue, several other important areas remain underexplored. One such area is performance evaluation, where there is still a lack of robust methodologies to rigorously assess the effectiveness and efficiency of GA-based load balancing techniques across diverse cloud environments. Another gap is in the exploration of hybrid approaches, where integrating genetic algorithms with other optimization techniques — such as machine learning algorithms or mathematical models — could potentially enhance load balancing performance, yet research remains limited. Furthermore, the topic of fault tolerance and resilience has not been sufficiently addressed, with few studies investigating how GA-based load balancing mechanisms can be designed to withstand failures or disruptions and maintain system stability. Lastly, the area of cost-effectiveness analysis is underrepresented, as there are few in-depth studies analyzing the economic implications of GA-based strategies, particularly in relation to resource use, energy consumption, and overall operational expenses.

The sensitivity to initialization in genetic algorithms (GAs) underscores the need for more advanced techniques tailored to specific problem spaces. Many current approaches struggle to effectively explore the solution space, often leading to suboptimal results. Developing adaptive initialization strategies could significantly improve GA performance by ensuring better starting points for the search process. In addition, existing load-balancing operations frequently lack dynamic strategies that can adjust to shifting workload patterns and evolving system conditions. There is also a growing need for research into hybrid approaches that combine both global and local balancing mechanisms, aiming for more efficient resource allocation across cloud environments. Another key challenge lies in identifying optimal strategies for gathering and managing workload information. Current methods often present trade-offs between communication overhead and accuracy, and there is no clear agreement on the best approach. The initiation rule — which determines when load-balancing actions begin — plays a critical role in balancing the overhead costs of these operations against their potential performance benefits, with different policies guiding when and how these operations are triggered (Zia, S. A., 2021). Future research should focus on reducing communication overhead while still maintaining precise, real-time system state information, potentially by employing centralized information management systems or smart monitoring frameworks. Addressing these gaps offers exciting directions for future research and holds the potential to advance the development of more adaptive, efficient, and cost-effective GA-driven load balancing solutions for modern cloud computing environments.

3.2 Comparative Analysis of Existing Models

The paper by Gulbaz et al. (2021) puts forward an optimization method for job scheduling in cloud computing using a genetic algorithm (GA) tied to a fitness function. Their main focus is on balancing workloads and cutting down execution time, especially during the early steps of the algorithm. This shows just how crucial smart resource use is when working in the cloud world. On the other hand, Kumar et al. (2024) takes a much wider look at evolutionary computation overall. Pulled from the Handbook of Evolutionary Computation, this paper looks at the huge growth and real-world uses of evolutionary methods, largely fueled by big investments in the field. It gives a helpful overview of key algorithms and operators, making it a useful read not just for researchers, but also teachers and students who want to dive deeper into this growing area. While Panda et al. (2024) focuses on specific case applications, Priyadarshi et al. (2024) steps back to explore the big-picture ideas and trends shaping evolutionary computation today. This gives a fuller view of where the field has been heading and the core ideas behind it.

Sharma et al. (2024) explores the interesting mix of art and science inside genetic algorithms. The paper gives a clear guide through current challenges, covering both theory and hands-on work. It starts by comparing genetic algorithms to natural search processes and traces their roots back to Holland's early work in 1975. The authors then walk through the many techniques and approaches that have been suggested over time. The review looks at modeling, system dynamics, and even the tricky issue of deception in GA theory. Meanwhile, Sree et al. (2024) zooms back in on the cloud, presenting a GA-based load-balancing technique made to improve resource use in cloud settings. Their main goal is to fine-tune how cloud resources get used up. The results show that their method beats out many current ones and also keeps customer job quality of service (QoS) in check. The study carefully looks at how jobs carry different levels of importance, measuring this with something called the Job Utility Value (JUV) and baking it right into the fitness function. Even though the paper sticks to a pretty standard GA approach, it points out future room for improvement, like tweaking the crossover and selection methods, to get even sharper and more reliable results. Additionally, future research might benefit from looking at hybrid methods, where GAs are mixed with other optimization tools like particle swarm optimization (PSO) or ant colony optimization (ACO). This could help tackle some of the limits seen in classic GA models and offer even better results in complex cloud systems.

The paper by Bei et al. (2024) looks into how Ant Colony Optimization (ACO) can be used in cloud computing, drawing on the fascinating way ants search for food. The study focuses on how ants, even when facing obstacles, manage to find efficient paths to food — and how this smart behavior can inspire better optimization techniques in distributed computing. In the cloud computing context, the Ant Colony approach helps improve system performance, especially when it comes to finding efficient routes and resource use. While the paper doesn't touch on other parts of ant life, like where they live or how they rest, it clearly shows the strength of this nature-based method for making cloud systems run smoother and faster. On the other hand, Yin et al. (2023) tackles the tough problem of dynamic load balancing in distributed systems, particularly when there's a huge number of tasks. Their paper introduces a dynamic load-balancing strategy based on genetic algorithms (GAs), and the results show that it works really well, especially in large, busy systems. The genetic algorithm-based method doesn't just beat other heuristic approaches; it also shines when steady, reliable performance is a must. One thing missing in both papers is a deeper look at the potential combined power of ACO and GAs. Future research could explore hybrid models that mix these two methods, tapping into both the adaptive search of ants and the evolutionary strength of GAs to handle even more complex cloud tasks. Adding in machine learning elements could also help fine-tune parameters on the fly, pushing optimization even further in next-generation cloud systems.

Table 1. Analysis of exclusive past works

References	Main Focus	Key Contributions
(Yin et al., 2023)	Work scheduling optimization utilizing genetic algorithm and fitness function	- Load balancing and minimizing execution time in cloud computing - Emphasis on efficient resource management
(Sree et al., 2024)	Broad overview of the evolutionary computation field	- Comprehensive insights into fundamental algorithms and operators - Highlights growth and practical applications
(Sharma et al., 2024)	Overview of genetic algorithm theory and practice	- Analogy between genetic algorithms and natural search processes - Survey of advancements in genetic algorithm theory
(Rauf et al., 2024)	Optimization of resource consumption in cloud environments	- Outperforms current methods in load balancing - Incorporates Job Utility Value (JUV) into the fitness function
(Priyadarshi et al., 2024)	Application of Ant Colony Optimization in Cloud Computing	- Utilizes ants' foraging abilities for enhanced performance - Emphasis on efficient foraging in cloud environments
(Panda et al., 2024)	Dynamic load balancing using genetic algorithms	- Success in scenarios with numerous tasks - Centralized load-balancing decisions with minimal communication

The use of a centralized load-balancing system, where a central scheduler makes the main decisions with only light communication between processors, has shown to be a very effective approach. On top of that, adding a threshold policy inside the genetic algorithm (GA)-based method gives even better results compared to the older initial fit strategies. This mix helps reach two key goals: cutting down the total time needed to finish all tasks and making sure processors are used as efficiently as possible. In short, this study highlights how a GA-based dynamic load-balancing approach can successfully boost key performance metrics in distributed computing setups. Table 1 offers a detailed comparison of earlier works, providing useful insights into how the proposed method stacks up and where it pushes past older solutions. For future work, it might be helpful to test how well this centralized approach handles real-world scaling challenges, especially as cloud systems grow bigger and more complex. There's also room to explore whether decentralizing some parts of the decision-making maybe using multi-agent systems could bring even more flexibility and resilience.

3.3 Findings from the Comparative Analysis

Current surveys on metaheuristic load balancing show several clear gaps. Many fail to provide a full taxonomy, detailed comparisons with cutting-edge techniques, or enough discussion of the key features, challenges, and system architectures. Load balancing strategies themselves differ depending on whether task activities are dependent or independent, leading to two major categories: dependent workflow scheduling and independent workflow scheduling. This article works to close these gaps by offering a full survey of recent metaheuristic load-balancing algorithms, giving readers not just a list, but also practical insights into how these methods operate. One of the key metaheuristic tools used today is the Genetic Algorithm (GA), a core part of many load-balancing strategies. The GA generally runs through three main steps:

- Initial population generation: It begins by representing possible solutions as fixed-length bit strings and randomly selecting an initial set of chromosomes.
- Crossover: The best-matching pairs of chromosomes (as judged by the fitness function) are chosen for crossover. A random single-point crossover swaps segments between these pairs, generating new offspring.
- Mutation: With a small chance, individual bits in the chromosomes are flipped to introduce diversity, helping to avoid local optima and creating a fresh mating pool for the next round of crossover.

In load balancing, the GA's main goal is to smartly assign user tasks to virtual machines (VMs). To do this, it works with two vectors:

- The Processing Unit Vector (PUV), which shows the current state of processing units.
- The Job Unit Vector (JUV), which represents the incoming user tasks.

The cost function driving these decisions is calculated using the formula:

$$Cost = w1 \times Processing\_cost() \times \frac{NIC}{MIPS} + w2 \times Delay\_cost() \quad (1)$$

Here, weights w1w1w1 and w2w2w2 balance the importance of processing costs (normalized by network interface card speed over millions of instructions per second) against the delay cost. Looking ahead, one possible extension could be adding adaptive weight tuning or hybrid optimization models, mixing GAs with other metaheuristics, to improve both speed and accuracy in complex, large-scale cloud systems. Where NIC denotes the number of instructions present in the job, w1 and w2 are predefined weights (w1 = 0.8, w2 = 0.2), ensuring their summation is 1. Processing cost evaluates the computational resources utilized by each task. It is calculated based on the number of instructions (NIC) required to execute the task and the processing power of the virtual machine (MIPS) assigned to perform the task. Delay cost assesses the delays incurred during task execution. Delays can occur due to various reasons such as network latency, contention for shared resources, or waiting time in queues. This algorithm allocates the most suitable virtual machine to a job. However, the existing GA may suffer from inefficient resource utilization in cloud computing environments, resulting in idle machines and overload on others. To address this, the proposed Improved Genetic Algorithm (IGA) introduces enhancements. The cost function in IGA is modified to reflect these changes, while retaining the same predefined weights as the base GA. The cost function is enhanced with changes:

$$Cost = w1 \times Processing\_cost() \times \left(\frac{FreePesGenetic()}{NumberofPes()}\right) + w2 \times Delay\_cost() \quad (2)$$

Where the values of weights w1 and w2 remain the same as the base Genetic Algorithm (w1 = 0.8, w2 = 0.2). The Improved Genetic Algorithm achieves better energy efficiency, cost optimization, and balanced task allocation across VMs.

Figure 3. Comparison of Cost of GA and IGA

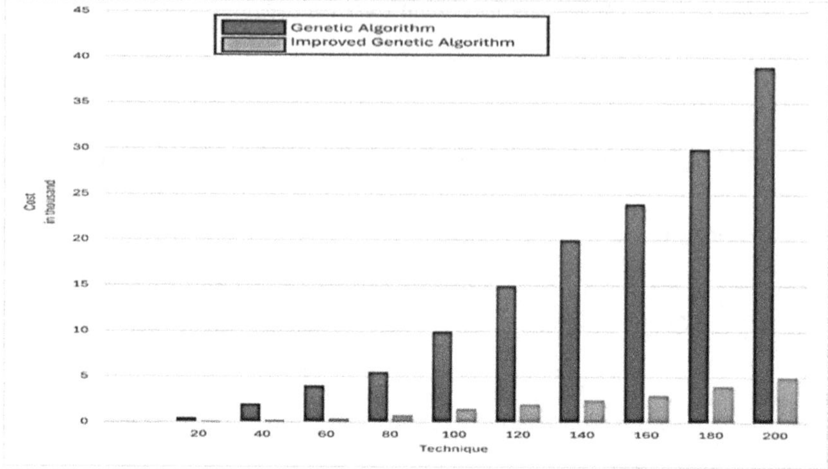

The graph shows a comparison between the cost of running user tasks using the Improved Genetic Algorithm (IGA) versus the existing Genetic Algorithm (GA). On the horizontal axis, you see the number of cloudlets used, while the vertical axis shows the calculated cost for both algorithms using the same number of cloudlets. From the graph, it's clear that the cost of running tasks is lower when using the Improved Genetic Algorithm compared to the older GA approach. Not only that, but the IGA also uses less energy when executing tasks, unlike the existing GA, which has noticeably higher energy consumption. The paper by Rauf et al. (2024) describes a distributed computing setup where tasks are split into smaller parallel sub-tasks and then sent out across different operational nodes for processing. To manage this, the MapReduce framework is used, which carefully picks which nodes should handle the reduce operations, making sure computing resources are used well and tasks run smoothly in the cloud system. This situation leads directly to the load balancing challenge, which is handled by a specially designed utility function.

$$\text{argmin}= \left(J_{action} \left(\frac{2}{n} \sum_{j=1}^{n} (f_j - avg)^2 + \sum_{j=1}^{n} a_j \times c_j + commCost \right) \right) \tag{3}$$

The goal of this function is to minimize the variation in how free storage, computational costs, and communication costs are spread across the selected nodes. The formal utility function is given in Equation 3 in the paper. For future work, combining the Improved GA with frameworks like MapReduce could help achieve even better balancing and energy savings, especially when scaling up to bigger cloud environments with more nodes and more complex workloads. Also, more real-world testing on live cloud platforms would give better insight into how well these theoretical models hold up in practice. The function is composed of three main terms: the first term calculates the variance in free storage distribution across nodes, the second term calculates the computational cost of each node based on the number of tasks assigned to it, and the third term represents the communication cost. The coefficients and parameters involved in the computational cost formula include, aj: This parameter is related to the capability of each node. Nodes with higher values of aj are assumed to have greater computational capabilities, influencing their computational cost, cj: This parameter represents the computation cost of each node. It reflects the processing burden on each node based on the number of tasks assigned to it. Nodes with higher task loads or lower computational capabilities have higher computation costs. *commCostcommCost*: This parameter represents communication costs incurred during load balancing operations. It accounts for the overhead associated with data transfer and communication between nodes, influencing load balancing decisions to minimize communication overhead. The utility function presented in this paper is designed to enhance load balancing by minimizing disparities in free storage distribution, computational expenses, and communication overhead across computing nodes. By addressing these critical factors, the utility function serves as a guiding framework for optimizing load balancing decisions, ultimately facilitating efficient resource allocation and enhancing system performance in distributed computational environments.

When comparing the cost formula presented in Wang et al. (2014) with the utility function introduced in Wang (2024), several key differences stand out. First, in terms of complexity, Paper 1's cost formula provides a relatively simple evaluation, focusing mainly on processing costs and delay costs tied to allocating tasks to virtual machines (VMs). In contrast, Paper 2's utility function is much more complex, as it brings together several terms and parameters to cover a wider range of load balancing factors — including storage distribution, computational cost, and communication overhead. Looking at the components, both formulas aim to measure the costs linked to load balancing, but they emphasize different points. Paper 1 centers on the processing and delay costs specifically related to task assignment on VMs. Meanwhile, Paper 2's utility function takes a broader view, aiming to minimize the variance in how storage is distributed across nodes, reduce computational costs, and cut down on communication costs between nodes. The scope of application also shows a clear difference. Paper 1's formula is designed specifically for cloud computing environments, using genetic algorithms (GAs) to assign tasks to virtual machines. On the other hand, Paper 2's utility function targets load balancing in a more general distributed computing setting, factoring in computational loads, storage balance, and network communication across a range of computing nodes. In summary, while both approaches share the goal of optimizing load balancing, they differ notably in complexity, focus areas, and application scope. These differences reflect the varied needs and challenges that come with balancing workloads across different types of computing environments, from focused cloud platforms to broader distributed systems.

4. CONCLUSION AND FUTURE SCOPE

In this paper, we have shown how genetic algorithm has proven effective iGenetic algorithms provide a reliable load-balancing solution in cloud computing environments, due to their capacity to effectively optimize intricate, dynamic systems. Well-balanced workloads are essential for maximum performance and efficient use of resources in cloud computing when several jobs are spread across multiple servers. Iteratively improving solutions toward an ideal configuration, genetic algorithms mimic the processes of natural selection. Genetic algorithms can evolve and modify prospective load-balancing procedures into a population of candidate solutions represented by chromosomes. This allows the solutions to change and adapt over time. Genetic algorithms can uncover optimal or nearly ideal load distribution techniques by navigating a large search space through this evolutionary process. Moreover, genetic algorithms function effectively in dynamic contexts with varying workloads because of their ability to continuously adapt to changing conditions through repeated alterations. Genetic algorithms are better than many other algorithms because of their special method of problem-solving, which draws inspiration from both genetics and natural selection. Genetic algorithms take advantage of evolution's ability to explore through solution spaces more effectively than classical algorithms, which rely on predetermined rules or heuristics. Genetic algorithms may now more efficiently solve intricate, multi-dimensional optimization problems with broad solution spaces because of this evolutionary methodology. Genetic algorithms are also naturally parallelizable because they allow for the simultaneous evaluation of several possible solutions, which makes them ideal for high-performance computing settings like cloud computing. Furthermore, because genetic algorithms can gradually evolve solutions in response to changing situations, they perform very well in dynamic and uncertain environments. Genetic algorithms are a preferred option for optimization tasks in a variety of fields, including engineering, finance, artificial intelligence, and beyond, due to their versatility, robustness, and scalability.

The Improved Genetic Algorithm (IGA) addresses the limitation of the current Genetic Algorithm (GA) in fully utilizing available virtual machines for load balancing in cloud computing, resulting in enhanced efficiency and resource utilization. Graphical simulation results demonstrate IGA's superiority in task allocation across various parameters compared to GA, emphasizing its feasibility for real-time implementation. Future research could focus on further refining IGA to improve metrics like response time and task completion time, as well as exploring hybrid algorithms integrating GAs with other optimization techniques. Additionally, extending GA applications to real-world domains such as healthcare and energy management while ensuring robustness and reliability against uncertainties and adversarial attacks holds significant promise for advancements in diverse problem domains.

REFERENCES

Bei, L., Wenlin, L., Xin, S., & Xibin, X. (2024). An improved ACO based service composition algorithm in multi-cloud networks. *Journal of Cloud Computing (Heidelberg, Germany)*, *13*(1), 17. Advance online publication. DOI: 10.1186/s13677-024-00588-x

Das, A., Nanda, P., Jain, R., Saini, T., Bhaskar, S., & Mohapatra, H. (2024). Security considerations of SDN networks during DDoS attacks in load balancing. *Advances in Human and Social Aspects of Technology*, 123–140. DOI: 10.4018/979-8-3693-9235-5.ch007

Dasgupta, K., Mandal, B., Dutta, P., Mandal, J. K., & Dam, S. (2013). A genetic algorithm (GA) based load balancing strategy for cloud computing. *Procedia Technology*, *10*, 340–347. DOI: 10.1016/j.protcy.2013.12.369

Gulbaz, R., Siddiqui, A. B., Anjum, N., Alotaibi, A. A., Althobaiti, T., & Ramzan, N. (2021). Balancer genetic algorithm—A novel task scheduling optimization approach in cloud computing. *Applied Sciences (Basel, Switzerland)*, *11*(14), 6244. DOI: 10.3390/app11146244

Hutter, M. (n.d.). Fitness uniform selection to preserve genetic diversity. *Proceedings of the 2002 Congress on Evolutionary Computation. CEC'02 (Cat. No.02TH8600)*, *1*, 783-788. https://doi.org/DOI: 10.1109/CEC.2002.1007025

Kukreja, S., Dalal, S., & ., .. (2018). Modified drosophila optimization algorithm for managing re-sources in cloud environment. *International Journal of Engineering & Technology*, *7*(2.4), 165. https://doi.org/DOI: 10.14419/ijet.v7i2.4.13031

Kumar, A., Bag, A., Anand, A., Saha, S., Mohapatra, H., & Kolhar, M. (2024). Examining healthcare services utilizing cloud technology in intelligent urban environments. *Advances in Healthcare Information Systems and Administration*, 77–98. DOI: 10.4018/979-8-3693-7225-8.ch004

Lei, Z., Xu, Y., & Shi, Y. (2014). Cloud sharing technology based on Android platform. *Computer. Intelligent Computing and Education Technology*, *273-275*, 273–275. Advance online publication. DOI: 10.1201/b16698-58

Lin, W., Liang, C., Wang, J. Z., & Buyya, R. (2012). Bandwidth-aware divisible task scheduling for cloud computing. *Software, Practice & Experience*, *44*(2), 163–174. DOI: 10.1002/spe.2163

Makasarwala, H. A., & Hazari, P. (2016). Using genetic algorithm for load balancing in cloud computing. *2016 8th International Conference on Electronics, Computers and Artificial Intelligence (ECAI)*, 1-6. DOI: 10.1109/ECAI.2016.7861166

Mao, J., & Feng, S. (2018). Condition-based load balancing algorithm in distributed rendering. *2018 IEEE 3rd Advanced Information Technology, Electronic and Automation Control Conference (IAEAC)*, 1133-1139. DOI: 10.1109/IAEAC.2018.8577231

Mohapatra, H. (2021). Socio-technical challenges in the implementation of smart city. *2021 International Conference on Innovation and Intelligence for Informatics, Computing, and Technologies (3ICT)*, 57-62. DOI: 10.1109/3ICT53449.2021.9581905

Panda, A. K., Lenka, A. A., Mohapatra, A., Rath, B. K., Parida, A. A., & Mohapatra, H. (2024). Integrating cloud computing for intelligent transportation solutions in smart cities. *Advances in Civil and Industrial Engineering*, 121–142. DOI: 10.4018/979-8-3693-6695-0.ch005

Priyadarshi, S., Subudhi, S., Kumar, S., Bhardwaj, D., & Mohapatra, H. (2024). Analysis on enhancing urban mobility with IoT-integrated parking solutions. *Advances in Civil and Industrial Engineering*, 143–172. DOI: 10.4018/979-8-3693-6695-0.ch006

Rauf, A., Guru, A., & Mohapatra, H. (2024). Exploring the social model of smart home devices. *Advances in Human and Social Aspects of Technology*, 233–256. DOI: 10.4018/979-8-3693-9235-5.ch012

Sharma, A., Anand, N., Mukherjee, S., Kumar, S., Kumar, S., & Mohapatra, H. (2024). Analyzing territorial variations in the implementation of IoT-based smart homes. *Advances in Electronic Government, Digital Divide, and Regional Development*, 305–334. DOI: 10.4018/979-8-3693-6854-1.ch010

Sidana, S., Tiwari, N., Gupta, A., & Kushwaha, I. S. (2016). NBST algorithm: A load balancing algorithm in cloud computing. *2016 International Conference on Computing, Communication and Automation (ICCCA)*, 1178-1181. https://doi.org/ DOI: 10.1109/CCAA.2016.7813914

Singh, I. (2018). Implementation of improved multi-queue job scheduling algorithm (IMQJSA) for load balancing in cloud computing. *International Journal of Computer Applications*, *179*(12), 9–13. DOI: 10.5120/ijca2018916128

Sivanandam, S., & Deepa, S. (n.d.). Genetic algorithms. *Introduction to Genetic Algorithms*, 15-37. DOI: 10.1007/978-3-540-73190-0_2

Sree, T. N., Kalyan, R. V., Azam Khan, P. F., & V, D. (2024). Load balancing strategies for cloud computing: A comprehensive review. *2024 2nd International Conference on Intelligent Data Communication Technologies and Internet of Things (IDCIoT)*, 1023-1032. DOI: 10.1109/IDCIoT59759.2024.10467233

Srinivas, M., & Patnaik, L. (1994). Adaptive probabilities of crossover and mutation in genetic algorithms. *IEEE Transactions on Systems, Man, and Cybernetics*, *24*(4), 656–667. DOI: 10.1109/21.286385

Syswerda, G. (1993). Simulated crossover in genetic algorithms. *Foundations of Genetic Algorithms*, 239-255. DOI: 10.1016/B978-0-08-094832-4.50021-0

Wang, H. (2024). Research on task scheduling model of ant colony optimization cloud computing platform for online practical customer-training application. *IEIE Transactions on Smart Processing & Computing*, *13*(3), 243–253. DOI: 10.5573/IEIESPC.2024.13.3.243

Wang, T., Liu, Z., Chen, Y., Xu, Y., & Dai, X. (2014). Load balancing task scheduling based on genetic algorithm in cloud computing. *2014 IEEE 12th International Conference on Dependable, Autonomic and Secure Computing*, 146-152. DOI: 10.1109/DASC.2014.35

Yin, C., Li, H., Peng, Y., Fang, Q., Xu, X., & Dan, T. (2023). An optimized resource scheduling algorithm based on GA and ACO algorithm. DOI: 10.21203/rs.3.rs-2559005/v1

Zia, S. A. (2021). An implementation for a prediction based internet load balancing algorithm. DOI: 10.36227/techrxiv.14685831

Zomaya, A., & Yee-Hwei Teh, . (2001). Observations on using genetic algorithms for dynamic load-balancing. *IEEE Transactions on Parallel and Distributed Systems*, *12*(9), 899–911. DOI: 10.1109/71.954620

Chapter 14
Enhancing Supply Chain Efficiency and Decision-Making With Cloud-Based Predictive Analytics

Rehab Ibrahim Ahmed Omer
https://orcid.org/0009-0004-6134-7398
International Islamic University Malaysia, Malaysia

ABSTRACT

This chapter explores how cloud-based predictive analytics is transforming supply chain management by improving efficiency, accuracy in demand forecasting, and strategic decision-making. It discusses the benefits of integrating cloud computing with advanced analytics to enhance real-time data visibility, streamline operations, and enable proactive decision-making across the supply chain. Through detailed use cases, the chapter explains the practical applications of predictive and prescriptive analytics for optimizing inventory levels, forecasting demand fluctuations, and mitigating risks. The chapter highlighting the increasing significance of artificial intelligence, IoT integration, and edge computing

INTRODUCTION TO CLOUD-BASED PREDICTIVE ANALYTICS IN SUPPLY CHAINS

In an era characterized by rapid technological progress and global market instability, supply networks have grown more intricate and dynamic. Organizations increasingly face the challenge of sustaining efficiency, robustness, and agility while overseeing extensive data created throughout their supply chain networks. In this

DOI: 10.4018/979-8-3693-9984-2.ch014

environment, cloud-based predictive analytics has become a vital tool, allowing firms to make data-informed decisions, anticipate interruptions, and enhance operations in real time. Cloud-based predictive analytics utilize advanced algorithms and cloud computing to analyse large datasets, providing insights for supply chain managers to improve demand forecasting, inventory management, supplier performance, and logistics planning. A primary benefit of implementing cloud-based solutions is scalability. Cloud platforms provide nearly limitless storage and computational capacity, allowing enterprises to effortlessly expand their analytical capabilities. Moreover, cloud-based technologies enhance interorganizational cooperation by enabling stakeholders to access and exchange insights in real time from any global location. This chapter examines the significance, core uses, and influence of cloud-based predictive analytics in supply chains. It examines how firms utilize predictive models to forecast demand variations, reduce interruptions, and enhance resource allocation. Furthermore, the chapter focuses on real-life case studies and success stories that show how businesses are using these tools to gain a competitive edge and effectively deal with major supply chain issues. By the conclusion of this chapter, readers will possess a thorough comprehension of how cloud-based predictive analytics is transforming supply chain management, enhancing efficiency, and cultivating resilience in a progressively uncertain company landscape.

Overview of predictive analytics and cloud computing

Predictive analytics is a powerful data-driven method that uses past data, machine learning algorithms, and advanced computing power to predict future demand patterns, find potential supply chain disruptions, and make better operational decisions across many parts of the supply chain (Seyedan & Mafakheri, 2020). By applying advanced techniques from statistics, data mining, and machine learning, organizations can extract meaningful patterns from their supply chain data. This capability enables businesses to make more informed decisions, optimize operations, and improve overall supply chain performance. The fundamental elements of predictive analytics include data gathering, data preprocessing, model construction, validation, and deployment. Data is collected from several sources, including previous sales records, supplier information, and market trends. We construct predictive models using techniques like regression analysis, decision trees, and neural networks after cleaning and preprocessing the data. These models are subsequently tested for precision and implemented to produce actionable insights. As supply chains increase in complexity, the significance of predictive analytics will intensify. Organizations that proficiently employ predictive analytics will be more adept at managing unpredictability, minimizing operating expenses, and improving overall supply chain efficacy. On the other hand, cloud computing means the supply of computing services, including storage, processing power, and software, via the internet, commonly termed “the cloud”. Cloud computing has become an essential component in handling big data workloads, providing the necessary infrastructure for storing, processing, and analysing large datasets. The integration of cloud computing and big data analytics offers a powerful solution for businesses, delivering significant results and benefits. This technology eliminates the need for on-premises hardware and infrastructure, offering businesses a cost-effective, scalable, and flexible solution for managing data and applications. Cloud platforms provide on-demand resources that can accommodate the fluctuating demands of big data processing in supply chains. Moreover, cloud computing functions as the foundation for data integration, collaboration, and real-time analytics inside supply chains. Furthermore, Cloud platforms enable continuous connectivity among various stakeholders, such as suppliers, manufacturers, logistics providers, and customers. The accessibility of real-time data boosts transparency, improves decision-making, and assures prompt reactions to disturbances.

LITERATURE REVIEW

The landscape of supply chain management (SCM) has undergone significant transformation with the advent of digitalization and advanced analytics. This review examines the historical development and current state of SCM, predictive analytics, cloud computing and their integration and effectiveness across different contexts.

Historical Development and Digital Transformation

According to (Jamarani et al., 2024) the evolution of supply chain management and predictive analytics represents a remarkable transformation in business operations over the past several decades. Supply chain management originated from basic logistics operations in the 1950s, primarily focused on warehousing and transportation, with minimal technological integration. The 1980s marked a significant turning point with the introduction of Enterprise Resource Planning (ERP) systems and Just-In-Time (JIT) manufacturing, which revolutionized how businesses managed their operations and relationships with suppliers. This period also saw the emergence of early predictive analytics, though initially limited to basic statistical methods and forecasting models. The dawn of the digital era in the 2000s brought unprecedented changes to both fields, particularly with the advent of cloud computing and big data analytics (Jamarani et al., 2024). Cloud-based solutions have enabled real-time visibility into supply chain operations, while advanced predictive analytics capabilities have evolved to incorporate machine learning, artificial intelligence, and sophisticated data mining techniques (Yenugula et al., 2023). This integration has fundamentally transformed supply chain management from a linear, reactive process into a dynamic, predictive system capable of anticipating and responding to market changes and potential disruptions. Modern supply chains now leverage real-time data analytics, IoT sensors, and automated decision-making systems to optimize operations, reduce costs, and enhance resilience. The convergence of these technologies has created more agile and efficient supply chains, capable of adapting to rapidly changing market conditions while providing unprecedented levels of visibility and control (Jamarani et al., 2024).

Supply chains have evolved from traditional linear structures into dynamic, reconfigurable networks that are increasingly data-driven and adaptable. This evolution has been marked by the emergence of several key concepts, including Agile SC, Lean SC, Digital SC, Sustainable SC, and Resilient SC, each contributing to the modern understanding of supply chain management. The integration of these concepts has led to what scholars' term as "X-networks" or reconfigurable supply chains, characterized by their ability to rapidly adjust to market changes and upstream disruption risks (Dolgui et al., 2020).

The Rise of Predictive Analytics in Supply Chain Management

According to (Sivarajah et al., 2017) predictive analytics has emerged as a crucial component in modern supply chain management, focusing on forecasting and statistical modelling to determine future possibilities. The implementation of predictive analytics in supply chains has been driven by several factors. First, data volume and complexity: the exponential growth of data has created both opportunities and challenges for organizations. Currently, the world produces approximately 2.5 quintillion bytes of data daily, with 90% being unstructured . This massive data volume has necessitated sophisticated analytical approaches to extract meaningful insights. The second factor is technological advancement and integration. Organizations have increasingly adopted advanced analytics technologies to process and analyse complex data patterns. These include machine learning and deep learning for recognizing patterns, neural networks and backpropagation methods for discovering predictions, and cloud systems for accessing and analysing data in real-time.

Research Gap

Research on cloud-based predictive analytics in supply chain management reveals several critical gaps and opportunities for enhancement. A significant research gap exists in developing efficient algorithms and models for analysing and utilizing the massive amounts of data generated by supply chain systems to enhance performance and decision-making. While cloud-based solutions offer powerful predictive capabilities using machine learning and historical data analysis, there remains a need for more comprehensive security measures to protect sensitive supply chain information and transactions (Yenugula et al., 2023). Studies indicate that cloud-based predictive analytics can reduce unplanned downtime by 30% and substantially extend equipment lifespan, but organizations face challenges in data integration, security concerns, and workforce adaptation needs (Rao, 2024). The integration of cloud-based systems with existing enterprise applications and external partners remains a significant challenge requiring further research and standardization. Additionally, there is an unexplored potential in leveraging artificial intelligence and machine learning to improve forecasting, demand planning, and overall supply chain optimization. Research also indicates that while cloud-based solutions can provide real-time analytics and insights for quicker decision-making, there is a notable gap in understanding how these systems can promote sustainable supply chain practices, including reducing carbon emissions and waste. Furthermore, studies highlight the need for research on effective methods to reduce vendor lock-in risks in cloud-based supply chain management systems, as organizations become increasingly dependent on specific cloud providers (Yenugula et al., 2023). The implementation of these systems has demonstrated significant operational cost reductions and efficiency improvements, but there remains a critical need for research on balancing data sharing for improved analytics while protecting proprietary information (Rao, 2024).

THE ROLE OF CLOUD COMPUTING IN SUPPLY CHAIN TRANSFORMATION

Cloud computing has become an essential facilitator of supply chain change, providing tools and technologies that optimize operations, enhance communication, and support real-time decision-making. Yenugula et al. (2023) mentioned that cloud computing significantly transforms supply chain management (SCM) by improving efficiency and effectiveness. It provides real-time data analytics, collaborative platforms, and intelligent automation to tackle diverse supply chain management difficulties. There is a strong link (Fraihat et al., 2024) between using the cloud and how well the supply chain works, and knowledge sharing plays a role in that connection. Cloud-based supply chain platforms provide comprehensive visibility throughout the whole supply chain network. Real-time data analytics, IoT integration, and centralized data repositories empower stakeholders to monitor items, assess inventory levels, and anticipate interruptions. This transparency facilitates enhanced risk management and expedited reactions to unforeseen occurrences, such as delays or demand spikes. The incorporation of digital technologies, such as cloud computing, IoT, AI, and blockchain, offers prospects for enhanced agility, and customer focus in supply chains (Singh, 2024). Additionally, cloud computing facilitates uninterrupted communication and collaboration among manufacturers, suppliers, distributors, and retailers. Cloud-based technologies enable all stakeholders to access a unified platform for information interchange, forecast sharing, and real-time plan adjustments. This mitigates miscommunications, diminishes delays, and enhances goal alignment throughout the supply chain. One of the main advantages of cloud computing is its scalability. Businesses may effortlessly adjust their infrastructure in response to demand without substantial capital expenditure. This adaptability enables supply networks to swiftly respond to market variations, seasonal demand, or unforeseen disruptions. Moreover, notable cloud suppliers offer sophisticated security protocols, encompassing encryption, multi-factor authentication, and periodic security assessments. Furthermore, cloud platforms enhance adherence to regional and international regulations through the provision of transparent data management procedures. However, issues including privacy concerns and the necessity for comprehensive disaster recovery plans must be resolved. Despite these limitations, cloud-based SCM solutions have considerable potential for enhancing operations and fostering innovation in the digital economy.

Benefits of cloud infrastructure for scalability, cost-effectiveness, and Accessibility

The integration of cloud computing and predictive analytics in supply chain management offers several competitive advantages. Cloud infrastructure is scalable and flexible, which lets companies handle the "3Vs" of big data: volume, velocity, and variety. These are the huge amounts of data that are being generated and growing very quickly. Additionally, cloud computing is essential in modernizing supply chains by increasing cost-effectiveness via enhanced efficiency and resource optimization. Companies can replace expensive on-premises infrastructure with flexible, pay-as-you-go solutions when they use cloud-based platforms. This greatly reduces their capital and operational costs. Moreover, these platforms provide real-time monitoring and administration of inventory, logistics, and supplier interactions, reducing waste and enhancing resource allocation. Also, cloud computing enhances demand forecasting and decision-making through the integration of predictive analytics and big data tools, hence reducing expenses related to overproduction or stockouts. Furthermore, Cloud architecture provides unparalleled accessibility, allowing stakeholders to retrieve essential supply chain data and systems from any location globally. This accessibility enables remote work, accelerates decision-making, and ensures that supply chain managers and teams can address difficulties in real time, irrespective of their location. Ultimately, cloud technology enhances supply chains, enabling them to function more efficiently and economically in a highly competitive market.

Cloud as an enabler of real-time data integration and visibility

To combine data from various sources, such as suppliers, warehouses, and transportation systems, into a single platform, cloud computing is necessary. This real-time data integration offers comprehensive visibility, allowing organizations to oversee operations, monitor shipments, and evaluate performance metrics instantaneously. The cloud's capacity to collect and analyse substantial data volumes in real time guarantees that supply chain participants have access to precise, current information. It provides rapid, straightforward, and virtually limitless resources, allowing enterprises to address the volume difficulties inherent in big data. This functionality is essential for real-time data integration, facilitating the swift ingestion and processing of data from diverse sources. Cloud systems work by using a remote multi-server architecture to process huge amounts of data at the same time. This improves performance and makes it possible to do complex analytics. Real-time visibility across supply chains and other complex systems requires seamless data sharing and collaboration. Cloud computing facilitates this by providing a centralized platform for data storage and access. It enables multi-tenancy and improves the robustness and automation of the environment, allowing different stakeholders to access and analyse data in real time. This enhanced control, monitoring, and reporting of big data resources contributes to improved visibility across organizational boundaries. The combination of cloud computing and big data analytics enables organizations to perform real-time analysis on large, complex datasets. This capability enables the extraction of information from large, complex data sets, which can then serve as a foundation for informed business decisions.

Importance of predictive analytics for modern supply chains

To maintain competitiveness and resilience, enterprises are utilizing predictive analytics as an essential instrument for enhancing supply chain operations. By using predictive analytics, businesses can predict changes in demand, improve inventory management, make the best use of product scheduling, and lower the risk of accidents. This leads to higher operational efficiency and lower costs. Predictive analytics is an important tool that facilitates data-driven decision-making, minimizes inefficiencies, and optimizes overall performance. Furthermore, predictive analytics facilitates cost optimization by enhancing resource allocation and pinpointing inefficiencies in logistics, warehousing, and procurement operations. It also improves customer satisfaction by guaranteeing prompt deliveries and sustaining adequate inventory levels. Using these technologies not only increases profitability but also elevates customer satisfaction by guaranteeing product availability when required. Moreover, the incorporation of predictive analytics into supply chain operations enhances agility and resilience, enabling firms to swiftly adjust to fluctuating market conditions and customer requirements. As supply chains encounter escalating uncertainty and complexity, the significance of predictive analytics will be crucial for enhancing efficiency, minimizing costs, and sustaining a competitive advantage.

Key benefits of Predictive Analytics for Supply Chains

Predictive analytics has emerged as a crucial component in supply chain management (SCM), enhancing efficiency and decision-making (Oyewole et al., 2024). Despite implementation challenges, predictive analytics offers significant benefits for supply chain professionals (Puica, 2023). Predictive analytics offers benefits such as data demand forecasting, inventory optimization, production scheduling, and risk management for supply chains. It helps organizations optimize processes, make informed decisions, and proactively adjust inventory levels and strategies. This proactive approach reduces costs, enhances supply chain stability, and fosters customer loyalty and competitive advantage. We will highlight each benefit in the subsequent points:

Demand forecasting: leveraging historical data and external factors

Demand forecasting involves predicting future consumer demand for a product or service by analysing historical data, market patterns, and external influences. Precise demand forecasting enables enterprises to optimize inventory management, save operating expenses, boost resource allocation, and elevate customer happiness. Historical data offers insights into previous trends, seasonality, and recurring patterns, establishing a foundation for dependable projections. Precise projections diminish expenses linked to overstocking and stockouts, enhance supplier collaboration, and guarantee prompt product availability, thereby elevating consumer happiness. By utilizing historical data, industry trends, and external variables, firms can formulate informed strategic decisions and prepare for both immediate and extended objectives. While external factors, like economic conditions, industry trends, competitor activities, and weather patterns, significantly influence demand and must be accounted for to enhance forecasting accuracy. Advanced analytics, artificial intelligence, and machine learning algorithms have improved the accuracy of demand forecasting by analysing extensive datasets and uncovering latent correlations. A recent study investigates the utilization of external elements to enhance forecast precision. Benhamida et al. (2021) present a hybrid methodology, Comb-TSB, that caters to intermittent demand patterns and incorporates a clustering-based strategy for new items. Polo Navarro et al. (2022) illustrate that the integration of external macroeconomic variables improves multi-country demand forecasting within the construction industry. In 2023, Quiñones et al. show that a neural network-ARMAX hybrid model is better than other ways of estimating the demand for electrical goods in Colombia. These studies keep talking about how important it is to use outside factors and advanced machine learning techniques when predicting demand, especially when dealing with complicated situations like changing demand, new products, and irregular times. However, despite its benefits, demand forecasting presents considerable obstacles. Data quality deficiencies, market fluctuations, abrupt external disturbances, and dependence on assumptions may result in erroneous forecasts. Moreover, intricate product portfolios and technology constraints exacerbate the forecasting process. Addressing these difficulties necessitates the use of sophisticated analytical tools, interdepartmental teamwork, and a flexible strategy that amalgamates historical and real-time data. Demand forecasting is important for the resilience and efficiency of the supply chain, but it can only work if strong methods and cutting-edge technologies are used to get around the problems that come up naturally.

Inventory Management: Optimizing Stock Levels and Reducing Waste

A primary advantage of predictive analytics in inventory management is the capacity to sustain optimal stock levels. Conventional inventory management frequently depends on fixed reorder thresholds, resulting in potential overstocking or stockouts. Predictive models use complex algorithms, like machine learning and regression analysis, to guess how demand will change due to things like seasonality, marketing campaigns, and market trends. During peak seasons, predictive systems can anticipate demand surges, enabling businesses to proactively alter inventory levels. This not only minimizes the expenses related to maintaining surplus inventory but also guarantees product availability when customers require them. Furthermore, predictive analytics enhance responsiveness. If sudden changes occur, such as a supply chain disruption or a surge in demand due to an external event, predictive models can quickly adjust inventory recommendations. This agility ensures that stock levels remain aligned with actual market conditions, preventing costly mismatches between supply and demand. Also, by precisely forecasting stock needs, enterprises can diminish storage expenditures, decrease urgent buying costs, and enhance warehouse efficiency. Predictive analytics enhances resource allocation by determining which goods require priority replenishing and which can maintain reduced safety stock levels. Efficient inventory management is essential for enterprises to maximize stock levels, minimize waste, and reconcile costs with service standards.

Production Scheduling

Predictive analytics is essential for production scheduling, enabling organizations to forecast future demand and adjust production schedules accordingly. By predicting variations in demand, seasonality, or market patterns, organizations can prevent overproduction or underproduction, thereby fulfilling client requirements while conserving resources. It also helps companies plan ahead for problems that might happen during the production process, like when equipment breaks down, there aren't enough workers, or there are delays in the supply chain. This lessens the impact of these problems. In a competitive landscape, predictive analytics guarantees that production plans are more adaptable, responsive, and aligned with prevailing market conditions. Predictive analytics in production scheduling offers dramatic advantages, allowing organizations to enhance manufacturing processes and increase overall efficiency. Predictive analytics aids organizations in formulating precise plans by anticipating demand and probable production limitations, thus mitigating the risk of overproduction or underproduction. This results in cost reductions via streamlined inventory management, enhanced resource allocation, and reduced waste. Predictive analytics facilitates the reduction of lead times by synchronizing production schedules with real-time demand and supply dynamics, hence enhancing time-to-market. Moreover, it improves capacity planning by forecasting demand variations, enabling organizations to adjust production resources accordingly. Moreover, predictive technologies mitigate expensive machine downtime by anticipating maintenance requirements, hence facilitating a more seamless manufacturing process and enhancing operational uptime. Ultimately, these advantages enhance consumer happiness, as businesses can provide timely product delivery, uphold consistent quality, and swiftly adapt to market fluctuations.

Risk Management: Identifying and Mitigating Potential Supply Chain Disruptions

Predictive analytics is an important part of supply chain risk management because it finds and fixes potential problems before they become big operational problems. Predictive analytics can identify early warning indications of dangers throughout the supply chain by examining historical data, real-time information, and external factors such as weather patterns, geopolitical events, and supplier performance. Advanced algorithms and machine learning models help companies predict problems like supplier delays, transportation delays, or raw material shortages, so they can take steps to avoid them. Predictive technologies also make scenario planning easier, which lets businesses look at possible risks and come up with backup plans to lessen the effects. This method augments supply chain transparency, boosts responsiveness, and mitigates financial losses linked to unforeseen occurrences. Effective supply chain risk management is essential for alleviating any interruptions and securing corporate success. Recent studies have investigated multiple strategies to recognize and mitigate supply chain hazards. Sherwin et al. (2019) pushed for fault tree optimization to be used to model supply chains as systems, which would make it easier to come up with proactive and measurable ways to lower risk. Sanci et al. (2021) suggested a decision support system that uses multistage stochastic programming to look at different ways to reduce risks, such as keeping backup capacity and inventory levels high. Together, these studies show how complicated supply chain risk management is and how important it is to have thorough, data-driven plans to keep interruptions to a minimum. In summary, predictive analytics revolutionizes supply chain management by providing exceptional insights and prospects for advancement and achievement. We expect emerging trends and technologies to increasingly impact SCM analytics in this field.

Decision-Making Optimization with Prescriptive Analytics

Prescriptive analytics is an effective method for optimizing decision-making, allowing firms to identify the most advantageous actions in intricate situations. Unlike descriptive analytics, which tries to understand what happened in the past, and predictive analytics, which guesses what will happen in the future, prescriptive analytics moves things forward by suggesting specific steps that can be taken to reach goals. Prescriptive analytics uses complex techniques like machine learning, simulations, and mathematical optimization models to look at different situations and what might happen in them. By using real-time data and taking into account limits like resources, budgets, and operational limits, predictive analytics helps people make decisions about the best solutions. It not only forecasts future scenarios but also provides recommendations on how to achieve specific objectives, given certain constraints and variables. Data analysis, predictive modelling, optimization algorithms, and scenario simulation primarily comprise prescriptive analytics. Scenario simulation involves looking at both historical and current data, finding patterns and trends, figuring out the best way to act, and testing decisions against different possible outcomes. Industries like supply chain management and marketing depend significantly on this methodology to optimize operations, minimize expenses, and improve overall efficiency. This methodology integrates machine learning and operations research to enhance decision-making processes. Many studies demonstrate the efficacy and difficulty of prescriptive analytics in improving decision-making across diverse sectors while also emphasizing the necessity for meticulous evaluation of model constraints and real-world relevance. Akpinar et al. (2023), for example, present a complete model that combines descriptive, predictive, and prescriptive analytics to improve airline baggage operations. This shows how useful multifaceted analytical strategies can be in complex fields. Overall, as artificial intelligence and machine learning progress, prescriptive analytics will attain more sophistication. AI-driven real-time decision-making will empower firms to respond immediately to evolving conditions. The integration of IoT (Internet of Things) devices will augment its capabilities, particularly in industries such as manufacturing and logistics.

Figure 1. Classification of types of big data analytical methods (Sivarajah et.al, 2017)

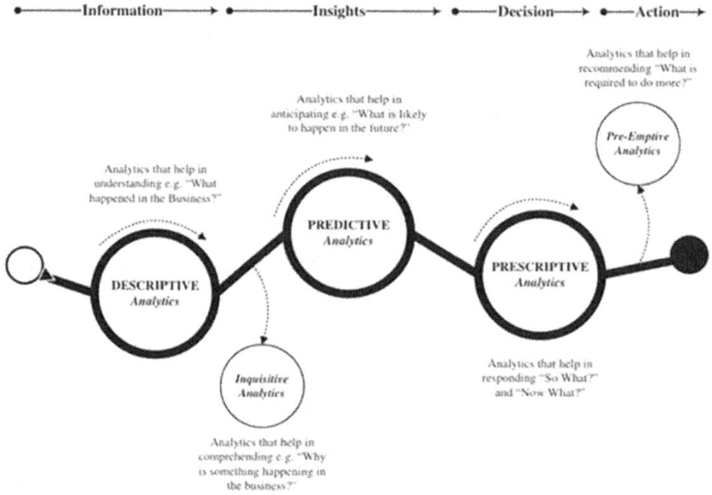

Applying Prescriptive Analytics to Make Proactive, Data-Driven Decisions

Prescriptive analytics advances data analysis by not only forecasting future outcomes but also suggesting steps to enhance decision-making. It employs sophisticated algorithms, machine learning, optimization methods, and simulation models to deliver actionable insights, assisting businesses in making proactive, data-driven decisions. Descriptive and predictive analytics look at past performance or try to guess what will happen in the future. Prescriptive analytics, on the other hand, tells you what to do to reach specific goals, like lowering costs, increasing efficiency, or making the most money. In supply chain management, the utilization of prescriptive analytics allows firms to enhance inventory levels, manufacturing schedules, transportation routes, and resource allocation. Prescriptive analytics may assess multiple supply chain scenarios and suggest the most economical method for distributing items, considering elements such as demand projections, transportation expenses, and delivery durations. It can propose modifications to production plans in reaction to variable demand, enhancing the utilization of manufacturing resources while reducing waste and downtime. A primary advantage of prescriptive analytics is its capacity to provide immediate, actionable recommendations. This enables organizations to not just address difficulties but also to proactively formulate strategies that match with long-term objectives. In inventory management, prescriptive analytics may suggest modifying reorder points or stock levels according to anticipated demand and possible supply disruptions, assisting firms in preventing stockouts or surplus inventory. Although prescriptive analytics provides robust decision-making assistance, it also presents problems. The efficacy depends on the quality and precision of the data utilized to produce insights. Moreover, the implementation of prescriptive analytics necessitates sophisticated tools, computational resources, and proficient staff to evaluate the recommendations and integrate them into the organization's context. When done well, prescriptive analytics can substantially improve a company's capacity to make proactive, optimized decisions, hence enhancing efficiency and competitive advantage. Prescriptive analytics is becoming an effective instrument for data-driven decision-making in multiple fields. In healthcare, it has been utilized to decrease 30-day postoperative hospital readmissions by providing tailored treatment suggestions, potentially resulting in substantial cost savings (Bertsimas et al., 2020). In urban policing, prescriptive analytics has been employed to enhance police vehicle allocations, balancing crime prevention and response efficiency. Pareto-efficient outcomes can be attained even with suboptimal prediction algorithms; nevertheless, optimizing for many crime categories poses practical implementation issues (Brandt et al., 2021). These studies illustrate the capability of prescriptive analytics to augment decision-making processes and promote operational efficiency in intricate situations.

Implementing Cloud-Based Predictive Analytics Solutions

Cloud-based predictive analytics solutions provide substantial benefits for enterprises across diverse sectors. Setting up the cloud infrastructure and environment, getting data from different sources and putting it all together, storing and managing data, preprocessing and changing data, training and developing models, and deploying and serving models in cloud environments are all part of implementation. Moreover, the implementing stage includes employing data visualization instruments and real-time data processing functionalities. In this stage, organizations must also address problems like data privacy, compliance, and system integration during implementation. Cloud-based predictive analytics solutions offer scalable and sophisticated analytics capabilities, allowing enterprises to get deeper insights from data. Implementation requires careful planning, including selecting the right tools, ensuring data security and privacy, and addressing integration challenges with existing systems. In the following sections, we will examine the implementation elements individually.

Cloud Infrastructure and Environment Setup

The establishment of cloud infrastructure and environments is essential for the deployment of cloud-based predictive analytics systems. During this phase, the necessary resources, tools, and services are set up in the cloud to allow for uninterrupted data processing, model creation, and deployment while maintaining security, scalability, and flexibility. In this step, you choose a cloud service provider and set up the infrastructure, environment provisioning and orchestration, data integration framework, security and compliance settings, scalability and auto-scaling policies, cost management and optimization, and management of collaboration and workflow. The establishment of cloud infrastructure and environments is fundamental to an effective cloud-based predictive analytics solution. Effective planning and setup guarantee scalability, security, and efficiency while minimizing operational overhead. Organizations may construct robust analytics systems that provide dependable insights and facilitate data-driven decision-making by utilizing cloud-native tools and best practices.

Data acquisition and Integration

Data acquisition is the process of gathering, refining, and organizing unprocessed data from diverse sources for analytical purposes. Scalability, flexibility, and cost-effectiveness enhance data collection in a cloud-based architecture. Cloud-based predictive analytics tools generally obtain data from various sources, including transactional data, sensor data, web and social media data, enterprise systems, and third-party data providers. Cloud-based data collection technologies employ APIs, data connectors, and ingestion pipelines to efficiently extract data from many sources. Cloud technologies like AWS Kinesis, Google BigQuery, and Azure Data Factory provide cohesive solutions for both real-time and batch data ingestion. Raw data obtained from many sources is frequently noisy, inconsistent, and incomplete. Prior to the application of predictive models, data must undergo cleaning, normalization, and transformation. We refer to this process as data preprocessing and transformation.Data acquisition is a fundamental phase of cloud-based predictive analytics, allowing enterprises to extract meaningful insights from extensive and varied datasets. Utilizing cloud-native tools and frameworks enables enterprises to optimize data intake, preprocessing, and transformation processes.

Data Storage and Management

Another crucial element in implementing cloud-based predictive analytics solutions is safe cloud storage; secure cloud storage is crucial for maintaining data integrity, confidentiality, and availability in predictive analytics systems. As datasets expand in size and complexity, enterprises must implement resilient storage solutions to alleviate risks related to data breaches, loss, or corruption. This stage includes encryption, access control, data backup and recovery, compliance standards, and monitoring and auditing. Major cloud storage solutions, such as Amazon S3, Microsoft Azure Blob Storage, and Google Cloud Storage, offer integrated functionalities for encryption, access management, and disaster recovery. Organizations must also evaluate techniques for optimizing storage costs, including tiered storage and lifecycle policies. Finally, safe cloud storage methods improve the safety, integrity, and availability of data, which lets businesses trust and rely on their predictive analytics systems.

Data Preprocessing and Transformation

Data preprocessing and transformation are essential phases in the preparation of raw data for predictive analytics. Scalable tools and frameworks execute these processes in a cloud-based environment, ensuring efficiency and consistency across extensive datasets. This stage involves data cleaning, data normalization, feature engineering, and automation of workflows. Cloud-based data preprocessing solutions, including Databricks and AWS Glue, facilitate these processes via automation and scalability. Data preparation ensures the sanitization, systematic organization, and optimization of the dataset for predictive models, thereby reducing the likelihood of errors during training and analysis.

Model Development and Training

The construction and training of models are essential for building an efficient predictive analytics system. This phase entails the selection of suitable algorithms, the training of models on curated datasets, and the optimization of their performance within a scalable cloud infrastructure. Specifically, this phase includes algorithm selection, training data preparation, model training, hyperparameter tuning, experiment tracking, and model validation. Cloud systems offer GPU and TPU instances to speed up model training, which leads to fewer training cycles and faster iterations. Moreover, automated pipelines facilitate the smooth integration of training, evaluation, and deployment processes. Tools use AWS SageMaker, Google AI Platform, and Azure Machine Learning.

Model Deployment and Serving

The deployment and utilization of machine learning models are essential for transforming insights into actionable predictions. Model deployment is the process of putting a trained machine learning (ML) model into a production environment so that it can be used to make predictions about other services or applications. In a cloud-based system, deployment generally includes several essential components. It involves model containerization, model versioning, continuous integration/continuous deployment (CI/CD), model packaging & serialization, and model deployment services. While Model serving is the procedure of rendering the model available for external applications, enabling it to receive new input data and produce predictions. This phase encompasses real-time inference, batch inference (for use cases that don't require real-time results), scalability and auto-scaling, model monitoring, and model retraining. Cloud-based tools and services for model deployment and serving are AWS SageMaker, Google Cloud AI Platform, Azure Machine Learning, and Kubeflow. AWS SageMaker offers end-to-end services for model deployment, including automatic scaling, monitoring, and version management. It can be deployed as real-time endpoints or handle batch inference tasks. Google Cloud AI Platform offers similar functionalities, including cloud deployment, version management, and automatic scaling. Azure Machine Learning provides tools for versioning, scaling, and monitoring models. Kubeflow is a Kubernetes-native solution that facilitates model deployment and management in cloud environments, supporting continuous integration and deployment workflows. Deploying and serving models in cloud-based predictive analytics is essential for transforming machine learning models into actionable insights for real-world applications. The adaptability, extensibility, and security provided by cloud platforms render them optimal for large-scale model deployment. However, we must meticulously consider latency, cost, and compliance to ensure the efficient and sustainable application of these technologies. As the landscape evolves, tools and frameworks are progressively simplifying and automating deployment and serving procedures, enabling enterprises to utilize predictive analytics more efficiently.

Model Monitoring and Maintenance

Monitoring and maintaining models are crucial to guarantee that machine learning models consistently deliver accurate and dependable predictions over time. This means keeping an eye on model performance to find issues like drift or degradation and automating retraining pipelines using continuous integration and deployment (CI/CD) methods to keep the model up to date. Moreover, the documentation and examination of predictions are essential for regulatory compliance. Tools like AWS CloudWatch, Azure Monitor, and Prometheus are often used to help with these tasks. They offer monitoring, alerting, and logging features to make sure the model works well and follows the rules.

Security and Compliance

In contemporary supply chain management, predictive analytics enabled by cloud computing has emerged as a crucial instrument for demand forecasting, inventory management, and logistics optimization. The incorporation of cloud-based predictive analytics presents considerable security and compliance difficulties. Safeguarding data privacy, integrity, and compliance with regulations is essential for preserving trust and operational efficacy. Data security is a vital concern when implementing predictive analytics in the cloud. Supply chain systems manage sensitive information, encompassing customer data, supplier contracts, and logistical details. Moreover, organizations must engage closely with cloud service providers to guarantee compliance with relevant laws and standards, undertaking frequent audits and evaluations. Besides that, strong data governance policies are necessary to manage data lifecycle, integrity, and ownership. Security and compliance in cloud-based predictive analytics are essential for sustainable and effective supply chain operations. Organizations must adopt a proactive strategy by establishing optimal data security policies, complying with legislation, minimizing vendor risks, and safeguarding AI models. By addressing these issues, firms may fully leverage predictive analytics while protecting sensitive information and preserving confidence within their supply chain ecosystems.

Insights and Visualization

Insights and visualization play a vital role in translating complicated predictive analytics data into usable insight for supply chain decision-makers. This stage involves converting raw data and predictive model outputs into actionable insights displayed via user-friendly dashboards and visualization tools. These insights assist stakeholders in making informed decisions, optimizing operations, and mitigating risks. Supply chains produce extensive datasets from sources such as IoT sensors, ERP systems, transportation logs, and inventory records. Analytical and visualization tools distill intricate facts into understandable formats, enabling decision-makers to recognize trends, patterns, and anomalies. Cloud-based platforms facilitate the real-time processing and display of data, enabling managers to monitor key performance indicators (KPIs) such as inventory levels, shipment delays, and demand changes. These real-time dashboards enable prompt corrective measures. In addition, predictive analytics frequently entails 'what-if' scenarios. Visualization tools allow supply chain managers to model different situations and comprehend their possible effects on logistics, procurement, and inventory management. Cloud-based predictive analytics platforms frequently incorporate robust visualization tools, such as Tableau, Power BI, or integrated dashboards offered by cloud service providers such as AWS, Google Cloud, and Microsoft Azure. These instruments provide insights via interactive dynamic dashboards, charts, and heatmaps. Key features include interactive dashboards, data storytelling, and collaborative tools. For supply chain management data-driven decisions to work as well as possible, the Insights and Visualization phase of cloud-based predictive analytics is a must. Utilizing appropriate technologies, firms can transcend just raw data analysis to attain operational excellence, agility, and resilience within their supply chains. As technology improves, there will be more focus on real-time, interactive, and AI-driven visualization. This will have an effect on the future of predictive supply chain analytics.

COLLABORATION AND WORKFLOW MANAGEMENT

Efficient cooperation and workflow management are crucial for the successful execution of cloud-based predictive analytics in supply chains. Essential practices encompass Enable seamless interaction and information sharing across teams; automating repetitive tasks enhances efficiency and reduces human error; encouraging collaboration between IT, analytics, and supply chain teams ensures alignment with business goals.

Common cloud platforms and tools (AWS, Google Cloud, Azure)

Cloud computing systems like Amazon Web Services (AWS), Microsoft Azure, and Google Cloud Platform (GCP) provide many services, including virtual machines, storage, databases, and serverless computing. Amazon Web Services (AWS), Google Cloud Platform (GCP), and Microsoft Azure are prominent cloud platforms that provide an extensive array of tools and services to assist enterprises in managing and extending their digital operations. AWS, the preeminent and most recognized platform, offers a comprehensive array of services, encompassing computing power, storage solutions, databases, AI/ML tools, and advanced analytics, rendering it appropriate for both startups and corporations. Google Cloud is distinguished for its proficiency in data analytics, machine learning, and AI services, featuring technologies such as BigQuery and TensorFlow, rendering it a favoured option for data-intensive tasks. Conversely, Microsoft Azure interacts effortlessly with Microsoft products such as Office 365 and Dynamics 365, providing hybrid cloud solutions, artificial intelligence capabilities, and enterprise-level support for enterprises deeply embedded in the Microsoft ecosystem. Each platform possesses distinct advantages, AWS excels in scalability, Google Cloud in artificial intelligence and data processing, and Azure in hybrid cloud capabilities, providing organizations with the choice to select the platform that aligns most effectively with their operational and strategic objectives. The platforms are evaluated according to criteria like cost, availability, security, and scalability. For instance, AWS is extensively utilized; yet, enterprises encounter difficulties in controlling cloud resources (Chauhan, 2020). Azure is investigating machine learning-oriented approaches to improve its platform functionalities (Bianchini et al., 2020). When choosing a cloud platform, enterprises must assess their particular needs and analyse the advantages of each provider (Chauhan, 2020). The selection of platform can profoundly influence an organization's IT architecture and operational efficacy. Organizations can utilize these platforms to expand their infrastructure, optimize performance, and enhance security. By leveraging the resources offered by these cloud platforms, enterprises can concentrate on innovation and expansion without the hassle of managing intricate systems independently.

Best practices for integrating predictive analytics into supply chain processes

To ensure accuracy, usefulness, and insights, adding predictive analytics to supply chain operations needs a well-thought-out plan. Organizations must commence by explicitly delineating their objectives, such as demand forecasting, inventory optimization, or risk management, and aligning these aims with overarching corporate plans. For making reliable prediction models, it's important to have clean, correct, and consistent data from both inside and outside sources, like past sales numbers, supplier performance indicators, and market trends. The cornerstone of predictive analytics is high-quality, dependable data. Inconsistent, incomplete, or obsolete data might result in erroneous forecasts and suboptimal decision-making. Predictive analytics depends on sophisticated technologies, such as machine learning algorithms, big data platforms, and cloud computing. Organizations ought to use scalable cloud-based solutions that provide flexibility, storage capacity, and processing capability for managing extensive datasets. Platforms like AWS, Google Cloud, and Microsoft Azure offer specific tools for predictive analytics, encompassing pre-built AI models and data visualization dashboards. Investing in these technologies enables firms to process real-time data, conduct sophisticated simulations, and produce actionable insights effectively. Moreover, utilizing sophisticated analytics tools and platforms capable of real-time data integration is essential for agile decision-making. Current supply chains function in dynamic settings, where instantaneous insights are crucial for prompt decision-making. When businesses combine predictive analytics with real-time data streams from IoT devices, RFID tags, and sensors, they can quickly spot problems and make changes. Moreover, automating standard supply chain procedures decreases manual involvement, mitigates errors, and improves operational efficiency. Furthermore, interdepartmental communication among supply chain, IT, and operations departments guarantees alignment and seamless execution. Finally, predictive analytics constitutes a continuous process rather than a singular application. Supply chain conditions, market dynamics, and external factors are always evolving, necessitating continual updates and adjustments to prediction models. Organizations must establish mechanisms to monitor, assess, and enhance analytics models over time to ensure their accuracy and usefulness. Organizations must constantly check, improve, and update predictive models to adapt to changing conditions and maintain their accuracy (Adewusi et al., 2024). Overall, incorporating predictive analytics into supply chain operations is essential for contemporary enterprises aiming to increase efficiency, save expenses, and boost responsiveness. Organizations can realize the full potential of predictive analytics by emphasizing data quality, implementing scalable technology, aligning analytics activities with business objectives, and promoting cross-functional collaboration. Ongoing surveillance, employee education, and a dedication to a data-centric culture further guarantee sustained performance. In a business world that is more uncertain and competitive, predictive analytics is an important tool for making smarter, faster, and more proactive decisions in the supply chain.

Real-World Use Cases of Cloud-Based Predictive Analytics in Supply Chains

Cloud-based predictive analytics has transformed supply chain management in many sectors such as retail, manufacturing, and logistics by facilitating data-driven decision-making and improving operational efficiency. In retail, predictive analytics enhances inventory management, minimizes stockouts, and accurately forecasts client demand. For instance, Walmart use cloud-based predictive analytics to examine extensive sales and logistical data, enhancing inventory management and guaranteeing product availability (Araf, 2024). In manufacturing, predictive analytics is essential for predictive maintenance, as it analyses machinery and equipment data in real-time to forecast possible problems, hence reducing downtime and maintenance expenses. General Electric (GE) employs predictive analytics in its industrial operations to enhance equipment reliability and maximize production efficiency. The deployment of AI-driven predictive maintenance solutions has led to a substantial decrease in unanticipated downtime. GE reports an approximate 30% decrease in unanticipated equipment failures and related downtime. This enhancement is ascribed to the prompt identification of possible problems and pre-emptive maintenance measures (Rao, 2024). In the same manner, Cloud-based predictive analytics in logistics is employed to enhance delivery routes, minimize fuel expenses, and accelerate delivery schedules. Companies such as DHL employ predictive analytics to anticipate cargo delays and adapt logistics operations accordingly (Soumpenioti et.al, 2023). These practical applications illustrate how cloud-based predictive analytics promotes agility, mitigates operational risks, and optimizes overall supply chain performance.

Figure 2. Adoption Rate and Benefits of AI-Driven Predictive Maintenance Across Industries (2020 2024), (Rao, 2024).

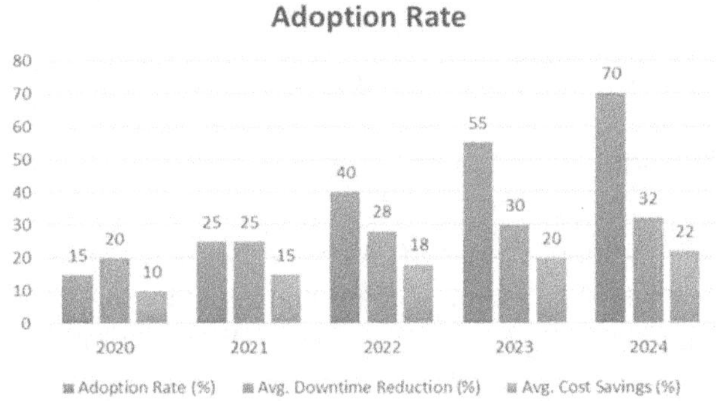

Cloud-Based Predictive Analytics Implementation Challenges in Supply Chain Management

The implementation of cloud-based predictive analytics in supply chain management offers significant benefits but also presents several challenges that organizations must address.

Data Security and Privacy Concerns

One of the primary challenges in implementing cloud-based predictive analytics is ensuring data security and privacy. As supply chain operations often involve sensitive information, companies must be cautious when storing and processing this data in cloud environments (Yenugula, Sahoo, et al., 2023).

Data Quality and Integration

The effectiveness of predictive analytics heavily depends on the quality and integration of data. In supply chain environments, gathering and integrating data from various sources can be challenging. Ensuring data quality and seamless integration is essential for accurate predictions and decision-making (Selvaraj & Lakshmanan, 2023).

Real-Time Decision-Making

Cloud-based predictive analytics systems in supply chain management often need to process and analyse data in real-time to provide actionable insights. Implementing systems capable of real-time decision-making can be technically challenging and resource intensive (Selvaraj & Lakshmanan, 2023).

Cost Considerations

While cloud-based solutions can offer cost benefits, implementing and maintaining predictive analytics systems in supply chain management may involve significant expenses. Organizations need to carefully consider the cost implications of adopting these technologies.

Technical Expertise

Implementing cloud-based predictive analytics requires specialized technical knowledge. Companies may face challenges in acquiring or developing the necessary expertise to effectively utilize these technologies in their supply chain operations (Oyewole et al., 2024).

Scalability and Performance

As supply chain operations grow and evolve, cloud-based predictive analytics systems must be able to scale accordingly. Ensuring consistent performance and reliability as data volumes and complexity increase can be challenging (Oyewole et al., 2024).

Despite these challenges, the potential benefits of cloud-based predictive analytics in supply chain management are significant. By addressing these implementation hurdles, organizations can leverage these technologies to enhance efficiency, improve decision-making, and optimize their supply chain operations.

DATA GOVERNANCE FRAMEWORKS

The integration of cloud computing and predictive analytics introduces complexities in data management, necessitating a structured approach to governance. Storing sensitive supply chain data, including customer information, supplier contracts, and financial records, in cloud environments raises significant security concerns. Organizations must ensure their cloud providers have strong security mechanisms to protect against cyber threats and unauthorized access. Beyond security, data privacy is a critical consideration, with a need for adherence to stringent compliance and data privacy regulations (Yenugula et al., 2023). The future of predictive analytics in supply chain management (SCM) hinges on establishing robust data governance frameworks to address these privacy and security concerns effectively. Practitioners are urged to prioritize data governance, and policymakers are encouraged to develop standards and regulations that foster innovation while ensuring the ethical use of predictive analytics (Adewusi et al., 2024).

Effective data governance frameworks in cloud-based predictive analytics for Supply Chain Management (SCM) are based on several key pillars. These include data quality, data security, data privacy, data ownership and control, and compliance and regulatory adherence. Data quality is crucial for accurate predictions and decision-making, while data security involves protecting data from unauthorized access, breaches, and cyber-attacks. Compliance with data privacy regulations like GDPR, CCPA, and HIPAA is non-negotiable, and data governance frameworks must incorporate policies and procedures to ensure compliance (Yenugula et al., 2023). Clear contractual agreements and service level agreements define data ownership, access rights, and control mechanisms.

Driving Supply Chain Sustainability through Cloud-Based Predictive Analytics

Cloud-based predictive analytics offers powerful capabilities to enhance the sustainability of supply chain operations across several key dimensions:

Optimized Resource Utilization

Predictive analytics can improve energy efficiency by forecasting energy demand throughout the supply chain, enabling businesses to integrate renewable energy sources, shift energy-intensive tasks to off-peak hours, and reduce energy waste. Cloud platforms provide scalable infrastructure for these models, enabling real-time adjustments. Predictive analytics also help in inventory management by minimizing overproduction and excess inventory, reducing waste from obsolete or spoiled goods, and reducing energy and resources consumed in warehousing, handling, and transporting unneeded products. Cloud-based supply chain management solutions streamline inventory processes. Predictive models can optimize delivery routes, select fuel-efficient transportation modes, and improve load consolidation, leading to substantial reductions in fuel consumption and greenhouse gas emissions. Real-time data processing capabilities of cloud platforms are crucial for dynamic route and load optimization (Yenugula, Sahoo, et al., 2023).

Waste Reduction and Emissions Control

Predictive analytics can significantly reduce material waste and spoilage of finished goods through improved demand forecasting and production planning. Cloud-hosted analytics can also prevent machinery failures, preventing material loss or environmental contamination. This leads to a smaller carbon footprint for the entire supply chain, as optimized energy usage, efficient transportation, and reduced waste result in a smaller carbon footprint. Cloud platforms facilitate comprehensive tracking and analysis of emissions across complex global networks, enabling targeted reduction efforts.

Enhanced Transparency and Support for Responsible Sourcing

Cloud-based platforms can significantly improve visibility into supply chain operations. This allows businesses to use predictive analytics to monitor and assess the sustainability practices of their suppliers, promoting responsible sourcing and helping to identify and mitigate environmental or social risks within their extended supply network.

The sustainability of cloud computing-based predictive analytics within the supply chain presents a dual-faceted scenario: while predictive analytics itself can drive significant sustainability improvements in supply chain operations, the underlying cloud infrastructure and the computational processes involved have their own environmental and resource implications that must be managed. Cloud-based predictive analytics offers substantial opportunities to make supply chains more sustainable across environmental, economic, and even social dimensions (Yenugula et al., 2023).

LESSONS LEARNED AND MEASURABLE IMPACTS ON EFFICIENCY AND PROFITABILITY

The implementation of cloud-based predictive analytics has imparted significant insights and quantifiable effects on operational efficiency and profitability for enterprises. One important lesson is how important it is to have good data and combine it with other data. Prediction models can't work well if the data isn't consistent or is kept separate. Moreover, enterprises have recognized that cross-functional collaboration among IT, data science, and operations teams is essential for optimizing the value of analytics programs. Advanced analytics technologies are successful only when individuals comprehend how to analyse findings and incorporate them into decision-making processes. Predictive analytics has markedly enhanced operational efficiency by improving resource allocation, reducing downtime, and streamlining supply chain procedures. Furthermore, cloud-based solutions provide flexibility and scalability, allowing businesses to manage substantial data volumes from many sources without considerable infrastructure expenditures. Finally Predictive analytics has empowered firms to recognize and mitigate possible risks, such as supplier disruptions or transportation delays, hence diminishing total supply chain vulnerabilities. Companies employing cloud-based predictive analytics estimate a decrease in operational costs of up to 30% and an enhancement in demand forecasting accuracy of 20%. Moreover, enhanced profitability frequently arises from superior inventory management, less waste, and heightened customer pleasure via individualized services and expedited response times. These quantifiable results indicate that cloud-based predictive analytics serves not simply as a technological investment but as a strategic driver for enduring corporate growth and resilience in competitive marketplaces. In summary, cloud-based predictive analytics has profoundly altered contemporary supply chain management. Organizations that prioritize high-quality data, foster cross-functional cooperation, and educate their staff to utilize analytical insights are experiencing notable enhancements in efficiency, cost reduction, and profitability. With the ongoing evolution of technology, predictive analytics will persist as a fundamental element of agile and resilient supply chains.

FUTURE TRENDS IN CLOUD-BASED ANALYTICS FOR SUPPLY CHAINS

Cloud-based analytics is becoming an essential trend in supply chain management (SCM), providing substantial benefits for enterprises. Businesses face many problems, but cloud computing makes it possible to solve them by providing real-time data analytics, collaborative platforms, and intelligent automation in supply chain management (Yenugula et al., 202`). The rising number of IoT devices and sensors in supply chain operations is driving the demand for real-time analytics. Cloud platforms will continue to improve so that they can collect and analyse huge amounts of real-time data. This will make it easier to make quick decisions and make changes to the supply chain that are more flexible. Moreover, data analytics is essential for enhancing supply chain processes, applicable in demand forecasting, product creation, logistics planning, and lean supply chain development. The incorporation of big data analytics and artificial intelligence in supply chain management is gaining significance, enabling firms to extract valuable insights from extensive data sets (Kuraishi, 2023). In the same manner, cloud-based supply chain management systems are swiftly advancing, enhancing the efficiency and efficacy of supply chain operations. Additionally, cloud-based analytics tools are increasingly collaborative, enabling various stakeholders, such as suppliers, manufacturers, and logistics providers, to securely share data. Improved integration features and collaborative dashboards are diminishing silos and promoting comprehensive visibility throughout the supply chain. Blockchain for Supply Chain Transparency is another future trend. Blockchain technology is being incorporated into cloud analytics platforms to improve traceability and transparency. This guarantees data integrity and offers an unalterable record of transactions, which is especially advantageous in sectors with rigorous regulatory mandates. Lastly, organizations employ cloud-based analytics to monitor carbon footprints, energy consumption, and resource optimization, as sustainability emerges as a paramount issue. Advanced analytical tools assist organizations in aligning their operations with sustainability objectives and adhering to environmental rules. Some problems still need to be fixed before cloud-based analytics can be fully used in supply chain management (Manideep Yenugula et al., 2023): data security, privacy issues; and the need for skilled professionals. The future of cloud-based analytics in supply chains is defined by more intelligent, expedited, and collaborative solutions. Companies that utilize these innovations will obtain a competitive advantage by improving efficiency, resilience, and sustainability throughout their supply chains. As technology advances, cloud analytics will persist as a fundamental element of contemporary supply chain tactics.

EMERGING TECHNOLOGIES: AI, MACHINE LEARNING, AND IOT IN PREDICTIVE ANALYTICS

When new technologies like Artificial Intelligence (AI), Machine Learning (ML), and the Internet of Things (IoT) are used, they make predictive analytics much more accurate, efficient, and scalable in many areas. AI makes predictive analytics easier by using complex algorithms that can handle huge amounts of data, find trends, and make accurate predictions. These algorithms are better than traditional statistical methods. AI systems may react dynamically to evolving data trends and provide real-time insights, enhancing decision-making processes. AI in predictive maintenance can foresee equipment breakdowns in manufacturing facilities, thereby minimizing downtime and repair expenses. Machine learning, a branch of AI, plays a crucial role in predictive analytics by automating data processing and improving prediction models. Machine learning algorithms derive insights from historical data and progressively enhance their predictions without direct programming intervention. Machine learning-driven predictive analytics frequently employs methods such as regression analysis, decision trees, and neural networks. The financial sector widely employs machine learning to forecast stock trends, evaluate credit risk, and identify fraudulent activity. A recent study underscores the revolutionary influence of emerging technology on predictive analytics across multiple domains. Artificial Intelligence (AI) and Machine Learning (ML) have transformed predictive modelling by improving accuracy and automating feature extraction (Sasmal, 2024). These technologies are extensively utilized in prediction, with random forests and support vector machines being prevalent methodologies. IoT devices provide vast quantities of real-time data from sensors, cameras, and various linked gadgets. In predictive analytics, IoT data functions as a crucial asset for comprehending operational trends and forecasting future occurrences. In the logistics industry, IoT sensors oversee fleet conditions and forecast repair requirements, facilitating prompt interventions and minimizing operational disruptions. The Internet of Things (IoT) is important for real-time data collection and early warning systems; however, obstacles like connectivity issues remain (Al-Rawas et al., 2024). The integration of AI, ML, and IoT establishes a solid foundation for predictive analytics. IoT devices gather and transmit real-time data; ML algorithms process and analyze this data to discern trends, and AI systems interpret the findings to produce actionable insights. This convergence in smart cities facilitates the prediction of traffic patterns, the optimization of energy use, and the enhancement of public safety. This amalgamation of AI, ML, and IoT offers novel business prospects but necessitates meticulous execution. However, for successful application across many industries, we must resolve issues pertaining to data quality and availability. Recent studies underscore substantial progress in supply chain optimization via artificial intelligence (AI) and other technologies. AI applications in demand forecasting, inventory management, and logistics optimization are improving efficiency, agility, and decision-making abilities (Joel et al., 2024). Machine learning, natural language processing, and robotics are fundamental AI technologies propelling these advancements. Supply Chain amalgamates artificial intelligence with the Internet of Things (IoT) and blockchain to facilitate real-time insights and automated decision-making. Notwithstanding these advancements, obstacles remain, such as data privacy issues, ethical dilemmas, and the necessity for proficient staff. Future research could look into how AI affects the long-term sustainability of supply chains, how to fix problems in closed-loop supply chains, and how to make technical and managerial aspects more aligned.

CONCLUSION

In conclusion, cloud-based analytics platforms give supply chain managers the tools they need to collect, analyse, and act on real-time data. This makes it easier to spot and respond to problems as soon as they happen. The implementation of cloud-based analytics can enhance supply chain resilience in multiple ways. The cloud-based infrastructure offers extensive computing capacity and storage, facilitating the processing and analysis of substantial data from various sources throughout the supply chain. Cloud-based predictive and prescriptive analytics are crucial tools for improving supply chain management efficiency and decision-making. Predictive analytics uses historical data and machine learning algorithms to forecast demand, anticipate disruptions, and optimize inventory levels. Prescriptive analytics provides data-driven insights and action plans for intricate scenarios. Cloud infrastructure allows real-time data sharing across geographically dispersed teams, ensuring quick responses to dynamic market conditions. Cloud platforms provide scalability and flexibility, enabling businesses to process large datasets efficiently without significant upfront investments. Both analytics approaches minimize operational costs by streamlining logistics, reducing maintenance downtime, and improving resource allocation. Predictive models identify potential risks, while prescriptive analytics suggest mitigation strategies. Real-time insights and prescriptive action plans enable supply chains to adapt quickly to market changes. The analytics tools optimize resource usage, reduce waste, and align with sustainability goals and regulatory requirements. Cloud-based analytics plays a crucial role in building a sustainable, responsive supply chain. By integrating data from multiple sources, such as suppliers, transportation, warehouses, and customers, it promotes real-time decision-making and improves transparency. This balances supply chain responsiveness with sustainability, reducing unnecessary resource consumption and aligning operations with environmental goals. Cloud-based analytics also optimizes resource allocation, highlighting areas for efficiency improvements. It also supports scalability and collaboration among stakeholders, facilitating seamless data sharing and promoting joint efforts to meet sustainability targets. Moreover, cloud-based analytics also enhances risk management by continuously monitoring disruptions and assessing their potential impact on the supply chain. It also makes it easier to use circular economy ideas in supply chains by keeping track of products' lifecycles and checking out whether reverse logistics for sending goods back into the chain is possible. In conclusion, cloud-based analytics is essential for building a sustainable and responsive supply chain, providing real-time visibility, predictive insights, and optimizing resource use. As organizations prioritize sustainability, the integration of cloud-based analytics will be essential for achieving long-term success.

REFERENCES

Adewusi, A. O., Komolafe, A. M., Ejairu, E., Aderotoye, I. A., Abiona, O. O., & Oyeniran, O. C. (2024). The role of predictive analytics in optimizing supply chain resilience: A review of techniques and case studies. *International Journal of Management & Entrepreneurship Research, 6*(3), 815–837. DOI: 10.51594/ijmer.v6i3.938

AKPINAR, M. T., HIZIROĞLU, K., & SEÇKİN CODAL, K. (2023). From Descriptive to Prescriptive Analytics: Turkish Airlines Case Study. *ADAM AKADEMİ Sosyal Bilimler Dergisi*. https://doi.org/DOI: 10.31679/adamakademi.1232332

Al-Rawas, G., Nikoo, M. R., Al-Wardy, M., & Etri, T. (2024). A critical review of emerging technologies for flash flood prediction: Examining artificial intelligence, machine learning, internet of things, cloud computing, and robotics techniques. *Water (Basel), 16*(14), 2069. DOI: 10.3390/w16142069

Araf, R. I. (2024). A Systematic Review of Data-Driven Insights in Retail: Transforming Consumer Behavior and Market Trend. *Innovatech Engineering Journal, 1*(01), 46–55. DOI: 10.70937/itej.v1i01.6

Benhamida, F. Z., Kaddouri, O., Ouhrouche, T., Benaichouche, M., Casado-Mansilla, D., & Lopez-de-Ipina, D. (2021). Demand Forecasting Tool For Inventory Control Smart Systems. *Journal of Communications Software and Systems, 17*(2), 185–196. DOI: 10.24138/jcomss-2021-0068

Bertsimas, D., Li, M. L., Paschalidis, I. Ch., & Wang, T. (2020). Prescriptive analytics for reducing 30-day hospital readmissions after general surgery. *PLoS One, 15*(9), e0238118. DOI: 10.1371/journal.pone.0238118 PMID: 32903282

Bianchini, R., Fontoura, M., Cortez, E., Bonde, A., Muzio, A., Constantin, A.-M., Moscibroda, T., Magalhaes, G., Bablani, G., & Russinovich, M. (2020). Toward ML-centric cloud platforms. *Communications of the ACM, 63*(2), 50–59. DOI: 10.1145/3364684

Brandt, T., Dlugosch, O., Abdelwahed, A., van den Berg, P. L., & Neumann, D. (2021). Prescriptive Analytics in Urban Policing Operations. *Manufacturing & Service Operations Management*. Advance online publication. DOI: 10.1287/msom.2021.1022

Chauhan, N., Agarwal, R., Garg, K., & Choudhury, T. (2020). Redundant Iaas Cloud Selection With Consideration Of Multi Criteria Decision Analysis. *Procedia Computer Science, 167*, 1325–1333. DOI: 10.1016/j.procs.2020.03.448

Dolgui, A., Ivanov, D., & Sokolov, B. (2020). Reconfigurable supply chain: The X-network. *International Journal of Production Research, 58*(13), 4138–4163. DOI: 10.1080/00207543.2020.1774679

Fraihat, M., Zowid, F., Ayasrah, F. T. M., Rababah, A., Ahmad, A. Y. A. B., & Othman, O. H. (2024). The impact of cloud computing on supply chain performance the mediating role of knowledge sharing in utilities and energy sectors. *Decision Science Letters, 13*(2), 377–390. DOI: 10.5267/j.dsl.2024.1.008

Gunasekaran, A., Kumar Tiwari, M., Dubey, R., & Fosso Wamba, S. (2016). Big data and predictive analytics applications in supply chain management. *Computers & Industrial Engineering, 101*, 525–527. DOI: 10.1016/j.cie.2016.10.020

Hashem, I. A. T., Yaqoob, I., Anuar, N. B., Mokhtar, S., Gani, A., & Ullah Khan, S. (2015). The Rise of "big Data" on Cloud computing: Review and Open Research Issues. *Information Systems, 47*(1), 98–115. DOI: 10.1016/j.is.2014.07.006

Joel, O. S., Oyewole, A. T., Odunaiya, O. G., & Soyombo, O. T. (2024). Leveraging artificial intelligence for enhanced supply chain optimization: A comprehensive review of current practices and future potentials. *International Journal of Management & Entrepreneurship Research, 6*(3), 707–721. DOI: 10.51594/ijmer.v6i3.882

Kırmızı, S. D., Ceylan, Z., & Bulkan, S. (2024). Enhancing Inventory Management through Safety-Stock Strategies—A Case Study. *Systems, 12*(7), 260. DOI: 10.3390/systems12070260

Kumar, P. (2024). Measuring the Broader Value Proposition of Digital Transformation in Supply Chains. *International Journal of Supply Chain Management, 13*(1), 16–24. DOI: 10.59160/ijscm.v13i1.6222

Kuraishi, Z. M. (2023). Role of Analytics in Supply Chain Management Industry in Lithuania. *Big Data Analytics & AI., 2*(4), 44–53. DOI: 10.55938/ijgasr.v2i4.65

Oyewole, A. T., Okoye, C. C., Ofodile, O. C., & Ejairu, E. (2024). Reviewing predictive analytics in supply chain management: Applications and benefits. *World Journal of Advanced Research and Reviews, 21*(3), 568–574. DOI: 10.30574/wjarr.2024.21.3.0673

POLO NAVARRO, L., SARASA RUBIO, M., CIPRES BAGÜESTE, D., & ESCUIN FINOL, D. (2022). MULTI-COUNTRY DEMAND FORECASTING FOR A COMPANY IN THE CONSTRUCTION SECTOR, BASED ON EXTERNAL MACROECONOMIC VARIABLES EXTRACTED FROM OPEN DATA SOURCES. *DYNA MANAGEMENT, 10*(1), [12 pp.]-[12 pp.]. https://doi.org/DOI: 10.6036/MN10356

Puica, E. (2023). Predictive Analytics Functionalities in Supply Chain Management. *Predictive Analytics Functionalities in Supply Chain Management.*, *17*(1), 986–996. DOI: 10.2478/picbe-2023-0090

Quiñones-Rivera, H., Rubiano-Ovalle, O., & Alfonso-Morales, W. (2023). Demand forecasting using a hybrid model based on artificial neural networks: A study case on electrical products. *Journal of Industrial Engineering and Management*, *16*(2), 363–381. DOI: 10.3926/jiem.3928

Rao, V. K. (2024). AI-DRIVEN CLOUD STORAGE SYSTEMS FOR PREDICTIVE MAINTENANCE IN MANUFACTURING. [IJRCAIT]. *INTERNATIONAL JOURNAL OF RESEARCH IN COMPUTER APPLICATIONS AND INFORMATION TECHNOLOGY*, *7*(2), 280–289.

Sanci, E., Daskin, M. S., Hong, Y.-C., Roesch, S., & Zhang, D. (2021). Mitigation strategies against supply disruption risk: A case study at the Ford Motor Company. *International Journal of Production Research*, *60*(19), 1–21. DOI: 10.1080/00207543.2021.1975058

Sasmal, B., Das, G., Mallick, P., Dey, S., Ghorai, S., Jana, S., & Jana, C. (2024). Advancements and challenges in agriculture: A comprehensive review of machine learning and IoT applications in vertical farming and controlled environment agriculture. *Big Data and Computing Visions*, *4*(2), 67–94.

Selvaraj, K., & Lakshmanan, L. (2023). The Machine learning for predictive maintenance in supply chain management. *Journal of Artificial Intelligence and Machine Learning*, *1*(1), 9–15. DOI: 10.55124/JAIM.V1I1.233

Seyedan, M., & Mafakheri, F. (2020). Predictive Big Data Analytics for Supply Chain Demand forecasting: methods, applications, and Research Opportunities. *Journal of Big Data*, *7*(1), 1–22. Springeropen. https://doi.org/DOI: 10.1186/s40537-020-00329-2

Sherwin, M. D., Medal, H. R., MacKenzie, C. A., & Brown, K. J. (2019). Identifying and mitigating supply chain risks using fault tree optimization. *IISE Transactions*, •••, 1–19. DOI: 10.1080/24725854.2019.1630865

Sinha Roy, D., Behera, R. K., Reddy, K. H. K., & Buyya, R. (2019). A Context-Aware Fog Enabled Scheme for Real-Time Cross-Vertical IoT Applications. *IEEE Internet of Things Journal*, *6*(2), 2400–2412. DOI: 10.1109/JIOT.2018.2869323

Sivarajah, U., Kamal, M. M., Irani, Z., & Weerakkody, V. (2017). Critical analysis of big data challenges and analytical methods. *Journal of Business Research*, *70*(1), 263–286. https://www.sciencedirect.com/science/article/pii/S014829631630488X. DOI: 10.1016/j.jbusres.2016.08.001

Soumpenioti, V., & Panagopoulos, A. (2023). *AI Technology in the Field of Logistics*. https://doi.org/DOI: 10.1109/SMAP59435.2023.10255203

Wang, Y.. (2020). Adoption of cloud-based technologies in supply chain management. *The Journal of Supply Chain Management*.

Yenugula, M., Goswami, S. S., Kaliappan, S., Saravanakumar, R., Alasiry, A., Marzougui, M., AlMohimeed, A., & Elaraby, A. (2023). Analyzing the Critical Parameters for Implementing Sustainable AI Cloud System in an IT Industry Using AHP-ISM-MICMAC Integrated Hybrid MCDM Model. *Mathematics*, *11*(15), 3367. DOI: 10.3390/math11153367

Yenugula, M., Sahoo, S. K., & Goswami, S. S. (2023). Cloud computing in supply chain management: Exploring the relationship. *Management Science Letters*, *13*(3), 193–210. DOI: 10.5267/j.msl.2023.4.003

Chapter 15

Unbundling Cloud Computing and Emergent Technologies: Construction Industry in Perspective

Sururah Apinke Bello
https://orcid.org/0000-0002-2689-9953
Obafemi Awolowo University, Nigeria

Mistura Laide Sanni
https://orcid.org/0000-0001-9206-4009
Obafemi Awolowo University, Nigeria

Lukumon Oyedele
University of the West of England, UK

Khadeejah Adebisi Abdulsalam
University of Lagos, Nigeria

Akinropo Musiliu Olajumoke
https://orcid.org/0000-0002-4571-1864
Obafemi Awolowo University, Nigeria

ABSTRACT

The construction industry, an important sector of the global economy, with large data generation and huge employment opportunities, requires automation for enhanced productivity and contribution to the Gross Domestic Products (GDP). The integration of Cloud Computing (CC) with Building Information Modelling (BIM),

DOI: 10.4018/979-8-3693-9984-2.ch015

however cannot deliver the future construction, hence, the need to explore the other specialised Emergent Technologies (ET). In this chapter, critical appraisal of existing literature to identify the application domain, problem areas and intersections between CC and ET were carried out. Case studies were cited to demonstrate the benefits of the adoption of CC and ET such as, BIM, Internet of Things (IoT) and Intelligent Analytics. The reluctance of this industry was also identified and some suggestions were proffered to mitigate the potential risks. However, the adoption is believed to have the potential to open up issues. Hence, the adoption is conjectured to be viewed as an asset.

1.0 INTRODUCTION

The construction industry contributes substantially to the world economy with its high volume of job opportunities. However, it is the second least digitised industry after Agriculture (Alaloul et al., 2022). This has made it difficult for the professionals in the industry to leverage on the versatility of computer application in the planning, materials acquisition and execution of projects. The industry with its low-profit margin desperately needs to improve on its efficiency and productivity for higher contribution to the Gross Domestic Products (GDP) of global economy (Blanco et al., 2016). In order to tackle this productivity problem, construction policy formulators have suggested the adoption of emerging technologies in the construction industry (Khahro et al., 2021). Since the construction industry has been adjudged by the (World Economic Forum [WEF], 2016) to account for approximately 13% of the global GDP, its transformation would be a significant developmental catalyst for enhanced productivity (Karim et al., 2023). It is conjectured that the adoption of such emerging technologies will turn around the construction processes (Uusitalo et al., 2024). This is particularly important to project managers who need to schedule the supply of materials, and manage the proper site layout. It should be noted that an ideal site layout will consider and integrate the functionality of site access, fencing, storage area, offices and accommodation; temporary services and plants. A typical construction site is shown in Figure 1.

Figure 1. Typical construction site layout

(Source:https://www.pobinc.com/wp-content/uploads/2017/08/POB_Site_Construction_Layout-Overview .jpg https://www.northatlanticconcrete.com/wp-content/uploads/2020/07/0005-essex-may-30-2020-1030x579.jpg)

The findings by (Sawhney et al., 2020; Hwang et al., 2022) have shown that cloud computing has become the delivery anchor for innovative and emergent technologies such as Building Information Modelling (BIM), 3D Concrete Printing, Internet of Things (IoT), Augmented Reality, Artificial Intelligence, Wearable Technology, Unmanned Vehicles or Robots, Radio Frequency Identification (RFID), Intelligent Analytics and Blockchain technology among others. To this end, embracing this pervasive digital revolution in the construction industry is a welcome development. However, the adoption of these emergent technologies will open up challenges/issues in the design, implementation, deployment and use of the projects.

Emergence of power tools has eliminated drilling of holes by hand, likewise heavy equipment substituted for laborious digging of trenches by shovels and elevators have made construction of many multi-storey buildings a possibility. The use of robots has also made it possible to mine precious stones at several kilometers below the ground level.

Emergent technologies are disruptive in nature as their essence requires a change in the original way and manner that businesses were conducted. Japanese construction industries are successful due to their technological superiority, whereas many of the third world countries are still lagging behind (Mutoh et al., 2020). The upsurge of various digital data generating devices in the construction industry has resulted in the availability of massive data, requiring real-time and secured access to these voluminous data for integration and decision making by the stakeholders. Optimising such voluminous, rapidly changing construction data requires latest computing technology for storage, processing and analysis for simulations and accurate predictions. Also, Zahoor et al. (2022) and Nawaz et al. (2012) observed that efficiency is further needed for construction management's schedule of work, cost negotiations and Request for Information. Furthermore, there is the need to share updated meaningful information for construction schedule and monitoring

(Kamat et al., 2011), to allow for collaboration. Thus, a platform is required, that could present a shared environment for data without duplication.

Cloud computing technology provides such shared computing facilities over the network, it is an emerging computing model that has revolutionized IT infrastructures by offering subscription-based computing service. Cloud computing is characterised with massive storage, high computing facilities with high speed, all available on a pay per use model, thereby eliminating upfront investment cost. However, there are attempts at justifying the need for the integration of cloud computing and BIM in construction, as opposed to file-based BIM for improved construction activities. This is because, cloud computing on its own cannot deliver the future construction. Hence, there is the need to further explore the application of cloud computing with BIM and other specialised technologies for optimised construction activities.

Thus, this study brings into forefront how BIM and cloud computing are being used together with other emergent technologies in the construction industries as well as consideration of possible future trend/implications for the industry. The study specifically pursues the following objectives:

(i) Explore the interception of cloud computing, emerging technologies and how they have influenced the construction industry.
(ii) Demonstrate/showcase some important application domains of cloud computing and other emerging technologies in the construction processes.
(iii) Understand how cloud computing has influenced the use of emerging technologies in the construction industry.
(iv) Develop an implementation framework for streamlining the adoption of cloud computing and emerging technologies for operational edge.
(v) Consideration of possible future trend/implications of this combination for the construction industry.

Thus, critical appraisal of existing literature to identify the application domain, problem areas and intersections between Cloud Computing (CC) and Emergent Technologies (ET) in the Construction Industry were carried out. Furthermore, case studies were employed to demonstrate the benefits of adopting CC and ET for competitive advantage and operational edge including challenges of its adoption. This study brings into forefront how BIM with the CC have been used together with other ET in the construction industries to achieve enhanced productivity. The study also demonstrates some application domain of CC and other ET in the construction industry. Additionally, it develops an implementation framework for streamlining the adoption of CC and ET for operational edge in the construction industry based on systematic and selection strategies.

2.0 OVERVIEW OF CLOUD COMPUTING

Cloud computing is an advanced technology where software and hardware are delivered as a platform for collaborative service through the Internet (Chong et al., 2014). According to the National Institute of Standards and Technology (NIST, 2011), "Cloud computing is a model for enabling convenient, on-demand network access to a shared pool of configurable computing resources (networks, servers, storage, applications, and services) that can be rapidly provisioned and released with minimal management effort or service provider interaction". It's categorised into Infrastructure as a Service, Platform as a Service and Software as a Service.

Infrastructure-as-a-Service (IaaS) is a service where the hardware is hosted by the service provider and the customer only pays for the use of the hardware (Zhang and Issa, 2012). The hardware infrastructure provided can be servers for storage or computing capability or network infrastructure. The provider presented the hardware, while the user configures it for appropriate use. Platform-as-a-Service (PaaS) provides a hardware and certain amount of application software to the user, e.g. for example, some PaaS services are Azure, GAE Bhardwaj et al. (2010). Then, the Software-as-a-Service (SaaS) model, enables users to access and use software provided as service by the cloud provider. It is the simplest cloud service as the users do not have to manage or control the cloud infrastructure or the operating systems. Example of SaaS are Office360, CRM, etc.

Generally, there is high level of global awareness on the use of cloud computing (Oke et al., 2021). The study used Relative Importance Index (RII) to show the most significant cloud computing with consideration to four Critical Success Factors (CSFs) of data storage, efficiency, usability and availability. The RII was determined by the use of Equation (1).

$$RII = \frac{\sum W}{A \times N} \tag{1}$$

Where, W = participant's weighting; A = largest value and N = number of respondents

3.0 CLOUD COMPUTING: ANNEXING THE CONTINGENCIES IN THE CONSTRUCTION INDUSTRY

The construction processes in the preliminary specifications and onsite activities may also benefit from deployment of ICT infrastructure with integration of cloud computing and including other positive technology disruption of emerging technologies that will boost the overall productivity. However, possible improvements accruing from such deployment include:

3.1 Economy Benefit/Massive Economy of Scale

Cost is a significant barrier in the adoption of IT solutions by construction companies because of its inherent low-profit margin resulting from prolonged completion period of the infrastructure. Whereas Cloud computing provides scalable computing services on a flexible pay per use model, the construction industry has not taken advantages of many of its benefits for enhanced productivity (Everett and Slocum, 1994). Cloud computing eliminates the upfront cost of owning computers infrastructure, installation cost, licensing cost including maintenance cost for IT professionals. Only consumed services will attract payment thus, reducing the total cost of a building project (Glover, 2018; Hay et al., 2011; Chen and Man, 2018).

3.2 Collaboration

The construction industry is made up of diverse professionals that are required to constantly pool resources and ideas together for successful delivery of a project. Hence, different data are generated continuously at every stage of a project life cycle. Accessibility to real-time construction information will enable collaboration, flexibility in design, otherwise, poor on-site coordination, planning and scheduling may result, with even dispute, project delivery delay, cost variation and eventual reduced Return on Investment (ROI) (Li et al., 2015; Yu et al., 2013). It should be noted that cloud computing is capable of providing an interoperable process for construction industry's application in a single repository platform (Hay et al., 2011). Cloud computing provides ubiquitous access to construction data that enables seamless connection of all stakeholders, thereby facilitating interaction in the construction team leading to an improved efficiency on the design and the construction (Du et al., 2016).

3.3 Secured Platform

The conventional practise of securing data within the construction industry gives rise to the fear of data breach due to exposure, as construction company's procedures on in-house data security are not robust enough to combat the current trend in cyber threats. Moreover, implementation of standard policies and procedures required to protect data from being breached may be too expensive for the construction industry all alone. Furthermore, implementing standard security measures on construction data in this premise, constitutes a diversion from the core construction operations.

Though, cloud storage service implements standard security practice that requires up-to-date security software, appropriate schemes for routine security check and certified data security employees need to be put in place.

3.4 Massive Storage

It is noted that the use of innovative technologies for construction activities generates voluminous data. Storing such data on site has been a problem as a result of the volume and the required hardware infrastructure for such on-site storage. With cloud storage, data can be easily saved and retrieved as at when needed. Even beyond convenience, the opportunity of restoring corrupted or loss data abound in the cloud, as loss of data could be a nightmare to construction industry procedures and activities.

3.5 Scalable IT Services

Cloud computing allows construction company to purchase its IT capabilities as services dictated with the specific requirements at that particular time. A short-term need for a higher capacity infrastructure that ties down huge capitals on computing facilities is no more fashionable. The unexpected high demand might not even give enough time for an infrastructure purchase and installation. With cloud computing technology, computing provision can be instantly increased or reduced depending on the actual need with ease. Thus, allowing Small and Medium Enterprises (SMEs) in the construction industry to be on the same level playing-field with the larger companies without tying down precious resources. Possibility of this method has been exhibited by the Chilean construction industry that utilises the cloud computing platform for knowledge management issues (Jiao et al., 2013).

4.0 BIM-CLOUD AND EMERGENT TECHNOLOGIES IN CONSTRUCTION INDUSTRY

Cloud computing has become the deployment baseline technique for the emergent technologies such as, Building Information Modelling (BIM), Internet of Things (IoT), Artificial Intelligence (AI) and other related software (Holt, 2015). This section describes cloud computing in combination with some of the emergent technologies described in the Hyper Cycle of Gartner group in 2017. However, these application areas are not yet exhaustive.

4.1 The BIM-Cloud Computing for Construction Industry

BIM is a modelling tool that produces a 5D design which includes time and cost projections in addition to the detailed 3D visualisations. In practice, BIM is meant to contain specialized documentations on architecture, landscape, construction and installation designs; scheduling, bills of quantities and cost estimates. Regrettably, BIM originally is not accessible in real-time, as traditional BIM is a standalone system, hence not widely adopted (Azhar, 2011). Cloud computing has been identified by Ghaffarianhoseini et al. (2017) as a key enabling technology for BIM to be accessed for collaboration. However, sharing BIM visualisations is not possible in its primary exchange format, unless it is extended with XML (Redmond et al., 2012; Jiao et al., 2014). Also, other that frameworks like cloud services have been developed such as SOA4BIM, Simplified Markup Language - SML, Open BIM, and Construction Business Social Network Service – CBSNS. These frameworks enable universal access to BIM paradigm, representation and exchange of partial geometric information; interoperability; dynamic splitting and merging of BIM information to capture social interaction (Jardim-Goncalves and Grilo, 2010, Redmond and Smith, 2011; Juan, 2013; Kuo et al., 2014; Merschbrock and Munkvold, 2015; Das et al., 2015; Jiao et al., 2012).

The concept of BIM is being expanded to infrastructure, building environment and sustainable cities, but the extremely complex workflows and big data management will require the cloud computing environment (Li et al., 2018). BIM-Cloud visualization model is able to store data through IFC using Apache Cassandra, hosted on Amazon EC2 in order to coordinate site activities; and as such translating it to software-as-a-service (SaaS) model with a web application (Getuli et al., 2016; Chuang et al., 2011). This allowed users to operate the 3D BIM models through the web without the limitations of time or distance; the SaaS on private cloud permits BIM over multiple servers via standard browser (Chen et al., 2016). Although there could be fragmentation and interoperability issues in the existing BIM usage, however, Cloud-BIM platform manages construction information for the realisation of green construction in China (Li and Ma, 2016).

Currently, BIM research with cloud computing is still a hot research area (Chen and Man, 2018), there is no doubt that unravelling the full potentials of traditional BIM requires its integration with cloud computing technology.

4.2 BIM-Cloud and IoT in Construction Industry

IoT in construction industry employs sensors to continuously gather data from the environment, which are then analysed for informed decision making and safety management at a reasonable cost (Fang et al., 2016; Sarkar et al., 2022). Atzori et al. (2010) has identified IoT in smart buildings as one of the domains for continuous improvement to human life. Meanwhile, complete IoT adoption in construction industry cannot be achieved without cloud computing, especially for real-time data storage and analysis, management system framework and IoT operations (Rui and Danpeng, 2015). IoT integration with big data analytics using Cloudera Hadoop Distributed Files System could control decisions for monitoring of environmental building data (Bashir and Gill (2016). On the other hand, a low-cost PaaS - based material tracking system with RFID solution monitors the workflow in materials management from factory to site (Ko et al., 2016; Fang et al., 2016).

Furthermore, integration of IoT with IaaS and SaaS solutions was to intelligently control energy in a building and share management services through the pay-per use mode among the companies involved in prefabricated construction (Khajenasiri et al., 2017; Jia et al., 2019; Xu et al., 2018; Wang et al., 2020). The integration of IoT with cloud storage for traceability in real-time was used to supervise on-site assembly processes; and for building's control system (Li et al.,2018; Wang et al., 2017). The case for Edge-IoT was presented for energy efficiency in public buildings (Sittón-Candanedo et al., 2019), real-time monitoring of early age of concrete (John et al., 2020), and smart industrial Internet of things (IIoT) designs based on unmanned aerial vehicle (Salhaoui et al., 2019). The integration of BIM, IoT and Cloud Computing was also exploited for price optimization platform and fabricated construction (Meerja et al., 2019; Hossein et al., 2020).

Generally, the use of BIM, IoT and cloud computing to process huge construction data in a building lifecycle is aimed at optimising decision making process in construction (Garyaev and Rybakova, 2018).

4.3 BIM-Cloud Computing Cybersecurity and Blockchain in Construction Industry

Construction industry is now managing vast amount of critical service data and information which predisposes the industry to a wide range of new-found threats and attack surfaces in the cyber space. In addition to holding valuable personal data of employees and payment details, intellectual property can also be of interest to the cyber criminals. A cyberattack on the design and detailing files for a bridge construction could cause devastating effects on its load carrying capacity, which may lead to its collapse, loss of lives and properties (Hay et al., 2011). Cyberattack relies on stealth and surprise to disrupt, destroy and steal, while, predictive security in the cloud operates in a counterintelligence fashion.

It should be noted that BIM, mobile Cloud, IoT, and Blockchain technologies were also deployed for handling security of construction information (Zheng et al., 2019). Blockchain technologies have found significant application in BIM and construction management mainly in the operations of built assets given the attendant resources and economic impact of the operation phase of construction (Li et al., 2018). These innovative next generation security approaches are capable of enhancing cloud computing to provide outstanding security against cyber-attacks on construction data. Blockchain technology with big data provided a point-to-point communication platform for smart city data on a trusted data sharing and information security platform (Ma and Yang, 2021). There is a have been cases of integration of BIM, mobile Cloud, IoT and Blockchain technologies for security of construction information with a 30% reduction in record keeping error rate, 17% reduction in casting cycle time and 50% reduction in transportation time (Zheng et al., 2019; Sarkar et al., 2022). These results showed that BIM, construction management, remote usage monitoring, equipment services and repair, construction tools and equipment tracking are areas where IoT is mostly being applied in the industry for now.

4.4 BIM-Cloud Computing and Immersive Technologies

Cloud computing technology has been identified by Chi et al. (2013) as one of the four pillars for wide adoption of Augmented Reality (AR) in the construction industry. Pan and Isnaeni (2024) proposed integration of BIM-Cloud with AR with a view to improving efficiency in the construction industry's operations while enhancing the management of data life cycle. Virtual Reality (VR) implemented in a SaaS cloud-based networking had been deployed for a shared immersive virtual experience during project communication (Du et al., 2016). Chu et al. (2018) integrated the AR in a cloud storage platform for retrieval and extraction of intensive construction information, with increased efficiency of 50%. Li et al. (2018) employed VR for visibility in real-time with cloud storage for efficient supervision of prefabricated construction. Energy efficient VR system was proposed for construction safety education and the development of intelligent environment for smart cities (Pham et al., 2018; Shirowzhan et al., 2020). Figure 2 illustrates a typical application of AR in the construction industry. AR can provide step-by-step guidance to workers during construction, showing where to place components through virtual cues or real-time instructions. Construction workers can follow instructions overlaid in their physical environment, thereby reducing errors and improving overall worksite efficiency.

Figure 2. Application of AR in Construction

4.5 BIM-Cloud Computing and Mobile Technologies in Construction Industry

The mobile devices user market has grown to become an important part of emergent technologies. Cloud and mobile service providers have collaborated to deploy applications in construction industry (Prasad et al., 2012). This enables most of the processing and data storage associated with the mobile BIM models' applications to be moved off the mobile devices to cloud computing platforms. The centralized applications are then accessed over the mobile Internet, thereby reducing the development and running time of mobile applications (Ferrada et al., 2016).

4.6 BIM-Cloud, Artificial Intelligence, and Robotics in Construction Industry

AI and robotics utilization in handling unhealthy and laborious risky construction tasks are projected to minimize incidences of hazards; save time and cost for workforce effectiveness, maximise output and quality. It has been discovered that the industry is presently at technology adoption stage, however, cases of risk inspection in overhead vantage points monitored by drones, robot masons for laying blocks, while a 6-axis robot arm is engaged for high precision block laying even at a millimeter accuracy (Avani and Bhavana, 2022; Faheem et al., 2024; Dörfler et al., 2016; Goessens et al., 2018). Additionally, many authors have equally reported successful use of robots in wall painting (Jayaraj and Divakar, 2018), concrete spraying (Więckowski, 2017), site inspection (Asadi et al., 2018; Rakha and Gorodetsky, 2018) and even demolition (Kasperzyk et al., 2017; Follini et al., 2020). The common metrics used in these specific construction scenarios include time, costs, productivity, quality, and safety of technology-augmented job sites to control groups (Faheem et al., 2024).

AI technologies have powered state-of-art intelligent decision-making processes in enhancing the capacity of professionals in the construction industry for analysis of very elaborate and complex datasets in order to obtain patterns from structured and unstructured data (Bhuiyan and Hammad, 2023; Waqar, 2024). Ars (2025) analysed the impact of project profitability risks using a deep learning model-based input metrics such as delay, financing and accident costs. The results showed that these factors are crucial in arriving at such informed decisions. Additionally, deep learning technique has been reported to be efficient in the determination of appropriate cement-water ratio for concrete mix in the construction process (Bello et al, 2020).

Cloud robotics and automation systems relies on either data or code from a network to support its operation with improved performance especially with access to global libraries, massive-parallel computation, collective robot learning and on-demand human guidance (Kehoe et al., 2015; Goldberg and Kehoe, 2013). Cloud computing has the capability to speed up many computationally intensive robotics and automation application systems (Riazuelo et al., 2014). Another central issue in robotics and automation is the uncertainty in sensing, modeling and control (Glover et al., 2009), which were solved by using cloud computing (Kehoe et al., 2012a; Kehoe et al., 2012b; Kehoe et al., 2015; Wong, et al., 2018). Integrating BIM for digital models with robotic construction for synchronous adjustment was developed in the works of (Kochovski and Stankovski, 2021). In another dimension, interacting with BIM using traditional interface of keyboard and touch screen is not convenient for construction worker on site (Azhar, 2011), thus, voice interfaced with BIM scenarios were developed including conversational AI (Akinade et al., 2017; Chui and Francisco, 2017; Li et al., 2014; Saka et al., 2024).

Despite these identified potential advantages of AI and robots in construction, the level of adoption of these two systems is still very low (Delgado et al., 2019; Bogue, 2018). Robotics and AI tools could facilitate better approaches in carrying out construction processes and even enabling redesigning of workflow to achieve disruptive digital services ranging from building material fabrication; real-time management; optimization of energy consumption; to scheduled maintenance.

4.7 BIM-Cloud Computing and Big Data Analytics in Construction Industry

The fast advancing technologies are chunking out incredible amount of data throughout the life cycle of a facility. BIM-captured 5D information is geometrically encoded, compute-intensive, compressed, with diverse proprietary formats (Jiao et al., 2014). Analytics is the art of establishing a useful pattern in data regarding the specified emphasis. The indispensable use of cloud platform for storage of construction data and its analytics were exhibited in the works of Alaka et al. (2018) to predict failure of construction business. While the technology is used to simulate energy performance of a building, and for rapid decision making on construction safety (Mansouri and Akhavian, 2018). The integration of IoT, Big Data and Cloud Computing was proposed to achieve automatic control, intelligence services for people and logistics in smart cities; manipulation of mass construction data and historical data (Li et al., 2015; Qian et al., 2021; Chen et al., 2016; Lei et al., 2020; Xiong and Ye, 2019).

4.8 BIM Cloud and Digital Twin in Construction Industry

The concept of digital twin technology involves the generation of virtual model from its physical twin with seamless transmission of feedbacks in real-time (Madubuike et al., 2022; Attaran and Celik, 2023). The ongoing transformation in the construction industry is a drive towards innovation where technology is employed to improve the competitiveness with digitization. However, digital twin technology application and adoption even in an important facet of construction cost management is still insignificant in Malaysia (Haron and Zafir, 2025). Moreover, simulation and visualization obtainable from the BIM component, could be exploited to address safety in the construction premises with the integration AI and other high-end devices. Furthermore, in digital twin for construction education, Wahbeh et al. (2020) reported the establishment of a bi-directional data exchange system between physical building components and their virtual BIM counterparts. This has enabled life-cycle information to be tracked, monitored and managed (Xing et al., 2020). Thus, leading to a decreased consumption of material resources, reduced generation of waste and a more sophisticated way of managing building assets. BIM and robots are employed to overcome the problem of unstructured and unstable site environment which usually obstruct the use of robots at construction sites (Follini et al. 2020). The instant feedback/real-time monitoring could be exploited for efficient management of construction processes including informed decision making, which are not obtainable in standalone BIM data. Although awareness issues, indecisiveness and cost concerns mar the adoption of digital twin especially in BIM-cloud (Haron and Zafir, 2025). Opoku et al. (2023) further classified the barriers that are challenging the fuller adoption of Digital Twin in the construction industry into four: Stakeholder-Oriented, Industry-Related, Construction-Enterprise-Related and Technology-Related Barriers.

5.0 CASE STUDIES OF BIM-CLOUD APPLICATIONS IN CONSTRUCTION

This section illustrates the use of BIM-Cloud in construction for collaboration, materials selection and enhanced design process as presented in Figures 3, 4 and 5. It also provides the cost benefit analysis of cloud-based system and On-Premise system.

5.1 BIM-Cloud Case Studies

(a) **Cloud-BIM for collaboration:** Figure 3 shows a typical case study of using BIM-Cloud for the expansion of Terminal 2 at the Helsinki Airport with several improvements. The 3D models were effectively utilised for visualization throughout the project stages resulting in better decision making. BIM was specifically used for collaboration among the vast project team.

Figure 3. Cloud-BIM for collaboration

Source https://www.novatr.com/blog/example-of-bim-projects-globally#11

(b) **Cloud-BIM for enhanced architectural design process**: In the Casa Piedra Blanca project in Figure 4, BIM was employed to integrate the project reports and Gantt charts into the architecture drawings. This provided the team with a clearer understanding of the physical reality of the project right from the design stage. Thereby eliminating uncertainties associated with construction projects.

Figure 4. Cloud-BIM for enhanced architectural design process

Source https://www.novatr.com/blog/example-of-bim-projects-globally#11

(c) **Cloud-BIM for insulation material selection:** In Figure 5, BIM was employed to evaluate the capacity of possible insulation material to be used for the renovation of the Silver Oak Winery after a fire outbreak. BIM compared the thermal and dimensional aspects of denim, fiber glass and foam and the team decided to use the recycled Levi's jeans afterwards. BIM 360 was further employed in cross-checking of the construction documentation against the model design.

Figure 5. Cloud-BIM for insulation material selection

Source https://www.novatr.com/blog/example-of-bim-projects-globally#11

5.2 Cost Benefit Analysis of BIM-Cloud in Construction

The Total Cost of Ownership (TCO) for maintaining on-premise infrastructure for construction software incorporates both the direct and indirect costs. Direct cost includes Capital Costs (CC) and Operational Costs (OC). CC encompasses software licensing, network infrastructure, storage environment, server and back-up systems installation. While OC cover support for servers and backup systems, storage warranty, data centre facilities, system administration, labour costs and IT staff training and retraining. In addition, for every dollar spent on infrastructure upgrade, an approximate $2 should be budgeted for managing and securing the extended infrastructure (Deochake 2023). On the other hand, indirect costs refer to loss due to unplanned server downtime, customer trust and reputation damage as a result of service disruption. However, cloud cost basically includes the cost of computer, network and storage facilities. Cloud users pay according to the consumption and duration patterns for the instances. This no doubt eliminates upfront cost and costs incurred during service downtime which cannot be estimated. Table 1 gives the basic items that constitute the cost of on-premise and cloud-based solutions for construction industry. The flexible pricing in cloud-based services enable construction company to calculate the IT utility cost and forecast IT budget using a usage history for proper project costing. Hence making the choice of cloud-based BIM services cost effective for construction companies.

Table 1. Constituents of On-Premise and Cloud-Based Solution Costs

On-Premise Cost	Cloud Cost
Infrastructure	compute instance
Maintenance and upgrade	network
Software license	storage
Software upgrade	
Data security solutions	
Downtime cost	
Staff training	

6.0 THE EMERGENT TECHNOLOGIES ECOSYSTEM

The rising interest in cutting-edge trends is primarily driven by cloud computing, as it serves as a boost for emergent technology initiatives. Cloud computing has become a foundational piece for modern IT architecture. In order to realise the full potentials of BIM, the visualisations have to be accessible in the cloud. The capabilities of the next generation BIM will be fully unleashed if it is cloud-based.

The intelligent analytics requiring powerful Central Processing Unit (CPU), is only available in the cloud. IoT devices will gather real-time data and push to the cloud for processing; the decision will then be communicated back to the provided data points to improve operations on site. With Immersive Technologies, information gathered will be forwarded to the cloud to promote effective collaboration. The IoT sensors collect and organize data and information by using wireless sensor and RFID which requires a high computing platform that is readily available on cloud computing platform to share and exchange data to control and manage the system (Zhu et al, 2010). Thus, the construction industry must embrace a centralised modern ecosystem, with cloud computing at the centre stage as shown in Figure 6 for a typical ecosystem in construction industry.

Figure 6. A typical Cloud-based emergent technology ecosystem in construction industry

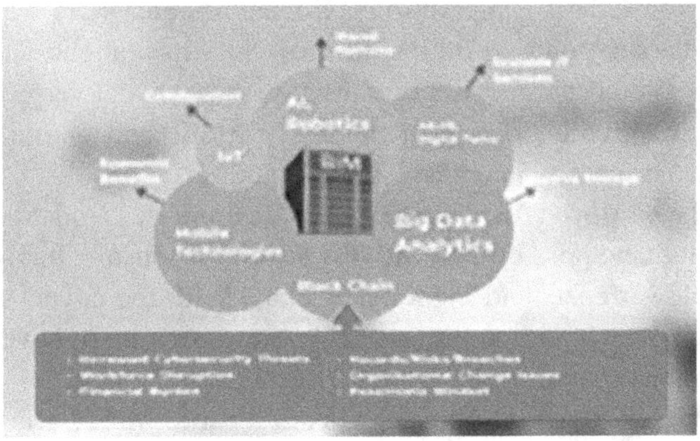

6.1 Opportunities/Motivations for Adoption of Emergent Technologies in Construction Industry

The emergent technology adoption will open up new possibilities and opportunities for the construction industry to meet up with the state-of-the-art approaches in doing business as will be seen in the up-to-the-minute methods of handling competition, labour shortage, high taste of clients among others.

(a) **Competition**: Many construction firms are finding it difficult to compete on price, hence the need to find a way to reduce project overhead costs and inefficiencies. The use of emergent technologies will increase efficiency and improve productivity.

(b) **Brain Drain (Labour Shortage)/Advent of Technological Age):** Seasoned professionals are getting retired with significant amount of institutional knowledge being lost with their exit. Thus, technology provides a way to capture experience and bridge the gap in knowledge. The upsurge in technology-related jobs lighten the hope of the younger generation for an enticing decade that allows application of creativity in the construction processes. The advent of technology savvy generation encourages the use of technology in the workplace even with the construction industry being noted for her reluctance to fully key into this change.

(c) **New/Evolving Client Expectations:** Clients nowadays are well informed of changing market trends resulting in growing expectations and demand for innovative tailored products in construction projects delivery. These requires construction activities to be modularized, specific and optimized on energy with enhanced security and health specifications.

(d) **Availability of powerful capacities in Technology**: Construction industry is witnessing new possibilities with the advent of sensors, hardware and software with lower costs and higher efficiency. With the advent of innovations in technology, construction professionals can exploit more novel and valuable transformations as a result of these emergent technologies.

(e) **Advent of Conducive/Supportive Legal Frameworks**: Digitalization has brought about an opportunity to reduce the environmental impact of construction projects. This is in line with the increasing government regulations on reduction of carbon dioxide (CO_2) emissions and efficient energy usage. Also, regulations on data usage and cyber security in building and infrastructures are becoming more popular. Thus, an opportunity to promote innovations in the construction industries.

(f) **Effects of the Pandemic:** A silver lining from the COVID 19 pandemic in 2020 triggered the adoption of emerging technologies in the construction industries. The adoption of emergent technology by industries was conservatively put at 3 years push by Esposito et al. (2021) while Blanco et al. (2016) reported a leap ahead by almost 6 years across the industries. In order to minimise the disruptions during the pandemic, the earlier stage of construction such as the design as well as some traditional site interaction processes such as site layout and material acquisition employed cloud-based digital platform to achieve remote participation and digital collaborations / interactions of workers. Scanning tools and various virtual platforms were used for site inspection and monitoring. Also, the use of advance safety wearables and planning tools witnessed a higher usage/adoption by the few workers on site. There is no doubt that the higher level of adoption of technology has come to stay in the construction industry and this will lead the industry to a higher growth globally.

6.2 Challenges and Mitigations to the use of Emergent Technologies in Construction

It is noted that despite the numerous identified potential advantages of adoption of the emergent software technologies in the construction industry, attention has to be paid to the mitigation of the potential threats of their adoption in order to reduce the possible losses in the industry. With that, these technologies will be embraced by the practitioners in the industry with more confidence. Some of these potential threats are discussed in this subsection.

6.2.1 Increased Cybersecurity Threats in Construction

As construction companies rely on digital means, cyber security threat is bound to be more pronounced than in the past years because construction businesses will be attractive to cybercriminal activities, spying and cyber terrorisms. The adoption of emerging digital technologies in pre-construction, construction, and facility management phases further predisposes the construction industry to increased attack surfaces or threats and vulnerabilities with respect to project stakeholders, equipment and processes. Detection and mitigation of cyber threats and vulnerabilities will protect sensitive data relating to work, workers, blueprints, financial and client matters (Naji et al., 2024). Hackers, ransomware, distributed /denial of service's (DOS/DDOS) will have phenomena effects on the construction industry. Government will come in form of General Data Protection Regulation, while construction companies will also require incorporation of cyber liability/protection insurance policies to progress. Benchmarks for cybersecurity management and technology-mediated countermeasures, such as the Blockchain-based systems, network virtualization and the organizational change-based integrated cyber risk management needs to be adopted (Salami and Ilbeigi, 2023).

6.2.2 Workforce Disruption_

The use of emergent technologies in the construction industry will no doubt change the nature of works and jobs, which could lead to displacement/loss of some workforce while some other new workforce may be created or emerge. Older technology and skills will become outdated and phased out. There will also be an increase in the use of new materials and approaches that will increase productivity in the construction industry. However, these new changes will be data driven which will require new skills and thus give birth to newer roles in the construction industry. There will also be the need for continuous training and retraining of the workforce not only on the proper usage of the adopted technologies but also on the risk of their misuse or abuse.

6.2.3 Financial Burden of New Technology

There is no doubt that the advancement in technology will be accompanied by financial responsibilities for the potential end users. This requires thinking about the future, as technology can become outdated quickly requiring frequent upgrades. This will translate to continuous/recurrent investment which may be a huge financial burden to both the service providers and the potential beneficiaries, if not well managed. It should be noted that, investing in a new technology also connote investment in skill development for the industry. There is no doubt that the cost of adopting the emergent technology in construction industry will be prohibitively significant, hence, a good financial model that will be able to accommodate this kind of disruption needs to be evolved.

6.2.4 Hazards/Risks/Breaches and Data Governance

Every stakeholder in the construction industry needs to understand how to properly use these innovative technologies as well as the handling/mitigation of the associated risks and breaches. Standard insurance policies may not be able to cover the associated liabilities with these new technologies. It is important that new and relevant risk management strategies are formulated to absorb any potential risk that may accompany the growing trend of adopting the emergent technologies in the industry.

Data governance frameworks has evolved overtime from the initial concept of managing data to establishment of protocols for data usage in digitization frameworks. In this case, it comprises of systematic strategies to optimize the value, access and including security of the strategic asset - data. The control and planning must ensure compliance with the regulatory authority and safety standards such as ISO 55000 series of protocols for asset management. For instance, ISO 55013, refers to protocol focusing Guidance on the Management of Data Assets, wherein ISO 55013 can be integrated with ISO 19650 for instance, on BIM data management. Therefore, security, performance, quality and privacy of data will be assured if data governance protocols be it Technical, Organization or Strategic protocols are embraced (Hua et al., 2025).

6.2.5 Organisational Change/Issues in Technology Adoption

Construction industry may adopt a technology because it is a cutting-edge and appears fascinating without being sure of its usefulness. In the same vein, the urge to attract some clients or win some contracts or jobs could also lead to the adoption of innovative technology (Construction Industry Training Board [CITB], 2018) which may not necessarily find efficient usefulness in the industry. Furthermore, organisational change management should encompass detail of what and how the changes are to be introduced (Maali, et al., 2020). DeJesus (2024) recommends the encouragement for open communication to assure stakeholders participation so as to drive job creation, and profitability at both micro and macro levels. Hence an all-round understanding of the implications of the new technologies to be adopted require investment in the capacity built around such technologies.

6.2.6 Pessimistic Mindset

Digital technologies are often viewed as disruptive technologies thus creating an unwelcoming mindset right from the start. There is the need to transform this mindset to that of an optimistic/asset atmosphere that is required to overcome the challenges associated with the implementation of the new technologies.

7.0 EMERGENT AND FUTURE TRENDS

These emerging technologies comes with promises of cost savings, processes and delivery efficiencies focusing on smart buildings, robots handling repetitive tasks, sustainable building, green construction, data quality and usage optimization. However, to properly estimate, control, and optimize the costs, construction industries need to understand the parameters that impact costs, assess their needs, design a strategic plan, continuously monitor and optimize usage and billing. The scalability of these cloud-based solutions could make resources to be run without understanding the long- and short-term implications. This makes it difficult to enforce policies about cloud usage costs. Thus, construction industry will require cloud management strategies to plan consumption and optimize costs of these cloud-based technologies to maximize Return on Investment (ROI) and increase efficiency.

It is conjectured that these emerging technologies will ride on the cloud-based platforms to achieve profound economic benefits, massive storage and shared platform opportunities; using automated collaboration tools for communication among stakeholders. In the future, the industry will combine edge computing (Saka et al., 2023) and conversational AI to further enhance its operations. Therefore, the transformed processes could gain wider adoption by the construction industry due to market pressure for faster project delivery with higher quality demands in the face of sustainable approaches throughout the project lifecycle. However, there is the need for cautions not to overstretch some of these expectations as excessive rush to completion may be disastrous in some construction projects. In particular, projects of concrete works usually require certain minimum curing days to develop adequate strength to be able to carry the expected design loads.

The adoption of emerging technologies has the potential for waste reduction and promote green construction through the use of digital blueprint, optimisation of supply chain as real-time tracking. While promotion of paperless communication and workflows, is geared towards environmental sustainability. In addition, energy efficiency through cloud computing is achievable as frequency of site visit is drastically reduced as well as optimisation of lighting, heating and cooling through real-time data. The use of renewable energy source by harnessing the solar and wind energy to power cloud computing infrastructure can promote greener future in construction industry.

It can also be anticipated that construction companies will invest in appropriate technologies to meet up with the digital transformation of construction processes. Hence it is projected that capacity building investment will also occupy topmost level of company budgeting to transform the workforce for best practices. This is because appropriateness of technology requires upskilled workforce.

It is presumed that market forces/pressures and the trend in investment on technology and workforce; will transform the processes and procedures; work ethics, handling of construction data and project delivery. Probably, there will emerge construction industry-specific solutions to upgrade the pessimistic mindset in technology adoption to optimistic level. Thus, it is hoped that there will be a general shift towards high-end automation in project management, data governance and the entire project lifecycle to achieve more sustainable cloud-based emergent technology ecosystem in the construction industry.

8.0 CONCLUSION

In this chapter, an overview of the cloud computing technology was given and its possible use together with the emergent technologies such as Building Information Modelling (BIM), Internet of Thing (IoT), Immersive Technologies (IT), Artificial Intelligence (AI), and others, for adoption in the construction industry. It was emphasised that the rising interest in the cutting-edge trends is primarily driven by cloud computing as it reinforces the emergent technology initiatives. Although cloud computing has ceded the spotlight to emerging trends such as AI or IoT, it has become a foundational piece for modern Information Technology (IT) architecture. It was identified that the potentials of the next generation BIM will be fully unleashed if it is cloud-based for easy accessibility of data which will enhance collaboration and affordability to improve the project lifecycle cost. It was also noted that the intelligent analytics of construction data, apart from requiring powerful CPU, is only available in the cloud. However, for effective utilisation, this requires data from different sources, such as subcontractors, material suppliers, design plans, even the site plan for historical data. IoT devices will gather real-time data and push it to the cloud for processing; the decision will be communicated back to the provided data points to improve operation on site. Virtual reality (VR) provides immersive and detailed virtual representation of construction project even before the construction commences and with cloud computing, this becomes interactive and shareable amongst the concerned professionals.

Therefore, the construction industry must embrace cloud computing for a centralised modern ecosystem of emerging technologies to manage projects from end-to-end for efficient and effective construction processes. However, the reluctance of the construction industry emanating from the fear of the associated risks with the adoption of the emergent technologies needs to be addressed. This can be done through the formulation of appropriate insurance policies and legislation to reduce the adverse effects of any potential breach of data from cyber criminals. Generally, it was opined that the emergent technologies are not to be viewed as just another costly exertion to disrupt the *status quo* in the industry, rather they should be viewed as an investment for a long-term sustainability of the construction industry.

REFERENCES

Akinade, O. O., Oyedele, L. O., Omoteso, K., Ajayi, S. O., Bilal, M., Owolabi, H. A., & Looney, J. H. (2017). BIM-based deconstruction tool: Towards essential functionalities. *International Journal of Sustainable Built Environment*, *6*(1), 260–271. DOI: 10.1016/j.ijsbe.2017.01.002

Alaka, H. A., Oyedele, L. O., Owolabi, H. A., Bilal, M., Ajayi, S. O., & Akinade, O. O. (2018). A framework for big data analytics approach to failure prediction of construction firms. *Applied Computing and Informatics*, *16*(1/2), 207–222. DOI: 10.1016/j.aci.2018.04.003

Alaloul, W. S., Musarat, M. A., Rabbani, M. B. A., Altaf, M., Alzubi, K. M., & Al Salaheen, M. (2022). Assessment of economic sustainability in the construction sector: Evidence from three developed countries (the USA, China, and the UK). *Sustainability (Basel)*, *14*(10), 6326. DOI: 10.3390/su14106326

Ars, M. M. M. N. (2025). Optimizing Risk Management Strategies in Mega Construction Projects Using Artificial Intelligence and Machine Learning Techniques. *Biomaterials Translational*, •••, 95–107.

Asadi, K., Ramshankar, H., Pullagurla, H., Bhandare, A., Shanbhag, S., Mehta, P., Kundu, S., Han, K., Lobaton, E., & Wu, T. (2018). Vision-based integrated mobile robotic system for real-time applications in construction. *Automation in Construction*, *96*, 470–482. DOI: 10.1016/j.autcon.2018.10.009

Attaran, M., & Celik, B. G. (2023). Digital Twin: Benefits, use cases, challenges, and opportunities. *Decision Analytics Journal*, *6*, 100165. DOI: 10.1016/j.dajour.2023.100165

Atzori, L., Iera, A., & Morabito, G. (2010). The internet of things: A survey. *Computer Networks*, *54*(15), 2787–2805. DOI: 10.1016/j.comnet.2010.05.010

Avani, P., & Bhavana, B. (2022, September). Building Information Modelling and Augmented Reality for building energy systems visualisation. [). IOP Publishing.]. *IOP Conference Series. Materials Science and Engineering*, *1255*(1), 012009. DOI: 10.1088/1757-899X/1255/1/012009

Azhar, S. (2011). Building information modeling (BIM): Trends, benefits, risks, and challenges for the AEC industry. *Leadership and Management in Engineering*, *11*(3), 241–252. DOI: 10.1061/(ASCE)LM.1943-5630.0000127

Bashir, M. R., & Gill, A. Q. (2016, December). Toward an IoT big data analytics framework: smart buildings systems. In *Proceedings of the 2016 IEEE 18th International Conference on High Performance Computing and Communications*. DOI: 10.1109/HPCC-SmartCity-DSS.2016.0188

Bello, S. A., Oyedele, L., Olaitan, K., Olajumoke, A. M., Olonade, K. A., Akinade, O., Akanbi, L., Ajayi, A., Sanni, M. L., & Bello, A. L. O. (2020). A Deep Learning Approach to Predict Required Water-Cement Ratio in Concrete Mix. *Results in Materials*, *15*, 100300. DOI: 10.1016/j.rinma.2022.100300

Bhardwaj, S., Jain, L., & Jain, S. (2010). Cloud computing: A study of infrastructure as a service (IAAS). *International Journal of Engineering and Information Technology*, *2*(1), 60–63.

Bhuiyan, M. M. A., & Hammad, A. (2023). A hybrid multi-criteria decision support system for selecting the most sustainable structural material for a multistory building construction. *Sustainability (Basel)*, *15*(4), 3128. DOI: 10.3390/su15043128

Blanco, J. L., Janauskas, M., & Ribeirinho, M. J. (2016). *Beating the low-productivity trap: How to transform construction operations*. McKinsey & Company.

Bogue, R. (2018). Exoskeletons–a review of industrial applications. *The Industrial Robot*, *45*(5), 585–590. DOI: 10.1108/IR-05-2018-0109

Chen, H. M., Chang, K. C., & Lin, T. H. (2016). A cloud-based system framework for performing online viewing, storage, and analysis on big data of massive BIMs. *Automation in Construction*, *71*, 34–48. DOI: 10.1016/j.autcon.2016.03.002

Chen, J., & Man, Q. (2018, August). A critical review on BIM research process and future trends at home and abroad. In *Proceedings of the International Conference on Construction and Real Estate Management 2018* (pp. 104-112). Reston, VA: American Society of Civil Engineers. DOI: 10.1061/9780784481721.012

Chi, H. L., Kang, S. C., & Wang, X. (2013). Research trends and opportunities of augmented reality applications in architecture, engineering, and construction. *Automation in Construction*, *33*, 116–122. DOI: 10.1016/j.autcon.2012.12.017

Chong, H. Y., Wong, J. S., & Wang, X. (2014). An explanatory case study on cloud computing applications in the built environment. *Automation in Construction*, *44*, 152–162. DOI: 10.1016/j.autcon.2014.04.010

Chu, M., Matthews, J., & Love, P. E. (2018). Integrating mobile building information modelling and augmented reality systems: An experimental study. *Automation in Construction*, *85*, 305–316. DOI: 10.1016/j.autcon.2017.10.032

Chuang, T. H., Lee, B. C., & Wu, I. C. (2011, June). Applying cloud computing technology to BIM visualization and manipulation. In *Proceedings of the 28th International Symposium on Automation and Robotics in Construction* (Vol. 201, No. 1, pp. 144-149). DOI: 10.22260/ISARC2011/0023

Chui, M., & Francisco, S. (2017). Artificial intelligence the next digital frontier. *McKinsey and Company Global Institute, 47*(3.6), 6-8.

Construction Industry Training Board (2018). *Unlocking construction's digital future: a skills plan for industry.*

Das, M., Cheng, J. C., & Kumar, S. S. (2015). Social BIMCloud: A distributed cloud-based BIM platform for object-based lifecycle information exchange. *Visualization in Engineering*, *3*(1), 1–20. DOI: 10.1186/s40327-015-0022-6

DeJesus, I. (2024). *Strategies for Implementing Organizational Change in the Construction Industry* (Doctoral dissertation, Walden University).

Delgado, J. M. D., Oyedele, L., Ajayi, A., Akanbi, L., Akinade, O., Bilal, M., & Owolabi, H. (2019). Robotics and automated systems in construction: Understanding industry-specific challenges for adoption. *Journal of Building Engineering*, *26*, 100868. DOI: 10.1016/j.jobe.2019.100868

Deochake, S. (2023). Cloud cost optimization: A comprehensive review of strategies and case studies. *arXiv preprint arXiv:2307.12479*.

Dorfler, K. (2016). *Mobile robotic brickwork, Robotic Fabrication in Architecture*. Art and Design.

Du, J., El-Gafy, M., & Lama, P. (2016). A Cloud-based shareable library of cooperative behaviours for Agent based modeling in construction. *Automation in Construction*, *62*, 89–100. DOI: 10.1016/j.autcon.2015.11.005

Esposito, D., Dipierro, G., Sonnessa, A., Santoro, S., Pascazio, S., & Pluchinotta, I. (2021). Data-driven epidemic intelligence strategies based on digital proximity tracing technologies in the fight against COVID-19 in cities. *Sustainability (Basel)*, *13*(2), 644. DOI: 10.3390/su13020644

Everett, J. G., & Slocum, A. H. (1994). Automation and robotics opportunities: Construction versus manufacturing. *Journal of Construction Engineering and Management*, *120*(2), 443–452. DOI: 10.1061/(ASCE)0733-9364(1994)120:2(443)

Faheem, M. A., Zafar, N., Kumar, P., Melon, M. M. H., Prince, N. U., & Al Mamun, M. A. (2024). AI and robotic: About the transformation of construction industry automation as well as labor productivity. *Remittances Review*, *9*, 871–888.

Fang, Y., Cho, Y. K., Zhang, S., & Perez, E. (2016). Case study of BIM and cloud–enabled real-time RFID indoor localization for construction management applications. *Journal of Construction Engineering and Management, 142*(7), 05016003. DOI: 10.1061/(ASCE)CO.1943-7862.0001125

Ferrada, X., Núñez, D., Neyem, A., Serpell, A., & Sepúlveda, M. (2016). A cloud-based mobile system to manage lessons-learned in construction projects. *Procedia Engineering, 164*, 135–142. DOI: 10.1016/j.proeng.2016.11.602

Follini, C., Magnago, V., Freitag, K., Terzer, M., Marcher, C., Riedl, M., Giusti, A., & Matt, D. T. (2020). BIM-integrated collaborative robotics for application in building construction and maintenance. *Robotics (Basel, Switzerland), 10*(1), 2. DOI: 10.3390/robotics10010002

Getuli, V., Ventura, S. M., Capone, P., & Ciribini, A. L. (2016). A BIM-based construction supply chain framework for monitoring progress and coordination of site activities. *Procedia Engineering, 164*, 542–549. DOI: 10.1016/j.proeng.2016.11.656

Ghaffarianhoseini, A., Tookey, J., Ghaffarianhoseini, A., Naismith, N., Azhar, S., Efimova, O., & Raahemifar, K. (2017). Building Information Modelling (BIM) uptake: Clear benefits, understanding its implementation, risks and challenges. *Renewable & Sustainable Energy Reviews, 75*, 1046–1053. DOI: 10.1016/j.rser.2016.11.083

Glover, J. (2018). *Unity 2018 augmented reality projects: build four immersive and fun AR applications using ARKit, ARCore, and Vuforia*. Packt Publishing Ltd.

Glover, J., Rus, D., & Roy, N. (2009). Probabilistic models of object geometry for grasp planning. *Robotics Science and Systems : Online Proceedings, IV*, 278–285. DOI: 10.7551/mitpress/8344.003.0040

Goessens, S., Mueller, C., & Latteur, P. (2018). Feasibility study for drone-based masonry construction of real-scale structures. *Automation in Construction, 94*, 458–480. DOI: 10.1016/j.autcon.2018.06.015

Goldberg, K., & Kehoe, B. (2013). Cloud robotics and automation: A survey of related work. *EECS Department, University of California, Berkeley, Tech. Rep. UCB/EECS-2013-5*, 13-5.

Goryaeva, N. A., & Rybakova, A. O. (2018). Cloud technologies of interaction in design and construction. *BST: Bulletin of construction equipment, 4*(1004), 28-31.

Haron, R. C., & Zafir, N. B. M. (2025). Digital Twin Application in Construction Cost Management. *Planning Malaysia, 23.*

Hay, B., Nance, K., & Bishop, M. (2011, January). Storm clouds rising: security challenges for IaaS cloud computing. In *Proceedings of the 2011 44th Hawaii International Conference on System Sciences* (pp. 1-7). IEEE. DOI: 10.1109/HICSS.2011.386

Holt, E. A., Benham, J. M., & Bigelow, B. F. (2015, June). Emerging technology in the construction industry: Perceptions from construction industry professionals. In *Proceedings of the 2015 ASEE Annual Conference & Exposition* (pp. 26-595). DOI: 10.18260/p.23933

Hossein Motlagh, N., Mohammadrezaei, M., Hunt, J., & Zakeri, B. (2020). Internet of Things (IoT) and the energy sector. *Energies*, *13*(2), 494. DOI: 10.3390/en13020494

Hua, Y., Kang, M., Yao, H., & Fu, Y. (2025). How to foster project organization resilience in the construction industry: The role of data governance capabilities. *Buildings (Basel, Switzerland)*, *15*(8), 1219. DOI: 10.3390/buildings15081219

Hwang, B. G., Ngo, J., & Teo, J. Z. K. (2022). Challenges and strategies for the adoption of smart technologies in the construction industry: The case of Singapore. *Journal of Management Engineering*, *38*(1), 05021014. DOI: 10.1061/(ASCE)ME.1943-5479.0000986

Jardim-Goncalves, R., & Grilo, A. (2010). SOA4BIM: Putting the building and construction industry in the Single European Information Space. *Automation in Construction*, *19*(4), 388–397. DOI: 10.1016/j.autcon.2009.11.009

Jayaraj, A., & Divakar, H. N. (2018, June). Robotics in construction industry. []. IOP Publishing.]. *IOP Conference Series. Materials Science and Engineering*, *376*(1), 012114. DOI: 10.1088/1757-899X/376/1/012114

Jia, M., Komeily, A., Wang, Y., & Srinivasan, R. S. (2019). Adopting Internet of Things for the development of smart buildings: A review of enabling technologies and applications. *Automation in Construction*, *101*, 111–126. DOI: 10.1016/j.autcon.2019.01.023

Jiao, Y., Baoming, Y., Liwu, W., & Wang, Y. (2014, July). FCL2-CloudBIM: Framework and applications for BIM-Based collaboration platform under cloud environments. In *Proceedings of the 21st European Group International Workshop on Intelligent Computing in Engineering*, Cardiff, UK, pp. 70-79.

Jiao, Y., Wang, Y., Yuan, L., & Li, L. (2012, May). Cloud and SNS supported collaboration in AEC industry. In *Proceedings of the 2012 IEEE 16th International Conference on Computer Supported Cooperative Work in Design (CSCWD)* (pp. 842-849). IEEE. DOI: 10.1109/CSCWD.2012.6221919

Jiao, Y., Zhang, S., Li, Y., Wang, Y., & Yang, B. (2013). Towards cloud augmented reality for construction application by BIM and SNS integration. *Automation in Construction, 33*, 37–47. DOI: 10.1016/j.autcon.2012.09.018

John, S. T., Roy, B. K., Sarkar, P., & Davis, R. (2020). IoT enabled real-time monitoring system for early-age compressive strength of concrete. *Journal of Construction Engineering and Management, 146*(2), 05019020. DOI: 10.1061/(ASCE)CO.1943-7862.0001754

Juan, D. (2013, December). The research to open BIM-based building information interoperability framework. In *Proceedings of the 2nd International Symposium on Instrumentation and Measurement, Sensor Network and Automation (IMSNA)*(pp. 440-443). IEEE. DOI: 10.1109/IMSNA.2013.6743310

Kamat, V. R., Martinez, J. C., Fischer, M., Golparvar-Fard, M., Peña-Mora, F., & Savarese, S. (2011). Research in visualization techniques for field construction. *Journal of Construction Engineering and Management, 137*(10), 853–862. DOI: 10.1061/(ASCE)CO.1943-7862.0000262

Karim, M. A., Abdullah, M. Z., Deifalla, A. F., Azab, M., & Waqar, A. (2023). An assessment of the processing parameters and application of fibre-reinforced polymers (FRPs) in the petroleum and natural gas industries: A review. *Results in Engineering, 18*, 101091. DOI: 10.1016/j.rineng.2023.101091

Kasperzyk, C., Kim, M. K., & Brilakis, I. (2017). Automated re-prefabrication system for buildings using robotics. *Automation in Construction, 83*, 184–195. DOI: 10.1016/j.autcon.2017.08.002

Kehoe, B., Berenson, D., & Goldberg, K. (2012, August). Estimating part tolerance bounds based on adaptive cloud-based grasp planning with slip. In *2012 IEEE International Conference on Automation Science and Engineering (CASE)* (pp. 1106-1113). IEEE. DOI: 10.1109/CoASE.2012.6386393

Kehoe, B., Berenson, D., & Goldberg, K. (2012, May). Toward cloud-based grasping with uncertainty in shape: Estimating lower bounds on achieving force closure with zero-slip push grasps. In *2012 IEEE International Conference on Robotics and Automation* (pp. 576-583). IEEE. DOI: 10.1109/ICRA.2012.6224781

Kehoe, B., Matsukawa, A., Candido, S., Kuffner, J., & Goldberg, K. (2013, May). Cloud-based robot grasping with the google object recognition engine. In *2013 IEEE International Conference on Robotics and Automation* (pp. 4263-4270). IEEE. DOI: 10.1109/ICRA.2013.6631180

Kehoe, B., Patil, S., Abbeel, P., & Goldberg, K. (2015). A survey of research on cloud robotics and automation. *IEEE Transactions on Automation Science and Engineering*, *12*(2), 398–409. DOI: 10.1109/TASE.2014.2376492

Khahro, S. H., Hassan, S., Zainun, N. Y. B., & Javed, Y. (2021). Digital transformation and e-commerce in construction industry: A prospective assessment. *Academy of Strategic Management Journal*, *20*(1), 1–8.

Khajenasiri, I., Estebsari, A., Verhelst, M., & Gielen, G. (2017). A review on Internet of Things solutions for intelligent energy control in buildings for smart city applications. *Energy Procedia*, *111*, 770–779. DOI: 10.1016/j.egypro.2017.03.239

Ko, H. S., Azambuja, M., & Lee, H. F. (2016). Cloud-based materials tracking system prototype integrated with radio frequency identification tagging technology. *Automation in Construction*, *63*, 144–154. DOI: 10.1016/j.autcon.2015.12.011

Kochovski, P., & Stankovski, V. (2021). Building applications for smart and safe construction with the DECENTER Fog Computing and Brokerage Platform. *Automation in Construction*, *124*, 103562. DOI: 10.1016/j.autcon.2021.103562

Kuo, R. C., Hsieh, S. H., Chen, Y. W., Yang, C. E., & Jean, T. F. (2014). Design and implementation of BIM collaboration cloud platform. *Journal of Chinese Institute of Civil and Hydraulic Engineering*, *26*(4), 309–321.

Lei, Y., Wang, L. H., & Wang, Z. H. (2020). Feasibility Exploration of "Multi-Conformity" under the background of Big Data. *The International Archives of the Photogrammetry, Remote Sensing and Spatial Information Sciences*, *42*(W10), 1261–1264. DOI: 10.5194/isprs-archives-XLII-3-W10-1261-2020

Li, D., Cao, J., & Yao, Y. (2015). Big data in smart cities. *Science China. Information Sciences*, *58*(10), 1–12.

Li, J., Deng, L., Gong, Y., & Haeb-Umbach, R. (2014). An overview of noise-robust automatic speech recognition. *IEEE/ACM Transactions on Audio, Speech, and Language Processing*, *22*(4), 745–777. DOI: 10.1109/TASLP.2014.2304637

Li, J., Greenwood, D., & Kassem, M. (2018, December). Blockchain in the built environment: analysing current applications and developing an emergent framework. Diamond Congress Ltd., Budapest University of Technology and Economics.

Li, M., Yu, H., & Liu, P. (2018). An automated safety risk recognition mechanism for underground construction at the pre-construction stage based on BIM. *Automation in Construction*, *91*, 284–292. DOI: 10.1016/j.autcon.2018.03.013

Li, Y., & Ma, X. (2016, September). Research on the informatization management of green construction based on Cloud-BIM. *In Proceedings of the International Conference on Construction and Real Estate Management 2016* (pp. 585-592). Reston, VA: American Society of Civil Engineers.

Ma, Q., & Yang, Y. (2021, April). Research on the construction of smart cities by the big data platform of the blockchain. [). IOP Publishing.]. *Journal of Physics: Conference Series*, *1883*(1), 012144. DOI: 10.1088/1742-6596/1883/1/012144

Maali, O., Lines, B., Smithwick, J., Hurtado, K., & Sullivan, K. (2020). Change management practices for adopting new technologies in the design and construction industry. *Journal of Information Technology in Construction*, *25*, 325–341. DOI: 10.36680/j.itcon.2020.019

Madubuike, O. C., Anumba, C. J., & Khallaf, R. (2022). A review of digital twin applications in construction. *Journal of Information Technology in Construction, 27.*

Mansouri, S., & Akhavian, R. (2018). The status quo and future potentials of data analytics in AEC/FM: A quantitative analysis of academic research and industry outlook. In *Construction Research Congress 2018* (pp. 90-100). DOI: 10.1061/9780784481295.010

Meerja, K. A., Naidu, P. V., & Kalva, S. R. K. (2019). Price versus performance of big data analysis for cloud based internet of things networks. *Mobile Networks and Applications*, *24*(3), 1078–1094. DOI: 10.1007/s11036-018-1063-6

Merschbrock, C., & Munkvold, B. E. (2015). Effective digital collaboration in the construction industry–A case study of BIM deployment in a hospital construction project. *Computers in Industry*, *73*, 1–7. DOI: 10.1016/j.compind.2015.07.003

Motawa, I. (2017). Spoken dialogue BIM systems–an application of big data in construction. *Facilities*, *35*(13/14), 787–800. DOI: 10.1108/F-01-2016-0001

Mutoh, T., Kotani, K., & Kakinaka, M. (2020). An overseas business paradox: Are Japanese general contractors risk takers? *PLoS One*, *15*(9), e0238570. DOI: 10.1371/journal.pone.0238570 PMID: 32915823

Naji, K. K., Gunduz, M., Alhenzab, F. H., Al-Hababi, H., & Al-Qahtani, A. H. (2024). A systematic review of the digital transformation of the building construction industry. *IEEE Access : Practical Innovations, Open Solutions*, *12*, 31461–31487. DOI: 10.1109/ACCESS.2024.3365934

National Institute of Standardse and Technology. (2011). The National Institute of Science and Technology definition of cloud computing. *National Institute of Science and Technology. Special Publication*, *800*, 145.

Nawaz, S., Efstratiou, C., Mascolo, C., & Soga, K. (2012, June). Social sensing in the field: challenges in detecting social interactions in construction sites. *In Proceedings of the 1st ACM Workshop on Mobile Systems for Computational Social Science* (pp. 28-32). DOI: 10.1145/2307863.2307872

Novatr (2025) https://www.novatr.com/blog/example-of-bim-projects-globally#11 accessed June 11th 2025

Oke, A. E., & Arowoiya, V. A. (2021). Evaluation of internet of things (IoT) application areas for sustainable construction. *Smart and Sustainable Built Environment*, *10*(3), 387–402. DOI: 10.1108/SASBE-11-2020-0167

Opoku, D. G. J., Perera, S., Osei-Kyei, R., Rashidi, M., Bamdad, K., & Famakinwa, T. (2023, January). Barriers to the adoption of digital twin in the construction industry: A literature review. []. MDPI.]. *Informatics (MDPI)*, *10*(1), 14. DOI: 10.3390/informatics10010014

Pan, N. H., & Isnaeni, N. N. (2024). Integration of Augmented Reality and Building Information Modeling for Enhanced Construction Inspection—A Case Study. *Buildings (Basel, Switzerland)*, *14*(3), 612. DOI: 10.3390/buildings14030612

Pham, H. C., Dao, N. N., Kim, J. U., Cho, S., & Park, C. S. (2018). Energy-efficient learning system using web-based panoramic virtual photoreality for interactive construction safety education. *Sustainability (Basel)*, *10*(7), 2262. DOI: 10.3390/su10072262

Prasad, M. R., Gyani, J., & Murti, P. R. K. (2012). Mobile cloud computing: Implications and challenges. *Journal of Information Engineering and Applications*, *2*(7), 7–15.

Professional, C. North Atlantic Concrete (2025). https://www.northatlanticconcrete.com/wp-content/uploads/2020/07/0005-essex-may-30-2020-1030x579.jpg accessed January 28th 2025

Qian, Z., Yang, X., Xu, Z., & Cai, W. (2021, March). Research on key construction technology of building engineering under the background of big data. []. IOP Publishing.]. *Journal of Physics: Conference Series*, *1802*(3), 032003. DOI: 10.1088/1742-6596/1802/3/032003

Rakha, T., & Gorodetsky, A. (2018). Review of Unmanned Aerial System (UAS) applications in the built environment: Towards automated building inspection procedures using drones. *Automation in Construction*, *93*, 252–264. DOI: 10.1016/j.autcon.2018.05.002

Redmond, A., Hore, A., Alshawi, M., & West, R. (2012). Exploring how information exchanges can be enhanced through Cloud BIM. *Automation in Construction, 24*, 175–183. DOI: 10.1016/j.autcon.2012.02.003

Redmond, A., & Smith, B. (2011, October). Exchanging partial BIM information through a cloud-based service: testing the efficacy of a major innovation. In *Proceedings of the IBEA Conference 2011.*

Riazuelo, L., Civera, J., & Montiel, J. M. (2014). C2tam: A cloud framework for cooperative tracking and mapping. *Robotics and Autonomous Systems*, *62*(4), 401–413. DOI: 10.1016/j.robot.2013.11.007

Rui, J., & Danpeng, S. (2015, June). Architecture design of the Internet of Things based on cloud computing. In *Proceedings of the 2015 Seventh International Conference on Measuring Technology and Mechatronics Automation* (pp. 206-209). IEEE. DOI: 10.1109/ICMTMA.2015.57

Saka, A., Bello, S., Kasali, A., & Agboola, A. O. AbdulRafiu, M., Ganiyu, S. A., ... & Ajayi, A. (2023). An Edge-Based Architecture for Personal Safety System on Construction Sites. In *Environmental Design & Management International Conference (EDMIC).*

Saka, K., Kasali, A. A., Sanni, M. L., Abdulsalam, K. A., Ayeni, S., & Bello, S. A. (2024). Design and Simulation of a Multilingual Safety System for Vehicles on Construction Sites. *In 2024, Faculty of Technology, Obafemi Awolowo University International Conference.*

Salami Pargoo, N., & Ilbeigi, M. (2023). A scoping review for cybersecurity in the construction industry. *Journal of Management Engineering*, *39*(2), 03122003. DOI: 10.1061/JMENEA.MEENG-5034

Salhaoui, M., Guerrero-González, A., Arioua, M., Ortiz, F. J., El Oualkadi, A., & Torregrosa, C. L. (2019). Smart industrial iot monitoring and control system based on UAV and cloud computing applied to a concrete plant. *Sensors (Basel)*, *19*(15), 3316. DOI: 10.3390/s19153316 PMID: 31357720

Sarkar, D., Patel, H., & Dave, B. (2022). Development of integrated cloud-based Internet of Things (IoT) platform for asset management of elevated metro rail projects. *International Journal of Construction Management*, *22*(10), 1993–2002. DOI: 10.1080/15623599.2020.1762035

Sawhney, A., Riley, M., Irizarry, J., & Riley, M. (2020). *Construction 4.0* (Sawhney, A., Riley, M., & Irizarry, J., Eds.). DOI: 10.1201/9780429398100

Shirowzhan, S., Tan, W., & Sepasgozar, S. M. (2020). Digital twin and CyberGIS for improving connectivity and measuring the impact of infrastructure construction planning in smart cities. *ISPRS International Journal of Geo-Information*, *9*(4), 240. DOI: 10.3390/ijgi9040240

Sittón-Candanedo, I., Alonso, R. S., Corchado, J. M., Rodríguez-González, S., & Casado-Vara, R. (2019). A review of edge computing reference architectures and a new global edge proposal. *Future Generation Computer Systems*, *99*, 278–294. DOI: 10.1016/j.future.2019.04.016

Spot (2025) https://spot.io/resources/cloud-cost/cloud-cost-models-management-strategies/ accessed June 11th 2025 accessed June 12th 2025

Uusitalo, P., Peltokorpi, A., Seppänen, O., & Alhava, O. (2024). Towards systemic transformation in the construction industry: A complex adaptive systems perspective. *Construction Innovation*, *24*(7), 341–368. DOI: 10.1108/CI-01-2024-0015

Ventures, C. (2025). https://www.cemexventures.com/how-augmented-and-virtual-reality-can-change-the-construction-industry/ accessed June 12th 2025

Wahbeh, W., Kunz, D., Hofmann, J., & Bereuter, P. (2020). Digital twinning of the built environment–an interdisciplinary topic for innovation in didactics. *ISPRS Annals of the Photogrammetry, Remote Sensing and Spatial Information Sciences*, *4*, 231–237. DOI: 10.5194/isprs-annals-V-4-2020-231-2020

Wang, M., Qiu, S., Dong, H., & Wang, Y. (2017, October). Design an IoT-based building management cloud platform for green buildings. In *Proceedings of the 2017 Chinese Automation Congress (CAC)* (pp. 5663-5667). IEEE. DOI: 10.1109/CAC.2017.8243793

Wang, X., Wang, S., Song, X., & Han, Y. (2020). IoT-based intelligent construction system for prefabricated buildings: Study of operating mechanism and implementation in China. *Applied Sciences (Basel, Switzerland)*, *10*(18), 6311. DOI: 10.3390/app10186311

Waqar, A. (2024). Intelligent decision support systems in construction engineering: An artificial intelligence and machine learning approaches. *Expert Systems with Applications*, *249*, 123503. DOI: 10.1016/j.eswa.2024.123503

Więckowski, A. (2017). "JA-WA"-A wall construction system using unilateral material application with a mobile robot. *Automation in Construction*, *83*, 19–28. DOI: 10.1016/j.autcon.2017.02.005

Wong, C., Yang, E., Yan, X. T., & Gu, D. (2018). Autonomous robots for harsh environments: A holistic overview of current solutions and ongoing challenges. *Systems Science & Control Engineering*, *6*(1), 213–219. DOI: 10.1080/21642583.2018.1477634

World Economic Forum. (2016). Shaping the future of construction, a breakthrough in mindset and technology. *In World Economic Forum* (pp. 11-16).

Xing, K., Kim, K. P., & Ness, D. (2020). Cloud-BIM enabled cyber-physical data and service platforms for building component reuse. *Sustainability (Basel)*, *12*(24), 10329. DOI: 10.3390/su122410329

Xiong, S., & Ye, B. (2019, March). Analysis on the development path of smart city in the era of big data. In *Proceedings of the 2019 IEEE 4th International Conference on Big Data Analytics (ICBDA)* (pp. 177-181). IEEE. DOI: 10.1109/ICBDA.2019.8713243

Xu, G., Li, M., Chen, C. H., & Wei, Y. (2018). Cloud asset-enabled integrated IoT platform for lean prefabricated construction. *Automation in Construction*, *93*, 123–134. DOI: 10.1016/j.autcon.2018.05.012

Yu, W., Xu, G., Chen, Z., & Moulema, P. (2013, October). A cloud computing based architecture for cyber security situation awareness. In *Proceedings of the 2013 iEEE conference on communications and network security (cNS)* (pp. 488-492). IEEE. DOI: 10.1109/CNS.2013.6682765

Zahoor, H., Khan, R. M., Nawaz, A., Ayaz, M., & Maqsoom, A. (2022). Project control and forecast assessment of building projects in Pakistan using earned value management. *Engineering, Construction, and Architectural Management*, *29*(2), 842–869. DOI: 10.1108/ECAM-11-2020-0989

Zhang, L., & Issa, R. R. A. (2012). Comparison of BIM cloud computing frameworks. *Computing in Civil Engineering (2012)* (pp. 389-396).

Zhang, Y., Meina, A., Lin, X., Zhang, K., & Xu, Z. (2021). Digital twin in computational design and robotic construction of wooden architecture. *Advances in Civil Engineering*, *2021*(1), 8898997. DOI: 10.1155/2021/8898997

Zheng, R., Jiang, J., Hao, X., Ren, W., Xiong, F., & Zhu, T. (2019). CaACBIM: A context-aware access control model for BIM. *Information (Basel)*, *10*(2), 47. DOI: 10.3390/info10020047

Zhu, H. B., Yang, L. X., & Yu, Q. (2010). Investigation of technical thought and application strategy for the internet of things. *Journal of China Institute of Communications*, *31*(11), 2–9.

Zhu, Q., Loke, S. W., Trujillo-Rasua, R., Jiang, F., & Xiang, Y. (2019). Applications of distributed ledger technologies to the internet of things: A survey. *ACM Computing Surveys*, *52*(6), 1–34.

About the Contributors

Aisha A. Hashim received her Ph.D in Computer Engineering (2007), M.Sc. in Computer Science (1996) and B.Sc. in Electronics Engineering (1990). She won the Best Graduating Ph.D Student Award during the IIUM Convocation ceremony in 2007. She joined IIUM in 1997 and is currently a Professor at the Department of Electrical and Computer Engineering. Professor Aisha has taught several courses related to Communication and Computer Engineering and is actively involved in curriculum development and programme accreditation. She has been a member of the Department Board of Studies for several years. She received the Best Teacher Award during IIUM Quality Day in 2007. Prof. Aisha has been appointed as external examiner/visiting professor/adjunct professor at different universities. Professor Aisha who is actively involved in research and postgraduate programmes, has published more than 200 journal/conference papers, and supervised/co-supervised more than 40 Ph.D/Master's students. She received the Promising Researcher Award in 2009 during IIUM Quality Day. She has also received many medals/awards in different national/international research exhibitions. One of her research exhibitions won the Promising Commercial Value Award (Second Runner Up) in IRIIE 2014. As a researcher, she has secured research grants from IIUM, Ministry of Higher Education (MOHE) and Ministry of Science, Technology and Innovation (MOSTI). She has actively contributed as a reviewer /technical committee member in many journals/conferences. Professor Aisha has established several teaching/research networks between IIUM and overseas universities. She has been appointed as IIUMÂ Internationalisation Ambassador to Sudan (October 2014) and has participated in initiating several MoUs as well as encouraging the PhD Student Mobility programme between IIUM and Sudanese Universities. Professor Aisha also participates in community services. She was appointed as a Board of Studies member at the International Islamic School, Malaysia. She also served as Parent/Teacher Committee member at the school for more than 10 years.

Zeinab E. Ahmed received her Ph.D. in Computer Engineering and Networks from the University of Gezira, Sudan. Dr. Zeinab has been working as an assistant professor in the Department of Computer Engineering at the University of Gezira, Sudan since June 2020. Currently, she is working as a postdoc fellow at the Department of Electrical and Computer Engineering, International Islamic University Malaysia, Malaysia. Dr. Zeinab has served as Head of the Department of Computer Engineering, Faculty of Engineering Technology, and the University of Gezira, Sudan. I've been engaged in some projects related to the field of computer engineering and networks. She has published more than eight research papers and book chapters on networking in peer-reviewed academic venues. Her areas of research interest are wireless communication networks. An experienced lecturer with a demonstrated history of working in the higher education industry. She is skilled in research, e-learning, programming, and lecturing.

Othman Omran Khalifa received his bachelor's degree in electrical and Electronic Engineering from Garyounis University, Libya in 1986. He obtained his Master's degree and PhD from Newcastle University, UK in 1996 and 2000 respectively. He worked in industries for eight years and he is currently a professor at the department of Electrical and Computer Engineering, International Islamic University Malaysia. Prof. Khalifa served as the head of department of Electrical and computer Engineering, IIUM from July 2005 until December 2014. He is a Charter Engineer (CEng) UK, a Senior member of IEEE USA, and a member IET UK. Prof. Khalifa was the chairman of the International Conference on Computer and Communication Engineering (ICCCE), 2006, 2010, 2012, 2014. Prof. Khalifa supervised more than 60 Masters and PhD students. He has extensively contributed through his writings in international journals, conferences and books. He published more than 500 publications including 14 books. In 2013, he received the highest citation in Citation Indexed Journal Award, in 2019 he got the TOKOH academic "Best Academician" award and last year in 2020, he Won the Murabbi "Best Teacher" award. In 2021, he got the publication (book publication) award. In 2022 won the National Best Book in Science and technology 2022.

Rashid A. Saeed received his Ph.D. in Communications Network Engineering, at UPM, Malaysia. Currently, he is a professor, Computer Engineering Dept, Taif University. He is also working in the Electronics Dept, Engineering Faculty, SUST, Sudan. He was a senior researcher in Telekom Malaysia™ R&D and MIMOS bhd sdn. He was Deputy director of the Scientific Research and Innovation Directorate at the MOHE, Sudan from 2015 to 2019 and Deputy dean for Scientific Research, SUST from 2012 to 2015. Rashid published more than 300 research papers, books, and book chapters in peer-reviewed academic venues. He is successfully awarded

13 WO, EP, CN, and MY patents in these areas. He supervised more than 50 MSc/Ph.D. students. Rashid is a Senior Member of IEEE, and a Member of IEM (I.E.M), Professional Accreditation as Consultant from SEC and SCE. Rashid is co-founder and Technical Committee Chair (TPC) of the International Conference on Computing, Electrical and Electronics Engineering (ICCEEE) in Sudan from 2013 to 2018, and General Chair for EAI AFRICOMM 2022 to 2024. He is an editorial board member Scientific African (SCIAF) journal. He is a guest editor in many journals.

***

Muhammed Zaharadeen Ahmed is a Post-Doctoral Fellow at the International Islamic University Malaysia, where he also earned his PhD in Engineering in 2022 and MSc in Computer and Information Engineering in 2017. He holds a BSc in Computer Engineering from the University of Maiduguri, Nigeria, obtained in 2014. His research interests include Networking, particularly Network Mobility (NEMO), Blockchain, and the Internet of Things (IoT). Dr. Ahmed currently serves as a Volunteer Senior Lecturer at the University of Technology and Arts of Byumba (UTAB), Rwanda, since February 2025. He has also held several notable academic leadership positions, including Head of the Computer Engineering Department at the University of Maiduguri, Nigeria (2023–2024), Head of the Cyber Security Department at Al-Ansar University, Nigeria (2022–2024), and Senate Member at Al-Ansar University in 2022. His professional journey also includes his role as a Research Engineer at the International Islamic University Malaysia and as a Computer Engineer at Zenith International Academy, Nigeria. Dr. Ahmed is an active member of several professional bodies, including the Nigerian Society of Engineers (NSE), the Council for Regulation of Engineering in Nigeria (COREN), the Board of Engineers Malaysia (BEM), and the Nigeria Computer Society (NCS). He is proficient in English and Hausa and has an intermediate command of Arabic.

Harishchander Anandaram completed a PhD in bioengineering, an M.Tech., and a B.Tech. in bioinformatics from the Sathyabama Institute of Science and Technology, Chennai, in 2020, 2011, and 2009. In his bachelor's and master's theses, he worked on analysing resistance in HIV protease inhibitors based on molecular mechanics and machine learning studies, a collaborative project with IIT Madras. In his PhD thesis, he worked on pharmacogenomics and miRNA-regulated networks in psoriasis, a collaborative project with Georgetown University, USA; JIPMER, India; CIBA, India; and ILS, India. His thesis illustrated a multi-disciplinary approach by combining computational biophysics and molecular biology machine learning. While doing a PhD, he had the opportunity to collaborate with international researchers and have publications in reputed international journals in bioinformatics and systems biology. He has received the prestigious "Young Scientist Award" from "The Melinda Gates Foundation" for his research abstract on "The Implications of miRNA Dynamics in Infectious Diseases.". To date, he has reviewed more than 200 manuscripts in systems biology.

Zainab Senan Attarbashi is an assistant professor at the Faculty of Information and Communication Technology, International Islamic University Malaysia (IIUM). She received her BSc (in Electronic and Computer Engineering), MSc, and Ph.D. (in Information and Computer Engineering) degrees from the International Islamic University in Malaysia. She Worked at School of Computing, Universiti Utara Malaysia (UUM). Her current research interests are Cyber Security, Info-Centric Networks, Network Mobility, blockchain and IoT Connectivity.

Wan Muhd Hazwan Azamuddin received his Ph.D from the National University of Malaysia (UKM), Malaysia in 2024. He obtained an MSc in Computer Science from the Technical University of Malaysia (UTeM) in 2016. Currently working as the head of the electrical department at Tangkak Industrial Institute. He has published several papers in peer-reviewed international journals. His research area includes networking, future internet technology, & mobility NDN

Salaheldin Mohamed Ibrahim Edam is an accomplished academic and researcher in the field of electronics and communications, currently serving as an Assistant Professor at the Sudan University of Science and Technology since July 2014. He has extensive teaching experience, having previously held positions as a Lecturer and Teaching Assistant in the School of Electronics Engineering. Edam earned his PhD in Engineering (Communications and Information Systems) from Beijing University of Posts & Telecommunications in China (2010-2014) and holds a Master's degree in Information Technology from Sudan University of Science and Technology (2008). His educational background also includes a Post Graduate Diploma in Advanced Information Technology from the International Institute of Information Technology in India and a Bachelor's degree in Electronics Engineering with honors. His areas of expertise encompass a wide range of topics, including MIMO systems, 5G and 6G technologies, machine learning applications in wireless communications, and the Internet of Things (IoT). Edam has supervised numerous graduate students and has held administrative roles, such as Head of the Communication Engineering Department and Coordinator of Graduate Studies for Electronics Engineering. Edam has contributed significantly to the academic community, with over 27 peer-reviewed publications focusing on wireless sensor networks, machine learning, and telecommunications. His work has been presented at various international journal and conferences, showcasing his commitment to advancing research in his field.

Hitesh Mohapatra received the B.E. degree in Information Technology from Biju Patnaik University of Technology (BPUT), Odisha in 2006, and the MTech. Degree in CSE from Odisha University of Technology and Research (OUTR) University, Odisha in 2009. He received his Ph.D. in Computer Science & Engineering in 2021 from Veer Surendra Sai University of Technology (VSSUT), Burla, India. He has contributed 30 SCI and Scopus indexed research papers, 21 international/national conferences and books on Software Engineering and C Programming respectively. He has 15 years of teaching experience both in industry and academia. He has served the research community with various capacities like session chair, technical chair, keynote speaker etc. His research interests include wireless sensor network, smart city, smart grid and smart water. Currently he is working as Associate professor at School of Computer Engineering, KIIT DU, Bhubaneswar, and Odisha.

Azana Hafizah Mohd Aman is a Senior Lecturer at the Research Center for Cyber Security, Faculty of Information Science and Technology (FTSM), Universiti Kebangsaan Malaysia (UKM), Malaysia. She holds a B.Eng., M.Sc., and Ph.D. in computer and information engineering from International Islamic University Malaysia. Her research focuses on computer systems and networking, with a particular interest in information and network security, the Internet of Things (IoT), cloud computing, and big data.

Rania Abdelhameed (IEEE member since 2003) received the B.Sc. degree in Electronics Engineering (Computer Engineering) from the Sudan University of Science & Technology (SUST), Khartoum, Sudan, in 2001, & the Postgraduate Diploma in Information Technology (Advanced Networking & Telecommunications) from the International Institute of Information Technology (I2IT), Pune, India, in 2003, & the M.Sc. & PhD. degrees from the University Putra Malaysia (UPM), Kuala Lumpur, Malaysia, in 2005 & 2010, respectively. In May 2009, she earned the IEEE Wireless Communication Professional (IEEE WCP) certificate of the Wireless Communication Engineering Technology (WCET) Exam. Currently, she is an associate professor and Director, Electronics System Research Centre, Faculty of Engineering, Sudan University of Science and Technology, Khartoum, Sudan. She has been award Elsevier Foundation Award for women in Engineering in 2017. She published over 30 scientific papers and two books.

Mamoon Mohammed Ali Saeed is Deputy Dean of the College of Engineering and Information Technology, and Director of the University Branch, and a

Lecturer at the Department of Communication and Electronics Engineering, UMS University, Yemen. received his Bachelor's degree in Communication and Electronics Engineering from Sana'a University, Yemen 2005, and his M.S. degree from the Department of Computer Networks and Information Security in Yemen Academy for Graduate Studies Yemen 2013. Recently, a Ph.D. in Alzaiem Alazhari University, Faculty of Engineering, Electrical Engineering Department, Khartoum, Sudan 2021. His research areas include cyber security, communication security, and artificial intelligence.

Maznifah Salam is a Malaysian academic and cybersecurity researcher based at Universiti Teknologi MARA (UiTM), Shah Alam. She holds a Master's degree in Computer Science and is currently pursuing a PhD focused on ICT security governance. Actively involved in UiTM's infrastructure and ICT development, she has contributed to several scholarly publications on cybersecurity maturity models for higher education, emphasizing governance, risk, human factors, and compliance. Her work bridges academic research and institutional policy, helping to shape cybersecurity frameworks within Malaysian universities and supporting national standards such as ISO 9001:2015.

C.V. Suresh Babu is a pioneer in content development. A true entrepreneur, he founded Anniyappa Publications, a company that is highly active in publishing books related to Computer Science and Management. Dr. C.V. Suresh Babu has also ventured into SB Institute, a center for knowledge transfer. He holds a Ph.D. in Engineering Education from the National Institute of Technical Teachers Training & Research in Chennai, along with seven master's degrees in various disciplines such as Engineering, Computer Applications, Management, Commerce, Economics, Psychology, Law, and Education. Additionally, he has UGC-NET/SET qualifications in the fields of Computer Science, Management, Commerce, and Education. Currently, Dr. C.V. Suresh Babu is a Professor in the Department of Information Technology at the School of Computing Science, Hindustan Institute of Technology and Science (Hindustan University) in Padur, Chennai, Tamil Nadu, India.

Srikanth Velpula received Ph.D. degree from Vellore Institute of Technology, Vellore, Tamilnadu, India in 2020. He received B.Tech and M.Tech degrees both from Jawaharlal Nehru Technological University, Hyderabad, India, in 2009 and 2012, respectively. He worked as an Assistant Professor in the Department of Electrical and Electronics Engineering at various engineering colleges in India during 2011-2022. Currently, he is working as Assistant Professor at SR University, Warangal, Telangana, India. His research interests include Power system stability, Converter controls, DFIG based systems, Electrical Vehicle Drives & Battery Management System, and the Integration of renewable energies into the power systems.

Index

A

B

C

D

K

L

M

N

O

P

Q

R

S

V

W

www.ingramcontent.com/pod-product-compliance
Lightning Source LLC
LaVergne TN
LVHW080350011026
849161LV00009B/2259